HOW ART WORKS

HOW ART WORKS

DK | Penguin Random House

Editorial Consultant
Aliki Braine

Senior Art Editor
Duncan Turner

Project Art Editors
Stephen Bere, Amy Child, Mark Lloyd

Illustrators
Ed Burn, Vicky Clarke, Natalie Clay, Mark Clifton, Mark Ruffle, Gus Scott

Managing Art Editor
Michael Duffy

Jacket Designer
Surabhi Wadhwa-Gandhi

Senior Jackets Coordinator
Priyanka Sharma

Senior Jacket Designer
Suhita Dharamjit

Senior DTP Designer
Harish Aggarwal

Production Editor
Kavita Varma

Art Director
Karen Self

Contributors
George Bray, Theodore Gordon, Alison Hand, Susie Hodge, Natasha Kahn

Senior Editor
Hugo Wilkinson

US Editor
Jennette ElNaggar

Editors
Anna Fischel, Ian Fitzgerald, Kathryn Hill, Natasha Kahn, Alice Nightingale

Editorial Assistant
Emily Kho

Managing Editor
Angeles Gavira Guerrero

Jackets Design Development Manager
Sophia MTT

Managing Jackets Editor
Saloni Singh

Production Controller
Laura Andrews

Associate Publishing Director
Liz Wheeler

Publishing Director
Jonathan Metcalf

First American Edition, 2022
Published in the United States by DK Publishing,
a division of Penguin Random House LLC
1745 Broadway, 20th Floor, New York, NY 10019

25 26 27 28 10 9 8 7 6 5 4 3 2
002–320523–Oct/2022

Published in Great Britain by Dorling Kindersley Limited

A catalog record for this book is
available from the Library of Congress.
ISBN 978-0-7440-5634-1

DK books are available at special discounts when purchased in bulk for sales promotions, premiums, fund-raising, or educational use. For details, contact: DK Publishing Special Markets, 1745 Broadway, 20th Floor, New York, NY 10019
SpecialSales@dk.com

Printed and bound in China

www.dk.com

FSC www.fsc.org MIX Paper | Supporting responsible forestry FSC™ C018179

This book was made with Forest Stewardship Council™ certified paper – one small step in DK's commitment to a sustainable future.
Learn more at www.dk.com/uk/information/sustainability

CONTENTS

DEFINING ART

MEDIA AND MATERIALS

SUBJECTS AND CATEGORIES

ELEMENTS OF ART

MOVEMENTS

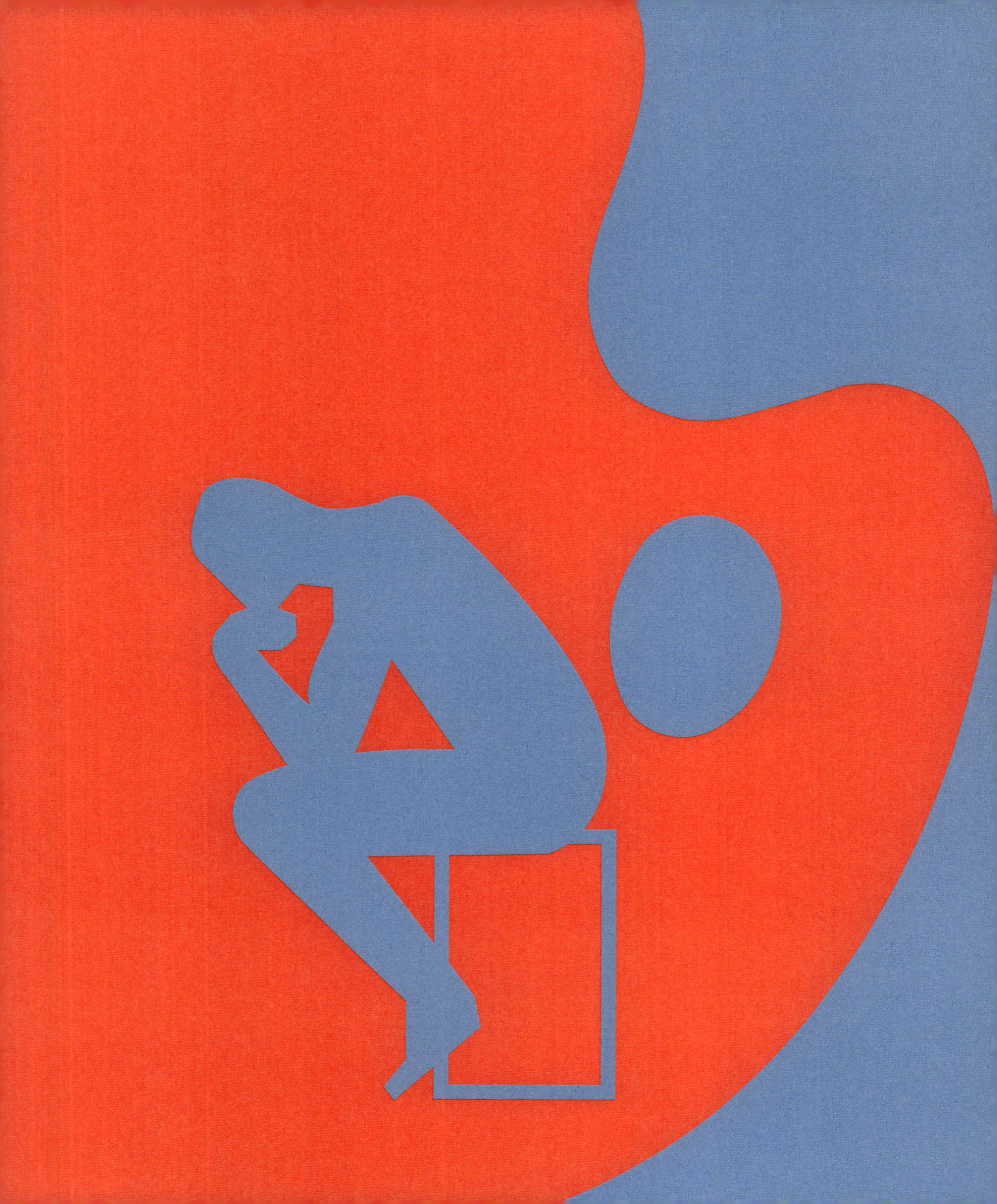

DEFINING ART

What is Art?

Art encompasses a diverse range of creative human expression and activity, which results in the production of works that variously display technical skills, aesthetic decisions, emotional power, intellectual theories, and conceptual ideas.

A way of thinking

Trying to explain in words the overwhelmingly visual medium of art is no easy matter—especially as there is no universally agreed definition of what art actually is. There have been attempts throughout history and across cultures, but these explanations have themselves shifted as times have changed. Art's elusive nature is partly due to its subjectivity—it means different things to different people. Artists themselves have different views on what art is, with some believing it is an inherently political undertaking, while others view it as an activity that has value in and of itself. Then there are those who see art as a process, the act of making forms and the expression of visual qualities.

It might be safer to say that art is a way of thinking. Artists are curious by nature and want to question the world. For the artist, art never stops; it is a lifelong commitment to learning and mastering a visual language and material vocabulary.

As a practice, it is separate from decorative arts and is often referred to as fine art because of its subject matter and aesthetic

FROM **1912 TO 1952**, **ART** WAS AN EVENT IN **THE OLYMPICS**

WHY IS SOME ART SO EXPENSIVE?

Artworks by a small number of famous artists have become a prestigious form of investment for the super-rich. However, most artists' work is sold for much smaller sums.

and conceptual content. Art appeals to the human need to make things and to express emotion. Art describes life and the imagination, poses philosophical questions, and communicates on a deep visual level.

A powerful force

Art can consist of crafted objects, such as paintings and sculptures, or it can be performed. Art can be made for a gallery, for the outdoor environment, for a domestic space, or for the digital world. It can be made to last or temporary.

Art may also be seen as dangerous, giving expression to powerful ideas. It has been suppressed by authorities for being "degenerate." Art can represent the ineffable and the intangible or turn an idea into something concrete and compelling. Art makes connections across cultures and across time, and it is carried ever forward by those who make it—and those who enjoy it.

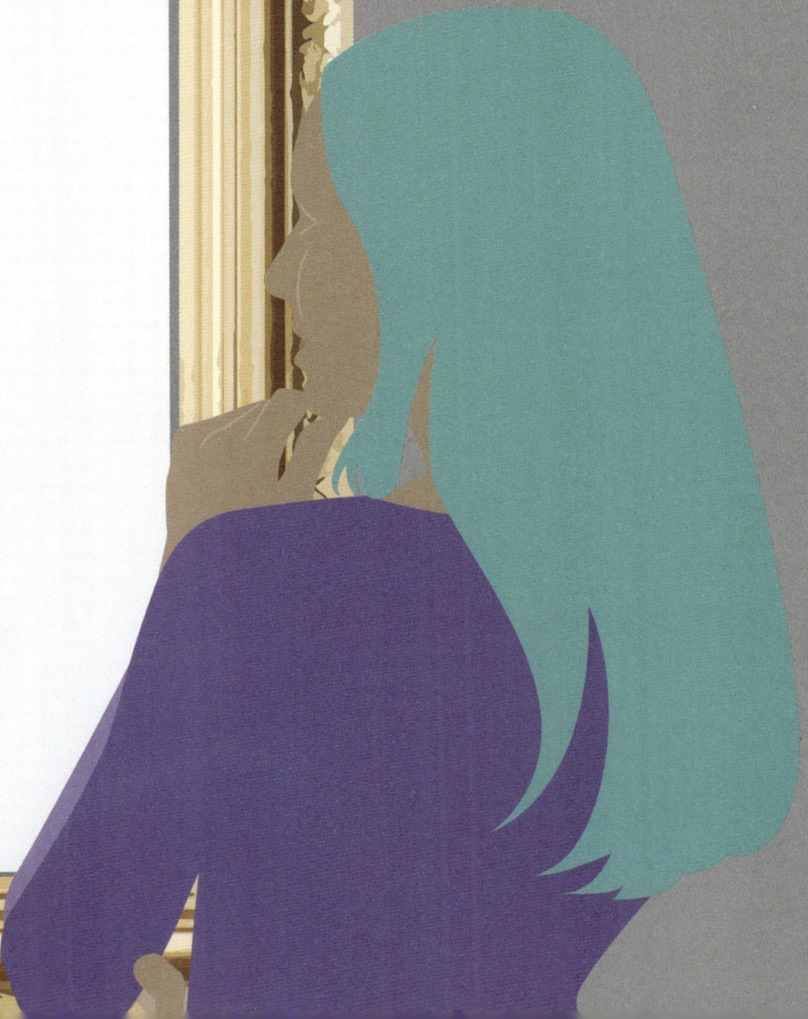

What Does Art Do?

A successful artwork is one that makes the viewer think and ask questions—about what the work means, what it is trying to say, and how it is saying it. More personally, it should provoke the viewer into thinking about their relationship with the work and why they are affected by it.

The role of art

Art is a complex language made up of visual qualities, material processes, and subject matter and content. It also incorporates the identity of the artist that makes it. Art can be mysterious or direct, beautiful or grotesque, but it always communicates in some way with the viewer. Some art is intended to be appreciated for the qualities of its form and its use of craft and skill, giving the viewer an aesthetic experience. Socially engaged art is meant to communicate a particular point of view to the audience and to effect change. Expressive artworks connect emotionally with the viewer and create a sense of empathy. Narrative artworks create worlds and scenarios that might be real or imaginary, but which draw in the viewer.

Tells a story
Art can tell a story and take the viewer into an imaginative, fictional world or an enhanced reality. Storytelling can be explored through a series of images, where the viewer "reads" the tale through sequential compositions or through the use of narrative imagery or metaphor in single artworks.

Conveys meaning
Art conveys meaning by the way it is made, its appearance, and its context. The exact meaning of an artwork can be difficult to identify, as artists often try not to be obvious or literal, aiming for a more subtle approach that encourages the viewer to spend time considering the work.

THE IDEA OF THE ARTIST

It was only from the early 1400s that artists began to be known by name and celebrated for their creativity. Before then, art was made by nameless artisans who were viewed as craftsmen rather than artists.

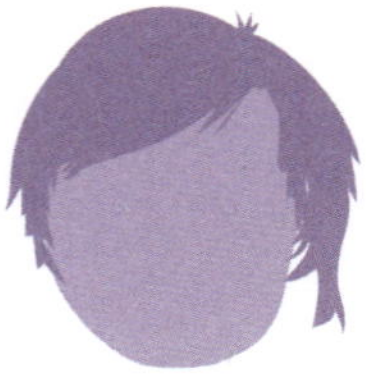

Expresses feeling
Art is particularly suited to expressing feeling and emotion as it communicates on a deep visual level. The artist might express their own emotions through the work, or suggest a particular mood, which the viewer can then feel through their experience of the piece.

SHOULD ART BE BEAUTIFUL?

Art reflects and comments on life, so it should be beautiful—but it should also be ugly, confusing, happy, sad, strange, and any other human quality it is possible to think of, too.

Provides aesthetic pleasure
Whilst some art is deliberately difficult, provocative, or "ugly", other art is intended to be experienced as beautiful or aesthetically pleasing. This gives the viewer a sense of pleasure, space to reflect, and a connection to the artwork.

Carries a message
Art can have a powerful voice. Public art is effective in conveying messages to a wide audience, while individual artists tend to use a more personal, allusive approach to share their concerns, engaging in more of a dialogue with viewers than state-sponsored or corporate art can offer.

Reflects the world around it
One of art's most powerful and useful qualities is that it can be used to hold a mirror up to society. Some art asks people to think about difficult subjects, such as death, loss, conflict, or poverty, often through creating or using confronting or disturbing images to provoke a response.

Explores pure line, color, or shape
Art does not have to contain a message. It can be purely formal, an exercise in exploring a work's visual or physical qualities and how they affect the viewer through elements such as the arrangement of shape, color, scale, and the materials used.

MIXED

The art of the material world

Textiles are now widely used in art, in "soft sculpture" processes such as quilting and sewing. Paper art includes the genre of artists' books, which artists often make and bind themselves, and paper sculpture. Installation art is where the artist creates an environment in which the viewer moves and interacts. Mixed media combines elements of different art forms into individual pieces or works.

TWO-DIMENSIONAL

Picturing the world

Two-dimensional art forms encompass mark making, color, line, gesture, and surface. Surfaces range from paper and canvas to wood and even walls. Painting and drawing have a spontaneous, immediate quality and are closely related, with artists often working with both media. Printmaking is more process-based, with the use of print presses. Murals can be large-scale indoor and outdoor works.

OTHER

Art as an experience

Conceptual art and performance art originated in the early 20th century but became more widespread in the 1960s, when artists questioned the meaning and the role of art itself in a time of intense social and political unrest. Performance uses the human body as a medium and can be interactive, and digital and film explore how cinematic processes and computer technologies can convey artistic ideas.

CAN SOUND BE ART?

In 1913–1930, the Futurist Luigi Russolo built the first sound art pieces—"noise machines." Since then, sound has been used in installations, performance art, kinetic sculptures, digital art, and more.

CRAFTS

Fine art was once distinguished from craft as it was seen as having an intellectual content that its more functional counterpart lacked. Today, it is agreed that utilitarian objects, whether it is a pot, a chair, or piece of embroidery, can have artistic merit, or simply be a work of art in their own right.

Forms of Art

Art can embody many forms, having evolved from ancient practices of painting, drawing, and sculpture, to encompass contemporary art forms such as performance and video. The 20th century produced a radical transformation and expansion in what could be considered art.

How artists choose their art form

Artists select their chosen media for many different reasons. For some artists, the idea or concept is the principle that decides the form that the artwork should take. Other artists feel an affiliation with a particular medium or material process, or they may prefer to work in two or three dimensions. Many artists work across media, using and even combining different art forms to create mixed media works or environments. Becoming skilled in any art form requires study and practice to build experience and facility.

HUMANS HAVE BEEN MAKING **FIGURATIVE SCULPTURES** FOR AT LEAST **35,000 YEARS**

THREE-DIMENSIONAL

Embodied art you can feel and touch
Sculpture can be made out of any material. Contemporary sculpture often combines different and unusual items, such as found objects or building materials. Traditional sculpting matter includes marble and stone, as well as bronze and plaster, which require a casting process. Once made as purely functional vessels, ceramics evolved into the creation of decorative and experimental pieces.

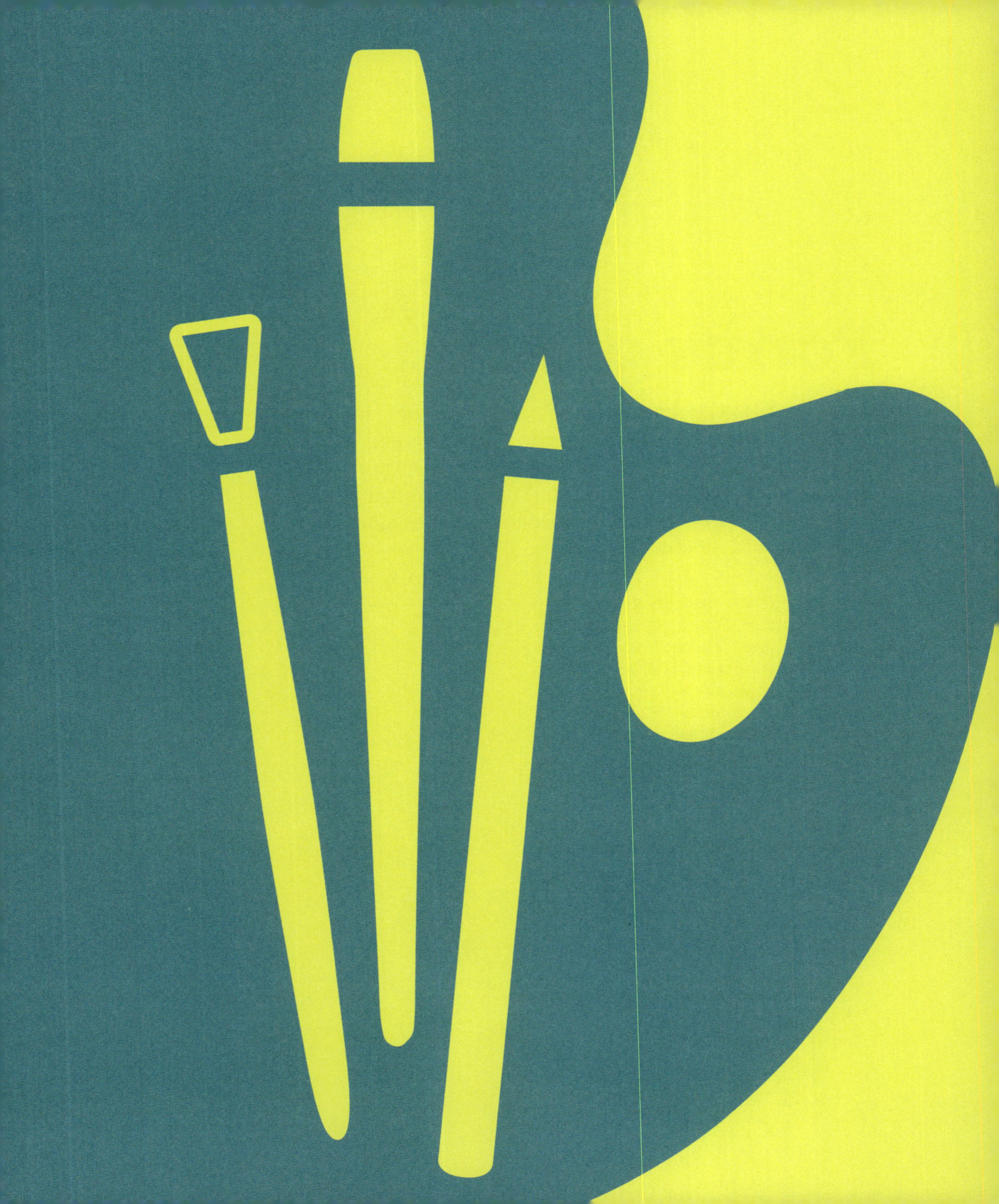

MEDIA AND MATERIALS

PAINT AND KNIVES

Although they are mainly used for mixing paint on palettes, paint knives can also be used to make marks by applying paint directly to a painting. This tends to create the kind of thick, heavy marks typically used in impasto, giving a work an expressive and heavily textured quality.

ABSTRACT ART OFTEN FEATURES EXPRESSIVE MARKS

Mark Making

Mark making describes the visible actions used in creating an artwork and how those actions are carried out through gesture and strokes.

Approaches to mark making

Mark making is inherent to both a work's overall style and to its emotional impact—marks are the tangible link between the artist and the viewer. Mark making expresses emotion and physical action: it can be spontaneous, showing speed and intuition, or planned, using line quality or repetition. With drawing materials such as charcoal (see pp.22–23), loose marks and smudges create immediacy, while pencil is often used for smaller, more detailed lines and patterns. In painting, mark making can incorporate poured paint, drips, or flatness as well as brushstrokes.

Mark making with oils

Oil paint has a versatility that embraces many types of mark making. A few examples are shown here, illustrating principles that artists can apply across a range of other drawing and painting media.

COARSE MARKS

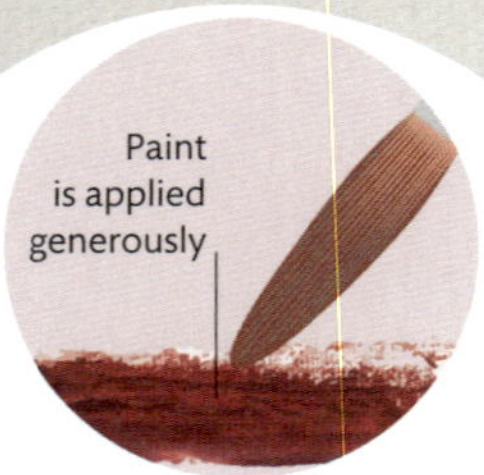

Gestural strokes using brushes with coarse hairs can be used to imply texture, solidity, or movement. This also helps establish the "core" elements of the image.

DRY BRUSH MARKS

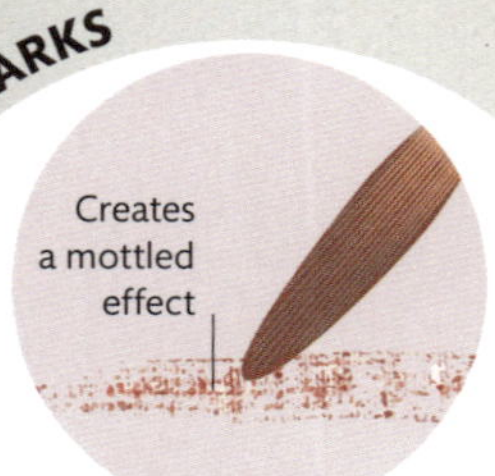

Dry brush marks can be made with coarse brushes, often using repetitive movements. This creates mottled, textured effects, with individual marks blending together.

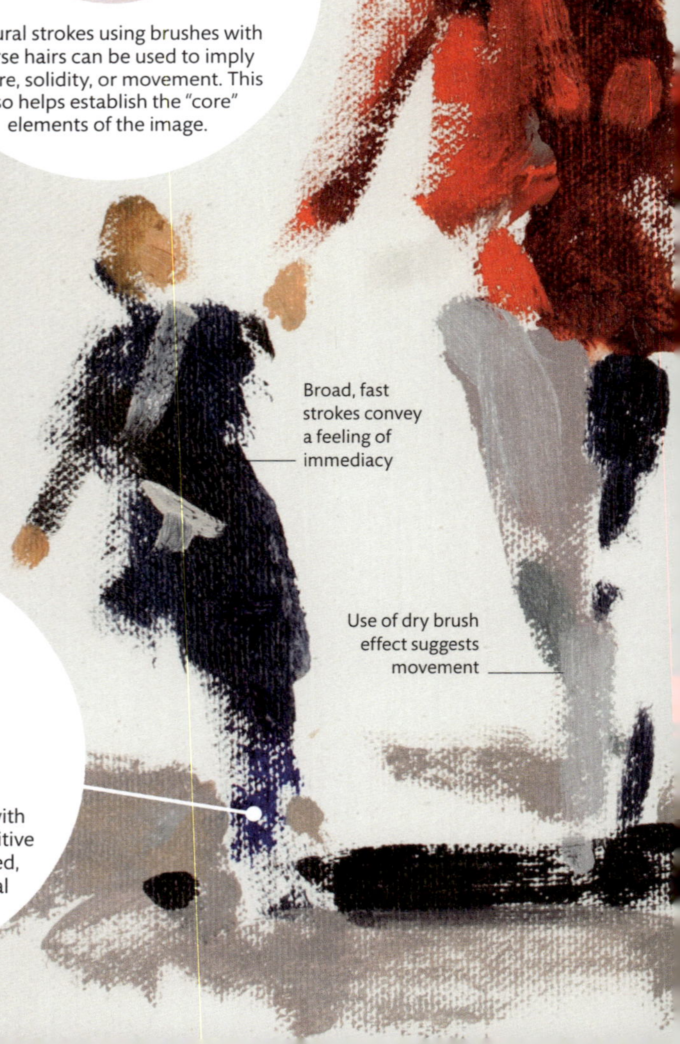

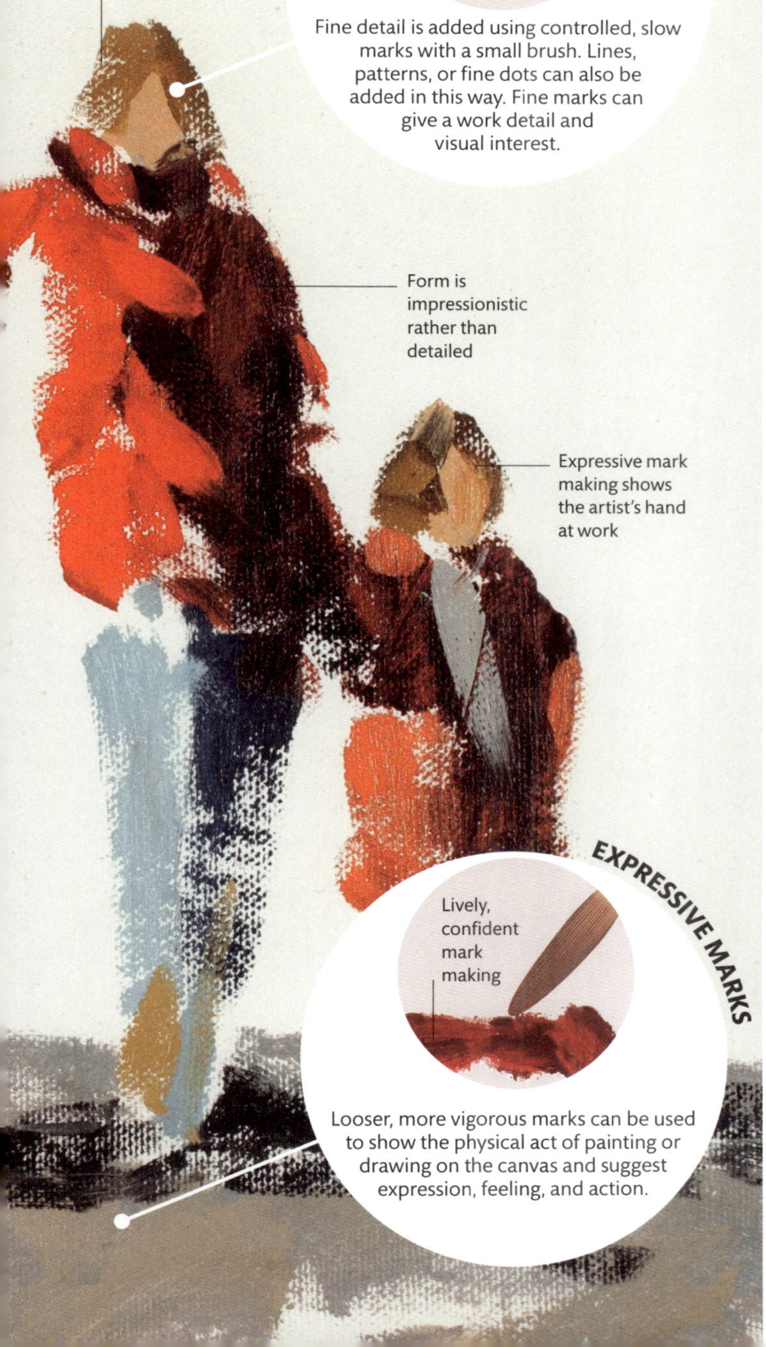

Fine detail is added using controlled, slow marks with a small brush. Lines, patterns, or fine dots can also be added in this way. Fine marks can give a work detail and visual interest.

Looser, more vigorous marks can be used to show the physical act of painting or drawing on the canvas and suggest expression, feeling, and action.

IS MARK MAKING PURELY VISUAL?

Mark making can be aural as much as visual. Sound artists often use particular sounds, noises, and "glitches" to enhance their work or make it identifiably theirs.

Mark making in sculpture

In sculpture, artists can choose whether to disguise the physical act of mark making or draw attention to it as part of the work. Movement can be implied by using visible marks, for example, leaving hand marks in clay or emphasizing rough carving marks in wood or stone. In structural processes such as welding or casting, the artist may leave their mark making in place or smooth it off to create a "cleaner" effect.

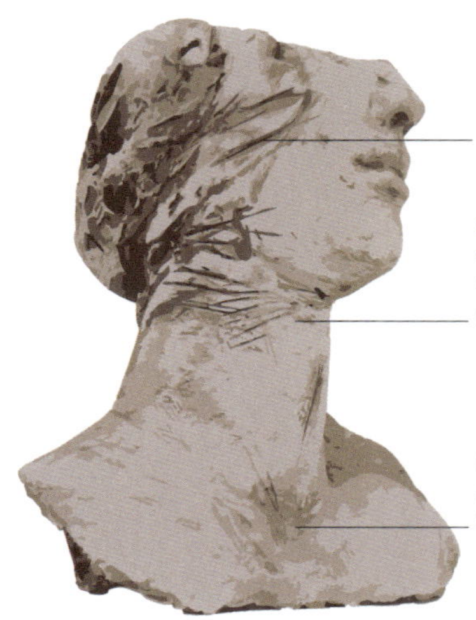

Scarring and sgraffito
Sculptor Henry Moore "scarred" some of his plaster works, cutting in lines to give the pieces a feeling of fragility. Sgraffito is where the sculptor scratches away a top layer of material to reveal a contrasting underlayer.

GOYA WAS ABLE TO PAINT AT NIGHT BY FIXING A CANDLE TO HIS HAT

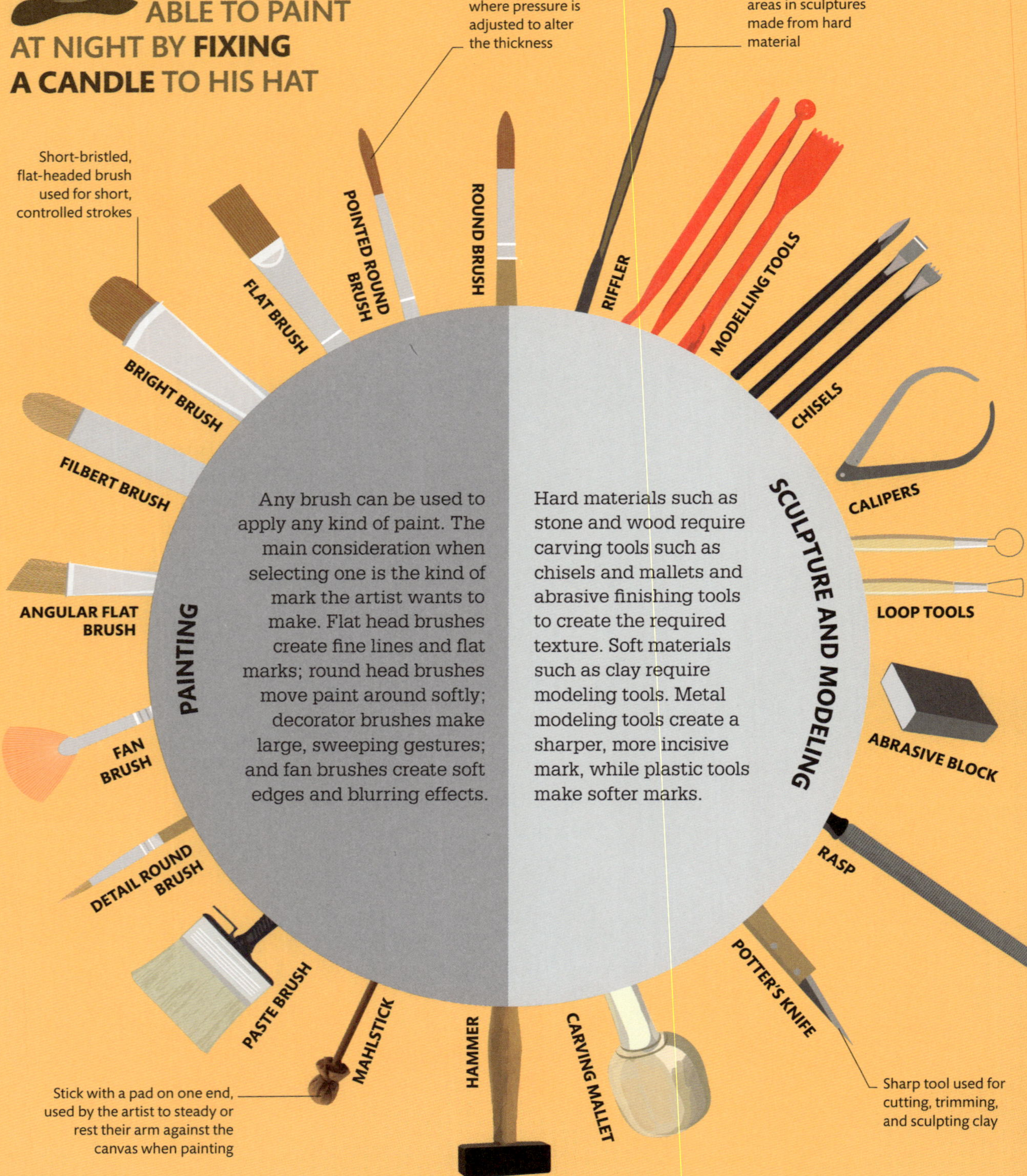

Any brush can be used to apply any kind of paint. The main consideration when selecting one is the kind of mark the artist wants to make. Flat head brushes create fine lines and flat marks; round head brushes move paint around softly; decorator brushes make large, sweeping gestures; and fan brushes create soft edges and blurring effects.

Hard materials such as stone and wood require carving tools such as chisels and mallets and abrasive finishing tools to create the required texture. Soft materials such as clay require modeling tools. Metal modeling tools create a sharper, more incisive mark, while plastic tools make softer marks.

Tools

There are certain key tools that traditionally form the backbone of an artist's toolbox. In practice, however, an artist can make use of any object that can be employed to make a mark.

From brushes to chain saws

It is useful to have a wide range of conventional tools when making art. A painter, for example, will usually have a wide selection of brushes, ranging from fine to large, decorator-style examples. Sculptors should have a selection of carving or modeling tools suitable for the materials they wish to use. Beyond these expected items, however, artists also use unconventional tools to help them in their work. Artist Helen Frankenthaler used large floor brushes and mops to create huge swaths of luminous color on canvas, and Germany's Georg Baselitz used a chain saw and axes to carve expressive large-scale heads and figures in wood.

DOES A BRUSH'S HAIR TYPE MATTER?

Natural hairs, especially sable, are porous and flexible, making them ideal for use with oil-based paints; synthetic fibers, being stiffer and less absorbent, work better for watercolors.

Using flat surfaces

Flat surfaces for painting and drawing provide support and resistance to mark making and brushstrokes. The particular type of surface helps determine the fluidity and texture of the paint applied. In addition to wood, canvas, and paper, unusual surfaces that have interesting textures or transparencies can be used, such as Perspex or acrylic sheets, glass, and even metal.

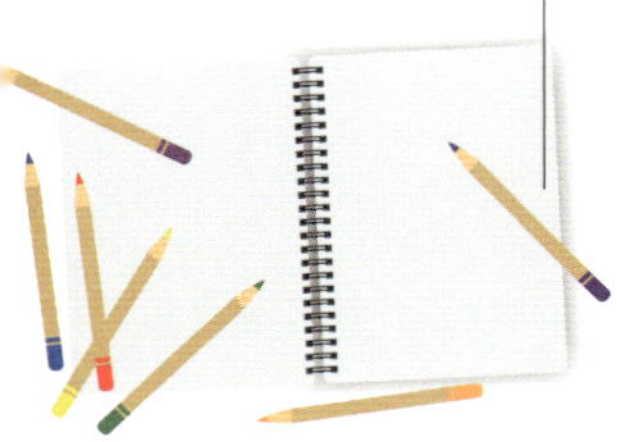

Sketch pads
Sketch pads are used to note ideas and jot down experiments. Charcoal, chalk, and pastels can smudge so require a fixative spray.

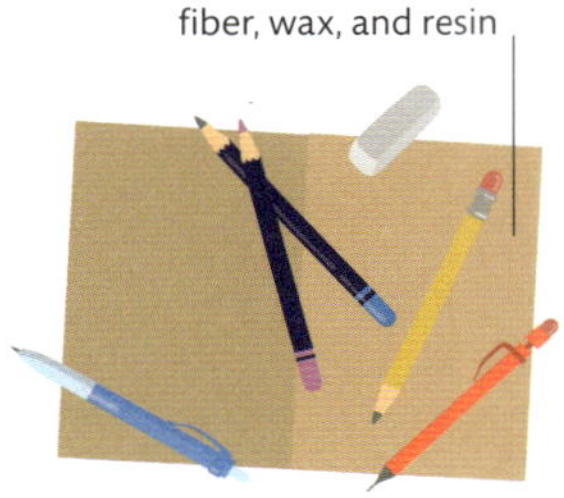

Board
MDF or wood is treated with a primer such a gesso to give a hard finish; unprimed MDF and wood have a raw feel and are more absorbent.

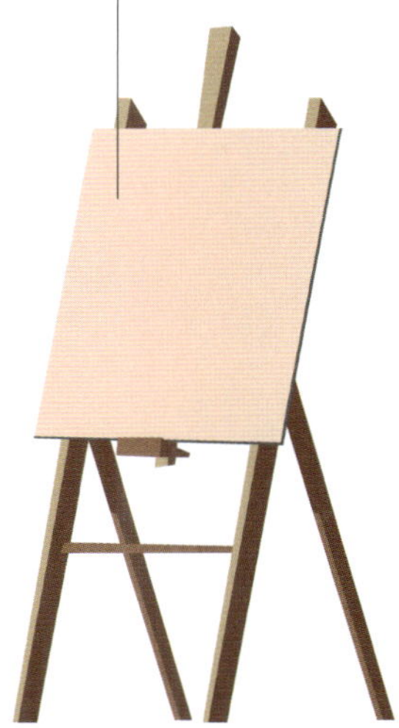

Canvas
Stretched and primed canvas has a good level of resistance and is very durable. Its absorbency helps protect against paint chipping.

HOUSEHOLD TOOLS

Household tools are an inexpensive and inventive way to create interesting marks. Large floor brushes, scourers, or steel wool can be used to create abrasions, texture, and surface details in painting and sculpture.

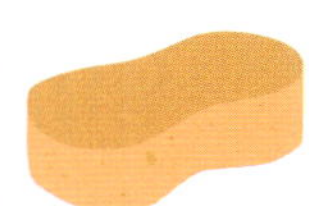

Sponges
Sponges create a mottled effect and can be used to erase or swipe paint.

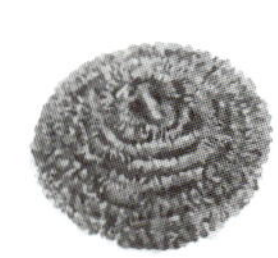

Scourers
Scourers create a scratchy texture that works with paint, clay, or plaster.

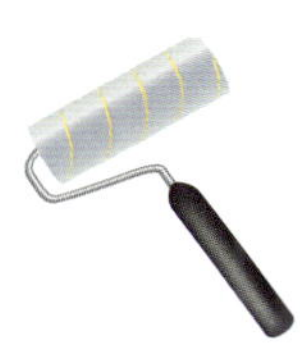

Paint roller
A roller covers large areas quickly, creating a flat surface without visible brushstrokes.

Pencils and Charcoal

Drawing is one of the oldest forms of visual art, with the first known charcoal sketches dating from the Paleolithic era, 30,000 years ago. The most common and widespread drawing tool today is the pencil, comprised of a graphite core enclosed in a wooden shell.

Instant marks

First developed during the 16th and 17th centuries, the pencil is a versatile drawing tool and provides the most immediate, responsive form of drawing. It instantaneously records the movements of the hand, leaving a physical mark that is water-resistant and reasonably durable but that can also be erased if required. Graphite comes in varying degrees of hardness (see right)).

Shading with hatching

Multiple lines can be used to create the illusion of shade, shape, depth, shadow, and more. Spacing can be increased or decreased to adjust how dark the area will be. This is typically done with dark, clear lines.

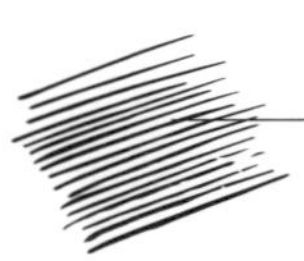

HATCHING

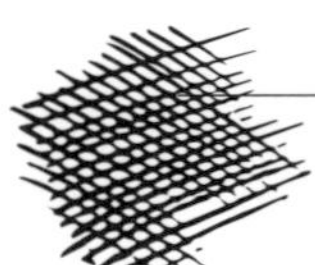

CROSSHATCHING

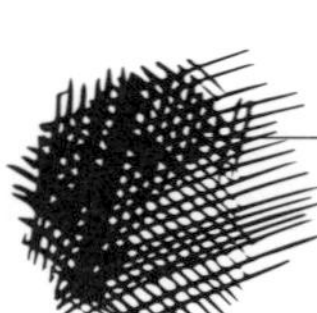

DOUBLE CROSSHATCHING

Line and texture
Initial sketches allow the artist to map out the composition, and lines can be easily erased and edited; later in the process, shading and crosshatching create shadow and volume to bring a subject to life.

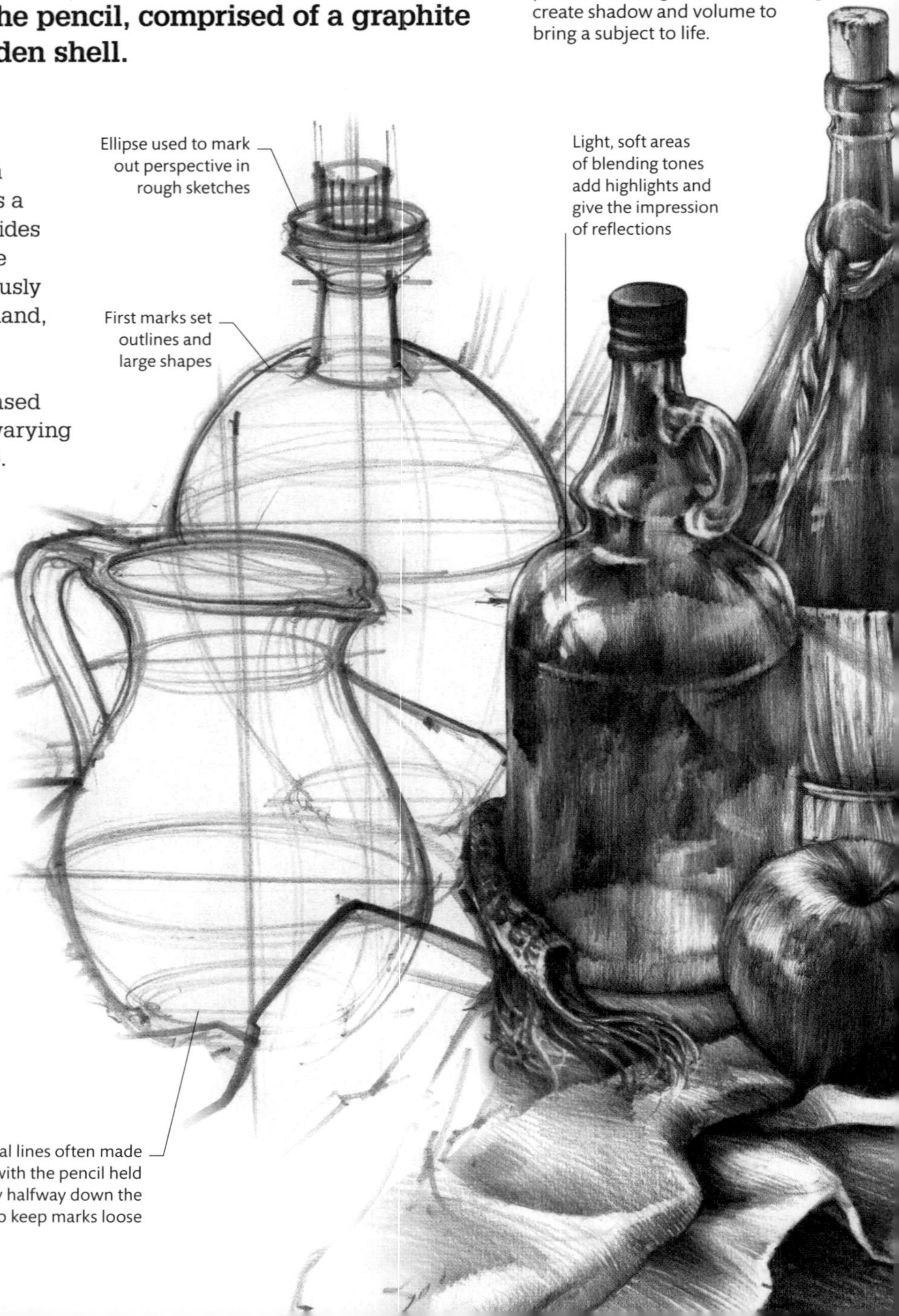

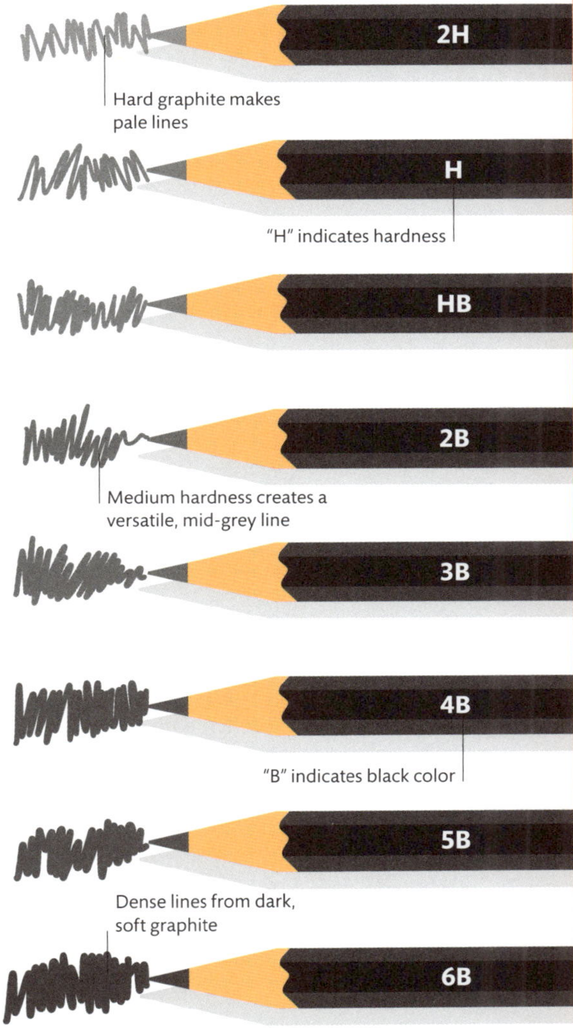

HOW WERE THE FIRST PENCILS MADE?

Graphite pencils were originally bound with string before hollow wood casings were invented and mass-produced during the Industrial Revolution.

ONCE FINISHED, CHARCOAL DRAWINGS MUST BE COATED WITH A FIXATIVE SPRAY; OTHERWISE, THEY WILL SMUDGE

Charcoal

The earliest drawing tools in the Paleolithic era (see pp.144–45) were made using whatever materials were on hand, and, as a by-product of wood fires, charcoal was widely available. It remains a key part of an artist's tool kit; its texture allows for a range of marks and makes it perfect for capturing the human form (see pp.68–69). Smudging effects ("sweetening") can be achieved with a tortillon (a tool made of rolled paper) or a finger, while highlights are made with a putty eraser.

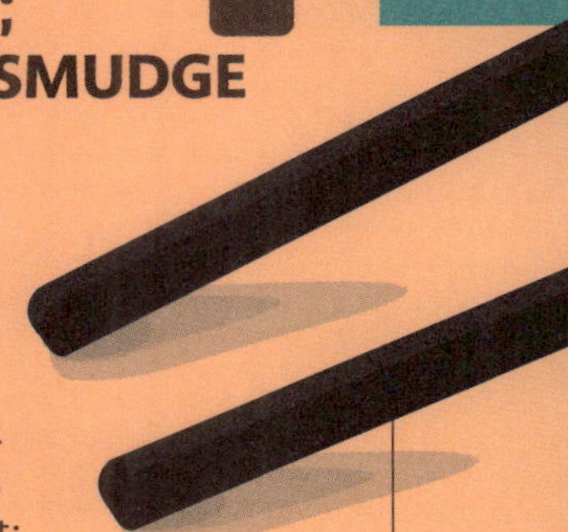

Mark making
Thin sticks held at the tip create fine lines, while rougher areas are made with the longer edge. Both can be smudged.

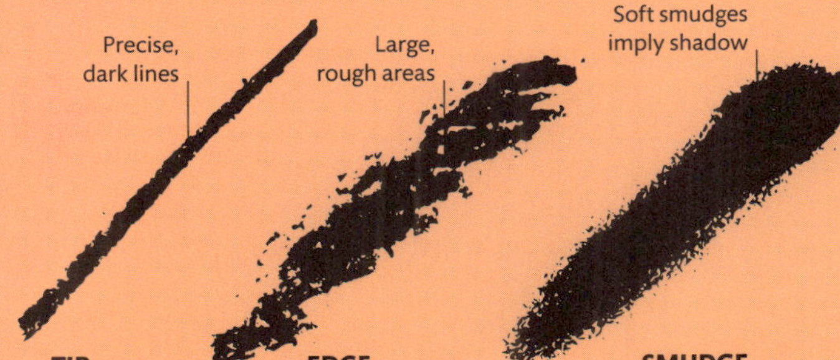

ROMAN STYLUS

The Roman stylus was an early precursor of the pencil. A pointed instrument made from lead, it could make marks on parchment, papyrus, or wax-coated tablets. A scraper at the other end was used for rubbing marks out.

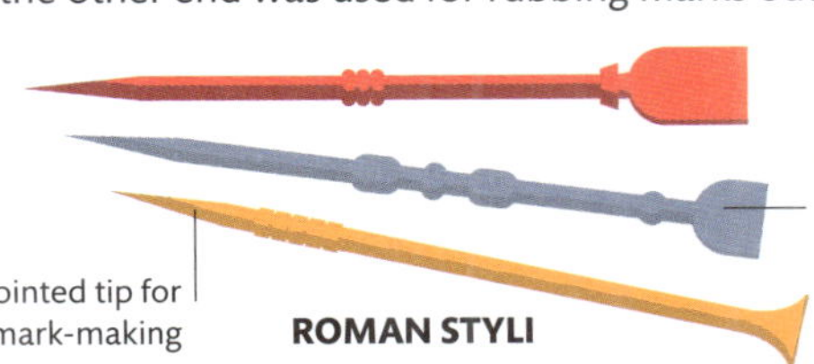

ROMAN STYLI

Inks

Inks have various uses in art, and painting with ink is mostly associated with the traditional art of east Asia, notably China, where it has been practiced for millennia. Mixed with water, the ink is applied using a brush.

Fine tradition

Calligraphy (the art of decorative writing) and painting were two traditional art forms that the Chinese scholar was expected to master. Both practices required ink, brushes, and an absorbent surface, such as rice paper or silk. The earliest surviving ink paintings date from around 700 CE. Subjects for traditional Chinese ink paintings include plants and flowers, landscapes, animals, and religious scenes, depicted in a variety of styles that accentuate the different marks and tonal variation the artist can make with the brush and ink.

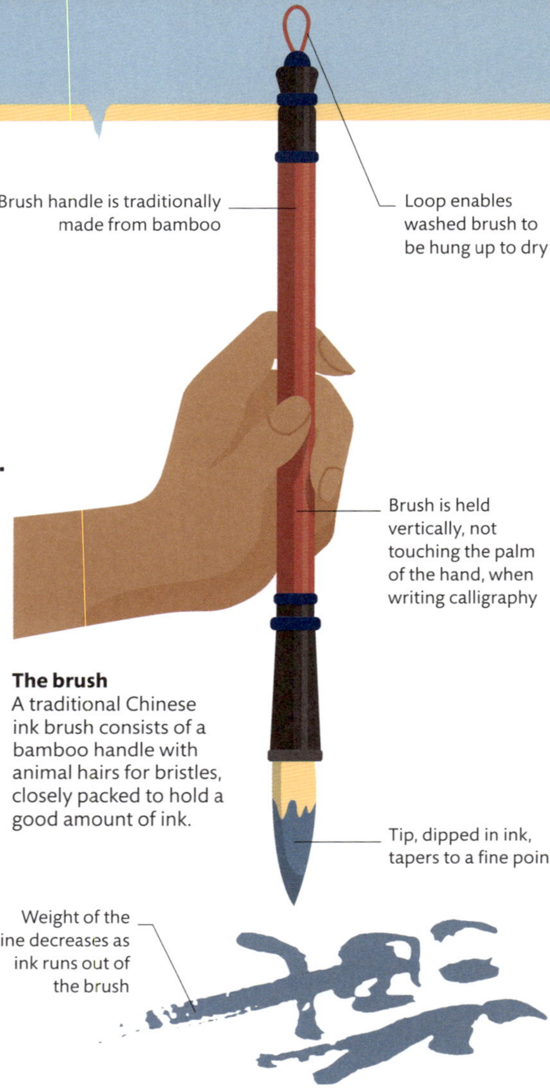

The brush
A traditional Chinese ink brush consists of a bamboo handle with animal hairs for bristles, closely packed to hold a good amount of ink.

Other uses of inks

The earliest inks were made from ground carbon dust mixed with a water-based animal glue, called size. Historically in Western art, ink and pen drawings were used for preparatory studies for painted works. Modern inks are produced from a wide range of organic and synthetic materials, often gum-based. When it is diluted with water, ink allows brushstrokes to be blended and a range of tonal gradation and transparency can be achieved.

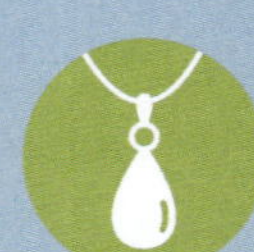

Glass and jewelry
Quick-drying, alcohol-based inks can be used to decorate nonporous surfaces, such as glass and jewelry—giving a stained-glass effect.

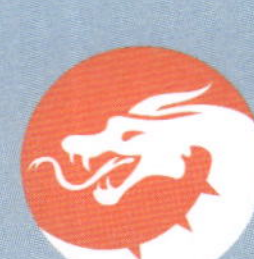

Tattooing
Tattoo inks use pigments such as iron oxide, metal salts, or liquid plastics. Mixed with a solvent, the ink is inserted into the dermis layer of the skin.

Printmaking
Thick printing ink is used to coat plates and blocks for wood block, engraving, lithograph, and monoprinting (see pp.42–47).

Fine line drawing
A dip pen or traditional quill dipped in ink is used to draw fine lines, usually on white paper. Crosshatching gives the impression of shading.

Using a seal
The artist may use two seals—one representing yin, the other, yang— to sign their name. They press each seal block into the red paste, then make a mark on the painting.

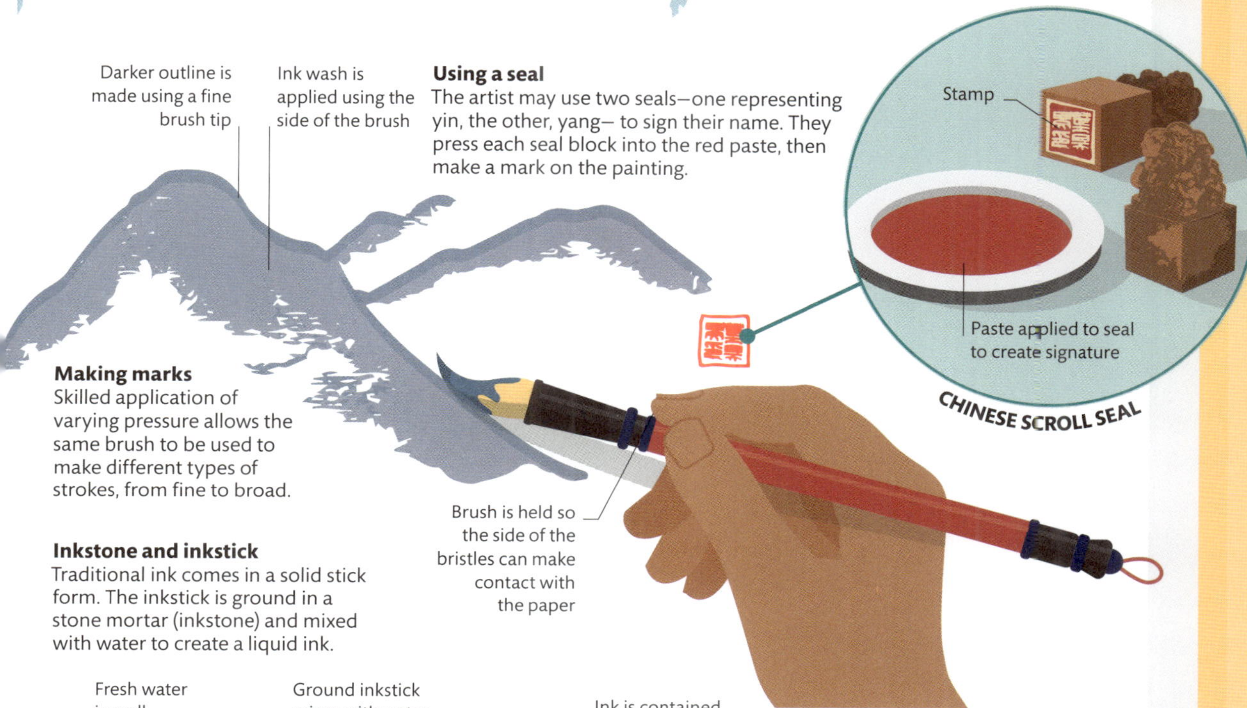

Making marks
Skilled application of varying pressure allows the same brush to be used to make different types of strokes, from fine to broad.

Inkstone and inkstick
Traditional ink comes in a solid stick form. The inkstick is ground in a stone mortar (inkstone) and mixed with water to create a liquid ink.

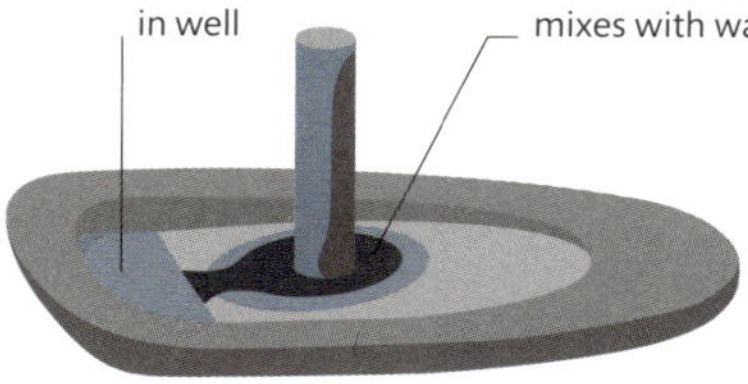

INKSTICK IN INKSTONE

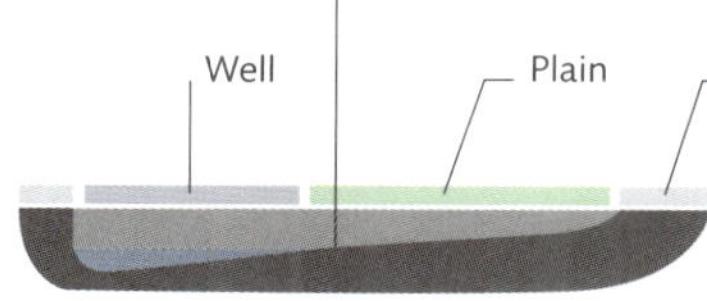

CROSS-SECTION OF INKSTONE

THE OLDEST INK BRUSH DATES FROM 475–221 BCE

WHEN WAS INK FIRST DEVELOPED?
It is thought that the first inks were invented by the Chinese and the Egyptians around the same time—approximately 2,500 BCE.

INK AND SCROLLS
Chinese ink paintings were not always designed to hang on walls; instead, they decorated everyday objects or were painted onto scrolls of silk or paper for private contemplation. These scrolls were read from right to left or top to bottom, or both.

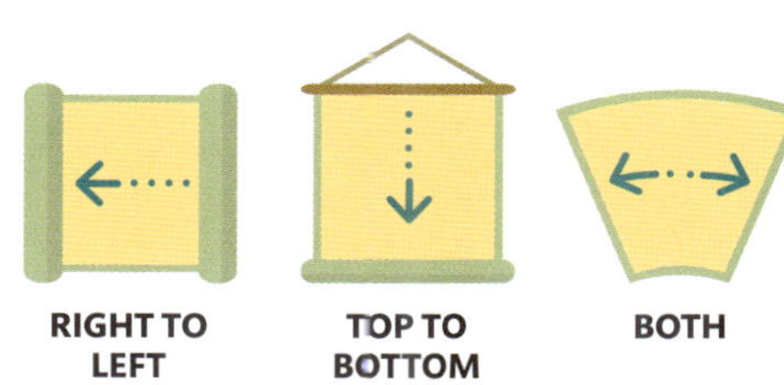

$70 million

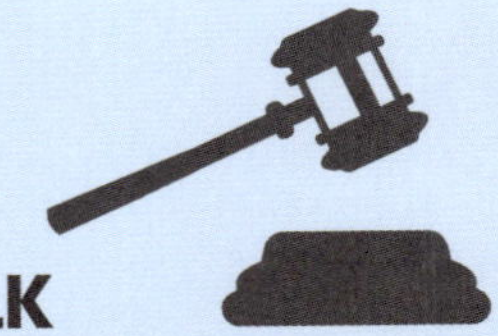

THE AUCTION PRICE IN US DOLLARS FOR A CHALK PAINTING BY CY TWOMBLY SOLD IN 2015

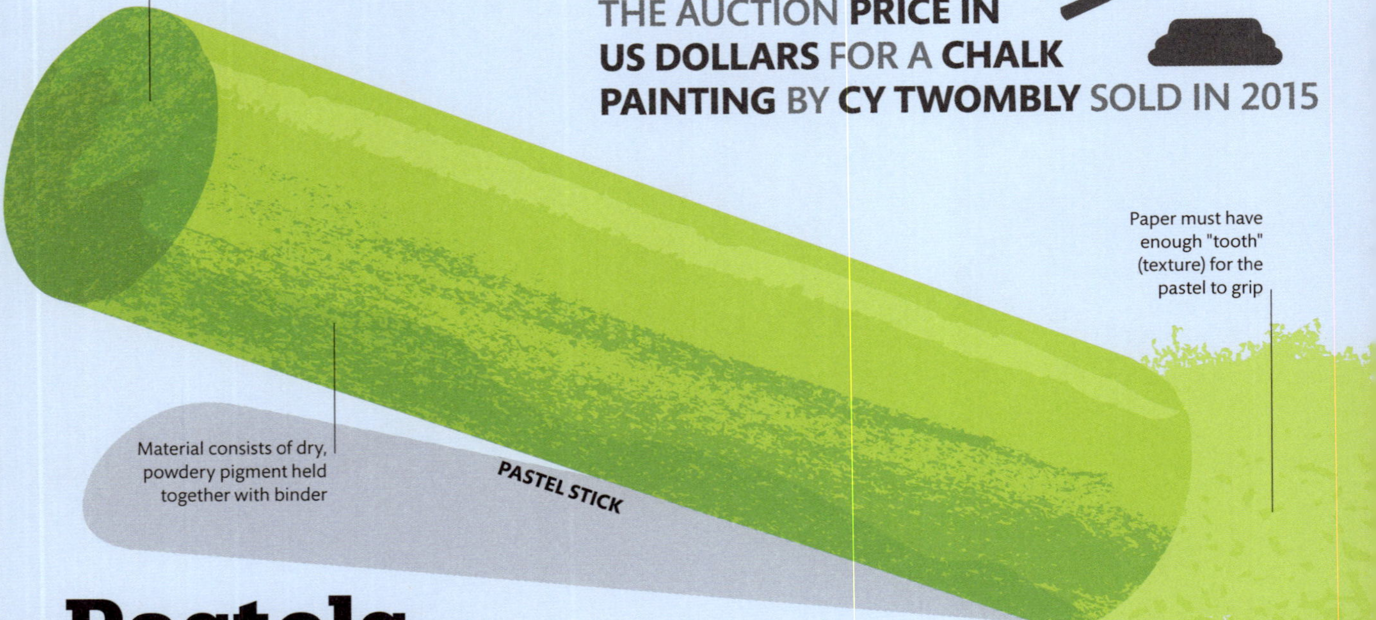

Pastels and Chalks

Chalk has been used to make artwork since Stone Age times, available as a naturally occurring mineral that leaves a crumbly white, red, or black mark. Pastels were developed during the Renaissance period, created by combining colored pigments with gum Arabic and fillers bound together to form a finger-size stick.

Uses and movements

Chalk's ready availability has made it a cheap and accessible drawing material for millennia (see pp.144–45). It was used by Renaissance artists (see pp.176–79) for preliminary studies on paper or vellum (treated animal skin). The colorful pastel became popular in the 1700s, particularly in French portraiture, and later with 19th century Impressionists (see pp.192–93).

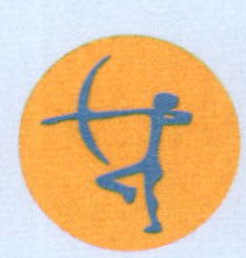

Stone Age
Natural deposits of chalk were abundant, making it a perfect drawing material to create cave art.

Portrait
The soft, saturated colors of pastel were well suited to capturing the skin tones in some 18th-century portraits.

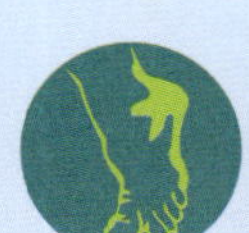

Renaissance
Subtle and erasable, chalk was used by the Renaissance masters to make rapid, working studies of form.

Impressionists
The broad color range and portability of pastels made them a favorite art medium among some Impressionists.

OTHER PASTELS

Named after its inventor, Nicolas-Jacques Conté, the conté crayon is a drawing material commonly used alongside pastels and chalk. Made from colored pigments mixed with graphite and clay, it is harder than both pastel and chalk and allows the user to create more defined, less crumbly lines.

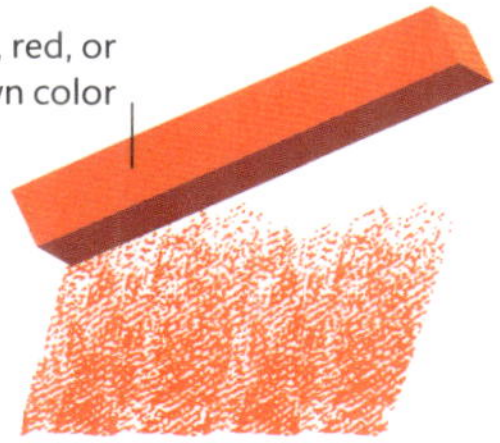

CONTÉ CRAYON

HOW ARE WORKS PROTECTED?

Pastel and chalk drawings can become easily blurred or smudged, which means finished works need to be protected by glass or a glue- or gum-based fixative spray.

Painting in dry color

Both pastels and chalk are quicker to use and easier to transport than paint, while allowing more painterly effects than pencil or charcoal, making them perfect for capturing subjects from life. With techniques such as layering, blending, and crosshatching, they enable the rapid buildup of form to create subtle, yet full-bodied, effects and are a popular medium among beginners and professional artists.

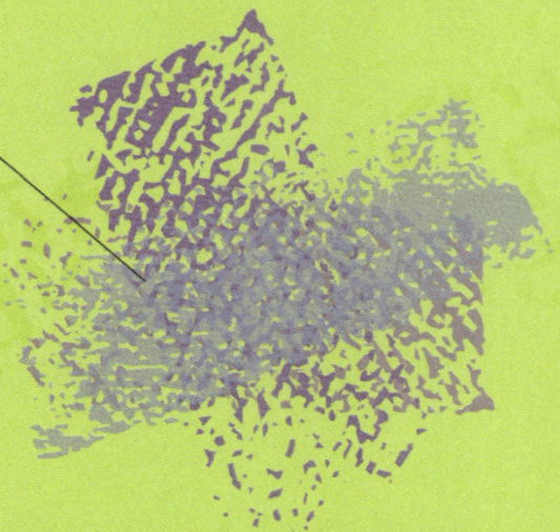

Layering
This technique involves holding the pastel or chalk on its side and dragging it across the drawing surface. It can be repeated using different colors to create a combination of hues that are not completely mixed.

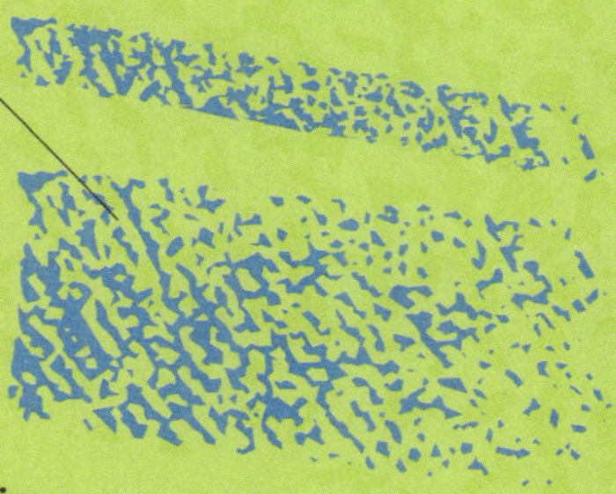

Edge or tip
Thinner, bolder, and more precise lines are achieved using the tip of the chalk or pastel. To cover greater areas of the drawing surface, the long edge of a large block of pigment can be used.

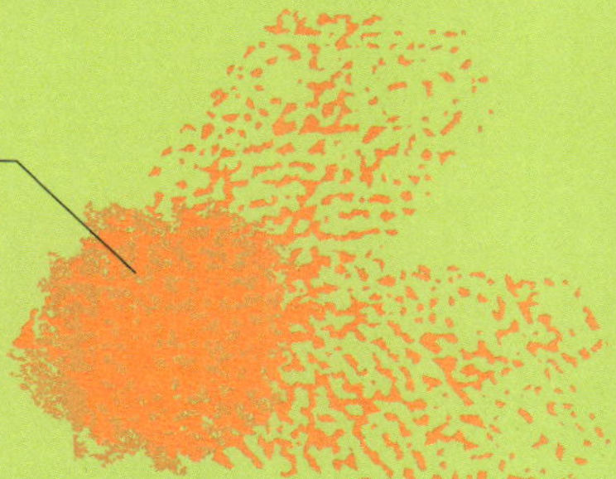

Blending ("sweetening")
This process is similar to layering and is achieved using a fingertip or the edge of the pastel or chalk stick to rub two or more colors together. The technique can create completely new hues.

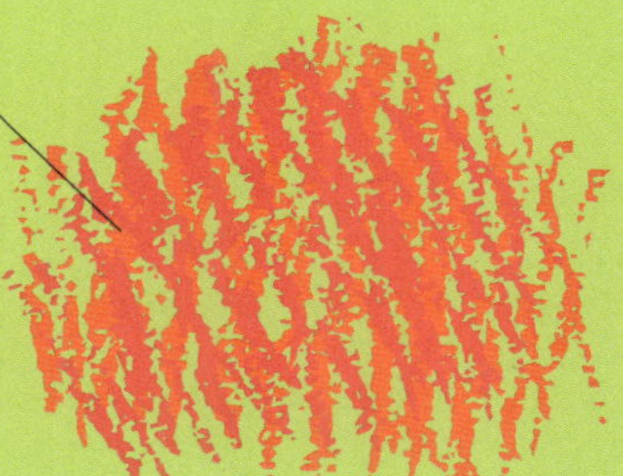

Crosshatching
This technique involves using the tip of the chalk or pastel to form a series of parallel lines (hatching). These lines are overlapped at an angle with other colors to create dense areas of color or shade.

Brushes and blocks

Watercolors can be applied with broad, flat, or fan brushes to create wide washes or with thin, pointed brushes for fine detail. Rougher brushes can be used to create a scratchy, stippled effect.

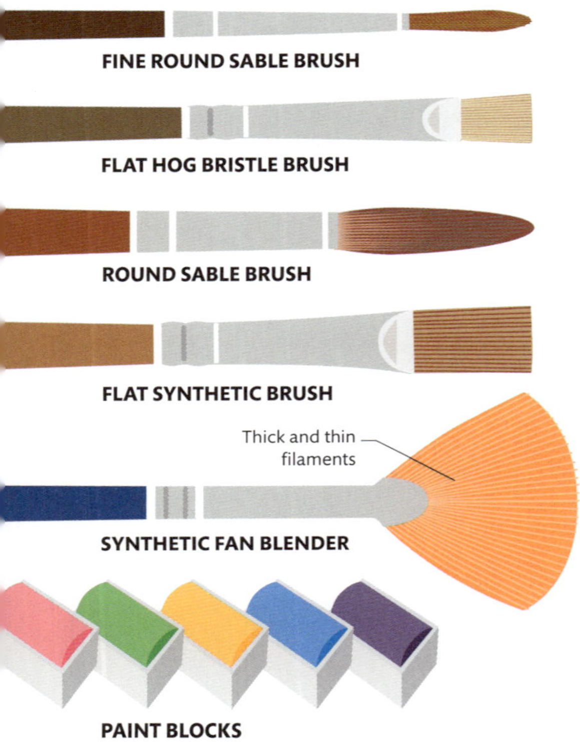

Paint pans
Liquid watercolor paint can be dried, stored in pans, then rewetted. This makes it a useful medium for working outside without the paint drying out.

WHEN DID WATERCOLORS BECOME POPULAR?

Watercolor gained popularity in the 1700s as new, portable equipment meant that artists could work outside their studios.

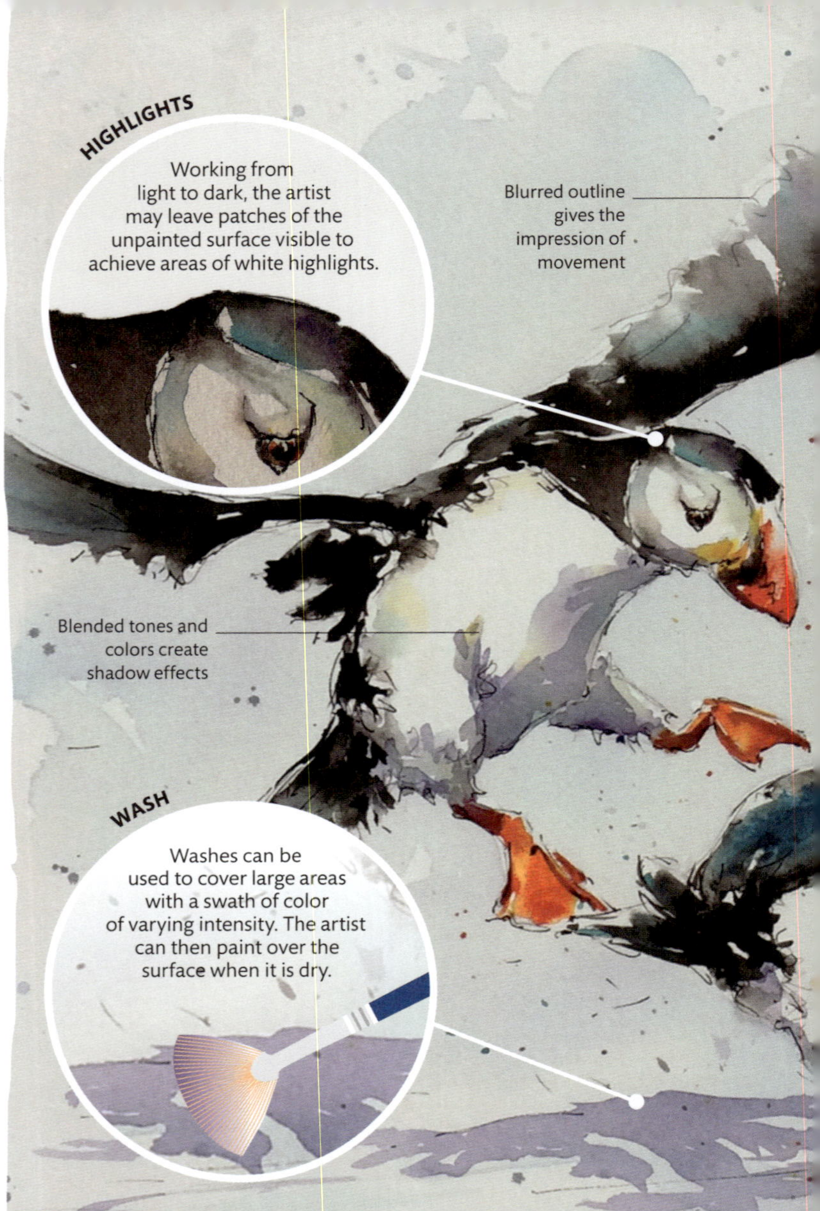

WATERCOLOR PENCILS

Watercolors can also be encased as pencils, combining their fluid versatility with the controlled precision of a drawing tool. They can be used directly on wet surfaces to create blended effects or applied dry, to create defined lines of color that can then be wetted by a brush later.

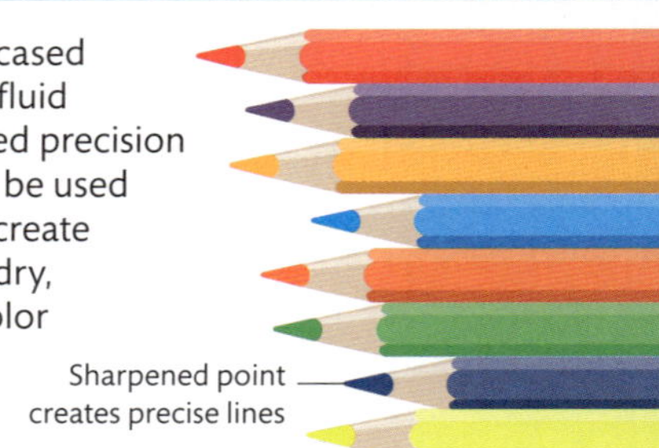

Watercolor

Used since medieval times, watercolor paint's fluid, translucent qualities make it a perfect medium for building up subtle layers of color.

SOME **TRADITIONAL WATERCOLOR** PAINT **RECIPES** CONTAIN **HONEY**

Semitransparent color

Watercolors are created by binding colored pigments with gum arabic, which can then be dissolved in water to create semitransparent paint. Varying levels of color saturation can be achieved by mixing this paint with differing amounts of water to create greater or lesser translucency. Artists apply watercolor paints to absorbent paper containing cotton fibers, preventing distortion when the paint dries. English painter J.M.W. Turner (see pp.188–189) was one of the most prolific watercolor painters, often using the wet-on-wet technique (see below).

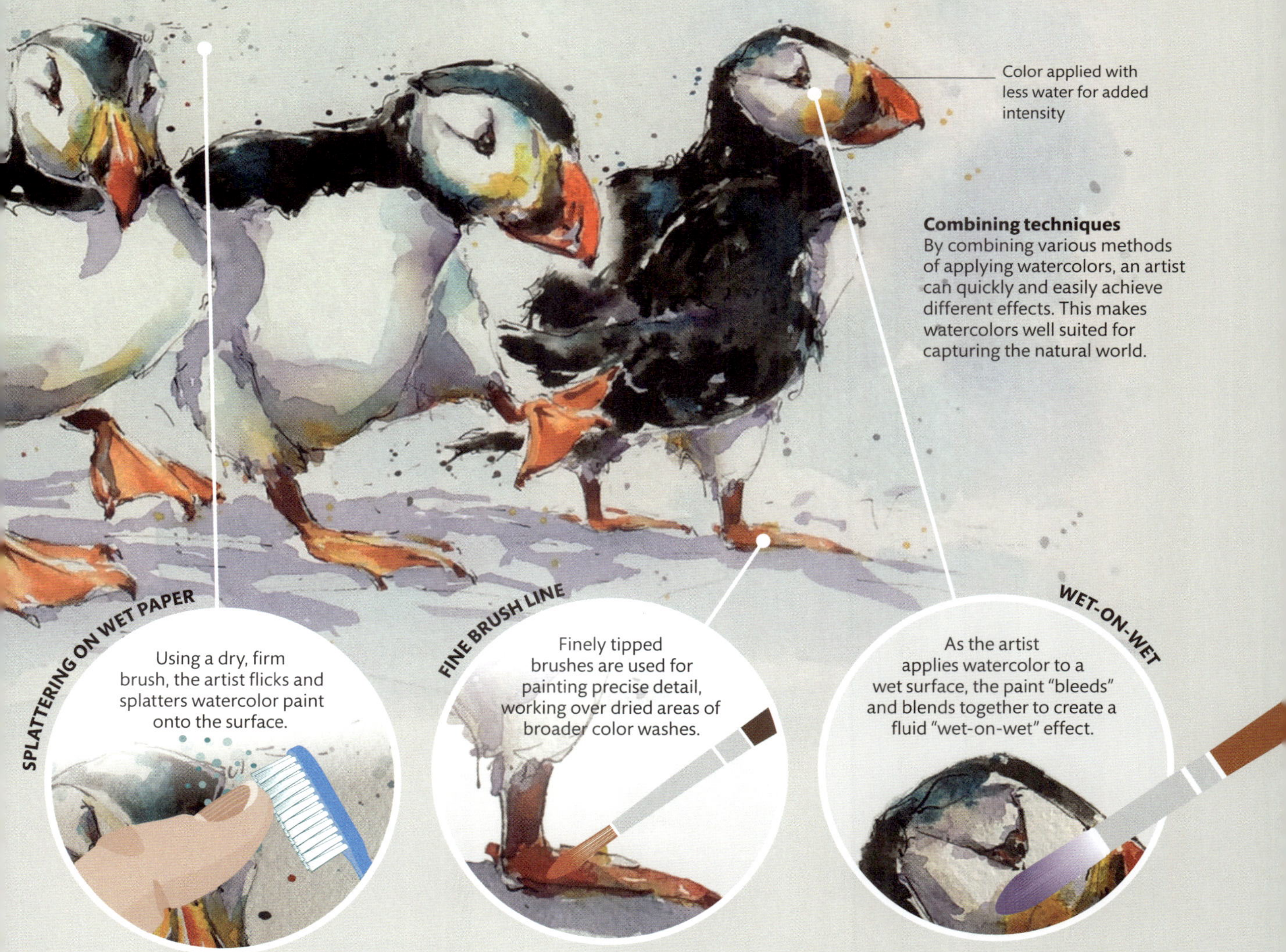

Gouache

Gouache paint is produced by mixing watercolors with white pigment and gum to create a paint that is more opaque than watercolor.

Properties of gouache

The opacity of gouache depends on the amount of water it is mixed with, so it can perform in a similar way to both watercolor and more opaque media such as oils and acrylics. Unlike acrylics, which cannot be reworked once dried, gouache paint can be "reactivated" with water. This versatile paint can be applied with a range of brushes on a variety of surfaces and worked alongside other mixed media.

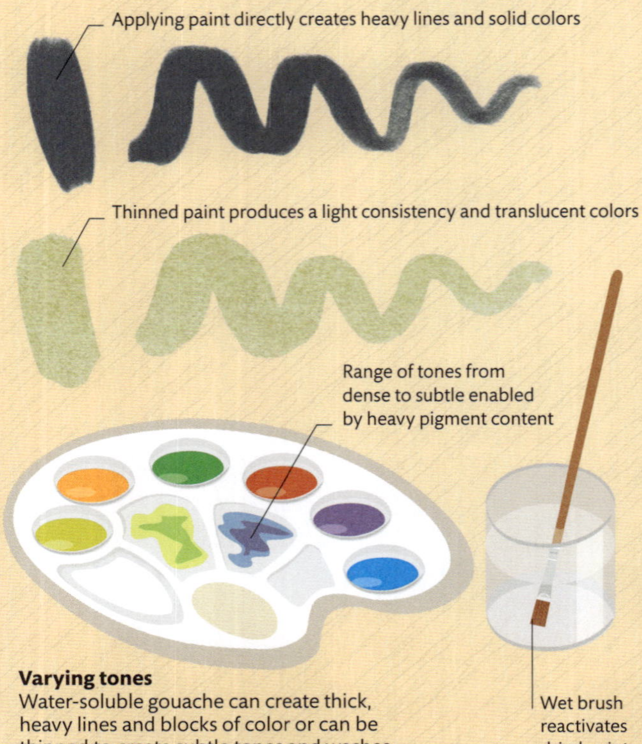

Varying tones
Water-soluble gouache can create thick, heavy lines and blocks of color or can be thinned to create subtle tones and washes that resemble watercolor.

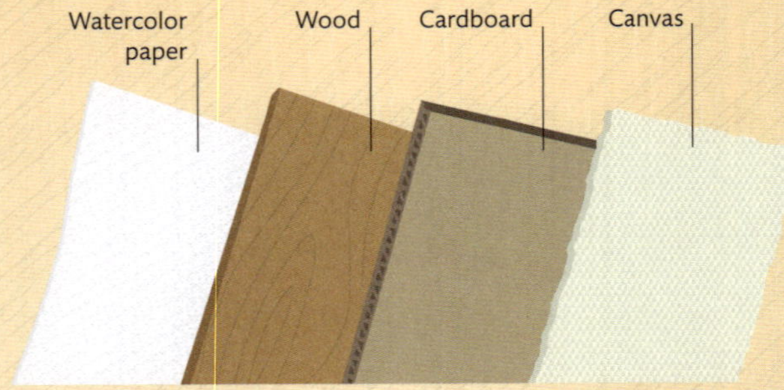

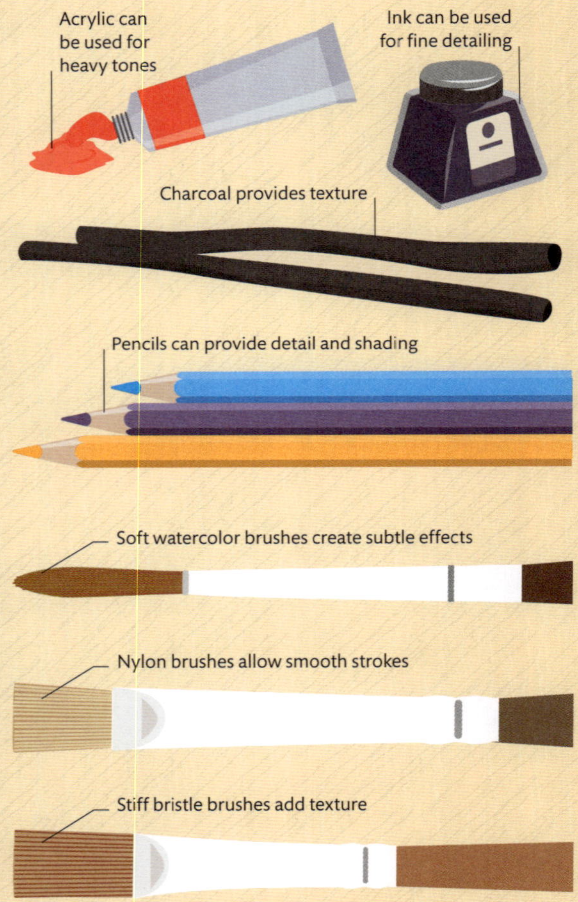

Surfaces, tools, and mixed media
Gouache works well on various surfaces and with a variety of tools. It is a popular paint for use in mixed media art, alongside inks, pencils, charcoal, and other paints.

Techniques

Gouache's versatility allows artists to implement a wider range of techniques than is possible with most other paints on their own. Gouache can be thinned to create watercolor-like washes, but it can also be applied in opaque layers of color like acrylics. With thickened gouache, the color lies on top in a continuous layer, allowing the artist to build up consistent opaque areas.

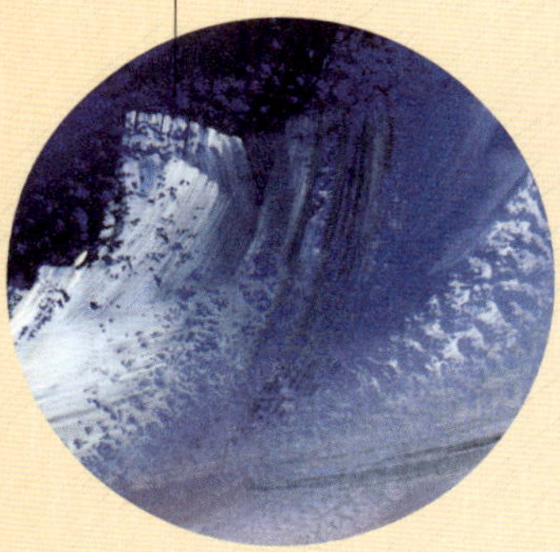

Highlighting
Unlike normal watercolors, gouache can be used to pick out highlights over the top of previous paint layers, once the earlier layers have dried.

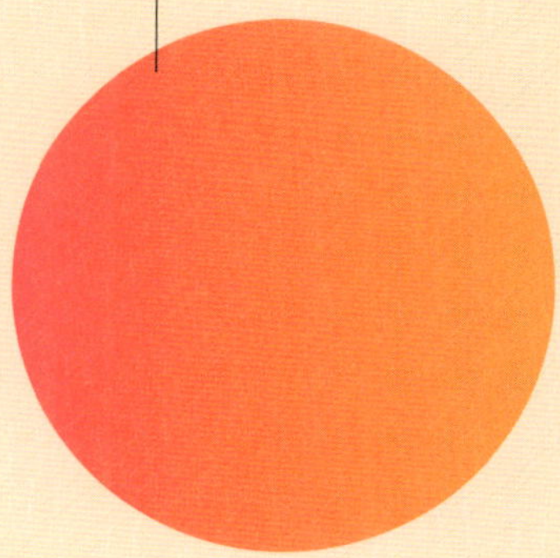

Gradients
Gouache can be thinned with different amounts of water to create gradients of translucency that range from opaque to almost entirely transparent.

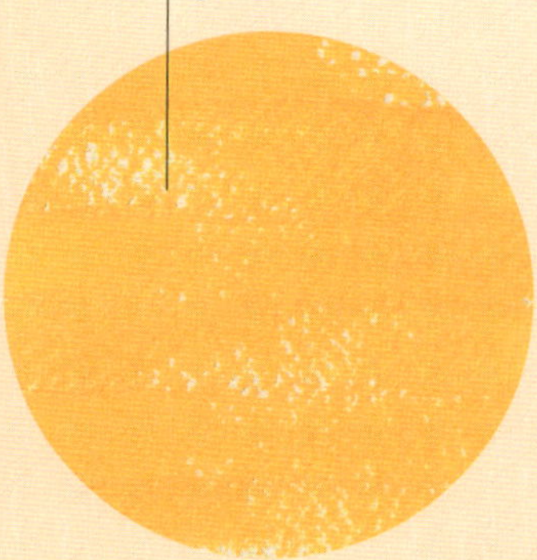

Dry brushing
When a minimal amount of water is used, gouache remains a very thick paint, perfect for dry brushing and building up areas of textured impasto.

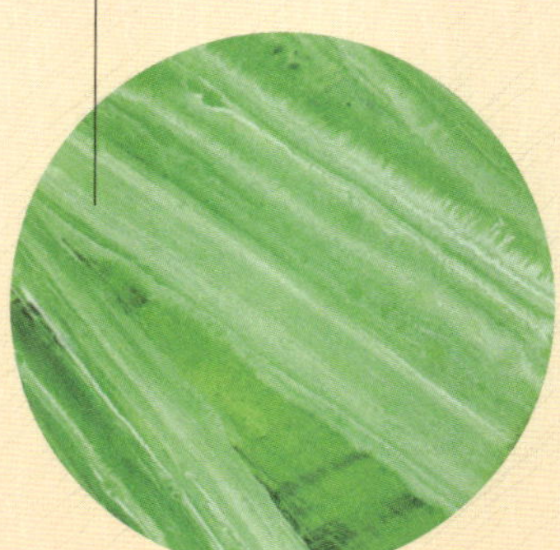

Washes
Once the desired level of translucency is achieved, gouache can be used to cover large areas of a surface, using washes applied with wide brushes.

WHERE DOES THE NAME GOUACHE COME FROM?

The French term gouache, which also used to known as "bodycolor," comes from the Italian word *guazzo*, meaning "puddle" or "pool."

HENRI MATISSE USED GOUACHE TO MAKE HIS FAMOUS CUTOUTS

SCIENTIFIC ILLUSTRATION

The flexibility and transportability of gouache make it a useful material to employ outside of a traditional artist studio. It was particularly favored by artists making scientific illustrations of the natural world, from the 1700s until the present day.

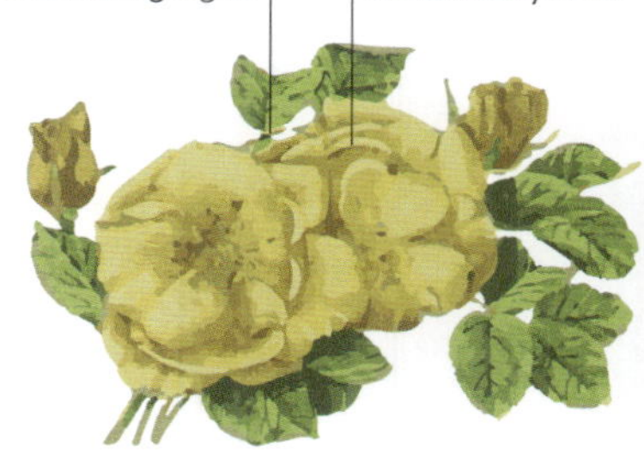

BOTANICAL ILLUSTRATION

A new kind of paint

Acrylic paint is durable, versatile, and, unlike oil paint, can be mixed with water. This gives it a faster drying time, allowing artists to work quickly without having to wait long periods to apply new layers of paint. Acrylics can be used on surfaces not suitable for oils and do not require chemical solvents to thin, making them safer and more convenient. They can also be mixed with additives and gels to achieve different effects.

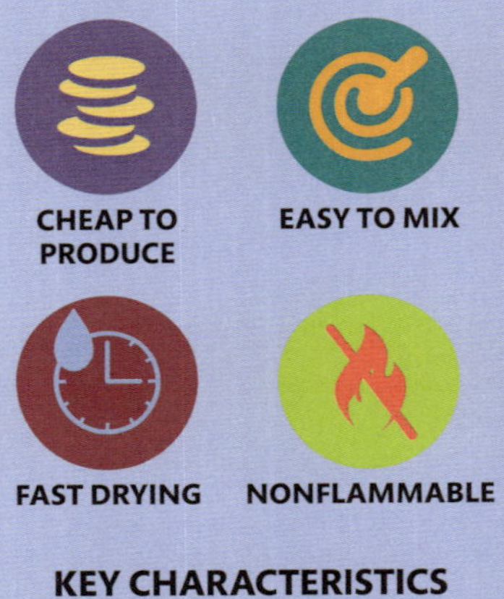

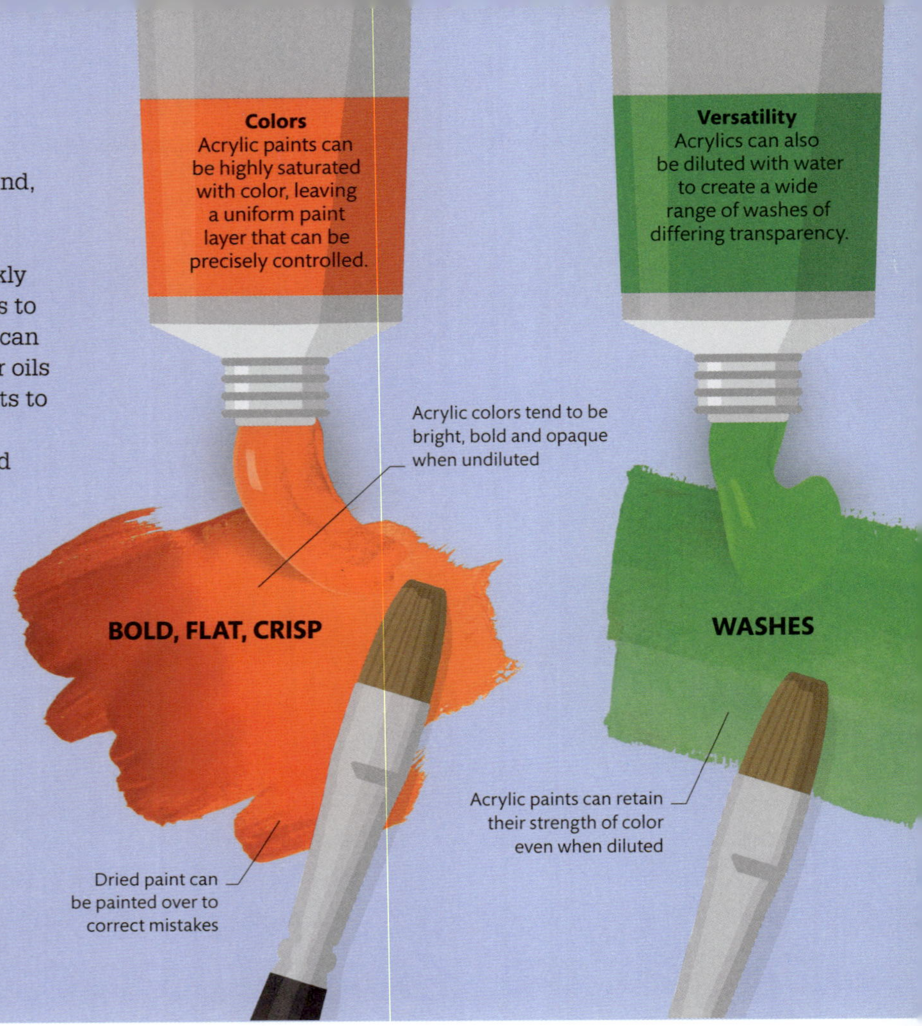

Acrylic Paint

Acrylic paints were developed in the 1940s and 1950s, initially for industrial use. They soon became popular with artists for their bold, flat colors, opacity, and crisp finish, as well as their versatility—they can be diluted to create large, watercolor-like washes or used undiluted like oil paints.

WHO INVENTED ACRYLIC PAINT?

German chemist Otto Röhm was one of the first to develop acrylic emulsions specifically for painting, introducing it commercially in the 1950s.

DAVID HOCKNEY WAS ONE OF THE **EARLIEST ARTISTS** TO USE **ACRYLIC PAINT** EXTENSIVELY

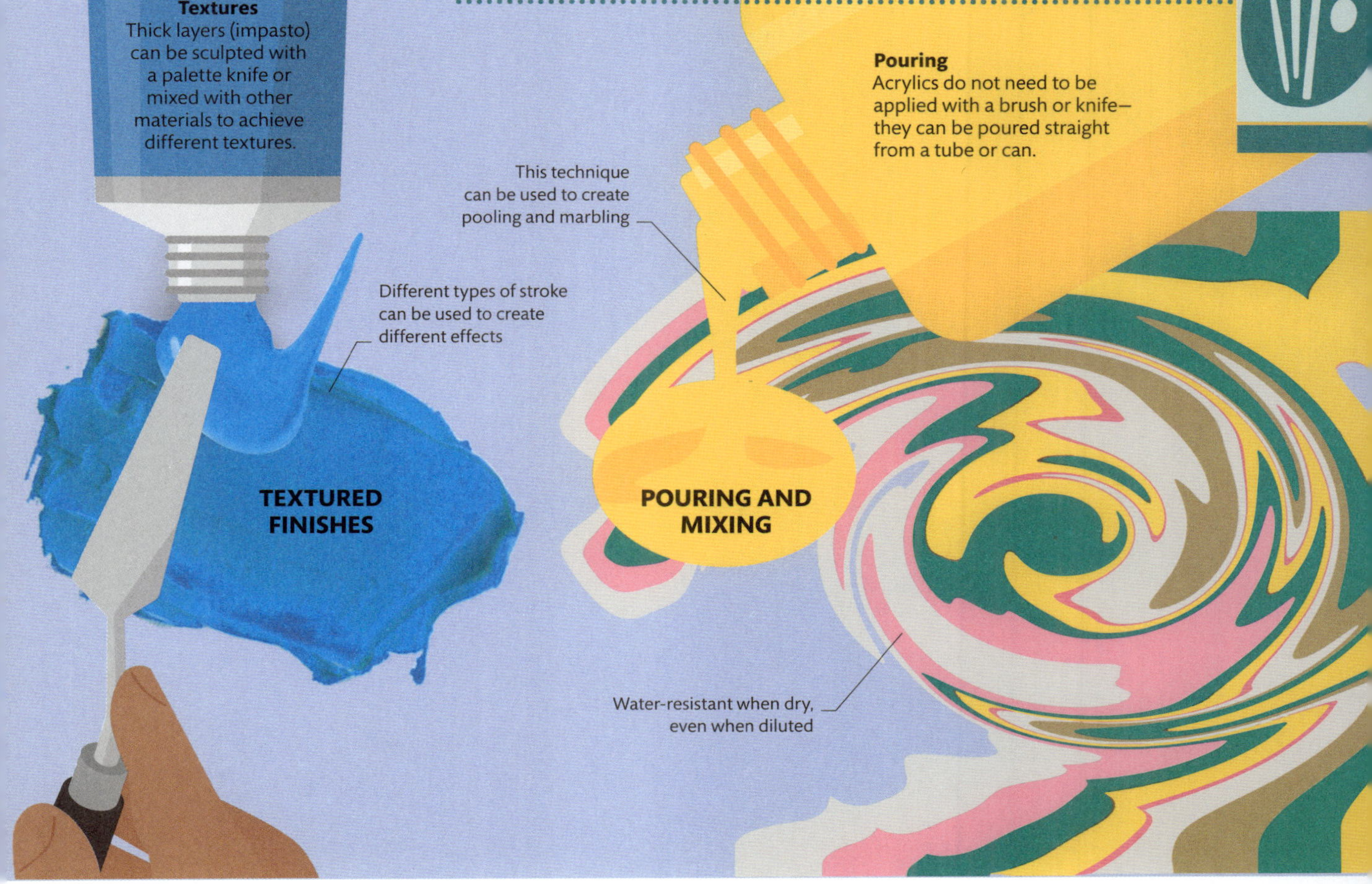

What's in acrylic?

Acrylic paints are made from a synthetic resin derived from acrylic acid, a by-product of gasoline production. The resin is bound with colored pigment to create a paint. Pigments are ground down to very small particles and then are combined with an acrylic polymer binder, both of which are carried in a vehicle (usually water) to create an emulsion. After paint is applied, the vehicle dries and evaporates, leaving a film of binder and pigment on the painting surface.

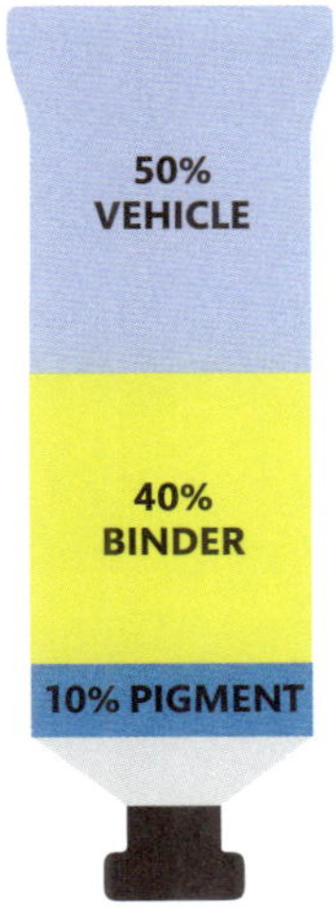

ACRYLIC COMPOSITION

LARGE-SCALE PAINTING

Acrylics are cheaper to produce than oil paints and are more resistant to changes in humidity and temperature. Their affordability and stability make them useful for working on a large scale, allowing 20th-century artists such as Bridget Riley to create striking, immersive paintings several feet in length and height without the surface cracking, as might happen with oils.

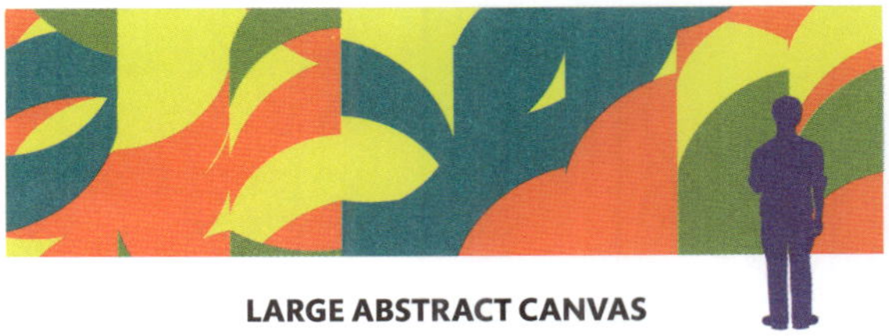

LARGE ABSTRACT CANVAS

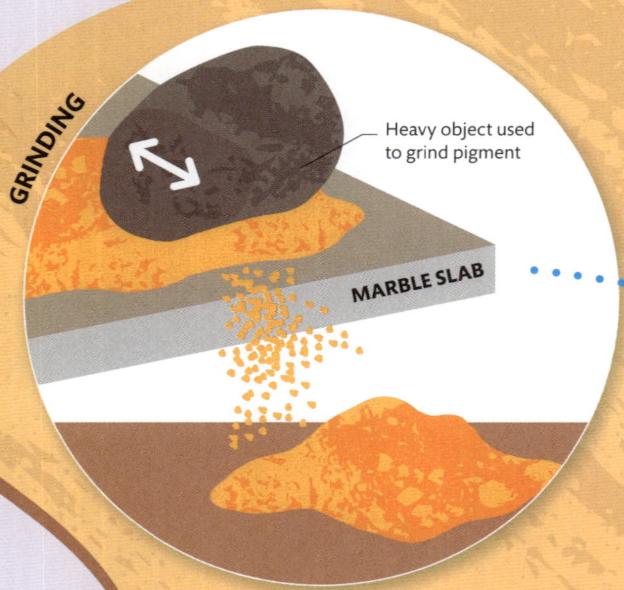

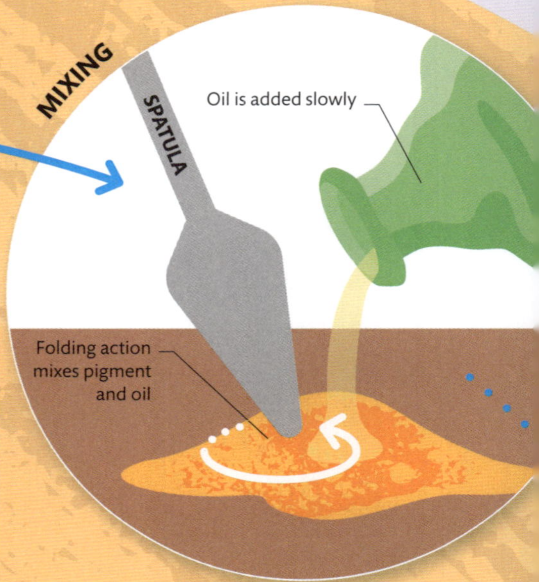

1 Grinding pigment
Historically, the artist would grind the pigments into fine particles on a marble slab; today, a mortar and pestle would be used. They mixed the color pigment with a small amount of oil to create a paste.

2 Paste into paint
The artist added more oil and kept folding with a spatula until the thick, doughy paste became buttery in consistency. In modern times, a flat glass mixing tool called a muller is used.

Paint-making then and now

Oil paints are created by grinding colored pigments and mixing them together with plant oils, such as linseed, poppy, or walnut oil, which are occasionally combined with additional chemical binders to help incerase the paint's stability. Properties such as the thickness, viscosity (fluidity), drying times, and transparency of the paint can be controlled by adjusting the relative amounts of these components.

Oil Paint

Popularized in the Netherlands during the 15th century, oil paints revolutionized painting, becoming the dominant medium in the following centuries. With water-based or egg tempera paints, an artist has to work quickly before they dry; however, the slower drying time of oil paints allows artists to gradually build up a picture in stages.

WHO FIRST MADE OIL PAINTS POPULAR?

Oil paints were pioneered by artist Jan van Eyck in the 15th century. His painting techniques soon spread throughout Europe.

1,470

YEARS: THE AGE OF THE OLDEST KNOWN OIL PAINTINGS DISCOVERED IN CAVES IN AFGHANISTAN

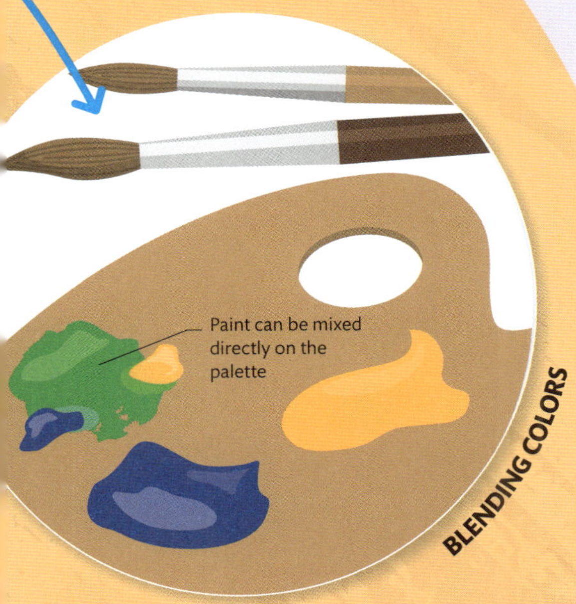

3 Adding colors to the palette The paint could be placed directly onto a palette without it drying out quickly. Alternatively, it was stored in a bag made from pig bladder—or in modern times, in paint tubes.

Techniques

Oil paints can be opaque or transparent, the latter quality allowing the artist to build up different layers of color to luminous effect. The flexibility and slow drying time of oil paint allows artists to represent nature in greater detail than ever before: from creating the effect of dark shadows to capturing the glint of light on metal; and from recreating the soft folds of fabric, to rendering lifelike skin tones.

Fine gradients
By thinning oil paints with a solvent such as turpentine, artists can apply paint in thin glazes to create delicate gradients of color.

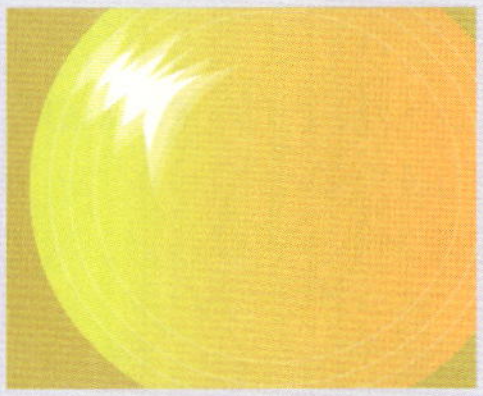

Depicting metal
The versatility of oil paints makes it possible for artists to create, for example, metallic-looking surfaces by adding precise highlights.

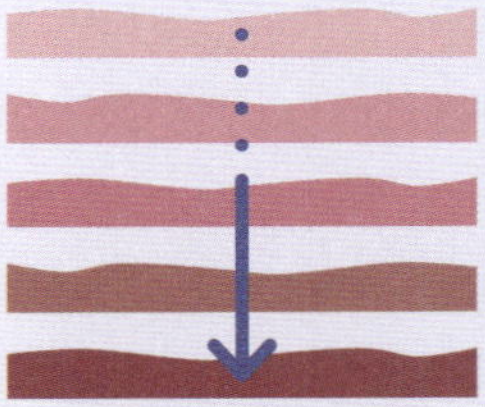

Dark to light
Using oil paints of varying opacity (lack of transparency), artists can build up combined layers of color, usually working from dark to light.

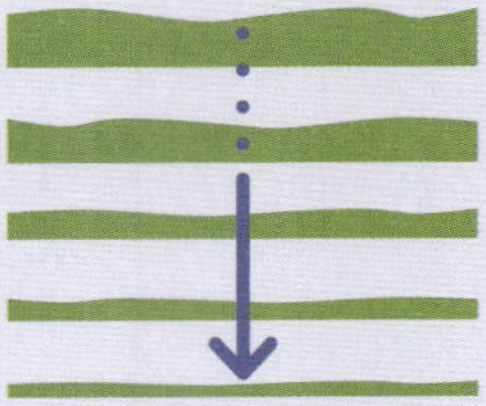

"Fat" over "thin"
As paints with a greater oil content ("fat") dry slower than paints mixed with turpentine ("thin"), artists paint thin layers first, so they dry more quickly.

VASARI ON OIL PAINT

Giorgio Vasari was a 16th-century Italian painter and writer who wrote biographies of many Renaissance artists and painters of the 1500s (see pp.176–179). Vasari compared the oil medium to alchemy that allowed pictures to be mirrorlike with huge amounts of detail.

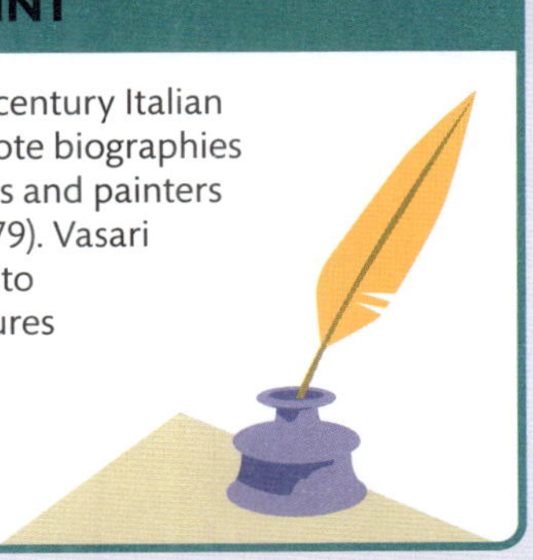

VISUAL ALCHEMY

Egg Tempera

Before the invention of oil paints, egg tempera was one of the most common painting mediums. Relatively simple to make with readily available ingredients, it was used in the ancient civilizations of Mesopotamia and Egypt and was employed in medieval European panel painting and the creation of Byzantine church icons. The 20th century saw a revival of the technique and it is still used today.

WHERE DOES THE WORD "TEMPERA" COME FROM?

Borrowed from Italian, "tempera" originally derives from *distemperare*, the Old Latin word for "soak" or "mix thoroughly."

Speed and detail

Egg tempera is made by mixing egg yolk with water and pigment to create a paint with a very fast drying time. Since it starts to dry rapidly soon after being mixed, it cannot be stored. This means that artists must work quickly but also methodically, applying very small amounts of paint at a time in layers, often using particularly fine brushes. As a result, paintings created in this way can take months to finish. Because of its fragility and tendency to flake, egg tempera requires a strong, inflexible painting surface, most commonly a wood panel, as a support. Artists paint directly onto this, creating a fine film.

CERTAIN EGGS ARE SOMETIMES USED FOR **DIFFERENT COLOURS** AS THEIR YOLKS ARE SAID TO **VARY IN HUE**

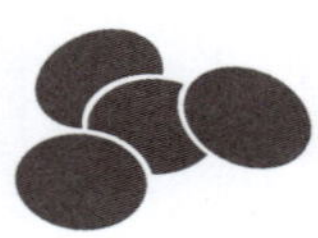

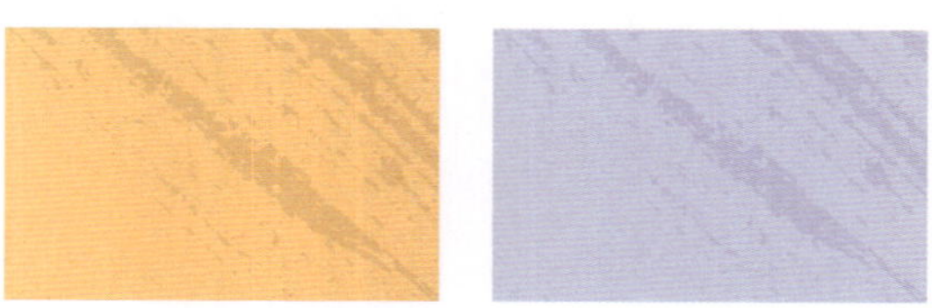

1 Preparing the panel
Purpose-made wood panels are coated with a smooth layer of white gesso (white pigment made from chalk or gypsum mixed with glue). The lightness of the base layer allows subsequently applied colors to retain their brightness and appear luminous.

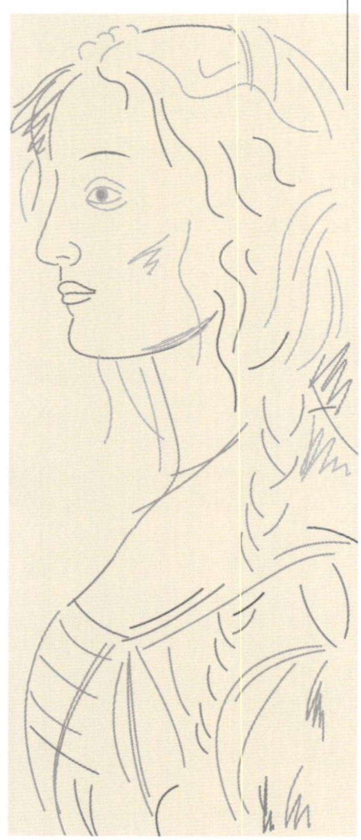

2 Transfer drawing
A transfer in charcoal, graphite or pencil is often necessary to show the artist where to paint, as they need to work quickly before their paint dries out.

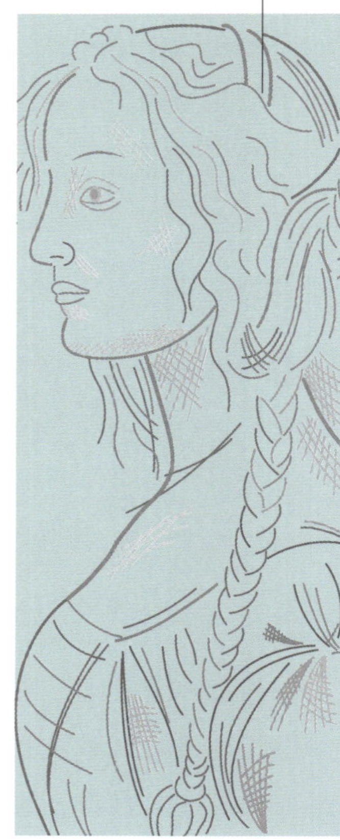

3 Crosshatching
Color can be mixed only on the painting surface by crosshatching in thin layers, so the tempera does not crack once it has dried. This can be very time-consuming for the artist.

ANCIENT METHOD

Egg tempera was used by the Ancient Egyptians (see pp.152–53) to decorate the interior walls of tombs, as well as sarcophagi. They used readily available eggs mixed with naturally occurring pigments, either sourced locally or imported from distant lands.

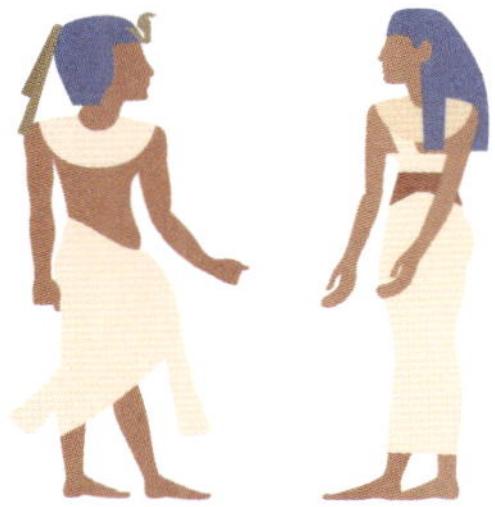

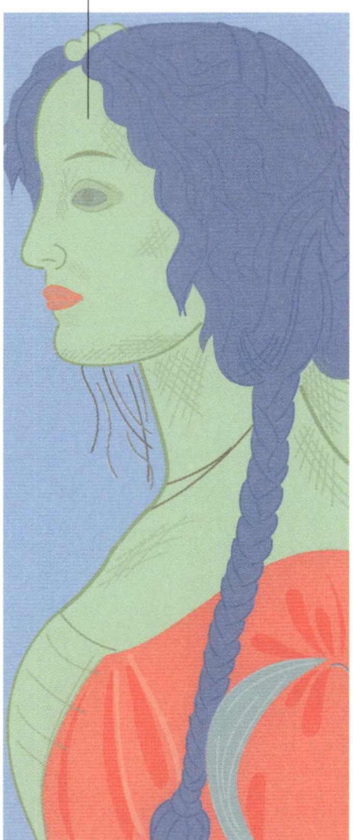

4 Underpainting Underpainting is used to create varying effects, such as a green earth underlayer to create lifelike skin tones. In older paintings, these have often discolored over time (see far left).

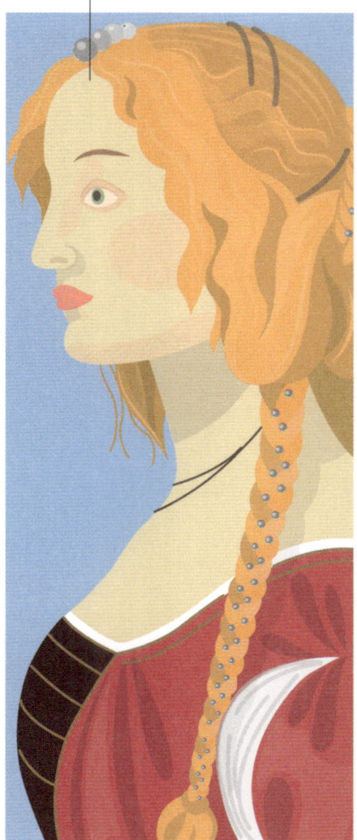

5 Applying final color Once the underpainting has dried, final layers can be applied, the slight translucency of the egg tempera allowing the undercolors to faintly show through.

Egg tempera ingredients and preparation

Egg tempera is made by separating a yolk from its egg white, draining it into a container, and diluting it with water. These elements are then combined with colored pigment to create the finished paint mixture. It must then be used very quickly before it dries, in small quantities at a time. Egg tempera must be prepared freshly before each use and cannot be stored, meaning it is a more process-intensive medium than other forms of paint.

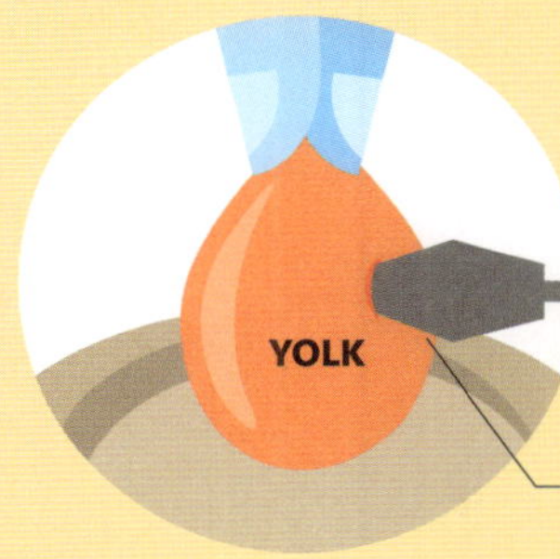

Yolk separated
The artist punctures the egg yolk to release the fluid and discards the membrane.

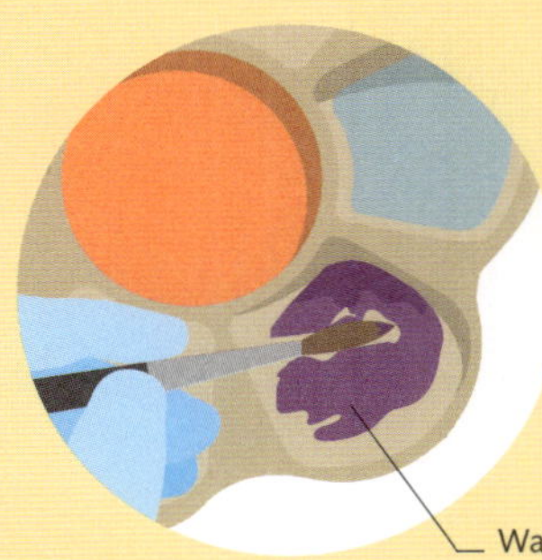

Mixing
Equal parts water, then pigment, are added to the yolk. This is then mixed to the desired consistency.

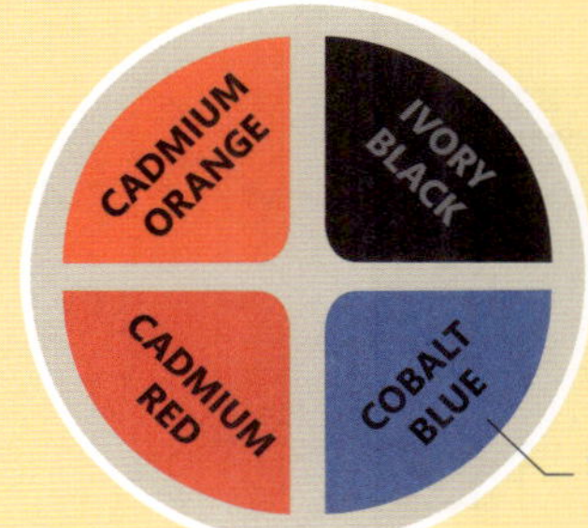

Tempera pigments
Medieval pigments were often highly toxic. Today they tend to be synthetic but still need to be stored carefully.

Sculptural materials

A sculpture can be made from anything that can be shaped in three dimensions. Bronze, wood, marble, and clay are traditional materials, while others such as Jesmonite have only recently come into use.

CLAY

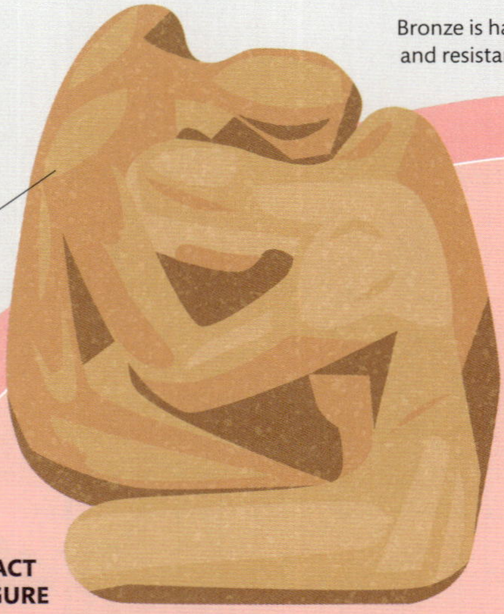

ABSTRACT CLAY FIGURE

Clay can be air-dried or fired in a kiln to make it permanently hard

Shaped by hand
One of the most common and easily available of all sculpture materials, clay is also one of the oldest known. It is very malleable, it's easily shaped by hand, and its surface can support intricate details.

BRONZE

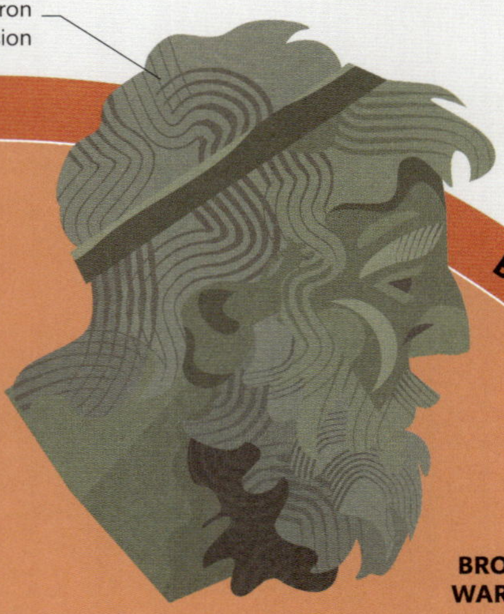

BRONZE WARRIOR

Bronze is harder than iron and resistant to corrosion

Cast for strength
Used as a sculptural material since antiquity, bronze remains popular. Modern bronze is usually 88 percent copper and 12 percent tin. Strong and flexible, it is good for casting figures in action.

MARBLE

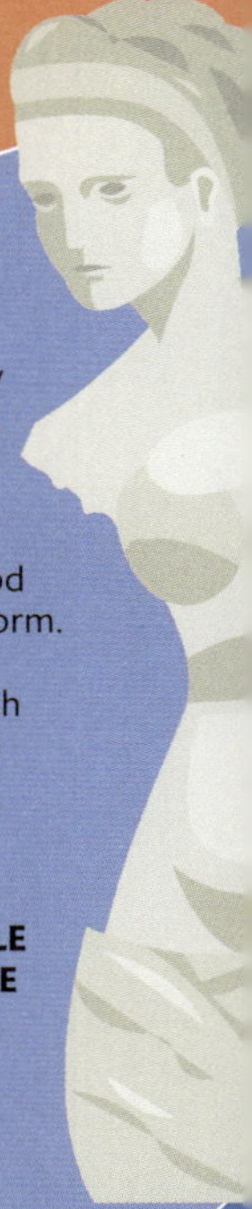

MARBLE STATUE

Classical beauty
Marble has been prized for its beauty since classical times, and its ability to absorb light gives it a translucent quality, making it especially good for sculpting the human form. It is durable and can be carved without too much difficulty, its fine grain making it easier to sculpt detail.

JESMONITE

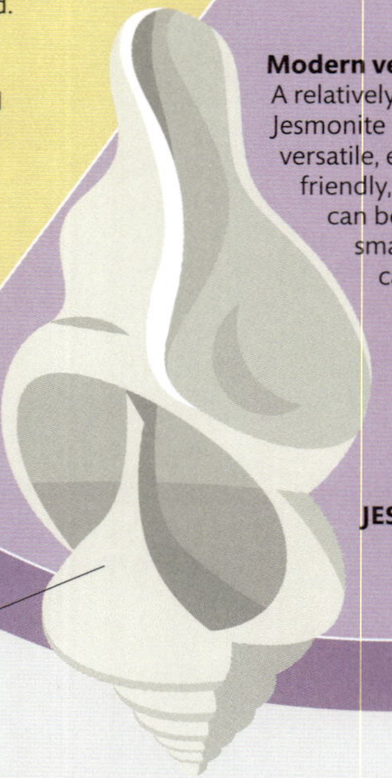

JESMONITE SHELL

Jesmonite is a composite material that was invented in 1984

Modern versatility
A relatively new material, Jesmonite is lightweight, versatile, environmentally friendly, and fire resistant. It can be used to construct both small and large objects and can be dyed with colored pigments or finished so it resembles plaster, stone, metal, and wood.

WOOD

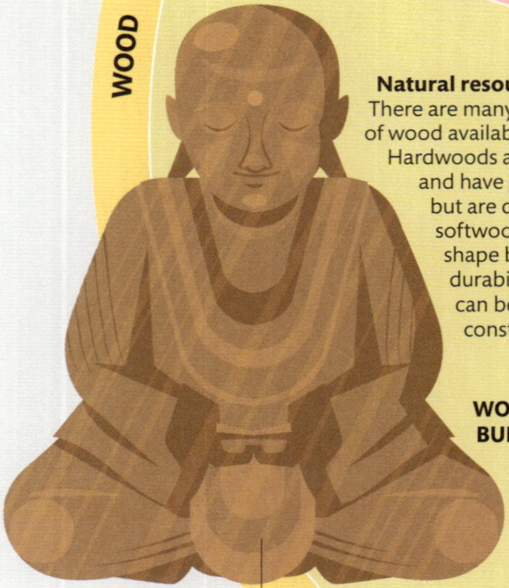

WOODEN BUDDHA

Wood is an anisotropic material, which means its properties depend on the direction of the grain

Natural resource
There are many different types of wood available for sculpting. Hardwoods are more durable and have greater luster but are difficult to carve; softwoods are easier to shape but have less durability. Wood can be carved or constructed.

Sculpture Basics

Sculpture is a three-dimensional art form made by carving, casting, modeling, or constructing hard or soft materials. A huge variety of media can be used to make sculpture, from the traditional marble, bronze, and clay to wax, fabric, and even "found objects." It is one of the oldest forms of visual art and also one of the most publicly visible.

Flexible forms

Sculptures are traditionally freestanding objects in space or reliefs that protrude outward from a background. However, contemporary sculptors now have an almost total freedom in materials and techniques. The type of material used will determine what process the work goes through; its location—indoors or outdoors—will also have a bearing on the materials used, as some are more durable than others. Colors can be natural or applied, and the final shape can take almost any form—from microscopic forms on top of a pin to ephemeral ice sculptures.

WHAT ARE FOUND OBJECTS?

From the French term "objet trouvé," or found art, found objects are usually repurposed, ordinary, everyday items that artists decide are art.

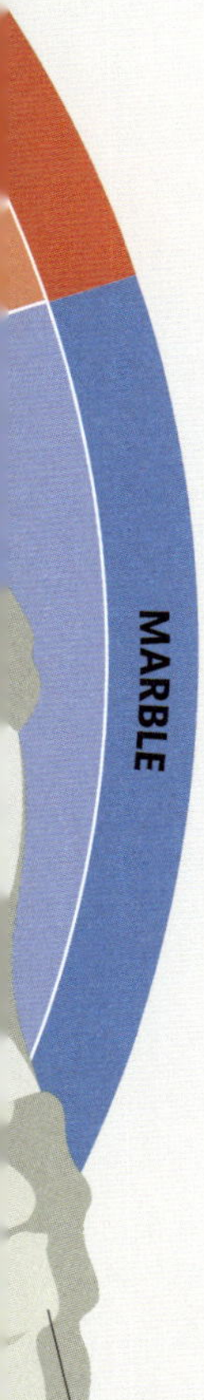

Finished marble sculptures can be polished to highlight patterns in the stone

A sculptural story

The earliest three-dimensional figurines date back to the Stone Age, with traditions of casting and carving emerging from the ancient Mediterranean civilizations. The depiction of the human form was a constant in Western art, and many sculptural masterpieces were created. In the 20th century, artists moved away from naturalism in favor of abstract shapes.

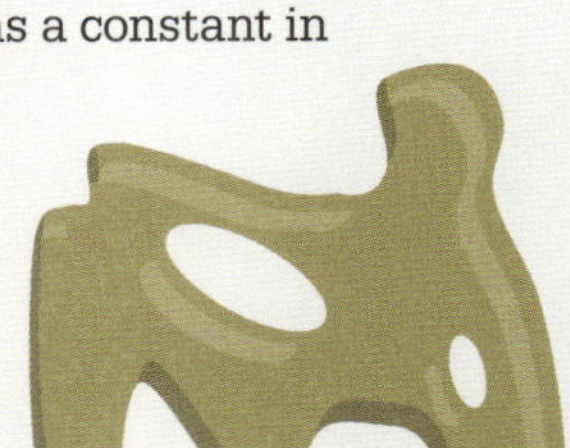

ABSTRACT SCULPTURE

THE **SMALLEST SCULPTURE** IN THE **WORLD** IS A CARVING OF AN EMBRYO **78 MICRONS TALL** AND **53 MICRONS WIDE,** MADE BY **WILLARD WIGAN**

RELIEF SCULPTURE

A relief is a sculpture of varying levels that projects from a background surface. High relief has a degree of definition that is almost three-dimensional; bas-relief has a relatively shallow projection and extends only slightly from the base.

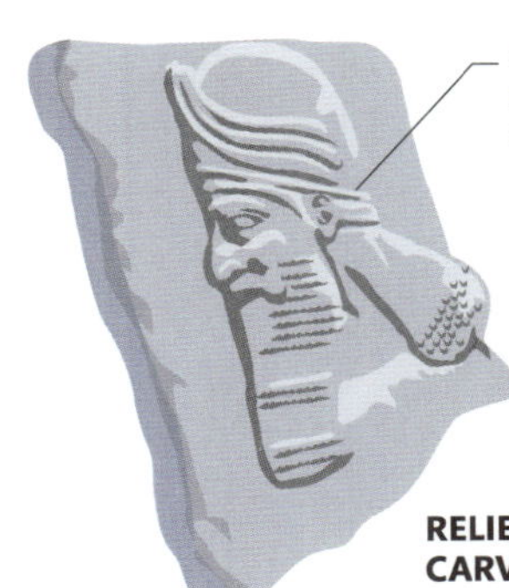

RELIEF CARVING

Sculpture Techniques

Sculptors may use one of two types of process: subtractive, where material is removed, or additive, where material is added. Casting, modeling, and carving are some of the most common techniques.

Casting

An additive process, casting involves pouring a liquid material such as plastic, molten metal, rubber, or fiberglass into a mold and allowing it to harden. The finished, solid form is the "cast." Flexible molds of rubber or silicone can be used more than once, so multiple impressions or "editions" of the same artwork can be made. The artist begins by shaping a model or "pattern" of the final piece in clay, wax, or plaster, which is then used to create a mold to cast from.

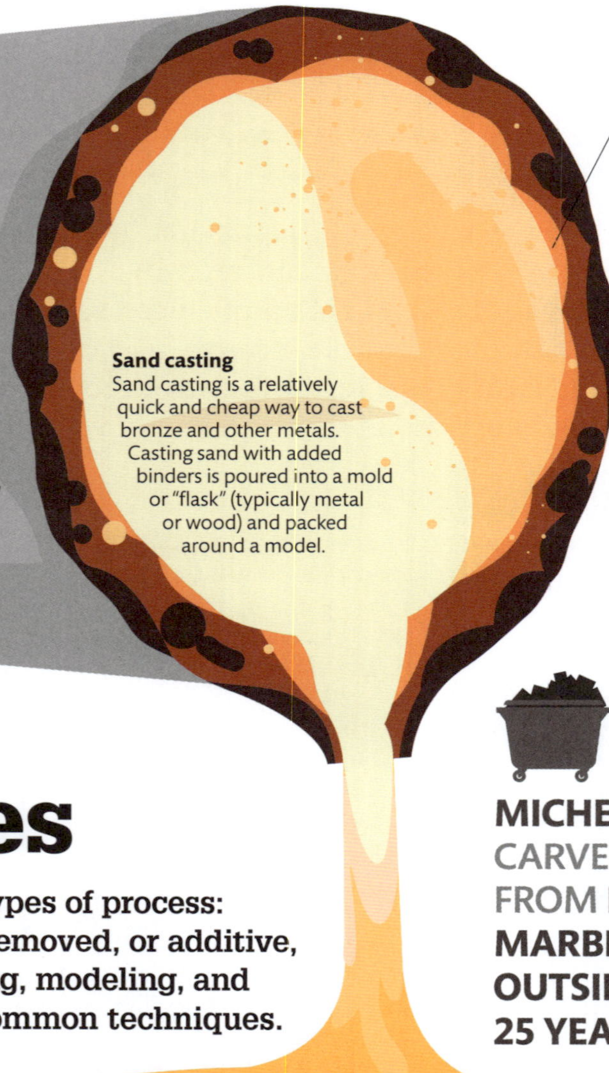

Sand casting
Sand casting is a relatively quick and cheap way to cast bronze and other metals. Casting sand with added binders is poured into a mold or "flask" (typically metal or wood) and packed around a model.

MICHELANGELO CARVED "DAVID" FROM REJECTED MARBLE, LEFT OUTSIDE FOR 25 YEARS

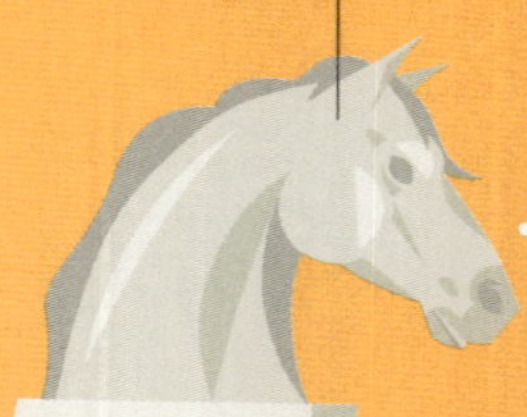

1 Cast model
The artist starts the process by making a replica of the finished artwork. The model needs to be slightly bigger to account for any shrinkage that occurs during the casting.

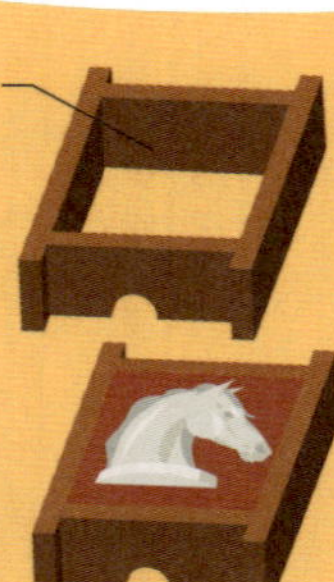

2 Making the sand mold
Casting sand is packed into one half of the flask, the model is laid on top, and more sand is packed around it. The two halves are joined and more sand added to fill.

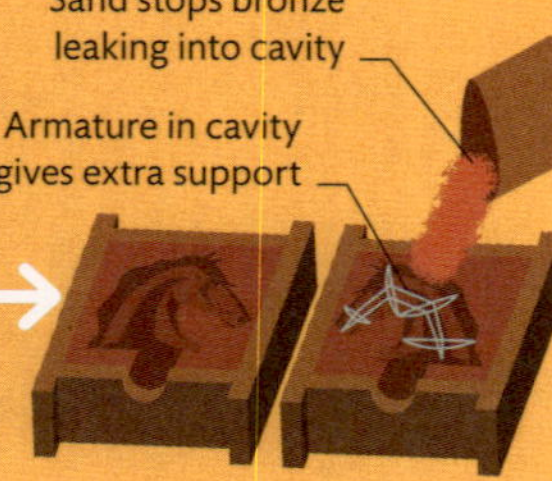

3 Finishing the mold
The flask is rotated and split, and the model is removed, leaving a negative mark from which a positive can form. An armature is fitted, draining channels are cut, and more sand added.

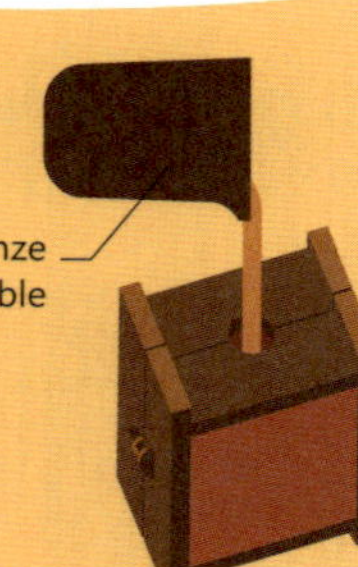

4 Pouring in the bronze
The two halves of the flask are reassembled and tightened up with threaded metal bars. Molten bronze is poured into the mold cavity and left to set.

Modeling

Modeling is an additive process in which a soft material such as clay or wax is worked by hand into the desired shape. Soft materials are pliable, so models can be altered and reshaped many times before they harden. Although not as permanent as wood or stone, models can be reproduced in metal by casting, or in stone by pointing (transposing measurements from the model's surface to a copy).

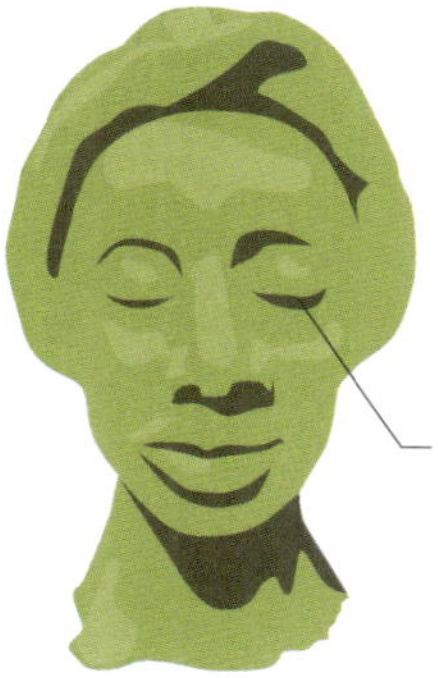

Clay modeling
Many clay models have an inner frame or armature that acts as a support. The clay is then gradually built up around it to form shape and detail.

WHAT IS ASSEMBLAGE?

Assemblage is sculpture made from elements such as everyday items, found objects, or scrap materials. It originates from Pablo Picasso's Cubist creations of 1912.

Carving

Carving is the act of chipping or cutting away at a shape from a block of stone, wood, or other hard material. It is a subtractive process, which means the block is progressively whittled down from the outside in. Large portions are knocked off first during the "roughing out" stage, and the excess is removed gradually and evenly. Some artists carve directly onto the material, without a model; others build a small maquette (see below) and transpose the form over using calipers. Once the approximate shape has been determined, the form is then refined using special tools to create details, before being polished.

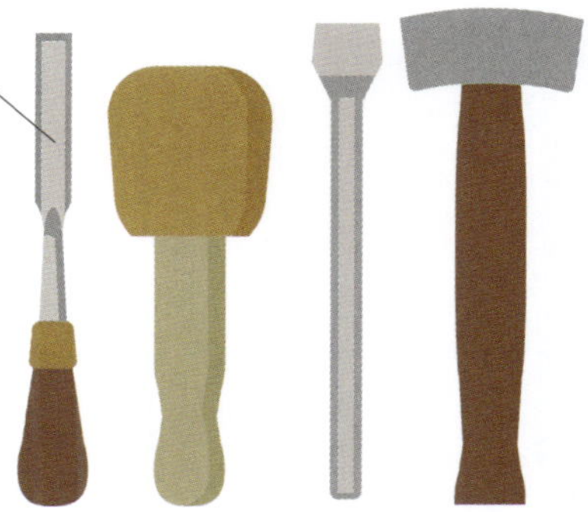

Carving tools
These vary depending on the material being carved. Flat chisels and hammers are needed to carve stone; for wood, mallets and chisels are used.

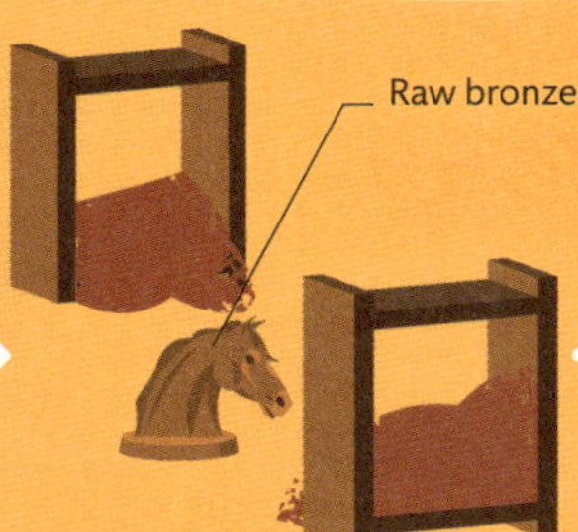

5 Fettling the bronze
Once the bronze is cold, the flask is taken apart and the sculpture is taken out. It then needs to be "fettled" (channels sawn off, any pits filled in, flaws made good, and cleaned up).

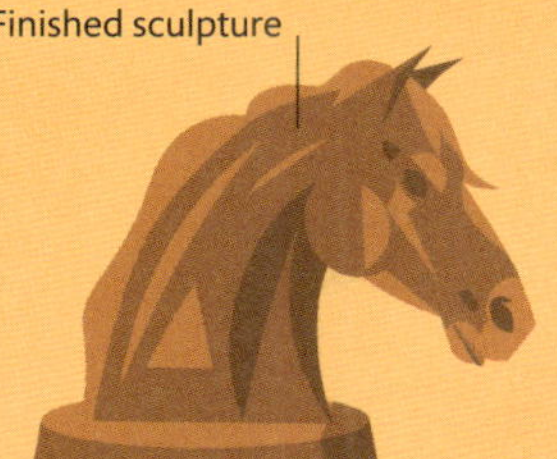

6 Patinating and polishing
Chemicals are painted onto the sculpture and bonded with heat to achieve the desired color. Once cooled, wax is applied and the sculpture is polished.

MAQUETTES

Artists often make three-dimensional sketches called maquettes before starting a larger piece of work. These serve as a way of figuring out different ideas and materials and allow the artist to visualize the final design.

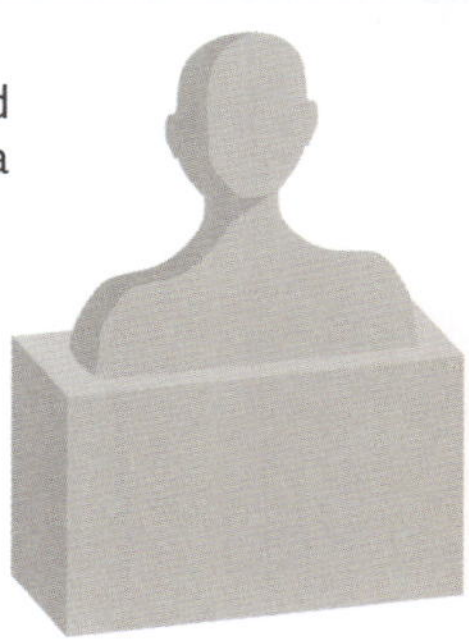

Different strokes

Various tools are required for cutting away at the woodblock. For bigger, empty areas, a large chisel with a straight edge is most efficient. Gouges work well for incising lines and for quickly removing wood, and tiny knives are useful for intricate details. Some printmakers prefer the feathery texture of the carved areas to show on the final print.

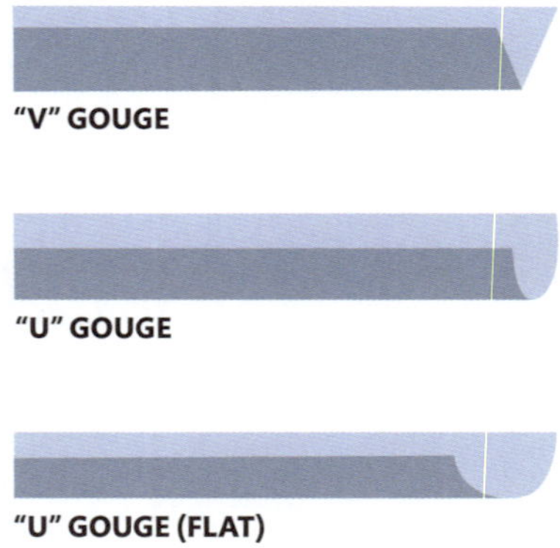

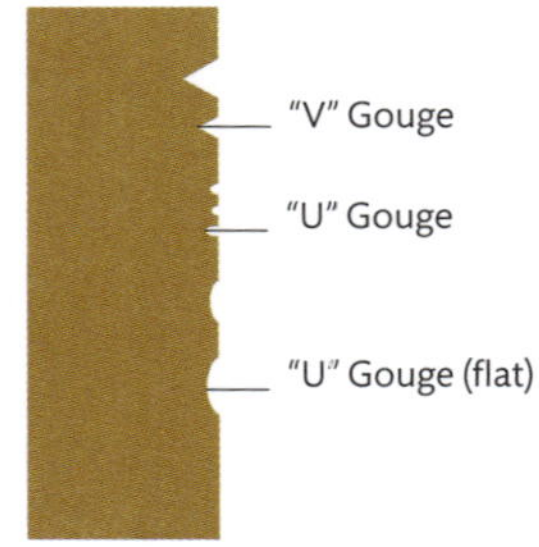

Carving lines
"V" gouges make precise lines; "U" gouges make broader lines; and flat "U" gouges carve out big areas.

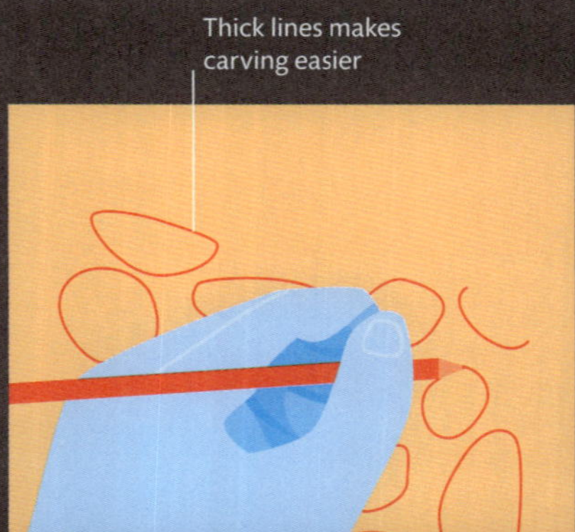

1 Transposing the image
The printmaker either draws the design directly onto the block or transfers it by tracing it onto the block using a sheet of carbon paper.

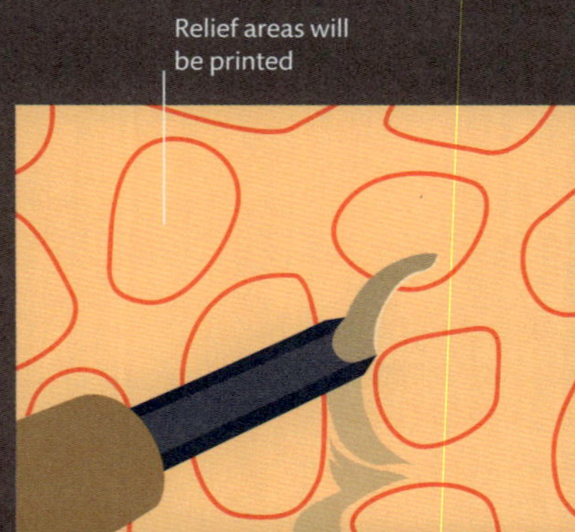

2 Carving away
Areas that will be blank on the final image are carved away with a gouge and other finer tools for more intricate details. These are the areas that will not be inked.

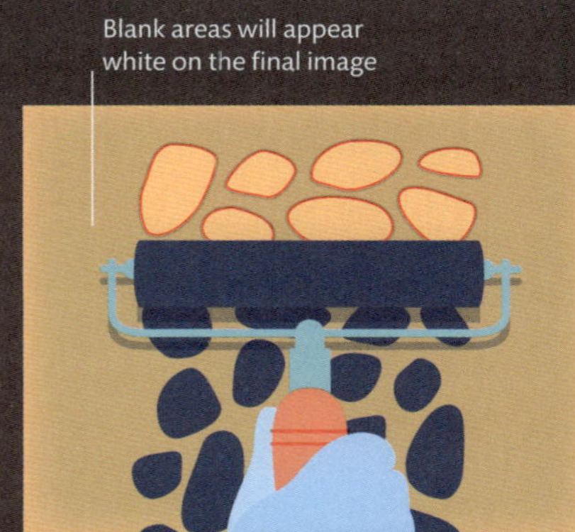

3 Inking up
The printmaker brushes away any excess shavings with a stiff brush and applies ink onto the relief areas of the block using a roller that is evenly covered with printing ink.

Woodcuts

The oldest known form of printing, woodcut prints are made by carving a wooden block (known as the "matrix") to create a raised image. This is then placed in a printing press with a sheet of paper, and pressure is applied.

Using the grain

Woodcut printing is an art of relief and reversal. Unlike etching or lithography, the image to be printed "stands up" on the matrix, and the final image will be the reverse of the design as it appears on the block. Woodcut prints show the interaction between mark making and the grain of the wood block, often exploiting this as a stylistic feature. It was used to produce images for early books, and as it is relatively cheap, quick, and durable, it played a vital role in the proliferation of illustrated newspapers in the 19th century.

Colourful depictions

Ukiyo-e are woodcut prints that were produced in Japan during the Edo and Meiji periods (1615–1912), depicting life in the racy inner cities during a period of peace and prosperity. In 1765, printers perfected a technique of using multiple woodblocks to layer colours, creating vibrant images that were cheap to reproduce (see pp.168–169). The print market burgeoned alongside domestic tourism, and Ukiyo-e prints went on to have a great influence outside Japan, including in Art Nouveau (see pp.200–201).

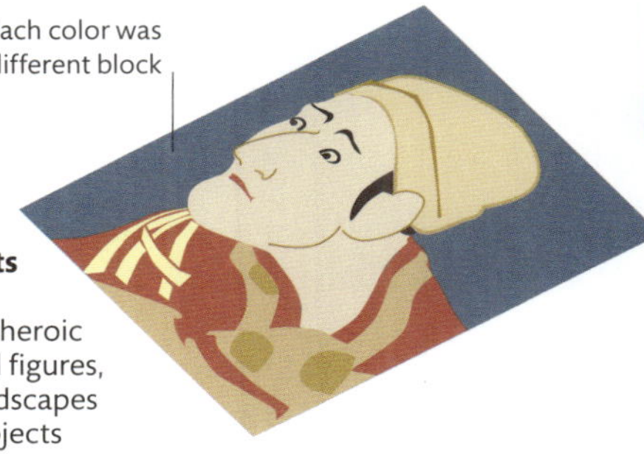

Multiple subjects
Images of actors, romantic scenes, heroic and mythological figures, and dramatic landscapes were popular subjects for Ukiyo-e.

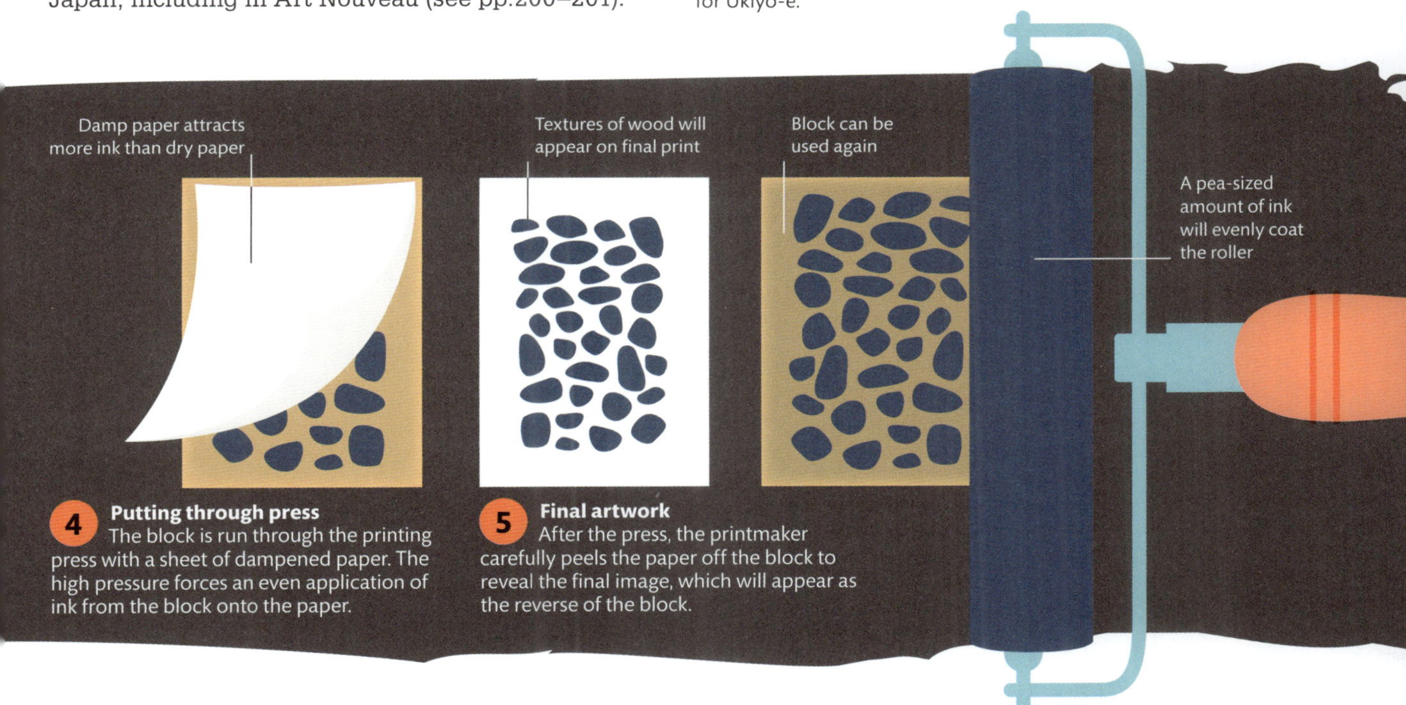

4 Putting through press
The block is run through the printing press with a sheet of dampened paper. The high pressure forces an even application of ink from the block onto the paper.

5 Final artwork
After the press, the printmaker carefully peels the paper off the block to reveal the final image, which will appear as the reverse of the block.

WHICH TYPES OF WOOD MAKE THE BEST BLOCKS?

Historically, hard fruit woods have been popular with printmakers: pear, cherry, and apple all allow for detailing, because of their fine grain.

AN **ALBRECHT DÜRER WOODBLOCK** WAS STILL BEING USED **100 YEARS** AFTER IT WAS FIRST **CARVED**

LINOCUTS

Similar to woodcuts, linocuts use a layer of linoleum in place of a wooden block. The artist carves into the lino to create a relief print, and as the lino is more flexible than wood, and does not have a grain, the results are sharper and less textured than woodcuts.

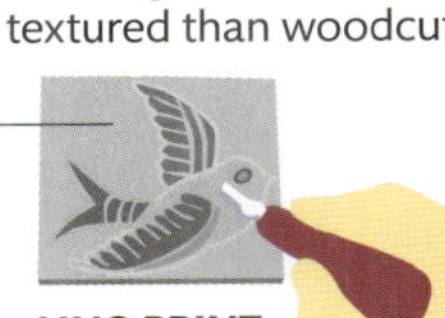

LINO PRINT

Etching

Etching is the most widespread "intaglio" process. Intaglio is a form of printmaking that involves carving an image into a metal plate, applying ink, and printing the plate under pressure. Other processes include engraving, drypoint, and aquatint.

WHO MADE THE FIRST ETCHING PRINTS?

In 1513, an artist from Switzerland named Urs Graf made the first known etched prints, using iron plates.

Metal plates

Etching first developed out of metalwork and decorative design on suits of armor in the 15th century. The process uses acid to incise or "bite" an image into a metal plate, which is then inked up and the surface cleaned, leaving the remaining ink in the depressed grooves. Unlike relief printing, which works by printing from raised areas, etchings can have very subtle tones, depending on how heavily the plate is inked.

Force of the press
Etching requires a roller press, which can exert tons of pressure. This creates a "plate mark," an outline of the plate on the paper, on the final image.

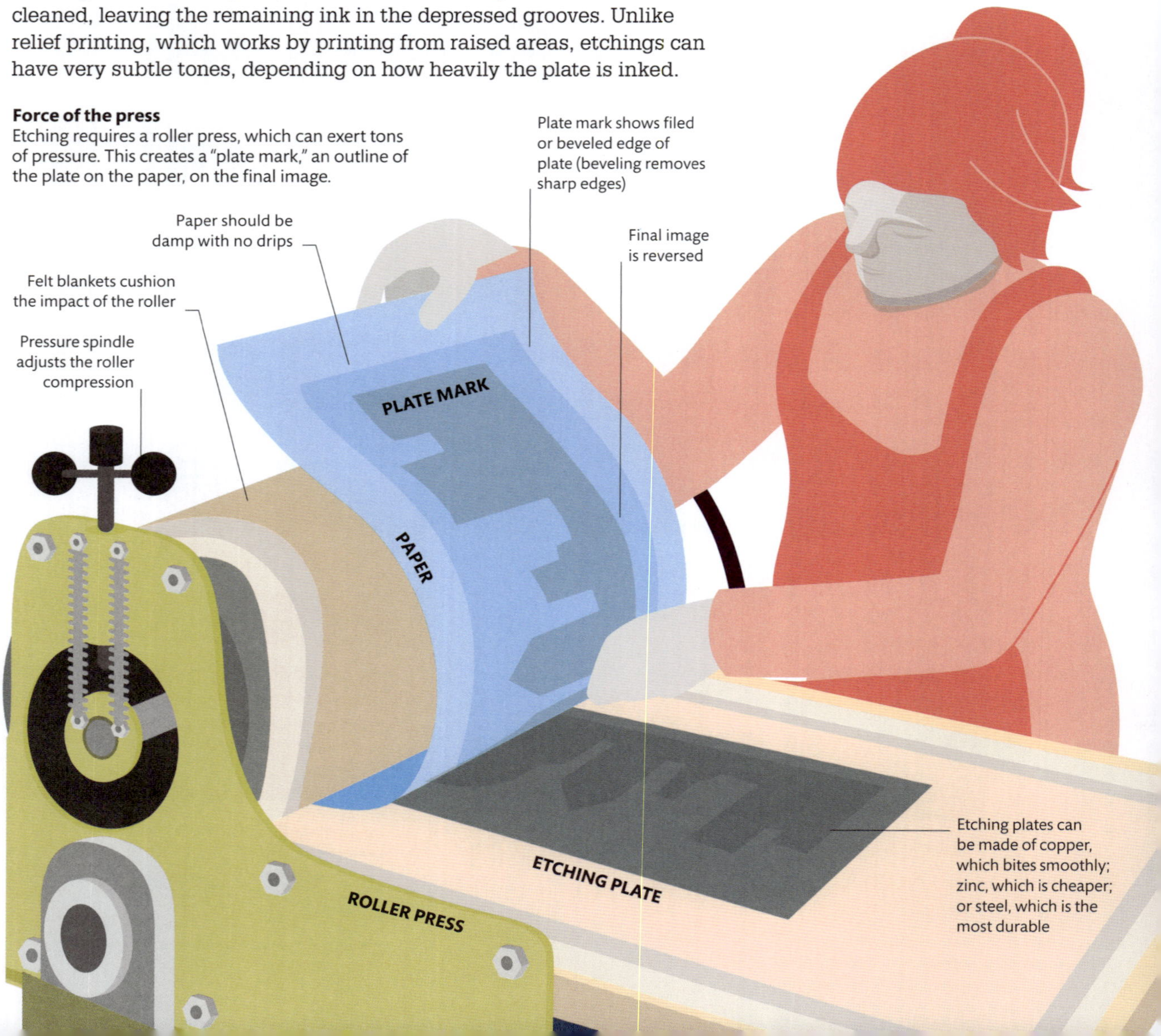

The etching process

The process of making an etching is detailed and methodical. It is crucial that the paper used for printing is damp, as this helps to pull out all the ink from the incised areas of the metal plate. The main stages are detailed here.

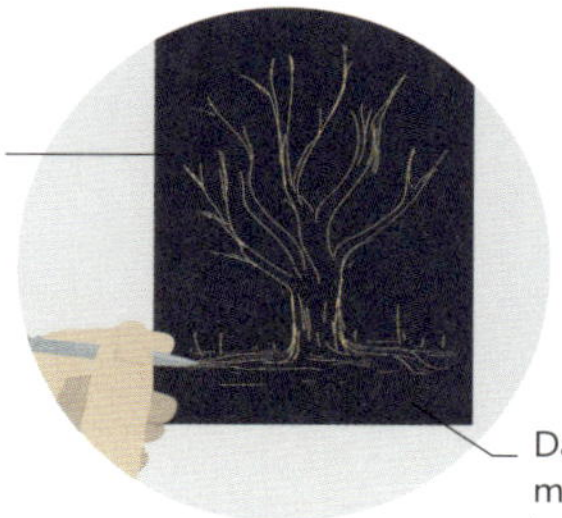

1 Prepare and etch plate
A plate of zinc, copper, or steel is cleaned and covered with a layer of beeswax. The artist then scratches into the wax using a burin, or stylus tool.

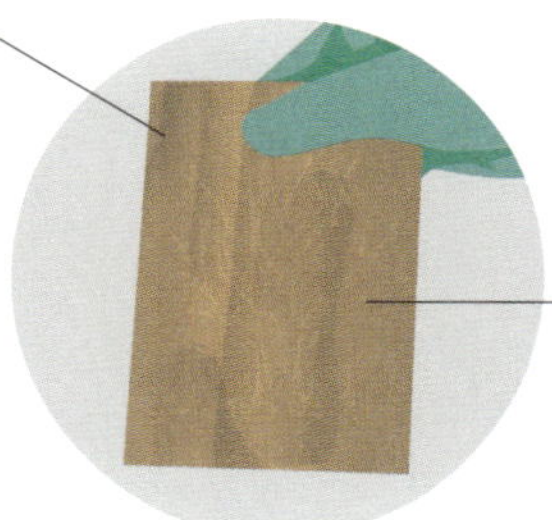

2 Submerge in acid
The plate is submerged in a bath of weak acid solution that eats away at the exposed areas. The plate is then washed and treated with solvent to remove the wax.

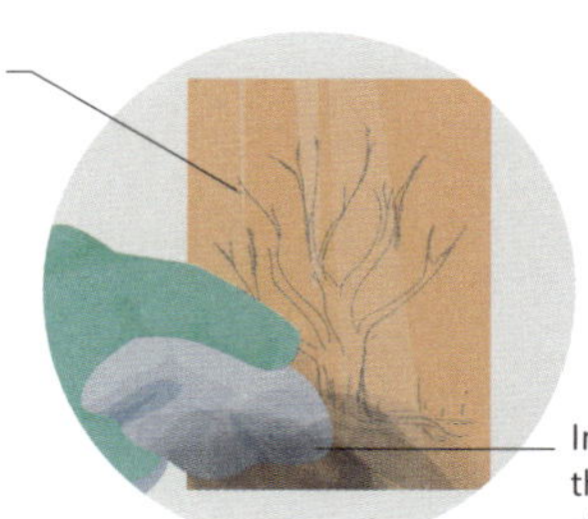

3 Ink up and rub off
The artist applies ink evenly across the plate then rubs the ink off, leaving it only in the scratched areas. The plate is ready to run through the press with a damp sheet of paper.

Engraving

A technique older than etching for making images with metal, engraving dispenses with acid and allows the printmaker to carve directly into the plate using a sharp metal tool with a beveled tip, known as a burin. French artist Claude Mellan's "Sudarium of Saint Veronica" (1649) is a notable example of this skilled process, as the entire plate was engraved with one continuous line.

Master of the plate

Rembrandt van Rijn (1606–69) was a pioneer of many experimental processes in etching and drypoint, producing over 300 plates between 1626–65. He would apply ink variably between each impression, producing atmospheric, painterly and unique printed works, and would often rework earlier plates with fresh drypoint to include new figures and details in scenes.

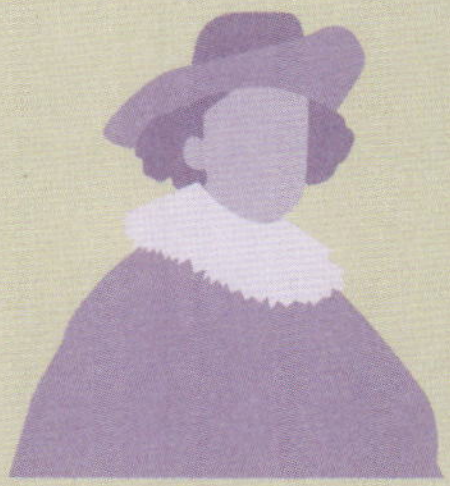

Etching virtuoso
Rembrandt's 32 etched self-portraits are famous as unique displays of human emotion.

REMBRANDT'S **ETCHINGS,** AS WELL AS HIS **PAINTINGS,** MADE HIM **FAMOUS** IN HIS **OWN LIFETIME**

DRYPOINT

Artists make drypoints by scratching with a pointed stylus directly into a copper plate. As the copper is a relatively soft metal, the scratches leave bits of metal behind. Known as the "burr," these raised edges catch extra ink, giving the print a soft appearance.

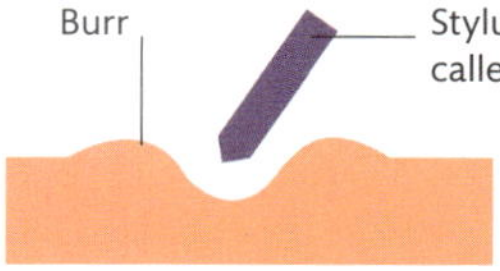

Short run
The pressure of the printing process will quickly deform the burr, meaning that drypoint print runs are short.

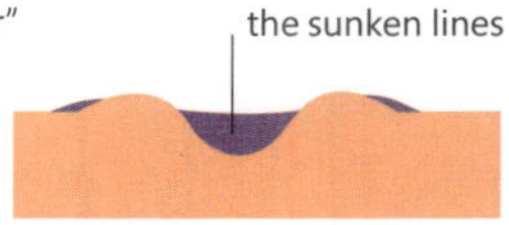

Ink wells
The incised depressions hold a large amount of ink, which during printing makes rich, deep lines.

Screen Printing and Lithography

These printing processes are planographic, meaning the surface used to print is flat. Screen printing uses stencils, while lithography uses a flat stone.

WHY IS SCREEN PRINTING KNOWN AS "SILK SCREEN PRINTING"?

Developed in around 1900, the name comes from the fine, woven silk that was fixed to the frame and used as a support for the paper.

Vibrant images

Screen printing is the process of transferring a stenciled image onto a surface such as paper or fabric using a screen, ink, and a squeegee. The method involves creating a drawing on a fine, mesh screen, and then pushing ink through to create an imprint of the image on the surface beneath. Screen printing is valued for its vivid colors and tactile qualities. Separate screens are needed for each layer of colored ink.

Exposing the emulsion

In this method, the artist creates a high-contrast image on acetate, which they will then place onto the mesh screen; the whole thing is then exposed under very bright light. Areas covered by the stencil are then washed away, leaving a clear image on the screen for the ink to pass through.

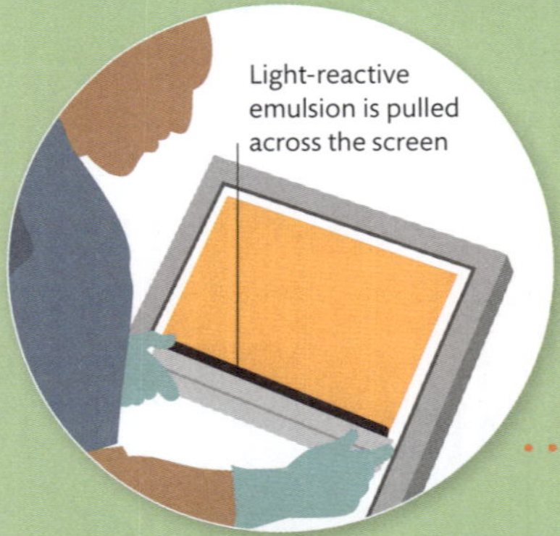

1 Coating the screen
The screen is covered with a thin, even layer of light-reactive emulsion. This can be household emulsion with added reactor for light-sensitivity.

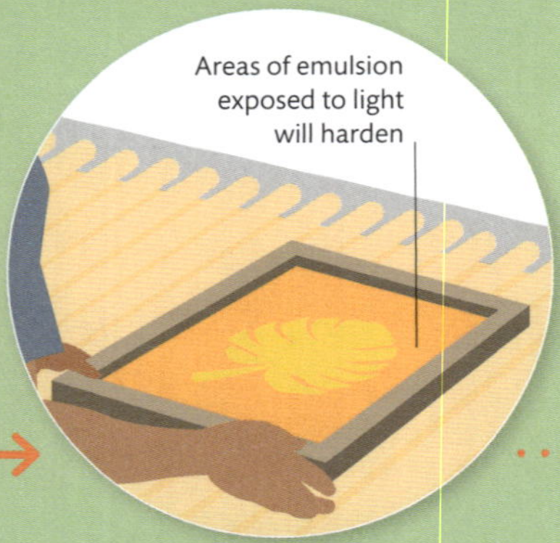

2 Revealing the image
The acetate stencil is placed onto the screen and both screen and stencil are put into an exposure cabinet to be exposed under bright light.

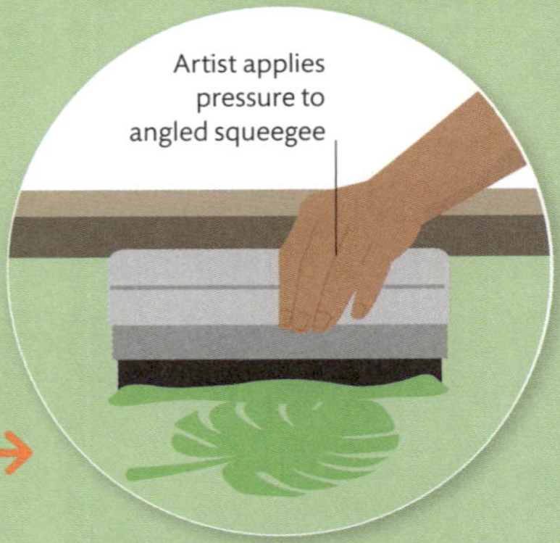

3 Ink applied
The screen is washed, removing any unhardened emulsion. Ink is poured along one edge. As it is pulled across, it seeps through the stencil onto the paper.

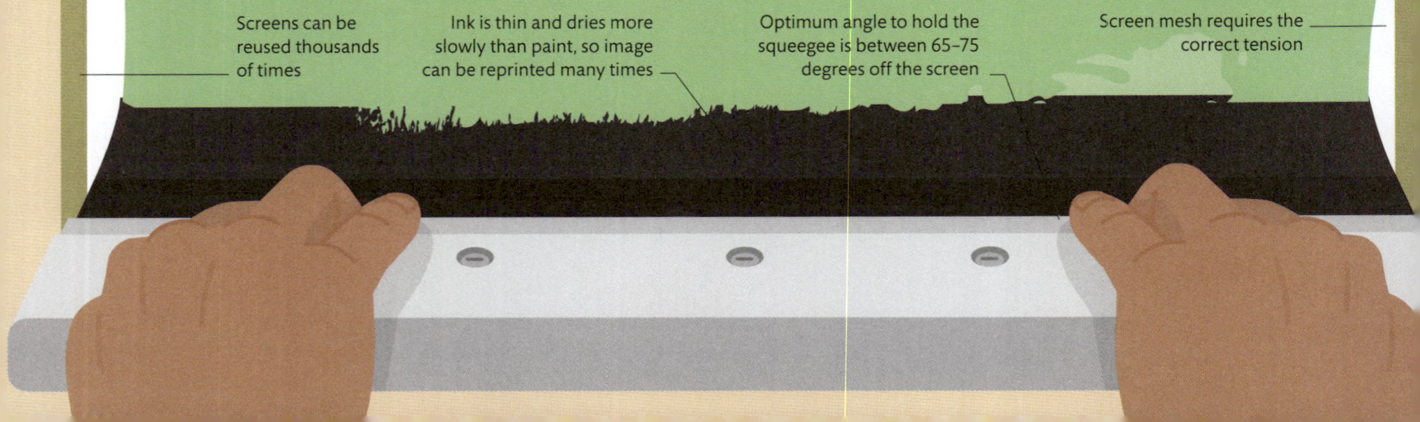

The lithography process
The image is drawn on the lithograph surface using a greasy medium, such as crayon or ink. The surface is then covered with gum arabic, and an oil-based ink is applied with a roller, adhering only to the drawing.

Lithography

Lithography is a printing process based on the premise that oil and water do not mix. It was favoured by Spanish Romantic painter and printmaker Francisco Goya (see pp.186–187). Lithography creates prints with a rich, softly textured look.

GRAINING

1 A slab of limestone, used as a printing surface, must first be "grained" (washed and ground down to remove previous image).

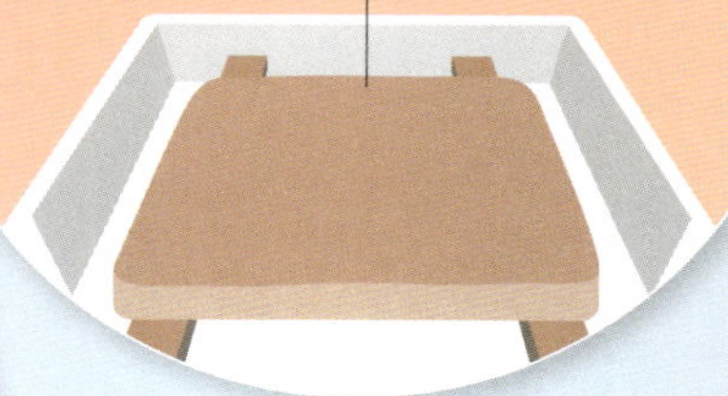

DRAWING

2 The desired image is then drawn or painted onto the surface of the stone using an oil-based ink or lithographic crayon.

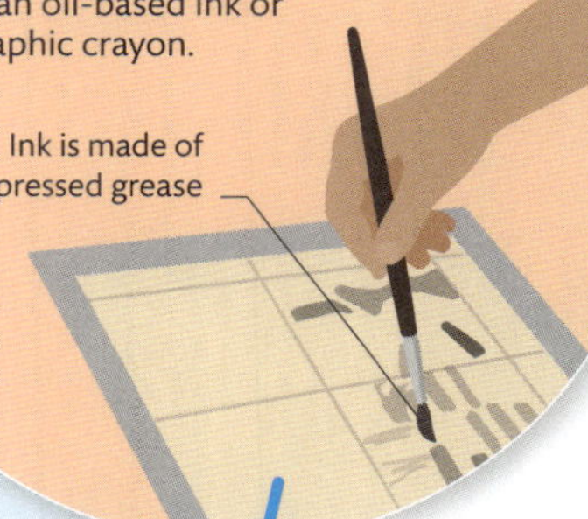

PROCESSING

3 Gum arabic mixed with water is applied to the stone creating a chemical reaction that etches the drawn image onto the stone.

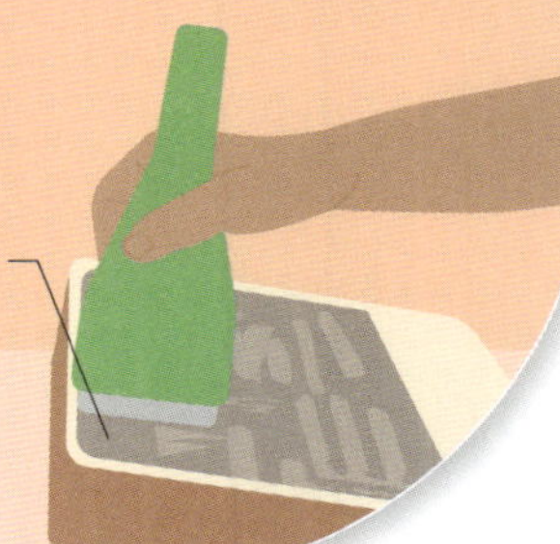

WASHING AND ROLLING

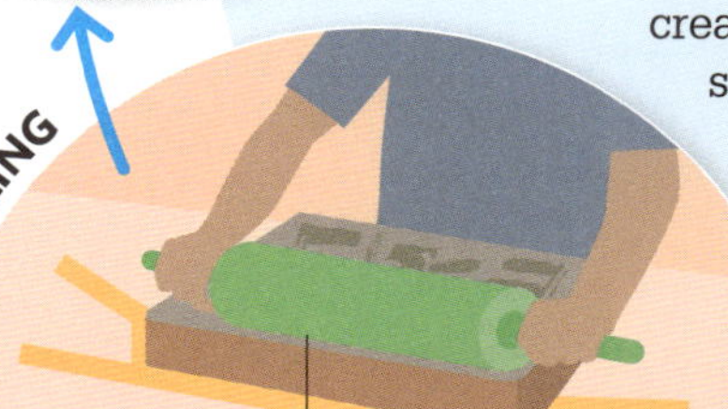

4 The greasy image is wiped off with a solvent and the stone is dampened with water. Ink is rolled on, sticking only to areas that were greased.

PRINTING

5 Damp paper is then placed on top of the stone, followed by a board, and the stone is run through the printing press.

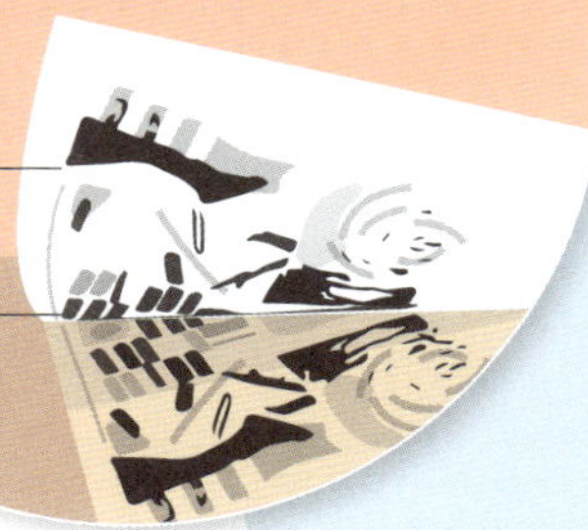

PRINT AND SOCIAL ISSUES

American artist and activist Corita Kent, also known as Sister Mary Corita, made around 800 screen prints. She used advertising slogans, biblical verses, literature, and song lyrics in her work, which became increasingly political during the 1960s.

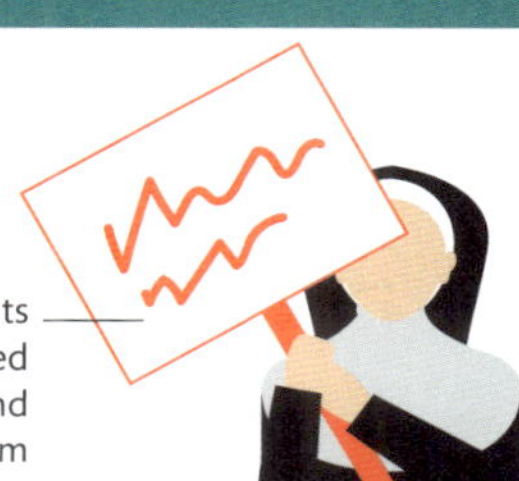

SCREEN PRINTING CAN BE EMPLOYED TO **DECORATE FOOD** USING **RICE PAPER** AND **CHOCOLATE "INK"**

Mixed Media

Mixed media describes art that combines multiple materials and techniques in the same work, creating complex and visually stimulating art. Collage, the cutting and pasting of paper, is a common example.

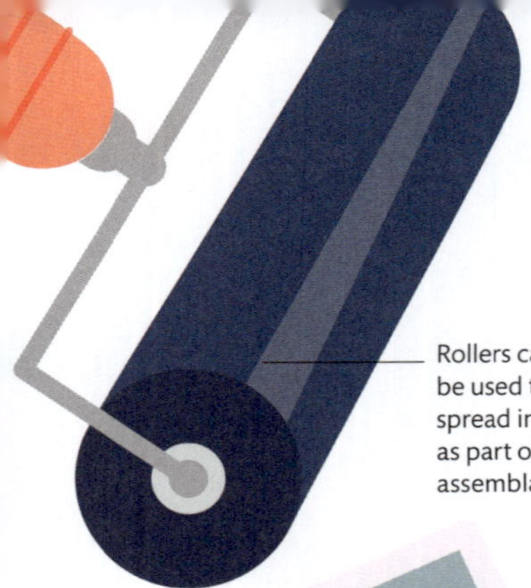

Combining fragments

Any material is potentially available for use in mixed media. Artists often use discarded "bits of the world," from newspapers and bus tickets to fabric and broken machines. They join these fragments together to make a new whole, which can act as a reference point for different times, places, and spaces. Mixed media can challenge or subvert the idea of the painted canvas or sculpted object, and artists have often turned to it in times of social and political crisis.

WHY IS MIXED MEDIA IMPORTANT IN AFRICAN DIASPORA ART?

Some African diaspora artists use items from different places in one visual space as a way of showing cross-cultural connection and identity.

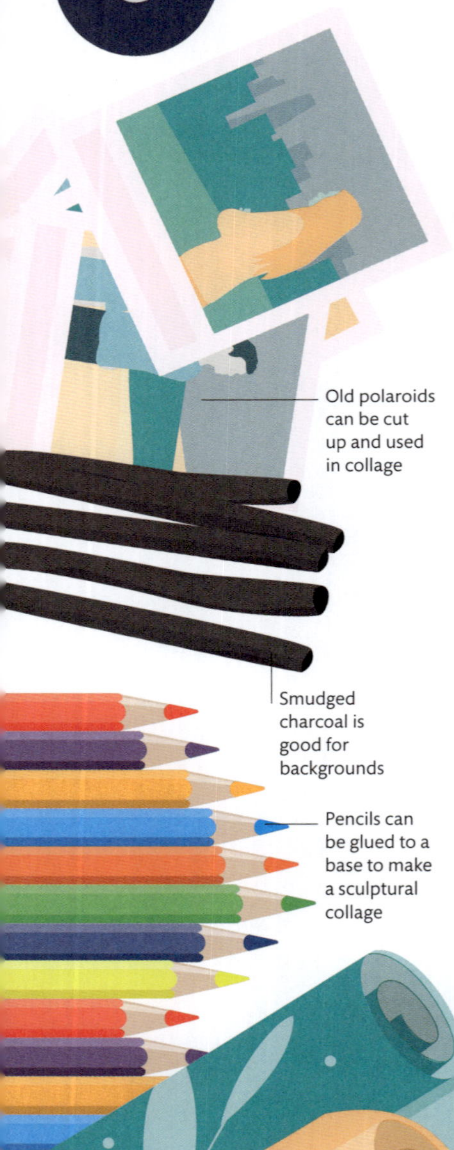

Mixed effects

Each painting medium has its own material properties so when combined, they either work with or against each other in interesting ways—oil resists water for example, so oil paint and watercolor will create interesting effects. Painters have learned to utilize these reactions and combinations to create new and original visual effects.

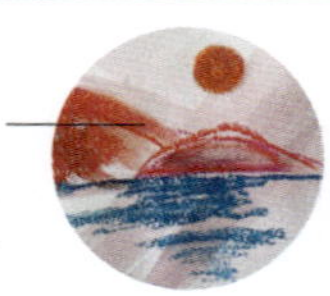

Watercolor and pastels
Once a watercolor painting is dry, high- and lowlights can be picked out with soft pastels.

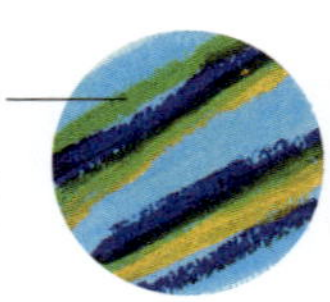

Acrylics and oil bars
Oil bars applied over dry acrylic paint can be especially vibrant and can be worked over impasto.

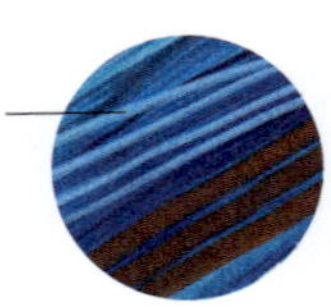

Acrylics and acrylic markers
Markers can add extra definition and detail to acrylic paintings.

Materials and meaning
Mixed media practice is all about juxtaposing and combining different materials together - many of which may mean something to the artist. The mixing of media combined with symbolism is what makes these works so powerful.

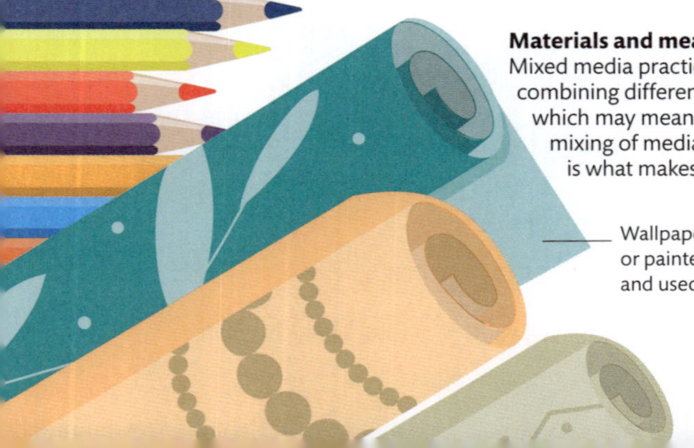

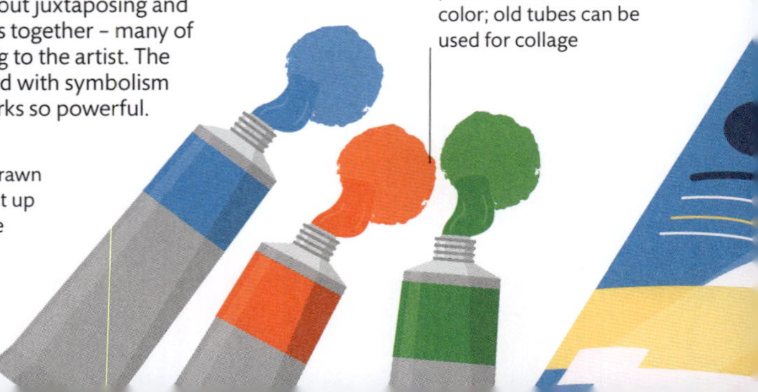

Assemblage

Used to describe mixed-media works constructed from disparate elements, assemblage can be traced back to Pablo Picasso's Cubist creations of 1912, and artists have explored its possibilities ever since. Robert Rauschenberg's "Combines" were part painting, part sculpture, and Phyllida Barlow creates temporary structures painted in bright colors.

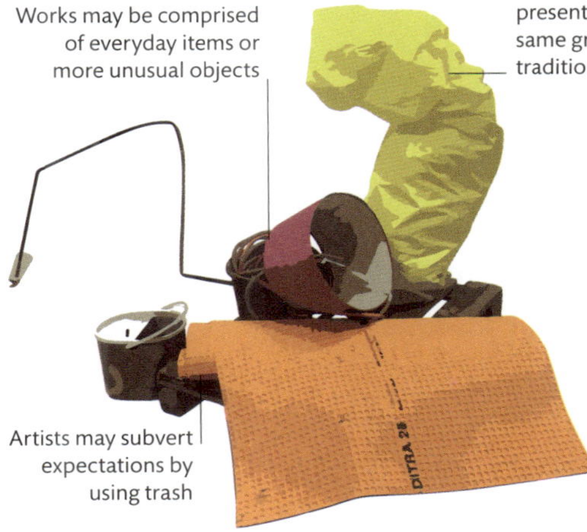

PAPER COLLÉ IS A FORM OF COLLAGE THAT IS CLOSE TO DRAWING

Ephemeral constructions
Assemblage can be put together in many ways, from nailing and welding to balancing and gluing. Many works are impermanent, and artists often recycle old pieces.

PHOTOMONTAGE

Artists in Weimar Germany (1918–1933), including Raoul Hausmann, Hannah Höch, George Grosz, and John Heartfield, pioneered photomontage (cutting and pasting together pieces of printed photographs). By montaging photographed objects together, the artists aimed not to portray reality but rather to visualize "invisible" social forces in turbulent interwar Germany and to use art as a weapon against Fascism.

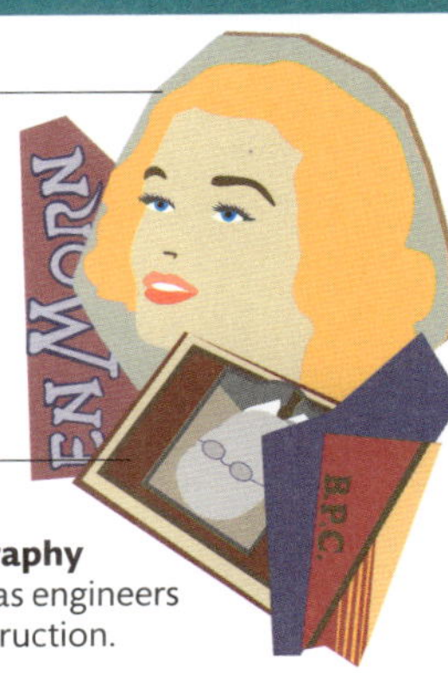

Architects of photography
Artists saw themselves as engineers and their work as construction.

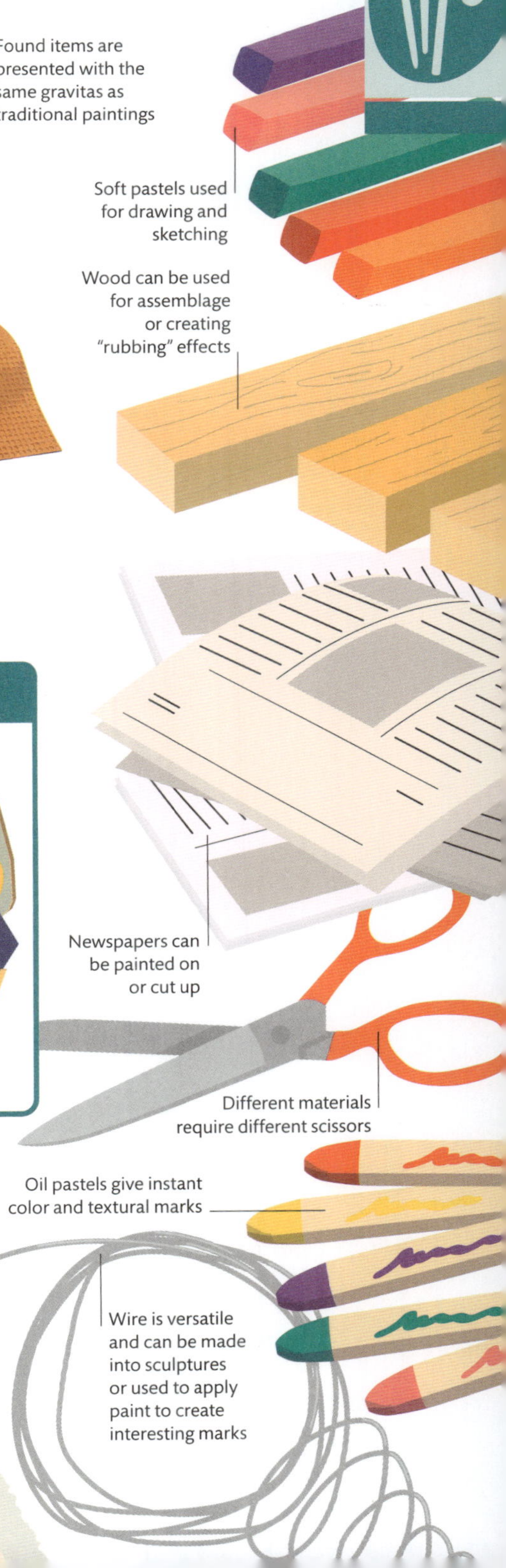

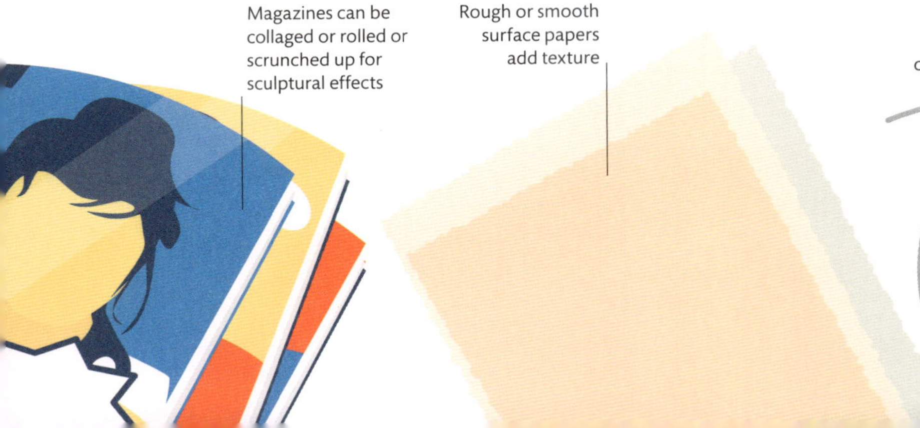

THROWING AN EARTHENWARE POT

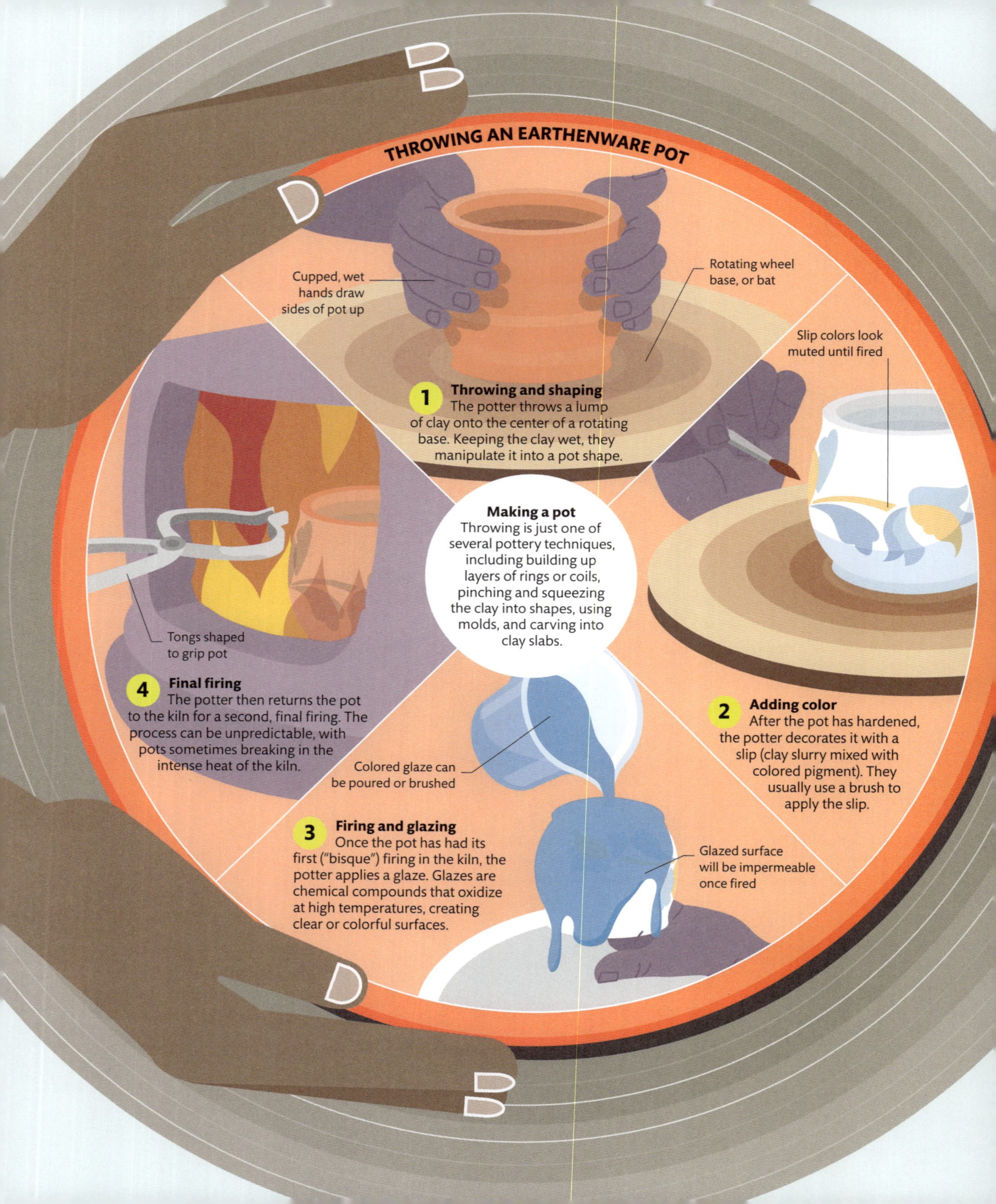

Making a pot
Throwing is just one of several pottery techniques, including building up layers of rings or coils, pinching and squeezing the clay into shapes, using molds, and carving into clay slabs.

1 Throwing and shaping
The potter throws a lump of clay onto the center of a rotating base. Keeping the clay wet, they manipulate it into a pot shape.

2 Adding color
After the pot has hardened, the potter decorates it with a slip (clay slurry mixed with colored pigment). They usually use a brush to apply the slip.

3 Firing and glazing
Once the pot has had its first ("bisque") firing in the kiln, the potter applies a glaze. Glazes are chemical compounds that oxidize at high temperatures, creating clear or colorful surfaces.

4 Final firing
The potter then returns the pot to the kiln for a second, final firing. The process can be unpredictable, with pots sometimes breaking in the intense heat of the kiln.

Ceramics

Ceramics are made by shaping and modeling clay, most commonly in the form of pots and other vessels; it can also take the form of sculptures or figurines. The clay is then dried and fired in a kiln (a special furnace) at very high temperatures. There are three main types of ceramics: earthenware, stoneware, and porcelain.

HOW OLD IS THE OLDEST KNOWN POTTERY?

Fragments of pottery found in a cave in Jiangxi province, southern China, are believed to be around 20,000 years old.

Earthenware and stoneware

Fired at temperatures up to 2,102°F (1,150°C), earthenware has a slightly porous surface and requires glazing to make it waterproof and durable. As well as in art, it is used in objects such as plant pots and roof tiles. Stoneware is fired at a higher temperature, up to 2,282°F (1,250°C), resulting in the clay vitrifying (achieving an almost glasslike quality). Stoneware pots can be used in cooking.

"WHITE GOLD" WAS THE NAME GIVEN TO PORCELAIN BY EUROPEAN TRADERS

Examples old and new

Humans have been making decorative and functional clay objects for thousands of years, from the terracotta army of the Qin dynasty (see p.167) to the distinctively styled Staffordshire potteries and beyond. Since the mid-20th century, pottery and ceramics have increasingly been seen as expressive practices. Decorative techniques include painting, where paint is applied with a brush; incision, where decoration is cut into the soft surface; and pouring, when paint is poured over the pot to create patterns.

SECRETS OF PORCELAIN

Petuntse (china stone) and kaolin (white china clay) are mixed, molded, and fired above 2,282°F (1,250°C) to create a strong, glassy ceramic. The Chinese kept its chemical composition (below) secret for years.

AU5INPD4

Chinese porcelain
This was developed in China during the Tang (618–907 CE), Song (960–1279), and Ming (1368–1644) dynasties.

Ottoman tile
Iznik, in modern-day Turkey, produced ornate, colorful tiles in the 16th and 17th centuries.

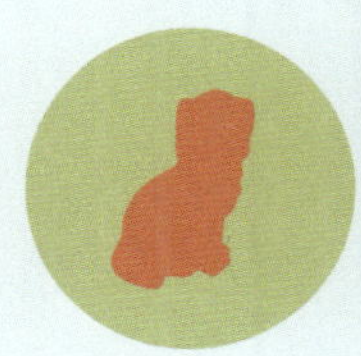

Staffordshire pottery
Stoke-on-Trent has been the home of English pottery for 300 years. Manufacturers such as Spode are based there.

Gillian Lowndes
Pioneering sculptor Lowndes (1936–2010) used clay and found objects, such as string, to create her sculptures.

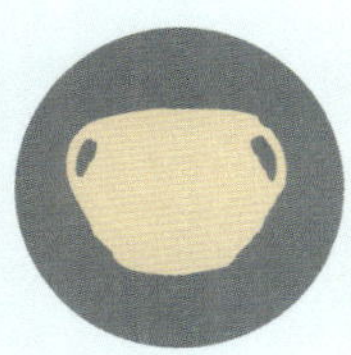

Shōji Hamada
Hamada (1894–1978) was a celebrated Japanese potter, with an influential studio in Mashiko.

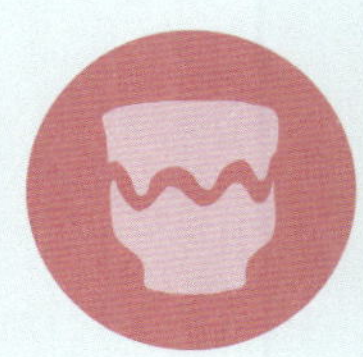

Ladi Kwali
Kwali (c.1925–1984) was an expert at traditional methods of coiling and pinching clay to create pots in Nigeria.

ALEXANDRA KEHAYOGLOU MAKES LANDSCAPE-LIKE ART USING YARN FROM A CARPET FACTORY

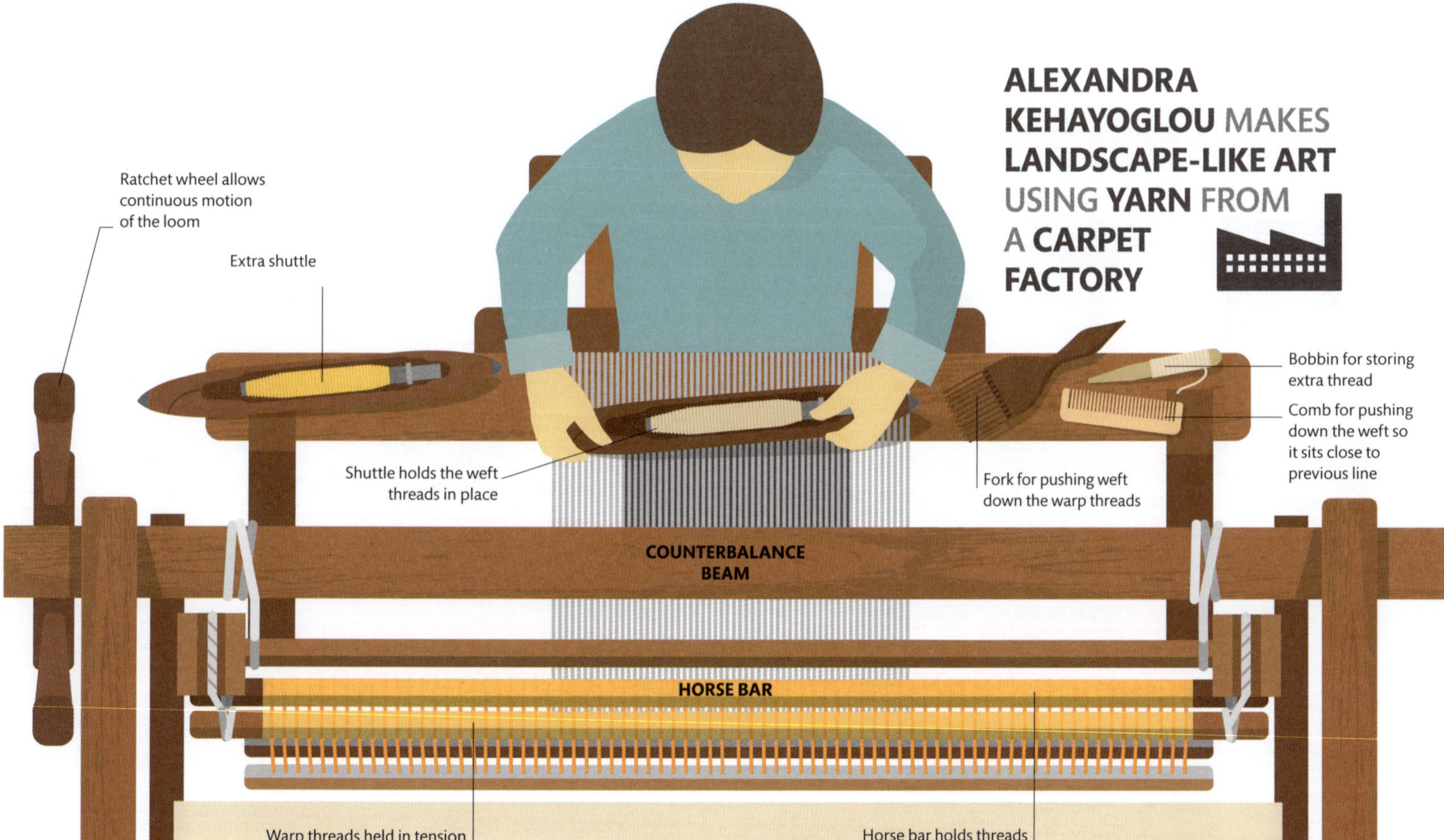

Textile Art

Textile art uses organic or synthetic fibers to make decorative or practical objects and includes the quilting and weaving of fabrics, embroidery, and contemporary sculptural installations.

From craft to art

Textiles have a rich history around the world, and textile designs are often an expression of identity, from Islamic rugs to African cloth to South and Central American panels and baskets. Since around the 17th century, the weaving of textiles in the West has been seen as a low-status form of craft. Contemporary Western artists, and feminists in particular, have seized on its historic "craft" status as the starting point for creating new, radical artwork.

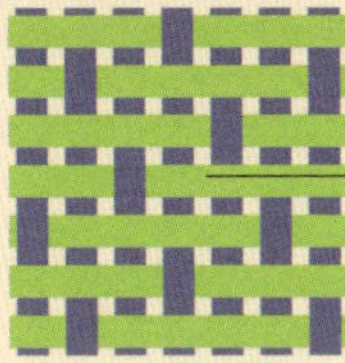
A satin weave gives a glossy top surface. Here, the warp runs over every four or more weft threads

SATIN

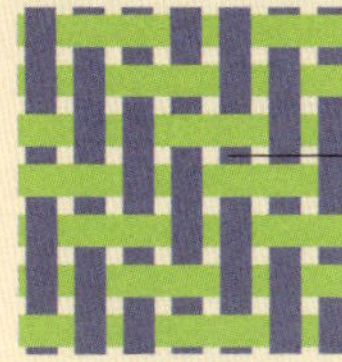
A traditional weave, twill has a diagonal pattern where the warp runs over two weft threads

TWILL

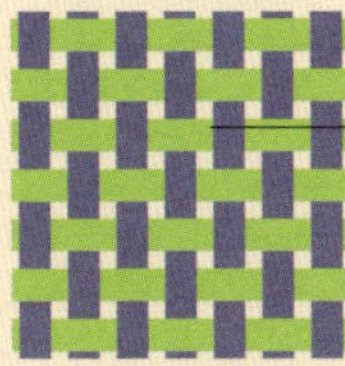
The simplest weave, plain weave has the warp and weft crossing regularly at right angles

PLAIN

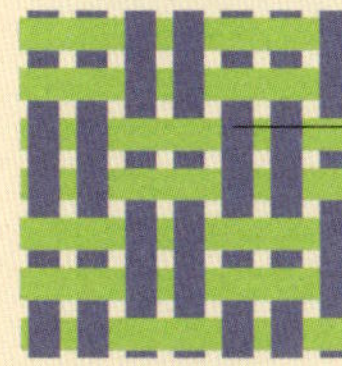
Basket weave is a regular crisscross, as two warp threads cover two weft, and vice versa

BASKET

Types of weaving

Weaving is the process of turning thread into fabric. Weaves are constructed from warp (vertical) and weft—from the old English word "to weave"—(horizontal) threads. The loom holds the warp threads tight, while the operator weaves the weft threads transversely, over and under the warp threads in a set pattern, depending on the desired type of weave. Weft threads are more flexible, moving over and under the tight, structural warp threads.

Fabric of dissent

Textiles are linked to politics—for example, their use in national flags. Artists have correspondingly used textiles to express political dissent. Dress and clothing can also be a powerful way to protest—by wearing another nation's colors in a show of support, or by subverting mainstream fashion trends, such as in the punk movement of the 1970s.

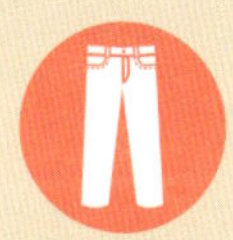

Denim
1960s Civil Rights activists wore denim to symbolize equality and solidarity.

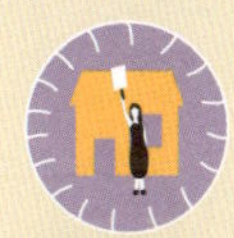

Arpilleras
Chilean women in the 1970s made these quilts as a form of protest.

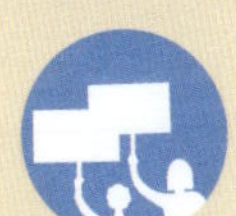

Trade unions
Banners with local designs are common across the British union movement.

Queer crafters
The HIV/AIDS Quilt was made as a way of mourning those who died.

SHEILA HICKS

Hicks (b. 1934), is an American artist known for creating large, colorful fiber installations of wool, woven thread, and flax. She studied ancient weaving and knotting processes in Chile and Mexico, and with Josef Albers at Yale, where she met Anni Albers, who used to run the weaving class at the Bauhaus art school.

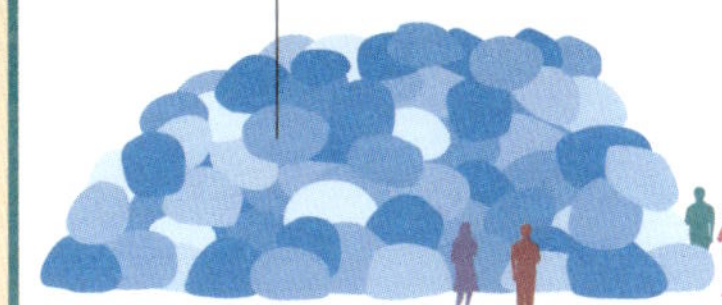
Hicks's large-scale, textile installations fill whole gallery spaces with texture and form

Breaking the boundaries
Inspired by her extensive travels, Sheila Hicks's work topples the barriers between art, architecture, and design.

WHAT IS BATIK?

The art of making decorative cotton cloth using wax and dye, and a penlike tool called a "canting," was developed in Indonesia and is also very popular in African textile design.

Paper Arts

For around 2,000 years, paper has been used as a medium on which to write, paint, draw, and print. In the modern period, artists have turned to paper as an expressive medium in its own right.

Dynamic medium

Paper is dynamic and variable. Even in drawings in graphite or ink where paper serves as a "ground" or surface, it is an active component in the creation of the work and can be used in highlights. Paper can be worked into sculptural forms through cutting, folding, embossing, layering, and engineering and treated with a range of materials, including washes and pastes, to make it malleable and textured. Below are some common cultural and artistic uses of paper.

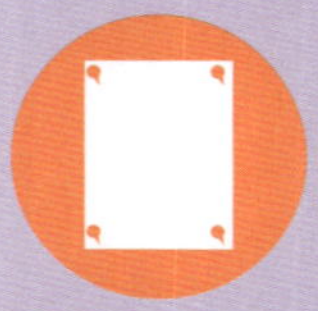

Posters
Paper graphic art and agitprop (propaganda) posters are pasted in civic spaces.

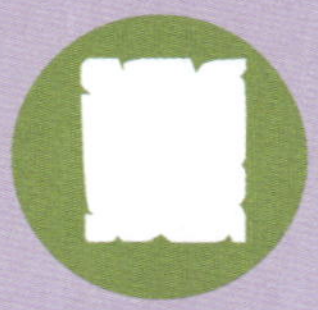

Papyrus
In Ancient Egypt, sheets of papyrus were prepared using the stems of an aquatic plant.

Newsprint
Cheap paper made from groundwood pulp is suitable for printing newspapers in large volumes.

Wallpaper
The first relatively high-quality wallpapers were produced using woodblock printing.

Origami
The ancient Japanese art of folding colored paper to make sculptural forms is still popular today.

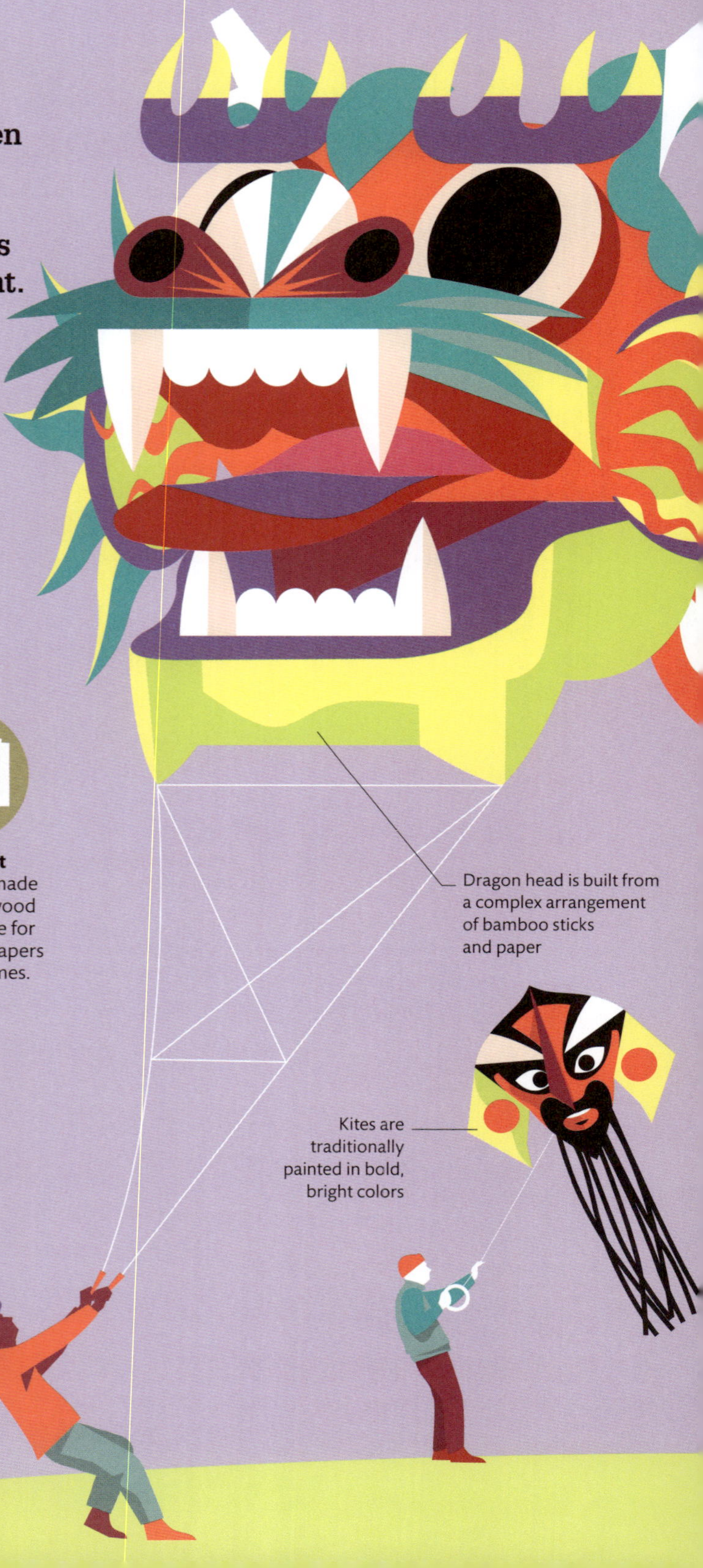

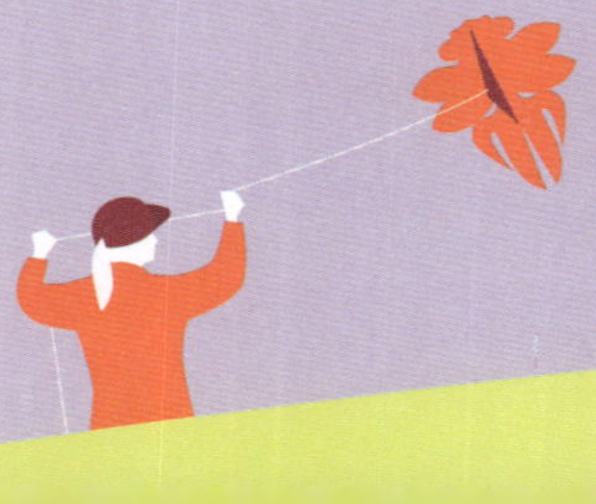

THE WORD **ORIGAMI** COMES FROM **"ORI"** MEANING **FOLDING** AND **"KAMI"** MEANING **PAPER**

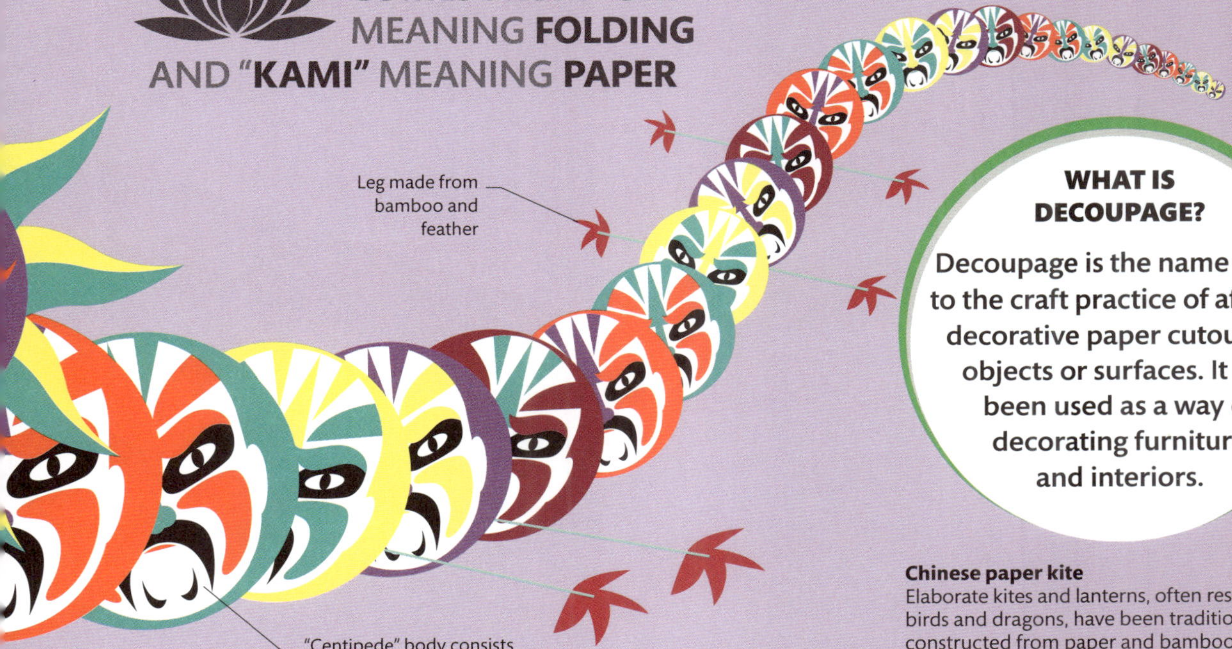

Chinese paper kite
Elaborate kites and lanterns, often resembling birds and dragons, have been traditionally constructed from paper and bamboo in China—especially during the Ming (1368–1644) and Qing (1644–1912) dynasties.

WHAT IS DECOUPAGE?

Decoupage is the name given to the craft practice of affixing decorative paper cutouts to objects or surfaces. It has been used as a way of decorating furniture and interiors.

Modern innovative art

Since World War II, modern and contemporary artists have worked with paper in innovative ways. Some examples of this include Brazilian artist Mira Schendel, who made sculptures she called *droguinhas* from damp, knotted rice paper; Robert Rauschenberg, who used newspaper in his artwork that featured a combination of painting and sculpture (dubbed "Combines"); and Mark Bradford, who uses found paper from street posters and hair salons.

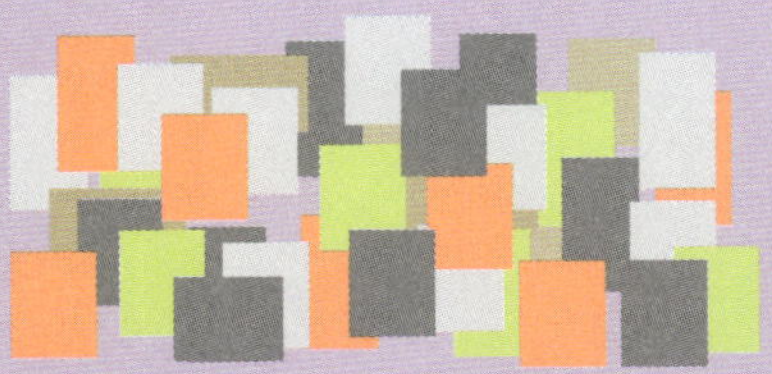

Found materials
Mark Bradford gathers the "end papers" from hair salons to create abstract paintings that reflect his early life as a hairdresser.

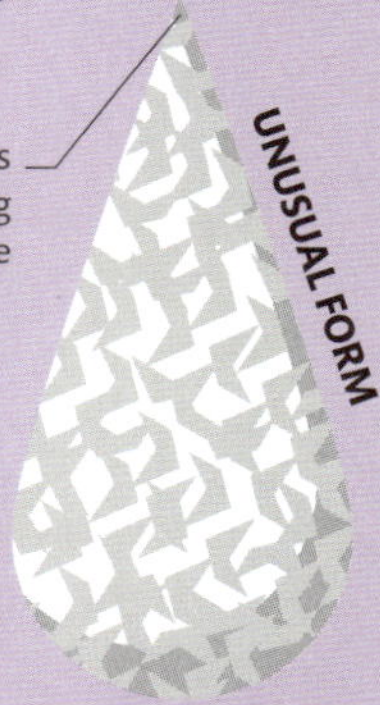

Droguinhas
Meaning "little nothings," Mira Schendel's *droguinhas* pieces use rice paper to explore the idea of fleeting things.

ART BOOKS

The art book, a piece of art in itself, is like an artist's workshop of ideas. In modern times, art books may consist of curated compilations of drawings, text, and prints. A notable example is *Twentysix Gasoline Stations* by Ed Ruscha.

Digital Art

Digital art can describe any art created using digital and computer technology. It relies on either hardware or software for production or display—for example, art that is created using a computer, displayed on a screen in a gallery, or created via 3-D printing. Some digital art in galleries is also now interactive and allows interaction with viewers.

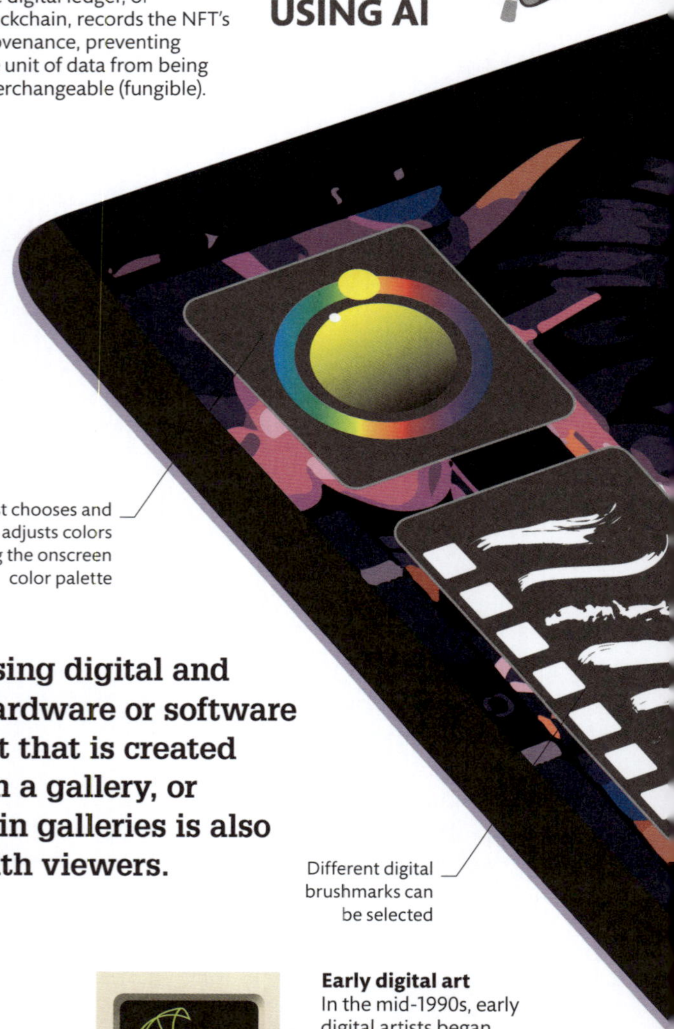

Artist chooses and adjusts colors using the onscreen color palette

Different digital brushmarks can be selected

New media

The earliest experiments with computer-produced art began in the 1950s and were, in fact, close to weaving (looms can also be "programmed" using a punch card). With the advent of home computers and the internet in the 1980s and '90s, digital art, or "new media art," became widespread. Today, artists use platforms such as Instagram (see p.67) and YouTube to reflect on digital processes of information transfer and to critique aspects of contemporary lifestyle, politics, and consumer culture.

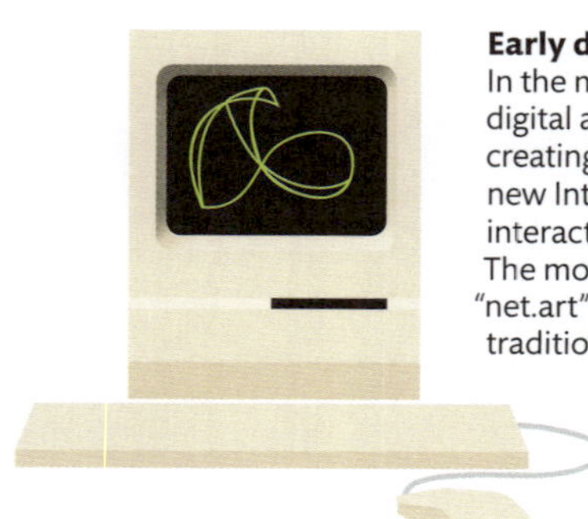

Early digital art
In the mid-1990s, early digital artists began creating works on the new Internet, often using interactive programs. The movement was called "net.art" and bypassed traditional gallery spaces.

Non-Fungible Tokens (NFTs)

An NFT is a unique, non-interchangeable piece of data that is stored on a public, digital ledger and is used as the certificate of ownership of a digital artwork. Any artwork that exists in digital form can potentially be sold as an NFT. NFTs have allowed artists greater autonomy when selling work but have also been criticized for contributing to the commodification of art and for their environmentally unfriendly energy usage.

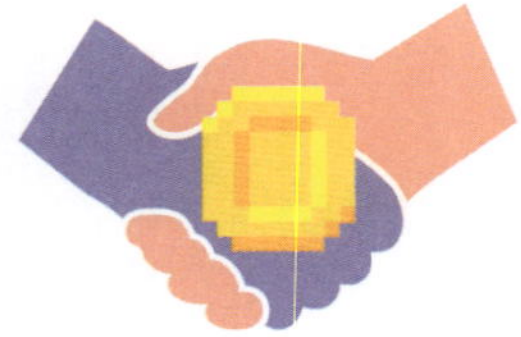

Digital exchange
The digital ledger, or blockchain, records the NFT's provenance, preventing the unit of data from being interchangeable (fungible).

AI-DA IS THE WORLD'S FIRST ROBOT ARTIST—IT MAKES ART USING AI

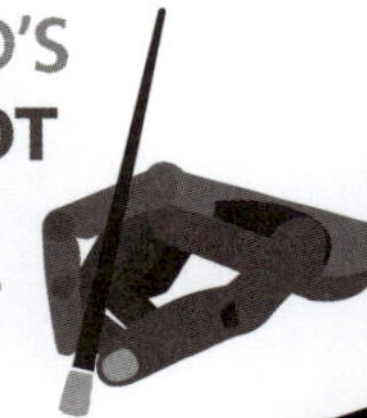

MODERN ADOPTERS

In recent years, traditional artists have started to embrace digital methods. British artist David Hockney "paints" using his iPad, choosing between different digital brushmarks. His paintings of the West Yorkshire landscape are made using this technology.

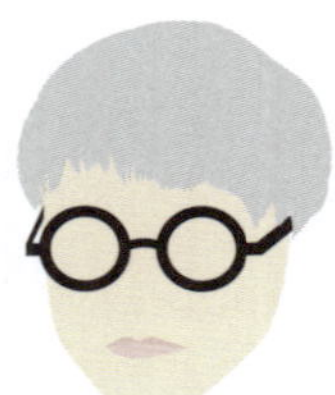

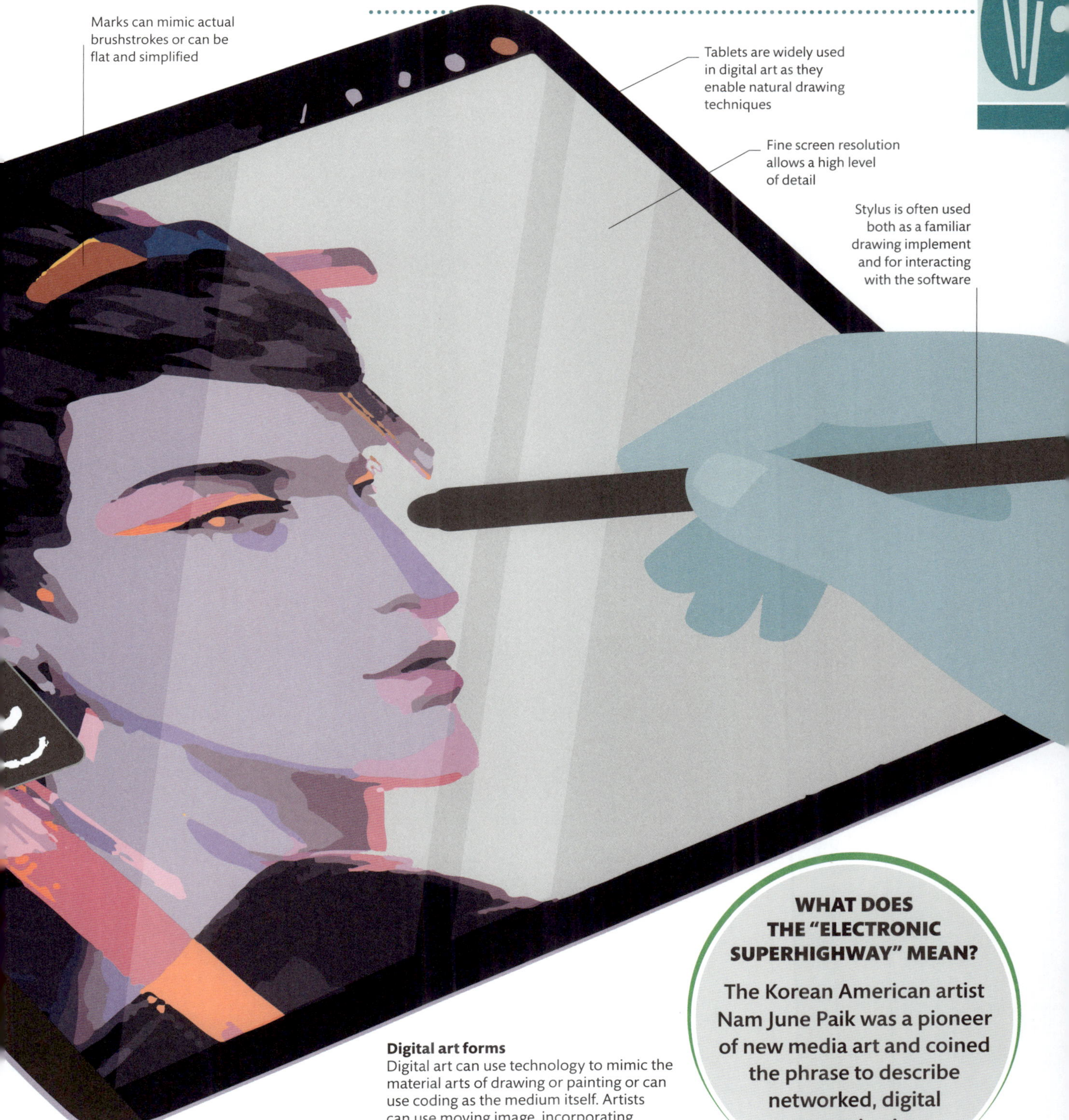

Digital art forms
Digital art can use technology to mimic the material arts of drawing or painting or can use coding as the medium itself. Artists can use moving image, incorporating digitized film and video.

WHAT DOES THE "ELECTRONIC SUPERHIGHWAY" MEAN?

The Korean American artist Nam June Paik was a pioneer of new media art and coined the phrase to describe networked, digital communications.

Mural Art

Murals are large-scale works of art, commonly paintings or mosaics, which can be found in royal palaces, government buildings, holy sites, public spaces, and private houses. The context of display determines the content and style of each mural.

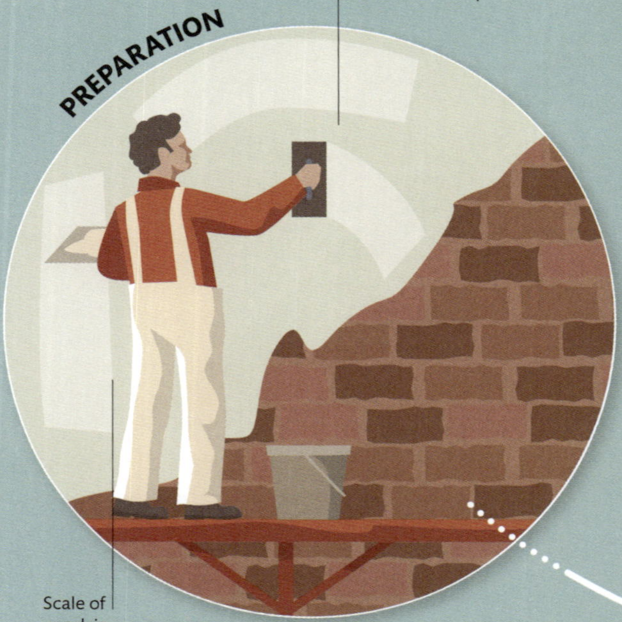

1 Preparing the surface
The artist prepares the wall surface with layers of plaster, which are left to dry and then brushed clean.

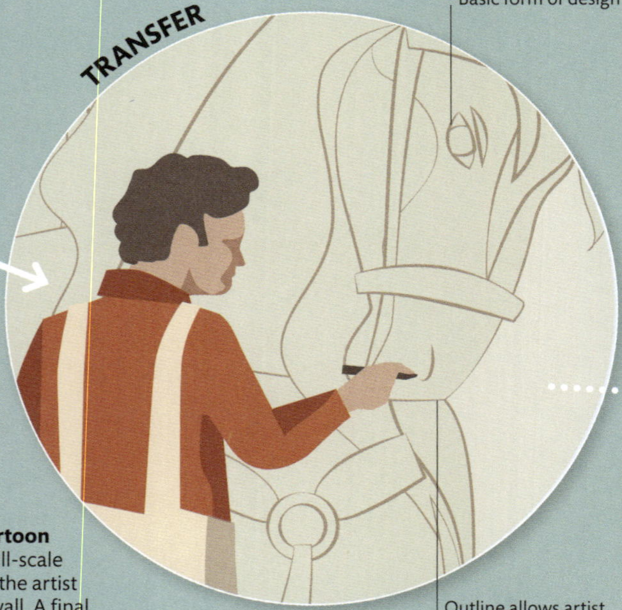

2 Transferring the cartoon
Using a cartoon—a full-scale drawing on transfer paper—the artist traces the design onto the wall. A final fresh layer of plaster is applied in small patches.

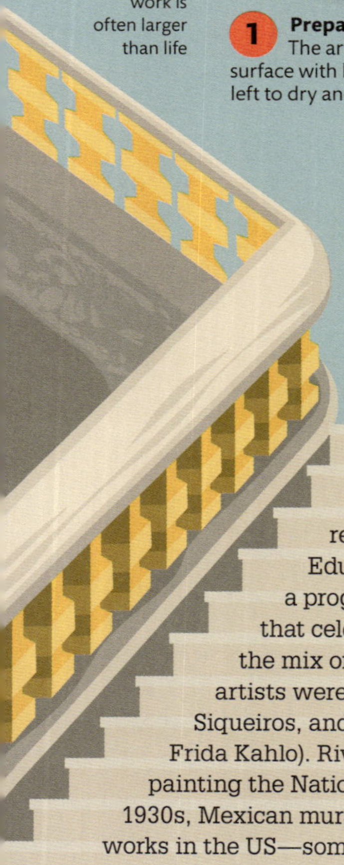

Mexican muralists

In 1921, following the Mexican revolution, the new Minister for Education, José Vasconcelos, sponsored a program of mural painting across Mexico that celebrated the power of workers and the mix of Indigenous and Latin cultures. Key artists were José Clemente Orozco, David Alfaro Siqueiros, and Diego Rivera (the husband of artist Frida Kahlo). Rivera worked in fresco, famously painting the National Palace in Mexico City. By the 1930s, Mexican muralists were commissioned to make works in the US—some of which sparked controversy.

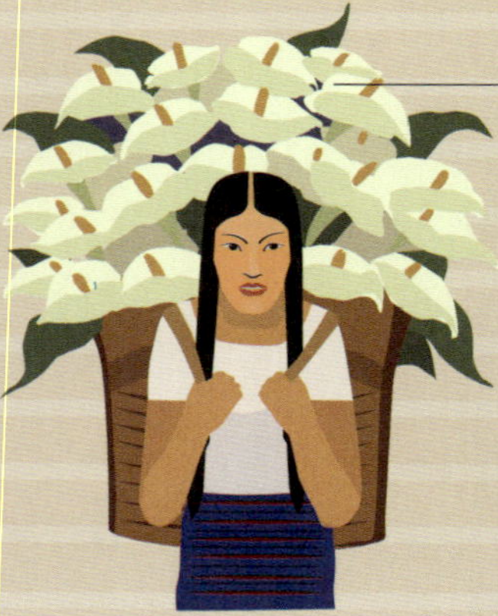

A new look at history
Although the new wave of murals was mainly historic in subject, the artists drew on modern influences, including European Modernism, Cubism (see pp.204–205), and Expressionism (see pp.202–203).

Imposing wall paintings

Murals can be painted on the interior or exterior walls of buildings. Artists need to design the mural to integrate with its surroundings, working with the architecture and available light and complementing the function of the space. Murals reflect the history, politics, and values of a particular area. The "buon" fresco technique, applying pigment onto wet plaster before it dries, was first developed in ancient Greece. Today, teams of artists may work together to complete complex murals.

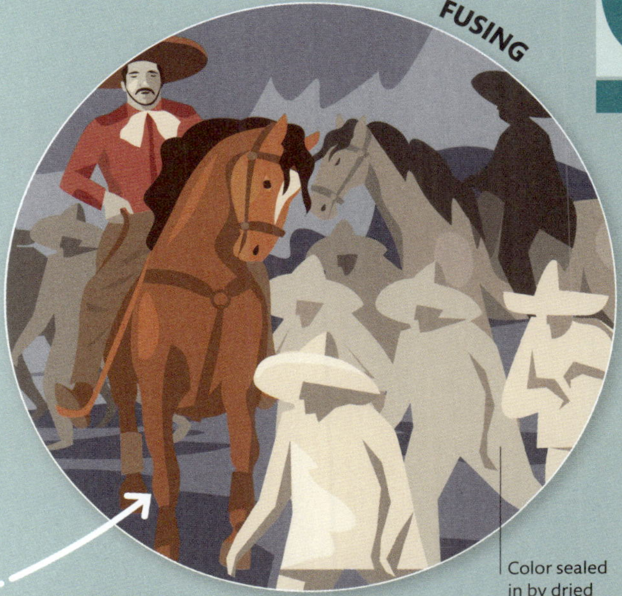

4 Drying and retouching
The pigment fuses with the plaster as it dries, binding the painting onto the wall and so making the fresco extremely durable. Retouches can be added after drying but will be much less durable.

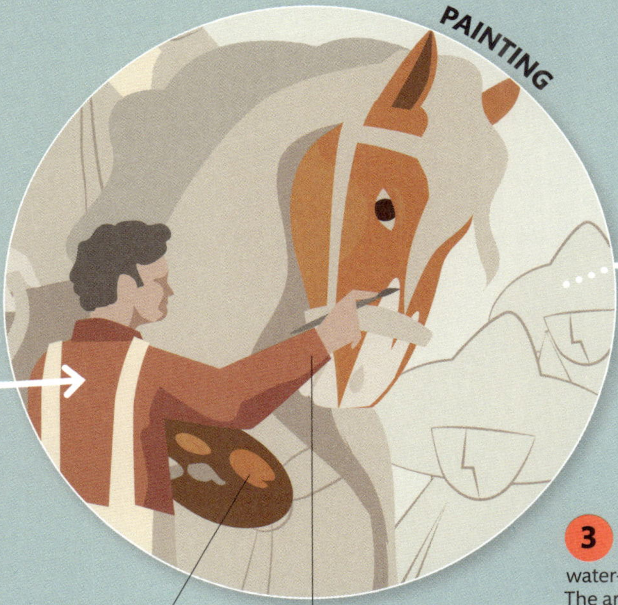

3 Painting onto wet plaster
Working quickly, the artist applies water-based pigment onto the wet plaster. The artist paints in sections; if the whole wall was plastered at once, parts of it would dry out before the artist could get to them.

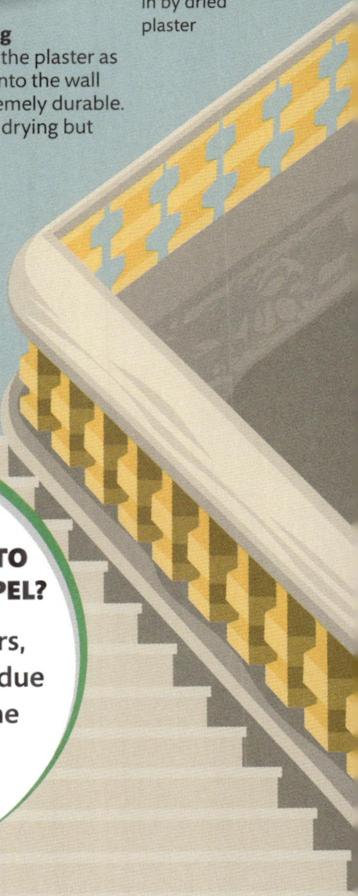

ITALIAN INSPIRATION

Some of the finest surviving works from the Italian Renaissance (see pp. 176–177) are frescoes, including works by Masaccio and Fra Angelico in Florence, and Michelangelo and Raphael in the Vatican City. Venetian painters did not make frescoes because of the humidity in Venice—the plaster would not dry properly.

ITALIAN CHAPEL

HOW LONG DID IT TAKE MICHELANGELO TO PAINT THE SISTINE CHAPEL?

The work took four years, between 1508 and 1512, due to its large scale, and the technical demands of fresco painting.

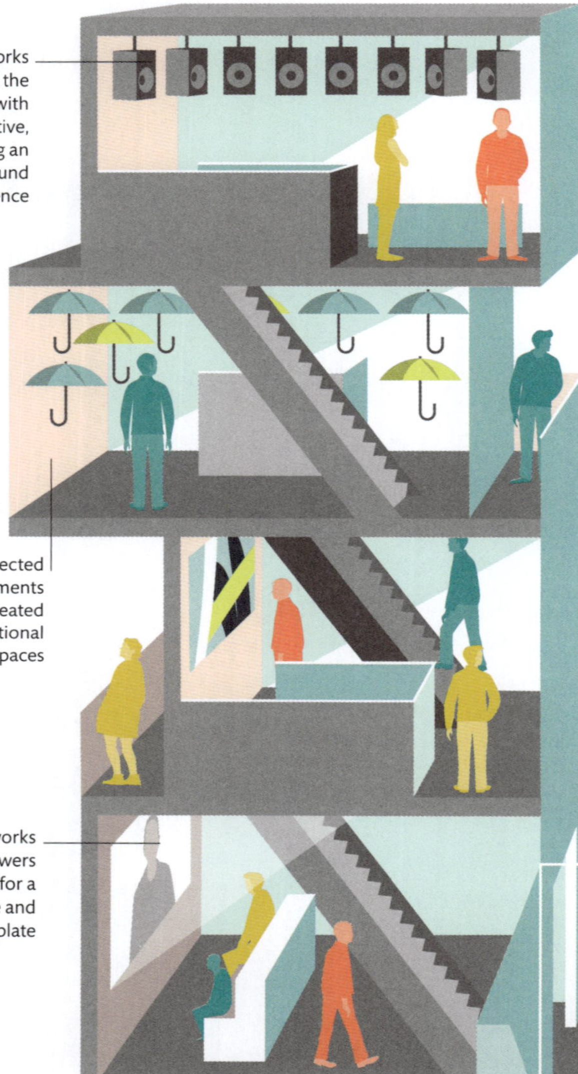

Interactivity or observation

Installation art can invite viewer interaction, and one strand of such work has been identified as "relational aesthetics," where viewers are encouraged to participate in the production of the work as a social event or experiment. In 1971, for example, Gordon Matta-Clark roasted a pig under a New York bridge, giving away 500 pork sandwiches as part of the performance.

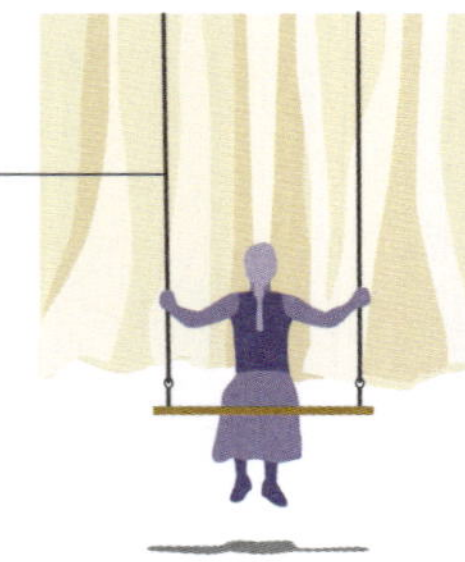

Playground piece
Ann Hamilton's installation invited people to revisit their childhood by riding swings in her 2012 ode to human relation.

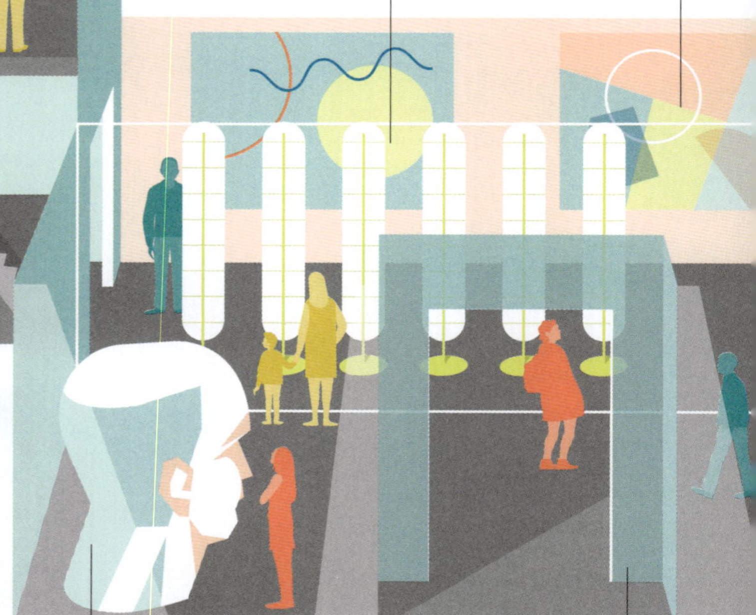

LAND ART INSTALLATIONS

In the 1970s, artists began to make installations by working directly with the earth, digging into it, and building works onto it, in a movement called land art, which was site specific. Key artists included Nancy Holt and Andy Goldsworthy.

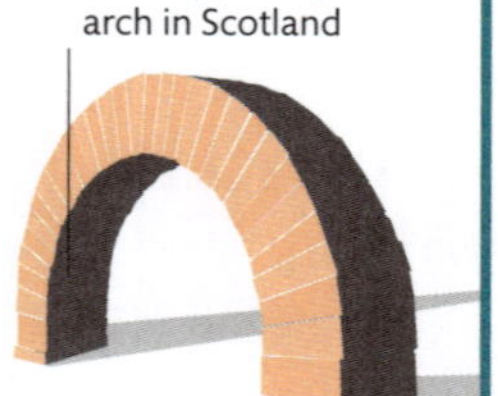

NATURAL INSPIRATION

Installation Art

Installation art is a temporary or permanent environment created using a varied range of materials, tools, and objects, which the viewer is invited to move through as an immersive experience.

Contesting the commercial

Installation art was pioneered by anti-war artists during World War I. They included Marcel Duchamp and Kurt Schwitters, who created his "Merzbau," an environment of junk, in his German house c.1923–37. In the 1950s and '60s, sculptors, performance artists, and conceptual artists began to focus on ephemeral installations to challenge the increasing commercialism of the art world. The crucial element of these works was that they were designed for a specific site; many were never remade, surviving only as photographs. Since the 1990s, works have become less site-specific, as artists often move them across the globalized art world.

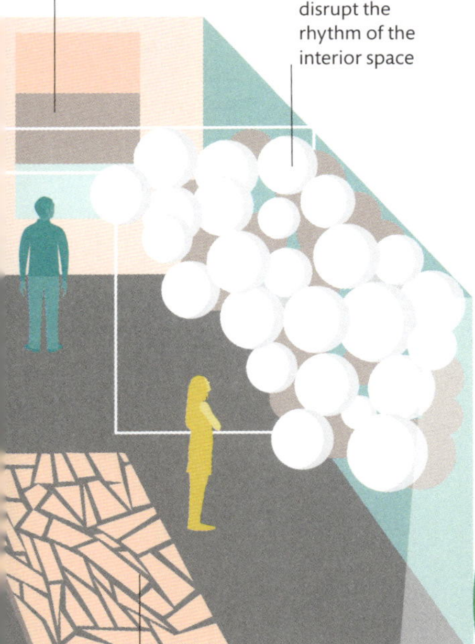

All-encompassing environments
Large spaces can accommodate epic works such as mirrors, light pieces, and even entire playgrounds, with visitors encouraged to navigate across and around displays. Light and sound effects are also a common feature.

ARTIST **ANDY GOLDSWORTHY** MADE **"RAIN SHADOWS"** BY LYING IN THE **RAIN**

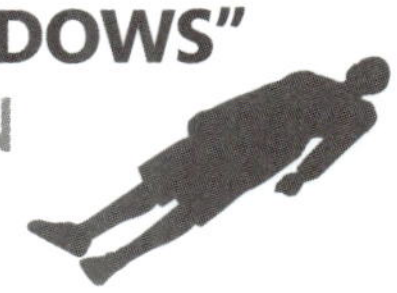

HOW DID YOKO ONO AND JOHN LENNON CREATE AN INSTALLATION?

The couple stayed in a hotel bed for two weeks in 1969 for a performance called "Bed-ins for Peace" in protest at the Vietnam War.

Performance art

In the 1970s, the modernist dominance of painting and sculpture gave way to more diverse art forms, where artists worked across a range of media. Performance was a crucial new form of artistic expression in this period, often reliant on the gestures of bodies (both the artist's, and others) in space.

Laurie Anderson
The artist pioneered performance in New York, once wearing ice skates frozen into ice while she played a violin.

Mierle Laderman Ukeles
Ukeles challenged the domestic role of women by focusing on "maintenance work" in society.

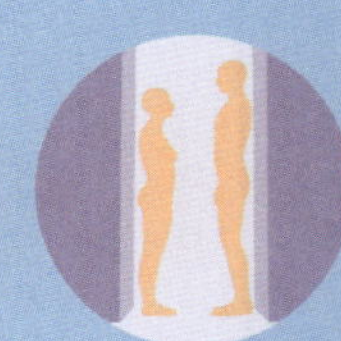

Marina Abramovic
Abramovic uses her body in interactive performances, such as "Imponderabilia" (1977), where viewers squeeze past naked bodies.

Joseph Beuys
In 1972, the artist gave an informal, 6.5-hour-long lecture at the Tate about democracy, while drawing with chalk.

Tania Bruguera
Bruguera's "School of Integration" (2019) had an eclectic curriculum of free classes that drew attention to diversity.

SUBJECTS AND CATEGORIES

Portraits

A portrait is an artistic representation of a single, real person or group of people and remains one of the most popular genres of painting, although it can also be expressed using other art forms. Famous portraits such as the *Mona Lisa* have captivated and mystified viewers for centuries.

WHY WERE PHOTO PORTRAITS POPULAR IN THE 19TH CENTURY?

In 19th-century Europe, photographic portraits were made of figures who, it was believed, had contributed to various fields of achievement.

Likeness and identity

A portrait is commonly understood as an artistic rendering of a sitter's likeness that also conveys aspects of their identity. Historically, some portraits were seen as having great power: in Roman times, portrait busts of the emperor were sent across the empire as a substitute for the ruler himself, as a physical extension of his authority. Today, subjects still sit with artists for painted portraits on occasion, even if smartphones allow casual photographic portraits to be taken and circulated rapidly.

Portraits through history
The meaning of a portrait is tied to its function, which has changed over the course of history, from images of divine power or aristocratic nobility to complex, modern explorations of subjectivity.

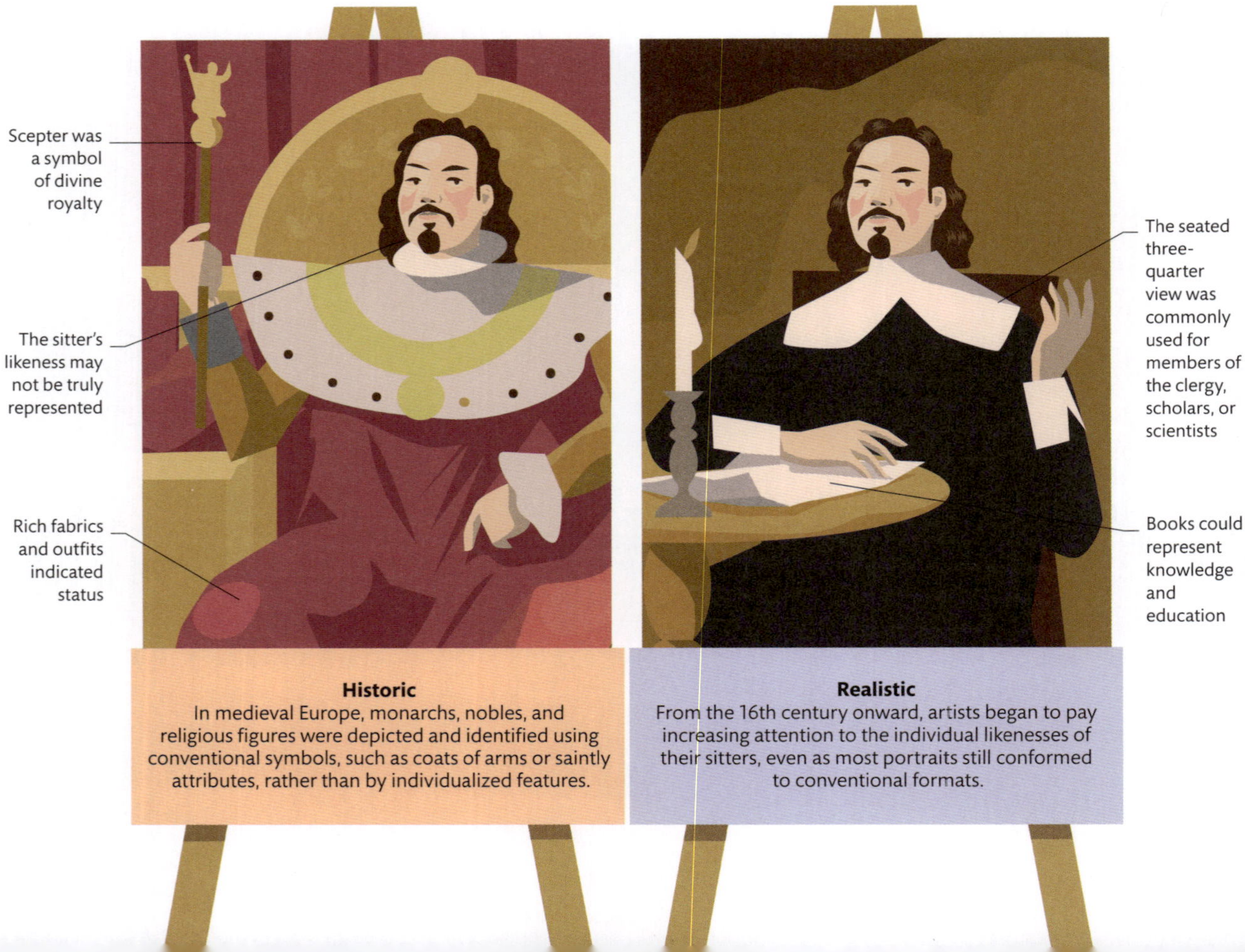

Historic
In medieval Europe, monarchs, nobles, and religious figures were depicted and identified using conventional symbols, such as coats of arms or saintly attributes, rather than by individualized features.

Realistic
From the 16th century onward, artists began to pay increasing attention to the individual likenesses of their sitters, even as most portraits still conformed to conventional formats.

Techniques and approaches

Portrait artists employ a wide range of techniques. Portrait galleries are full of honorific portraits, designed to emphasize the dignity and power of the sitter, which usually follow set formal conventions: bust, half-length, three-quarter length, and full length. Caricature is a popular type of portraiture, used subversively to mock the authority of politicians and other figures of power, by exaggerating and emphasizing certain facial or bodily features. The mood, pose, and intended meaning of the portrait all contribute to its overall impact.

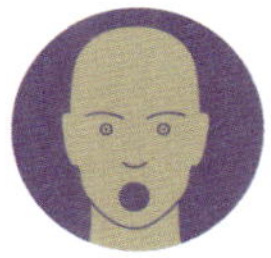
MOOD

POSE

MEANING

NON-REPRESENTATIVE PORTRAITS

Cuban American artist Félix González-Torres made portraits out of piles of sweets, the overall weight matching that of the sitter, as a comment on the AIDS crisis. Viewers were offered a free sweet, meaning the pile gradually diminished.

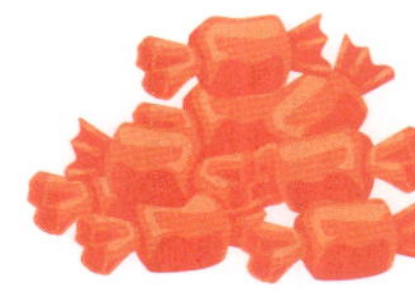
SWEETS AS MEDIUM

PORTRAITURE FLOURISHED IN **ANCIENT EGYPT** AROUND **5,000 YEARS AGO**

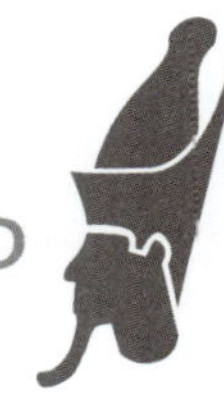

Sitters often posed against plain backgrounds

Formal pose was typical of early photograhic portraits

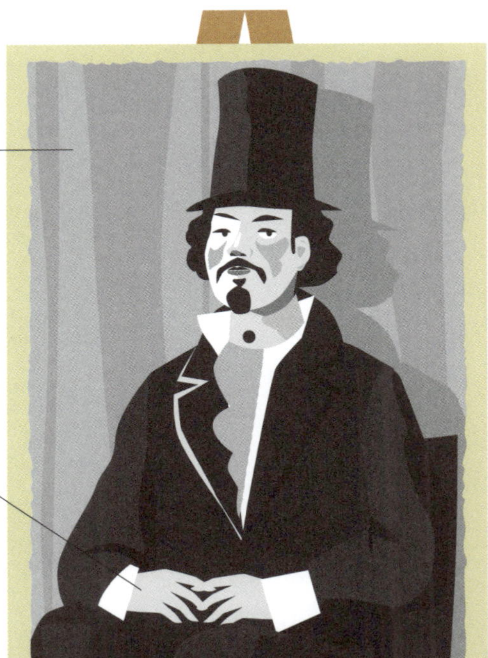

Photographic
Photographic portraits, which were first popularized in the 1850s, can appear to offer an objective representation of the sitter but are as equally based in conventions, such as framing or pose, as painting.

Sitter may be represented in unrecognizable ways

Simple shapes combine to give the impression of a likeness

Facial features may be arranged in strange configurations

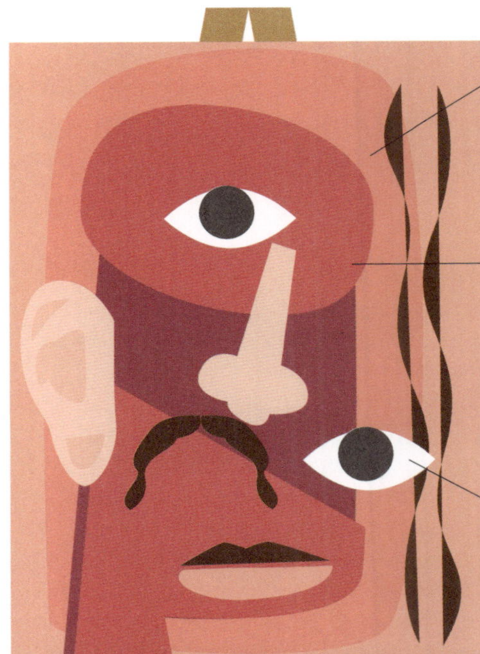

Deconstructed
The move away from lifelike depictions in art after 1900 and the advent of conceptual art (see pp.216–217) prompted a modern mode of portraiture that deliberately avoids naturalistic resemblance.

Religious themes

Artists have historically used their faces to model character types in Biblical and mythological narrative paintings – even, once, using the artist's face as a model for Christ (Dürer, famously in his 1500 self-portrait). The "insertion" of the artist as a figure into religious paintings can have various different meanings; perhaps to please a particular patron, to represent their own devotion, to convey an allegorical message, or simply to bulk out the crowd in a scene.

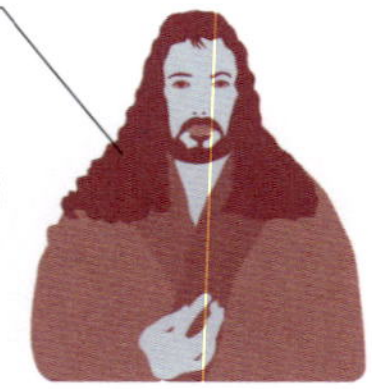

Messianic image
Albrecht Dürer (1471–1528) was a pioneering and prolific painter of self-portraits, who portrayed himself as a Christ-like figure.

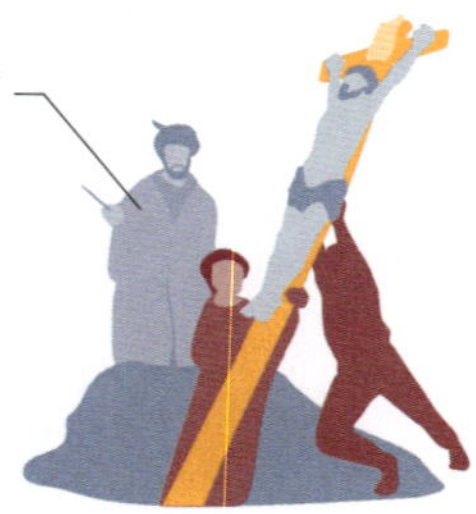

Religious scenes
Rembrandt van Rijn (1606–1669) created over 80 innovative self-portraits, including Biblical scenes.

VINCENT **VAN GOGH** PAINTED **SELF-PORTRAITS** BECAUSE HE COULD **NOT AFFORD** MODELS

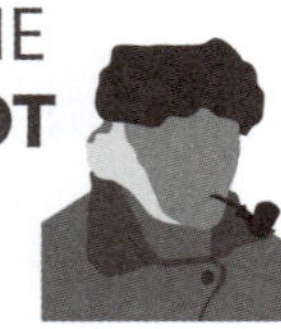

Self-portraits

A self-portrait is an artist's portrait of their own figure. This outwardly simple exercise can lend itself to a wide range of different styles, representational conventions, and media and can convey complex meaning.

The figure of the artist

Self-portraits emerged as an artistic genre during the Renaissance (see pp.176–179), when artists were increasingly viewed as significant social figures endowed with particular attributes, such as creativity, ability, vision, and "genius." Artists would insert self-portraits into painted narrative scenes, often as a figure in the crowd turning to look at the viewer (see above). Artists have since used self-portraits for many purposes—to figure out their particular style and experiment (the artist's own figure is the most readily available model), to promote their own status and interests, and to contemplate subjectivity, selfhood, and perception.

Particular configurations of apparatus and tools are needed to make self-portraits. For paintings, the artist will often use a mirror. For chemical photography, the artist needed to hold the camera's shutter release; digital cameras now often have a timer. For sculpture, the artist may work from photos of themselves.

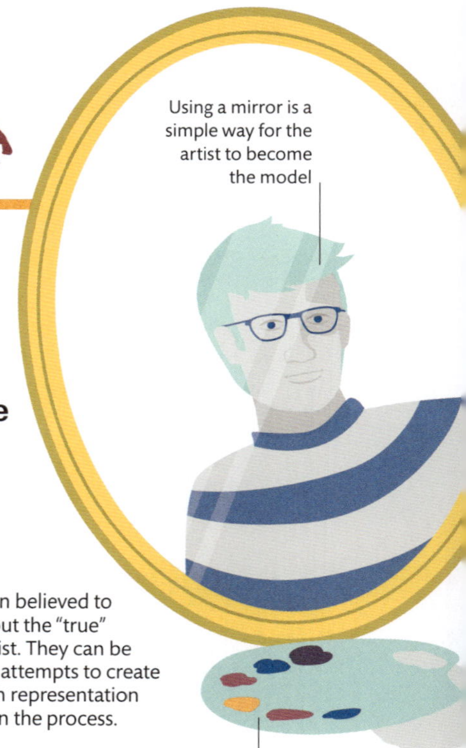

Reflecting the self
Self-portraits are often believed to reveal something about the "true" psychology of the artist. They can be better understood as attempts to create an artistic self through representation and to find meaning in the process.

WHO WAS THE MOST NOTABLE SELF-PORTRAIT ARTIST OF THE 20TH CENTURY?

Frida Kahlo painted around 55 self-portraits, many of which addressed themes of feminine subjectivity and Mexican politics and identity.

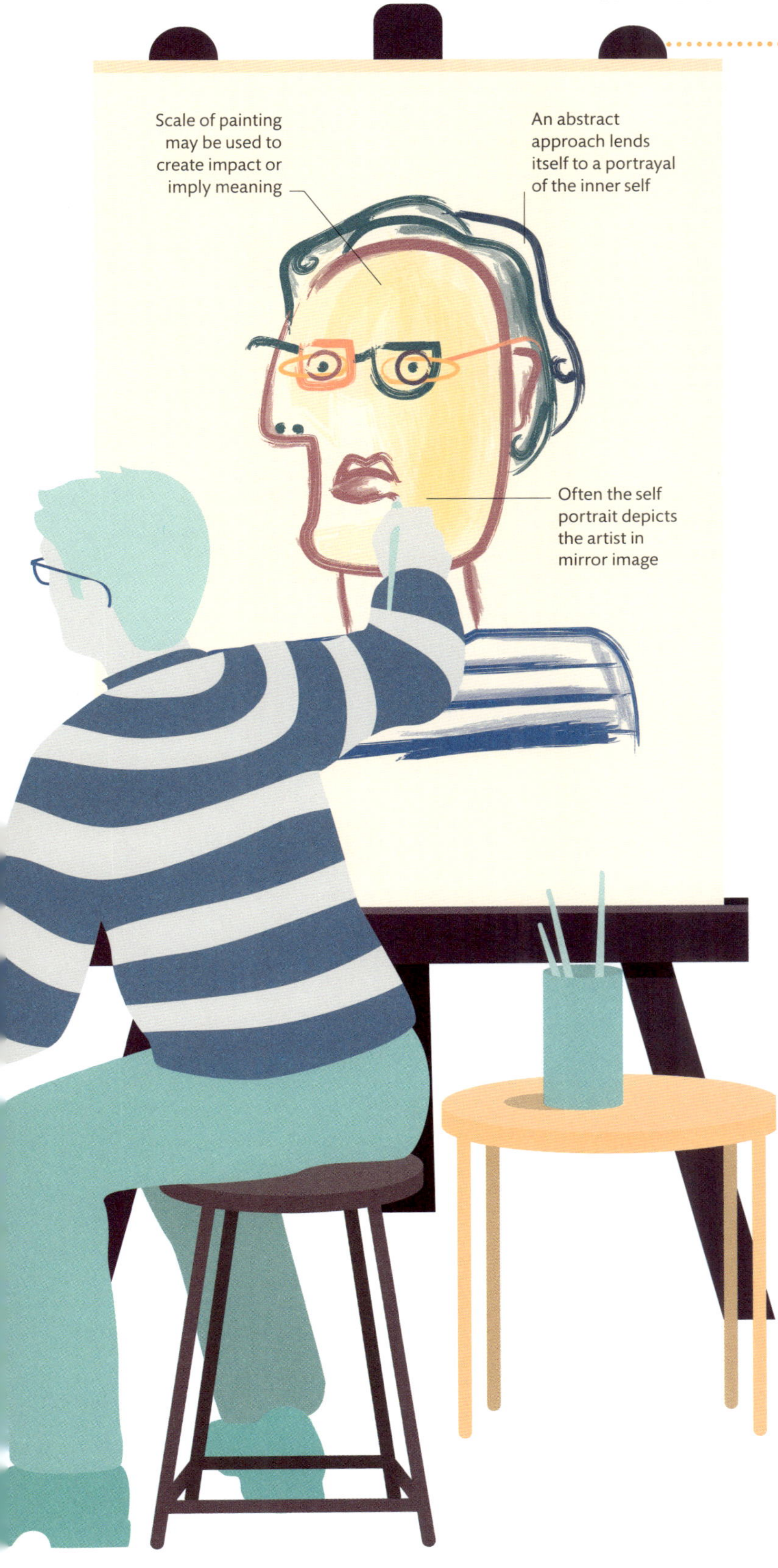

Other types of self-portraits

Self-portraits may take various different forms, with the artist creating coded likenesses, abstract representations, or allegories of their own self. Since 1900, alternative self-portraits have become increasingly commonplace in art and feature more forms.

Sculpture
Helen Chadwick's *Ego Geometric Sum* is a series of wooden blocks with photographs of significant objects printed on the sides.

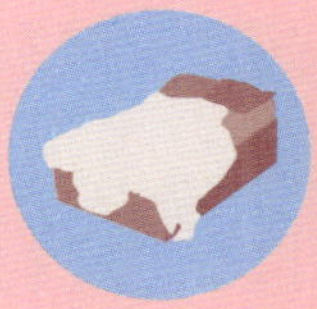

Personal objects
In her installation *Bed*, Tracey Emin displayed detritus from her life (dirty clothes, empty vodka bottles) from a bout of depression.

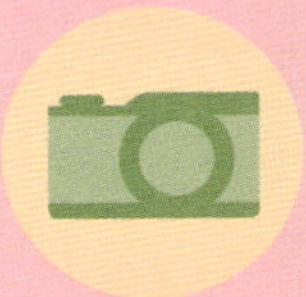

Photography
Oladélé Bamgboyé uses multiple exposures, which comment on the complexity of identity constructed in the African diaspora.

"SELFIES"

Modern smartphone and digital camera software means that most people are able to take good self-portrait photographs ("selfies") easily. Artists have addressed how selfies on social media can create relatively autonomous digital identities. In her work *Excellences & Perfections*, photographer Amalia Ulman "staged" a lifestyle makeover over several months on Instagram by manipulating selfies using Photoshop.

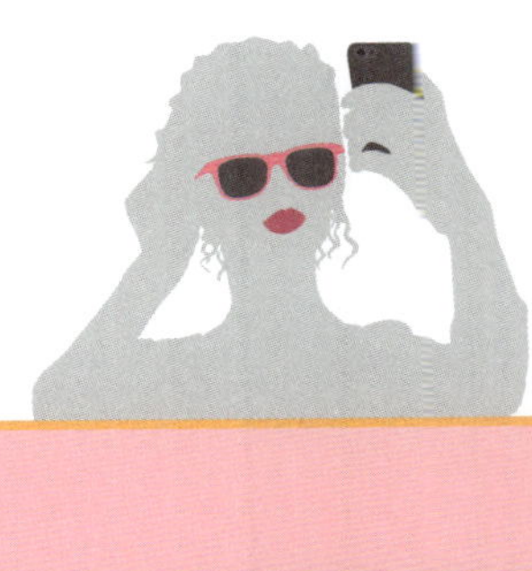

Life Drawing

The practice of observational drawing using fully or partially nude human models is known as life drawing. Since the 15th century, students in art schools have studied life drawing to improve their ability to record the human body realistically. Life drawing remains one of the key ways that artists gather together to practice their drawing skills.

Observing the human figure

In the 15th century, Renaissance artists including Albrecht Dürer, Leonardo da Vinci, and Michelangelo Buonarroti (see pp.176–79) began to observe and draw nude figures in an attempt to understand and reproduce what they believed to be God's finest achievement—the human body. Observational drawing became prized as a method of both reproducing the divine and understanding form and structure, and was made central to art education.

A model's role
The model is an integral part of the life-drawing process. Experienced life models are able to hold poses that show the body in tension—enabling the artist to observe muscles and tendons.

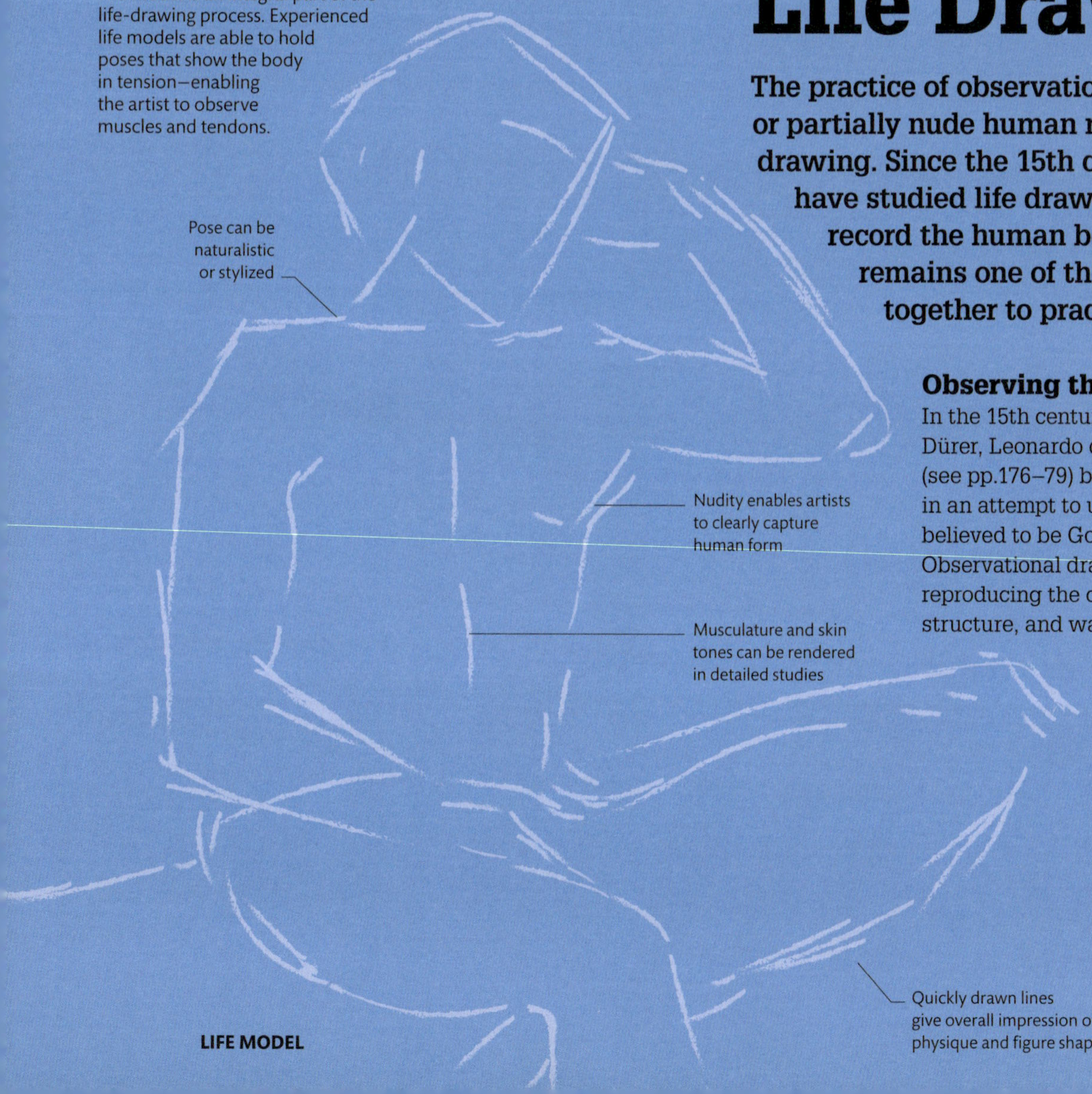

LIFE MODEL

HOW OLD IS LIFE DRAWING?

The two earliest known sets of figure drawings (at Lascaux Cave, Dordogne, France, and Kimberley, Western Australia) are thought to be around 20,000 years old.

Approaches and process

Instructors may use a range of techniques and materials to challenge and expand drawing practice, which are intended to hone observation skills and help the artist find new ways to translate what they see into marks on the paper. The value of life drawing often lies in exploration and process, and the final drawing may not be as important as this process of discovery.

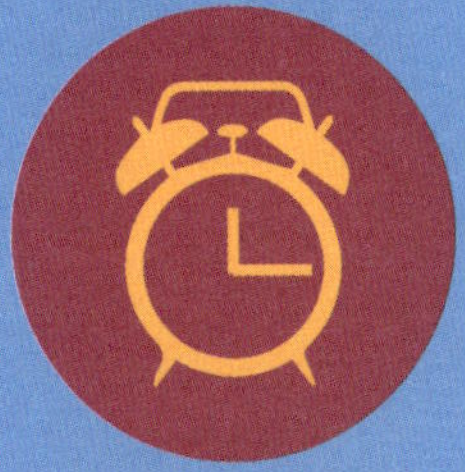

Speed drawing
As a warm-up exercise, the artist tries to draw the model in as much detail as possible in a short amount of time.

Continuous pencil
The artist makes a single, long continuous mark—without the pencil leaving the paper—resulting in overlaid lines.

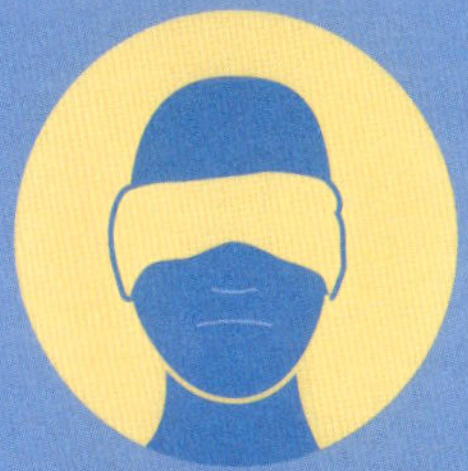

"Blind" drawing
Without looking at the paper, the artist draws the figure by observing their form and structure.

Eraser drawing
Using an eraser as a drawing tool, the artist rubs out shaded areas of the paper and fills in darker tones with a pencil.

Stick and ink
The artist dips a stick into Indian ink, then makes marks on the paper. The ink may run, creating interesting effects.

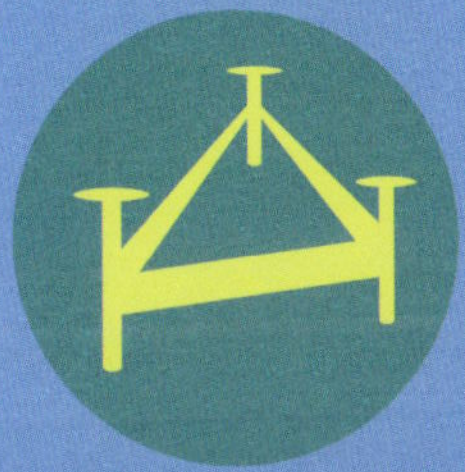

Nails and rubber bands
To help figure out perspective and proportion, the artist stretches rubber bands around nails fixed to the paper.

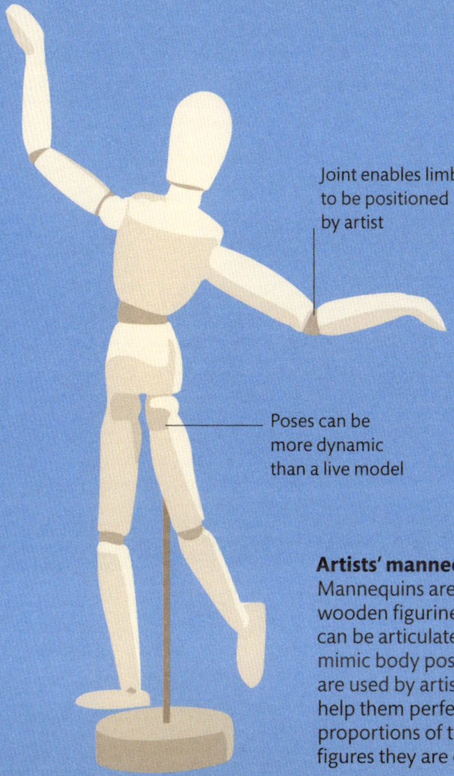

Artists' mannequins
Mannequins are typically wooden figurines that can be articulated to mimic body poses. They are used by artists to help them perfect the proportions of the figures they are drawing.

A POPULAR **US ANIMATION STUDIO** PROVIDES **REGULAR LIFE DRAWING CLASSES** FOR ITS IN-HOUSE **ARTISTS**

LEONARDO'S NOTEBOOKS

Leonardo da Vinci recorded an array of notes, scientific diagrams, and sketches of people and animals on sheets of paper that were bound into notebooks after his death. Leonardo's incredible life drawings are often a mixture of observation and deduction; he sometimes imaginatively based aspects of human anatomy on animal dissections.

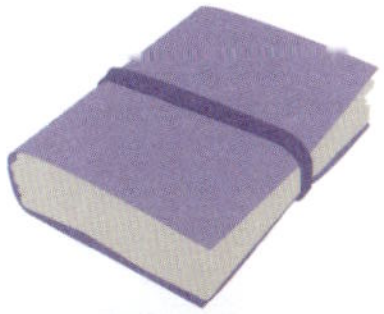

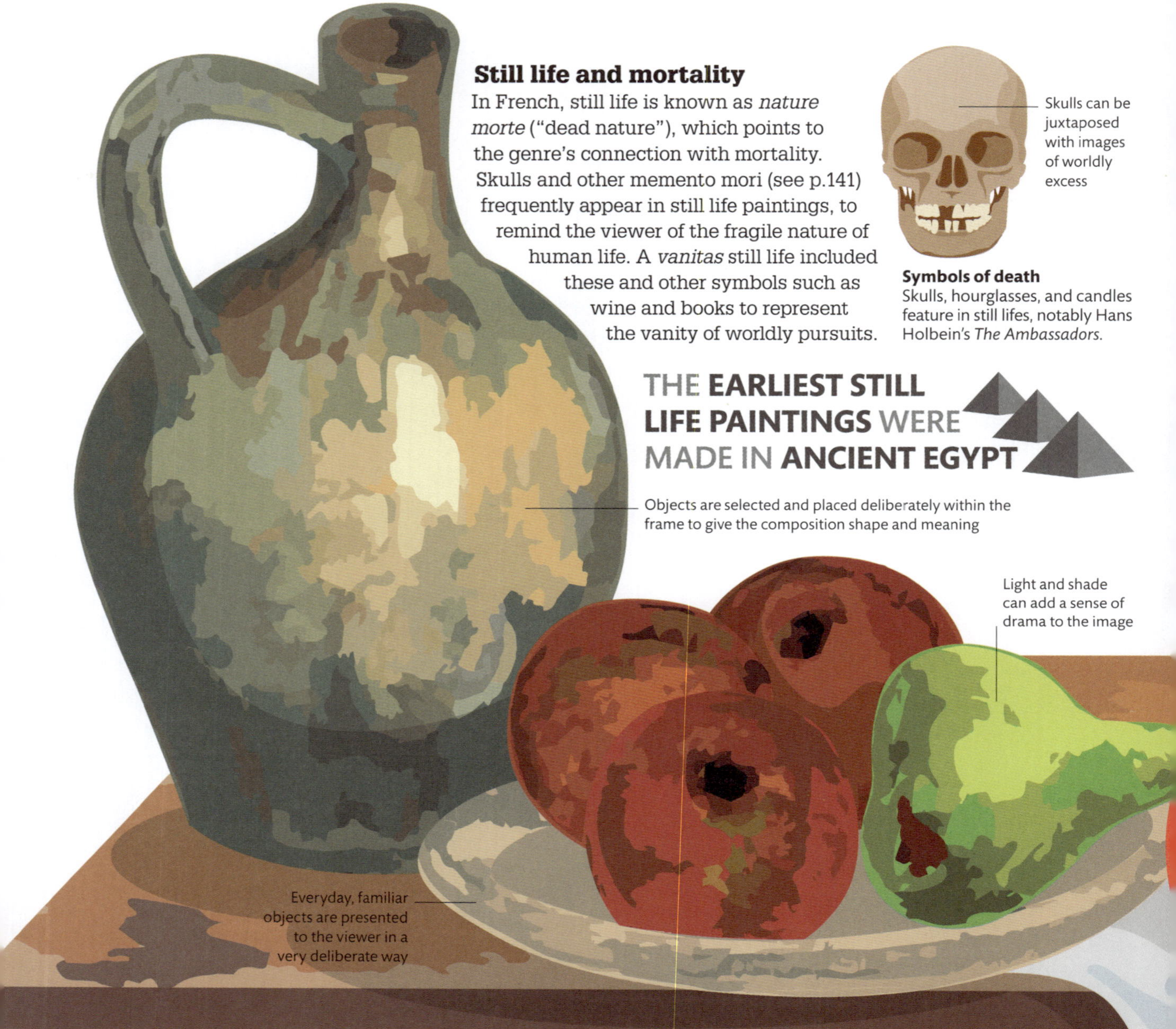

Still life and mortality

In French, still life is known as *nature morte* ("dead nature"), which points to the genre's connection with mortality. Skulls and other memento mori (see p.141) frequently appear in still life paintings, to remind the viewer of the fragile nature of human life. A *vanitas* still life included these and other symbols such as wine and books to represent the vanity of worldly pursuits.

Skulls can be juxtaposed with images of worldly excess

Symbols of death
Skulls, hourglasses, and candles feature in still lifes, notably Hans Holbein's *The Ambassadors.*

THE **EARLIEST STILL LIFE PAINTINGS** WERE MADE IN **ANCIENT EGYPT**

Commodities and symbolism

Still life grew in popularity as global patterns of trade were becoming established from the 17th century. Exotic commodities flowed into the prosperous Low Countries of colonial Europe and began to appear in paintings. The meaning of any particular object depends on its place in a painting's system, but some have more general symbolic meanings.

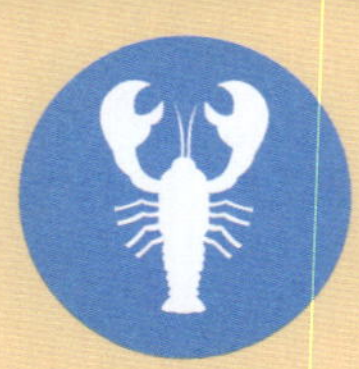

Lobster
Lobster was expensive, so signified wealth. It also hinted at a patron's link with sea trade.

Gold cup
Manufactured objects testified to wealth and global trade, as well as to decadence.

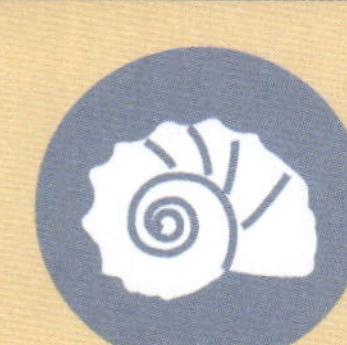

Shell
Exotic but empty, shells could mean tension between wealth and spiritual vacuity.

Still Life

Still life describes a type of image making that developed as a genre in early modern Northern Europe, in which a group of inanimate objects, man-made or natural, are depicted together.

Relationship between objects

A still life is best understood as a system, or the relationships between a selection of objects set in a particular space. Still life was initially considered inferior to historical and religious painting, portraiture, and landscape. However, artists in the 17th and 18th centuries began producing beautiful still lifes, exploring techniques and meaning. By the end of the 19th century, avant-garde painters were trying to push boundaries and break norms and turned to still life to experiment with form and content. Modern and contemporary artists have used collage, assemblage, readymades, industrial objects, and sculptures.

MODERN STILL LIFE

The post-World War II boom in consumption in North America provoked artists to contemplate the social ubiquity of commodities. Mass-produced consumer goods became the subject of works of Pop Art, from tins of soup to road signs and hamburgers (see pp.212–213) and can be understood as a modern form of still life painting.

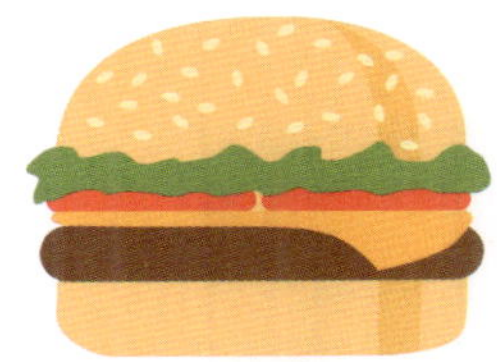

MASS-PRODUCED GOODS

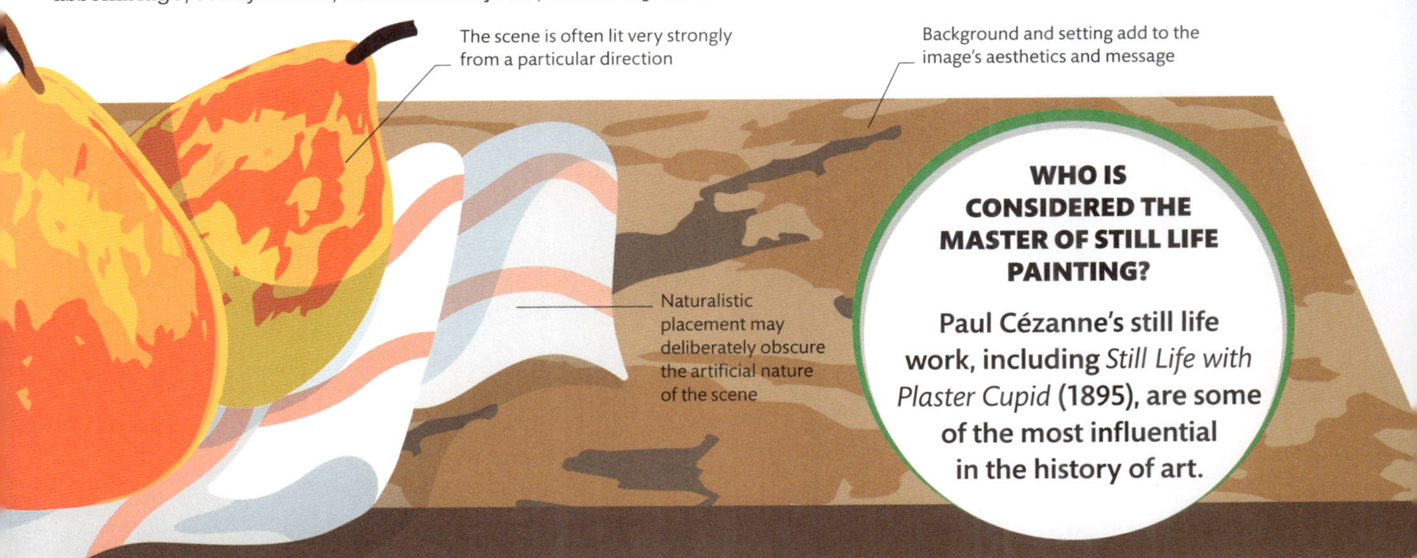

WHO IS CONSIDERED THE MASTER OF STILL LIFE PAINTING?

Paul Cézanne's still life work, including *Still Life with Plaster Cupid* (1895), are some of the most influential in the history of art.

Butterfly
Butterflies could symbolize resurrection and the emergence of new life.

Apple
Fresh produce often symbolized earthly beauty, fecundity, and life—even if fleeting.

Flower
Flowers' fertility and quick decay linked sexual pleasure with life's fragility.

Candle
Burning candles, with the implication of time-bound, finite light, are memento mori.

Wine
A Christian symbol, wine also implied wealth and trade, and pleasure and excess.

Landscapes

Art depicting landscapes can use almost any medium, but painting remains its most popular form. Artists may depict a landscape to convey a particular message or feeling, or they may simply be inspired by the beauty of the land.

Capturing a scene

Chinese artists have been painting landscapes since the 4th century CE, and it is part of the art of many cultures. Landscape as a genre developed in the West in the 17th century in history and mythological painting, with artists reimagining contemporary views to depict classical locations. The industrialization of Europe saw a reworking of the genre by J.M.W. Turner and the Impressionists (see pp.192–193), who depicted the changing meaning of "nature." In the US, artists such as George Inness depicted the wild terrain.

Location
Landscapes may show fields, forests, mountains, coasts, or lakes and can include man-made structures

Season
Some artists paint the same landscape view through different seasons, to show the changes.

Time of day
Many Impressionist landscapes try to capture particular times of day, often dawn or dusk.

Weather conditions
Depicting different weather conditions and light can help artists create depth and mood.

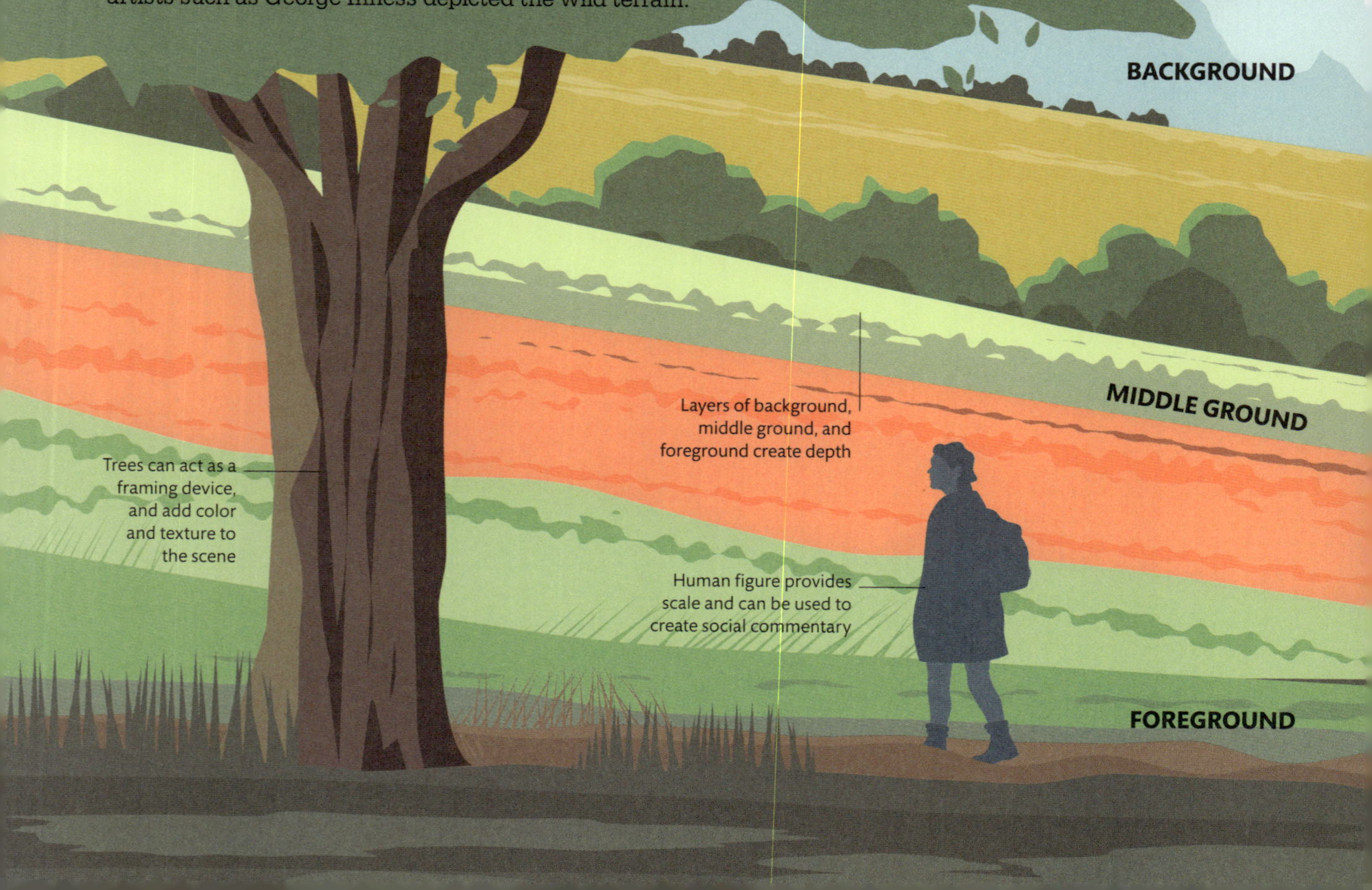

WHAT IS A SURREALIST LANDSCAPE?

Surrealist artists attempt to represent the landscape of the mind by depicting uncanny imagery and fantastic symbols populating invented outdoor scenes.

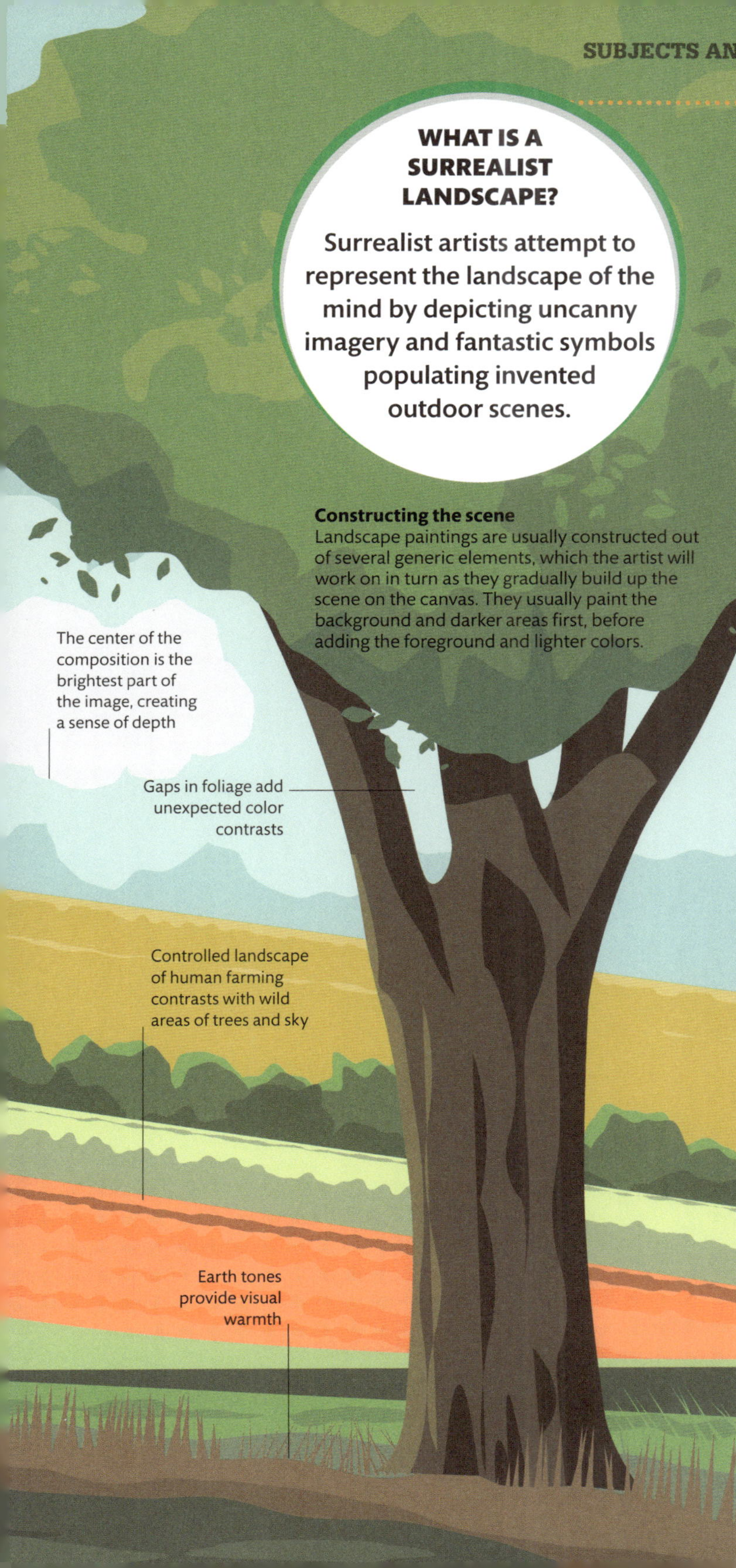

Constructing the scene
Landscape paintings are usually constructed out of several generic elements, which the artist will work on in turn as they gradually build up the scene on the canvas. They usually paint the background and darker areas first, before adding the foreground and lighter colors.

Rückenfigur

The German term *Rückenfigur* (meaning "figure from behind"), describes the use of a figure in a landscape painting with its back to the viewer, looking out at the scene. The *Rückenfigur* positions viewers as spectators to the act of contemplating the landscape. The trope was first popularized by German Romanticism, in particular the painter Caspar David Friedrich, and has since been adopted across other genres of art.

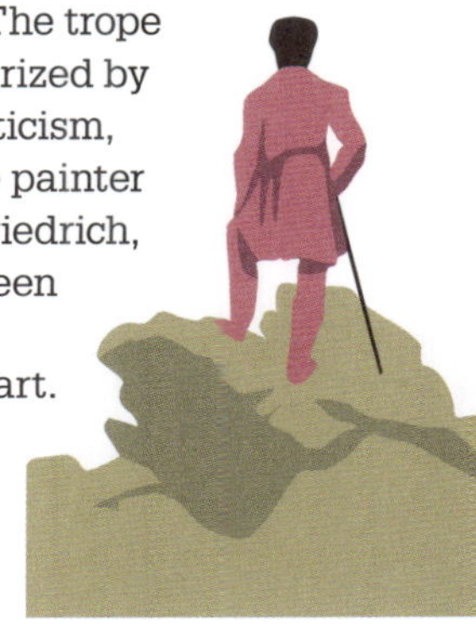

Contemplative figure
Landscape painting, especially during the Romantic movement, often aimed to depict massive scenes of nature and turbulent weather. This contrasted with the tiny scale of the individual, who may be watching in awed and overwhelmed contemplation.

THE **AMERICAN** ARTIST **GEORGIA O'KEEFFE** HELPED PIONEER THE **CITYSCAPE**

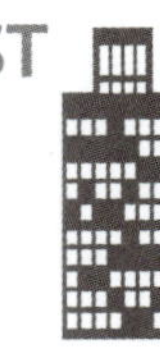

MAN-MADE STRUCTURES

Artists can make man-made objects central to a landscape. British artist Tacita Dean has created films that archive redundant human structures in landscapes. *Sound Mirrors* (1999) features obsolete concrete "sound mirrors" designed to detect aircraft.

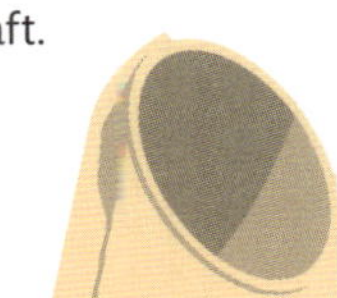

FABRICATED OBJECTS

Fine and Decorative Art

The difference between "fine" and "decorative" arts was established during the Renaissance—fine art was seen as the work of an enlightened individual (the artist), while decorative art was concerned with beauty and function. Both require craftsmanship, skill, and ingenuity.

Functional but aesthetic

Decorative arts refer to the use of design and ornament in the production of a range of aesthetic, but functional objects. In his 1931 essay "Ornament and Crime" Adolf Loos, an Austrian architect, denounced ornamentation as a sign of excess and degeneracy. Fine art, in contrast, refers to traditionally highbrow art forms such as painting and sculpture, as well as architecture.

ROCOCO

A highly ornamental, sumptuous and intricate style, Rococo (from the French *rocaille*, referring to the use of seashell and rock motifs), emerged in France in the 1720s. Rococo style embellished ceramics, furniture, silverware, and interior design. It influenced the style of many paintings, such as "The Swing" (1767) by Fragonard.

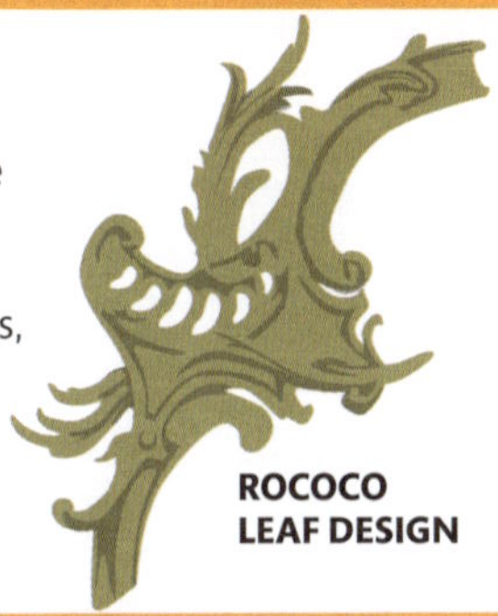

ROCOCO LEAF DESIGN

THE **ANCIENT GREEK MEANDER** PATTERN WAS WIDELY USED IN **DECORATIVE ARTS**

Fine art
Working in Florence, the polymath Leon Battista Alberti (1406–72), defined the three main categories of fine art by writing a treatise on each. Alberti's works were crucial to art education in Europe, leading to the contemporary division between "fine" art and "decorative" art.

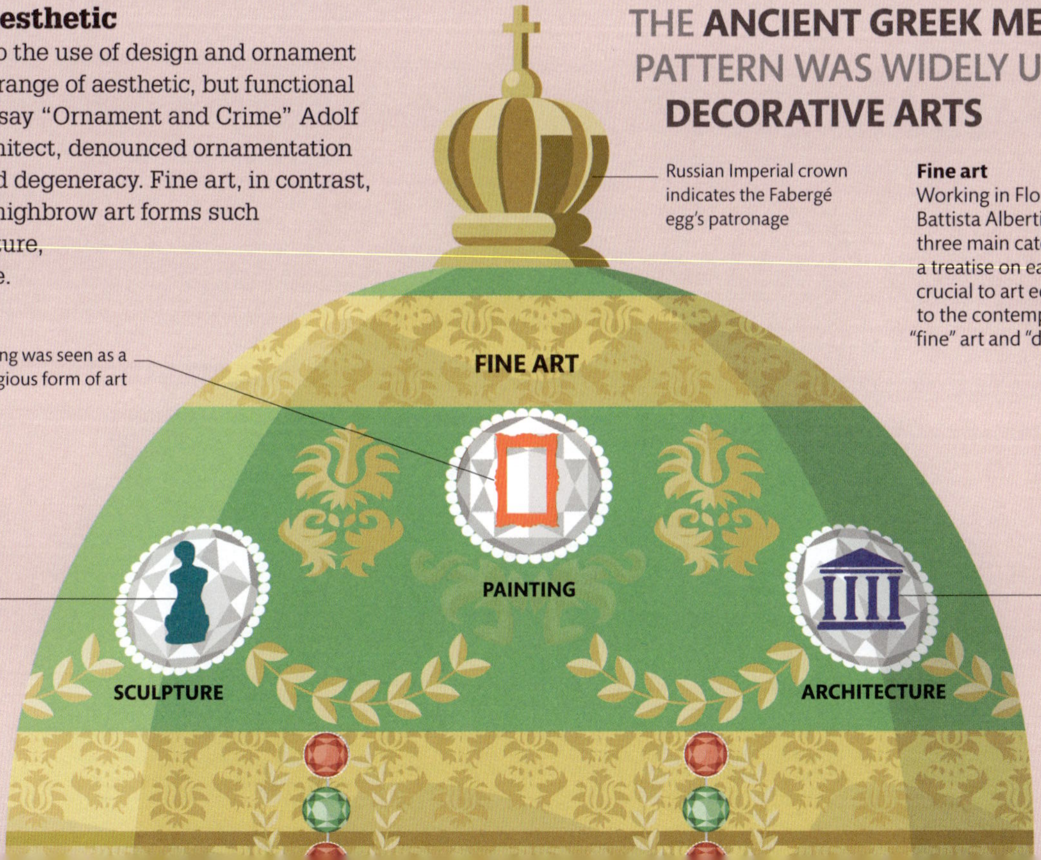

Russian Imperial crown indicates the Fabergé egg's patronage

Painting was seen as a prestigious form of art

Sculpture often depicted classical notions of beauty in the human form

Practicality was taken into consideration for architecture, as well as aesthetic beauty

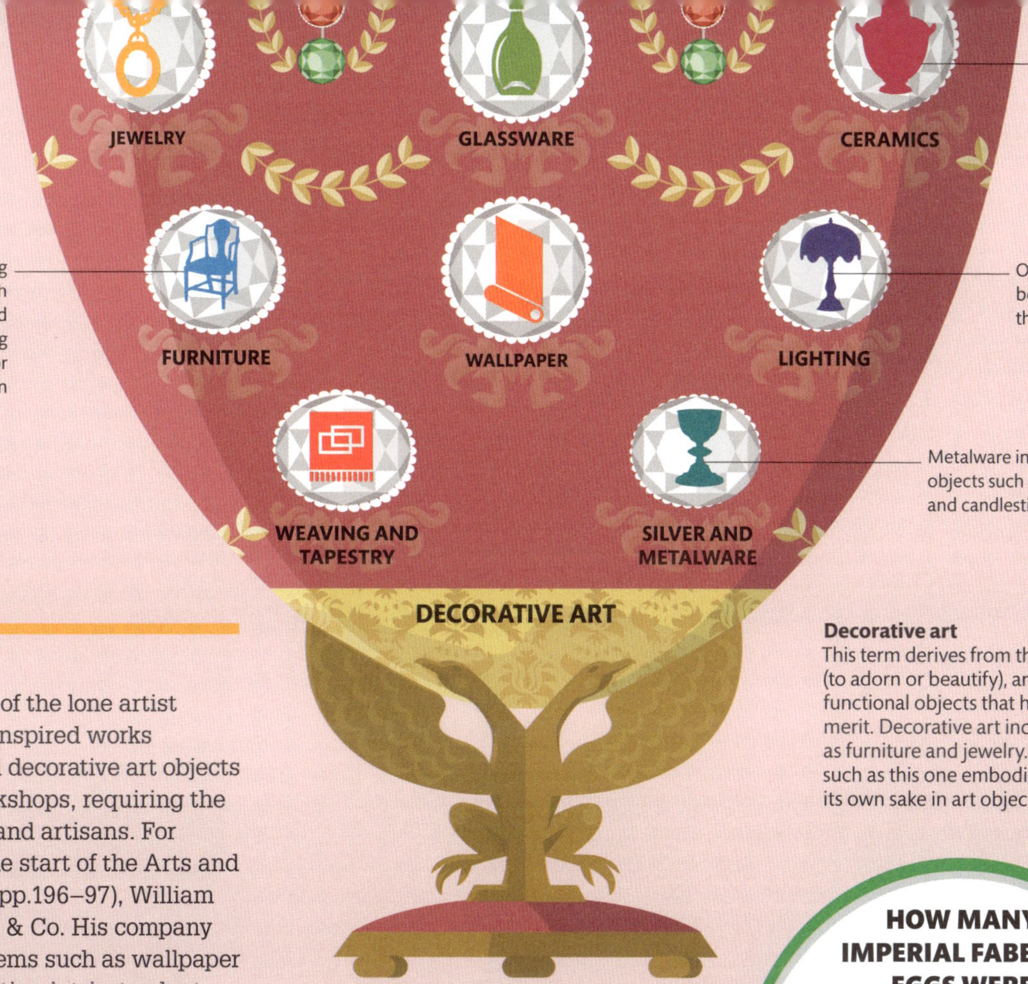

Decorative art
This term derives from the Latin *decorare* (to adorn or beautify), and describes functional objects that have aesthetic merit. Decorative art includes items such as furniture and jewelry. Fabergé eggs such as this one embodied decoration for its own sake in art objects.

Workshops

In contrast to the idea of the lone artist producing personally inspired works of fine art, applied and decorative art objects are often made in workshops, requiring the skill of several artists and artisans. For example, in 1861, at the start of the Arts and Crafts movement (see pp.196–97), William Morris founded Morris & Co. His company made decorative art items such as wallpaper and textiles, incorporating intricate plant and animal motifs.

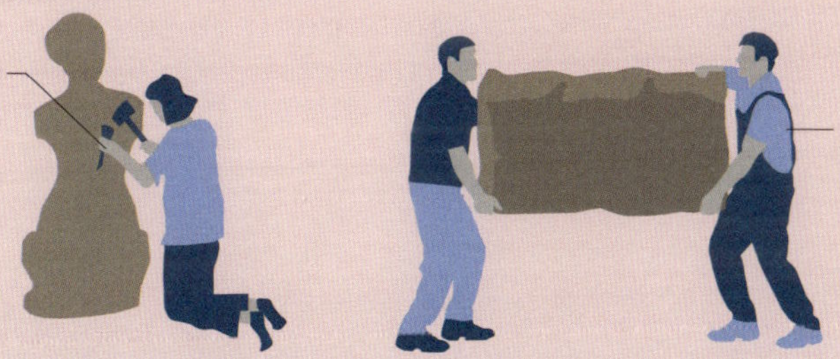

HOW MANY IMPERIAL FABERGÉ EGGS WERE MANUFACTURED?

Between 1885 and 1917, Carl Fabergé, based in St. Petersburg, made 50 Imperial Easter eggs for the Russian court; 44 of these survive today.

Types of realism

The use of realism has fluctuated throughout the course of history. In the medieval period, painting and sculpture depicted more detail and facial expression than before—although the main focus was on symbolic images—and this carried through into the Renaissance. However, it was in the mid-1800s that true realism in art began.

19th-century Realism
Gustave Courbet painted people's daily lives instead of religious themes (see pp.190–91)—the Realism movement referred to subjects, not depictions.

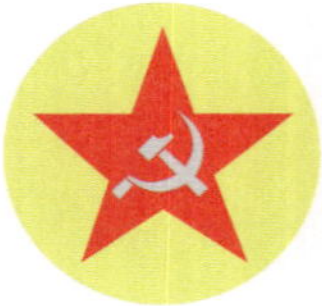

Socialist realism
Soviet artists practiced "constructed realism," portraying workers and citizens in naturalistic but very idealized ways.

Photography
Photography and other lens-based media capture the real world but can also be used to make social, political, or artistic points.

HOW DO ARTISTS PLAY WITH REALISM?

A work such as Édouard Manet's *Bar at the Folies-Bergère*, with lifelike figures shown in impossible symmetry and unfeasible angles, implies that even realistic art is never truly real.

TRUTH AND TECHNOLOGY

In the 19th century, the new process of photography was claimed to provide a purely objective and neutral reproduction of subjects. It went on to have a huge impact both in society and in the art world; however, both artists and photographers in general soon realized that it could be used to misrepresent and distort what was "real" just as much as any other visual medium.

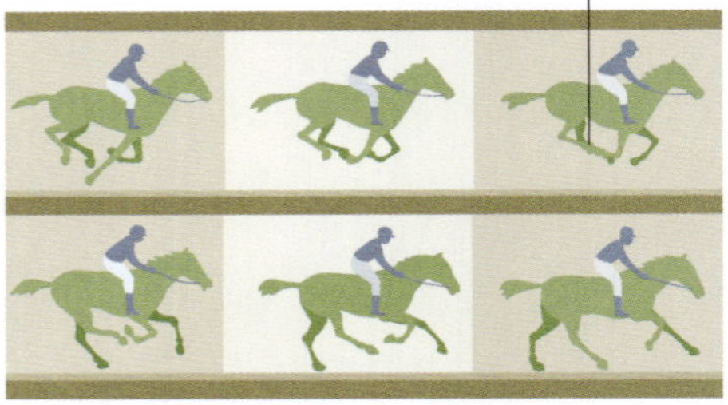

Capturing motion
In 1878, Eadweard Muybridge used photography to accurately capture a horse in motion for the first time.

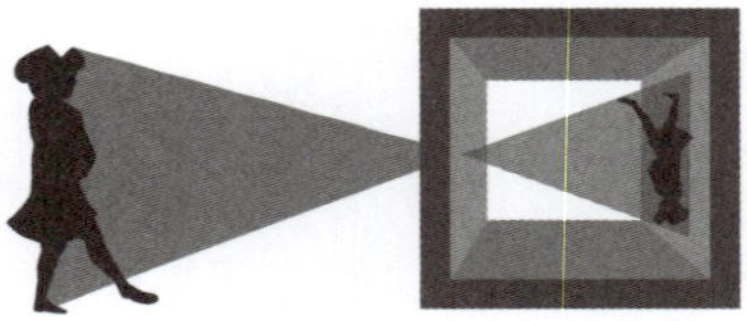

FRENCH SCIENTIST JOSEPH NICÉPHORE NIÉPCE TOOK THE FIRST PHOTOGRAPH IN 1826

Contemporary realism

In the 1990s, "critical realism" emerged as an art movement that questioned the truth of visual imagery and used text alongside photography to prompt viewers to question what they were seeing. Contemporary artist Trevor Paglen uses military and intelligence agency images to challenge perceptions of reality. Other artists have used techniques such as drone photography of landscapes to explore new methods of depicting reality.

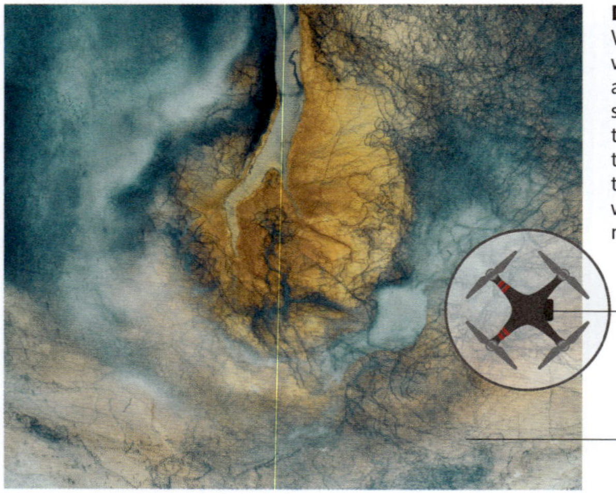

Drone landscape
While most realism works are figurative and focus on people, some artists have turned their attention to landscapes and how to represent the natural world honestly and meaningfully.

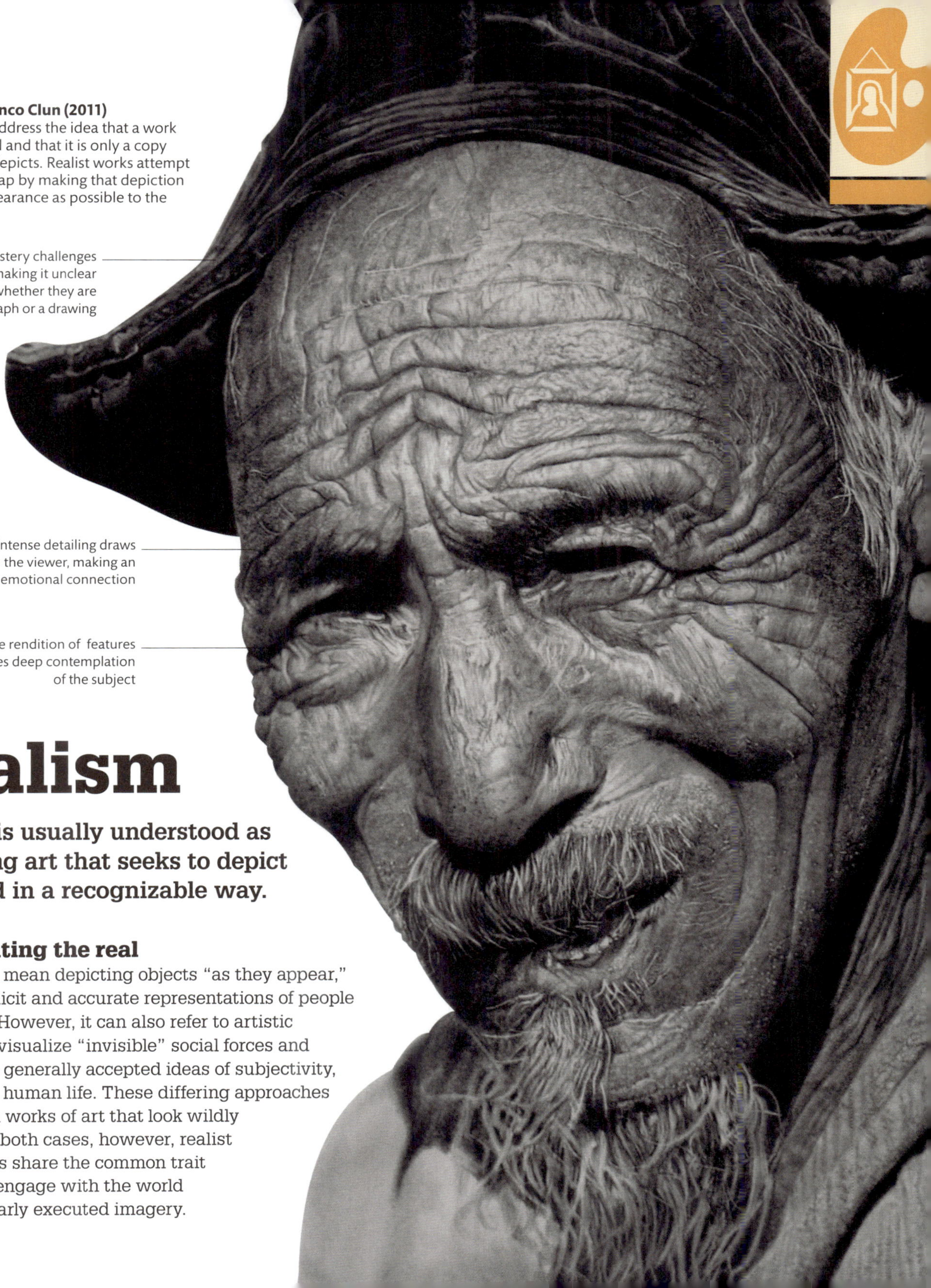

"Old Man", Franco Clun (2011)
Realism must address the idea that a work of art is not real and that it is only a copy of the thing it depicts. Realist works attempt to bridge this gap by making that depiction as close in appearance as possible to the original object.

Realism

Realism is usually understood as describing art that seeks to depict the world in a recognizable way.

Representing the real

Realism can mean depicting objects "as they appear," making explicit and accurate representations of people and things. However, it can also refer to artistic attempts to visualize "invisible" social forces and to challenge generally accepted ideas of subjectivity, politics, and human life. These differing approaches can result in works of art that look wildly different. In both cases, however, realist compositions share the common trait of trying to engage with the world by using clearly executed imagery.

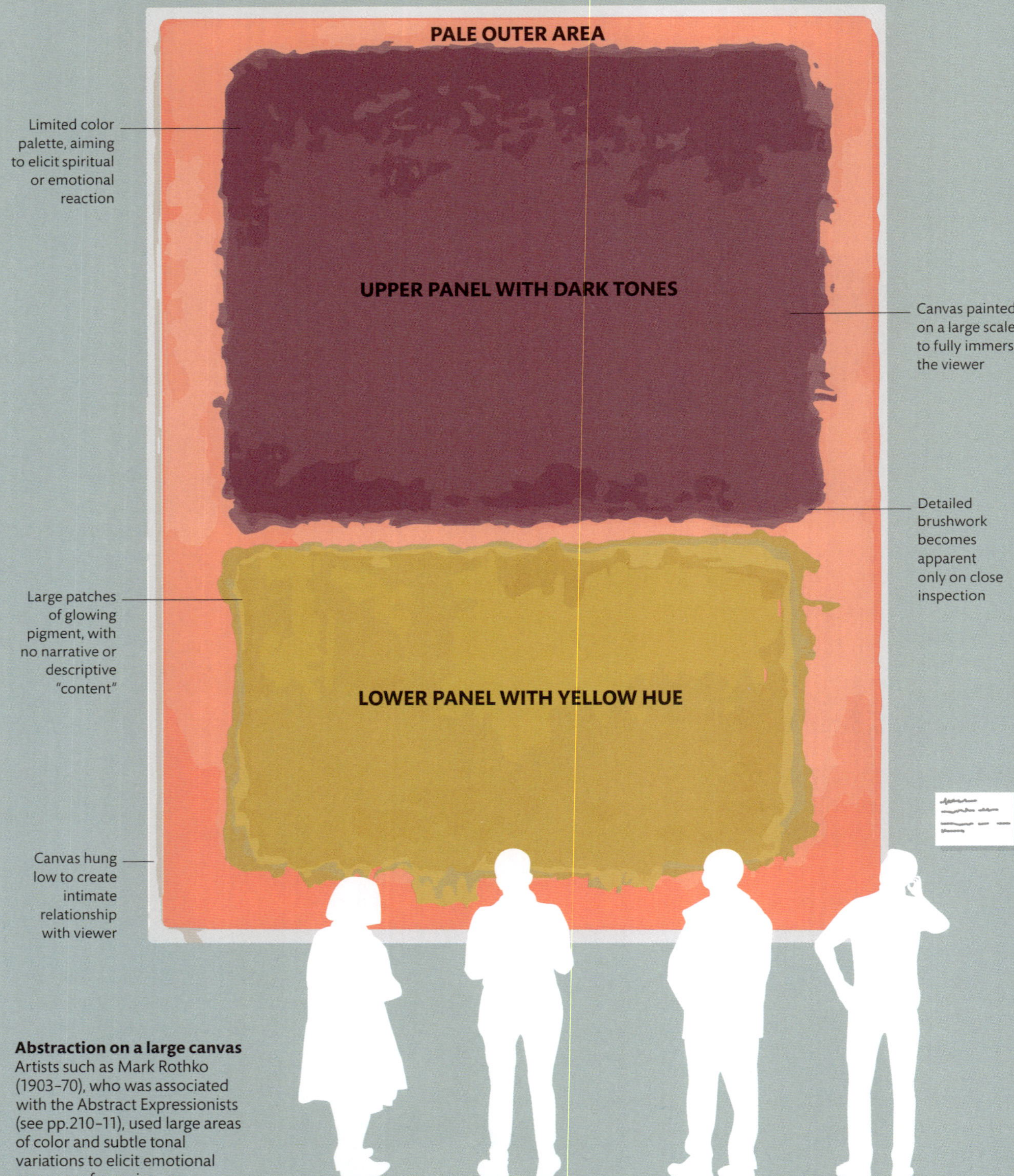

Abstraction on a large canvas
Artists such as Mark Rothko (1903–70), who was associated with the Abstract Expressionists (see pp.210–11), used large areas of color and subtle tonal variations to elicit emotional responses from viewers.

Abstraction

Abstraction describes art that does not represent things, objects, and people in recognizable form but rather foregrounds formal elements, including shape, line, color, pattern, composition, texture, and surface. "Abstract art" encompasses an extraordinary range of practices that are not unified by any single theory, use of material, or sociopolitical intention.

WHAT KIND OF UNCONVENTIONAL MATERIALS HAVE BEEN USED IN ABSTRACT ART?

In 1970s New York, Howardena Pindell used chads (hole-punch offcuts) and perfume to create her abstract paintings.

Nonrepresentational art

Abstraction is defined in opposition to figuration or representation. Abstract patterns have been used to embellish objects and buildings around the world for thousands of years, and many mosques are decorated with abstract designs in Islamic art (see pp.164–65). Modern and contemporary abstract artworks, however, are frequently closer to representation than they might like to admit; for example, Helen Frankenthaler's poured color field canvases flirt with landscape painting.

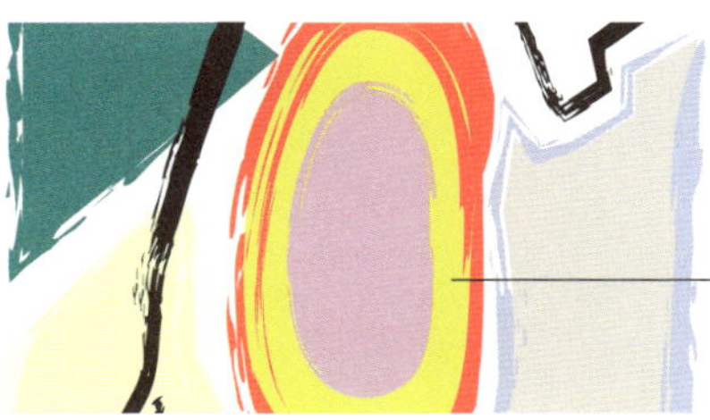

Real vs abstract
Abstract art may seem far from reality, but can be closer to representation than first appears.

Abstract painting resembling a sun going down over a field

Selected elements found	Elements not commonly found
Form: emphasis on the material construction of the work	Figuration: representation of figures and objects from the world
Composition: the relationship of parts to each other, and to the whole	Narrative: abstract art does not generally tell stories in the way that other forms of art may do
Connotation: shapes, marks, and colors may have particular associations or meaning	Denotation: elements of the work in abstract art do not represent specific objects

YAYOI KUSAMA

Japanese artist Kusama uses repetition of abstract forms, famously dots. In 1969, she painted dots on naked, dancing performers, during a "happening" on Wall Street to protest the Vietnam War.

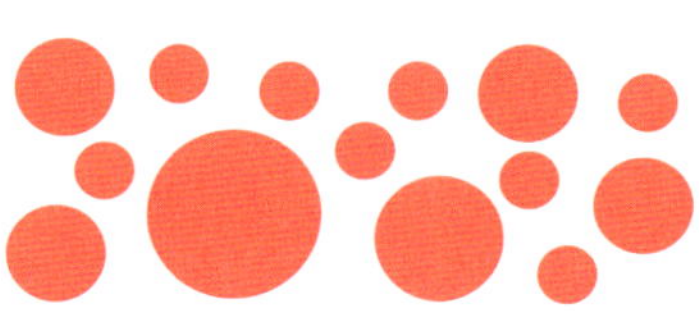

The origins of abstraction

Rather than having a single "inventor", modern abstraction developed in multiple locales at once, in the wake of Cubism and Futurism (see pp.204–05). In Russia, artists turned away from depicting "nature" toward pure shape, color, and line to find a new anti-elitist aesthetic, matching the aims of the 1917 October Revolution. Dada artists in Zurich, such as Hans Arp and Sophie Taeuber-Arp, rejected representation in disgust at what they saw as the bourgeois values that had caused the mindless slaughter of World War I. Debates between artists over realism and abstraction at particular moments have been decisive for the development of modern art.

"Black Square", Kazmir Malevich, 1913
In 1915, Malevich exhibited this piece at the exhibition that launched Suprematism, or what he called "nonobjective" art.

Religious Art

Across history, religions around the world have used art to express their systems of belief, using various forms, including architecture, sculpture, dance, and music.

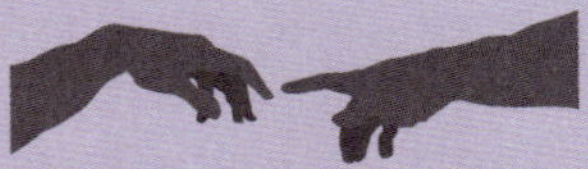

MICHELANGELO TOOK **FOUR YEARS** TO PAINT **343 BIBLICAL FIGURES** IN THE **SISTINE CHAPEL**

Devotion and ritual

To understand religious art, it is crucial to consider any particular object in its context of devotion and ritual. Spaces, objects, smells, and sounds are often experienced all at once in practices of worship, unlike the experience of viewing individual pieces of art in museums. Shown below are the six most populous world religions, which all use art in this way.

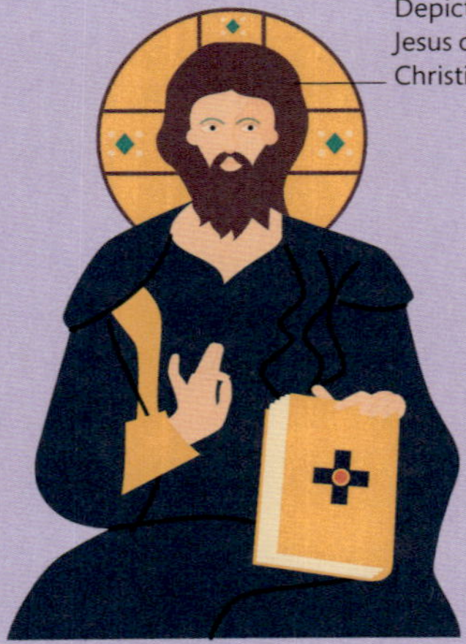

Christianity
Christian art is defined by church architecture, prayer books, and figurative representation of holy figures, notably Christ and the Virgin Mary, as aids to worship.

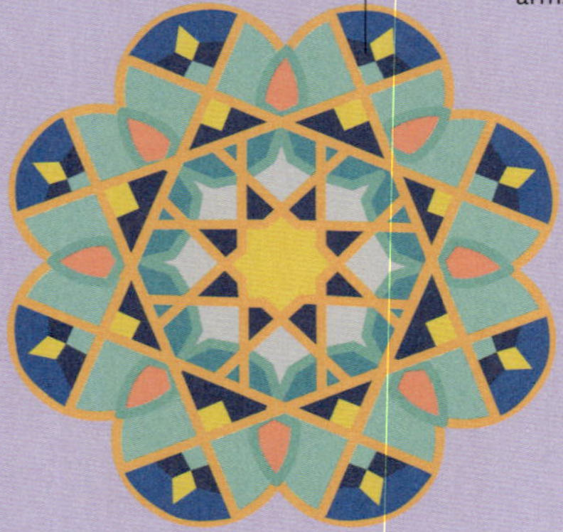

Islam
Geometric patterns, calligraphy, and pottery are common in Islamic art (see pp.164–165). Figurative images are rare, but Sunni and Shi'a Muslims have varying views on this.

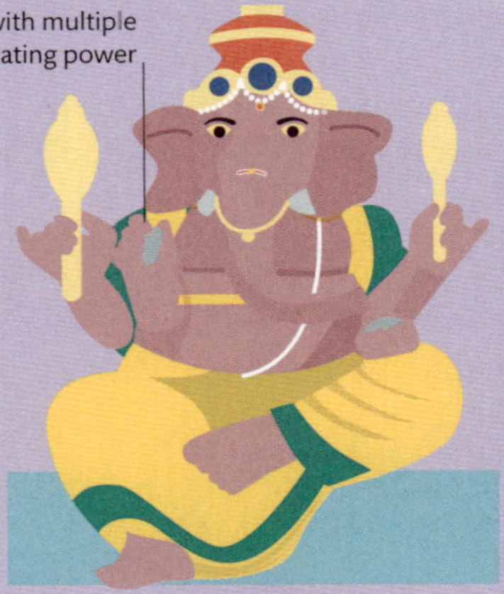

Hinduism
Hindu's myriad deities are represented using vibrant color and ornamentation and are designed to enable *darshan*, direct communion with the divine (see pp.160–161).

Other religions

Many religions around the world have developed artistic practices to convey beliefs and spread messages. Some of these are now entirely historic, such as Ancient Greek and Roman, Aztec, and Mayan religions, and remain as relics only. However, living religious art practices continue to have a huge influence on the contemporary art world. A nonexhaustive selection of these is shown here.

Jainism
Temples and sculpted figures of *jinas*, worshipped souls freed from perpetual reincarnation, scatter the Indian subcontinent.

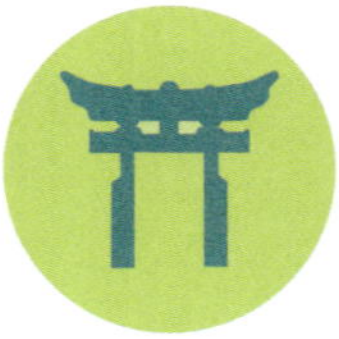

Shinto
Developed in Japan, Shinto shrines, buildings, and monuments enable connection and harmony with *kami*, supernatural spirit-beings.

Taoism
Originating in China, Taoism uses calligraphy, architecture, and symbols, such as the yin yang, to promote balance and harmony.

WHERE IS THE WORLD'S OLDEST KNOWN TEMPLE?

The 11,000-year-old Göbekli Tepe in Turkey was possibly designed to worship Sirius, the "dog star." Its pillars are carved with vultures, lions, and scorpions.

CHILA KUMARI BURMAN

Chila Kumari Burman, a Punjabi-Liverpudlian, uses gods and stories from Hindu mythology to address issues in the postcolonial world, in paintings, installations, photography, and printmaking. For example, she models herself in photographs as Kali, the goddess of power, to represent her own commitment to feminism.

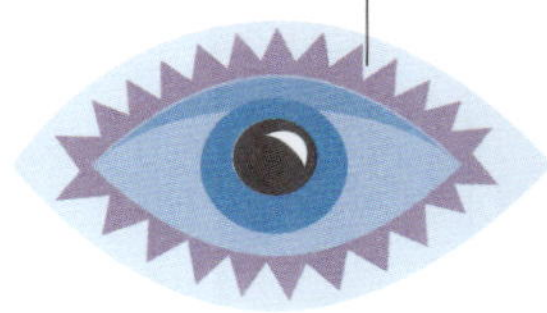

EYE OF SHIVA

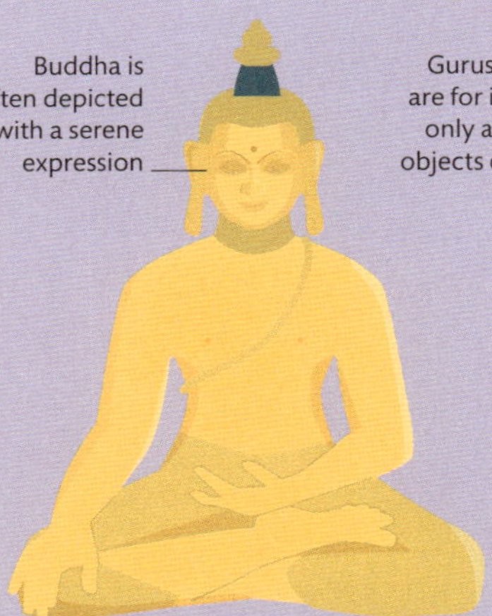

Buddhism
Buddhist art is incredibly diverse; initially characterized by symbols of journeying and enlightenment (trees, wheels, footprints, and lotus), images of the Buddha now proliferate.

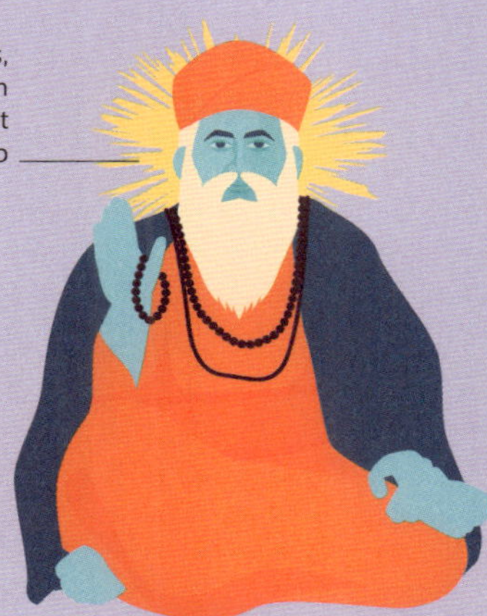

Sikhism
Sikh art centers on symbols but also includes portraits of prominent gurus, illuminated manuscripts, as well as coinage, jewelry, and clothing.

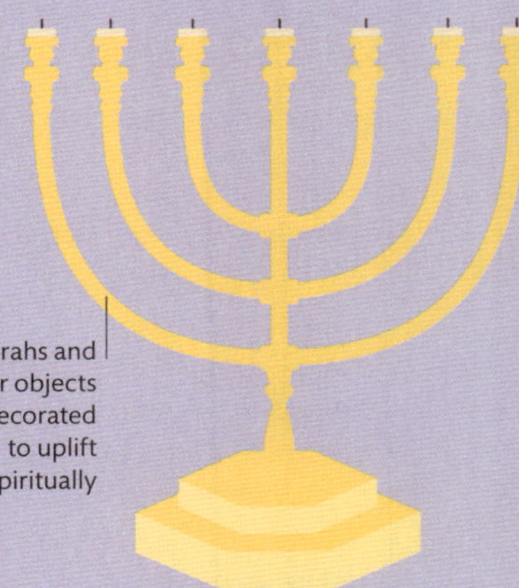

Judaism
The Ten Commandments forbid the reproduction of icons. However, synagogues, and objects are often beautifully constructed and decorated with fine ornament.

Baha'i
Emerging out of Iranian Shi'ite Islam, the monotheistic Baha'i faith understands art as spiritually uplifting and promoting world unity.

Zoroastrianism
This religion from ancient Iran has no art associated with it. Its religious symbol is the Faravahar, a bearded figure with wings.

Cao Dai
Caodaism uses the eye of God in a triangle as its main symbol. Its central, colorfully ornamental temple is based in Vietnam.

Confucianism
Confucian art includes calligraphy, paintings, and ceramics and uses symbols to promote ethics, such as the orchid for morality.

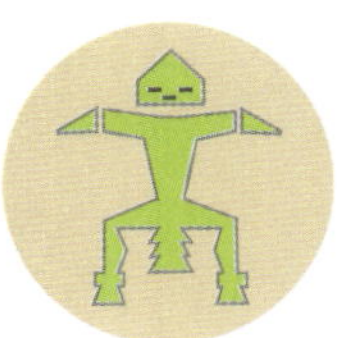

Navajo
The Navajo use sand paintings in rituals. The paintings have an active role in soliciting the gods' help for healing and harvest.

The Art of History

Civilizations across the world have used art to represent events and figures from history. In Western art in the 15th–19th centuries, history painting was regarded as the highest genre of art.

Illustrating history

History exists mainly in the form of stories. This includes artistic representations, which play an active role in how we see the past. History paintings are narrative paintings of historic, Biblical, or mythological events—large-scale, complex compositions of multiple figures, illustrating moments of drama and significance. Often they reveal more about the political conditions at the time of their creation than about the events they depict.

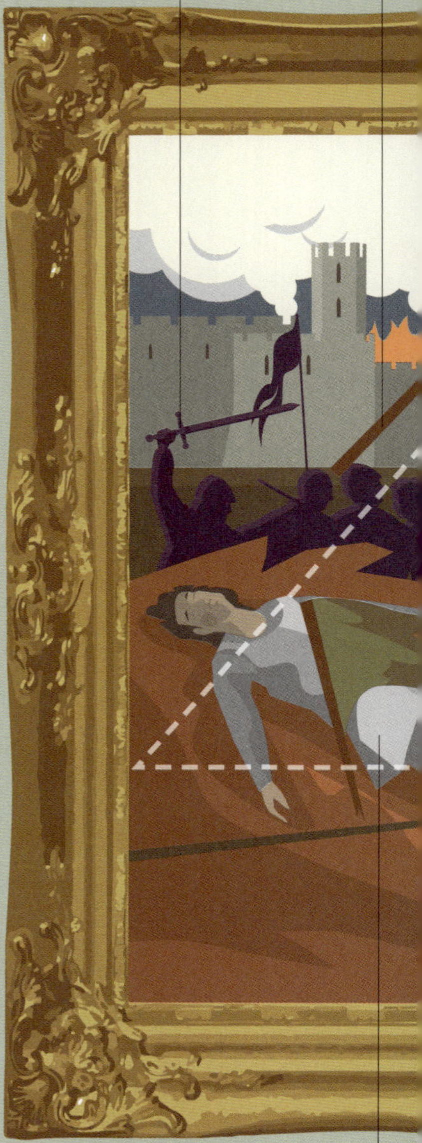

Glorified scene
The painted depiction of scenes encourages viewers to see historical events—often battles or other violent acts—from a particular point of view.

HOW DO MODERN ARTISTS MAKE HISTORICAL ART?

Contemporary artists such as Tessa Boffin and Isaac Julien use photography and film to recreate fantasy versions of histories that have been marginalized.

A **FATAL SHIPWRECK IN 1816** WAS PAINTED AS AN **IDEALIZED SCENE** IN **"THE RAFT OF THE MEDUSA"**

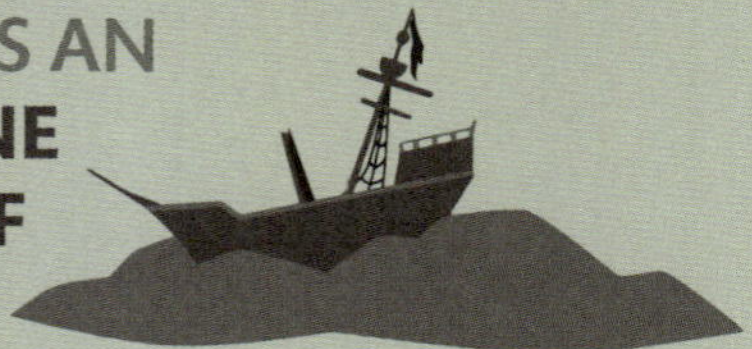

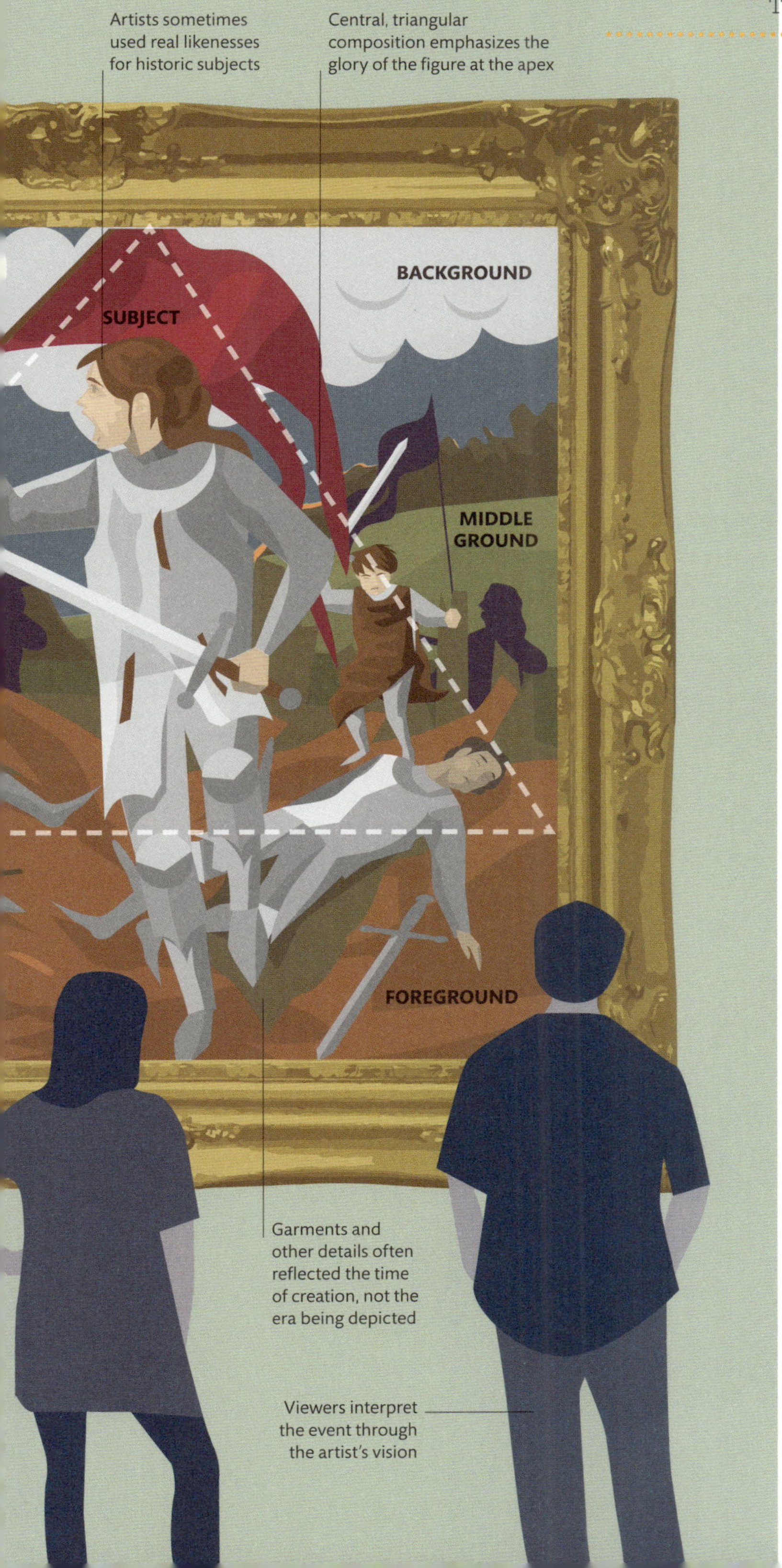

Sculptures and history

Sculpture has been a vital medium for depicting historical and other stories, scenes, and figures in many cultures; one of the most famous examples is Michelangelo's "David," completed in 1504. Classical styles of sculpture are often used to represent civic figures as public statues. These works exemplify the stories that a society wishes to tell about itself, and some statues of controversial figures (for example, those involved in the slave trade) have sparked backlash and protest.

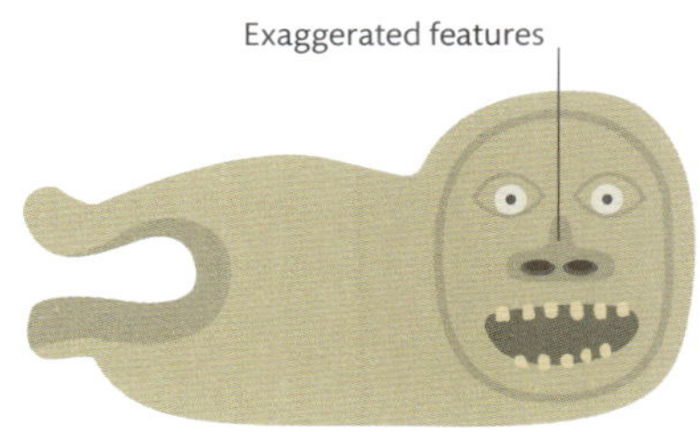

Inuit stories
Inuit peoples have been making carvings for thousands of years from whalebone and other materials. Modern Inuk artist Karoo Ashevak adopted an expressionistic style and made many pieces inspired by Inuit tradition and stories.

TV AND NEWS MEDIA

The representation of a historical event on television can enter people's minds as their own visual memory (for example, the assassination of US president J. F. Kennedy). News media plays an active role in constructing the stories of modern history.

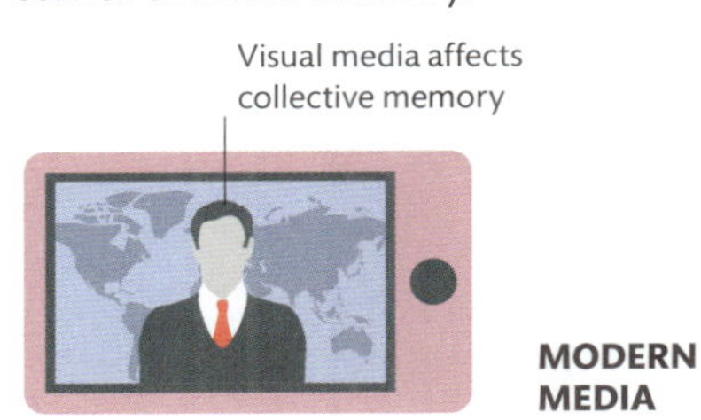

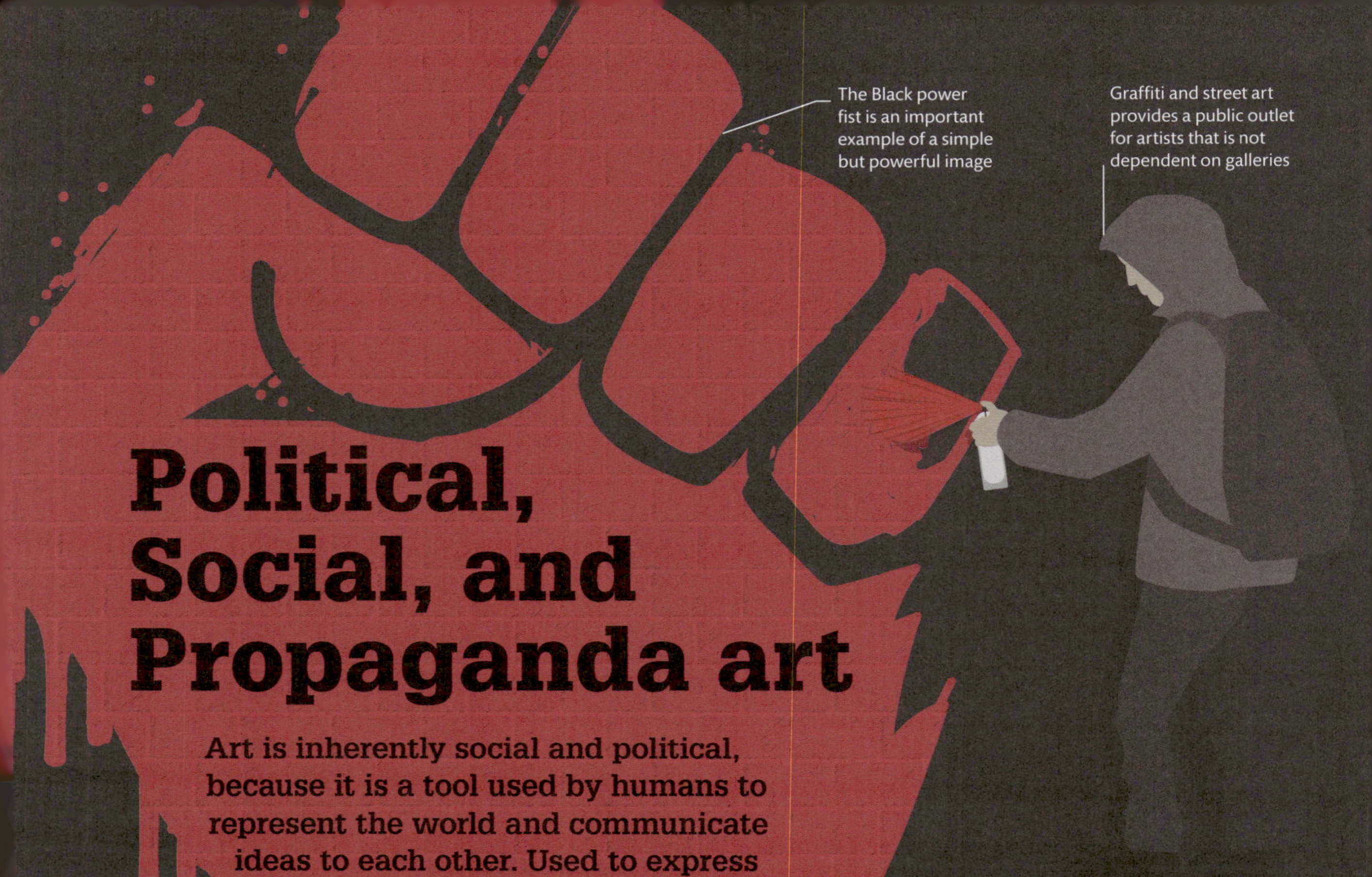

The Black power fist is an important example of a simple but powerful image

Graffiti and street art provides a public outlet for artists that is not dependent on galleries

Political, Social, and Propaganda art

Art is inherently social and political, because it is a tool used by humans to represent the world and communicate ideas to each other. Used to express political discontent, create slogans of solidarity, and promote social change, art has been at the heart of protest and revolution for hundreds of years.

Artistic revolutions

Artists are often also activists. For example, Dadaism emerged in Europe and North America in protest at the horrors of World War I. Marcel Duchamp's *Fountain* (see pp.216–217), one of the most famous works of modern art, has also been interpreted as a protest work. The Situationist International was a group of artists and intellectuals who were involved in protests in Paris in 1968, and in 1969, the Art Workers' Coalition withdrew works from a Paris museum in protest against the Vietnam War.

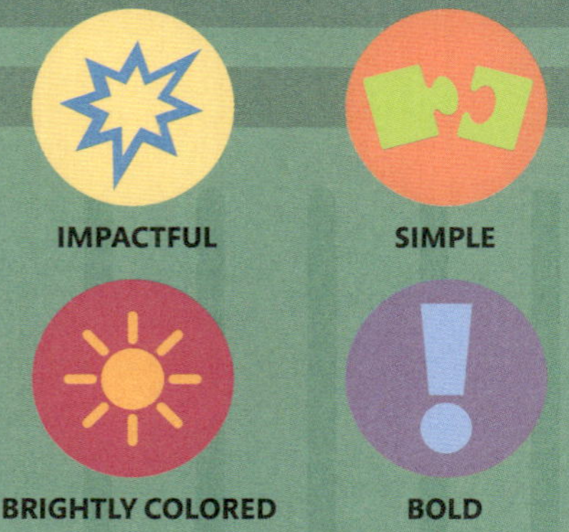

Characteristics
Protest art and activism often rely on simple and powerful graphics to convey their message. In the age of the internet, such graphics can spread very quickly.

HOW CAN ART TACKLE SPECIFIC ISSUES?

American photographer Nan Goldin founded Prescription Addiction Intervention Now (P.A.I.N.) in 2017, a group that uses performance art to protest the opioid industry.

ACTIVISTS **THE GUERRILLA GIRLS** OFTEN USE **STATISTICS** TO PROTEST **SEXISM** IN THE **ART WORLD**

Types of protest art

Effective protest art works through using familiar methods of communication. Posters in civic spaces have been widely used, but since the advent of television and the internet, art activism has also had to concentrate on the production of actions and graphics that can reach audiences through these channels of communication. Artists may also use more traditional formats and spaces—American artist and AIDs activist Keith Haring exhibited his paintings and drawings widely in galleries and created murals and sculptures.

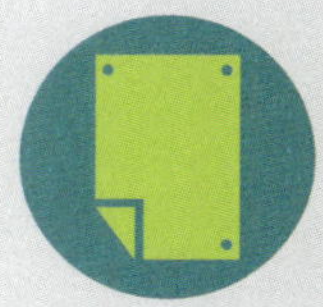

Posters
Posters are publicly visible, effective, and cheap to make.

Installations
Interactive and immersive, installations can evoke strong emotions.

Projections
Large images can be projected onto public buildings.

Graffiti
Painted in public spaces, graffiti reaches a broad audience.

Protest media
Activist art can potentially come in any medium but works best when made and distributed in a way that will reach large numbers of people.

Modern protest art

Contemporary climate activist groups, such as Extinction Rebellion or Wretched of the Earth, have become known mainly through the power of their visual campaigns. Extinction Rebellion's graphic logo is reminiscent of that of the Campaign for Nuclear Disarmament (CND), and they have engaged in performance art protests, including blocking the streets of London with a pink boat and ghostly figures.

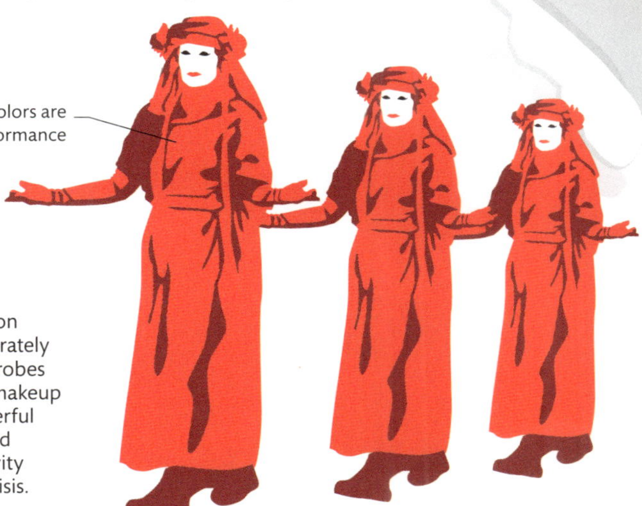

Art protest
In 2019, Extinction Rebellion deliberately used blood red robes and white face makeup to create a powerful visual impact and impress the gravity of the climate crisis.

EXILED ARTISTS

Many political artists work in exile from their home countries. In 1973, Cecilia Vicuña was exiled from Chile when the dictator Augusto Pinochet took power. Vicuña continues to make feminist work with poetry, paintings, and textile installations in protest against dictatorship.

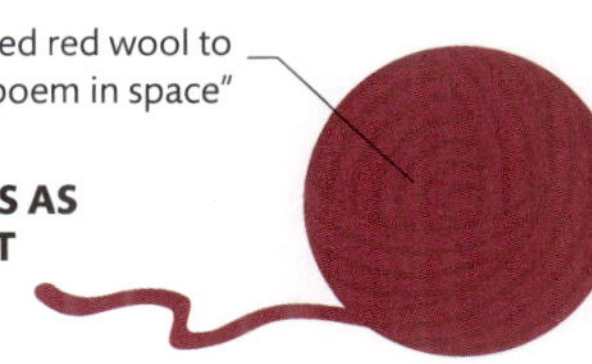

TEXTILES AS PROTEST

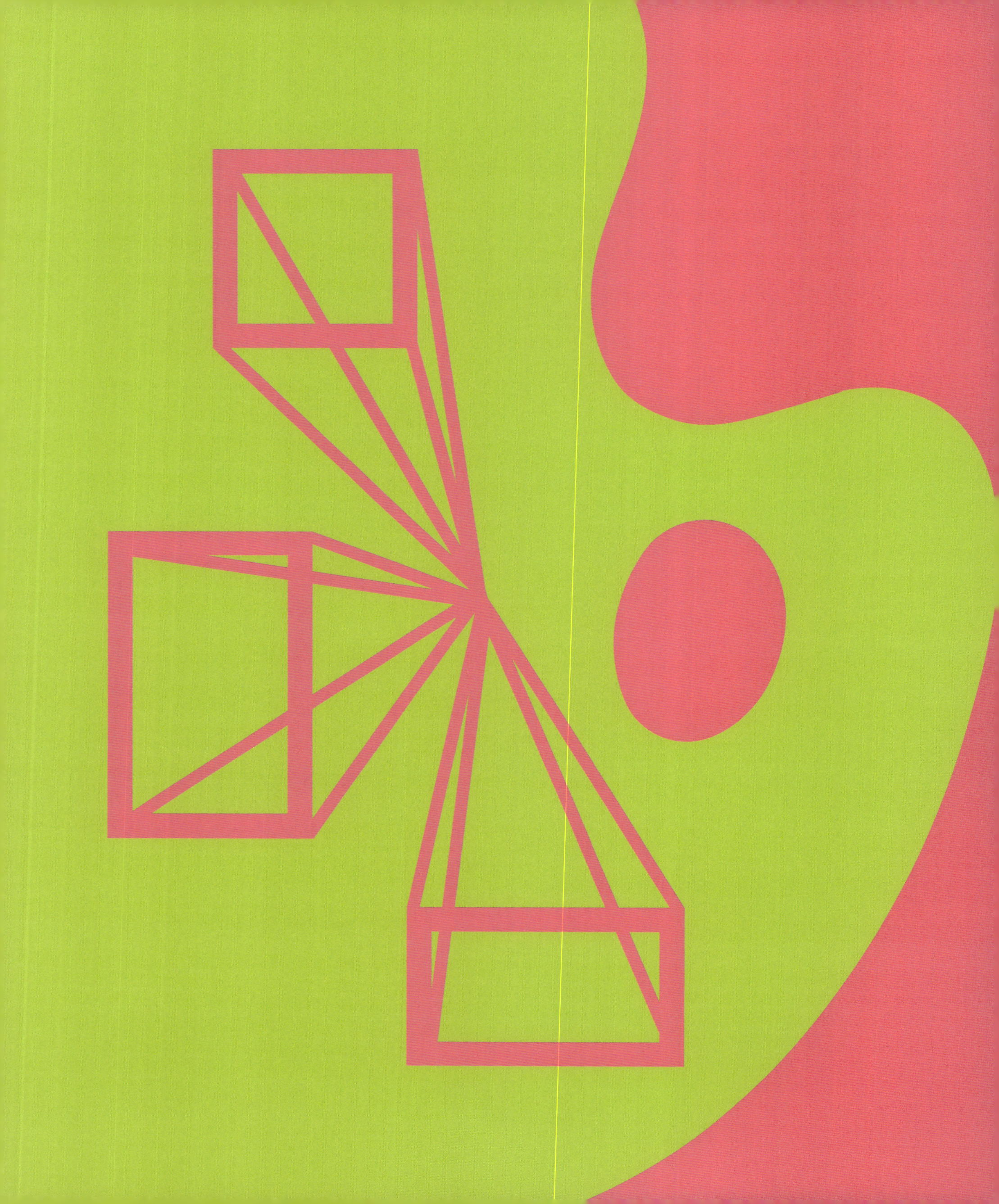

ELEMENTS OF ART

How Color Works

In the mid-1600s, English scientist Isaac Newton discovered that white light is composed of seven visible colors—the visible spectrum. Each color has a different wavelength, detectable by receptors in the human eye. As objects reflect these wavelengths to different degrees, they appear as different colors to our eye. This knowledge has informed how artists understand and use color.

1,000,000

THE AVERAGE NUMBER OF **COLORS** THAT CAN BE **DETECTED BY THE HUMAN EYE**

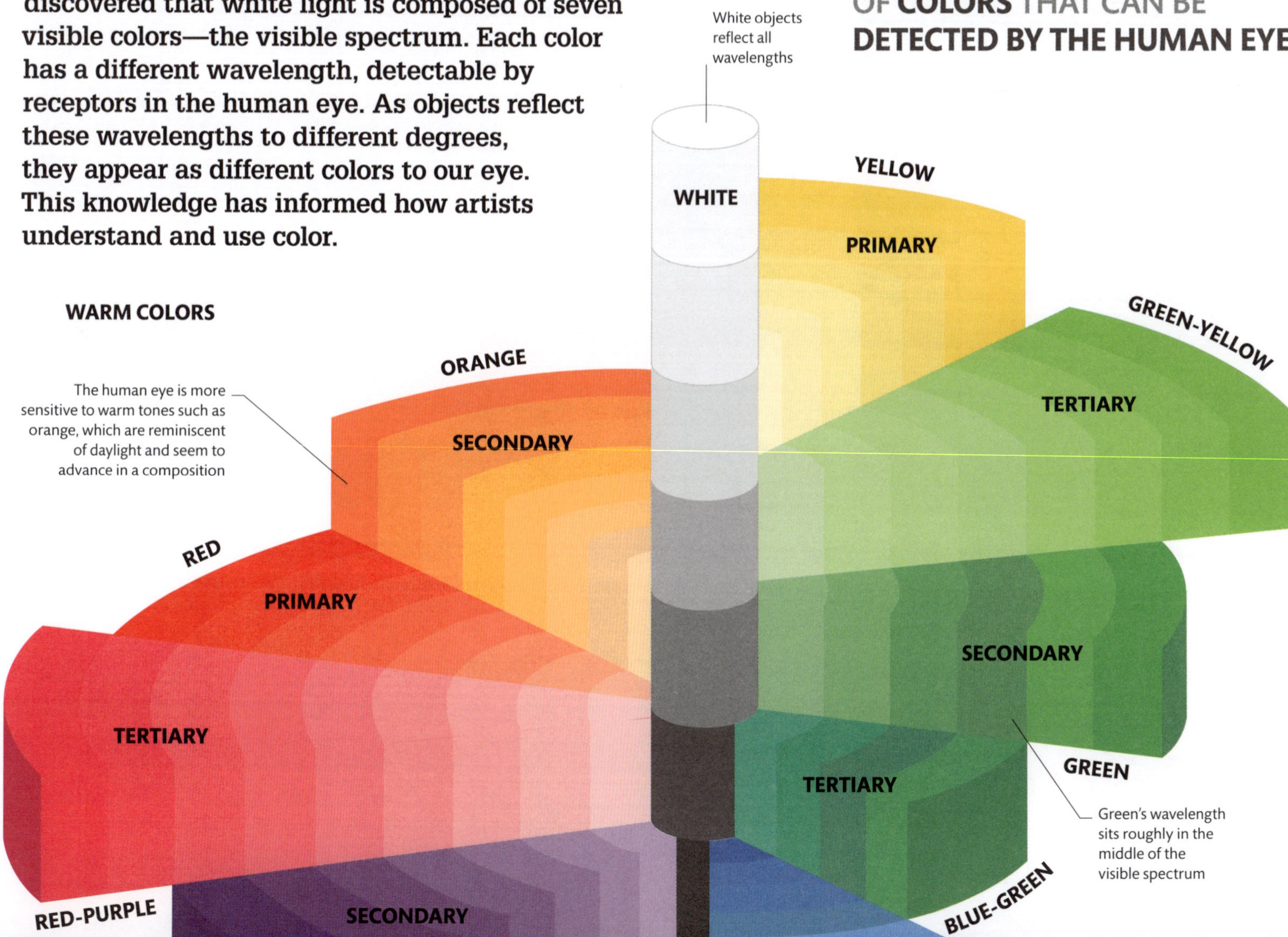

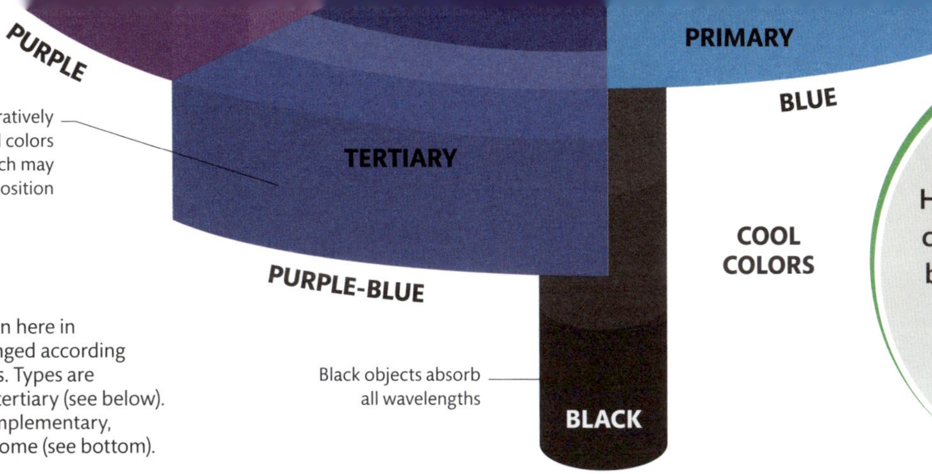

The eye is comparatively less sensitive to cool colors such as purple or blue, which may seem to recede in a composition

Black objects absorb all wavelengths

The color wheel
This circle of colors, shown here in three dimensions, is arranged according to types and relationships. Types are primary, secondary, and tertiary (see below). Relationships include complementary, analogous, and monochrome (see bottom).

WHAT ARE HUE, TONE, AND TINT?

Hue refers to the dominant color family, such as red or blue; tint is hue with white added; and tone is hue with pure gray (equal amounts black and white) added.

Primary, secondary, tertiary

In the 17th century, Irish chemist Robert Boyle (1627–1691) identified red, yellow, and blue as primary colors—colors that cannot be created by mixing other colors together, but from which all other colors can be made. When two primary colors are mixed, they create secondary colors of green, orange, and violet. Tertiary colors are created by combining one primary with one secondary color, such as red–purple (magenta), or blue–green (teal). Pointillist artist Paul Signac (1863–1935) used dots of contrasting primary and secondary color paint to create intense, vivid color in his paintings.

COLOR AND WAVELENGTHS

White light contains all the wavelengths, and when it is directed through a glass prism, it splits into its component colors of varying wavelengths. Red has the longest wavelength and violet has the shortest.

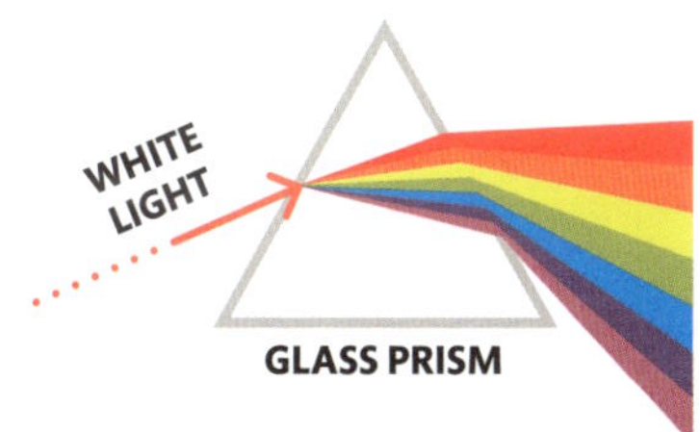

Complementary and more

On the color wheel, complementary colors sit directly opposite each other. They comprise one primary color and the other two primaries mixed together. For example, the complementary of red is green (yellow mixed with blue). Complementary colors especially contrast with each other and make each other appear brighter when used together. Colors that sit next to each other on the wheel are known as analogous colors, and they seem to match and blend together. Monochromatic colors are those that consist purely of varying shades of the same color.

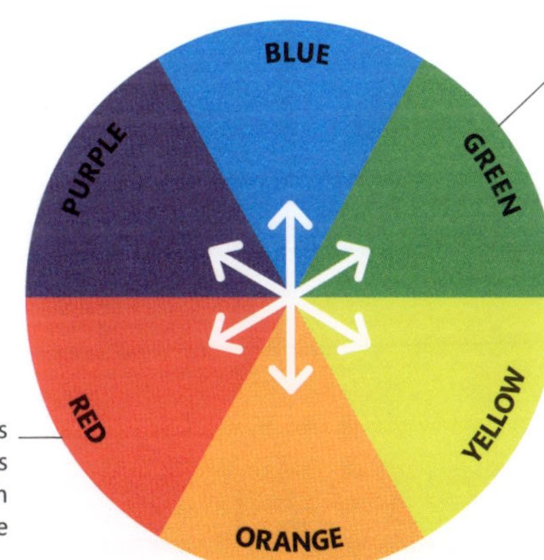

Red complements green and is analogous with orange and purple

Green complements red and is analogous with blue and yellow

Complementary relationships
Each of the double-headed arrows on this color wheel indicates colors that have a complementary relationship—for example, green and red, or yellow and purple.

Pigments

Pigments are substances that impart color to painting mediums. They can be natural or synthetic in origin and consist of insoluble particles mixed in a water- or oil-based binder and applied to surfaces.

NAPOLEON IS SAID TO HAVE **DIED** FROM THE **ARSENIC** IN HIS **GREEN WALLPAPER**

Symbolic color

Colors can have symbolic meanings, which may vary between cultures. White may represent hope or purity. Black can suggest despair or death. Red implies anger or danger, while blue may mean calm or holiness. Purple can symbolize royalty, magic, or power. Green can signify fertility, growth, or healing, while yellow may mean warmth, happiness, or positivity.

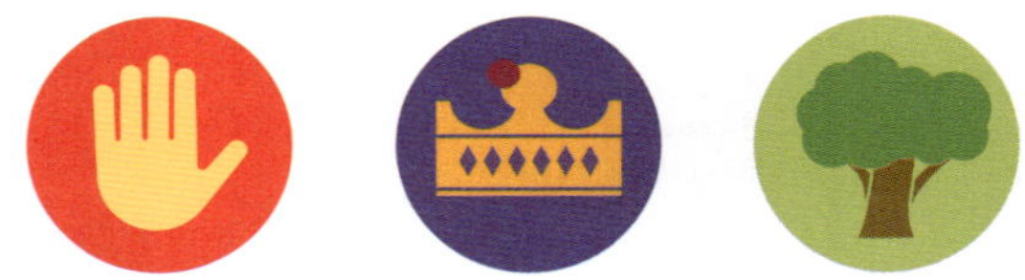

DANGER ROYALTY NATURE

The lifeblood of art

The discovery of color pigments has been key to the evolution of art. The earliest artists' pigments came from easily accessible natural sources. These could be inorganic, such as clay, rocks, and charcoal, or organic, which includes snail shells, plant parts, and insects. Today, pigments may be of either natural or synthetic origin. Most modern pigments are mostly either inorganic or synthetic organic (made in a laboratory). Several early pigments contained dangerously toxic substances.

PAINTS	BLUE	YELLOW
NAMES	Egyptian blue, cobalt, ultramarine, Prussian blue, cerulean, indigo, IKB (International Klein Blue).	Lemon yellow, cadmium yellow, yellow ocher, chrome yellow, aureolin (or cobalt yellow).
SOURCES	Ultramarine was made from lapis lazuli; indigo came from a crop grown in India and Egypt; Prussian Blue, the first synthetic, was created in 1708.	The first yellow color was yellow ocher, an earth pigment; gold was used in some cultures; orpiment (or King's yellow) was made using arsenic.
USES	Prussian blue was used by Japanese ukiyo-e artists and Picasso during his Blue Period from 1901 to 1904.	Yellow pigment made from gold leaf was used in Egyptian, Roman, Byzantine, medieval, and Renaissance art and in Japan in the 16th and 17th centuries.

WHICH INVENTION HAD AN EFFECT ON THE PRACTISE OF PAINTING?

Metal paint tubes meant that artists could leave their studios and paint outside; they also meant that paint could be mass-produced.

THE MAUVE DECADE

Discovered by chemist William Henry Perkin in 1856 as he sought a treatment for malaria, mauveine was one of the first synthetic chemical dyes to be mass-produced. Its popularity led to the 1890s being called "The Mauve Decade."

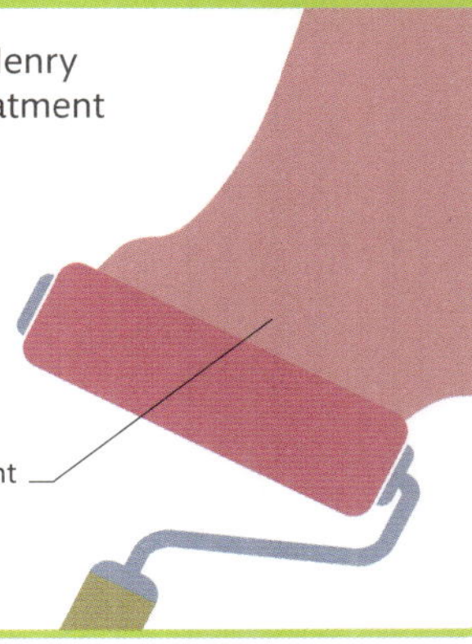

MASS-PRODUCED COLOR

RED	GREEN	ORANGE	PURPLE
Vermilion, carmine, rose madder, alizarin crimson, red iron oxide, madder, magenta, maroon, minium, cinnabar.	Cobalt green, emerald green, green earth, malachite, verdigris, viridian.	Orange ocher, realgar, cadmium, and cobalt orange.	Manganese, Tyrian purple, cobalt violet, mauve.
Red ocher is an earth pigment from France; cinnabar is a mineral with high mercury content; carmine was made from cochineal beetles.	Green pigments from earth and the mineral malachite were used by the ancient Egyptians; arsenic was used in early green pigments.	Ancient Egyptian and medieval artists used realgar; other orange pigments were made from highly toxic orpiment.	Tyrian purple was made from the mucus of murex snails; in the 19th century, mauve was named after the purple French mallow flower.
Mughal artists in India and Persia in the 17th and 18th centuries used minium; some paintings became known as "miniatures" after the pigment.	Impressionists used green extensively, partly due to the development of new, brighter synthetic green pigments.	Orange was popular with Pre-Raphaelites. Impressionists and Post-Impressionists often placed orange next to complementary blue, to create vibrancy.	Around 15,000 BCE in France, artists used sticks of manganese and hematite powder to draw on cave walls. This rare colour became associated with royalty.

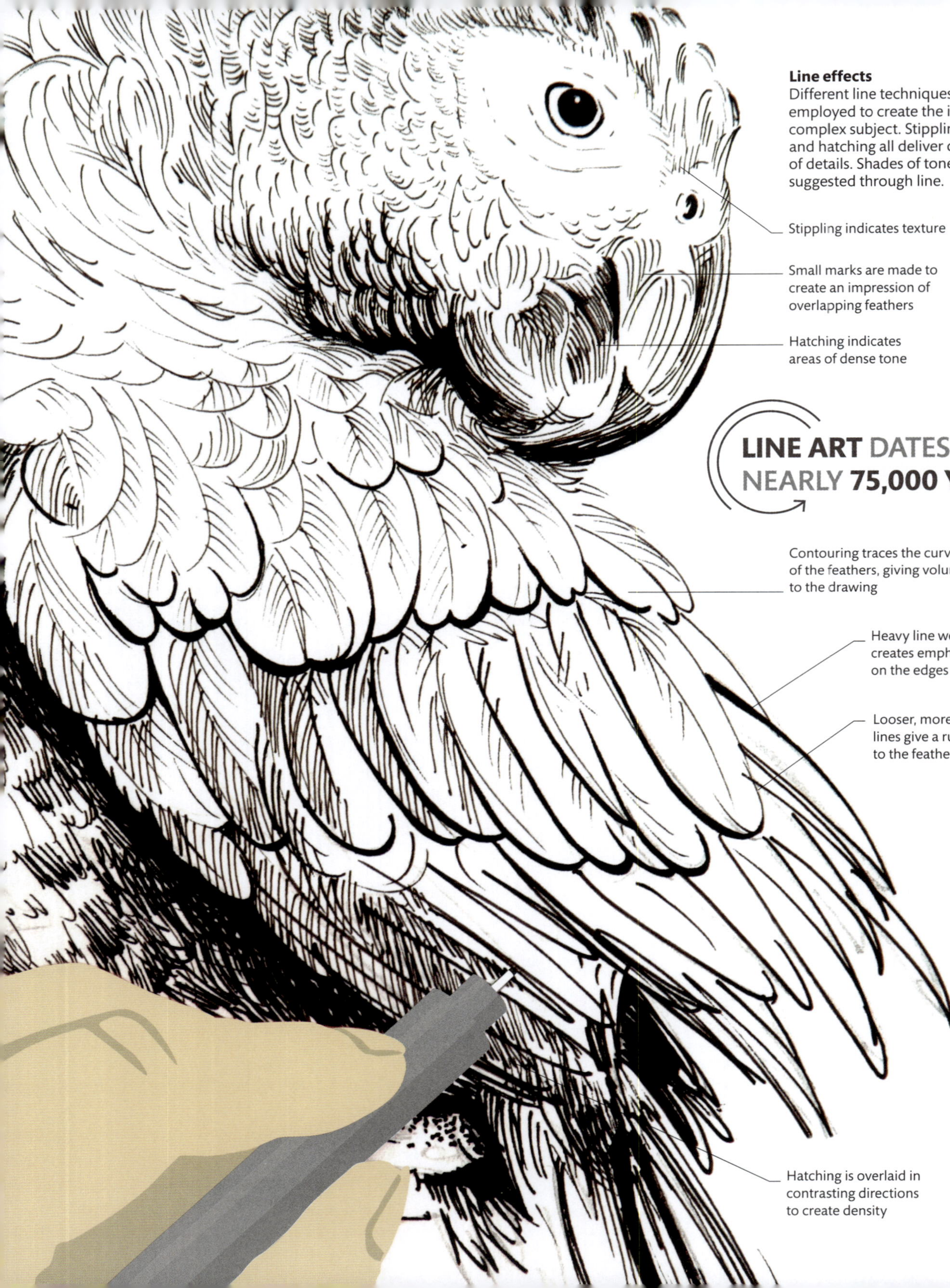

Line effects

Different line techniques can be employed to create the impression of a complex subject. Stippling, contouring, and hatching all deliver different types of details. Shades of tone can also be suggested through line.

Stippling indicates texture

Small marks are made to create an impression of overlapping feathers

Hatching indicates areas of dense tone

LINE ART DATES BACK NEARLY **75,000 YEARS**

Contouring traces the curves of the feathers, giving volume to the drawing

Heavy line weight creates emphasis on the edges

Looser, more sketch-like lines give a ruffled feel to the feathers

Hatching is overlaid in contrasting directions to create density

Line

The use of line is a way of articulating and defining form and space and is an expressive, gestural action. Line is an important consideration in all mediums.

Line drawing

Line drawing can be used to trace contours, create space and structure, and suggest tonal variation. The materials used, techniques employed, and choice of line weight each give drawings different qualities. Pencil and graphite produce accuracy of form, while charcoal creates a suggestive line that can be blurred and layered (see pp.22–23). Monoprinting gives a soft line, and ink creates a calligraphic and expressive line (see pp.24–25). Working within constraints helps to develop skills—for example, in continuous line drawings, where the drawing implement stays on the page surface throughout.

CONTOURING HATCHING STIPPLING

Techniques
Contouring and hatching create density and fluidity; stippling adds texture. Using a flat brush or card edge varies line quality.

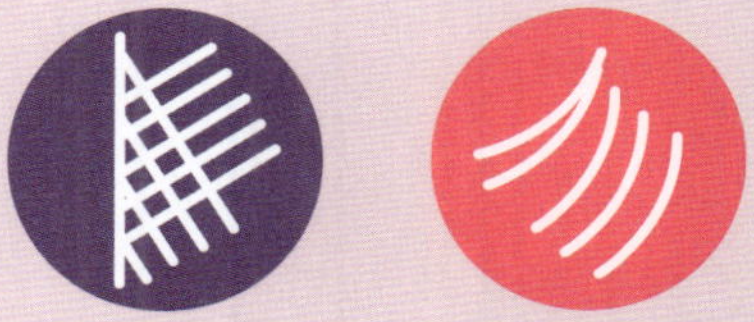

CARD EDGE FLAT BRUSH

Line weight
The darkness or thickness of the line is referred to as the weight. A thicker line suggests strength.

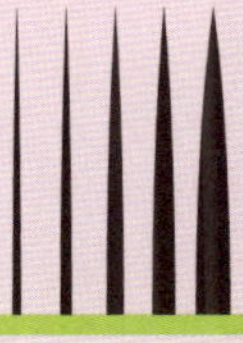

Line quality
The feel of the line, which could be rough, smooth, soft, or hard, is described as the line quality.

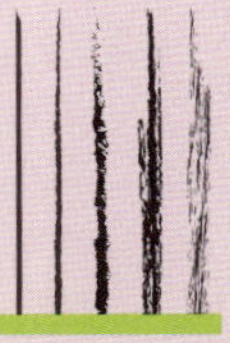

Actual vs. implied line

Actual line is a physical, linear mark on the page that makes a solid connection between points. It is the direct result of putting a drawing implement in contact with a page surface and moving it to make a continuous mark. With an implied line, marks are made to *suggest* contours and tonal changes. The variation in strength and proximity creates an impression of a line, with the viewer's visual mind filling in the gaps.

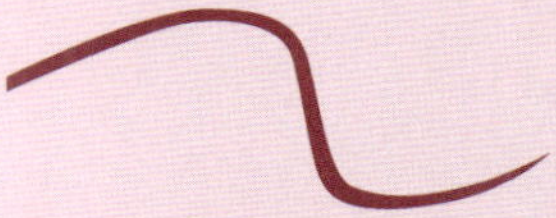

Actual line
The artist Sol Le Witt stated that "A drawing of a person is not a real person, but a drawing of a line is a real line."

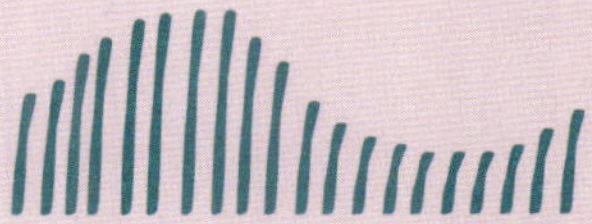

Implied line
Small, repeated strokes create zones of positive and negative space that are shaped to suggest a line.

WHY ARE PICASSO'S LINE DRAWINGS SO POPULAR?

Picasso's deceptively simple line drawings capture a playfulness and simplicity that express joy through intuitive, dextrous marks.

2D TO 3D

Line can be taken from two dimensions into three dimensions. Using wire or a similarly fine material, an artist can take a line drawing and realize it as a spatial object. The Venezuelan artist Gego is noted for wire drawing installations.

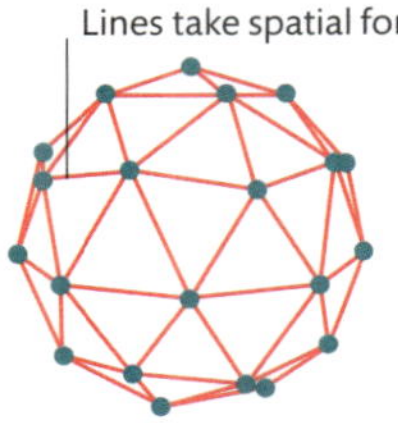

LINE IN 3D

HOW DID MATISSE USE SIMPLE SHAPES?

At the end of his career, Henri Matisse began to use paper shapes as a way of drawing directly in color, using simple cutouts as a joyful and immediate form of expression.

Abstraction and geometry

In the 20th century, some artists freed shape from form and investigated the abstract juxtaposition of geometric shapes, playing with their qualities and symbolism. Russian-Ukranian artist Kazimir Malevich created a new language he called "suprematism", using only geometric shapes. Russian artist Wassily Kandinsky had a condition, synaesthesia, where senses become entwined and to him his combination of organic and geometric shapes often evoked music.

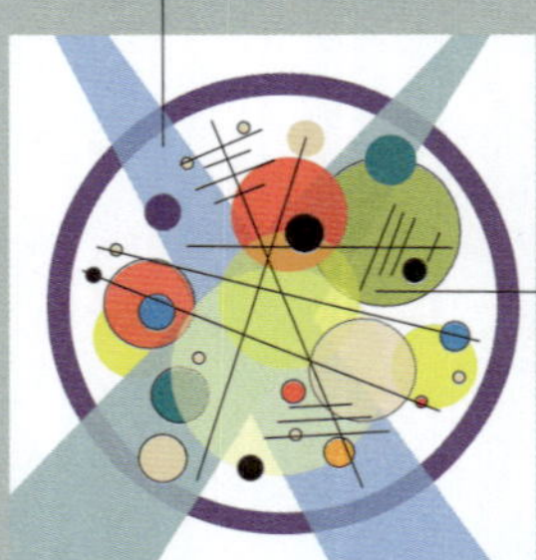

Abstraction
Artists often employ geometric shapes in abstract works, as they can be used to create a sense of abstract visual space, and a disconnection with the observed world.

Organic shapes

Organic shapes can be defined as freeform shapes that often relate to natural forms, including the body. They can be irregular, curved, and flowing, giving an asymmetrical and unpredictable feeling to a work. French-American artist Louise Bourgeois' drawings use organic, interlocking shapes to convey movement, connection, and a sense of nature and the body. The paintings of English abstract artist Gillain Ayres play with flowing, entwined organic shapes that deny background and foreground.

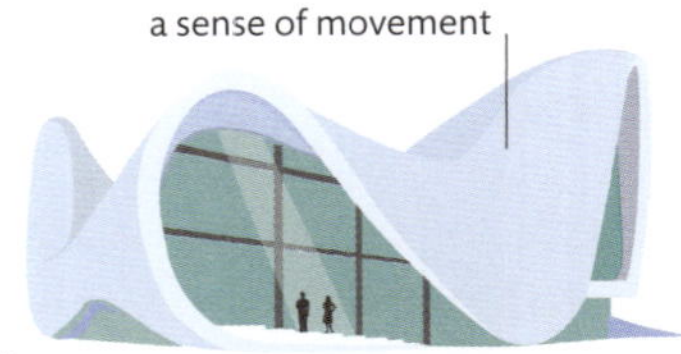

ORGANIC ARCHITECTURE

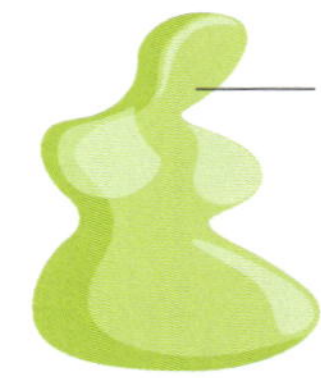

ORGANIC SCULPTURE

Simplified shapes
An effective way to understand structural shapes within complex forms is through simplification. Distilling observed forms, space, and objects into their basic shapes helps to show how they fit together. When drawing figures, simplifying complex anatomy into basic shapes is a good way of understanding proportion.

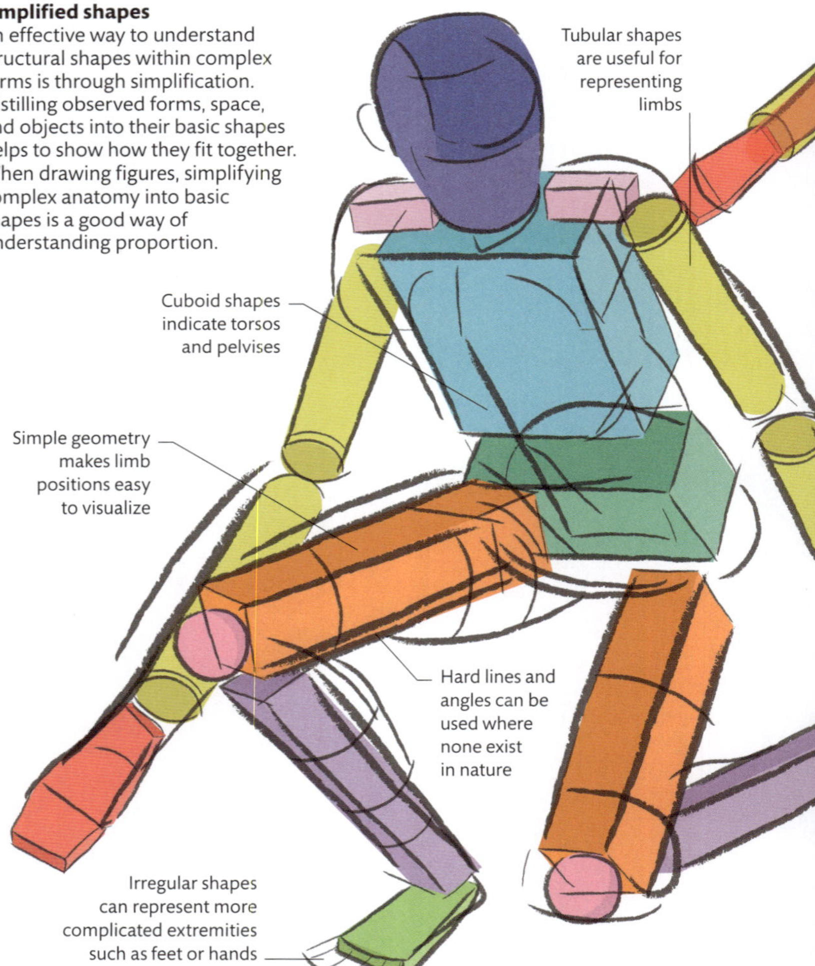

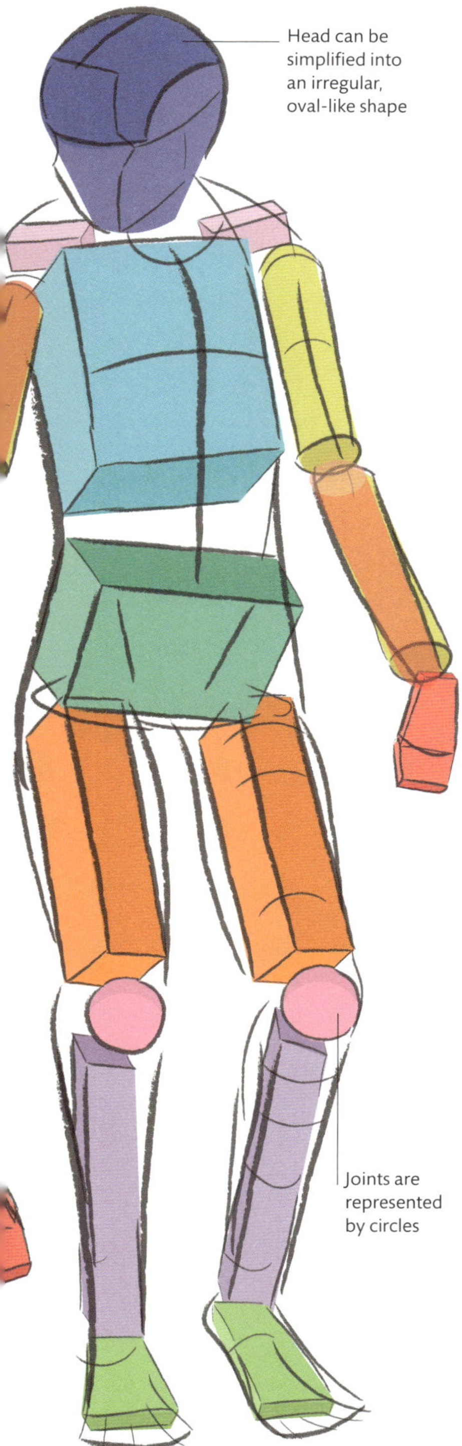

Shape

A shape can be defined in art as a two-dimensional, enclosed space. It can be geometric and mathematically defined, such as a circle, square, or triangle, or organic, asymmetrical, and free flowing.

Organic and geometric

Whether geometric or organic, shapes embody specific qualities, such as structure, symmetry, fluidity, or spontaneity, which the artist can use in a representational or abstract work. In abstraction (see pp.78–79), geometric and organic forms can be combined to create different visual velocities across the work. In representational art, shapes play an integral role in how the artist understands what they are observing, and how they translate this into the artwork. Shapes that are formed by objects are positive shapes, and the space around objects is referred to as negative shapes or space. By observing and recording negative shape as well as positive shape, the artist can gain a better understanding of how forms occupy space. Shape is related to form (see pp.96–97), with form combining both shape and three-dimensional properties.

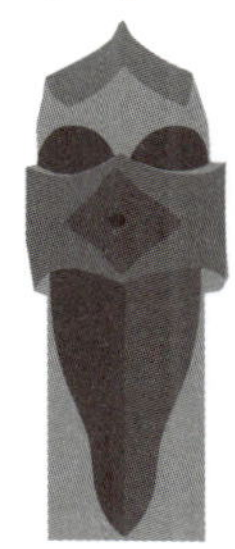

ANTONI **GAUDÍ'S ARCHITECTURE** WAS INSPIRED BY **NATURE** AND ITS **ORGANIC SHAPES**

SHAPED SURFACES

Some artists question the conventional rectilinear shape of the canvas itself, exploring other shapes that draw attention to the edges of the work, and the relationship of the canvas to the surrounding space. The canvases of American artist Ellsworth Kelly pushed painting towards sculpture, and created an extra dimension of shadows on the wall.

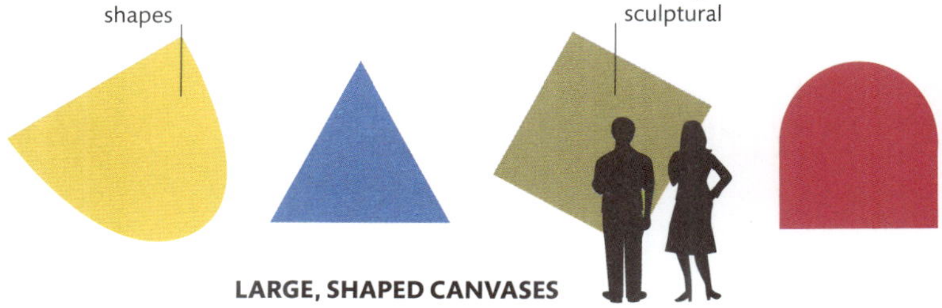

LARGE, SHAPED CANVASES

Form

Form in artwork is related to shape but also encompasses mass and volume, weight, and structure. There are two ways of understanding form—first, as the overall form and physical nature of the artwork itself, and second, as the expression and description of forms within the work.

WHAT IS FORMALISM?

Formalism is a movement that states that form and visual quality are the most important aspects of a work. It emphasizes the composition of formal elements—line, shape, space, and form.

Working with form

A form is a shape (see pp.94–95) in three dimensions, either suggested in painting and drawing, or realized in sculpture. In two-dimensional artwork, form can be described using tone, modeling, scale, and spatial relationships. Artists employ the effects of light and shadow to suggest form, using the contrast of varying degrees of lightness or darkness to create the sense of a three-dimensional form. Form in sculpture is a solid object that is created by its shape, structure, and size and the arrangement of components such as length, width, and depth.

Scale
A 1:1 scale favors realism, while scaling up considerably increases the impact of the form.

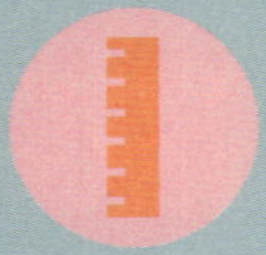

Contrast
Using the contrast of light and shadow on a form increases the sense of solidity and presence.

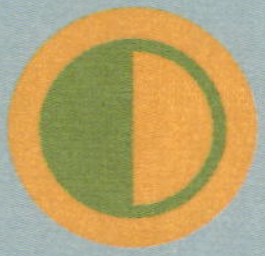

Juxtaposition
In painting, juxtaposing forms against flat areas of paint increases their three-dimensional quality.

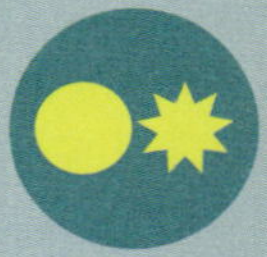

Found objects
Artists draw attention to the form of ready-made objects to highlight cultural associations.

Modelling from life
Working from life in painting and sculpture gives the artist a direct connection with the subject's form (see right).

Abstract forms
In abstraction, form is non-representational. Abstract art uses shape, color, and gesture to denote forms.

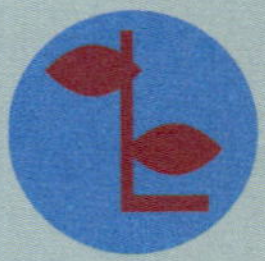

DISRUPTING FORM

Some sculptors play with perceptions of form by manipulating materials to behave in unexpected ways. British sculptor Julian Wild uses industrial materials such as stainless steel to depict forms and colors found in nature, bending metal into sinuous knots or peeling it away from the central form to reveal a hidden color.

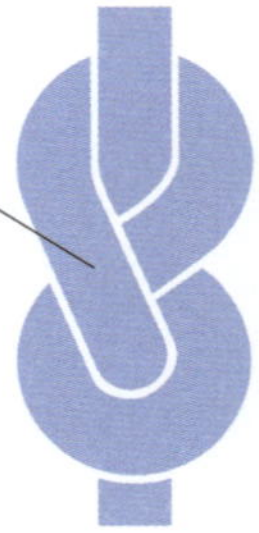

KNOTTED STEEL

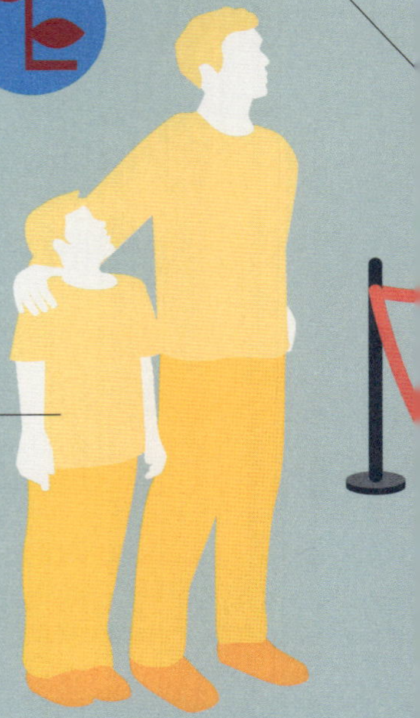

Sculptural form
This partial depiction of a figure is rendered in three dimensions at a great scale, creating visual impact. A sculptural form's physical presence in a space affects the way people interpret it.

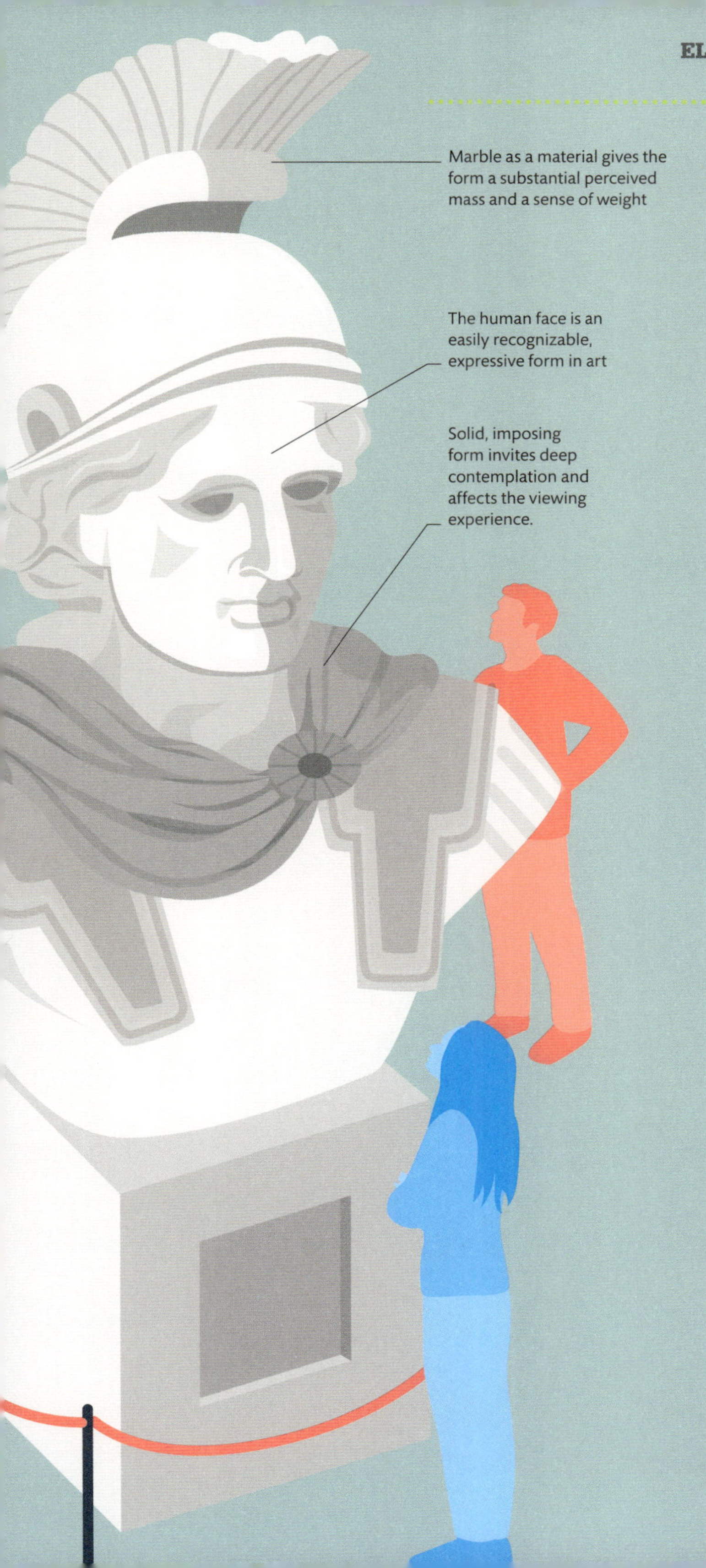

Drawing from observation

Drawing from life helps artists to understand form and how forms occupy space. Still life painting (see pp.70–71) is a study in drawing from observation—a meticulous, detailed examination and representation of three-dimensional form in two dimensions, rendered realistically or in abstract. Drawing an object or figure from different angles increases understanding of its form, and identifying negative space helps situate it in its environment.

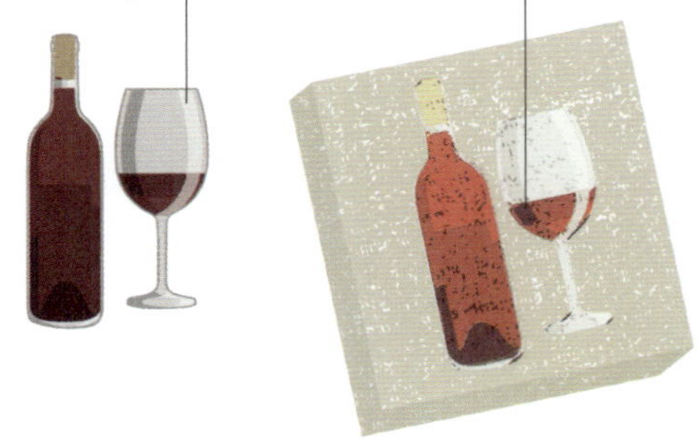

Still life and form
Carefully depicting how shadow falls on an object or figure, or concentrating mainly on shadows and reflected highlights, can enhance the three-dimensional appearance of a drawing.

PATTERNS AND **COLORS** CAN BE USED IN **THREE-DIMENSIONAL ART** TO **DISGUISE** OR **CONCEAL** AN OBJECT'S **VOLUME** AND **MASS**

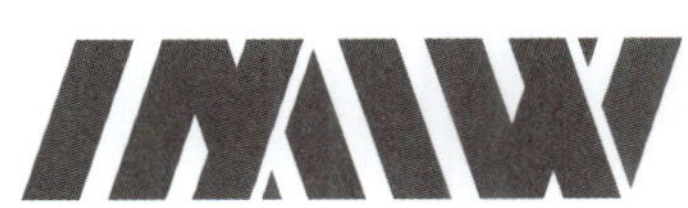

Implied texture

In painting, implied texture can be created through illusion, where the artist paints the look of a texture. For example, using drips of solvent through oil paint can create the look of a rough surface such as a wall; using small strokes and blurring techniques can create a feeling of fur; and using semitransparent acrylic layers can create the impression of glass. This approach allows the artist to suggest texture without adding substances or materials to the paint.

ANNI ALBERS USED WEAVING TO CREATE REVOLUTIONARY TEXTURED ARTWORKS IN THE 1920S

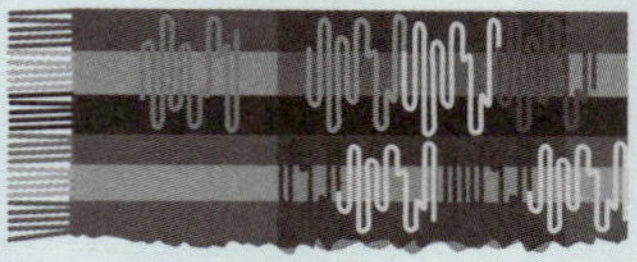

ORGANIC

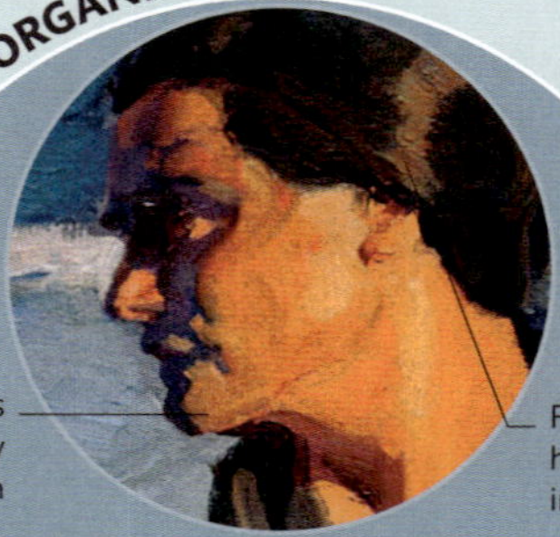

Hair texture is suggested through highlighted sections, which follow the implied contours of the head. Smooth skin texture is created by blending warm tones.

WET

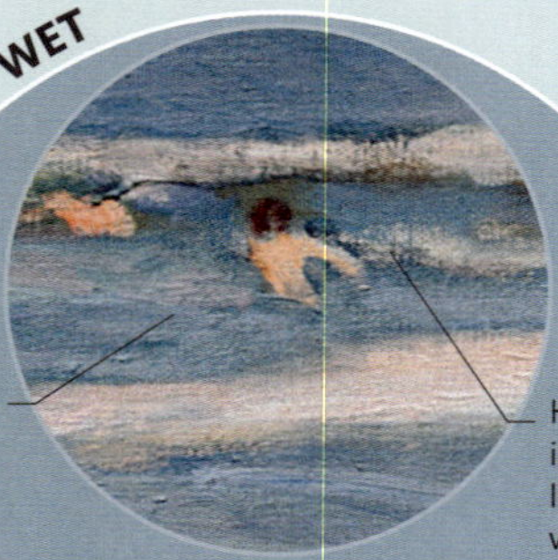

The liquidity of sea is implied through lighter ripple and wave shapes contrasted against the blue of the ocean. The brush strokes indicate movement in the surface.

ROUGH

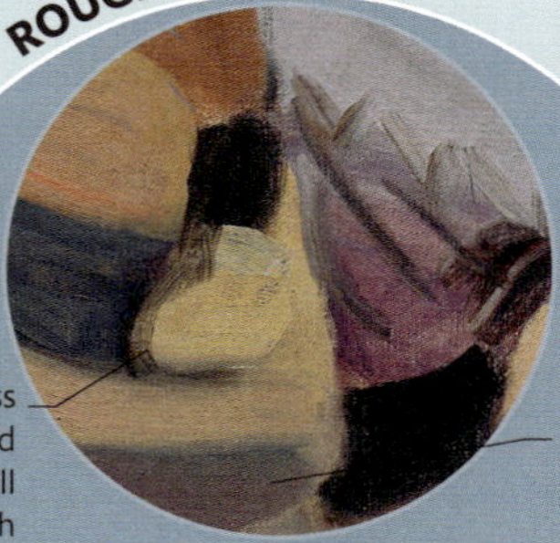

The rough yet even texture of the sand is suggested through layering dry brushstrokes, leaving visible traces of the underlying color.

FLOWING

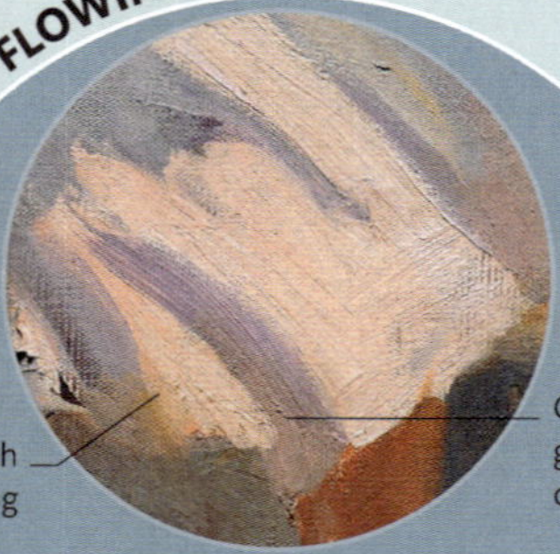

The artist has created the impression of a flowing white fabric using soft blending and contrasting highlights and shadows. The fabric itself appears smooth.

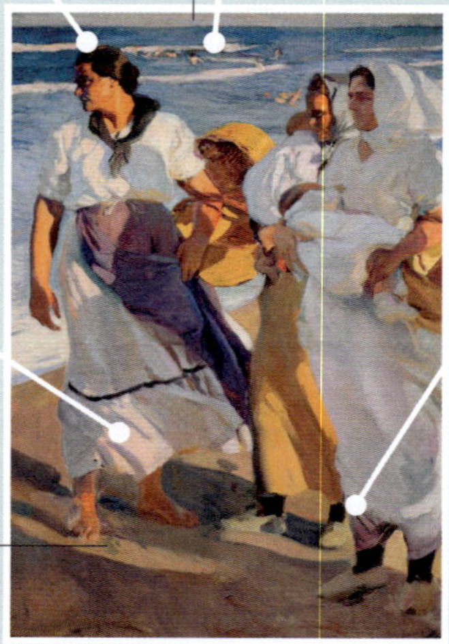

Cloud is suggested using a soft texture with sweeping brushstrokes

The grainy sand texture is made with rough brushstrokes

Combining textures
This painting shows a variety of implied textures, with subtle differences between each texture and the way it is painted. This ensures that the painting "reads" as a whole, while still creating a sense of illusion and atmospheric place.

Texture

Texture is the appearance or sensation of a surface—for example, rough and abrasive, or smooth and flat. It can be implied or physically created, depending on the type of artwork and the desired effect.

Actual texture

Actual texture is using the real, tangible texture of objects and surfaces in an artwork to convey emotions, ideas, and sensations. Sculptural materials each have their own "language." For example, clay can be modeled but also suggests immediacy as it picks up the impression of the hand; plaster has a cool quietness and can be used to pick up fine details in casting; metals such as steel can be mirror polished or left with an industrial feel.

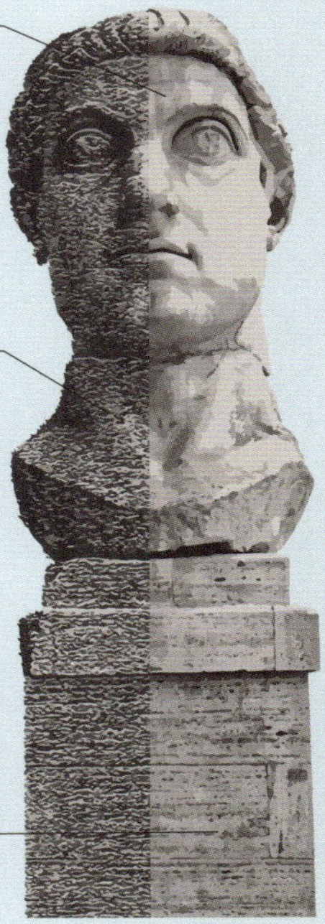

Fine texture and detail can create a sense of realism

Visble marks may allow the viewer to feel connected to the artist's process

Smoothness in geometric planes and angles can suggest industrial objects

Rough vs. smooth
The artist's use of texture in a sculpture can affect how the viewer "reads" it. A smooth, polished texture can create a sense of serenity or blankness, while a rough texture can suggest dynamism and immediacy.

ABSTRACT OR UNUSUAL

Texture can also be used in an abstract way to create unexpected effects. The transition across an abstract painting between impasto (see below) and flat areas creates the feeling of different visual speeds. In sculpture, abstract texture suggests tactile sensations.

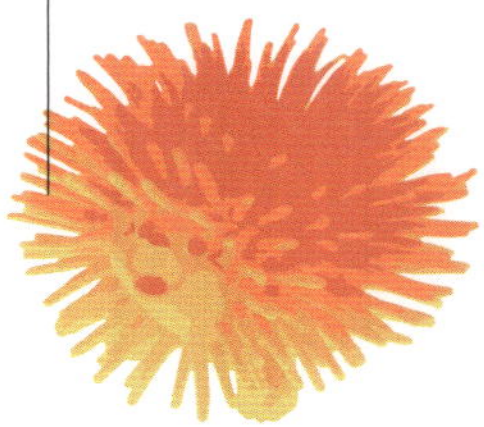

Visual impact caused by unusual material

UNEXPECTED TEXTURE

Materials and effects

In painting, a range of tools can be used to create different actual surface textures. Palette knives, scourers, and sandpaper are used to scrape and erase paint. Substances such as marble dust and beeswax can be added to paint to create body.

Palette knife impasto
Impasto is thickly applied paint, and palette knives are often used for layering in impasto oil painting.

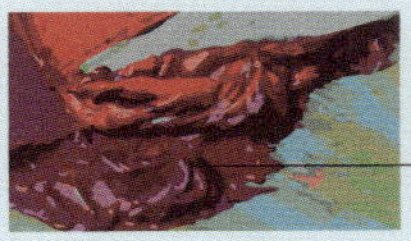

Thick paint projects from the canvas

Sand and grit
Sand, fine grit, and even cement can be added to paint to create an architectural feel.

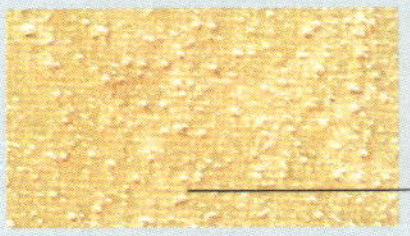

Granular texture suggests stone surfaces

Combing
Readymade or bespoke brushes and combs can be raked through paint, creating parallel grooves.

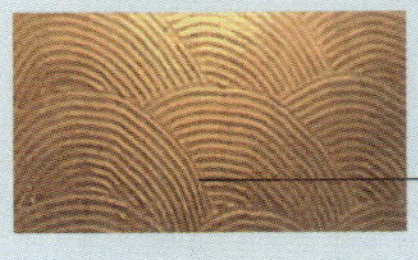

Dense, repeated lines create uniformity

Paper and cloth
Textiles and papers absorb paint differently, creating texture—from fine silk to rough handmade paper.

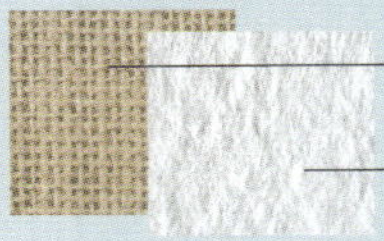

Cloth

Paper

HOW DID VINCENT VAN GOGH CREATE HIS TEXTURED WORKS?

Van Gogh used small brushstrokes with impasto paint in complementary colors to create paintings full of movement.

IT IS HARDEST TO DISTINGUISH DISTANCE AT DUSK AS THE TONAL CONTRAST IS AT ITS LOWEST

LIGHT IN INSTALLATIONS

Installation artists often use light directly as well as projection to transform objects. English artist Cornelia Parker dramatized her sculpture of an "exploding" shed using directional lighting to enhance the cast shadow.

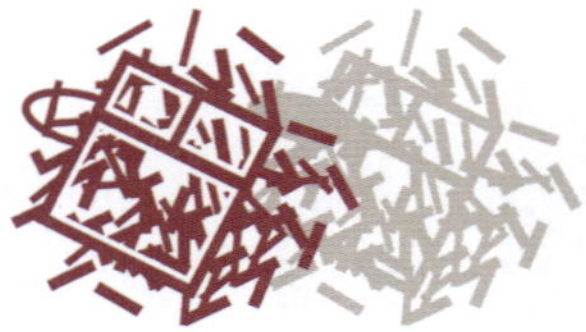

LIGHT SOURCE AT CENTER

High contrast

The use of high contrast shows how drama and expression can be created through strongly juxtaposed light and shade. The dark staircase leads down to the highly lit area, drawing on Expressionist composition that uses strong light and dark and unusual angles to create tension. The figures are, therefore, in silhouette against the strong light, which creates mystery and implied narrative.

Dramatic scene
This image shows a simple urban scene of figures approaching a staircase. However, due to the use of high contrast, the scene becomes dramatic and foreboding, suggesting an event is about to happen.

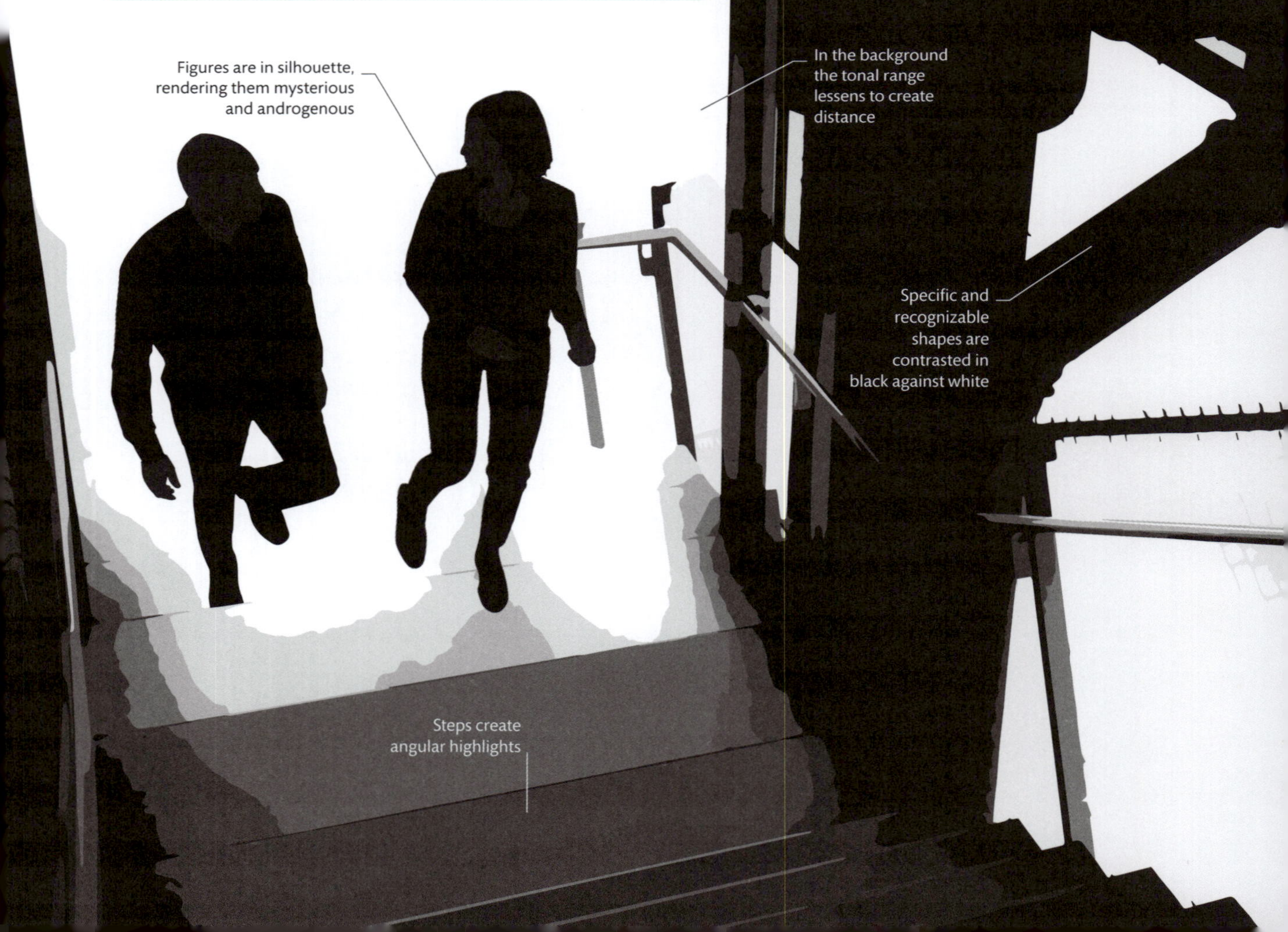

Light, Shade, and Contrast

Light, shade, and contrast can be used across all art forms to variously create form, drama, illusion, and atmosphere. Some materials are particularly suited to creating strong contrasting effects such as charcoal and chalk, as well as spray paints and stencils. Digital manipulation of images can also be used to exaggerate contrast.

WHAT IS CHIAROSCURO IN ART?

Chiaroscuro is the use of light and shadow to define three-dimensional objects. In painting, it was made famous by Renaissance (see pp.176–177) and Baroque artists (see pp.182–183).

Expanding tonal range

In drawing and painting, it is important to explore the power of light and shadow and to move beyond a limited tonal range. When drawing from observation, an effective way for the artist to perceive the tonal differences is to half close their eyes. These differences can then be exaggerated to create drama. Identifying the darkest and lightest areas of the scene, then working between these parameters, is a great way of expanding the tonal range. Working with silhouettes, strong directional lighting onto a scene, or a lit object within a dark space all help explore the range.

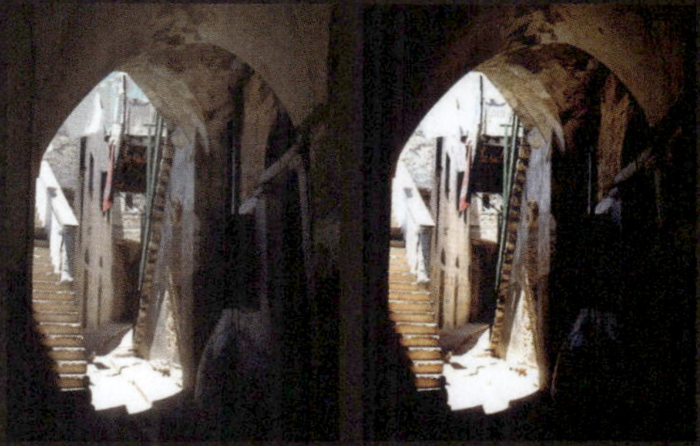

FLATTER SCENE **MORE DEPTH**

Light and dark
Here, the contrast between light and dark is exaggerated across the two images. The second image creates more of a sense of depth and invites the viewer into the scene through the use of light at the center.

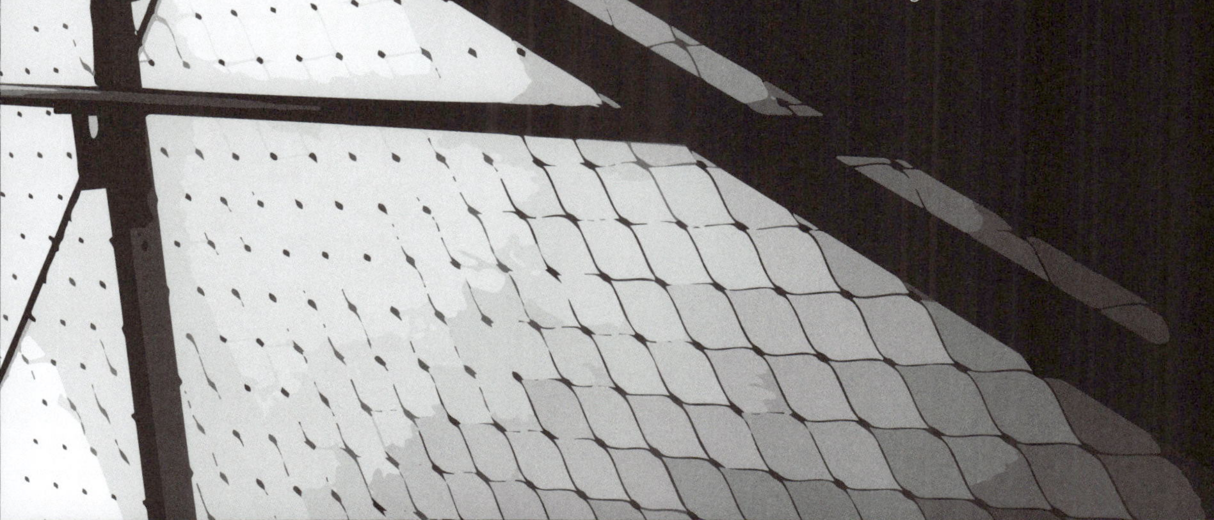

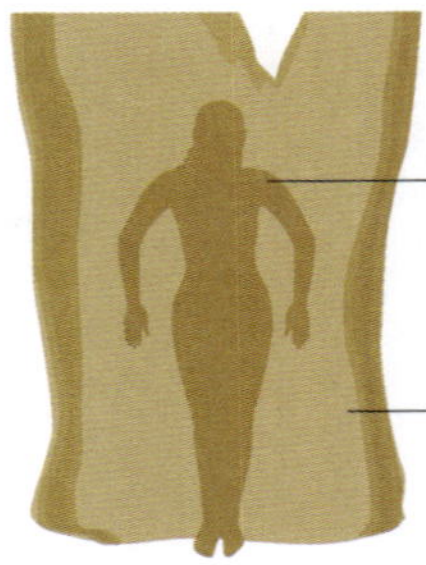

ENVIRONMENTAL SPACE

Space and environmental art
Artists may use the natural world as a space for making work, even using the landscape and outdoors as a medium in itself (see p.115). Often drawing attention to environmental issues, artists can use the landscape as a way of expanding the conventional scale of an artwork into epic proportions, and of changing expectations about how an artwork is seen and experienced. Artists may also explore space using the body. Multi-disciplinary artist Ana Mendieta created over 200 works in which she placed herself in an outside environment, using space and her surroundings as sculptural and performance mediums.

Space

The creation, suggestion, and manipulation of space is used across all art forms. Space can be used to create the illusion of depth and can be a medium in itself within three-dimensional art.

Pictorial space
"Pictorial space" describes the suggestion of space created within the flat picture plane, which is the surface of the picture as if transparent, held parallel to the artist's face, showing imaginary space. The depiction of illusory space in painting emerged following the development of geometric perspective in the 15th century. In modern and contemporary art, space can be constructed in ways such as using perspective, creating a distinction between foreground, middle ground, and background; using layers of recessive and dominant colors; overlapping, and using objects of relative size.

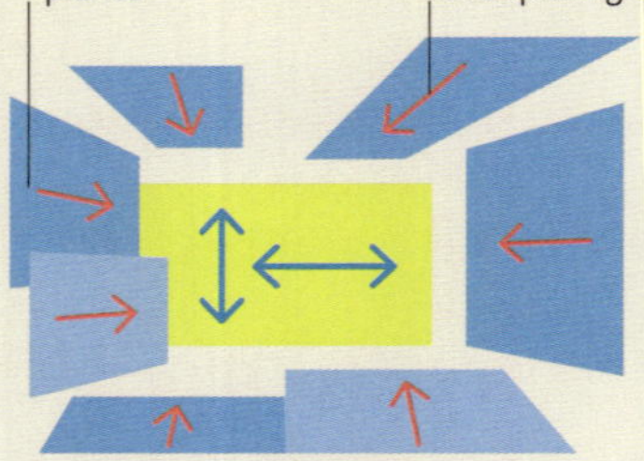

Creating space with planes
Planes organized at different perspectival angles create a sense of space and distance by receding into the picture plane.

Geometric perspective
Artists may use elements such as perspective, varying planes, patterns, and shapes to create pictorial space in a painting or other two-dimensional work. Figures can lend the space tension and meaning.

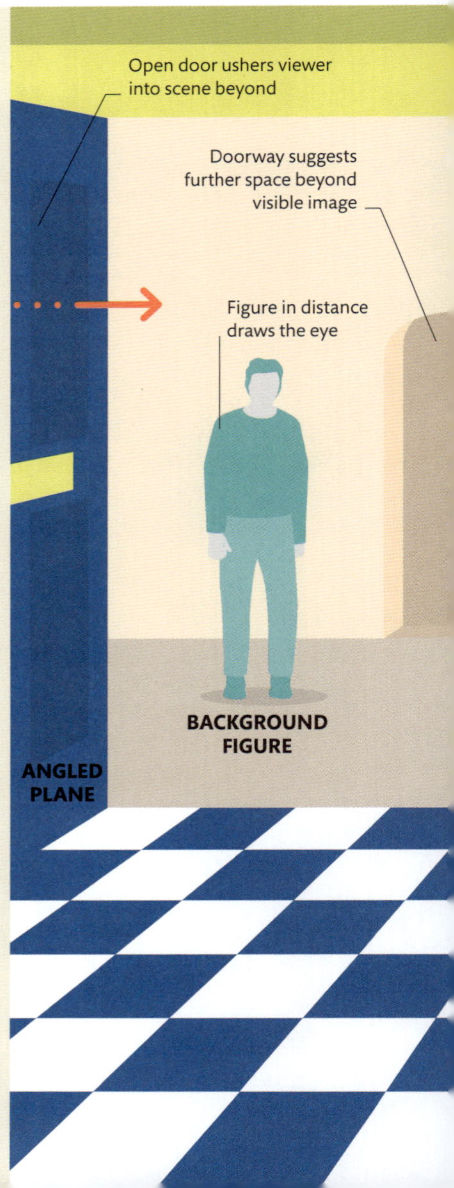

ART INSTALLATIONS PLAY WITH CONCEPTS OF **SPACE,** IMMERSING THE **VIEWER** FOR A **FULLER EXPERIENCE**

INTERIOR AND EXTERIOR SPACE

Installation artists often explore and highlight the feeling and character of particular spaces, and the relationship between interior and exterior. James Turrell creates spaces for contemplation by framing the sky from within a calm, minimal interior.

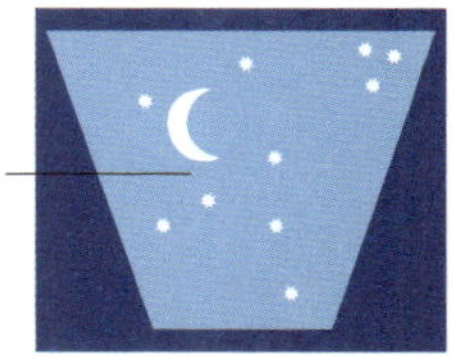

FRAMING THE SKY

HOW IS SPACE USED IN SCULPTURE?

Sculptures may contain areas of negative space, such as the holes formed in Henry Moore's figures. Alternatively, works may interact with the space they inhabit.

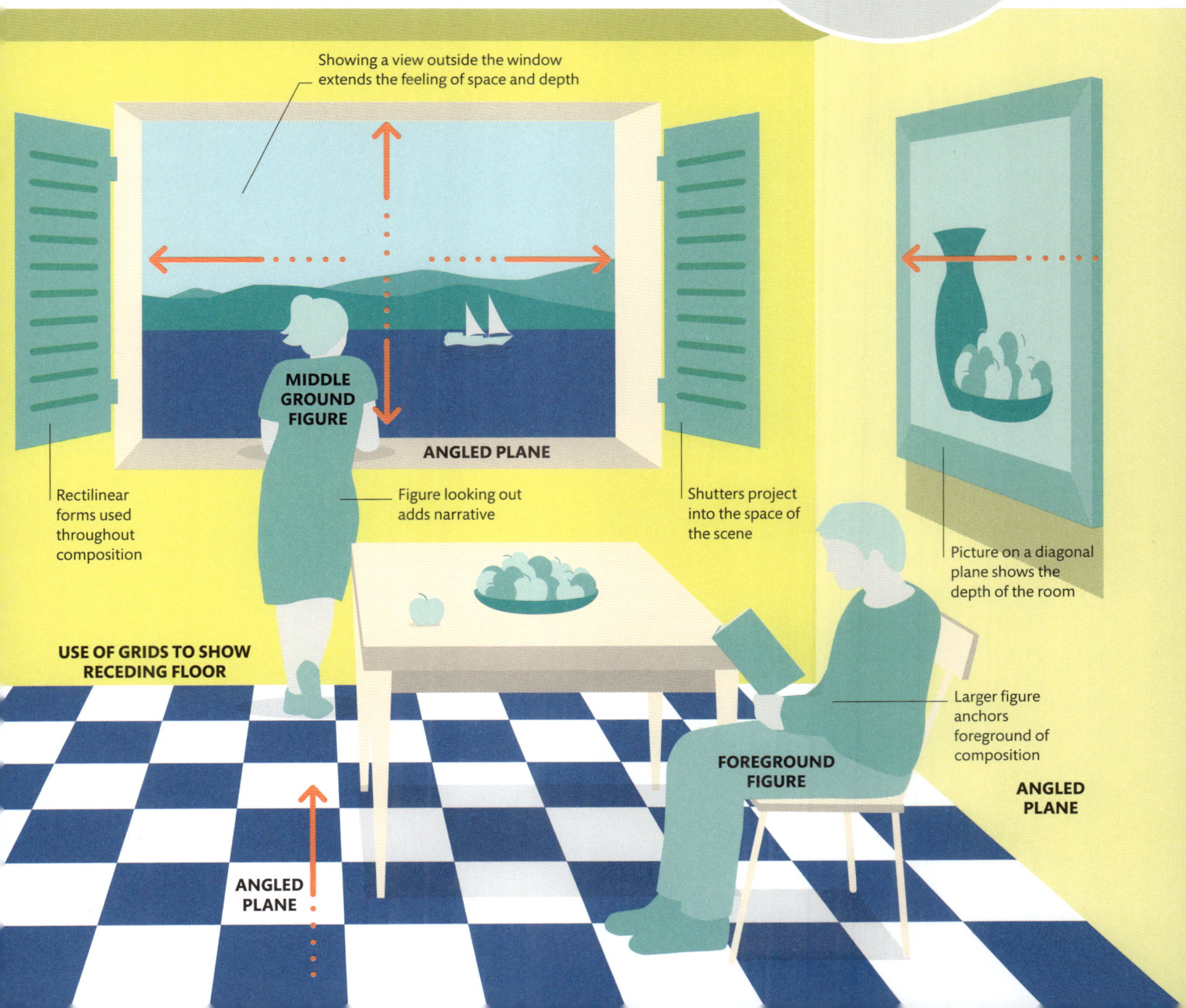

ALBRECHT DÜRER FIRST DEMONSTRATED **TWO-POINT PERSPECTIVE** IN HIS **1525 BOOK**

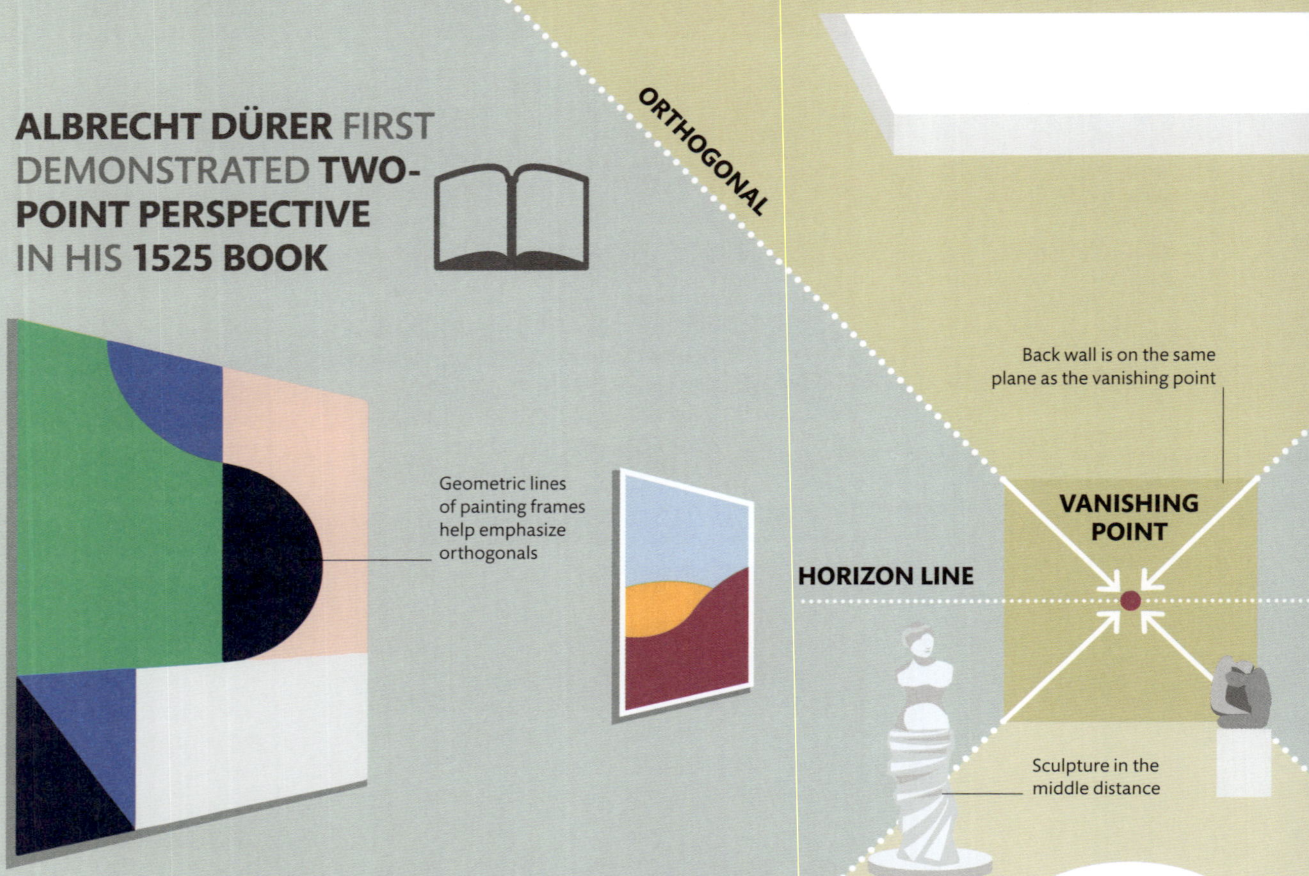

Linear Perspective

Creating the illusion of depth in a painting or drawing relies on particular techniques and the skillful use of perspective. Artists use the system of linear perspective to convey the illusion of spatial depth in scenes with straight lines, enabling them to accurately translate the real world onto paper or canvas.

How linear perspective works

In perceiving depth, objects closer to the viewer appear larger than those further away. For example, a tree in the foreground of a painting might be larger than a mountain in the distance. On a two-dimensional surface this disparity in size gives the impression of receding space, and in order to replicate this artists need to employ three components: a horizon line, which acts as a divide between the sky and ground, orthogonals (diagonal lines) that recede into the distance, and a vanishing point, which is the point at which all orthogonals converge.

Vantage point
The vantage point is the point from which the scene is viewed. The height of the horizon line affects the vantage point. If the horizon line is higher, the viewer has the feeling of being able to walk into the scene; lower, and the viewer could be looking down into it. A central horizon line gives balance to a composition.

VIEWER

ORTHOGONAL

Multiple perspectives

Pictures that have only one vanishing point on the horizon line use the one-point perspective system. An artist would use this method if they wanted to accurately render a road, corridor, or a building with the front directly facing them. Early perspective methods used one vanishing point, and more were added later to create more realistic scenes.

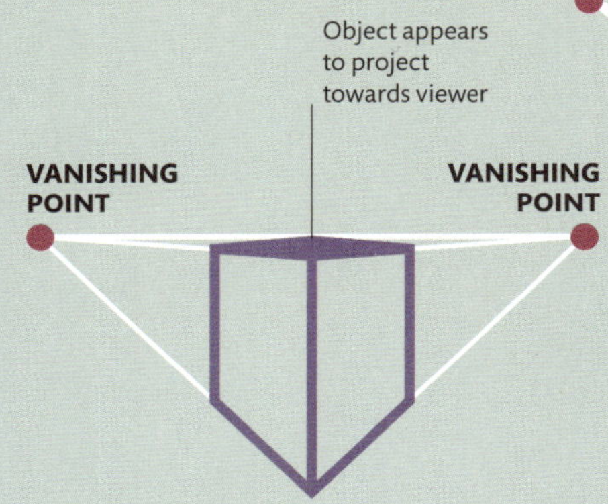

Two-point perspective
This method uses two receding points on the horizon line to create an advancing view—ideal for architectural landscapes.

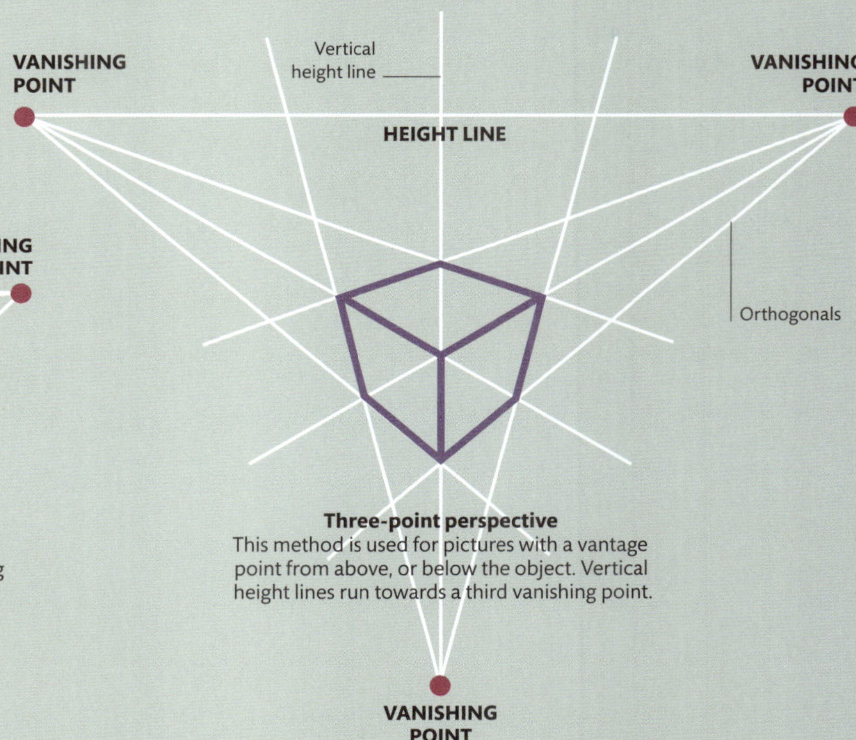

Three-point perspective
This method is used for pictures with a vantage point from above, or below the object. Vertical height lines run towards a third vanishing point.

WHICH ARTISTS USED BRUNELLESCHI'S FINDINGS ON PERSPECTIVE?

Renaissance artists such as Michelangelo, Leonardo da Vinci, and Botticelli used this system to create celebrated paintings.

FILIPPO BRUNELLESCHI

Perspective was known to the ancient Greeks and Romans, but lost during the Middle Ages. The Italian Renaissance architect Filippo Brunelleschi theorized linear perspective around 1415, when he demonstrated the concept of a single vanishing point by accurately rendering Florence Baptistery in two paintings. Brunelleschi's findings changed painting, ushering in an era of increased realism.

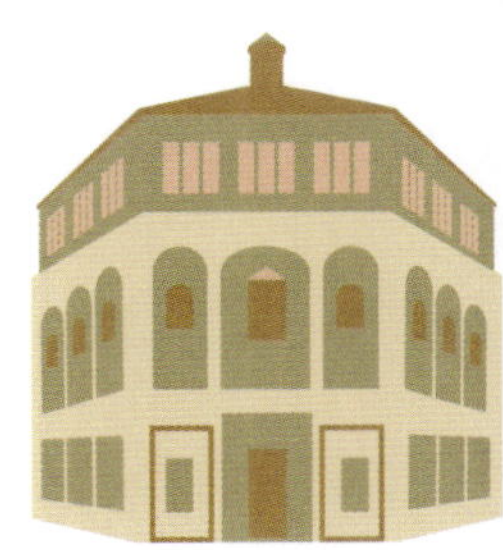

FLORENCE BAPTISTERY

Perspective Illusions

Leonardo da Vinci was one of the first to note that when a landscape recedes into the distance, its appearance changes in tone and color. In painting and drawing, this is called aerial or atmospheric perspective. Objects and figures are also susceptible to distortion in the form of foreshortening and other optical illusions.

WHAT MEDIA CAN BE USED IN AERIAL PERSPECTIVE?

Oil paint can be used for thin glazes for the gradual changes in tone, with impasto for the foreground textures. Watercolour can create washes of color.

Aerial perspective

When viewed from a distance, buildings, trees, and other elements in a landscape look hazy, outlines and details are indistinct, and colors become weaker and veiled in a bluish hue. With subtle adjustments of color, combined with a gradual change in tone between the warm foreground and cooler background, artists can replicate the phenomenon of aerial perspective and create the illusion of depth in a painting or drawing.

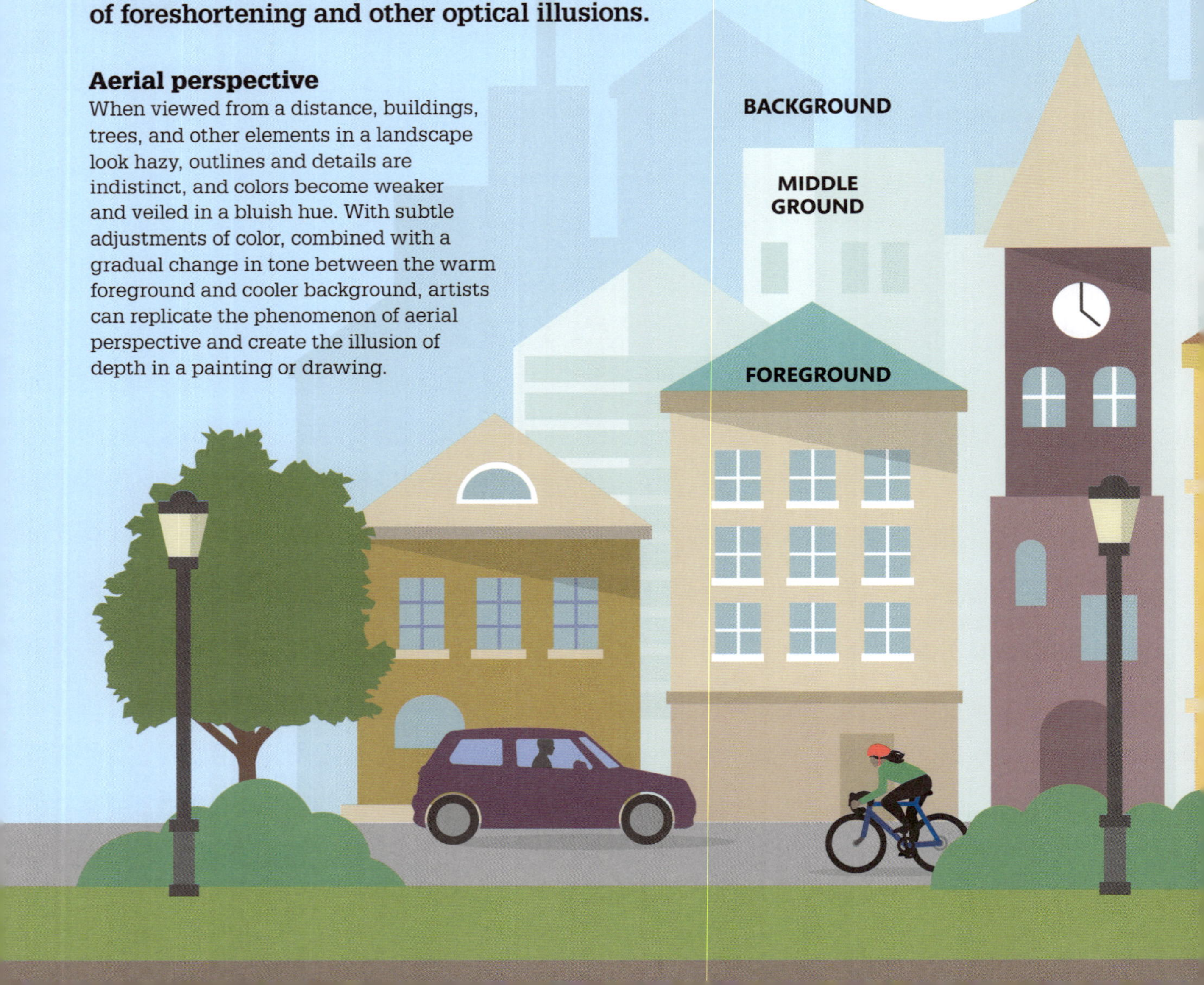

Foreshortening

The technique of foreshortening is used to depict an object or figure in depth. It is the distortion perceived by the eye when something is viewed from afar or from an odd angle. For example, if a reclining figure is depicted with the feet closest to the viewer, the feet will appear abnormally large; the parts of the body farthest away, unnaturally small.

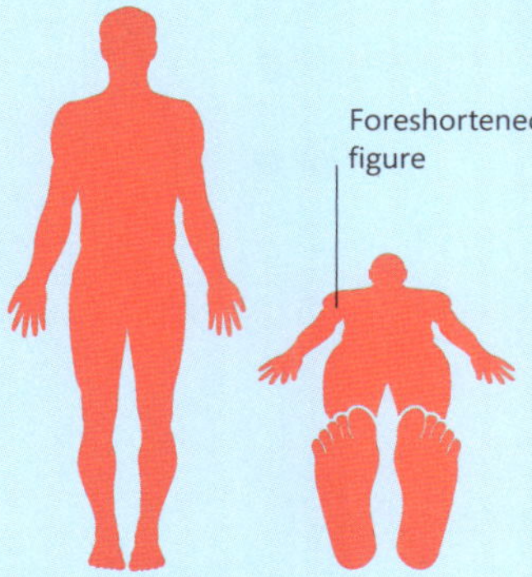

Sense of space
A foreshortened figure's legs and chest appear shorter, creating an impression of depth.

IMPOSSIBLE FIGURE

Designed by Oscar Reutersvärd in 1934, the Penrose triangle is an impossible figure—an inconsistent shape that gives a disorienting sense of perspective. The bars appear to be going in opposite directions, but they seem to connect.

THE PENROSE TRIANGLE

ARTIST J.M.W. TURNER TAUGHT PERSPECTIVE FOR 30 YEARS

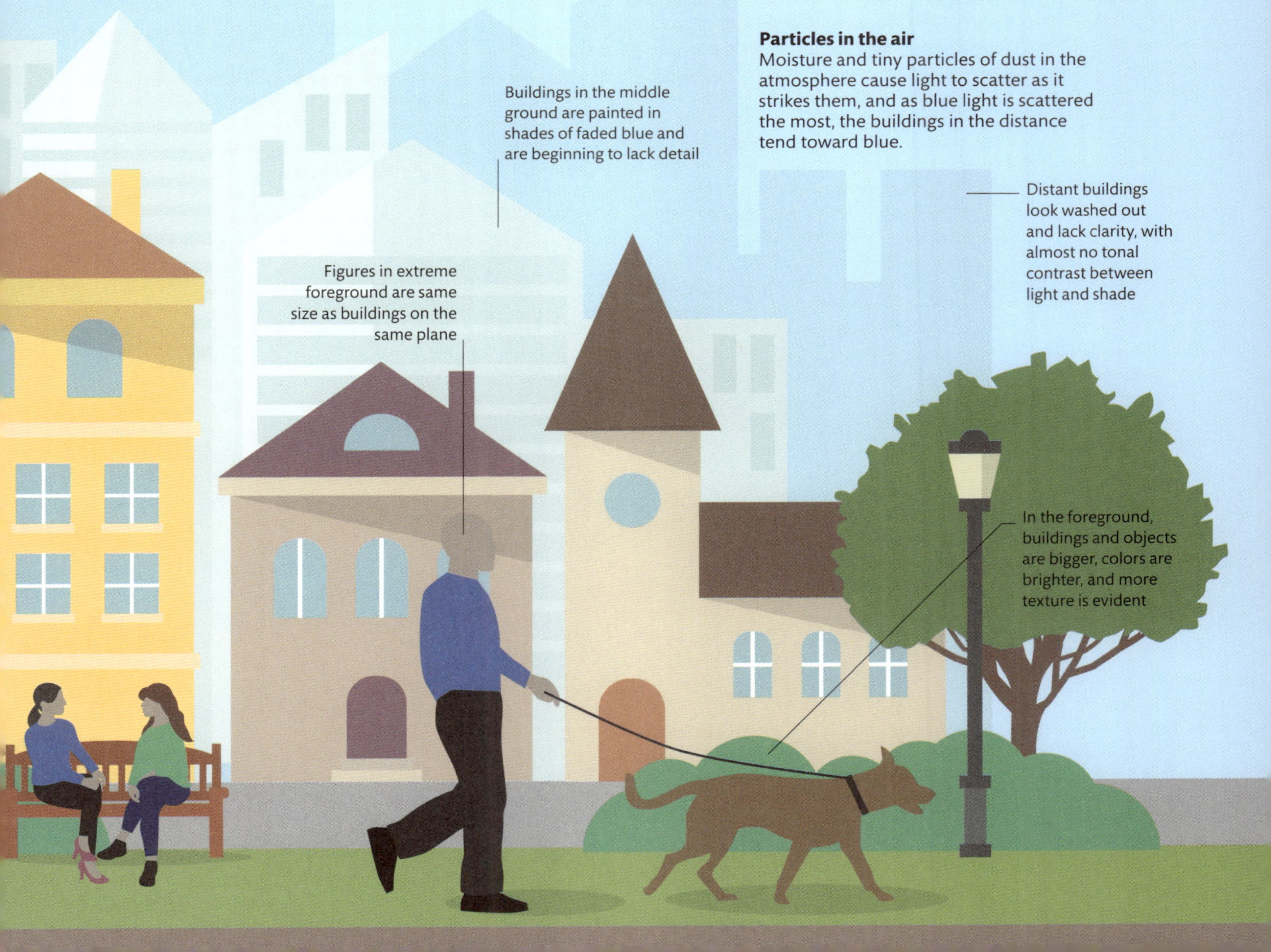

Particles in the air
Moisture and tiny particles of dust in the atmosphere cause light to scatter as it strikes them, and as blue light is scattered the most, the buildings in the distance tend toward blue.

Subject

Subject is the main element that an artwork depicts. It can shape the work in terms of materials, visual language, scale, and viewer experience and is what distinguishes a studio exercise from a meaningful artwork.

Main types of subject matter

Artists may choose the subject of their work by asking themselves questions about the issues and interests that concern them. Some artists combine autobiography with wider themes, for example, connecting their identity and past with issues such as race and gender. Other artists may be politically motivated or make artworks that draw from history. Some artists consider the nature of the materials they use to be the subject and explore ideas of time or transformation through the action of the materials themselves. Analyzing the visual language that the artist employs can help the viewer understand the subject matter more clearly.

HOW DO TITLES RELATE TO SUBJECT MATTER?

The title of an artwork may be directly descriptive, or it may be deliberately ironic, atmospheric, or obscure. A title may even add another layer of meaning to a work.

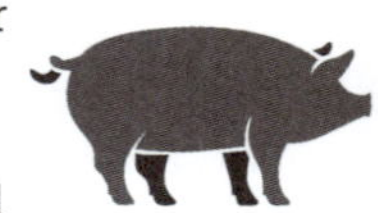

ANIMALS ARE AMONG THE **FIRST KNOWN ART SUBJECTS**, PAINTED ON **CAVE WALLS**

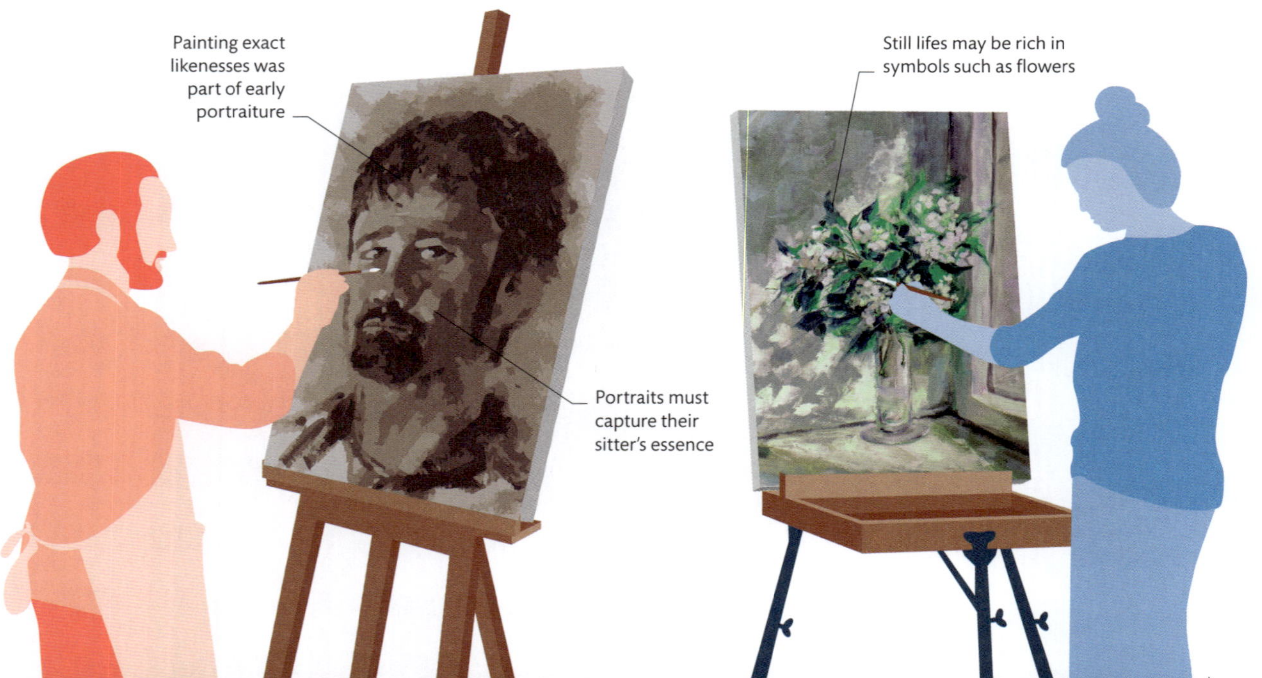

Portrait
Portraiture (see pp.64–65) has historically been used to reinforce hierarchies, such as in the representation of royal figures, while also being a window into human experience. Portraits offer a glimpse of the artist's view of their subject, sometimes including visual clues such as objects or clothing.

Still life
Still life (see pp.70–71) is a style often used allegorically, to suggest ideas such as prosperity or mortality, for example, by Dutch 17th century painters. In the 20th century, artists including Georges Braque and Paul Cézanne used still life as a vehicle to explore the idea of composition itself.

Historical subjects

Historically, subject matter tended to be drawn on commonly known legendary themes and stories. Gradually, artists widened their horizons, embracing more everyday subjects and nonnarrative themes, a development that allowed them to better express their own identities and make more inclusive art.

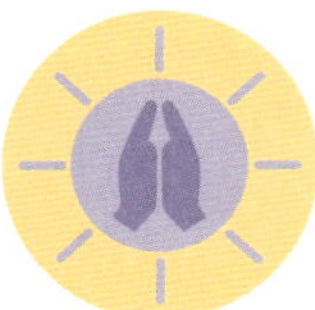

Devotional
This art was a way of conveying religious ideas through images to a mostly nonliterate audience.

Narrative
Historical, mythical, or religious subjects were tackled in works that told an easily identifiable story.

Genre
Paintings showing scenes of normal, everyday life became popular from the 1600s onward.

LIFE INFLUENCES ART

Artists are the products of their environment. External factors such as the media they consume, the people they interact with, and the places they live, combine with internal influences, including their memories, thoughts, and psychological state, to inform their work.

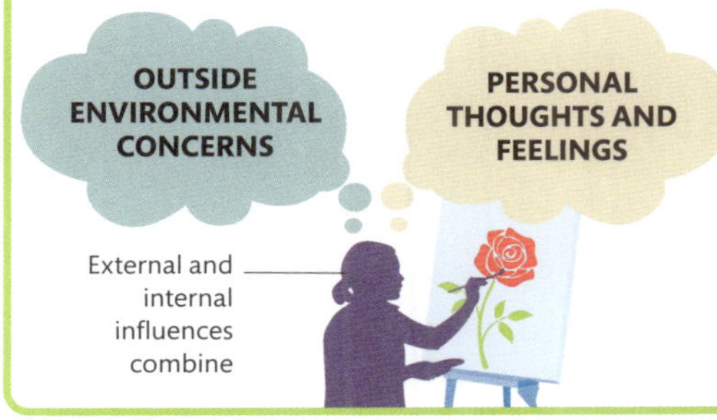

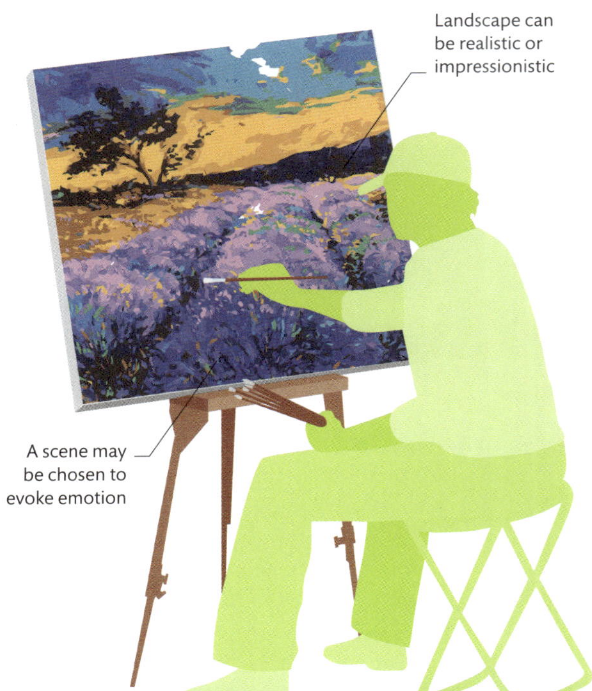

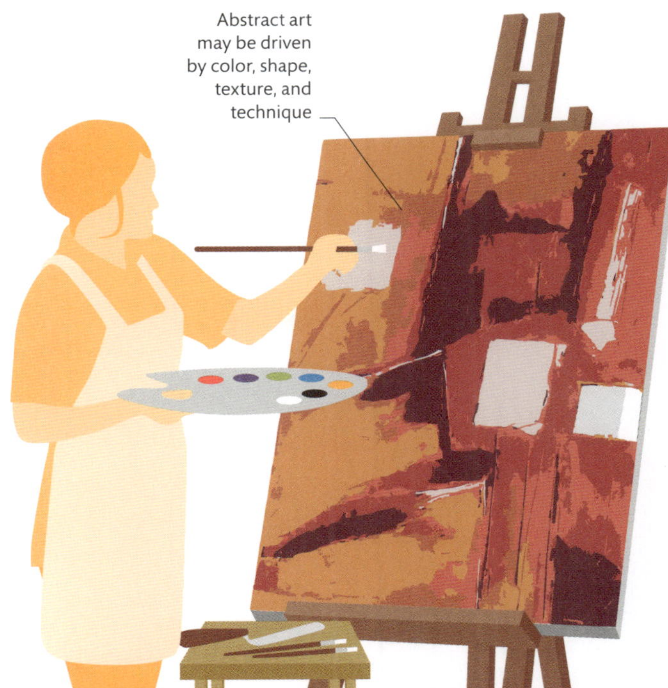

Landscape
Not simply depictions of nature, landscape paintings reflect the attitudes of their time: ordered and calm in the Classical era, for example, or wild and intense in the Romantic age. They can also carry social or political messages, as in Paul Nash's World War I battlefields suggesting the horrors of war.

Abstract
Some artists reduce forms from life to geometric or organic abstract shapes, while others use subject matter such as new philosophical and revolutionary ideas that they feel can be depicted only through abstraction rather than figurative, identifiable images.

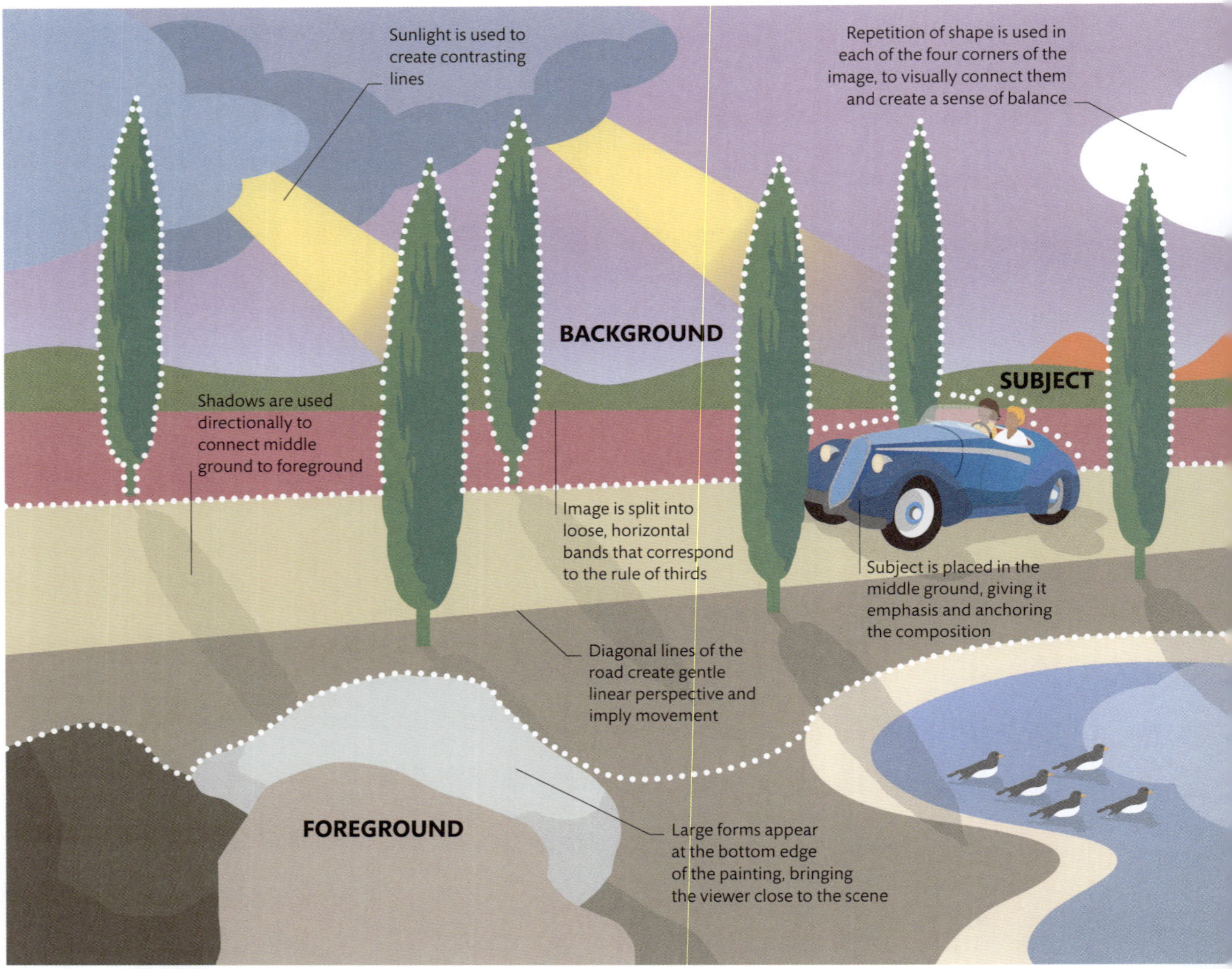

THE RULE OF THIRDS

The rule of thirds is a simple compositional tool for two-dimensional artwork. To use it, the artist splits the image into a hypothetical three-by-three grid and arranges the focal points of the piece to follow this structure. This creates a balanced, intriguing, and visually pleasing arrangement of elements.

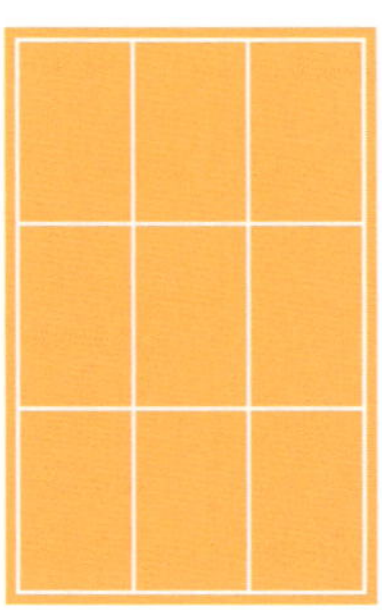

SIMPLE GRID

Compositional devices

A number of fundamental compositional devices, or strategies, have been used in art through the ages. These strategies create the main structure of the painting, with other elements such as figures or objects, colors, and space placed within this structure. Modern composition sometimes incorporates or subverts these techniques, or adopts a combination of different strategies within the same painting.

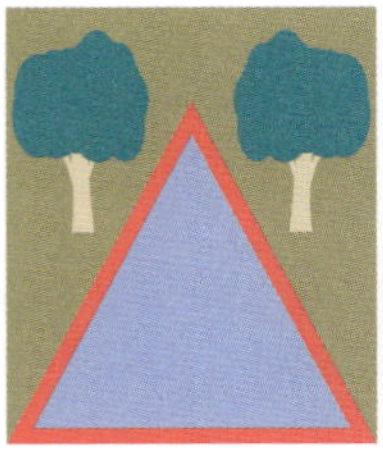

Triangular
Often seen in Renaissance painting, the triangle is the organizing principle around which elements are placed to create a dynamic composition.

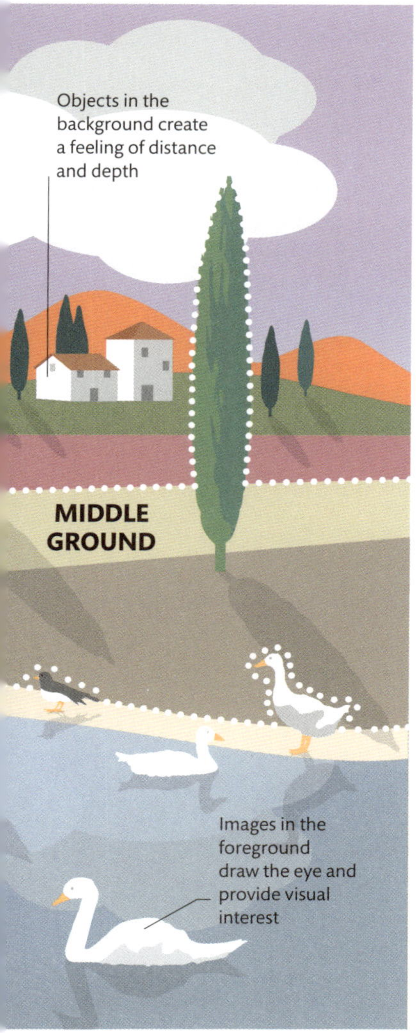

Composition

The term composition describes how an artwork is structured and how individual elements within it are arranged and organized to create an overall visual impression. An artist will consider the composition of a piece before they begin work.

Deliberate structure

Most commonly used to describe two-dimensional work, composition is the artist's way of guiding the viewer around the work, using the structure of pictorial space to create movement and deliberate points of interest. Composition encompasses more than the arrangement of elements on a surface and includes structure in terms of how a painting is put together and the relationship between the illusion of depth and surface.

HOW DO ARTISTS USE COMPOSITION WHEN WORKING FROM REAL LIFE?

When drawing or painting a real scene, an artist may use a rectangular viewfinder to "frame" different views to find the best composition.

Combining elements

Composition combines different elements to create the desired effect. Perspective, planes of depth, contrasting sizes, and angled lines all help give a scene drama and visual impact.

BALANCED COMPOSITIONS CREATE A FEELING OF HARMONY

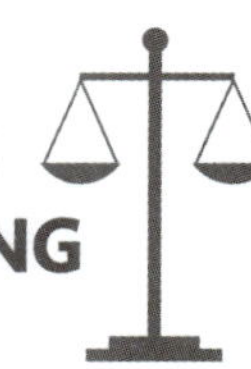

Centered
A common method of composing a portrait, this style of composition is simple and the attention is drawn to the figure through its placement in the center.

Diagonal
Diagonals are used to create dynamic forces across the artwork. They lead the eye from corner to corner and suggest that the image continues beyond the edges of the painting.

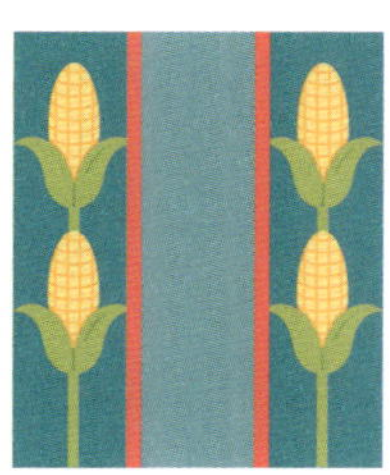

Vertical
Elements of the painting are arranged to emphasize vertical lines, creating the impression of height or length, which can be either unsettling or imposing.

Focal point
Using perspective or sense of distance can draw the viewer's eye deliberately toward a focal point. This can become more complex and involve multiple focal points.

Asymmetry
A feeling of irregularity can create an exciting composition that forces the eye to move around the painting at different speeds and suggests disruption or change.

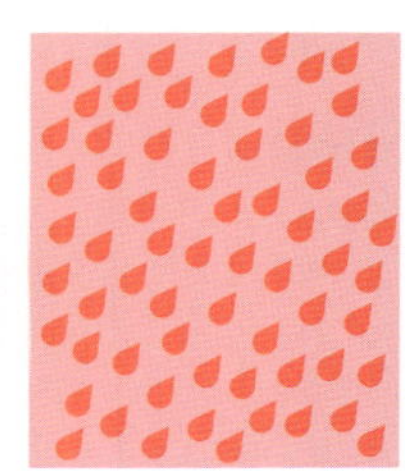

No focal point
This composition becomes surface-based rather than spatial. The repetitive mark making across its surface creates the impression of movement.

Viewpoint

Viewpoint refers to the way the artist presents a work and its subject in relation to the viewer. This can be both within the work, for example, implied viewpoints in a painting, and also the placement of the art object itself.

Deliberate positioning

The angle from which a viewer sees can be manipulated by the artist to create a particular effect in an artwork. In painting and drawing, devices such as geometric perspective, cropping, and multiple images can be used to create specific viewpoints within the frame of the artwork itself. In sculpture and installation art, the viewer's approach to the work and the way they move around it in three-dimensional space become key parts of the way they experience it.

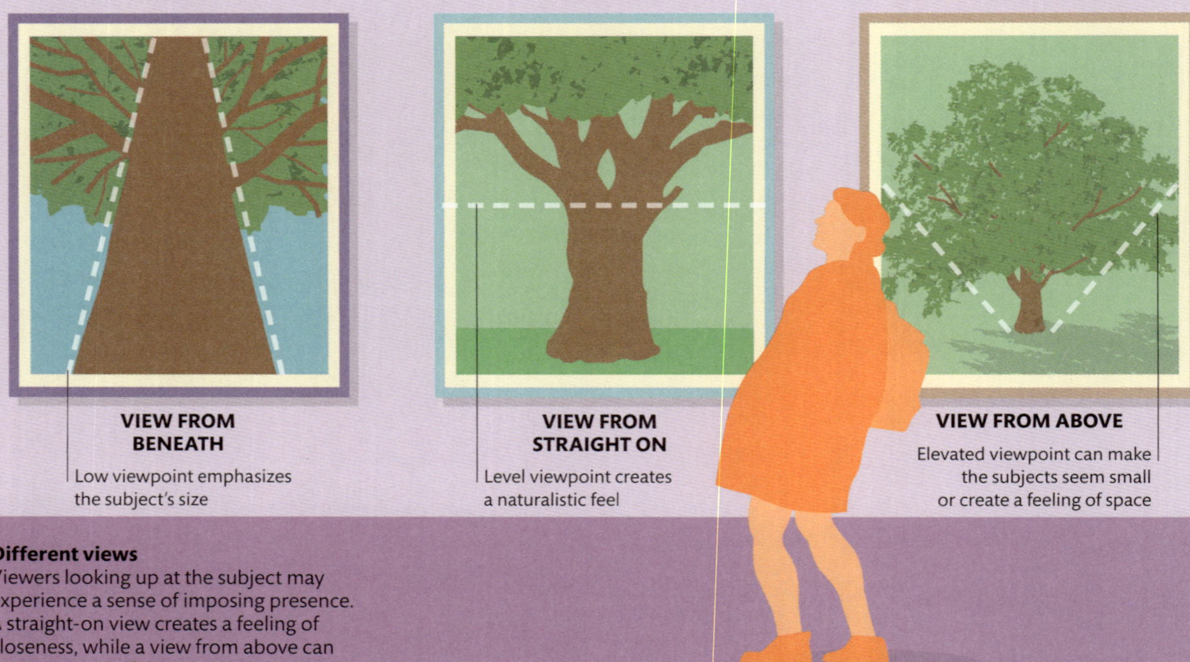

Different views
Viewers looking up at the subject may experience a sense of imposing presence. A straight-on view creates a feeling of closeness, while a view from above can create a sense of dizzying altitude.

Unusual viewpoints

Viewpoint in painting and drawing is closely linked to the use of perspective (see pp.104–107), which can be manipulated to create a distorted sense of space or multiple viewpoints. Depicting different spaces in the same painting can shift the viewpoint around the composition, subverting conventions of foreground, middle ground, and background. Some artists use inventive viewpoints such as cropping or framing the main view with a closer object to add narrative or a sense of drama to the art piece.

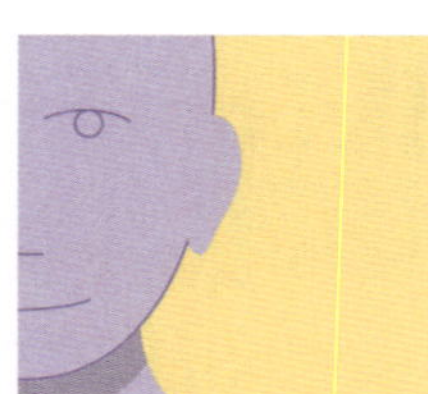

Close crop
Close cropping or zooming in can suggest a fragment of a wider scene, creating a dramatic and cinematic viewpoint.

View past
Shifting the viewpoint past the foreground and into the distance helps place the viewer in the space.

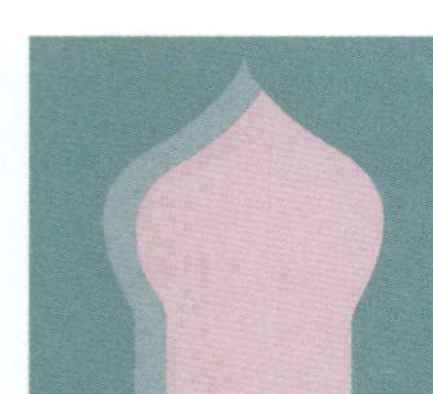

View through
Highlighting the space behind or beyond draws the viewer to the painting by creating a feeling of layers.

ANAMORPHOSIS REFERS TO A **DISTORTED IMAGE** THAT LOOKS NORMAL FROM A **SPECIFIC VIEWPOINT**

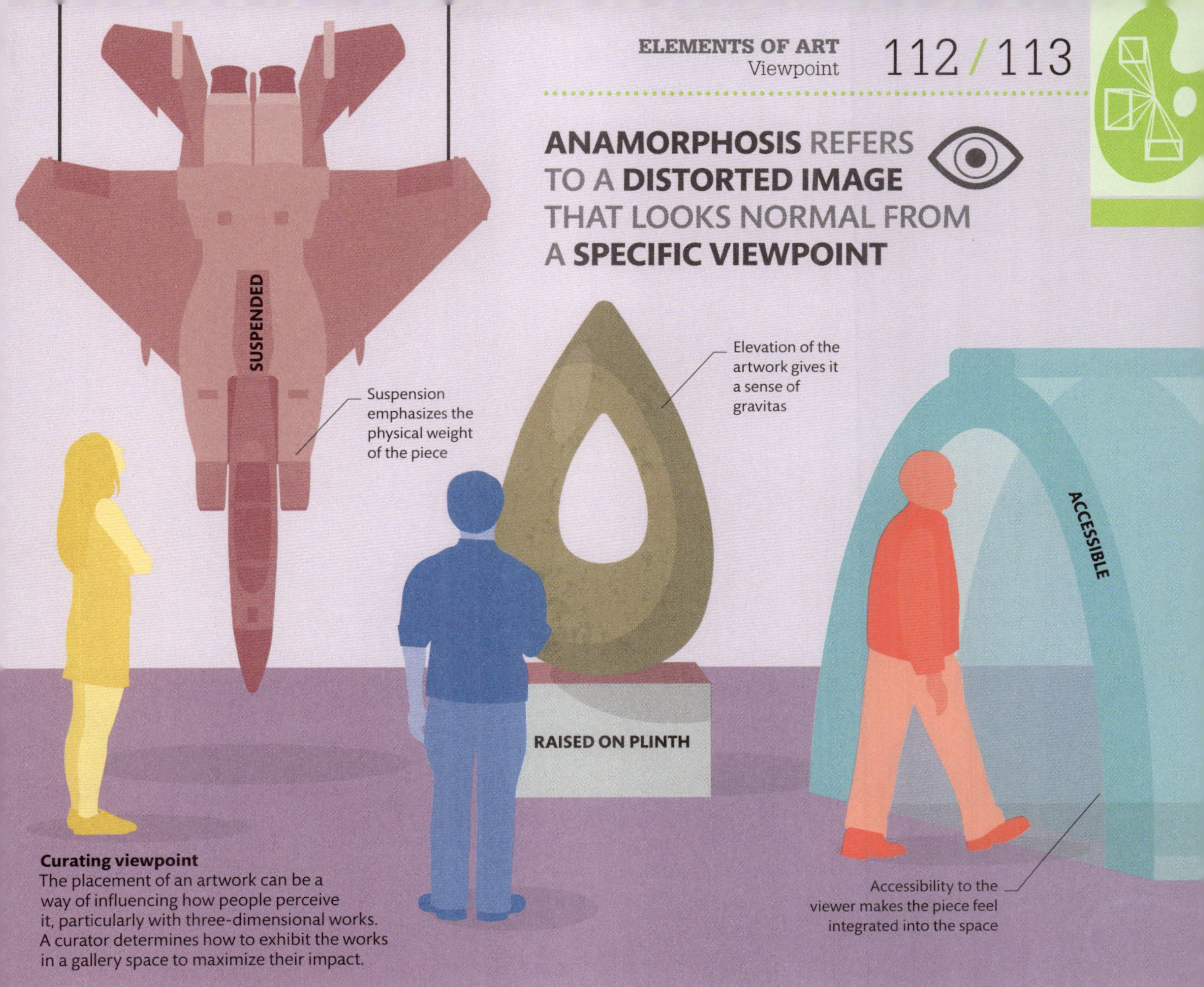

Curating viewpoint
The placement of an artwork can be a way of influencing how people perceive it, particularly with three-dimensional works. A curator determines how to exhibit the works in a gallery space to maximize their impact.

SHIFTING VIEWPOINTS

In installation art (see pp.60-61), artists often have more scope to play with viewpoint. As the viewer moves around the work, the viewpoint changes and creates a shifting experience. Visual artist Pipilotti Rist creates immersive environments with hanging sheets of organza onto which images are projected. The viewer experiences a dreamlike sense of changing viewpoints that challenges their sense of space.

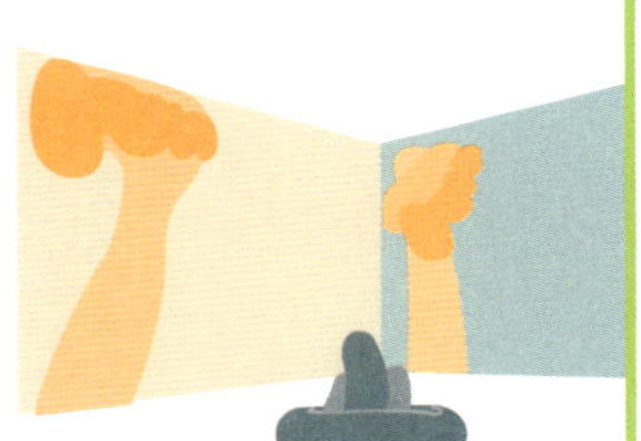

HOW DID VERMEER ACHIEVE SUCH REALISTIC VIEWPOINTS?

Vermeer may have used a camera obscura to project an image of a space onto his canvas, allowing him to capture the scene with accuracy.

Atmosphere and Weather

Depicting weather can be an effective way for an artist to capture and communicate mood. Atmospheric light and darkness can be used to set the scene for a narrative, to create feelings of elation or turmoil, or to express a specific landscape or place.

Weather into paint

Paint's fluidity makes it an ideal medium for conveying weather and its effects on a landscape. Capturing subtle atmospheric conditions, such as dusk, can be achieved using gentle variations of color and tone, while bright sunlight can be suggested using high contrast and juxtapositions of color. Atmospheric perspective (see pp.106–107) uses tonal variation to create a sense of distance.

Sun
Effects of sunlight, such as dappled light or strong shadow contrasts, can be depicted in colors varying from cool and acidic to warm and glowing, depending on the season (see right).

Rainbows
Watercolor is a popular medium for capturing the luminosity and blur of a rainbow. Using the illumination of a white ground, the colors may merge together to create an ephemeral visual quality.

Mist and fog
The effect of mist and fog over a landscape is often achieved by layering with acrylic or oil glazing. It can convey a sense of uncertainty or otherworldliness in an otherwise ordinary scene.

Wind
Wind can add dynamism and movement (see pp.126–127) to otherwise static scenes. Elements such as trees may be shown at an angle, or figures may seem to be battling the wind.

THE ROMANTIC PERIOD SAW A SURGE OF INTEREST IN **ARTISTIC AND PERSONAL DEPICTIONS** OF WEATHER

WHAT IS "SKYING" IN PAINTING?

The term "skying"—looking at clouds—was coined by 19th-century painter John Constable, who made hundreds of studies of clouds.

Reflections
Reflections on water give a distorted but recognizable imprint of familiar surroundings, which may be rendered in detail or reduced to simple shapes or even swashes of color.

Night
A nighttime atmosphere can be rendered through layering acrylic or oil glazes in dark colors, such as blue and green. An artist may use more than one block of color, giving a sense of depth.

Rain
Rain is often evoked through colors such as inky blues and grays painted as straight, diagonal lines. Some artists brush water across a wet painting. White highlights can suggest rain splashes.

Storms
Stormy conditions may signify turmoil or the power of nature. Artists may use colors such as Payne's gray, indigo, and Prussian blue mixed with burnt umber to create a brooding atmosphere.

ENVIRONMENTAL ART

Land artists such as Andy Goldsworthy use natural forms—leaves, wood, or stones—to create pieces within the landscape. Some artists, such as Milton Becerra, use environmental art to raise awareness of ecological issues.

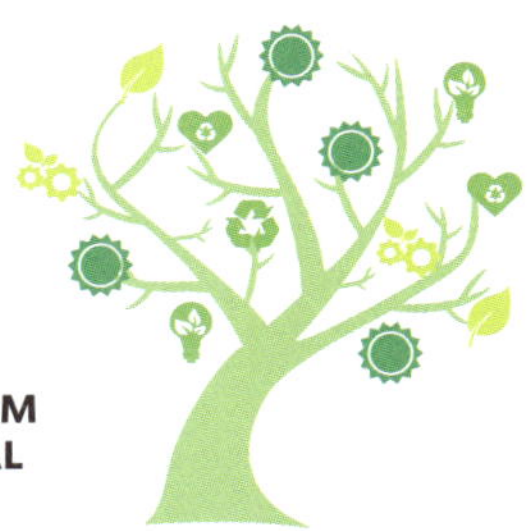

ART FROM NATURAL FORMS

Seasonal palette

The seasons have been depicted by artists as a way of evoking a specific time, place, and attitude toward the landscape. Artists may choose from a range of colors typically associated with a particular season, as seen in the rich, fall hues in the paintings of the Canadian wilderness by the Group of Seven. Other color choices may be surprising, however. In his snowscapes, Claude Monet (see pp.192–93) used a wide range of purple and blue hues to render snow and ice. During the winter of 1874–1875, Monet painted 18 snowy scenes in Argenteuil, France.

Spring
Acidic colors such as lemon yellow, cerulean blue, and sap green suggest freshness and new life emerging in spring.

Summer
Strong colors such as magenta, cobalt blue, and cadmium yellow convey the heat of summer.

Fall
Rich, warm colors of yellow ocher, burnt umber, and crimson take the palette into the deeper shades of fall.

Winter
Inky colors such as Payne's gray, Prussian blue, and lamp black contrasted with lilacs suggest the coolness of winter.

Playing with scale

Large-scale work offers a sense of immersion and can relate to space and architecture. At the opposite end, working in miniature creates an intimate viewing experience, and a fictional quality or suspension of belief reminiscent of a dollhouse. Varying the scale of subjects within a composition can be used to convey emphasis or imply relationships.

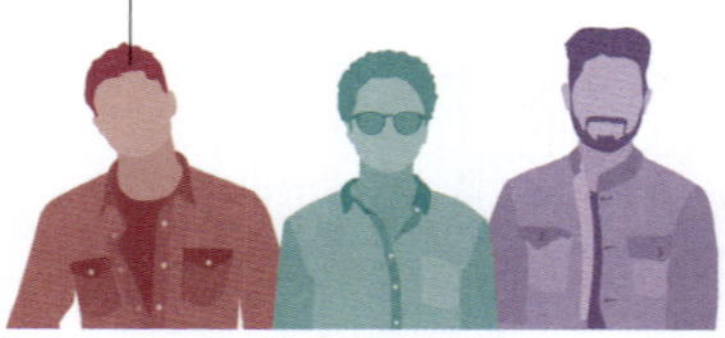

Equal scale
A consistent scale is used to create equality between figures and a simple composition.

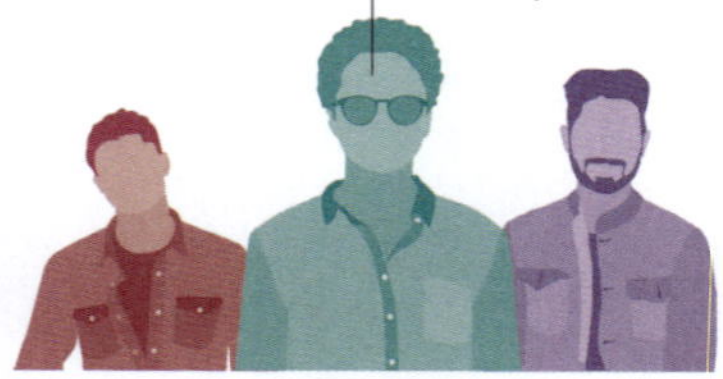

Altered scale
Scale is altered here to exaggerate the middle figure for emphasis and a dynamic composition.

SCALE IN SCULPTURE

In sculpture, working at large scale can be used to invite or overwhelm the viewer. Australian sculptor Ron Mueck plays with the scale of the body, often making his figures larger than life, which creates a contradiction between their realism and their strange proportions.

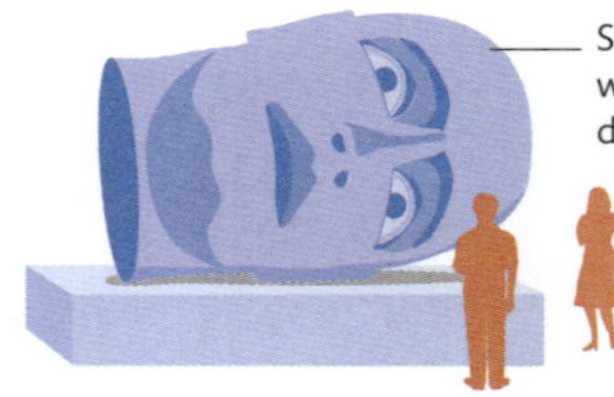

HEAD SCULPTURE

Plumb lines and proportion

Life drawing (see pp.68–69) is a good way of developing a sense of proportion, through observation. Plumb lines—threads with a weight attached—can be used to give a true vertical against which to measure a figure's proportion and alignment. To measure proportions more roughly by eye, a pencil held out at arm's length can be used.

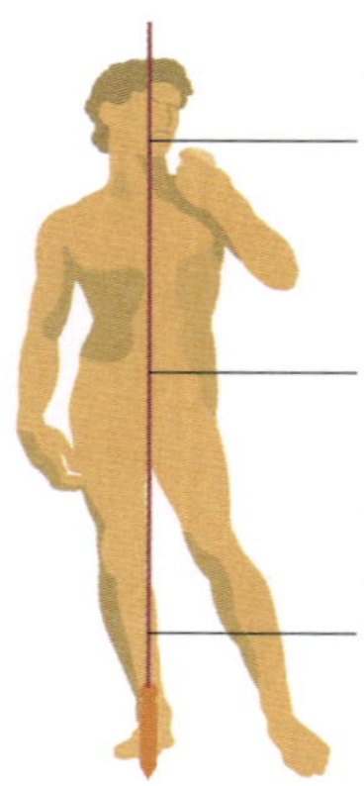

PLUMB LINE CENTER

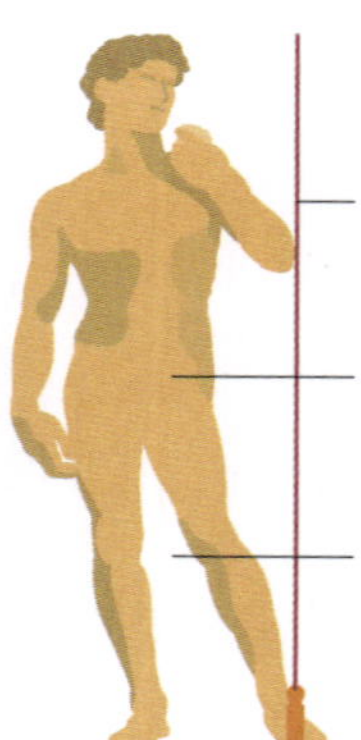

PLUMB LINE OFF-CENTER

WHAT IS CONTRAPPOSTO?

Contrapposto is an Italian term that describes a human figure bearing their full weight on one leg, with different elements of the body facing in opposite directions.

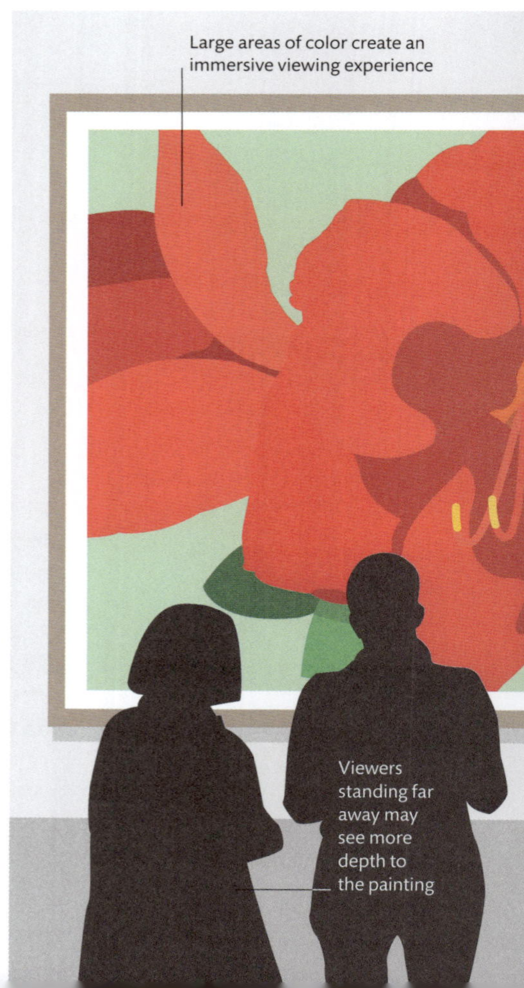

Size, Scale, and Proportion

Size, scale, and proportion are key aspects that an artist must consider when creating an artwork, as they determine how a viewer physically and psychologically relates to the piece of work.

Relationship to the body

People perceive scale, size, and proportion as relative to their own size, and so a viewer's experience of art has a relationship to the body, as well as to the dimensions of the surrounding space. Size refers to the physical dimensions of an artwork; scale is the relative size of an object in relation to another object, person, or a space; and proportion describes the relationships between height, width, and depth, for example, of a figure. Artists can adjust or manipulate these elements to achieve a particular quality, narrative, or feeling.

Large scale
When a painting is made at a scale larger than the body, the experience becomes physical as well as optical, and there is a sense of "walking into" the work. The Abstract Expressionists (see pp.210–211) embraced scale in painting, creating immense works that presented pure color as form and large gestures that embodied the movement of the artist's hand.

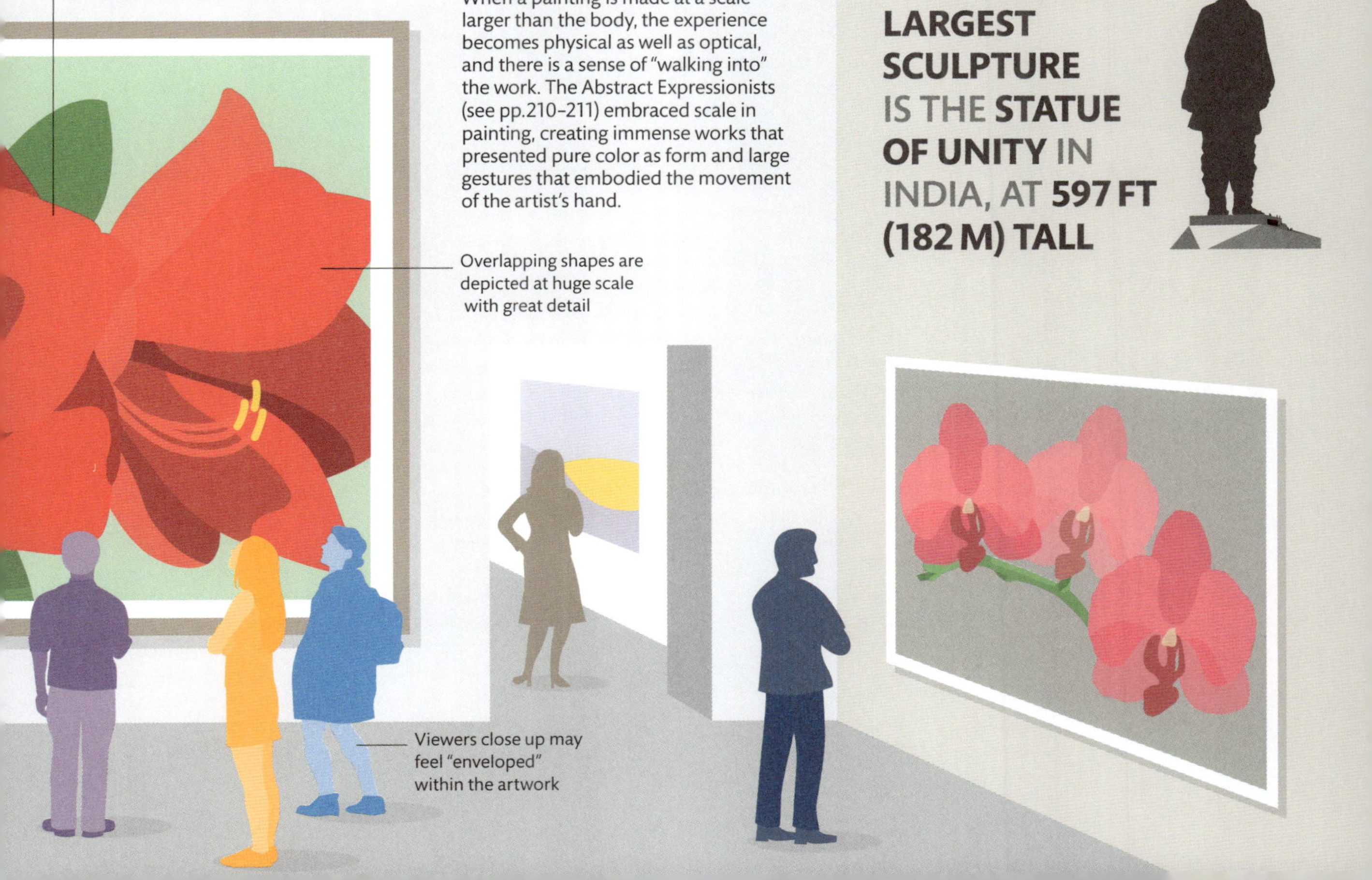

THE WORLD'S **LARGEST SCULPTURE** IS THE **STATUE OF UNITY** IN INDIA, AT **597 FT (182 M) TALL**

POSITIVE BECOMES NEGATIVE

Freeing it from its traditional role as a secondary compositional element, artists across various disciplines have adapted the use of negative space and made it the focal point in their work. Wolfgang Tillmans used positive space in photographs as a frame for the negative space; Ana Mendieta made sculptures by leaving negative traces of her body in sand; Rachel Whiteread cast the interior of houses.

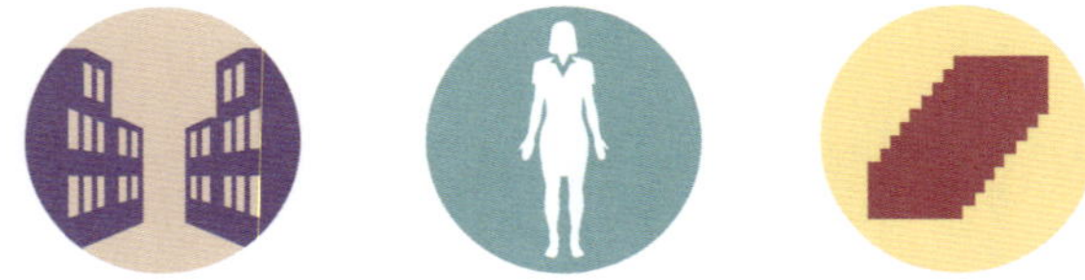

SPACE BETWEEN BUILDINGS | **SHADOW OF A PERSON** | **CAST OF THE SPACE AROUND A STAIRWELL**

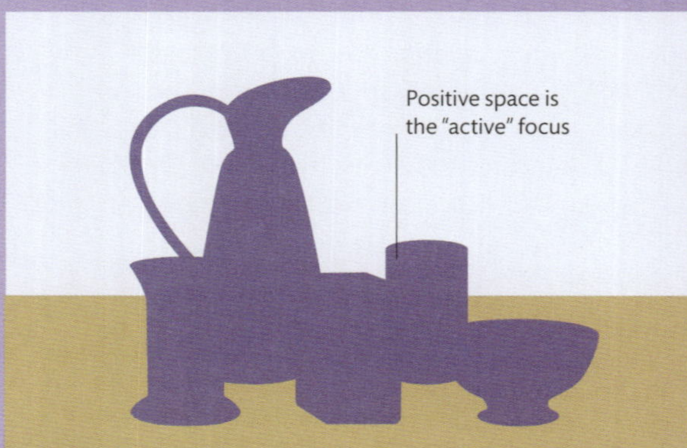

Positive space
A viewer's eye is usually pulled automatically toward the busy area of positive space. It tends to be more dynamic and interesting than negative space, and the eye is naturally drawn to it.

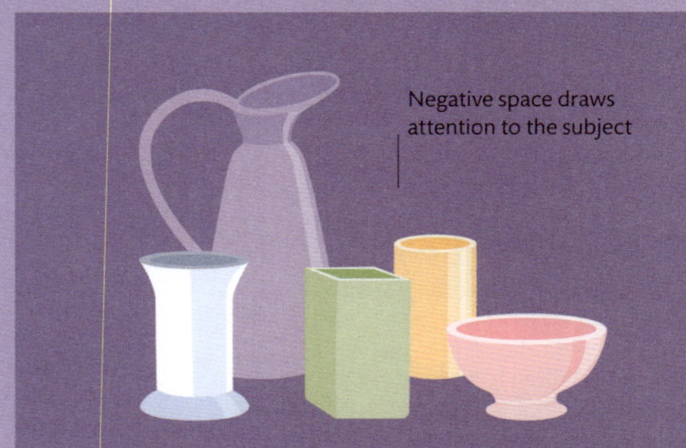

Negative space
Negative space gives the viewer's eye a place to rest and creates a sense of spaciousness within the picture. Too much negative space can make the subject appear insubstantial, or may create a sense of emptiness.

Positive and Negative Space

Positive space is the main subject in an artwork, and negative space is the area around it. Both elements are needed to form a balanced composition.

Guiding the gaze

Positive space is the positive, definable part of a picture, such as a tree in a landscape or a person in a portrait, and is usually the first stopping point for the viewer's eye. Negative space is the area around the positive space, for example, in between the leaves of the tree or around a figure. Its presence activates the positive space and gives it context, and an artist may use it as a tool to guide the viewer's eye toward the subject.

HOW DO ARTISTS DRAW NEGATIVE SPACE?

An artist may focus on the space between the objects in the frame—for example, the space between the leaves of a plant, not the leaves themselves.

SCULPTOR RACHEL WHITEREAD'S CAST OF A HOUSE INTERIOR WAS DISMANTLED AFTER ONLY A FEW MONTHS

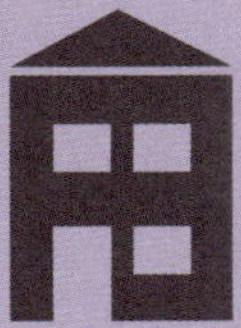

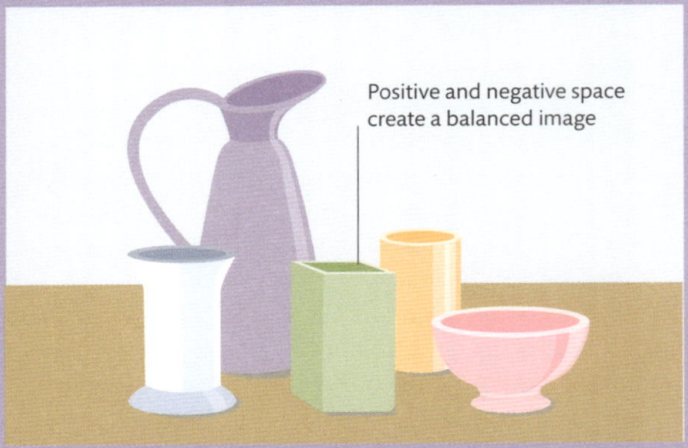

Compositional balance
Positive and negative space should work together to bring balance and tension to a composition. Both elements are inextricably linked and one does not exist without the other.

Negative space in sculpture

In sculpture, the positive space is the object itself, and the negative space can be found in the empty areas around the form. The sculpture may have a hole in the middle, for example, or its shape may create hollows of negative space. The 20th-century sculptor Barbara Hepworth explored these ideas in her work, carving holes in stone, wood, and plaster to create abstract spaces.

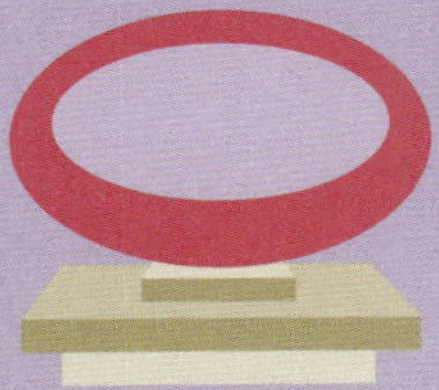

SPACE IN SCULPTURE

Rubin's vase

Around 1915, psychologist Edgar Rubin illustrated how positive and negative space can manipulate perception when he developed this optical illusion (see pp.120–121). If the central shape is seen as positive space, it appears to be a vase, but if that same shape is viewed as negative space, the profiles of two faces appear in black—the curves of the vase creating the illusion of a forehead, nose, and mouth.

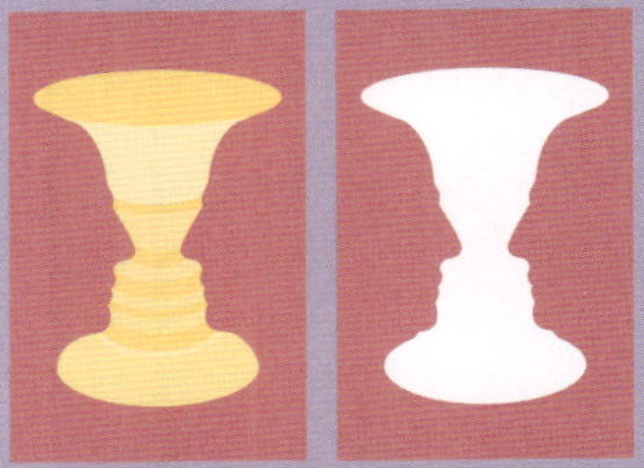

Light and dark
The brain sees positive shapes as dark and negative as light because forms appear dark against the sky. When a shape can be seen as both, it is called figure/ground reversal.

Illusion

By its very nature, much representational art is a form of illusion. However, in some works, the artist deliberately sets out to use illusion to trick or amuse the viewer, display technical proficiency, or produce interesting visual effects.

Why use illusion in art?

Illusion in art is employed to achieve different effects, for example, to transport the viewer to an imaginary place, to play with perception of an object or space, or to create an optical illusion. Perhaps most famously, *trompe l'oeil* is the name for the creation of illusions through highly rendered simulations of objects or architectural spaces. This can be achieved with photorealism—rendering the scene in minute detail—but does not rely on this. The artist's brush marks can be expressive on the surface, but when observed from a distance, they can form a figurative, convincingly realistic illusion. Sculptures may also use realism to create illusion or may experiment with form and perspective, such as in anamorphism (see above).

Hand implies the illusion that an external figure is disrupting the scene, evoking a playful and subversive feel

Illusion is created by three-dimensional rendering of the hand, and by breaking out of the frame

Unexpected brick background provides humor, which is often used in illusory art

Subverting expectations
Illusion in art relies on creating a sense of "cognitive dissonance" in the viewer by convincingly combining contradictory elements into a seemingly coherent whole.

Image uses a combination of two- and three-dimensional elements

Realistically depicted fabric is part of the illusory nature of the scene

ANAMORPHISM

Anamorphism describes images or artworks that are distorted so they can be understood only when seen from a certain angle. A work may at first appear random but, when viewed from the right angle, resolves itself into a coherent image. It is highly technical, relying on a deep understanding of perspective and visual perception on the part of the artist.

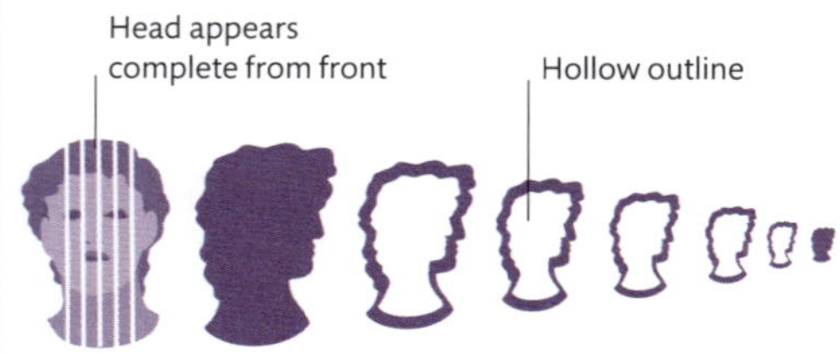

Anamorphic sculpture
From the side, this sculpture appears as "slices" of a face. Viewed head-on, it "becomes" a complete head.

"TROMPE L'OEIL" TRANSLATES AS "DECEIVES THE EYE"

Op art

Op art was a 1960s painting movement that used geometric forms to create complex optical effects. It also used color theory to explore how color juxtapositions create visual disturbance and how gradually changing shapes suggest movement, distortion, and three-dimensional space. Bridget Riley, the best-known of the group, was inspired by the Impressionists, who, rather than mix colors on the palette, put them directly onto the canvas so that they would blend in the viewer's eye.

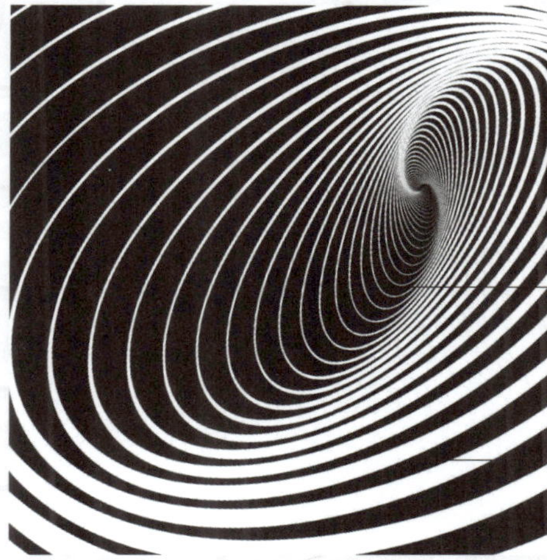

Illusion of movement
In this piece, the suggestion of a vortex is created through the changing gradation of asymmetric and off-center black strips against white.

White bands close in to create the illusion of compression

Strips become wider as they appear to advance toward the viewer

WHAT IS A KEY EXAMPLE OF ANAMORPHIC ART?

A famous use of the technique occurs in Hans Holbein's *The Ambassadors*, a dual portrait that contains a skull image that can only be seen from an angle.

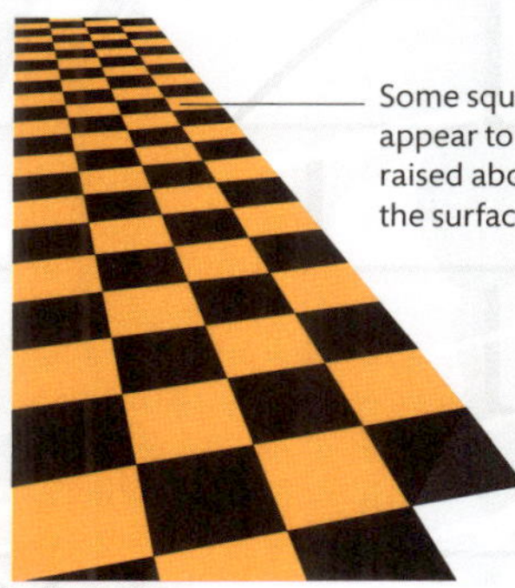

Some squares appear to be raised above the surface

Using perspective
Straight, angled lines and alternating colors suggest the idea of convergence.

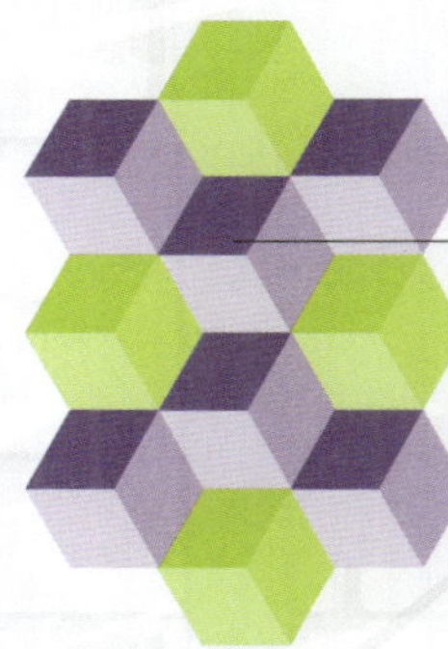

"Cubes" are created using a pattern of angled diamonds

Challenging perception
A pattern suggests cubes that appear to change dimension due to the color placement.

Basic techniques

Artists use six basic techniques to create illusion. These apply to painting and drawing in particular, although some of these approaches are equally valid when making sculptural works. Another, slightly more advanced method for manufacturing illusion is the production of three-dimensional maquettes or collages as source material, to convey a more direct sense of both depth and space.

Perspective
One-, two-, and three-point perspectives create illusion by replicating three-dimensional space.

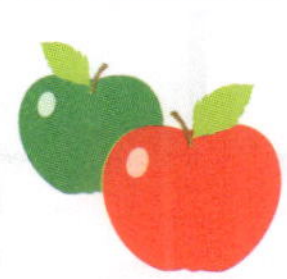

Overlapping
Placing one element overlapping another creates a sense of viewpoint and depth.

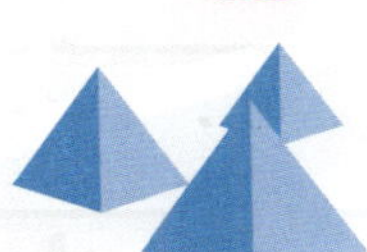

Size
Depicting objects of similar form at different sizes produces a believable idea of scale.

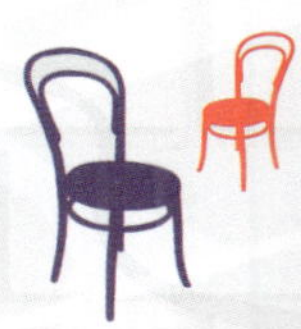

Placement
Positioning objects low down in a picture makes them appear closer than those placed higher up.

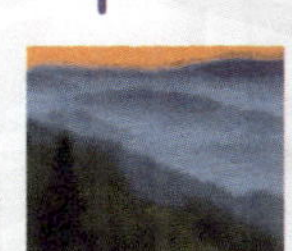

Color and texture
Using graduating colors suggests depth, while adding texture can create foreground.

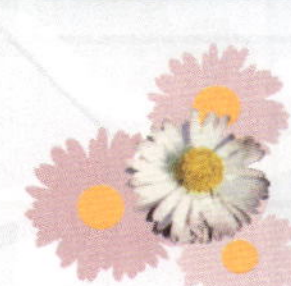

Detail
Adding detail causes the eye to focus on an area of the picture and makes it appear closer..

Symmetry and Asymmetry

Symmetrical balance occurs within a two- or three-dimensional work when there is equal visual weight on both sides of a composition.

Balanced or unbalanced

Bilateral symmetry in an artwork (see below) results in a mirroring effect, where no single part of the composition is dominant. The effect is harmonious and the viewer's eye moves around the artwork at a measured and constant pace. Symmetry in an artwork is often associated with order, structure, or clarity, while asymmetry may represent disorder, disruption, and imbalance and can also be visually dynamic. When considering symmetry in a work, an artist must question whether they want to create a balanced or unbalanced composition and how effectively this communicates their ideas.

SYMMETRY

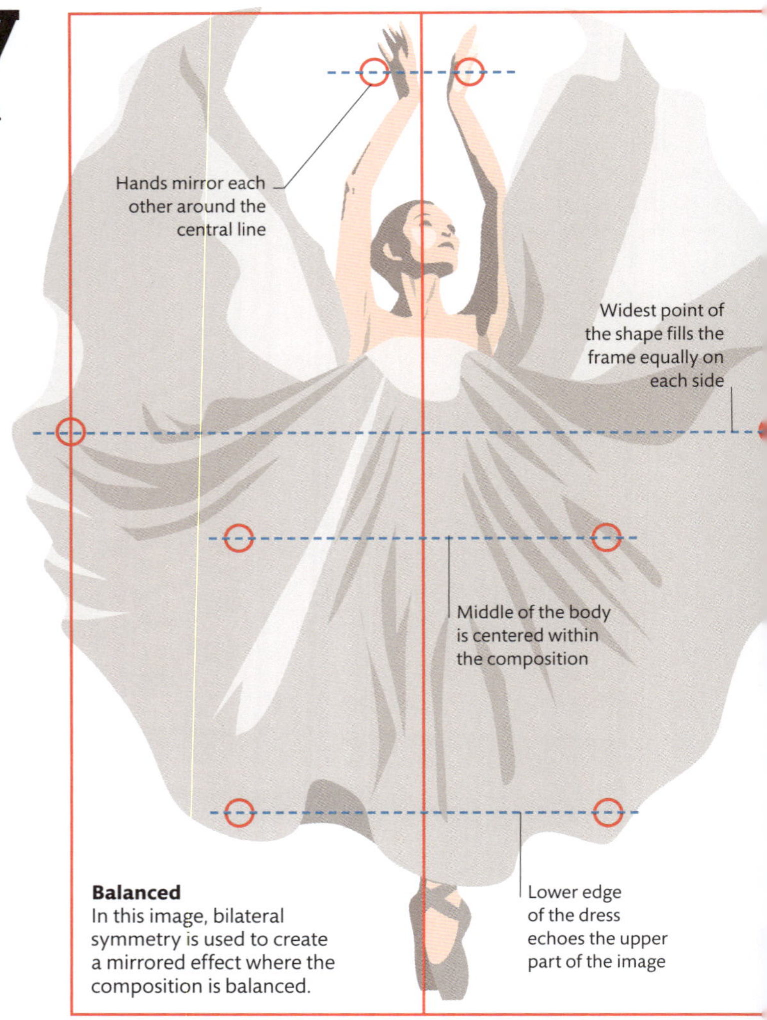

Balanced
In this image, bilateral symmetry is used to create a mirrored effect where the composition is balanced.

THE PARTHENON IN ATHENS IS AN **EARLY EXAMPLE** OF THE **USE OF BILATERAL SYMMETRY**

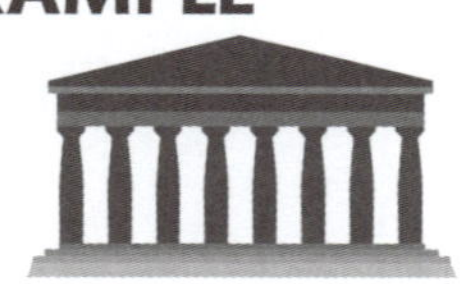

Types of visual balance

Artists and philosophers throughout history have investigated and debated symmetry and asymmetry, some believing that the structure of symmetry equates with beauty; others that it is rigid and unrepresentative of the true form of the world around us. Different types of symmetry and visual balance can be employed in artworks to create varying effects.

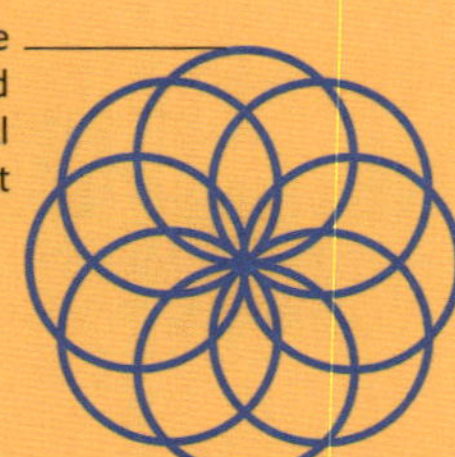

Radial symmetry
Elements radiate from a central point. Ripples in water around a dropped stone are an example of radial symmetry.

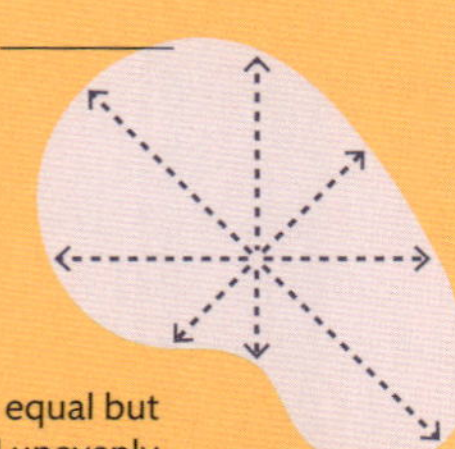

Asymmetrical balance
The two halves of an image may be different but have equal visual weight and interact to create a sense of balance.

ASYMMETRY

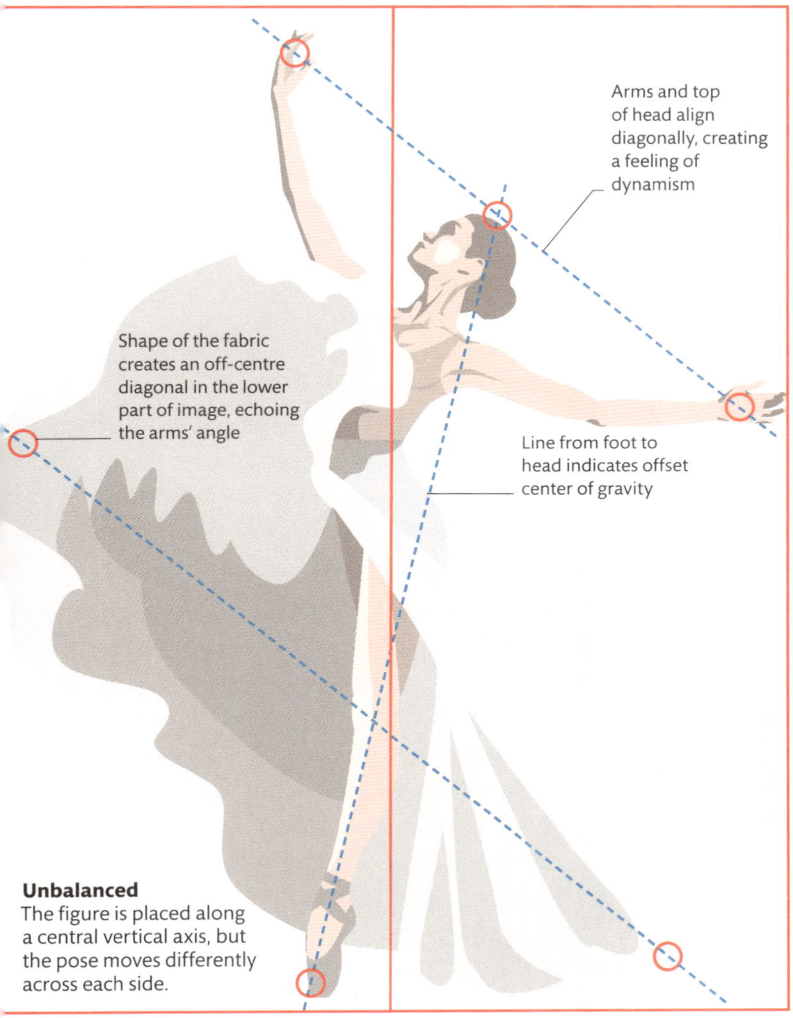

Unbalanced
The figure is placed along a central vertical axis, but the pose moves differently across each side.

THE GOLDEN RATIO

Also known as the divine proportion, the golden ratio is a mathematical proportion of 1.168. In visual form, a rectangle is continually subdivided into these proportions, creating a natural spiral. In artistic compositions, elements can be placed at key points within the partitions, lending a harmonious and infinite feel to the image.

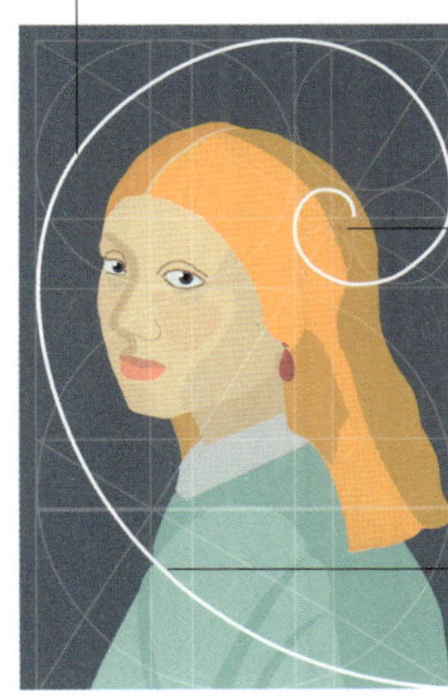

A visual tool
Although commonly used in paintings, the golden ration can be employed in almost any visual medium.

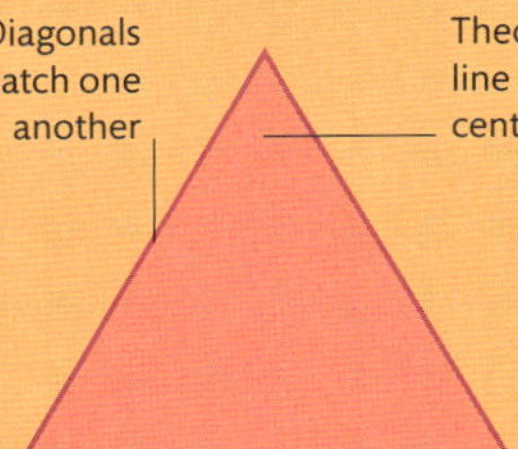

Bilateral symmetry
An image or object is mirrored equally across an imaginary vertical line. The visual weight is balanced.

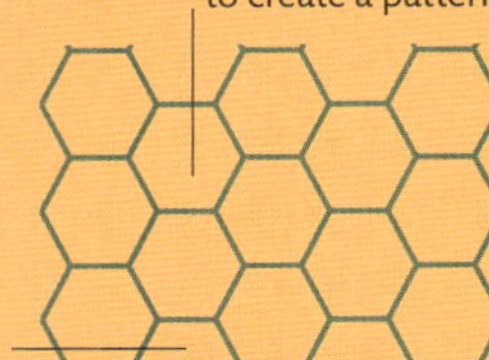

Translational symmetry
Elements are repeated over different locations in space. This can create a sense of rhythm, motion, and speed.

WHAT ARE THE ORIGINS OF THE GOLDEN RATIO?

The ancient Greek mathematician Euclid was the first writer to mention the golden ratio in a published work, *Elements*.

HERRINGBONE PATTERN DATES BACK TO ROMAN TIMES AND WAS USED IN MASONRY

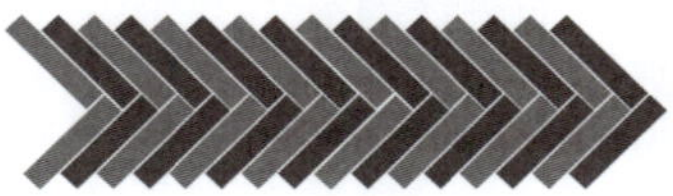

ORGANIC PATTERNS

Some artists draw upon observable patterns in nature such as crystalline forms, webs, or snowflakes. Many patterns in nature are fractals, which repeat at increasingly fine magnifications. Digital art forms use computer-generated fractals.

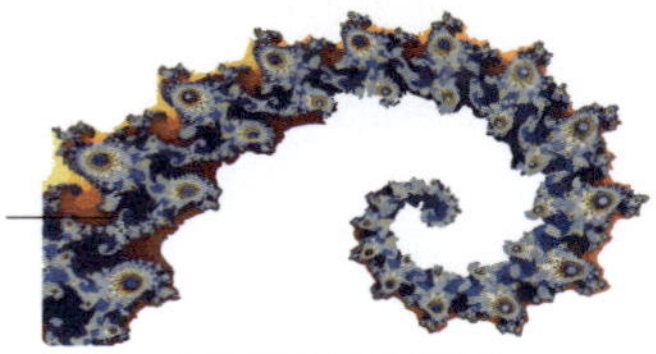

DIGITAL FRACTAL

Pattern

The use of pattern in art is ancient and global. Pattern is used variously as a decorative device, to create optical effects, and to suggest philosophical ideas.

Search for patterns

Pattern is the visual arrangement of elements in a sequence or repeated design. Pattern recognition is a human trait: viewers search for patterns in nature, in human behavior, and in art. Patterns can also reflect sequences from the natural world. They can be used in all mediums, including textiles, painting and drawing, and sculpture.

HOW HAVE ISLAMIC PATTERNS INFLUENCED OTHER ART FORMS?

Dutch artist M. C. Escher developed his ideas for optical illusions from sketching the tiles in the mosaics in the Alhambra.

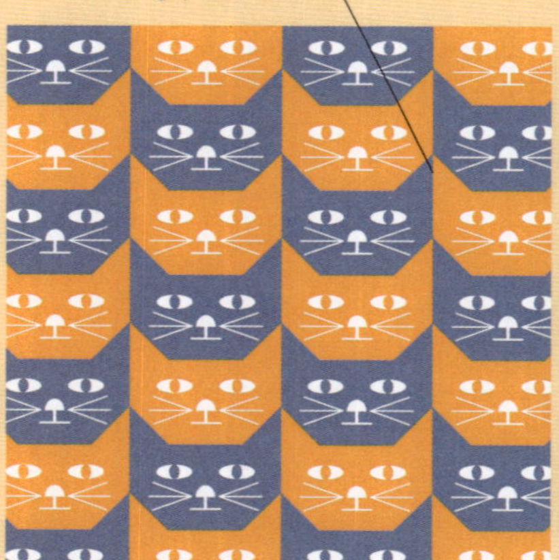

Repeating objects
Here, a recognizable image is repeated and overlapped to create a "motif." The motif can then be altered by using different colors or by changing the orientation.

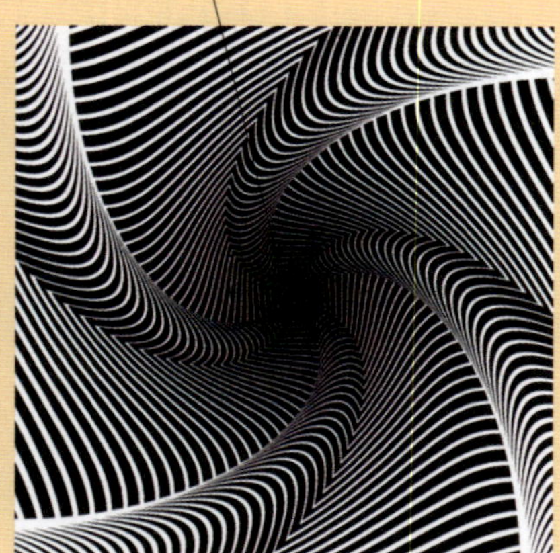

Central point
Using a central point to generate a pattern in an outward trajectory creates an illusionistic 3-D effect (see pp.120–121) rather than appearing two-dimensional.

Line patterns
In repeated line pattern, line weight and trajectory guide the visual quality of the pattern. Lines that gradually change across a surface can create an optical illusion.

Domestic patterns

Patterns in domestic forms such as textiles, wallpaper, and furnishings can be used by artists to express ideas around gender, the home, and memory. Some contemporary artists work with existing patterned textiles, appropriating their form or adding to them, involving images or other patterns. Historically, artists have used such patterns as a way of exploring and questioning perspective and depth. The Post-Impressionist Jean-Édouard Vuillard's paintings of interior scenes were influenced by Japanese prints and used domestic patterns to blend figures into spaces, creating strange perspectives.

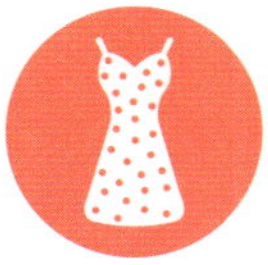

CLOTHING

WALLPAPER

CROCKERY

FURNITURE

Cultural approaches

Patterns are frequently culturally significant and can be used to carry specific meanings. Islamic art (see pp.164–165) uses pattern as a way of depicting the infinite, without using iconography or imagery, for example, the beautifully repeated patterning of the space within the Alhambra Palace in Spain. Artist Yinka Shonibare uses Dutch-produced patterned African textiles to draw attention to colonialism.

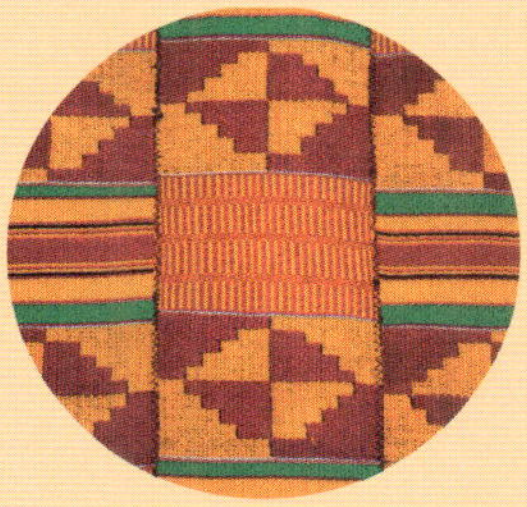

Kente cloth
Handwoven cloth made in Ghana, it originated as cloth for royals. Each pattern has a specific name and meaning.

Kente weaving
The colors and symbols chosen for each cloth can signify common motifs, religious beliefs, and political commentary.

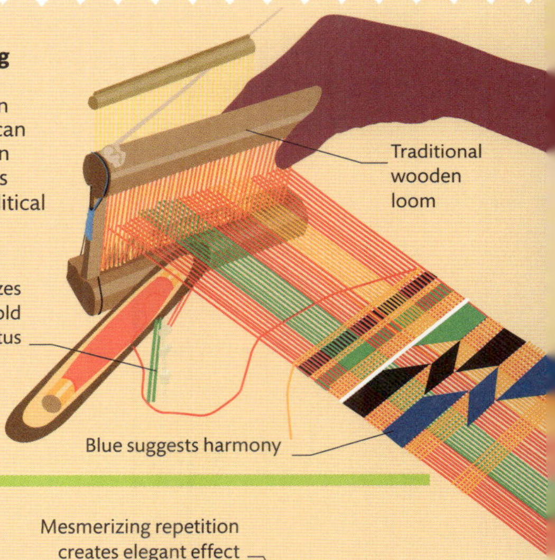

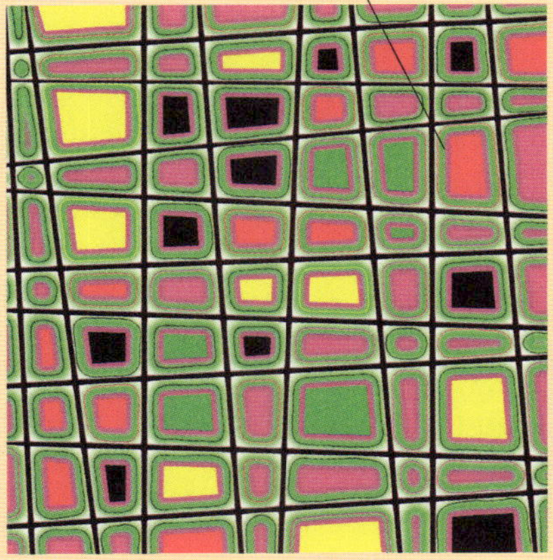

Repeating colors
Color juxtaposition is important as colors behave differently according to their place on the spectrum. Analogous or harmonious colors create different visual sensations.

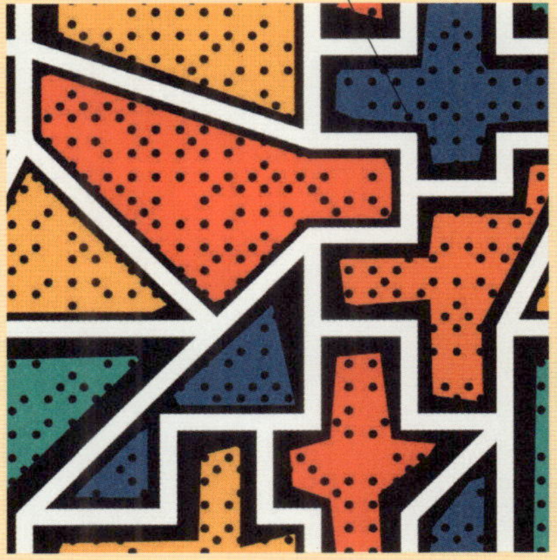

Irregular patterns
An irregular pattern creates a surface of interlocking shapes that tessellate together and suggest complexity rather than order. The way it is repeated may be unpredictable.

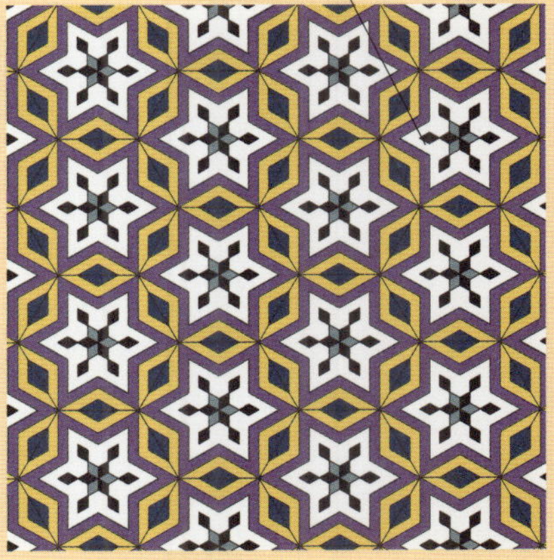

Repeating shapes
Repetition is a way of creating a feeling of order, symmetry, and infinity. The repetition can become mesmeric and psychologically calming for the viewer.

Creating Movement

The visual depiction of movement within an artwork is intended to capture an impression of an action, event, or dynamic force and can also be a way of leading the viewer through the pictorial space. It is achieved using a few simple compositional and technical elements.

Techniques used

Artists often suggest movement through a combination of rhythm, line, color, and structure. Rhythm can be suggested by using a repeated element or motif as a visual echo across an artwork. Dynamic lines that run diagonally to the edge of the picture plane, or are irregular or expressive, evoke movement by creating imbalance within the composition. Juxtaposing complementary colors (see pp.88–89) can also create the visual sensation of movement, as can expressive brush marks.

Implied motion

Motion can be implied by the particular positioning of a figure or form. Capturing a figure in motion is an effective way of suggesting movement in art, and this can be emphasized by using directional lines or brushstrokes to describe the form. Impressionist artist Edgar Degas created many studies of dancers using quick pastel or paint strokes that captured a sense of fleeting movement and anticipation.

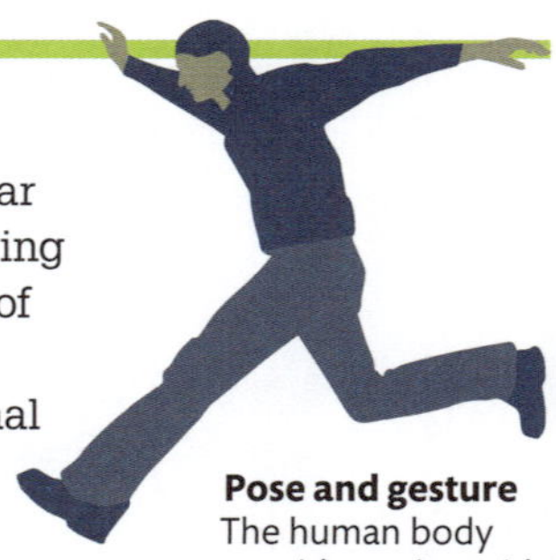

Pose and gesture
The human body provides artists with a familiar form that can be arranged to imply motion.

KINETIC ART

Kinetic art is an art form that uses kinetic energy, or actual motion, as a medium. Movement is generated by using mechanical elements that can be powered in various ways, including touch, wind, water, gravity, or balance.

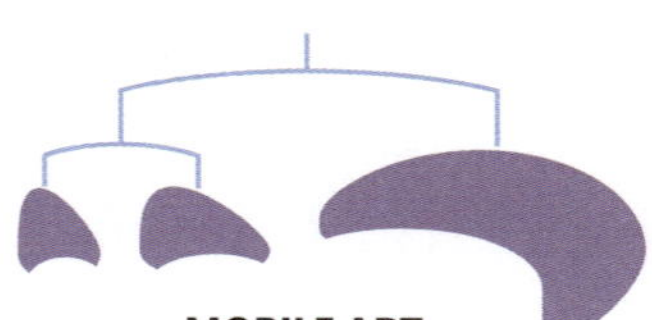

MOBILE ART

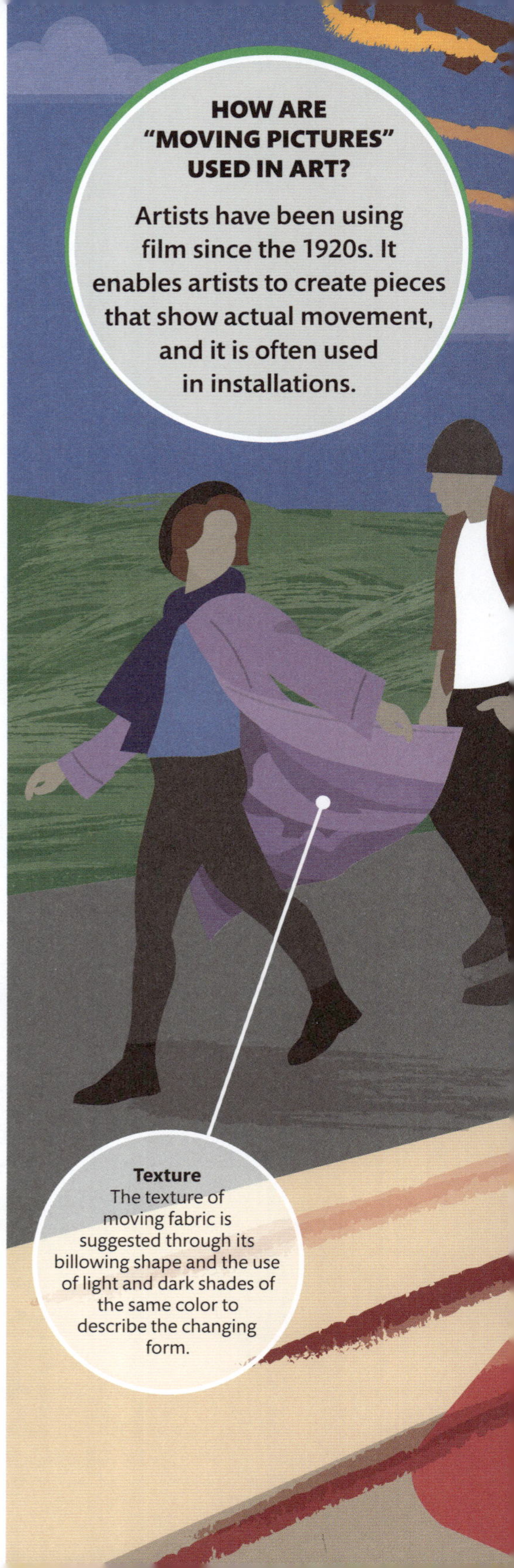

HOW ARE "MOVING PICTURES" USED IN ART?

Artists have been using film since the 1920s. It enables artists to create pieces that show actual movement, and it is often used in installations.

Texture
The texture of moving fabric is suggested through its billowing shape and the use of light and dark shades of the same color to describe the changing form.

ALEXANDER CALDER CREATED THE FIRST MOBILE ART IN THE 1930S

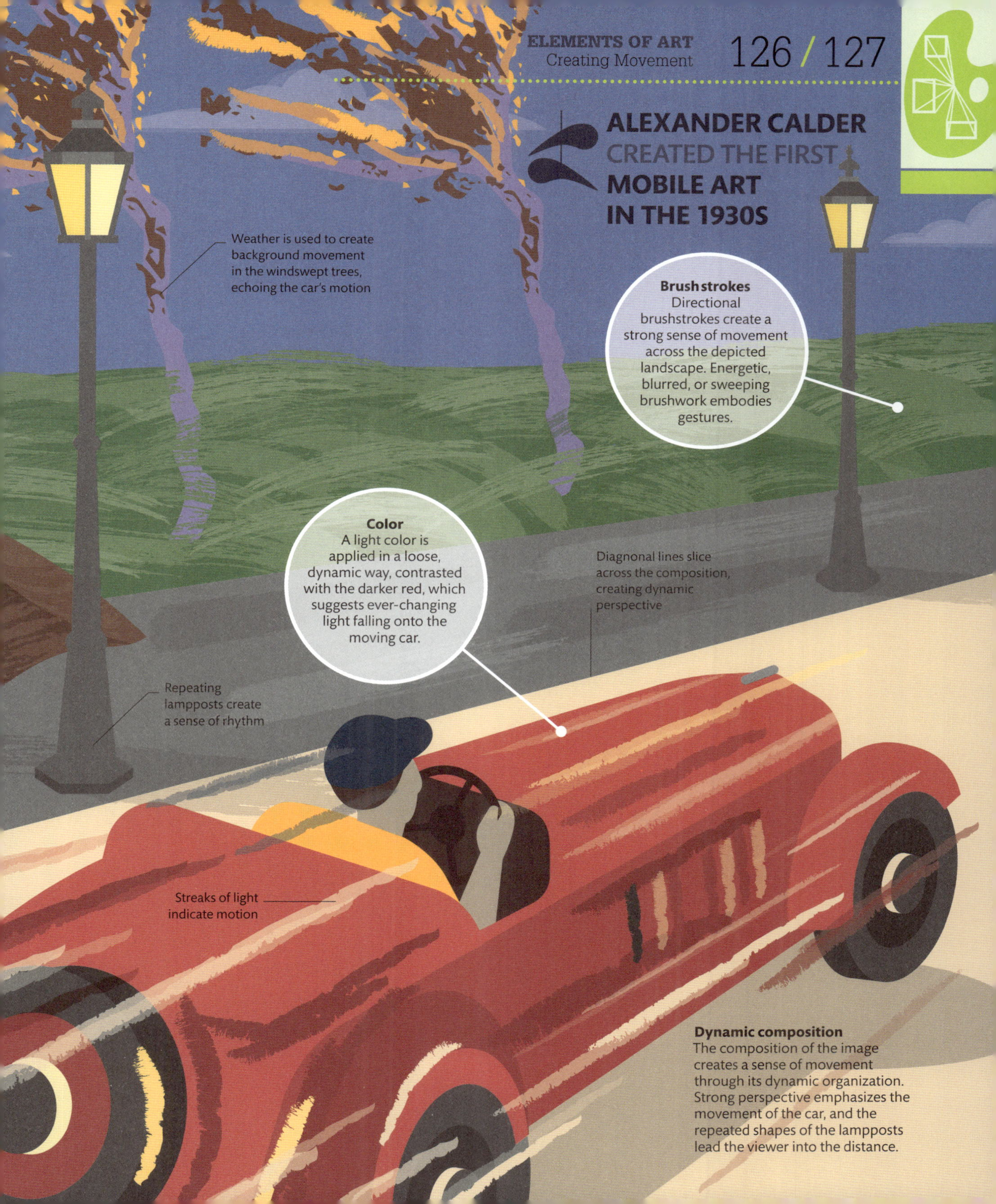

Atmosphere and mood

Mood is intrinsic to an artwork and expresses the artist's feelings using the work's components (see right). Using imagery with a psychological or metaphorical impact can help convey a specific mood, while establishing ambiguity can create intrigue and encourage the viewer to question what they see.

PLAYFUL

OMINOUS

AMBIGUOUS

MELANCHOLY

Components

Visible marks, contrast, and exaggerated shadows are often components of expressive artworks. Artists may use colors to express emotions—for example blue, Payne's gray, and black to suggest sadness, or primary hues such as cadmium red and yellow to indicate joy. Tonal contrast and heavy light and shadow can be used expressively.

COLORS

CONTRAST

MARKS

TEXTURE

MEDIA

LIGHTING

Basic elements

In artworks, the subject informs both the way the work is structured and the narrative that the artist wishes to incorporate. The subject may be portrayed in a distorted or unnatural way in order to convey emotion, while fragmentation or disruption of the composition help show emotional subjectivity.

SUBJECT

COMPOSITION

NARRATIVE

AUTOBIOGRAPHY IN ART

Artists may draw on their own experiences to create expressive artworks. They transform autobiographical subject matter into something universal to which a wider audience can relate. British artist Tracey Emin uses her personal history to make raw artworks that question gender expectations and stereotypes.

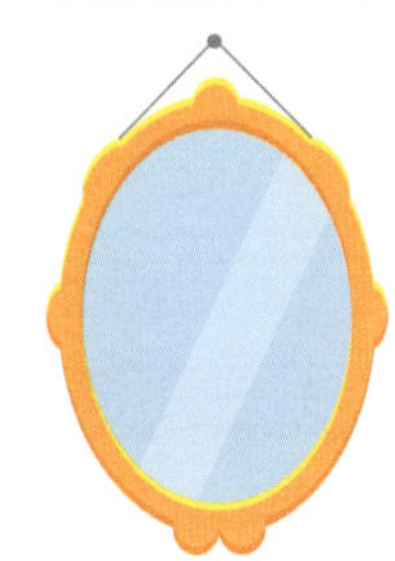

ART REFLECTS THE SELF

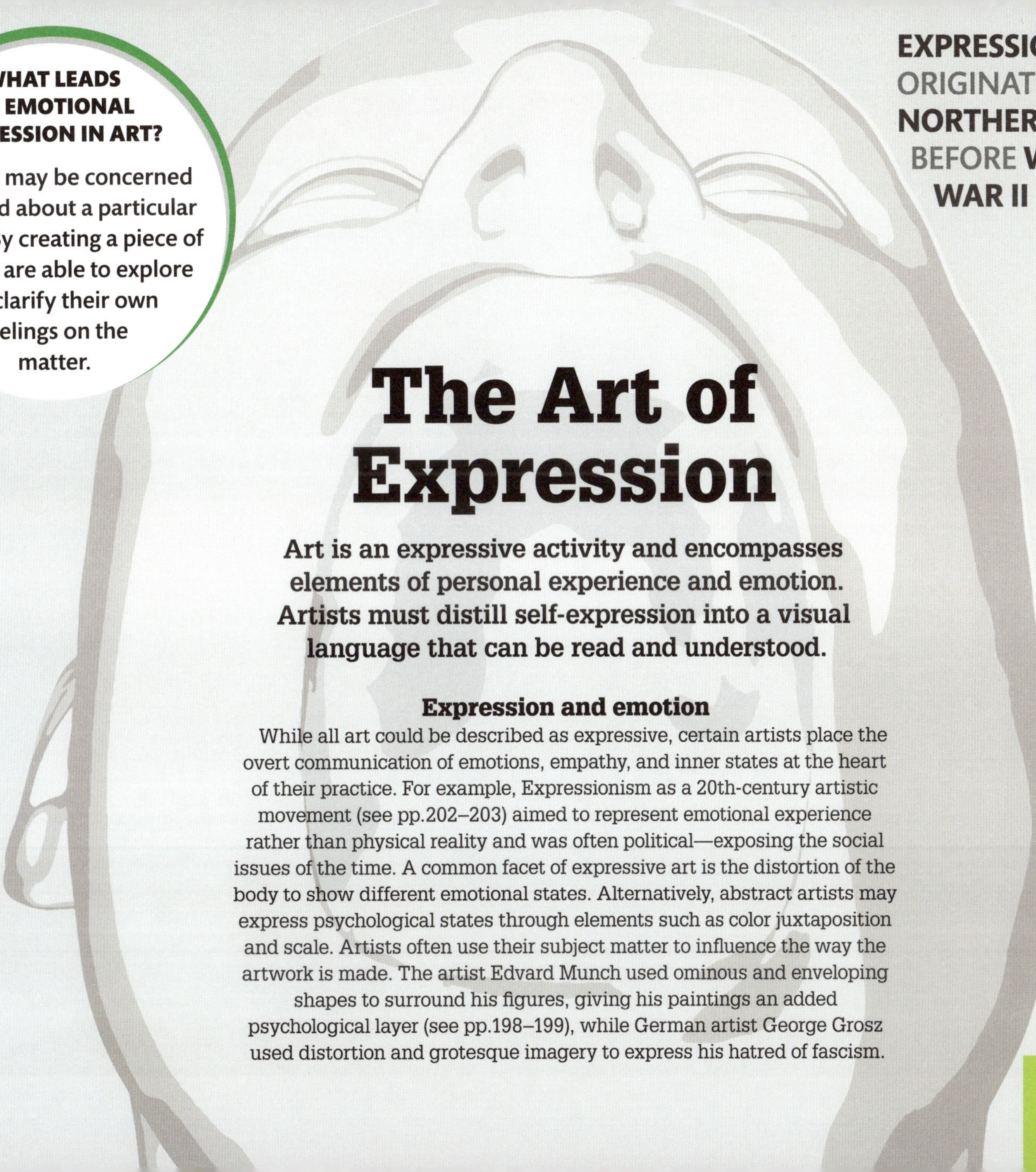

WHAT LEADS TO EMOTIONAL EXPRESSION IN ART?

An artist may be concerned or excited about a particular subject. By creating a piece of art, they are able to explore and clarify their own feelings on the matter.

EXPRESSIONISM ORIGINATED IN NORTHERN EUROPE BEFORE WORLD WAR II

The Art of Expression

Art is an expressive activity and encompasses elements of personal experience and emotion. Artists must distill self-expression into a visual language that can be read and understood.

Expression and emotion

While all art could be described as expressive, certain artists place the overt communication of emotions, empathy, and inner states at the heart of their practice. For example, Expressionism as a 20th-century artistic movement (see pp.202–203) aimed to represent emotional experience rather than physical reality and was often political—exposing the social issues of the time. A common facet of expressive art is the distortion of the body to show different emotional states. Alternatively, abstract artists may express psychological states through elements such as color juxtaposition and scale. Artists often use their subject matter to influence the way the artwork is made. The artist Edvard Munch used ominous and enveloping shapes to surround his figures, giving his paintings an added psychological layer (see pp.198–199), while German artist George Grosz used distortion and grotesque imagery to express his hatred of fascism.

Perception

Perception is the subjective experience of the world and how we interpret the information we receive through our senses. For most artists, this means translating their own perception of the world into something that can be shared and interpreted.

Understanding perception

The Cubist artist George Braque once argued that “a thing cannot be in two places at once. You can’t have it in your head and before your eyes.” However, this broadly describes perception, in which the brain needs to make the connection between the visible object and what the viewer understands it to be. This is done via a set of cognitive processes that draw on memories, knowledge, and emotions. In art, these processes are complicated by a painting or a sculpture being both an object in itself and a representation of something else, making the brain work harder in order to perceive it fully.

IS IT POSSIBLE TO “TRICK” OUR PERCEPTION?

Yes—this is known as an optical illusion and describes an image that has been made visually ambiguous so that the brain cannot fully perceive it.

LEONARDO DA VINCI DISSECTED HUMAN EYES TO UNDERSTAND HOW BOTH SIGHT AND **PERCEPTION WORKED**

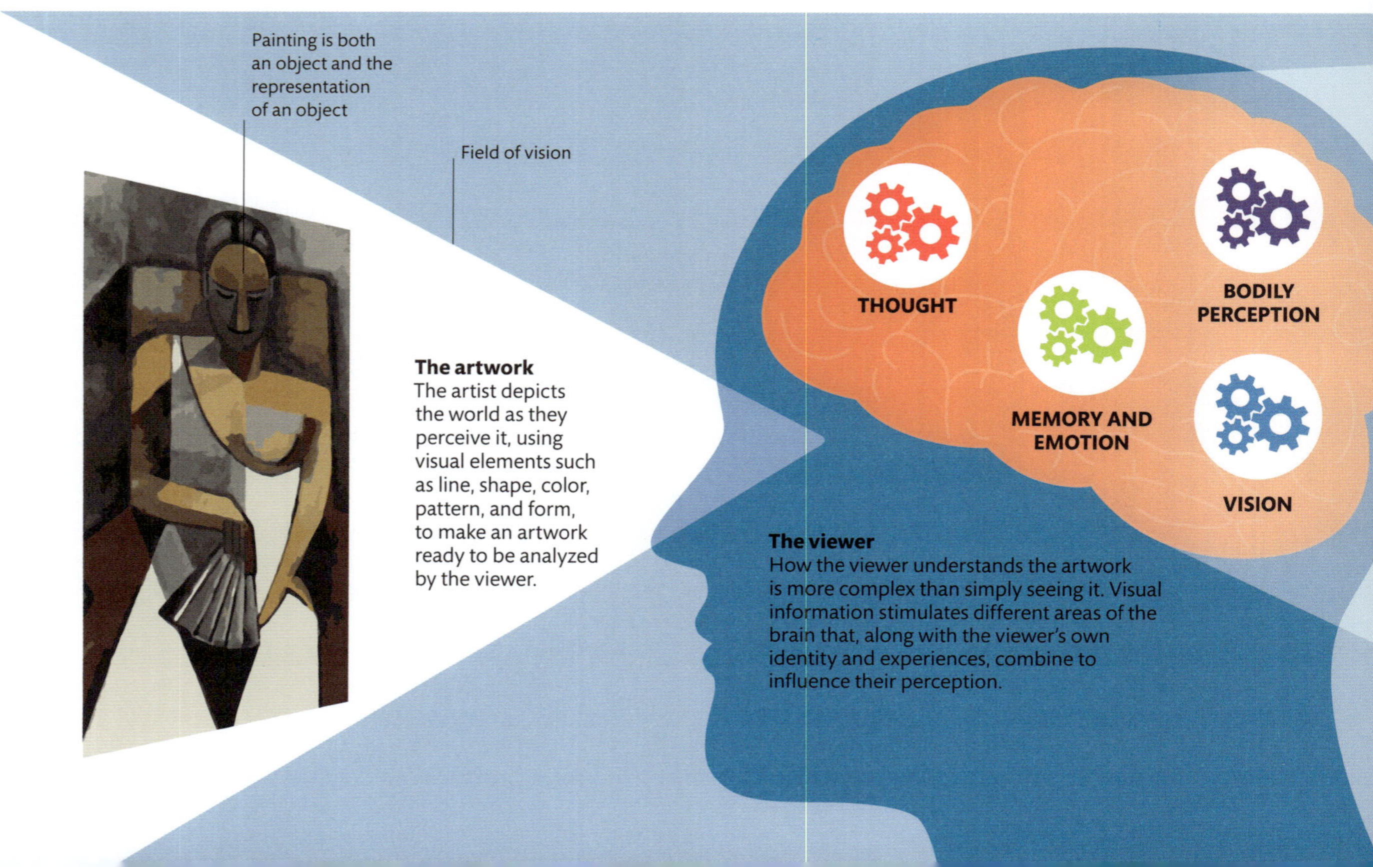

Field of vision

When we perceive the world, we use central vision to focus on the main details of a scene and peripheral vision to gather data about the surroundings. Some artists use this to create effects in their work. The Impressionists (see pp.192–193) were interested in peripheral vision, using dashes of color away from their paintings' central images to draw the eye and expand the field of vision. Some modern artists create works with no central main image and several focal points spread across the painting. This leads the viewer to shift their field of vision as they view the work.

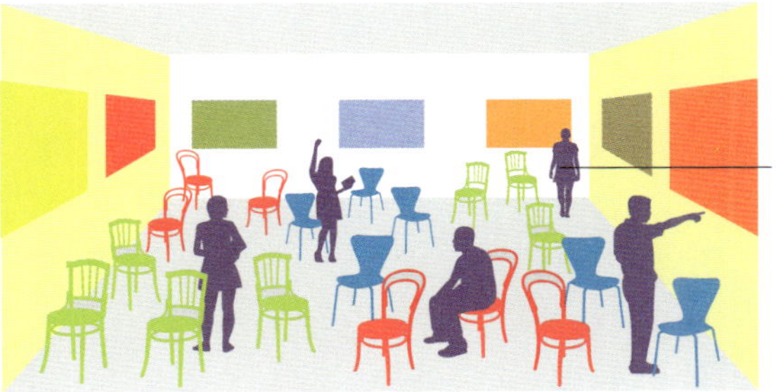

Human figures create multiple natural focal points within the composition

Points of focus
A viewer's field of vision—and their experience of the image—changes with each focal point.

MULTIPLE FOCAL POINTS

ALTERED PERCEPTION

Artists sometimes use perception-altering substances to influence their work. Surrealist Jean Cocteau took opium when making some of his drawings, as did his friend Pablo Picasso. The psychedelic paintings and poster art of the 1960s were inspired by hallucinogens such as LSD.

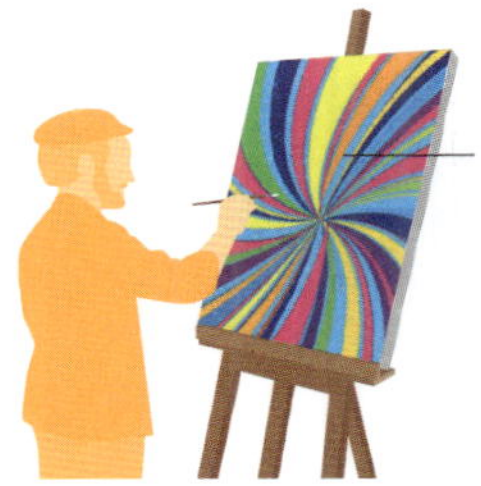

Bright colors and swirling shapes

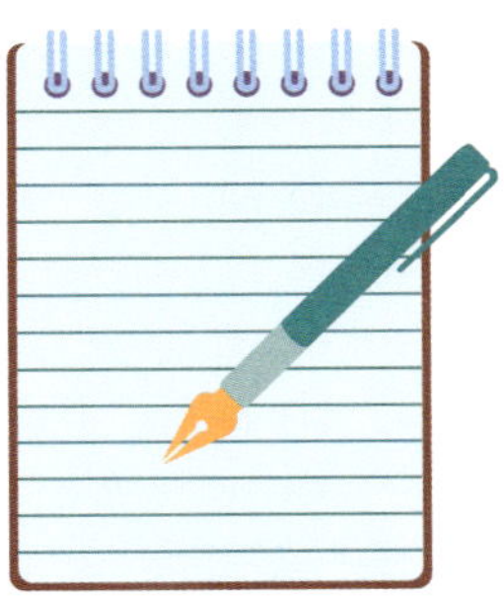

Telling a story
The artist can arrange the work so that the viewer perceives a narrative. This may draw on personal, cultural, or historical information, transmitted in visual cues that the viewer must understand and translate.

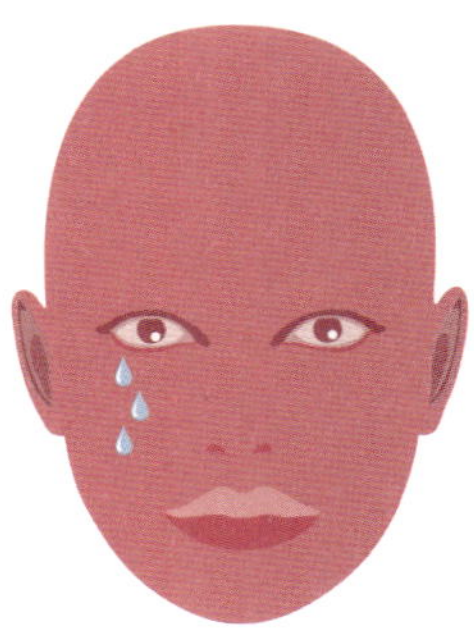

Evoking emotion
Some visual imagery can be used to engage with the viewer's feelings and provoke emotional responses. This can be achieved with elements perceived by the viewer such as colors, expressive marks, composition, and light and shade.

Delivering a message
Artists may translate their perception of the world into a specific message or idea, for example, personal or political. To do this, they must engage with the viewer's own perceptions by using familiar subjects or themes.

Telling a Story

Storytelling in art is often referred to as creating a narrative. To do this, elements of a static artwork can be arranged to suggest a wider series of events.

Why tell stories in art?

Historically, storytelling was seen as the main function of art; it is still used to play with the ways viewers see the world. An artwork may give shape and character to real events, imagined realities, or social systems and behavior. Stories may be suggested through the arrangement of figures or the representation of an action, or through mood, atmosphere, and the use of recognizable imagery and symbols. Although narrative was rejected by some modern styles such as abstraction (see pp.78–79), storytelling remains widely used to convey meaning in art. By presenting familiar scenarios, storytelling allows the viewer to "read" a work and gain a sense of it having a beginning, an end, and—perhaps—a meaning.

STORIES CAN BE TOLD **IN SERIES**, SUCH AS IN HOGARTH'S **"THE RAKE'S PROGRESS,"** A MORALITY TALE IN **EIGHT PRINTS**

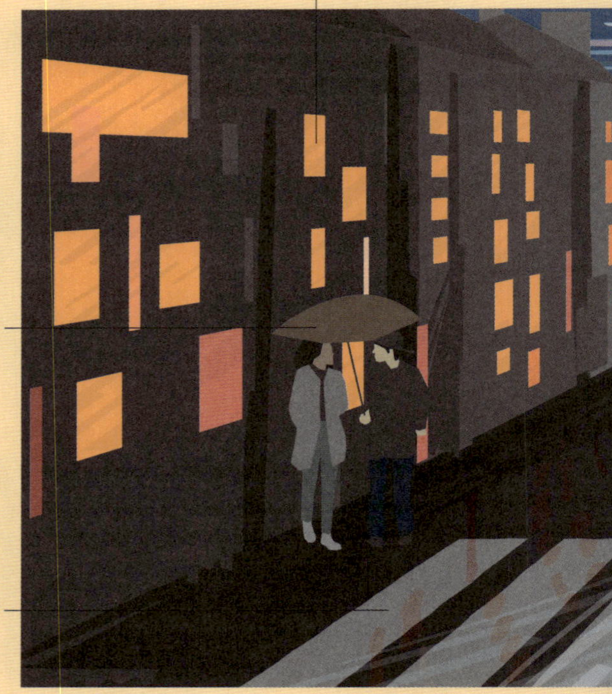

Street scene at night
This image uses the subject of a woman crossing a city street to imply a wider narrative, emphasized by the dusky urban landscape and use of steep, one-point perspective.

Types of storytelling

Storytelling was one of the first forms of art, and our earliest ancestors used cave walls in prehistory (see pp.144–145) to record stories through imagery long before they developed writing or literacy, or lived in settled societies. This communal and narrative aspect of art taps into the fundamental human need to share experiences and interpret or make sense of the world by visually representing it. As an artistic method, storytelling can be grouped into four main categories.

Mythic
Ideas such as Greek myths and religious stories were often retold through statues and large, symbolic paintings.

Historical
Historical art may depict an event via a specific interpretation, designed to influence the viewer (see pp.82–83).

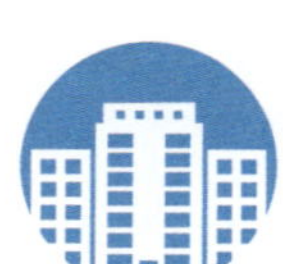

Contemporary
Today's artists may tell stories using modern forms of expression such as performance and digital media.

Personal
Telling personal stories in art relies on using expression to forge a bond with viewers, creating a feeling of empathy.

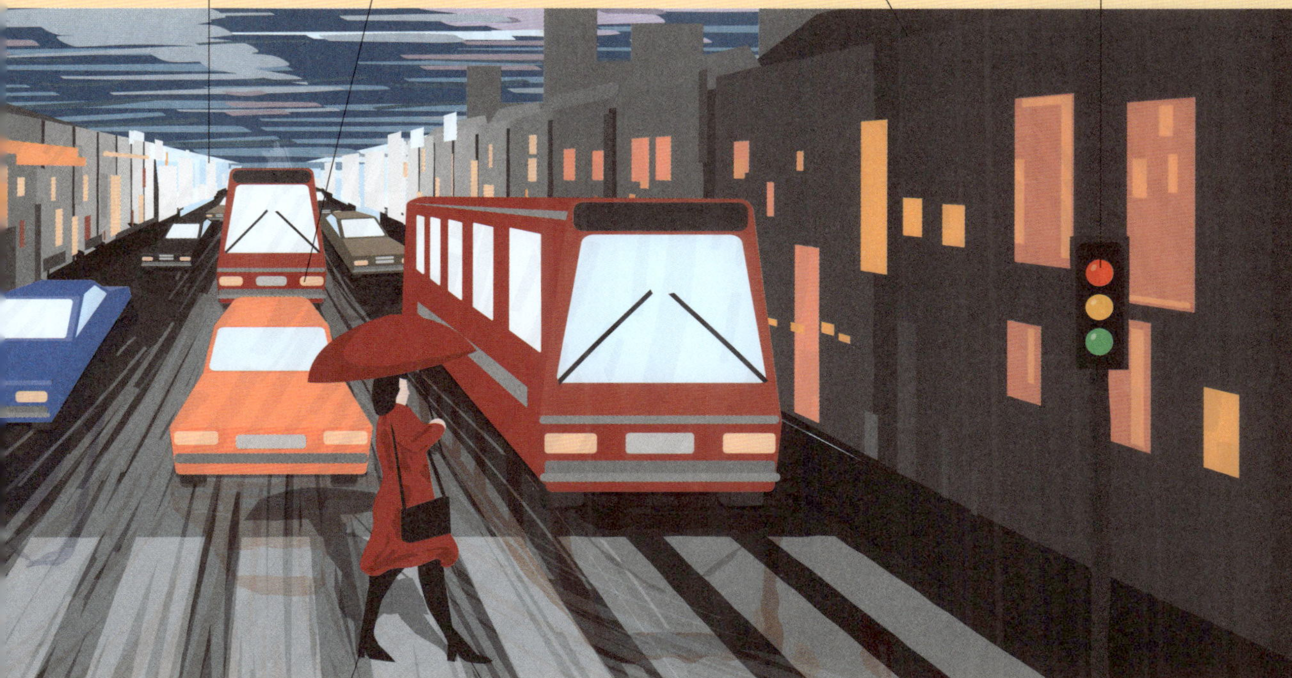

AMBIGUITY IN STORYTELLING

Ambiguity is a way of intriguing the viewer with alternative possibilities, forcing them to question their interpretation of a particular scenario. Portuguese-British artist Paula Rego, for example, creates ominous drawings and paintings that simultaneously present both a sense of violence and a fairy-tale atmosphere.

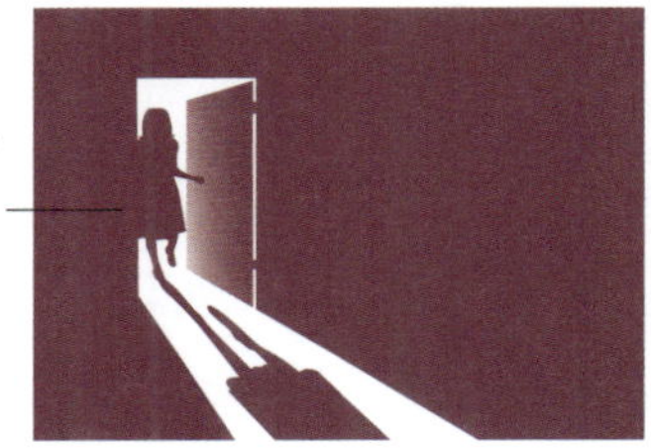

Facing the unknown
Ambiguity can use deliberate uncertainty to create tension.

HOW HAS CINEMA INFLUENCED ART?

Edward Hopper's film noir–inspired paintings suggest suspenseful stories by using cinematic devices, such as cropping to imply action taking place just out of view.

Depicting Emotion

Creating emotion in art is a way of connecting with the viewer on a fundamental and intuitive level. Artists create empathy in their work by accessing and representing emotions visually, using elements such as expression, color, narrative, gesture, and technique.

Ways of showing feeling

Artists have always depicted emotions in different ways. Expressionism (see pp.202–203) placed the representation of feeling at the forefront of the work, with artists such as Käthe Kollwitz using color, distorted forms, and expressive mark making to convey emotions such as despair and introspection. Francisco Goya (see pp.186–187) used darkness and strange, inhuman characters to portray the horror of persecution, while Henri Matisse used simple cutouts of brightly colored paper to give the viewer a childlike sense of joy.

USING **LIGHT AND SHADE,** KNOWN AS **CHIAROSCURO,** IS A TECHNIQUE FOR CONVEYING **DRAMA IN ART**

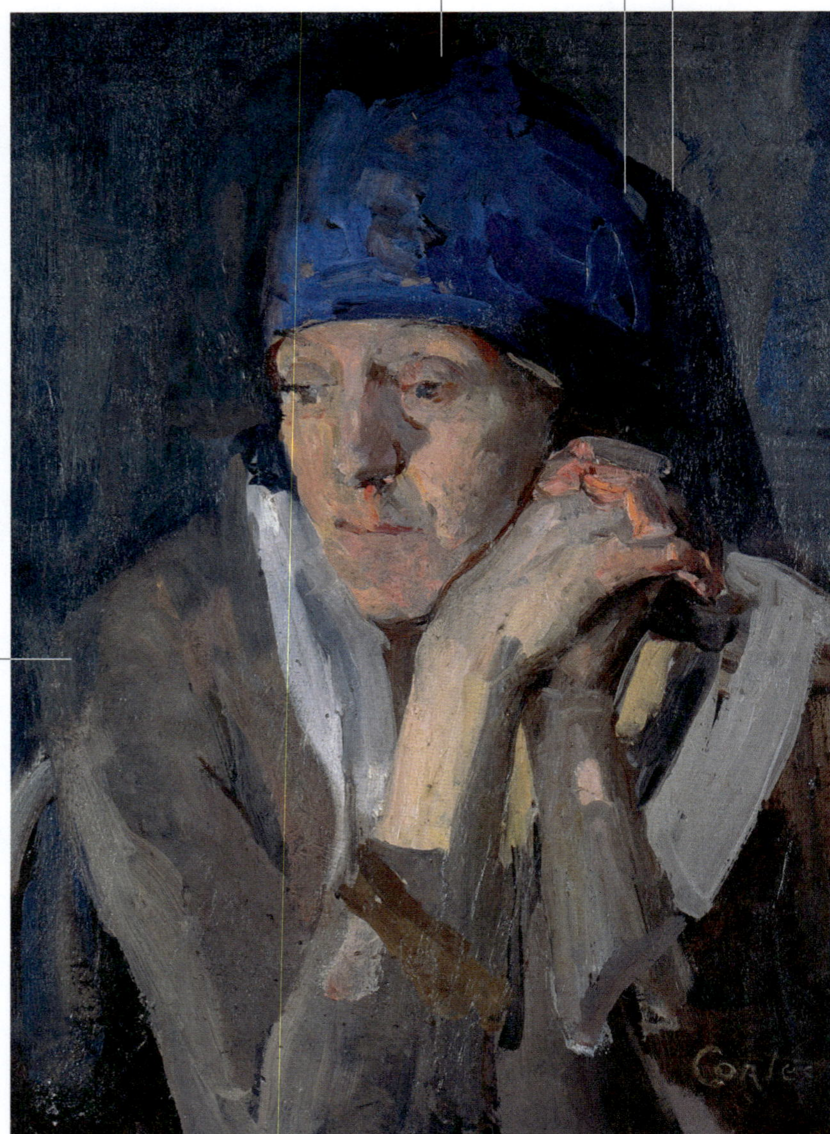

"Memories," George James Coates (1926)
This painting is full of expressive emotion, and the artist has managed to create a sense of empathy between the viewer and the painted figure.

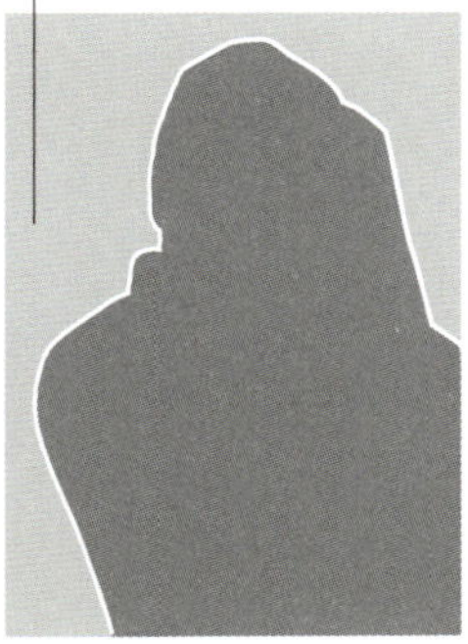

Composition
The composition is centralized, focusing the viewer's attention on the figure and her face and hands.

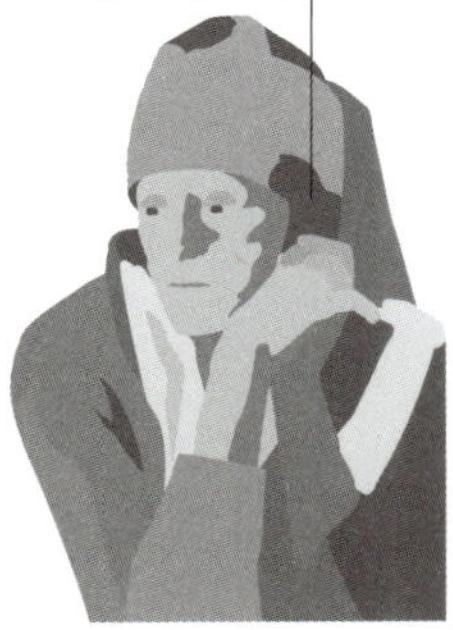

Light and shade
The face is lit from an angle as if by candle or gaslight, creating an introspective mood. The darkness closes in, suggesting solitude.

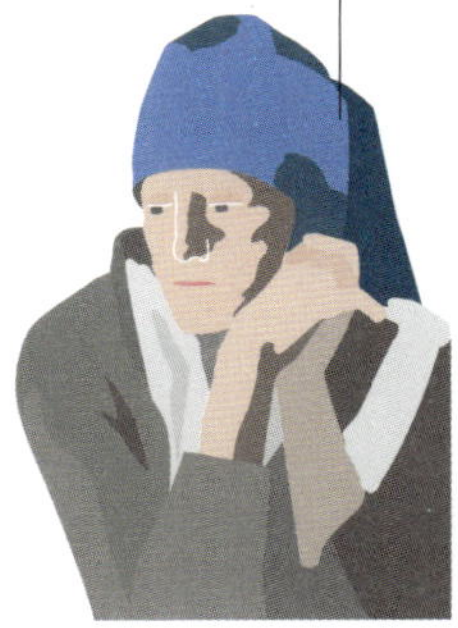

Colors
The palette is melancholy, with blues and grays contrasting with the warm skin tones. The pale collar helps frame the face.

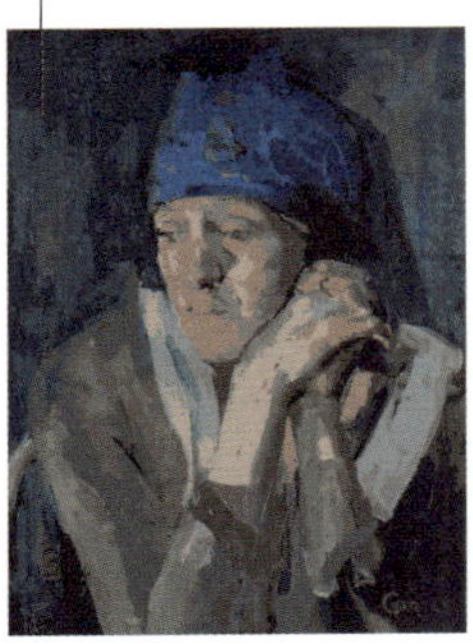

Brushstrokes or marks
The brushstrokes are loose, suggesting a softness and sensitivity. The scene is depicted with compassion through the mark making.

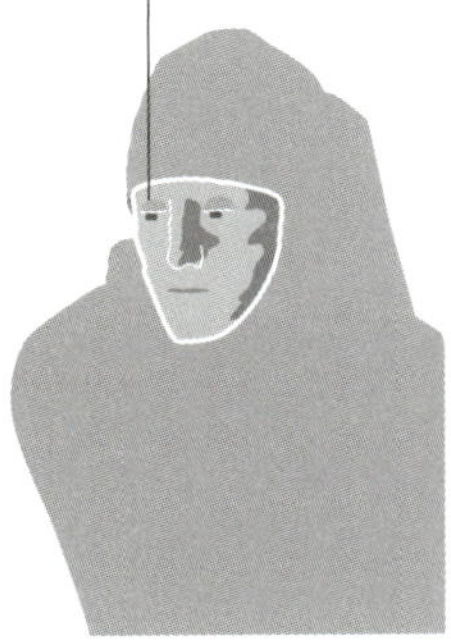

Expression
The face is pensive and angled slightly downward, suggesting contemplation. The downcast eyes may signify sadness or regret.

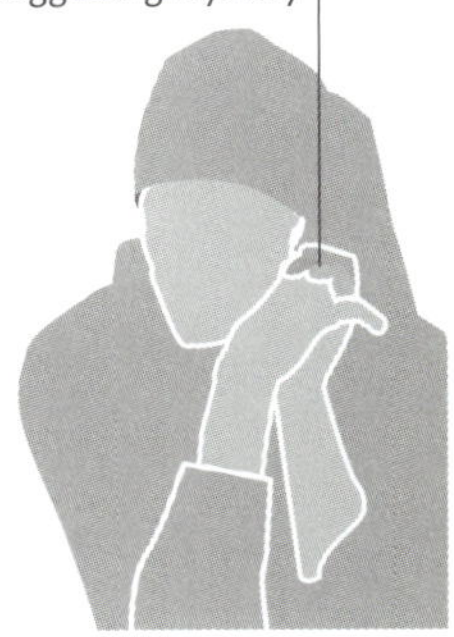

Pose
The hunched shoulders indicate vulnerability, while the clasped hands resting below the face imply deep thought.

Abstract emotion

There is a strong history of emotional expression through nonfigurative forms of art. Abstraction (see pp.78–79) often explores the power of pure color, composition, and shape and uses the juxtaposition of color, light, and shade to create mood. The Abstract Expressionists (see pp.210–211) used gesture to communicate emotion; Mark Rothko painted soft, dark rectangles against deep reds that conveyed strong emotions such as sadness. Wassily Kandinsky's paintings depicted joyous, energetic emotions by creating a "dance" between luminous color and shape, influenced by music.

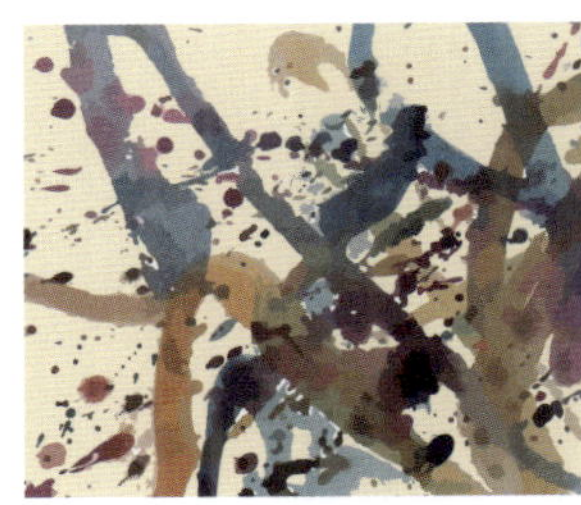

Emotion without a face
Feeling can be depicted without using figures or characters, created instead by suggesting a sense of expression and the use of color and light.

THE ART OF WAR

Artists' works concerning war often carry powerful emotional weight. In 1917, Christopher Nevinson's war paintings were banned in Britain for their upsetting content, while Peter Howson's work on the 1990s Bosnian conflict is noted for its impact.

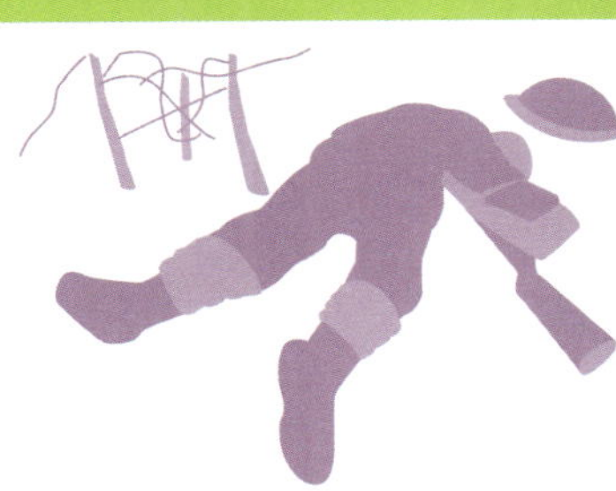

DEPICTIONS OF CONFLICT

DOES COLOR AFFECT EMOTION?

Blue and purple are cool, calming colors, while red, orange, and yellow can evoke strong emotional responses. Green is the most balanced color.

Conveying Information

An artist communicates with the viewer through their artwork. Conveying information involves choosing subject matter, developing the visual language to describe and convey the content, and deciding on the medium, materials, size, and other aspects of the work.

Subject and inspiration
Subject matter describes what the artist chooses to be the thematic content underpinning the artwork (see pp.108–109). The artist draws on their own interests to find subject matter about which they feel passionate. This could be personal, political, or philosophical (see pp.112–113), and they may look to art history for inspiration.

Figurative imagery
Stories can be communicated effectively through figurative work, where the viewer imagines relationships between figures.

The natural world
Landscape or organic forms can be used to express concern for the environment or to explore philosophical ideas about nature.

Humanity
Human activity can be explored through visual metaphors such as architecture and urban space, and social or community scenes.

Imagination
Dreams and memories can be communicated through visual language such as surreal juxtaposition and fragmentation.

Media and materials
The medium, materials, and the ways in which they are used are all intentional. The material itself might have inherent suggestions, such as the malleability of clay or the hardness of metal. Painting materials also have their own identity, and the artist's choice of paint in a work can affect its mood and meaning.

Painting
Visual properties of paint types can be used to convey information.

Sculpture
Sculpting materials can convey an idea, such as lightness or heaviness.

Visual language
Related to media and materials, visual language is the way these materials are used by the individual artist to create their own unique visual vocabulary. This may focus on shape, colour, lines, or a combination of elements, to convey the relevant information.

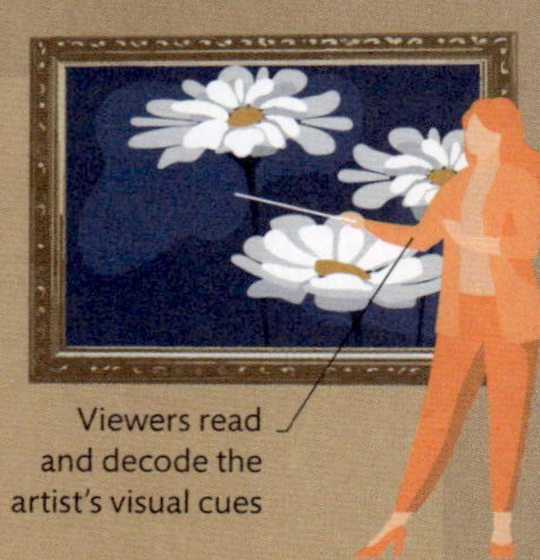
Viewers read and decode the artist's visual cues

PATRONAGE

In the past, people in powerful positions, such as royalty or the Church, would fund artists to create artwork for them. The artist would often include visual information referring to their patron.

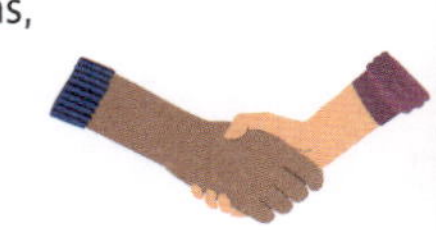

Fusing content and technique

In artworks, content and technique are inextricably linked. The way an artwork is made can communicate as much information to the viewer as the visual content or story of the work. The technical crafting of a piece helps convey and shape the experience the viewer has of the artwork. The artist might, for example, use gestural marks, hard edges, smooth or rough surfaces, or a particular color palette—these elements should all be considered in terms of how they help convey the content of the work.

Scale and presentation
These are key considerations in how the artwork is interpreted (see pp.116–117). With a small-scale artwork, either painting or sculpture, a more intimate viewing experience is created in contrast to the more immersive quality of a large-scale work. Two-dimensional art can be framed for a formal feel, or left with raw edges for an informal effect.

Large
Large size can be used for dramatic effects.

Small
Small artworks encourage detailed scrutiny.

Techniques
Some artists consider techniques to be the most important communicative element of their work. They may impart information using compositional techniques or through brushwork and mark making or by the use of lighting within the artwork.

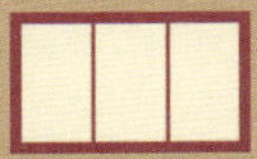

COMPOSITION

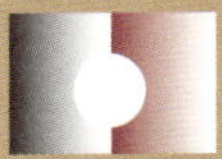

LIGHT AND SHADE

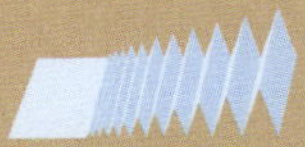

TEXTURAL SURFACES

The subject and composition is literal, but the use of color gives pause for thought

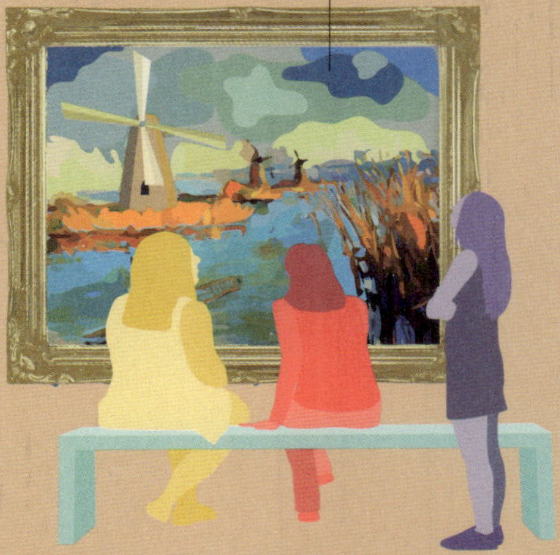

Engaging the viewer
An artist may choose to communicate information in ways that are literal and obvious, demanding little of the viewer. Alternatively, a subtle approach may create a richer artwork that encourages the viewer to consider the piece carefully, and question what might be behind it.

ARTIST **ANSELM KIEFER** USES **HEAVY MATERIALS** SUCH AS **LEAD AND CLAY** TO CONVEY THE **WEIGHT OF HISTORY**

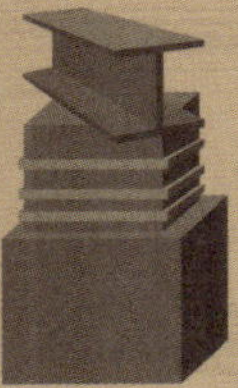

ON AVERAGE, HOW LONG DOES A PERSON SPEND LOOKING AT A PIECE OF ARTWORK?

The average time a gallery visitor spends looking at each artwork is estimated to be between 15 and 30 seconds.

ADVERTISING AND ART

Advertising and art influence each other, dating back to the Art Nouveau movement (see pp.200–201). Art uses the language of advertising to explore themes such as leisure, consumer culture, propaganda, and gender. Advertising, meanwhile, borrows heavily from art in its imagery and visual styling.

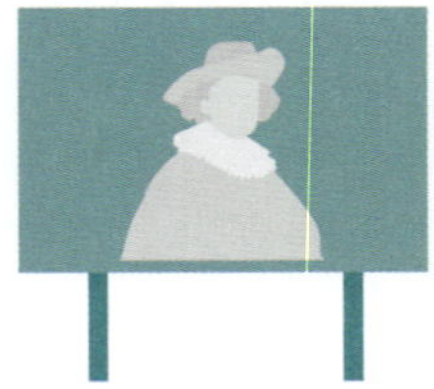

Communicating Ideas

Communicating ideas in art involves transmitting often complex concepts to the viewer, whether in a direct or a more subtle way.

How can artists convey ideas?

Most artworks consist of a number of different elements combined into a whole. Some or all of these components can be used by the artist to communicate a nuanced message or idea that transcends the work's superficial appearance. Such elements may be simple and visual, or they may require a deeper contemplation or understanding.

THE **DADA** ART MOVEMENT USED THE IDEA OF **ABSURDITY** TO **OPPOSE WORLD WAR I**

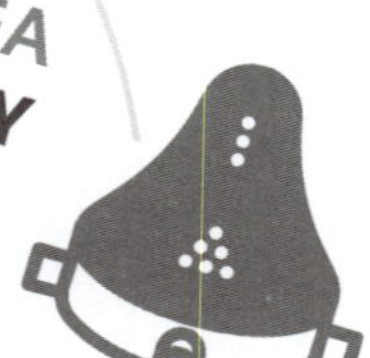

DOES ALL ART HAVE A MESSAGE?

Art exists in its purest form as an exercise in creativity and self-expression—"art for art's sake." An artist is free to choose whether to include a message in their work, or not.

Combining visual elements
The message of the artwork, as well as its mood and intended emotional impact, can be imparted through the combination of its basic visual elements. This may include the subject and the visual language, the artwork's size and scale, its composition, and the use of color. Taken together, these elements can also indicate how the viewer is meant to "read" the work.

Materials and media
The materials selected and the processes used to create a work contribute to the way in which the artwork communicates its message. The physical appearance of a work can make an impact. Scoring, cutting, or deliberately damaging a canvas, for example, can serve as a political or personal statement, while an unusual or deliberately limited choice of materials can be used to impart meaning.

Coded messages
Artists have long included allegorical or coded messages in their work across many cultures (see pp.140–141). Famously, paintings such as Hans Holbein's *The Ambassadors* and many Dutch still-life works of the 17th century are filled with symbols that explain the work's meaning. In this era, an empty glass suggested the fleeting nature of life, and musical instruments stood for peace and harmony.

Context
The physical context in which art is curated—how and where people see it—can be used to convey ideas. For example, viewing art in a gallery is a different experience from seeing it in other settings. Since the 1960s, more emphasis has also been placed on the social context of art. Artists are now more aware of the language they use to communicate ideas and how it might be understood now and in the future.

What kind of ideas may be communicated in art?

Any idea can be communicated through art. Artists often combine personal or autobiographical elements with wider themes, which could be topical or political issues of the time, or broader philosophical and historical ideas. Art is the perfect medium to tackle big ideas, and artists frequently question society with curiosity and a creative and open mindset. Artists often try to communicate these ideas in nonliteral ways, believing that the viewer's engagement and interpretation will be richer and more rewarding if the work is less obvious and has layers of content to work through.

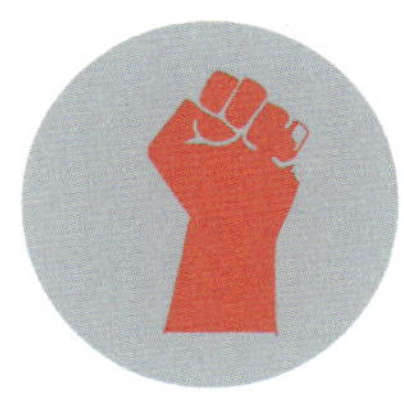

Political and social
Art is influenced by society and is often used as a means of reflecting and commenting on it.

Philosophical
Art offers a means of discussing the big, complex ideas of life in a visual, more accessible way.

Religious
Historically focused on messages of faith, today's religious art also asks spiritual questions.

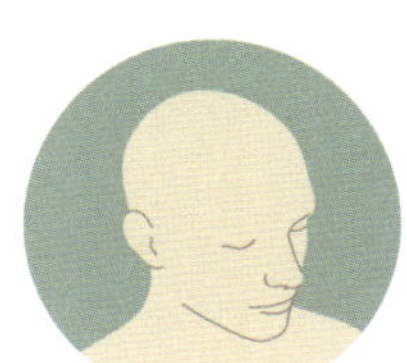

Personal
An artist's own story can connect individual and universal messages in resonant, meaningful ways.

Signs and Symbols

Since ancient times, signs and symbols have been used as a tool in art to communicate ideas that go beyond surface appearances or language barriers. Imagery such as animals, birds, and vegetation, or colors, shapes, and even human gestures are often used.

THE ART HISTORIAN **ERWIN PANOFSKY** HAS COMPARED **ARTISTIC SYMBOLS** TO **GESTURES BETWEEN PEOPLE**

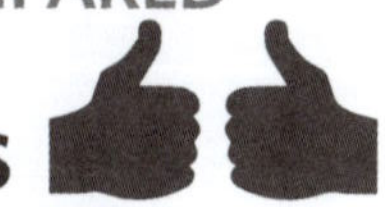

Symbolic meanings in art

Symbols in art are often based on stories that have their roots in religion, culture, or mythology. By using such symbols in an artwork, an artist can ground the work in an existing narrative framework or can use the symbolism to draw comparisons or suggest contrasts. Symbols can be vehicles for artists to communicate directly with viewers, offering a deeper comprehension and interpretation of the art. Some common symbols used in art are shown below.

Self-reflection

Mirrors in art have, for centuries, been used to signify insight, self-knowledge, truth, deception, wisdom, vanity, and introspection. In the 16th century, they replaced the use of water, polished metal, or obsidian as a means of seeing one's reflection, and since then, myths have told of magic being held in mirrors. They can reflect hidden truths, provide a way into the soul, or allow entry into another world.

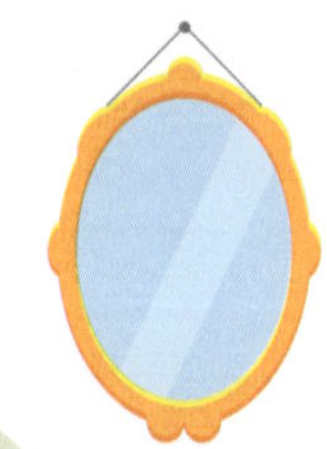

MIRROR AS TRUTH SYMBOL

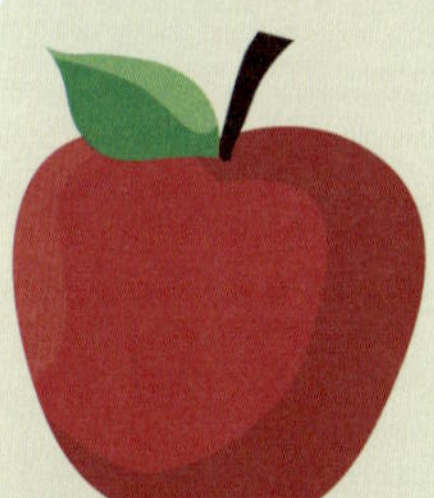

Apple
Apples symbolize health, well-being, knowledge, wisdom, immortality, perpetual youth, or the Biblical fruit of the forbidden tree.

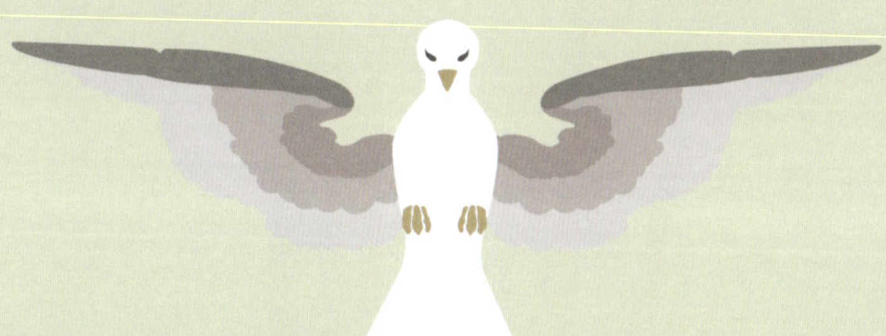

Dove
Depicted in many cultures and religions, doves can symbolize peace, healing, spiritual purity, innocence, hope, happiness, motherhood, harmony, or love.

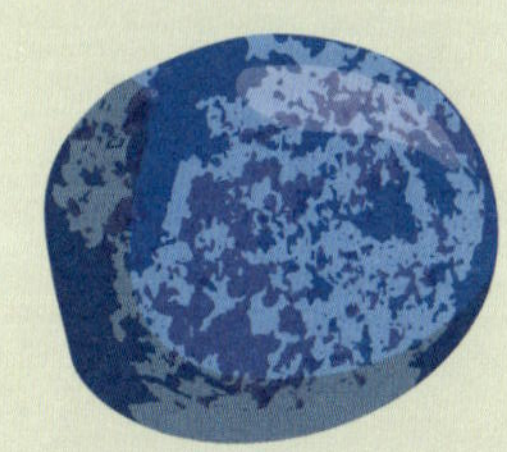

Blue (Lapis lazuli)
Traditionally a symbol of truth, clarity, and heaven, blue has also been associated with Christianity's Virgin Mary and with spirituality.

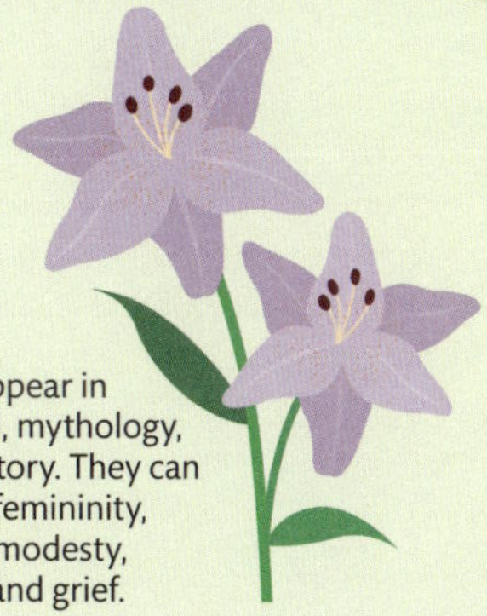

Lily
Lilies appear in religion, mythology, and history. They can signify femininity, purity, modesty, death, and grief.

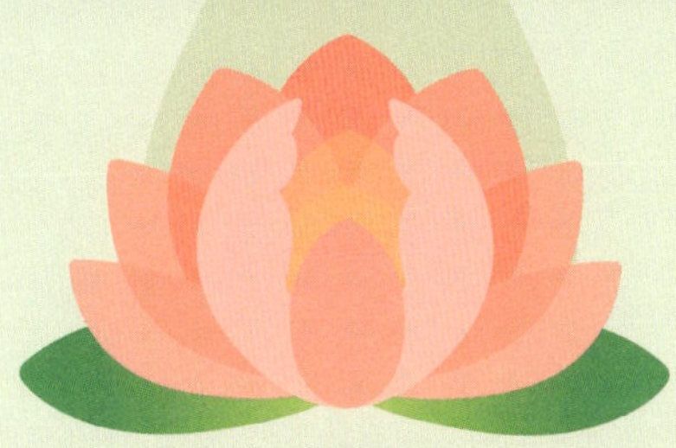

Lotus
In Hinduism, the lotus flower symbolizes the goddess Lakshmi. In other cultures, it represents wisdom, enlightenment, and beauty.

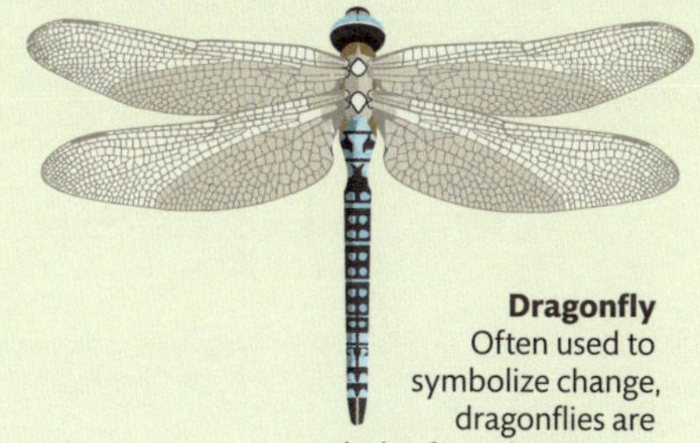

Dragonfly
Often used to symbolize change, dragonflies are symbols of new beginnings and opportunities, growth, maturity, and wisdom.

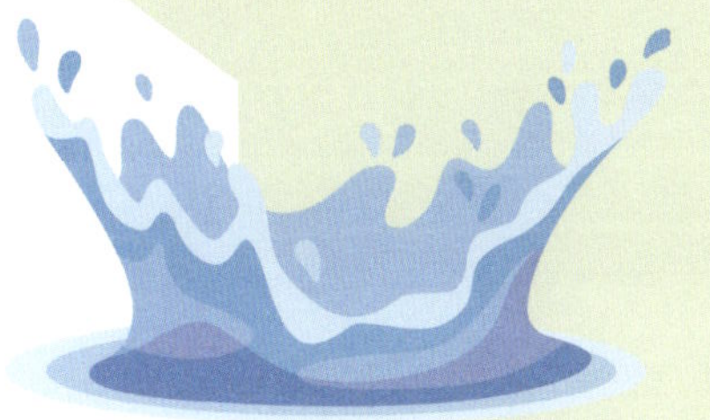

Water
Often associated with purity and sanctification, water also signifies change, or a new beginning. If turbulent—power and chaos.

Triangle
In Christianity, a triangle implies the Holy Trinity. In pagan symbolism, a triangle pointing up denotes fire; pointing down, a chalice or water.

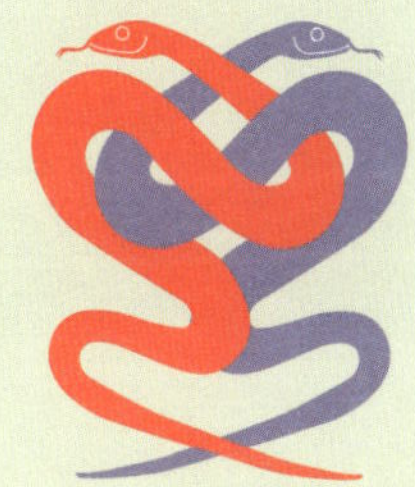

Snake
Snakes can represent evil, temptation, wisdom, or rebirth. In Chinese culture, they can symbolize elegance, nature, and good luck.

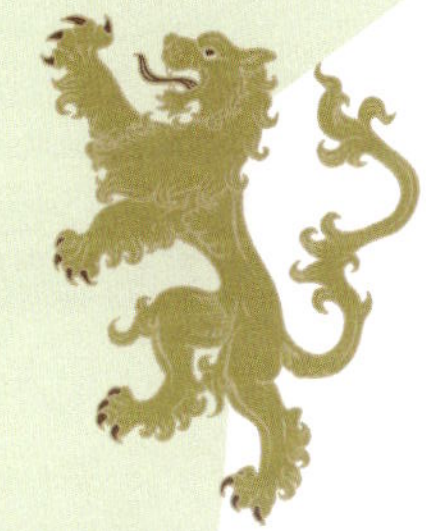

Lion
In several cultures, lions are symbolic of rulers. They also commonly appear in art to denote strength, courage, majesty, and fortitude.

MEMENTO MORI PAINTINGS

Latin for "remember you must die," a memento mori aims to remind the viewer of their mortality and the fragility of human life. Popular in the 17th century, these paintings often feature hourglasses, clocks, snuffed or sputtering candles, skulls, decaying fruit, and fading, dying flowers.

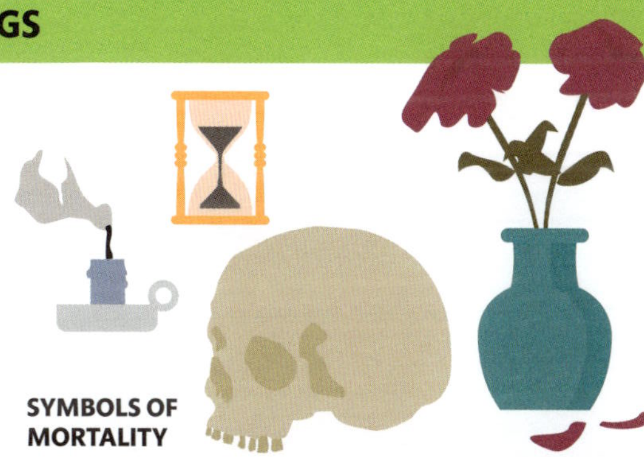

SYMBOLS OF MORTALITY

WHAT IS THE STUDY OF SIGNS CALLED?

Semiotics is the name for the study of symbols and signs, often used in philosophy. Iconography is the name for a system of signs and their meanings.

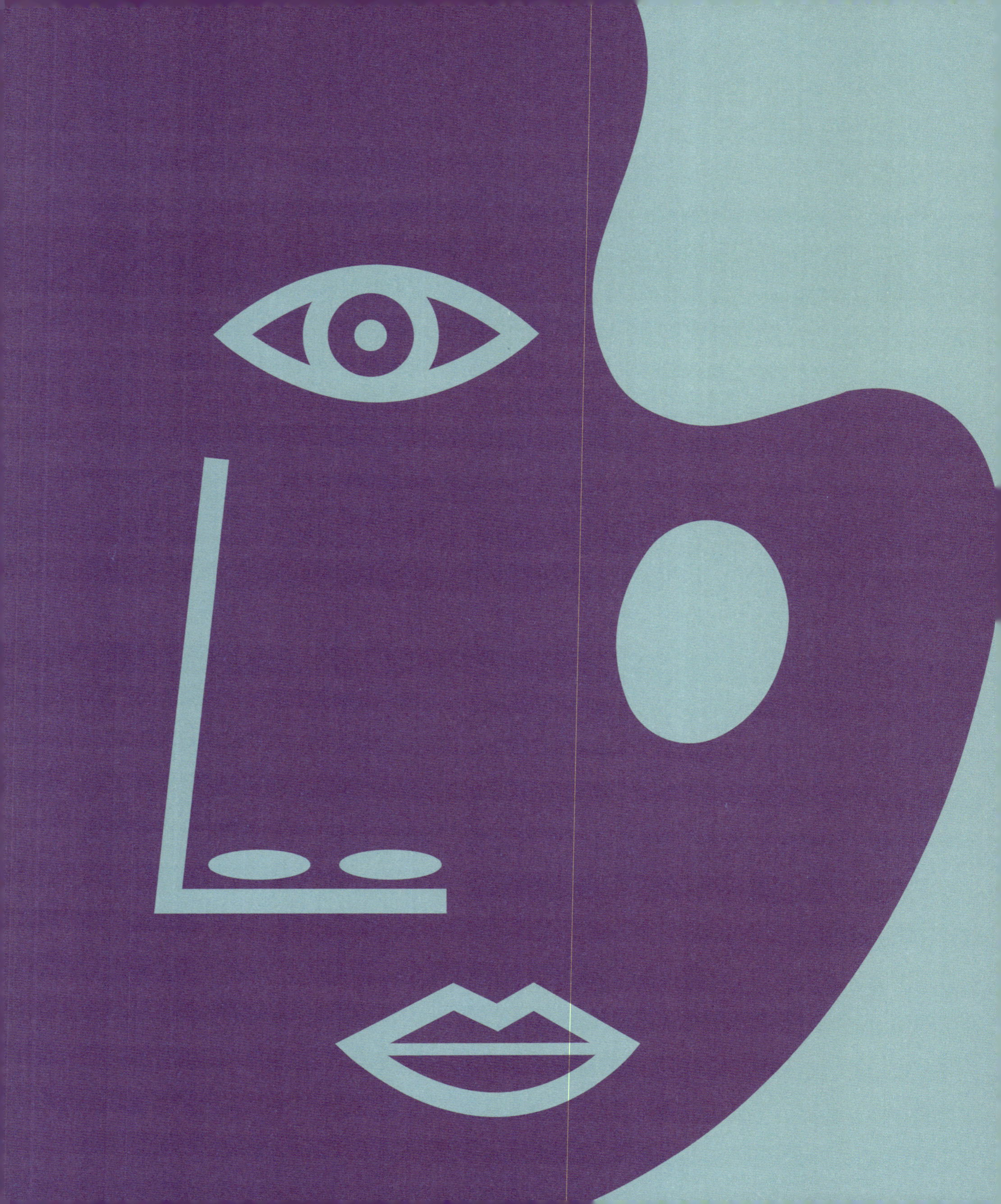

MOVEMENTS

Stone Age Art

What we know about Paleolithic, or Stone Age, art comes mainly from examples of rock paintings that have survived for thousands of years preserved deep in sheltered caves.

Cave art

Early prehistoric cave paintings were discovered in Spain in the 1860s, and since then, other sites have been discovered as far afield as Argentina, Indonesia, and the US. Despite being thousands of miles apart, many of these paintings were made using similar tools and materials. Early artists are believed to have employed readily available materials to create richly symbolic imagery of the animals they encountered in their daily lives. Some artworks were created using the simplest form of stencil available—by blowing pigment around a hand placed on a wall.

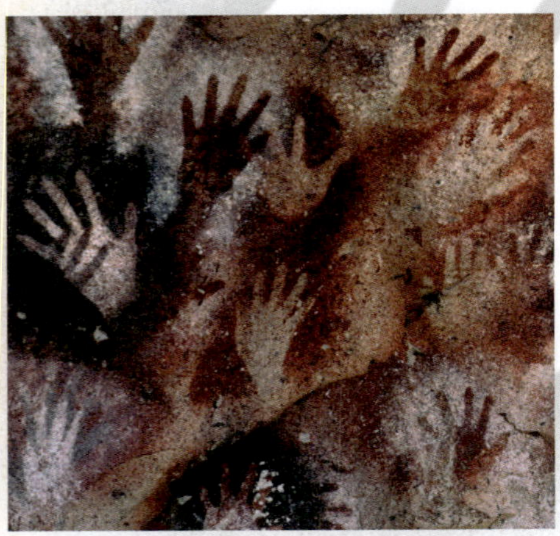

Cave of the Hands
This cave in Argentina is filled with painted stencils of hands. Most of the prints are of left hands, suggesting the early artists may have held blowpipes in their right hands. Making these stencils is thought to have been a way of marking presence in a place.

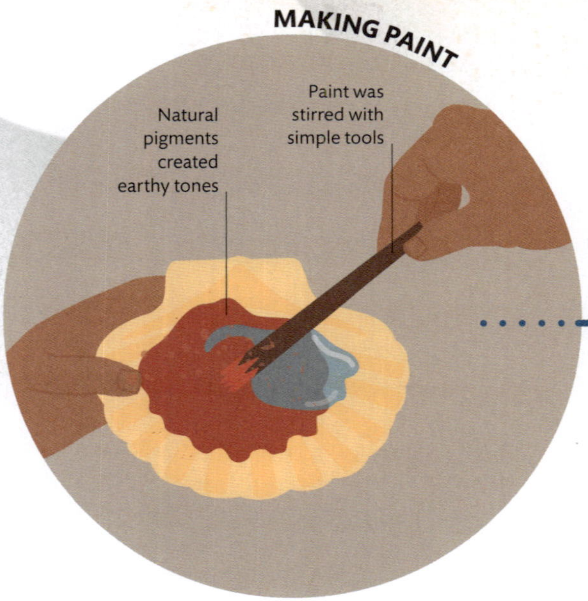

1 Making paint
Rudimentary paint is believed to have been created by mixing ground-up natural clays or minerals from the earth (called earth pigments) with water, animal fat, or saliva to create a thin, malleable paste.

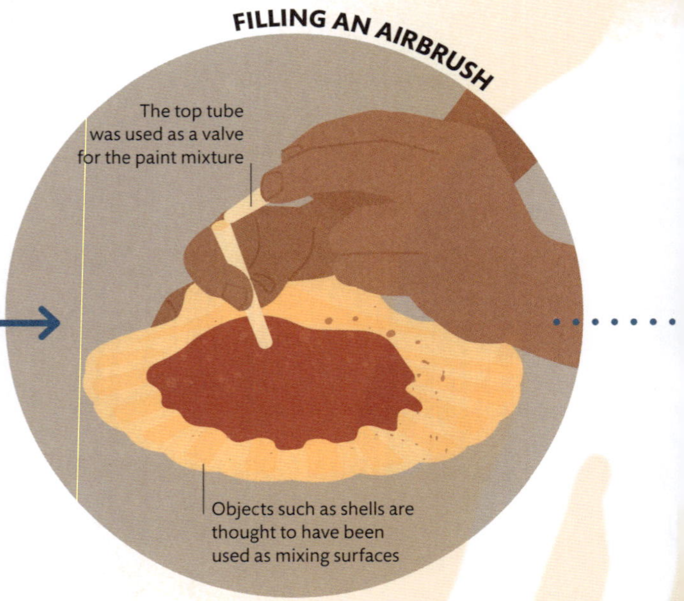

2 Filling the airbrush
It is thought that the artist may have used a pair of hollow reeds or bird bones as a basic airbrush. One of the tubes was filled with the paint mixture from the palette and held with its base dipped in the paint.

Tools and materials

Stone-age artists used naturally occurring materials that would have been integral to their lives, such as flint, which was also used for tools and arrowheads, and charcoal from fires. Some works used naturally occurring shapes in the rock face as starting points for paintings of animal forms. While the earliest painters used their hands and fingers, later painters employed simple tools like paint brushes made from feathers, or sharpened chalk.

Natural elements
Prehistoric art makers used charcoal sticks left over from fires or naturally occurring earth pigments from the ground to create early forms of colored paint.

HOW OLD IS STONE AGE ART?

The earliest recorded artworks date from around 45,000 years ago. A picture of a wild pig, discovered in Indonesia, is believed to be the oldest known figurative artwork in the world.

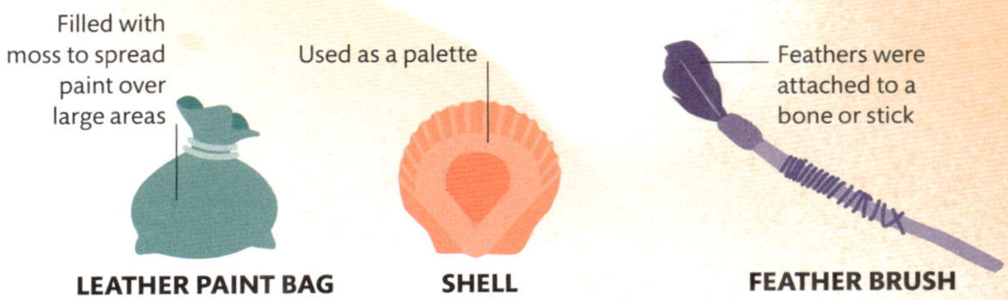

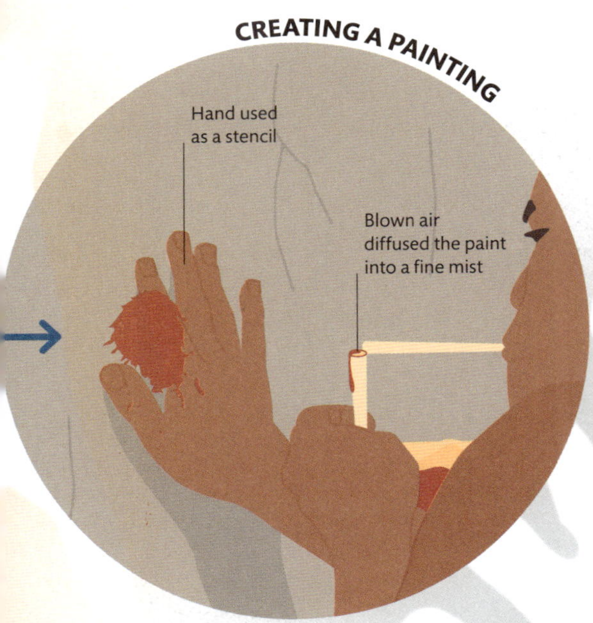

3 Creating the painting
Finally, the artist would place their hands on the cave surface and blow air across the top of the paint tube, spraying pigment to leave a very personal stencil record of themselves.

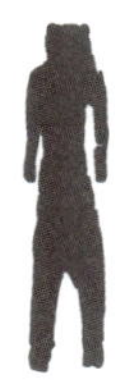

THE 40,000-YEAR-OLD "LIONMAN" SCULPTURE IS THOUGHT TO BE THE EARLIEST EXAMPLE OF RELIGIOUS ART

SUBJECTS

The creators of the earliest known artworks mostly turned to the natural world in the subjects they depicted. It is impossible to be sure of the original purpose of Stone Age art. Prehistoric wall decorations predominantly depict the wide variety of animal life that coexisted alongside early humans, and it is believed that these images had a ritual or sacred significance.

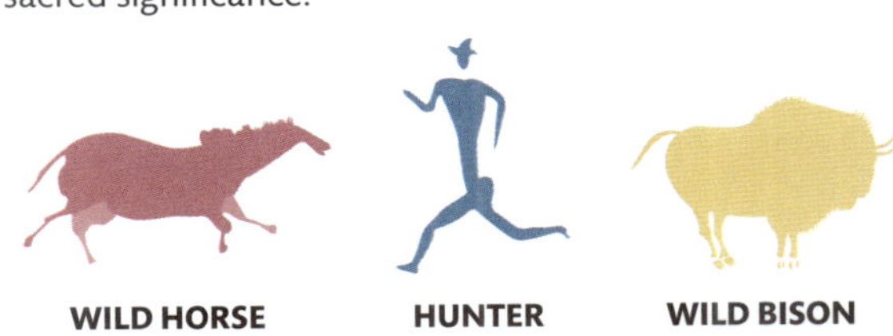

First Australian Art

Rock art is integral to Indigenous culture in Australia, with a continuous tradition dating from prehistory to today. There are an estimated 100,000 significant rock art sites around Australia.

ARTISTS CANNOT PAINT A STORY THAT IS NOT FROM THEIR FAMILY LINEAGE

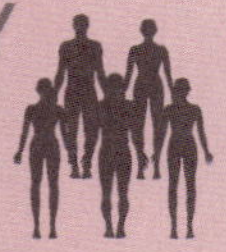

Stories of the past

From the time they first inhabited Australia approximately 45,000–50,000 years ago, First Australians were using artwork in symbolically important sites to tell the stories and creation myths of their past. Rock art was a way of passing these narratives down through the generations, with subsequent artists adding to or altering works over the centuries, a process that continues to the present day.

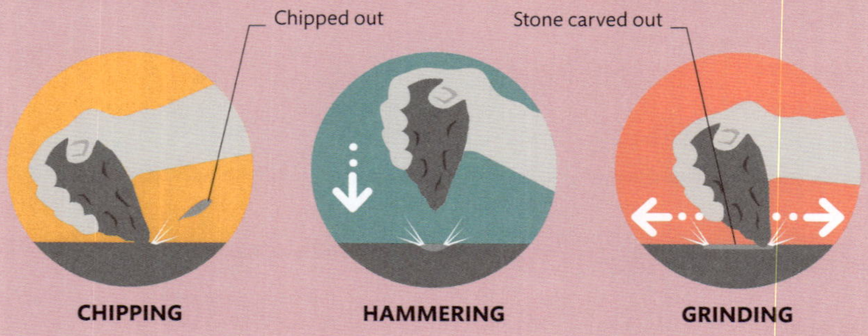

PETROGLYPHS

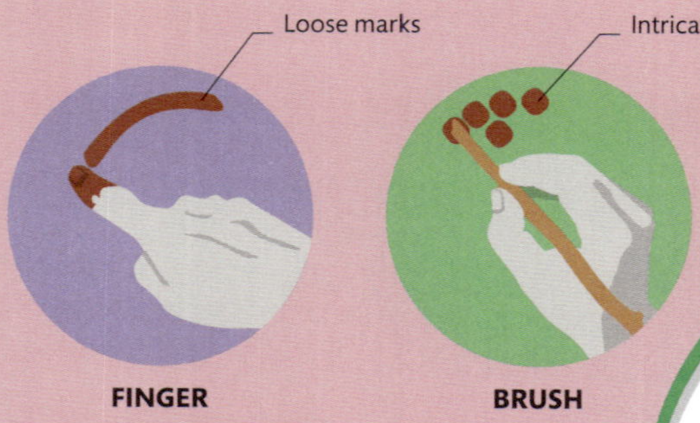

PICTOGRAPHS

Petroglyphs and pictographs
The two main types of First Australian rock art are petroglyphs, engravings carved into the rock, and pictographs, drawings made using natural pigments. Artworks mainly consist of geometric forms, such as circles, arcs and dots, or figurative human or animal forms.

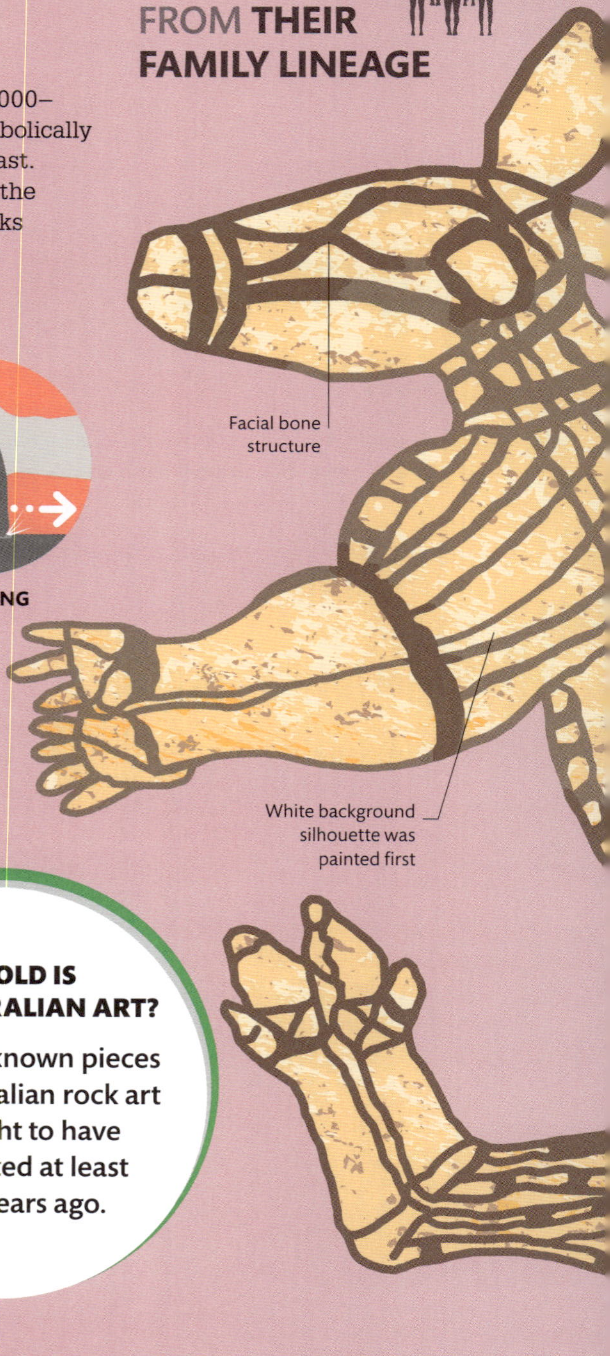

HOW OLD IS FIRST AUSTRALIAN ART?

The earliest known pieces of First Australian rock art are thought to have been created at least 30,000 years ago.

DOT PAINTINGS

Aboriginal Australians have been making "Dot paintings" for thousands of years. Richly colored earth pigments are applied in rhythmic dots and dashes on to the body and are used to make rock art. Artists today also utilize modern acrylics and canvases to create works that are exhibited internationally in museums and galleries, far away from the land and desert rituals that inspired them.

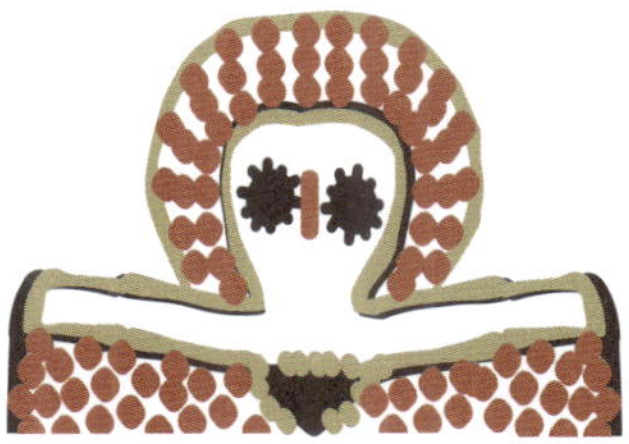

MODERN DOT PAINTING

"X-ray" style
The earliest dated examples of rock art date from 2000 BCE. Some drawings depict slender figures or animals with their skeletons and internal organs visible in an "x-ray" style and demonstrate an understanding of human and animal anatomy.

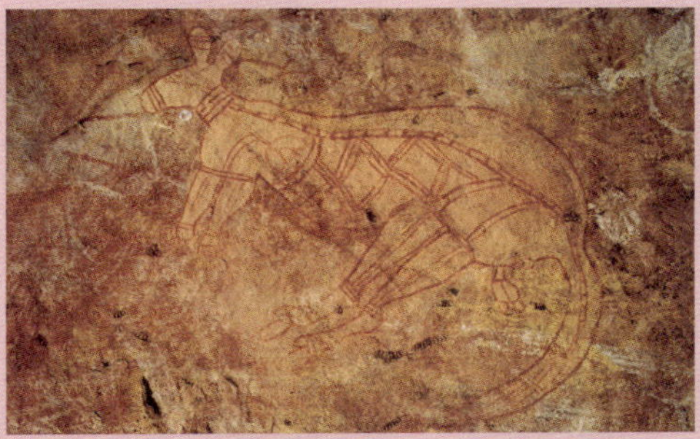

ABORIGINAL ROCK ART PAINTING OF A KANGAROO, AT YIRGALKGALK, AUSTRALIA

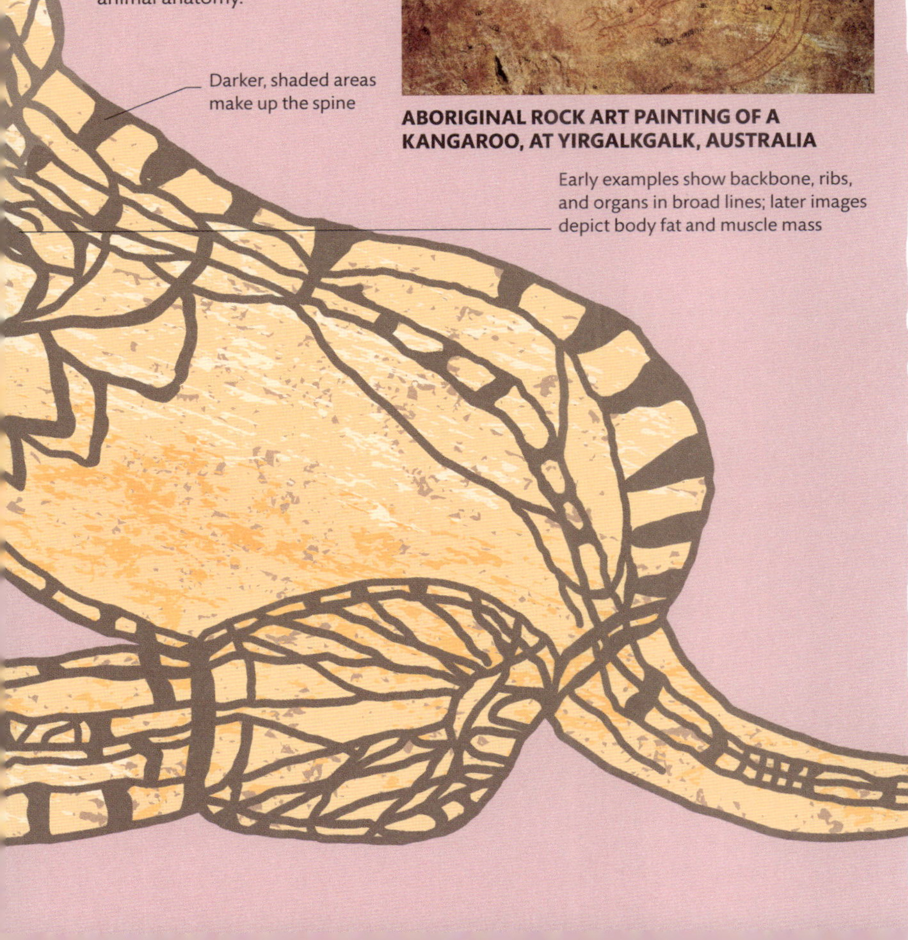

Symbols and their meanings

First Australian art encompasses traditional iconography passed down through hundreds of generations. This rich symbolism is rooted in the concept of "the Dreaming," a time in which the world was shaped by spirits who took the forms of animals and humans—a belief that still governs life today.

PERSON

PEOPLE SITTING

EMU

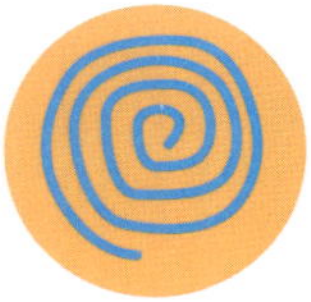

WATERING HOLE

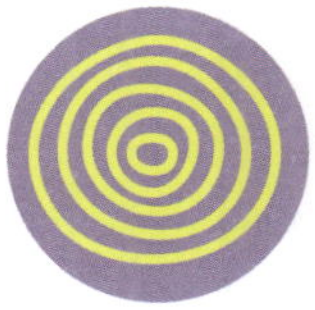

CAMPSITE

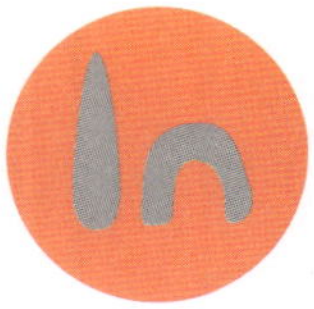

WOMAN

KANGAROO

Mesopotamian Art

Ancient Mesopotamia was a region in what is now the Middle East. Thanks to its fertile land, early development of irrigation systems, and organized farming, it saw the emergence of the world's first cities around the fourth millennium BCE.

Religious artifacts

Urban societies produced elaborate stone carvings and decorated ornaments in metal, terracotta, and wood. Surviving art from Mesopotamia is mainly sculptural—as materials such as textiles perished over time—and most of it was created to serve a religious purpose. Many artifacts carved in the shape of animals have been found, including sheep, goats, lions, and cows.

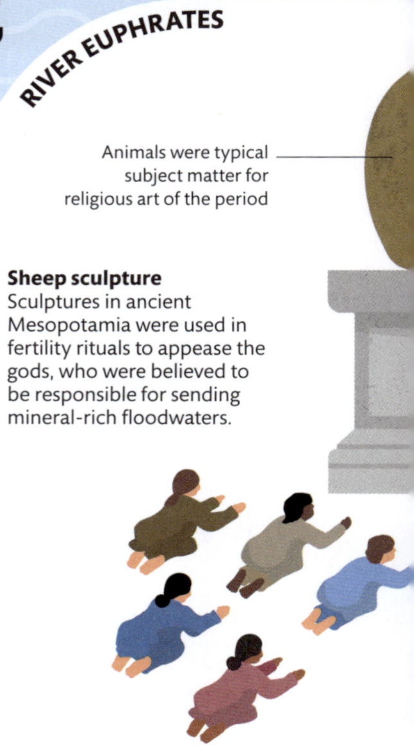

Sheep sculpture
Sculptures in ancient Mesopotamia were used in fertility rituals to appease the gods, who were believed to be responsible for sending mineral-rich floodwaters.

Cylinder seals

Mesopotamian art has also survived in the form of engraved stone cylinder seals, which, when rolled across wet clay, left an impressed design. These designs, depicting patterns and images of gods, humans, and animals, were unique to the seal's owner and could be used to mark property or make legal agreements.

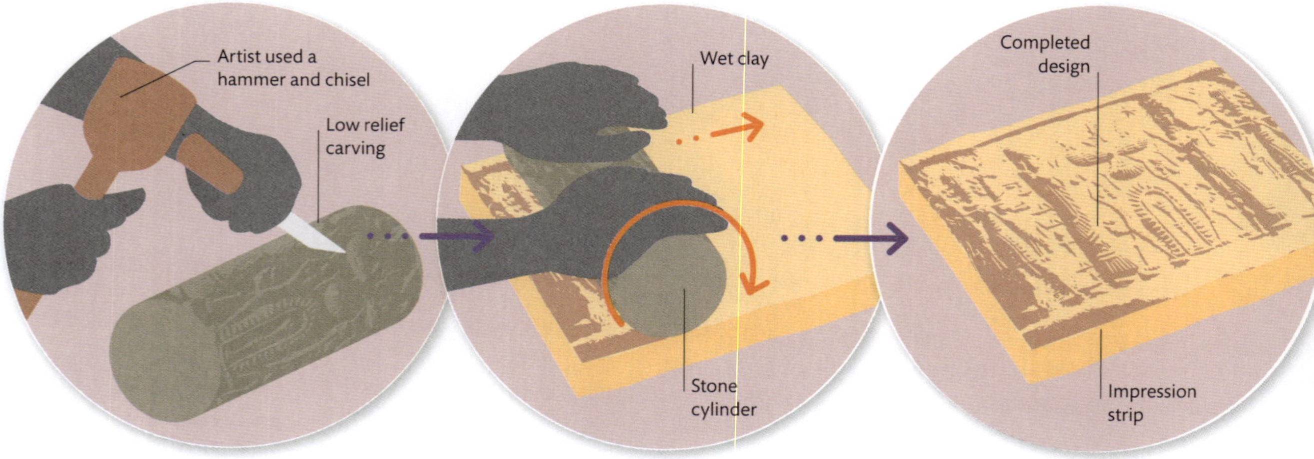

1 Engraving The artist chisels and carves out a unique design into a stone cylinder, creating a hollow relief.

2 Rolling The artist firmly rolls the engraved seal over a thick sheet of wet clay, leaving the design impressed on the surface.

3 Drying As the clay dries, the relief image hardens into an unalterable, long-lasting impression.

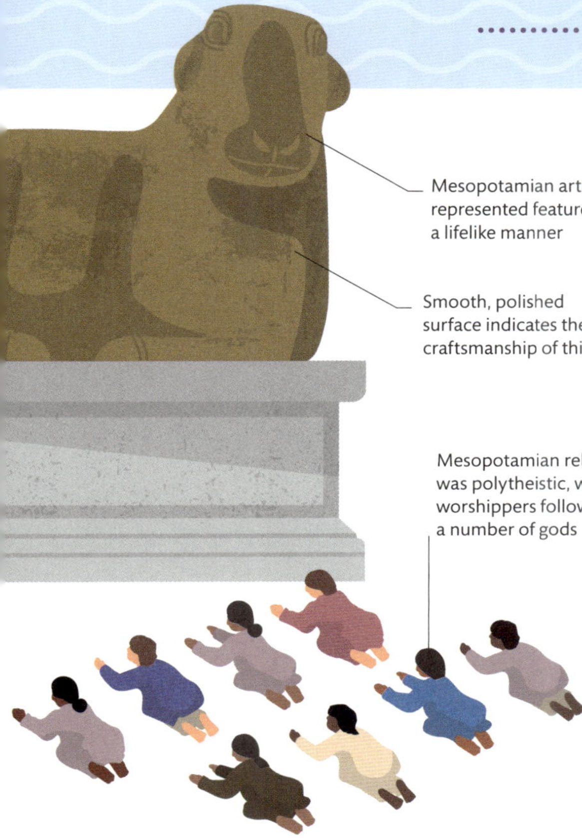

THE CITY OF UR

Ur was one of the most important cities in Ancient Mesopotamia, with an impressive ziggurat, or stepped tower, at its center. In the 20th century, archaeological digs at the city's Royal Cemetery revealed key art treasures.

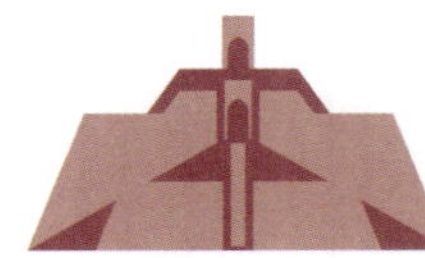

GREAT ZIGGURAT OF UR

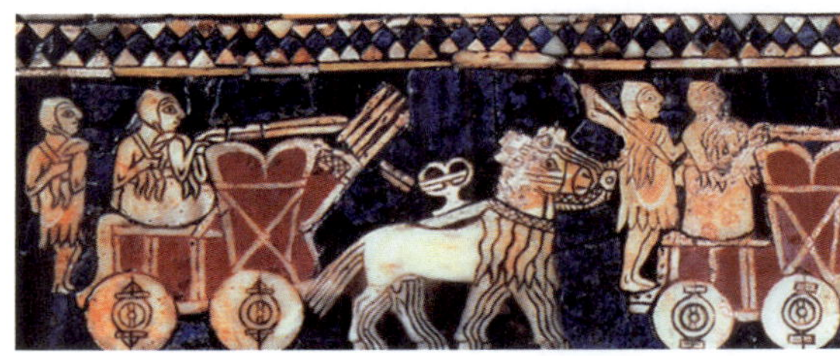

Detail from the Standard of Ur
Discovered in the 1920s, the Standard of Ur is a wooden rectangular object decorated with lapis lazuli (a bright blue stone) and shells, depicting the spoils of war.

DATING FROM **c.9000 BCE**, THE **URFA MAN** IS SAID TO BE THE **OLDEST** LIFE-SIZE HUMAN STATUE

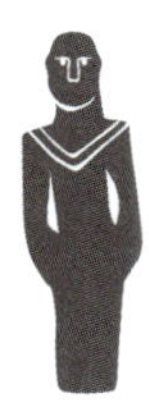

WHAT DOES THE NAME "MESOPOTAMIA" MEAN?

"Mesopotamia" literally means "the land between the rivers"—the Tigris and the Euphrates rivers.

Trading materials

Stone and wood were scarce in the floodplains of the fertile crescent, so many materials used in the creation of sculptures needed to be imported. Mesopotamia was the hub of an important trading network linking East and West, exporting agricultural produce, such as fruit, nuts, and animals, in exchange for metal ores, semi-precious stones, and timber.

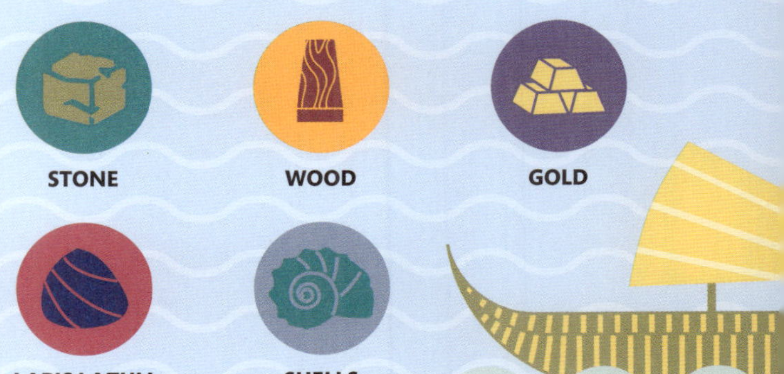

RIVER TIGRIS

Polynesian Art

The islands of the Pacific were settled by people over thousands of years. While different societies share linguistic and cultural similarities, as well as a traditional connection to the natural world, the artworks produced in each region have distinct aesthetic identities.

Natural legacy

Early settlers of the Pacific were master navigators, traveling vast areas of ocean using the stars, weather patterns, and wildlife to guide them. This connection to nature has been passed down through generations and is embodied in the art of the islands, cemented by the widespread belief in the ongoing spiritual presence of ancestors, which many Polynesian cultures hold to be key to maintaining social order and a harmonious community life. Artworks, from small, crafted items worn daily and passed down through families to ceremonial objects created for a specific event recall deceased loved ones and their ongoing link with nature.

WHAT STONE WAS USED TO MAKE THE RAPA NUI "HEAD" STATUES?

Most of the carvings were made of the volcanic rock, tuff. It erodes easily, so much detail has been lost.

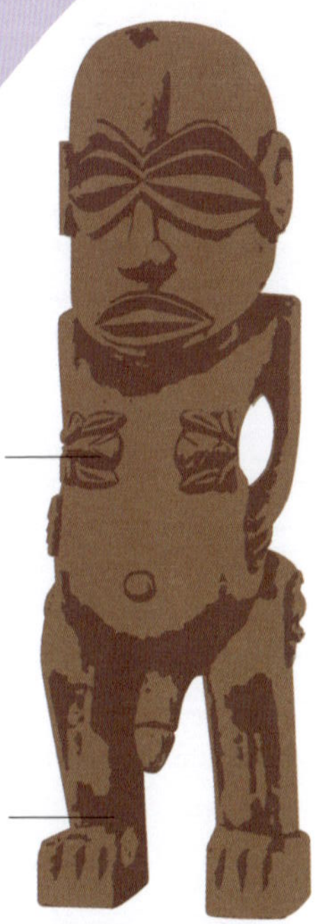

MANGAIA STATUE OF RONGO, GOD OF CROP CULTIVATION

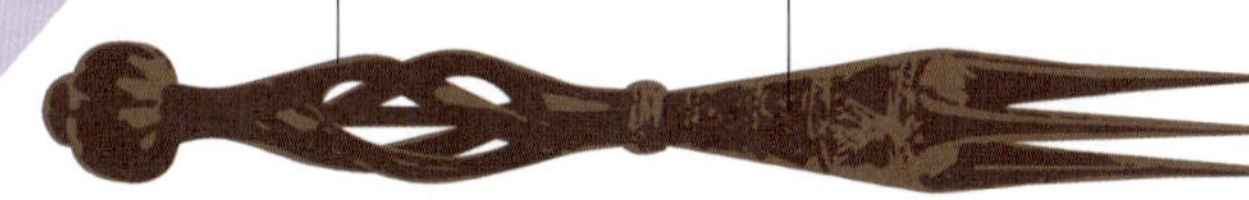

FIJI FORK, PROBABLY USED BY CHIEFS AND ELDERS

POLYNESIAN ISLANDS

Polynesia covers a vast, triangular-shaped area between New Zealand, Hawaii, and Rapa Nui (formerly Easter Island). It includes over one thousand Pacific islands spread out over millions of square miles of ocean.

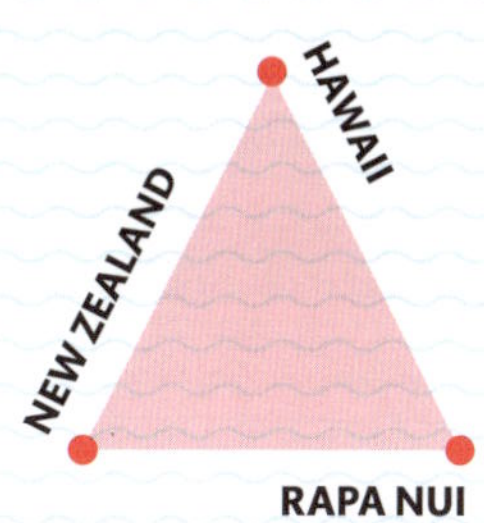

Status and heritage

Across the islands, artworks are primarily carvings and may indicate the status and rank of individuals both living and dead. Among the most famous pieces are the giant stone sculptures of enlarged, stylized heads and torsos known as *moai* on Rapa Nui (formerly Easter Island). More than 887 statues were carved and erected facing inland. These are believed to represent revered ancestors and were said to grant local chiefs divine power.

Māori art

The Māori people of New Zealand have a long and varied art history that typifies many aspects of Polynesian art. Carved *pounamu* (greenstone) pendants called *hei tiki* often share similar visual characteristics inspired by natural forms but are typically used to represent a unique personal history connected to a specific ancestor. Wavelike swirls carved into the face and body of the *hei tiki*, known as *moko*, convey complex genealogical histories.

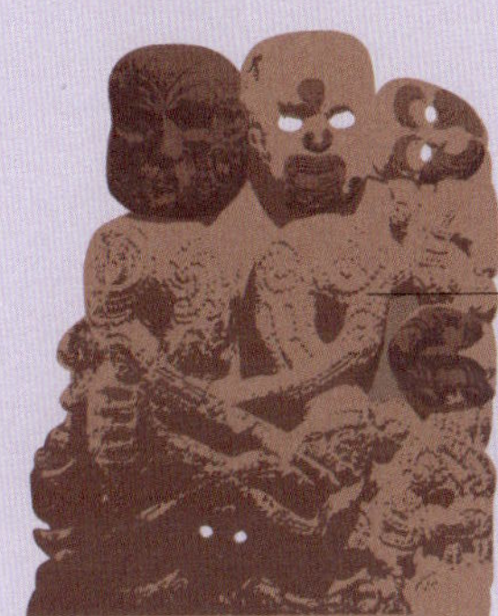

One of 70 male children who became Māori gods

Original Māori gods
This carving depicts the first gods: Rangi, the sky father and Papa, the Earth mother. They had 70 children.

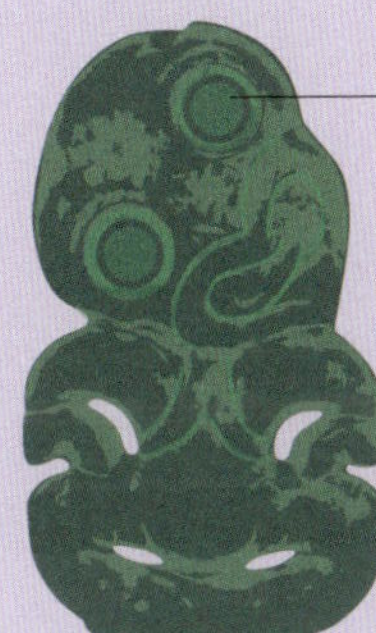

Eye shape would be inlaid with shell

Māori pendant
It would take several months for a master carver to chisel and carve a sacred *hei-tiki* such as this.

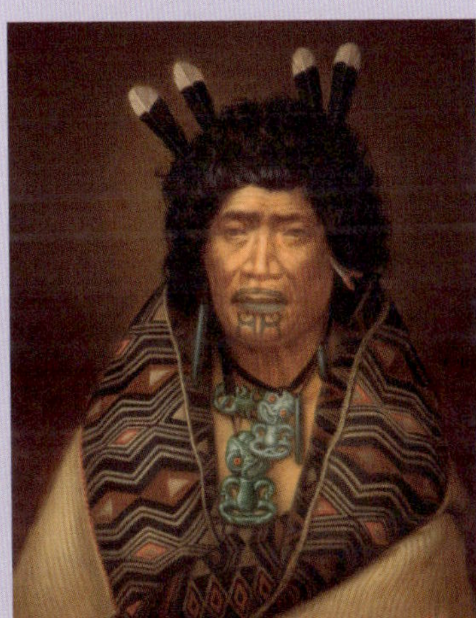

Tribal leader Rangi Topeora
Known as the "Queen of the South," Rangi Topeora was a composer and Māori tribal leader. In this portrait, she wears three *hei tiki* pendants.

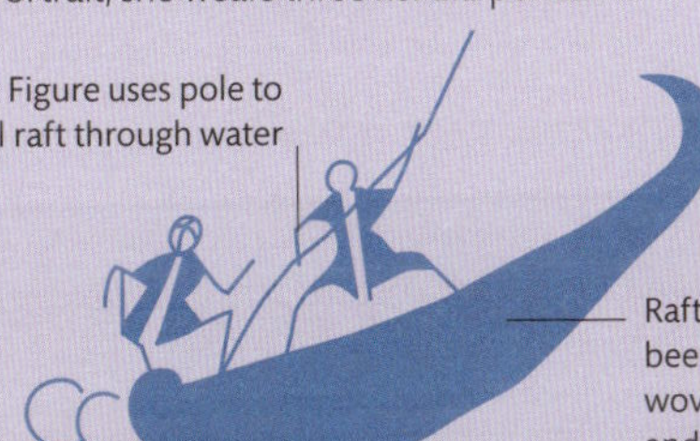

Figure uses pole to propel raft through water

Raft would have been made from woven rushes and flax

Rock drawing
A Māori drawing, thought to be from around 1400 CE, was discovered close to the Opihi River in New Zealand. It shows two figures on a raft called a *mokihi*, which was used for hunting lake birds.

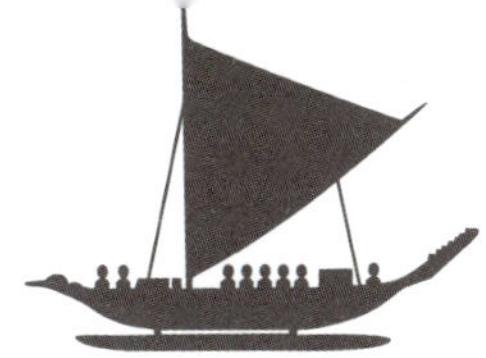

MĀORI SETTLERS CAME TO NEW ZEALAND IN 1250–1300 CE

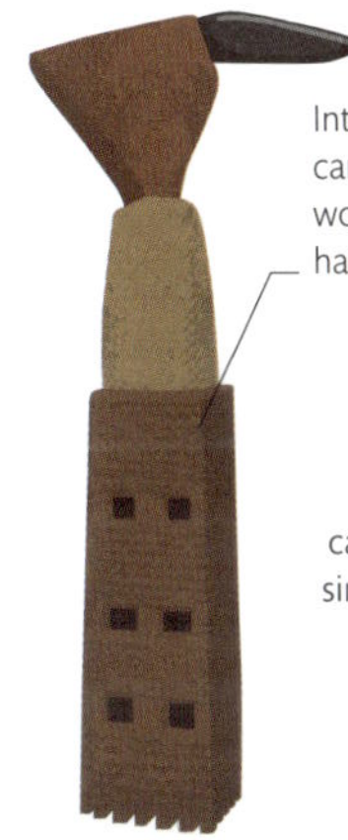

Intricately carved wooden handle

MANGAIA ISLAND CEREMONIAL ADZE (AXE)

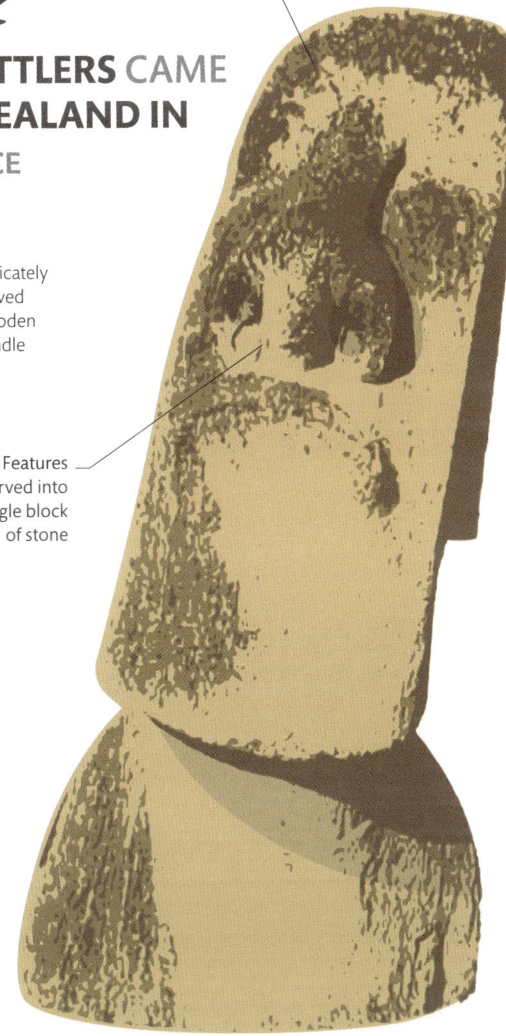

Eye sockets originally inlaid with coral and red stone

Features carved into single block of stone

MOAI HEAD FROM RAPA NUI

A king's tomb paintings
Tomb paintings adhered to specific rules—figures were shown in their entirety, in profile, with the relative size of the person, god, or animal depicted depending on their importance. The north wall of Tutankhamun's tomb shows the king in three scenes ranged right to left.

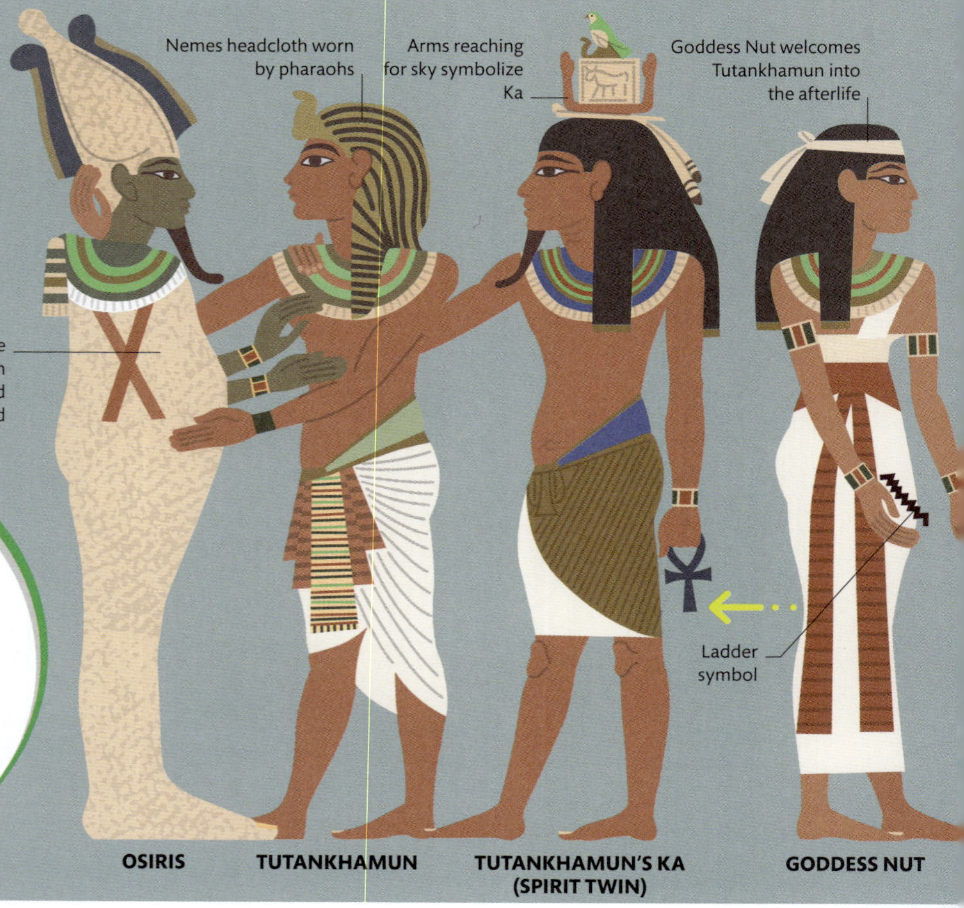

WHAT TOOLS DID EGYPTIAN ARTISTS USE?

Tomb decorations usually combined carvings with paints made from local pigments and applied with palm brushes.

Egyptian Art

Dating from as early as 3000 BCE, the tomb paintings of the Egyptian elite were not intended for human eyes but for the spirit realm of the gods. They followed strict conventions that endured for three millennia.

MOST EGYPTIAN ART BURIED IN TOMBS WAS STOLEN BY **GRAVE ROBBERS** OVER **THOUSANDS OF YEARS**

Honoring the dead

Egyptian tomb art mainly revolved around honoring the dead and depicting the objects they required to navigate their journey into the afterlife. Colors had various symbolic meanings, and conventionally men were shown with red skin, women with cream skin, and gods with yellow skin.

SYMBOLIC COLORS

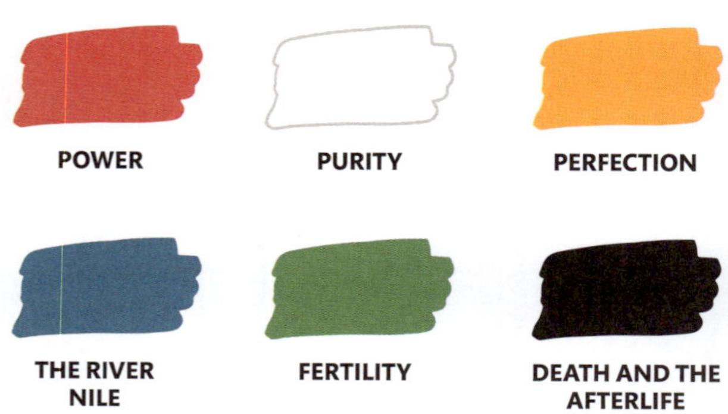

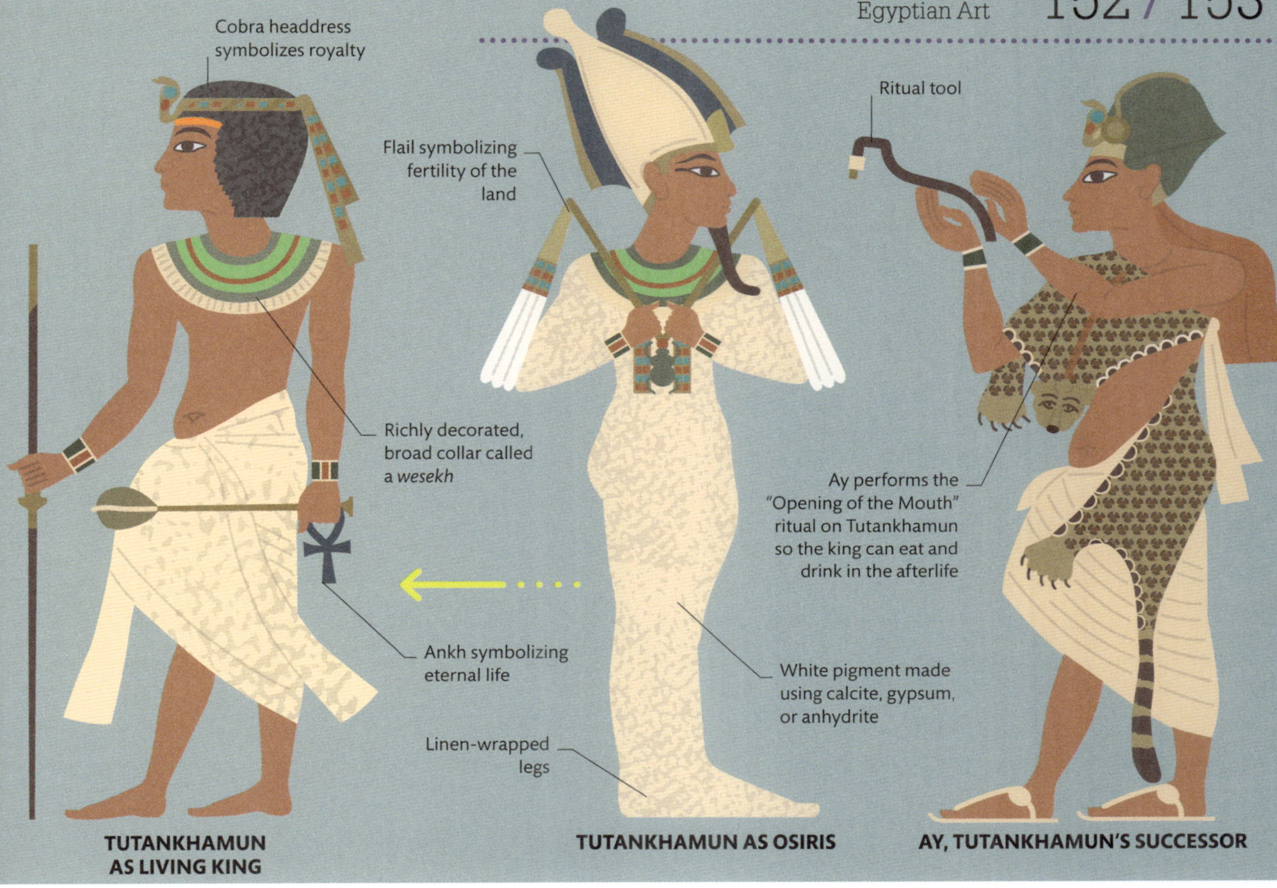

Fayum art

In the 1st and 2nd century CE, around 3,000 years after the first tomb paintings, Egyptian art became more naturalistic. Fayum portraits of the dead were influenced by the Roman desire for realism after Egypt fell to the Roman Empire in 30 BCE. Named after the city of Fayum, southwest of Cairo, these encaustic (hot wax and pigment) or tempera (see pp.36–37) portraits were intended to depict the deceased as realistically as possible. They revealed an awareness of anatomy and made skilled use of light and shade to give a three-dimensional appearance.

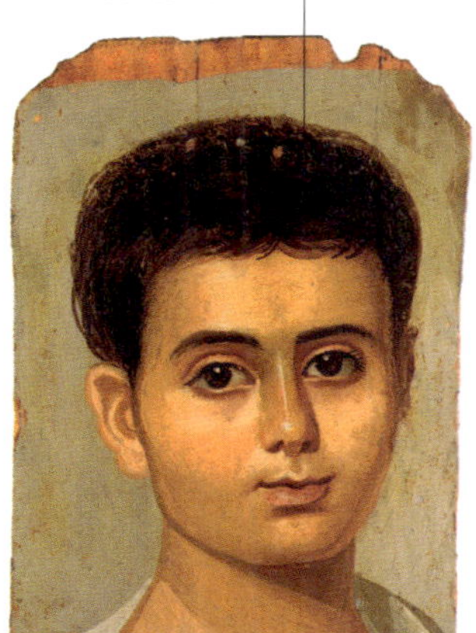

Fayum portrait
These realistic portraits were painted on wooden death masks placed over the face of the deceased.

PACKING FOR THE AFTERLIFE

The images in tombs represented everything the deceased person would need in the afterlife. From their spouses, children, and servants, to animals and even foodstuffs—all were depicted in carvings and paintings on the walls of the tomb and on stone sarcophagi.

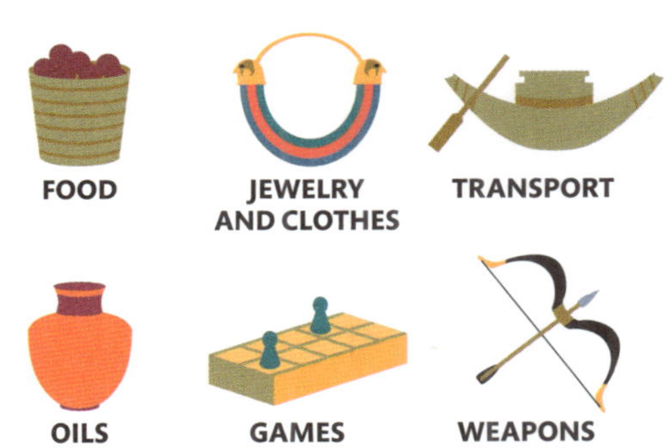

Greek Art

Much of what historians know about the art of Ancient Greece has come through its decorative pottery (paintings existed but have not survived). However, it is predominantly Greek sculpture, which today the world knows mainly through Roman copies alone, that has had a lasting influence on ideas of beauty throughout the following centuries.

Rules of proportion

The sculptors of Ancient Greece's Classical Age tried to calculate the dimensions of the perfect human figure using rules of proportion, writing about how each part of the body should ideally relate to another, and illustrating these perfectly proportioned figures in statues carved from stone or cast in bronze. The ratio of 1:7 between the head of a figure and the rest of its body was considered the ideal by sculptors such as Polykleitos.

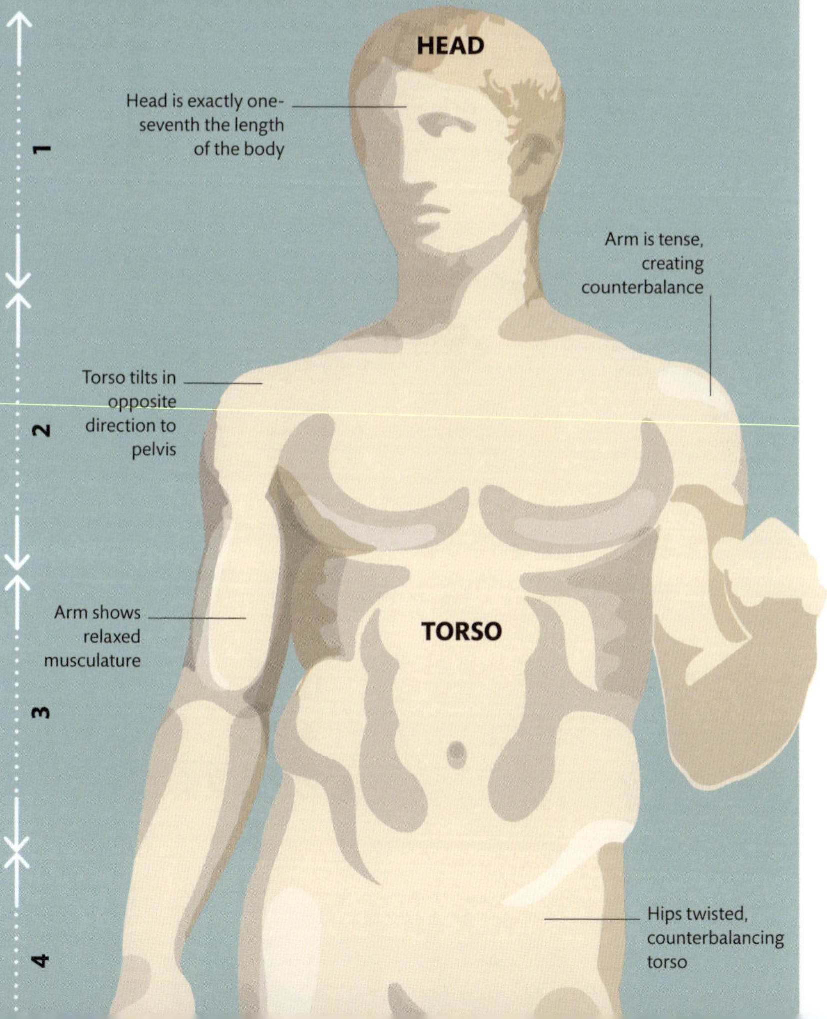

Mathematical beauty

Ancient Greek artists were aiming for mathematical perfection in their portrayal of the human form (see left) and devised formulas for ideal proportion. They also applied this pursuit of perfection to their architecture, seeking beauty, unity, and harmony in the designs of their religious and municipal buildings. This attempt to temper realism with idealized forms ingrained a standardized idea of "classical" beauty in the European consciousness that has influenced art ever since.

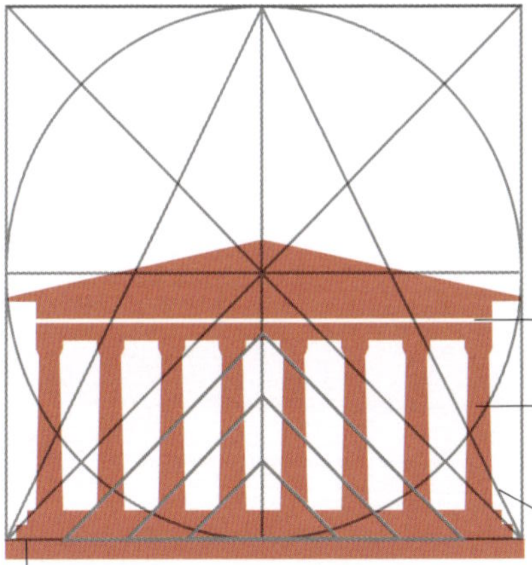

Temple of balance
The Greeks used the rules of proportion to create the Parthenon in Athens. The temple uses the ratio of 9:4 in various areas, and the vertical and horizontal lines create a harmonious design.

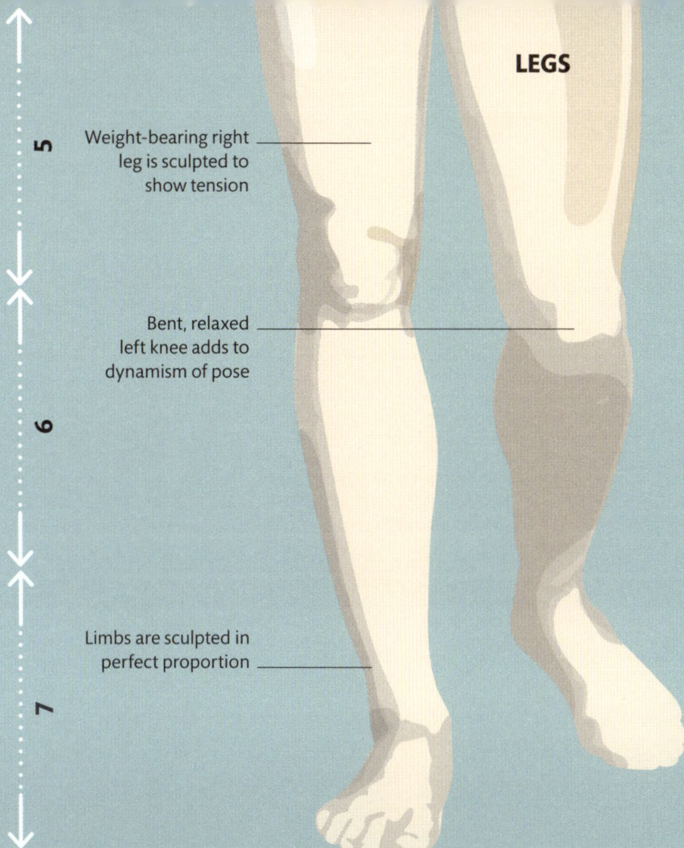

"Doryphoros", Polykleitos (450–440 BCE)
Although the exact details of his "canon" were lost (see opposite), Polykleitos' sculpture "Doryphoros" is a physical demonstration of his system. The body is divided into equal parts all related proportionally, with the figure depicted in a dynamic "contrapposto" pose where the weight is resting on the right leg, leaving the left one free. The counterbalance of the body evoked the idea of a perfectly balanced mind.

WHY HAVE SO FEW ANCIENT GREEK STATUES SURVIVED?

Many Ancient Greek statues were made from bronze, a precious material that was valuable and highly-prized, and so often melted down and recycled.

POLYKLEITOS

Polykleitos was a Greek sculptor who established a "canon" (a series of mathematical laws) for the ideal human proportions. He created the Classical style and was the first sculptor to have a school of followers, all observing his system of balance and proportion.

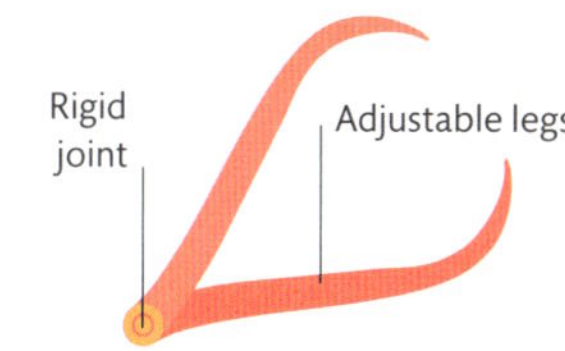

CALLIPERS USED TO MEASURE PROPORTIONS

Terracotta vessels

Pottery made from terracotta was an important part of everyday life, and surviving vases provide a rare insight into Greek culture. Earlier pots were incised with designs; later vases were painted with liquefied clay or "slip." Shapes remained constant for practical reasons—volute kraters for mixing wine and water; hydria for storing water; kylikes for drinking.

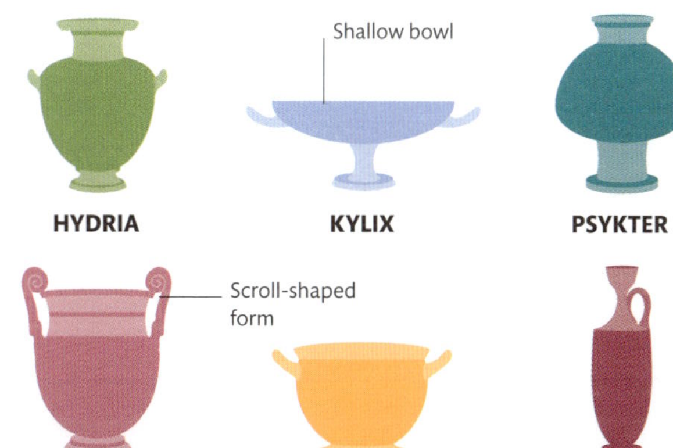

POTTERY WAS THE MOST **COMMON** ITEM **BURIED IN GREEK TOMBS**

Roman Art

Most of what we know of Roman art comes through its statues, though a few rare examples of Roman painting also survive, as well as fragments of mosaic. Some of the best-preserved mosaics have been found in Pompeii, a Roman settlement near Naples that was buried beneath volcanic ash.

Realism and illusionism

The Romans' art was influenced by the Greeks, whose statues they copied, and by the Etruscans—skilled metalworkers who populated central Italy before the rise of the Roman empire. Unlike the sculptures, most Roman paintings are believed to have been lost as they deteriorated over time. What has survived reveals some of the earliest known experiments with illusionism—the attempt to portray subjects as accurately and realistically as possible. This can be seen in the fragments of floor mosaics and wall frescos that have been discovered—particularly in places buried by the eruption of Mount Vesuvius in 79 CE. These offer an insight into Roman tastes and lifestyles and also show a desire for realism in art.

WHAT IS TROMPE-L'ŒIL?

The Romans were among the first to pioneer the technique of trompe-l'œil (French for "deceive the eye"), creating the optical illusion of objects existing in three dimensions.

Buildings in distance give sense of perspective

Ornate pillar helps frame the view beyond

Bronze shield in foreground painted to look shiny

Trees and blue sky make viewer feel like they are looking outside

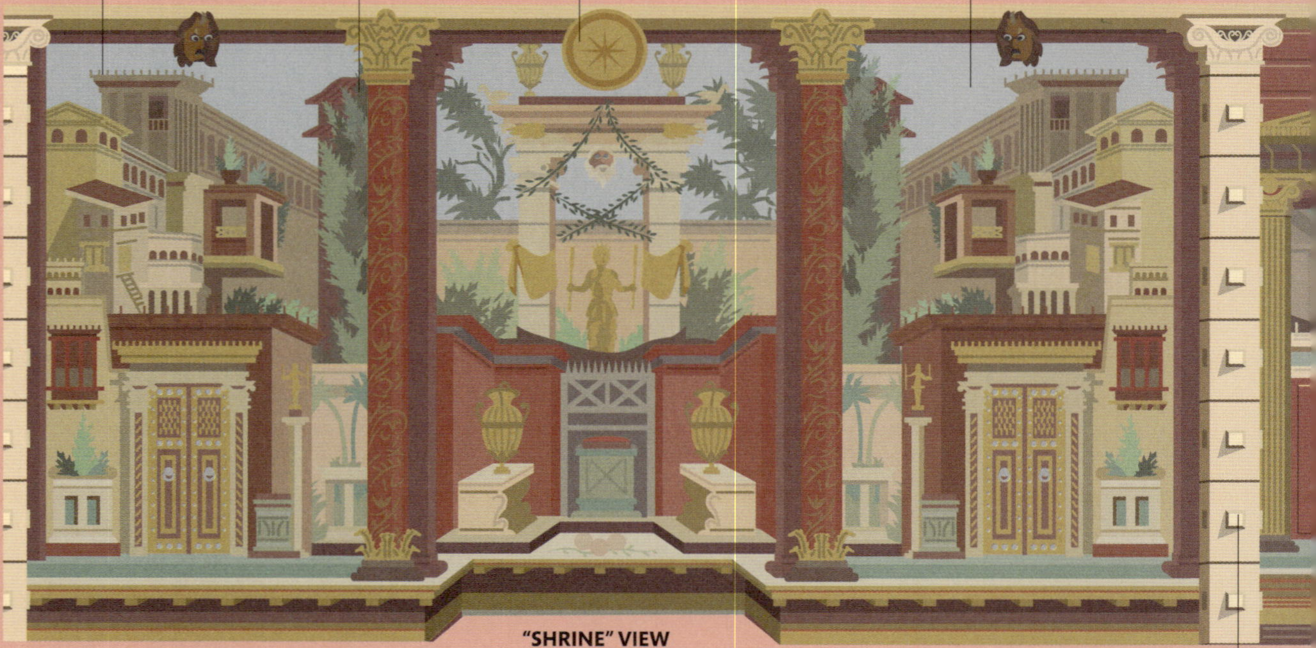

"CITY" VIEW

"SHRINE" VIEW

"CITY" VIEW

Features on column cast realistic shadows

"UNSWEPT FLOOR" MOSAIC

Mosaics made from colored tiles of stone and glass adorned the floors and walls of the villas of the Roman elite. One famous mosaic motif depicts discarded food items, shells, and bones appearing as though they had recently been dropped on the floor—each one casts a shadow for that extra touch of realism.

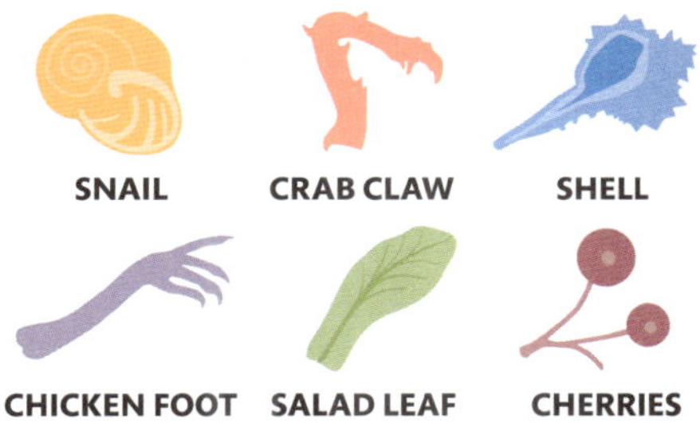

THE ERUPTION OF MOUNT VESUVIUS ALMOST 2,000 YEARS AGO PRESERVED THE FRESCOES UNDER LAYERS OF VOLCANIC ASH AND PUMICE STONE

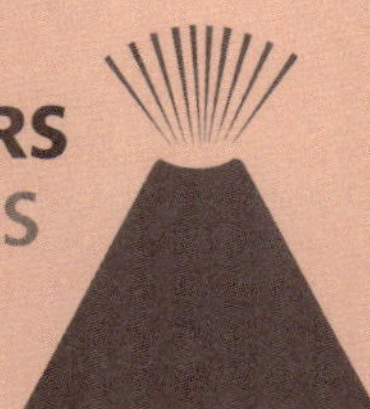

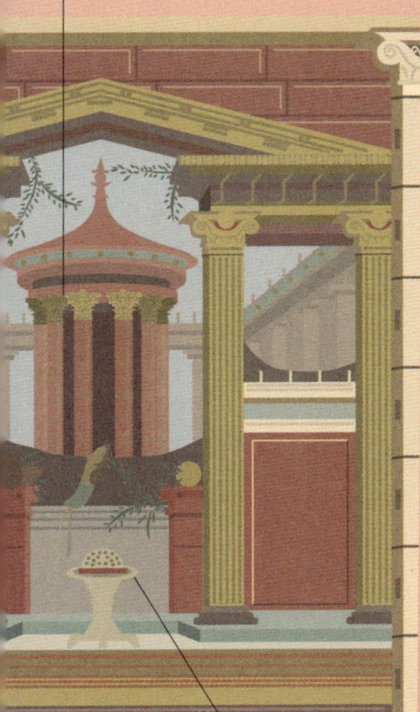

"TEMPLE" VIEW

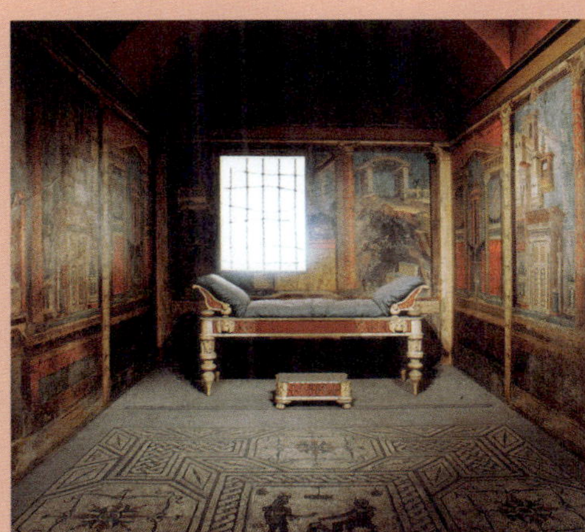

FRESCOS IN THE VILLA OF P. FANNIUS SYNISTOR AT BOSCOREALE, 40–30 BCE

Wall paintings
The volcanic eruption, although disastrous for the occupants of the nearby towns of Pompeii and Herculaneum, played a vital role in preserving key examples of Roman painting. Frescos (see pp.58–59) were found in the villas of the wealthy or in public buildings. They depict exotic feasts or grand vistas, often painted as though viewed through a window.

Cultural influences

With the expansion of the Roman Empire, Roman art began to be influenced by the styles and art forms of different cultures. Statues reflected the Greek desire to emulate physical perfection, while portraiture took on a realism often seen in Etruscan art.

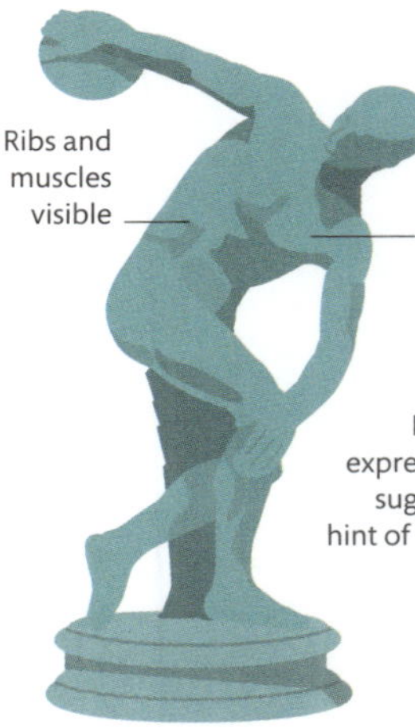

ROMAN STATUE OF GREEK ATHLETE

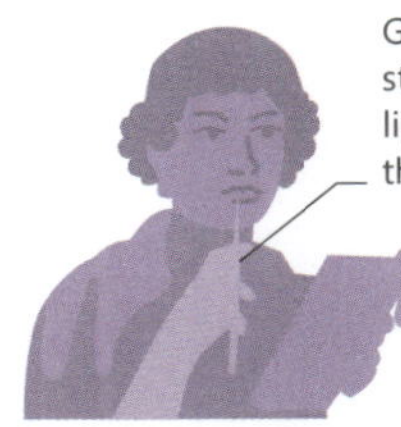

ROMAN PAINTING OF THOUGHTFUL GIRL

Different styles
These examples of Roman art show three different approaches to depicting the human form: the perfection of the Greek-inspired statue; the expression of the girl; and the realistic evening shadow of the Etruscan boy.

ETRUSCAN BRONZE OF BOY TITLED "EVENING SHADOW"

West African Art

West Africa covers a vast area of many differing countries—which today include Nigeria, Benin, and Mali—with a rich variety of cultures, each with their own complex traditions of art. Much of this art takes the form of sacred statues created over the past 1,000 years.

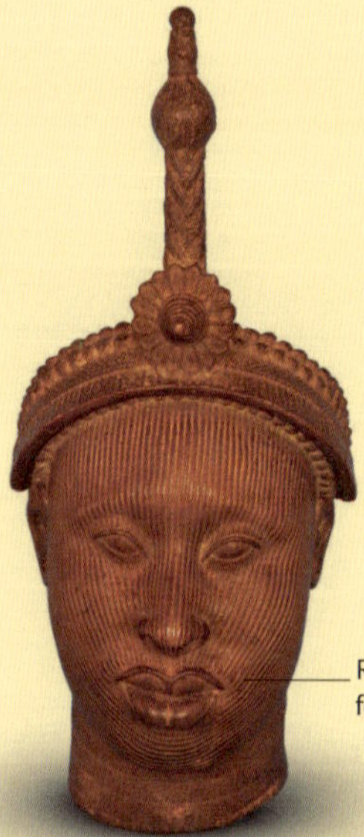

Olokun head
The ancient Yoruba and Benin kingdoms of Nigeria created a tradition of royal art that venerated the heads of ancestors, past monarchs, and gods. Their features were captured in naturalistic detail, first in clay, then later in a copper-alloy.

Sacred statues

The materials used in the art of West Africa reflect its role as a center of trade for centuries. Its wealth of stone, iron ore, and sumptuous hardwoods led many of its cultures to produce figurative statuary, which were integral to the daily lives of the community. Many West African statues depict the human figure, from leaders and skilled individuals of great prowess, to archetypal male and female sculptures with idealized physical attributes. Many of these were sacred items used to connect to a spirit world and were continuously altered or added to over many years of ritual use—rubbed with oil; adorned with fabric, beads, and amulets; pierced with blades; or worn down through touch as a sign of devotion.

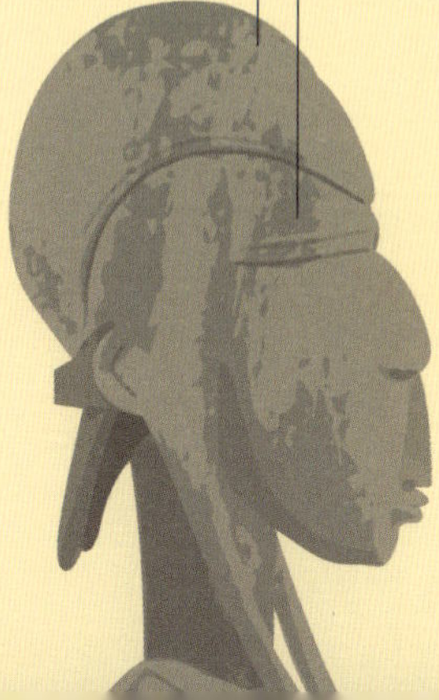

THE **OLOKUN HEAD** WAS USED IN 1973 AS A **SYMBOL** FOR THE **ALL-AFRICA GAMES**

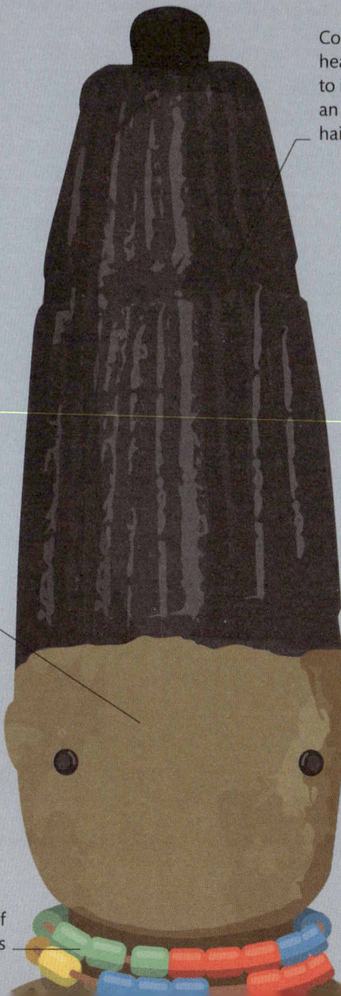

Ere ibeji figure
This sacred, wooden figure originates from southwestern Nigeria and represents the soul of a deceased child that needs caring for as if they were still alive. They are ritually washed, fed, adorned with jewelry, and carried.

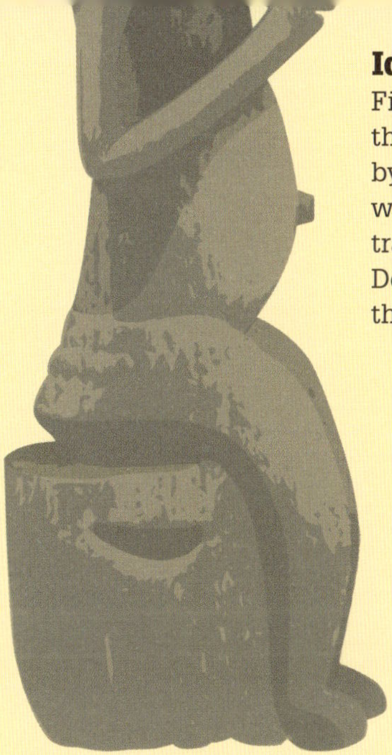

SEATED WOODEN STATUE CARVED BY BAMANA PEOPLE

Idealized role

Figurative sculptures of couples, typified by the Gwandusu and Gwantigi statues produced by the Bamana people of southern Mali, show women and men in the prime of life, fulfilling traditional roles of rearing children and hunting. Depicted with stout bodies and elongated heads, the figures represent cultural ideals of beauty.

WHY WERE SACRED STATUES CREATED?

Often statues were commissioned by parents who had lost a child so that the child's soul would be cared for in the next life.

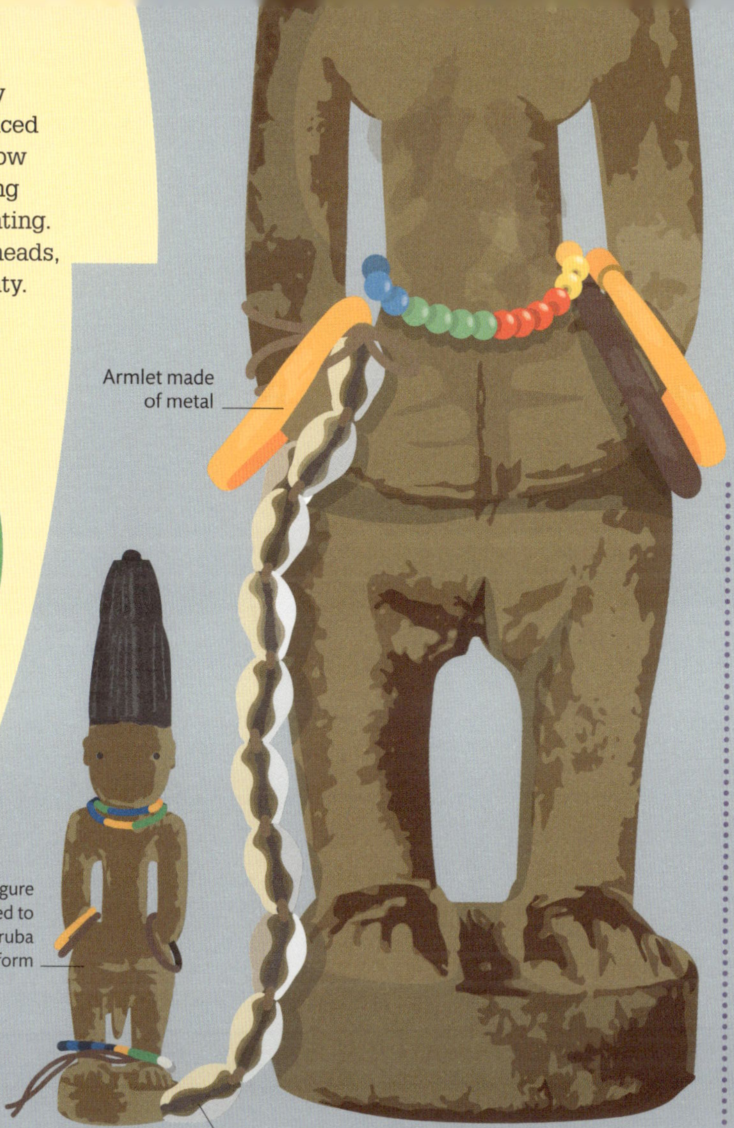

MALE ERE IBEJI FIGURE

FEMALE ERE IBEJI FIGURE

NIGERIAN BRONZE

The craftspeople of Igbo-Ukwu, an ancient culture of the Lower Niger (now Nigeria), became expert casters around the 9th or 10th century CE. They used the "lost latex" technique to create decorative swirl-patterned pots. Designs were sculpted in latex before being coated in clay to make an impression that, once the latex was removed, could be cast with molten bronze. Pots were cast in sections, with intricate designs of ropework and knots.

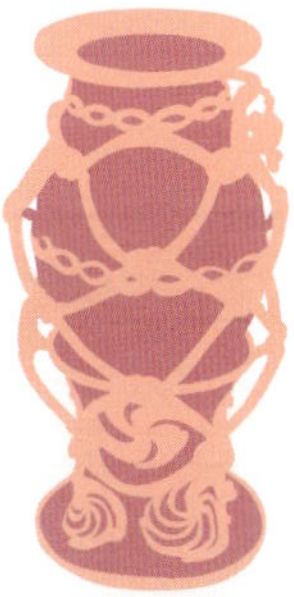

ROPED POT OF IGBO-UKWU

Indian Art

The art of the Indian subcontinent reflects a multitude of overlapping territories and cultural influences. Various different Indian art forms exist, including paintings, textiles, and sculptures. Much of it is influenced by the world's major religions originating in South Asia.

Divine attributes

In the art of many Indian faiths, the aim is to capture idealized characteristics of a god or goddess, which accentuate their divine attributes and communicate their story in vivid detail. A frequent element of this is a sensuous, stylized approach to the human figure that uses symbolic exaggeration, elaborate design, and ornamentation. The goddess Lakshmi, for example, is often shown with four hands, each representing an aspect of Hindu life. Sculptures may be carved in stone or cast in bronze and are decorated with ornaments as offerings to the gods.

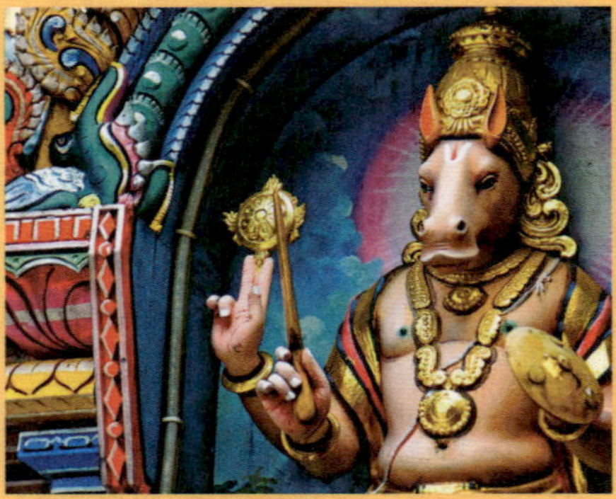

Temple decoration
Over the centuries, Indian temples and sacred sites have been adorned by many religious symbols and deities, such as this Hindu sculpture of Hayagriva.

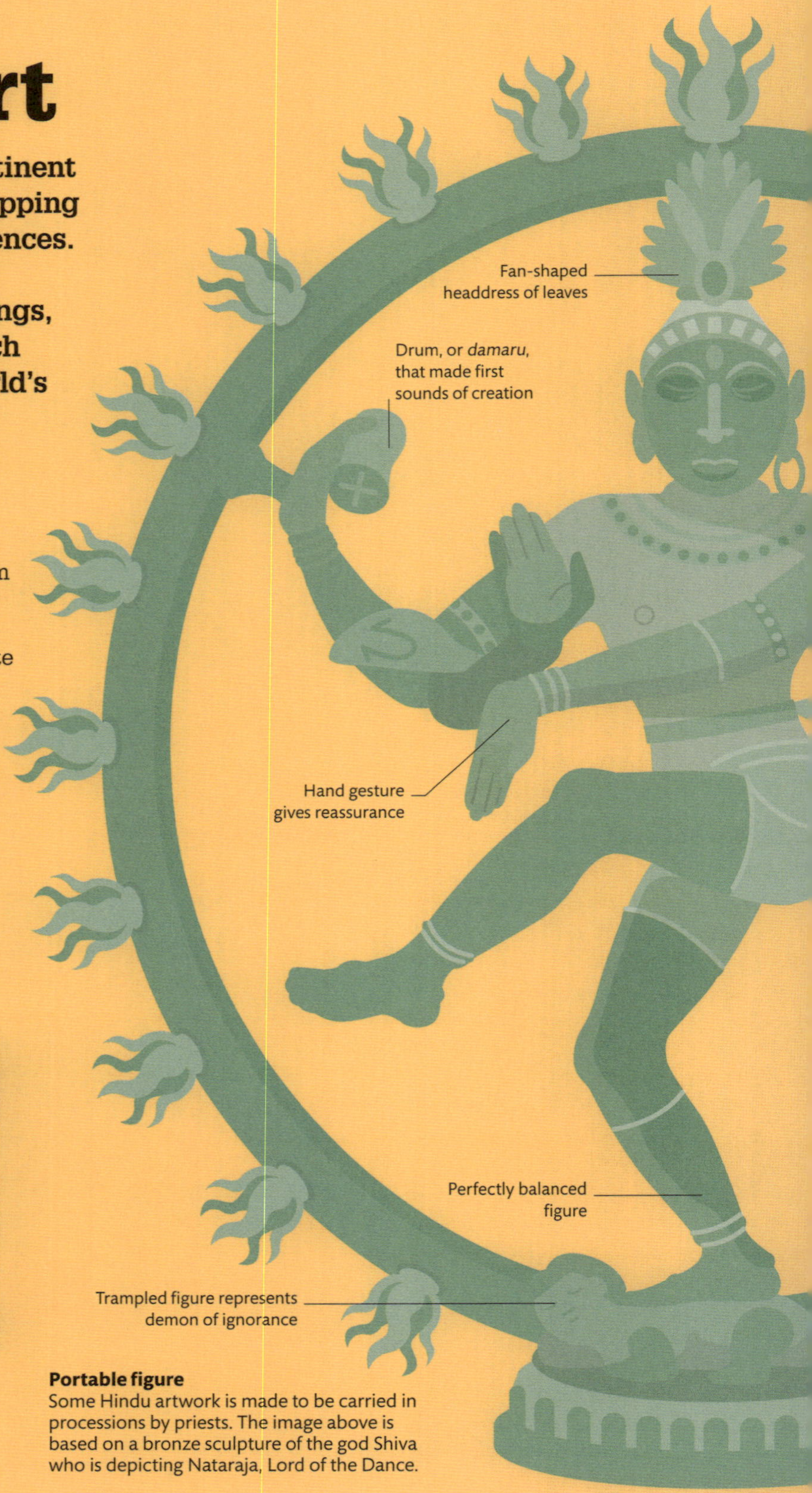

Portable figure
Some Hindu artwork is made to be carried in processions by priests. The image above is based on a bronze sculpture of the god Shiva who is depicting Nataraja, Lord of the Dance.

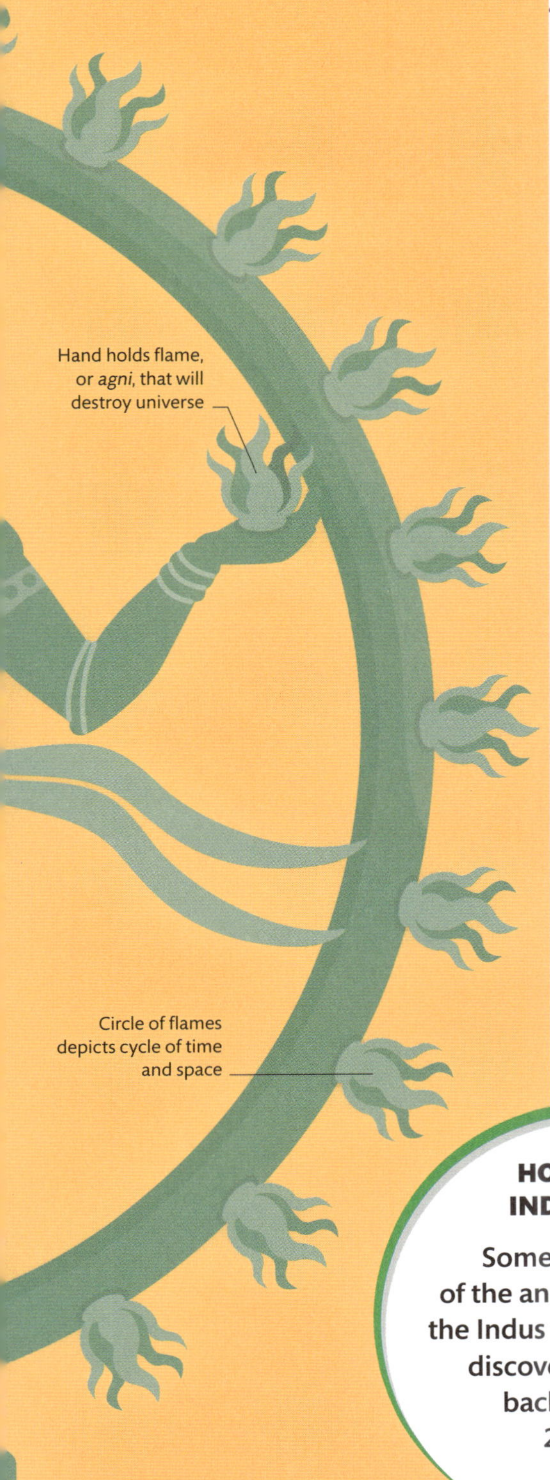

Art in Indian religions

A multitude of philosophies, deities, and technologies are expressed through Indian art (see pp.80–81). Religious artworks are often the focus of worship, teaching stories to believers via images and helping understand a world beyond the material. Images follow specific descriptions of gods and their cosmic world from religious texts.

Sikh art
Emerging in the 1400s in Punjab (around northern India), Sikh art portrays the teachings of its founder, Guru Nanak (1469–1539), usually in the form of brightly colored paintings, often in miniature.

Buddhist art
Mandalas are complex patterns that were traditionally used by Buddhist monks to aid meditation. As trade routes developed around India, this Buddhist art form was introduced to countries in the Far East.

Jain art
One of the oldest Indian religions, Jain temple art focuses on its tenets of nonattachment, nonviolence, and belief in the multifaceted reality of life. Other forms include murals, illustrations, and mandalas.

Hindu art
Hindu art revolves around the belief in a personal connection with the divine, concentrated through the devotional depiction of gods and goddesses, manifestations of the one true God, the Brahman.

BRIGHT COLOR IN INDIAN ART TRADITIONALLY IMPLIES NATURE

HOW OLD IS INDIAN ART?

Some sacred seals of the ancient cultures of the Indus valley have been discovered that date back to at least 2500 BCE.

GUPTA BUDDHAS

Around 450 CE, during the Gupta Empire that covered northern, central, and western India, artworks from that time portrayed Buddha with downcast eyes, resting features, and short, curly hair—presenting an image of peace and calm reflection.

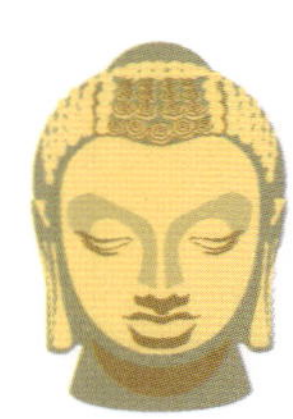

HEAD OF BUDDHA

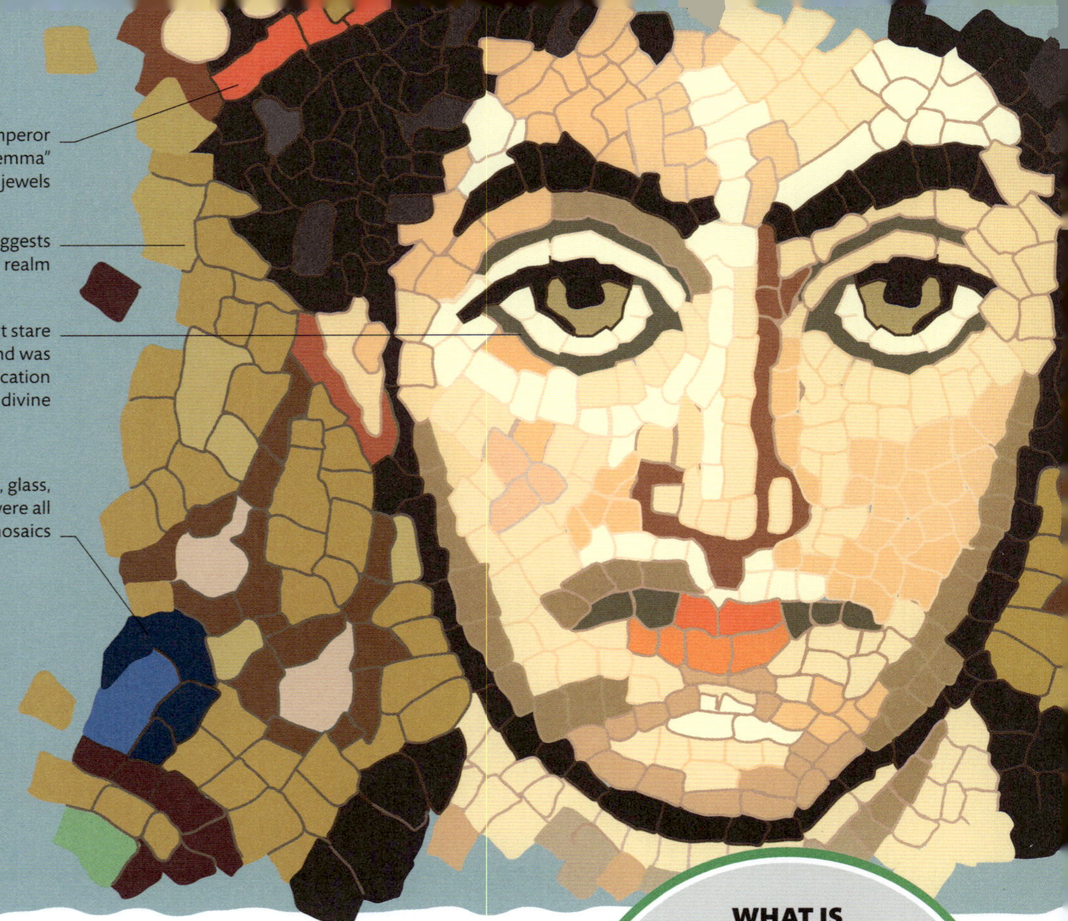

The mosaic shows the emperor wearing a crown or "stemma" adorned with jewels

A gold surround suggests a heavenly realm

An intense, direct stare engaged the viewer and was thought to aid communication with the divine

Mother-of-pearl, glass, and gold leaf were all used for mosaics

Mosaic art
Earlier Byzantine art bypassed the controversy surrounding prohibited "graven" images (idols worshipped as gods) by creating mosaics and decorating cathedrals with vivid, gold-studded scenes of religious or imperial subjects.

Byzantine Art

After the splitting of the Roman Empire and the loss of its western territories, the eastern city of Byzantium, became a "New Rome"—the center of a Byzantine Empire that fostered a wealth of religious art controlled and funded by the Christian church.

Veneration art

Following the conversion of the Roman emperors of Byzantium to Christianity beginning c.300 CE, the city was renamed Constantinople (modern-day Istanbul). A new religious art spread throughout the empire, involving the production of icons of Christ and other figures for veneration in churches, cathedrals, and later in the home. The icons followed strict rules, and despite earlier Roman attempts at realism, they became more stylized over time, with elongated hands, flowing bodies, and penitent facial expressions.

WHAT IS AN ICON?

From the Greek "eikon" (image), icons were sacred images in various media intended to be conduits that channeled worshippers to Christ or the saints.

HAND RAISED **FIGURE WITH HALO** **FRONTAL POSE**

Rules of depiction
Icons are copies of an original image, believed to have been made before the subjects themselves. As a result, artists followed strict rules dictating pose, gesture, and more.

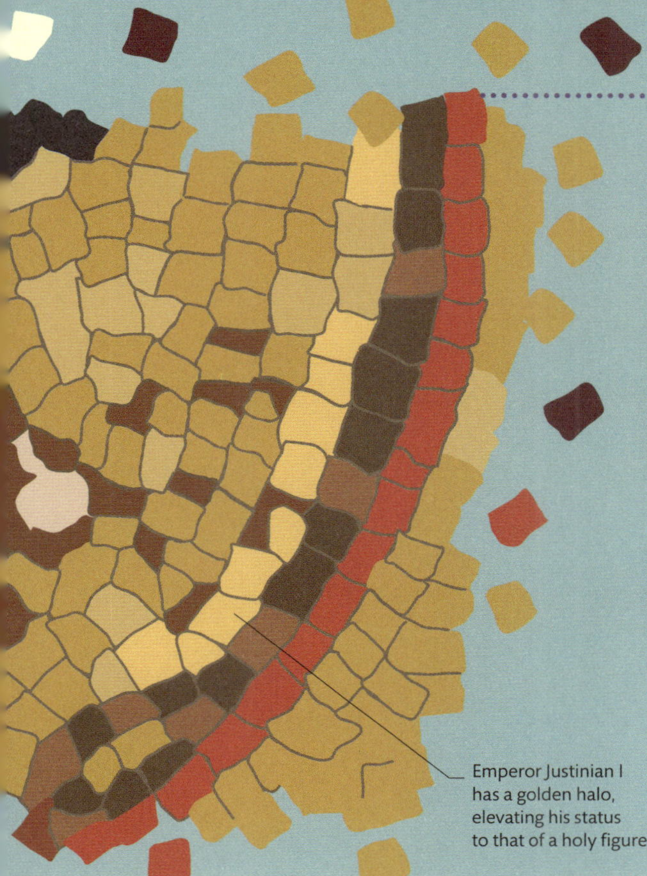

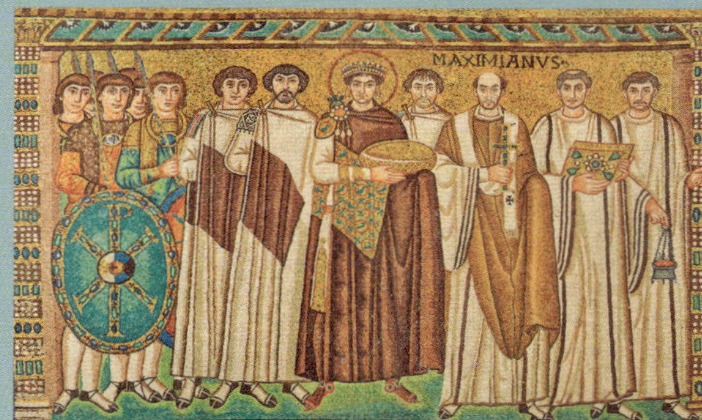

MOSAIC, SAN VITALE, ITALY (6TH CENTURY CE)

CONTROVERSIAL IMAGES

The veneration of icons split the church, causing fierce debates, and the Byzantine Empire witnessed periods of iconoclasm in the 8th and 9th centuries CE ("image breaking") during which icons were banned or destroyed.

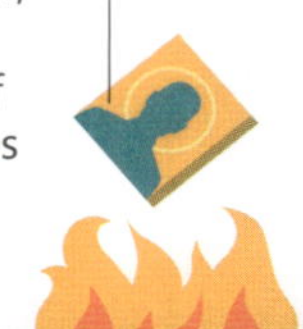

Encaustic technique

Some early Byzantine artists used encaustic, wax-based painting that involved applying a mixture of pigment and melted beeswax to wooden panels. The resulting surface was heavy and thickly colored, with a luminous quality akin to oil paint, and its matte finish could be polished to a shine.

ENCAUSTIC COMES FROM THE GREEK WORD **ENKAUSTIKOS** MEANING **"TO HEAT OR BURN IN"**

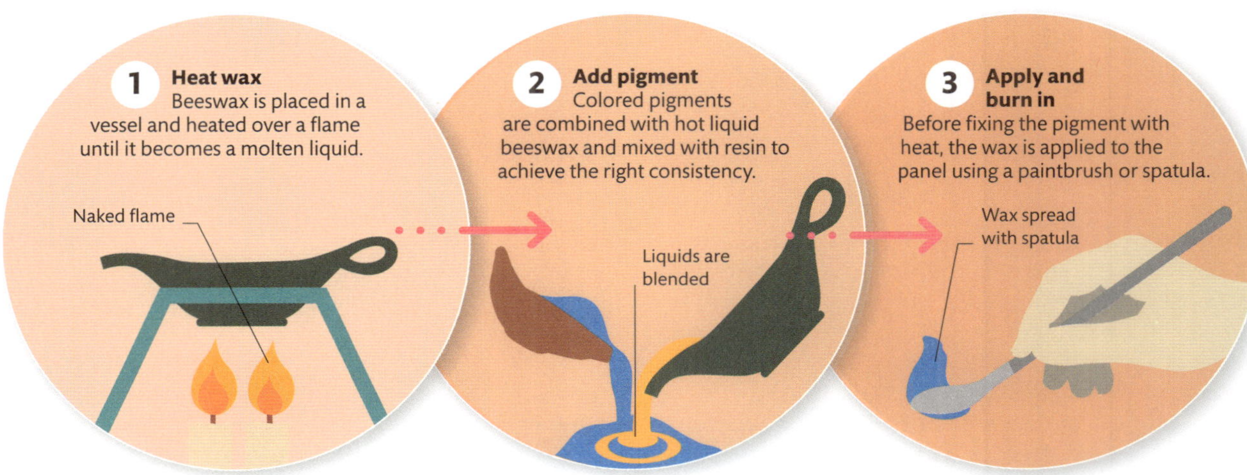

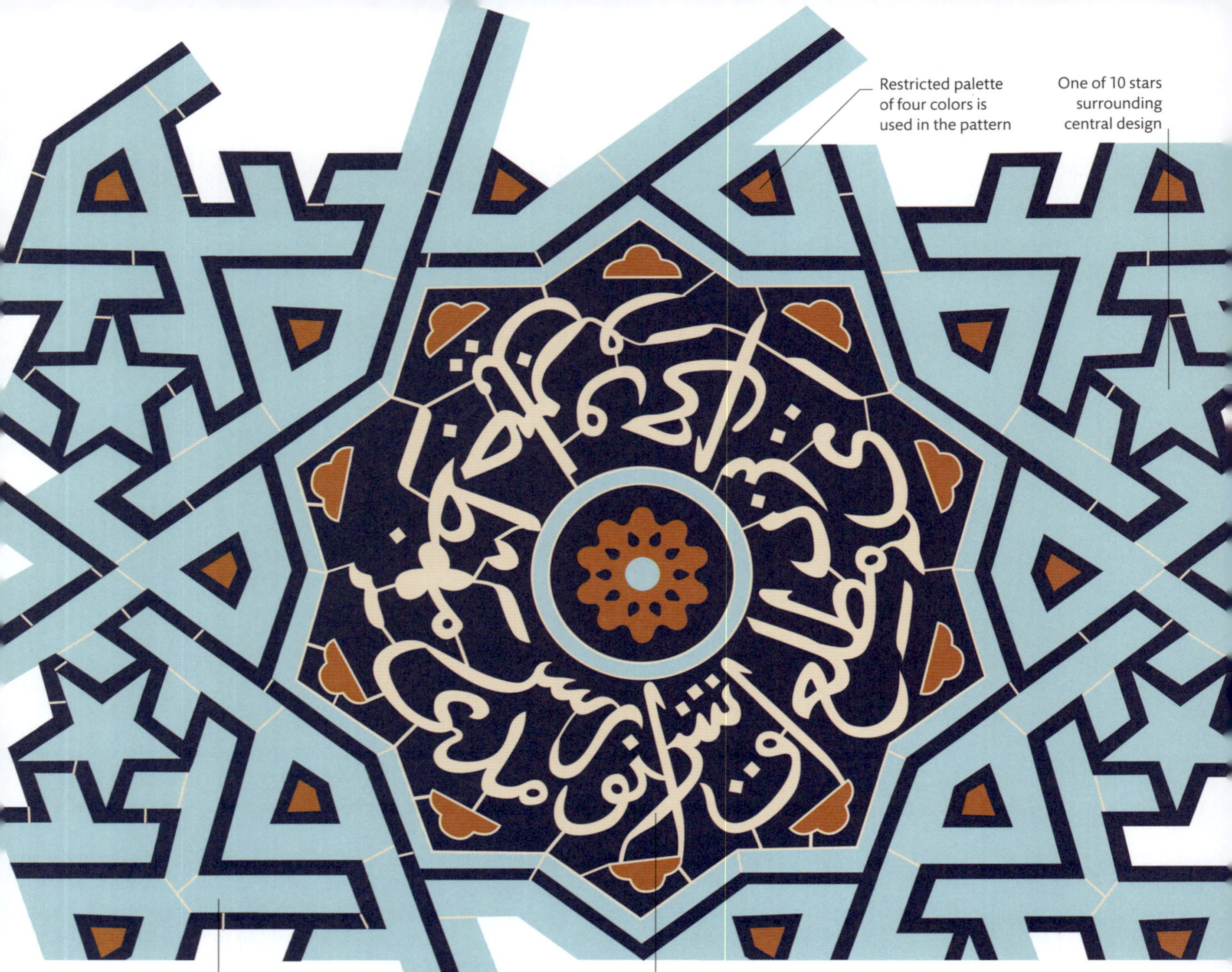

Mosque tiling
Many mosques contain excellent examples of Islamic mosaics, created using brightly colored ceramic tiles laid in complex, repeating geometric patterns and floral designs.

Favored art forms

As Islam expanded to new territories and absorbed ancient centers of culture, the Islamic world became a powerhouse for intellectual thought—mathematics, science, and philosophy all flourished from the early medieval period (c.8th century CE) onward. These scholarly pursuits influenced Islamic art, which was expressed through art forms that included calligraphy, ceramics, and jewelry, as well as textiles such as carpets.

Calligraphy
Over the centuries, calligraphic motifs became steadily more intricate and ornate to the point of abstraction, with artists striving to achieve beauty of overall design and harmony of color.

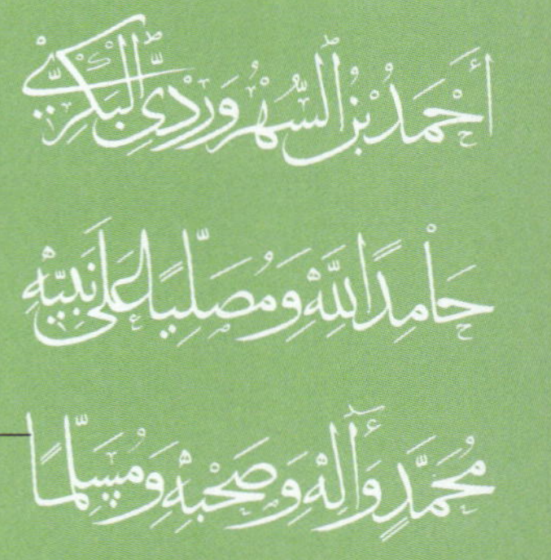

Islamic Art

Produced from the 7th century CE onward, Islamic art soon developed its own distinctive style and conventions across various disciplines. As Islam spread, it assimilated cultural influences from the Middle East and beyond.

Use of pattern

Although not specifically prohibited in Islam's holy book the Quran, for many periods of Islamic art the depiction of people was banned. This resulted in artists creating imagery that did not revolve around depictions of the human body, as can be seen in much Western art. Instead, Islamic art featured abstract, geometric designs of intense colors, often based on interlocking polygons; natural motifs suggestive of flora and fauna, often referred to as arabesque design; and religious text.

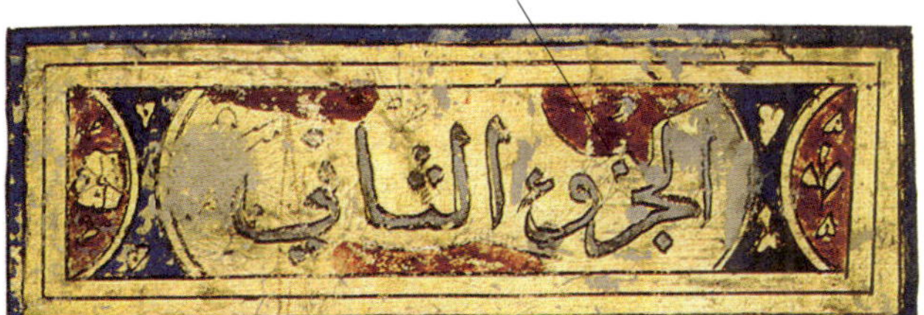

Detail from the Quran, 14th century
Designs based around calligraphic text were among the art forms held in highest regard in Islamic art. Often passages from the Quran were embellished with ornate decorative patterns.

MUGHAL MINIATURES

The courtly art of the Islamic Mughal dynasty of India, which ruled large parts of the subcontinent from the 16th to the 19th century, moved away from abstraction to depict human forms in bold, vivid colors in miniature paintings, as illustrations in manuscripts and books, or as stand-alone works of art. Influenced by Persian paintings, Mughal miniatures were exquisitely detailed works—fine lines were painted using a brush made from a single hair.

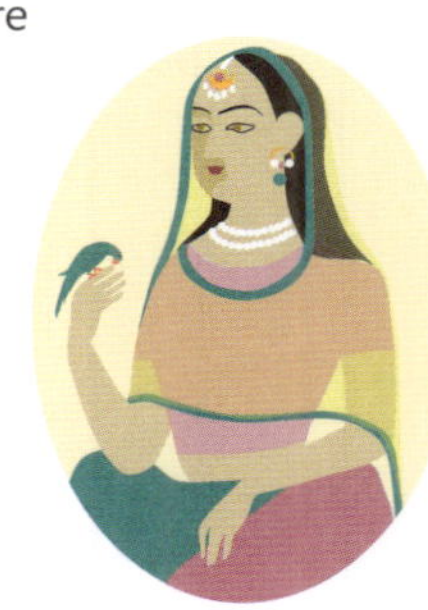

MINIATURE PORTRAIT OF AN EMPRESS

WHY ARE PEOPLE OFTEN NOT DEPICTED IN ISLAMIC ART?

The Qur'an forbids idolatry, which many people have interpreted as banning the production of images of living things.

Ceramics
Much Islamic pottery features traditional blue-and-white color schemes. Early Islamic potters made innovations in the glazing and painting of ceramics.

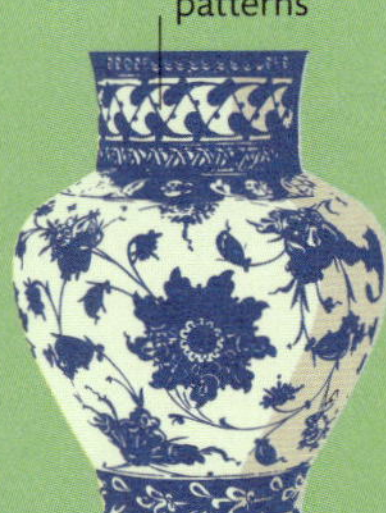

Jewelry
Islamic jewelry is often lightweight, hollow, and boxlike and is typically made from gold. It may feature filigree work (when a fine piece of the precious metal is twisted into curly, arabesque motifs).

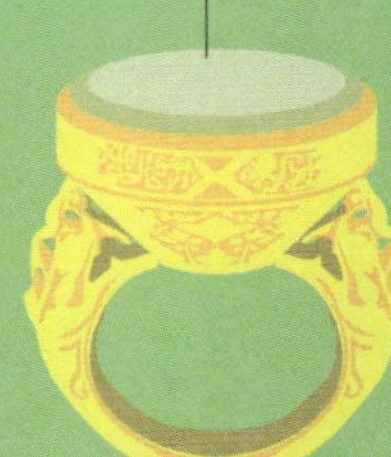

FROM C.**1540 CE,** THE **ARDABIL CARPET** IS ONE OF THE OLDEST **EXISTING ISLAMIC CARPETS**

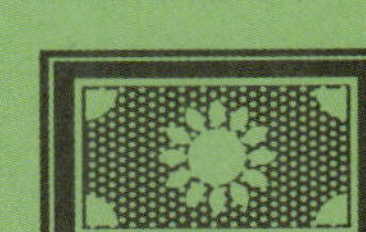

Chinese Art

Chinese civilization is responsible for a range of artistic innovations that have shaped not just its own art but also that of other cultures around the world.

Rich tradition

Art in China has flourished since prehistoric times and has seen the development and refinement of technologies such as paper, ceramics, inks, silk, and more. The religious and philosophical influences of Confucianism, Daoism, and Buddhism have influenced the style of many of the nation's artworks created over the last two millennia, while its materials, inventions, and artifacts spread to the West through the interlacing trade routes of the Silk Road. A few examples of Chinese art are shown here.

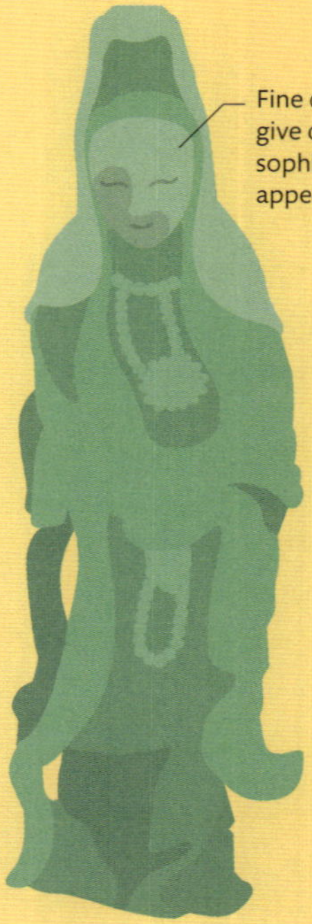

Jade
Also known as "The Emperor's Stone," jade is a rare and highly prized material in China. Jade ornaments and jewelry are venerated in Chinese art, its hardness and durability representing longevity and immortality.

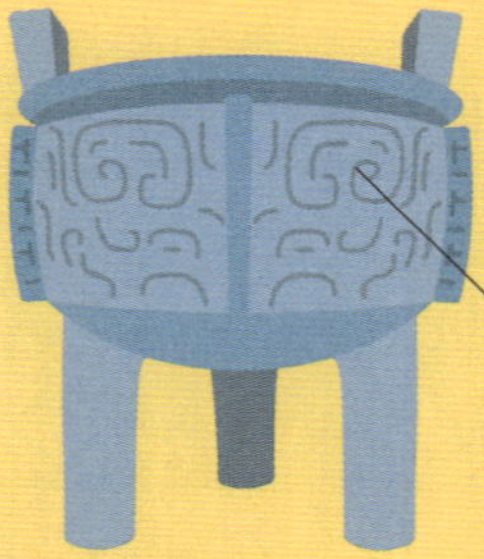

Bronze Age art
During the Chinese Bronze Age (2000–256 BCE), many Ding (ritual vessels) were made for the aristocracy to communicate with their ancestors.

Porcelain
Chinese porcelain, with its characteristic blue and white glazing, was highly sought after in Europe throughout the Renaissance and beyond, a demand exacerbated by China's bans on exports in the 14th to 17th centuries.

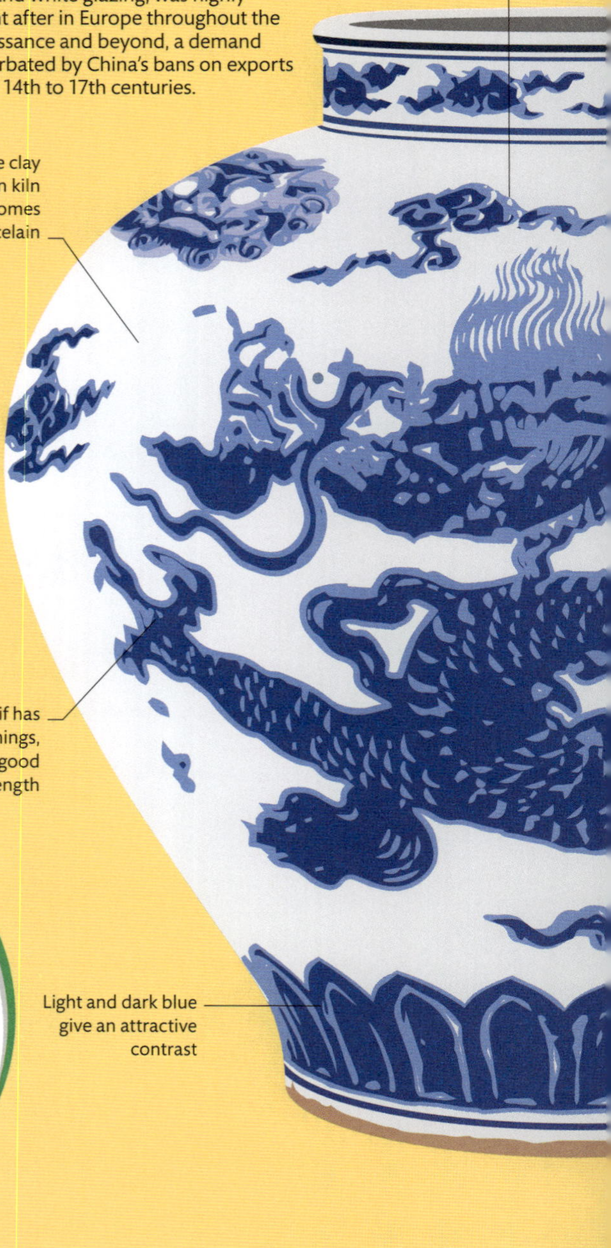

WHY ARE CHINESE CERAMICS BLUE AND WHITE?

Cobalt oxide pigment was first used for Chinese porcelain in the Tang dynasty (618–907 CE). The color can withstand the high temperatures needed to fire porcelain.

THE TERRACOTTA ARMY WARRIORS WERE BURIED WITH REAL BRONZE WEAPONS

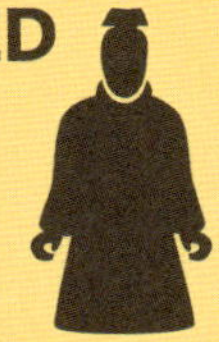

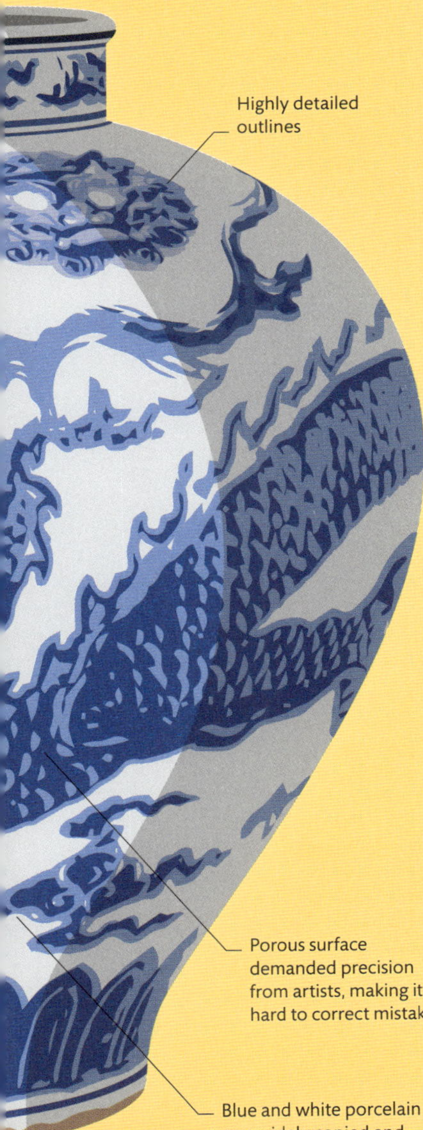

Highly detailed outlines

Porous surface demanded precision from artists, making it hard to correct mistakes

Blue and white porcelain was widely copied and by potters worldwide

Ink brushstrokes

Painting has a particularly revered place in Chinese art, dating back over 2,500 years. Subjects have varied over time, but the methods and materials have remained relatively constant, mainly painted on silk, and later paper scrolls, using black Mo ink.

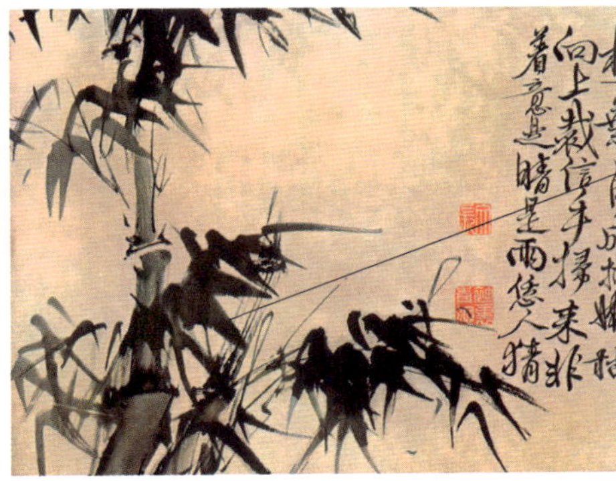

The art of calligraphy was intertwined with painting

Delicate brushstrokes of ink evoke rustling bamboo leaves

"Bamboo," Xu Wei (c.1540)
The most valued paintings, intended for contemplation in private, were considered on par with the greatest works of poetry and philosophy.

Brushes
The traditional Chinese painting brush is made from bamboo, with animal-hair bristles, and comes in many shapes and styles for different uses.

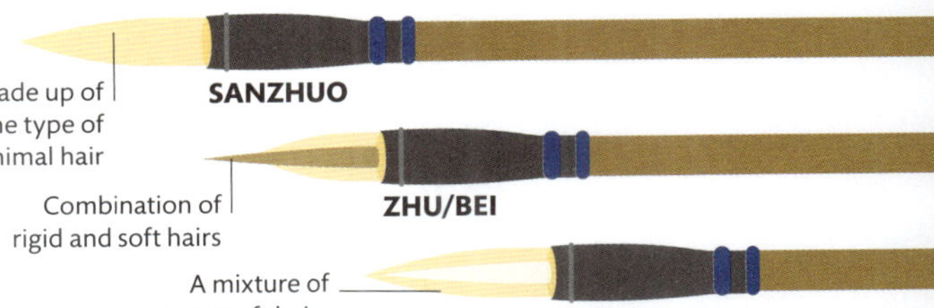

Made up of one type of animal hair

SANZHUO

Combination of rigid and soft hairs

ZHU/BEI

A mixture of very soft hairs

JINHAO

Style of painting
Chinese painting developed different schools or styles over time, including the "boned" style, which refers to outlines, and the "boneless" style, which relies on washes of ink to suggest form.

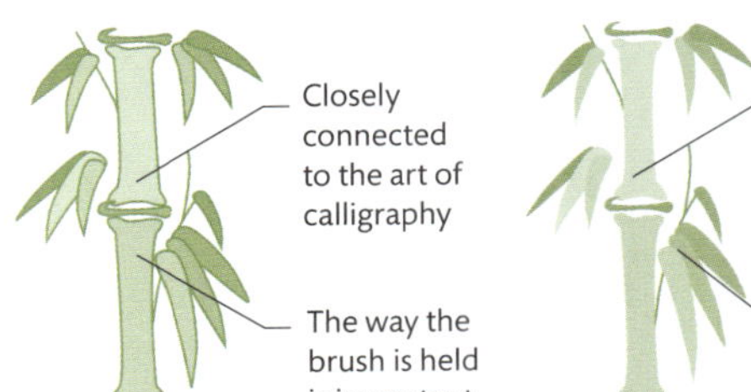

Closely connected to the art of calligraphy

The way the brush is held is important

BONED

Loose brush marks create shapes

No solid lines are visible

BONELESS

TERRACOTTA ARMY

An insight into the development of human sculpture in China was revealed in 1974 with the discovery of the Terracotta Army, a group of terracotta sculptures buried in 210–209 BCE next to Emperor Qin Shi Huang, to serve him in the afterlife. Thousands of statues show a rare attention to lifelike detail.

Japanese Art

The people of Japan developed a rich artistic tradition over thousands of years. Inspired by the native Shinto religion, they combined an esteem for exceptional craftsmanship with a deep spiritual connection to the landscape.

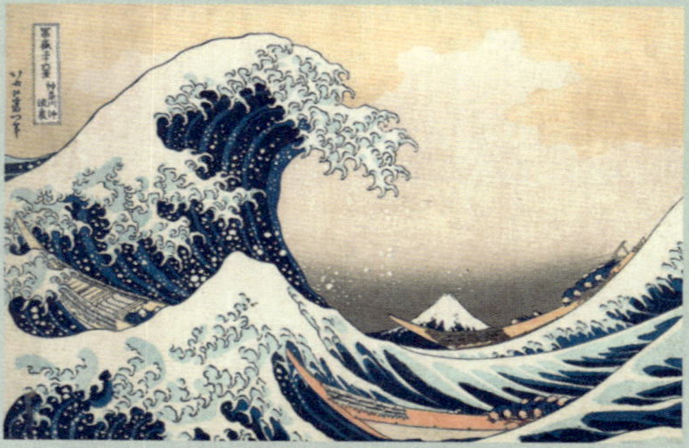

"THE GREAT WAVE OFF KANAGAWA" KATSUSHIKA HOKUSAI (1831)

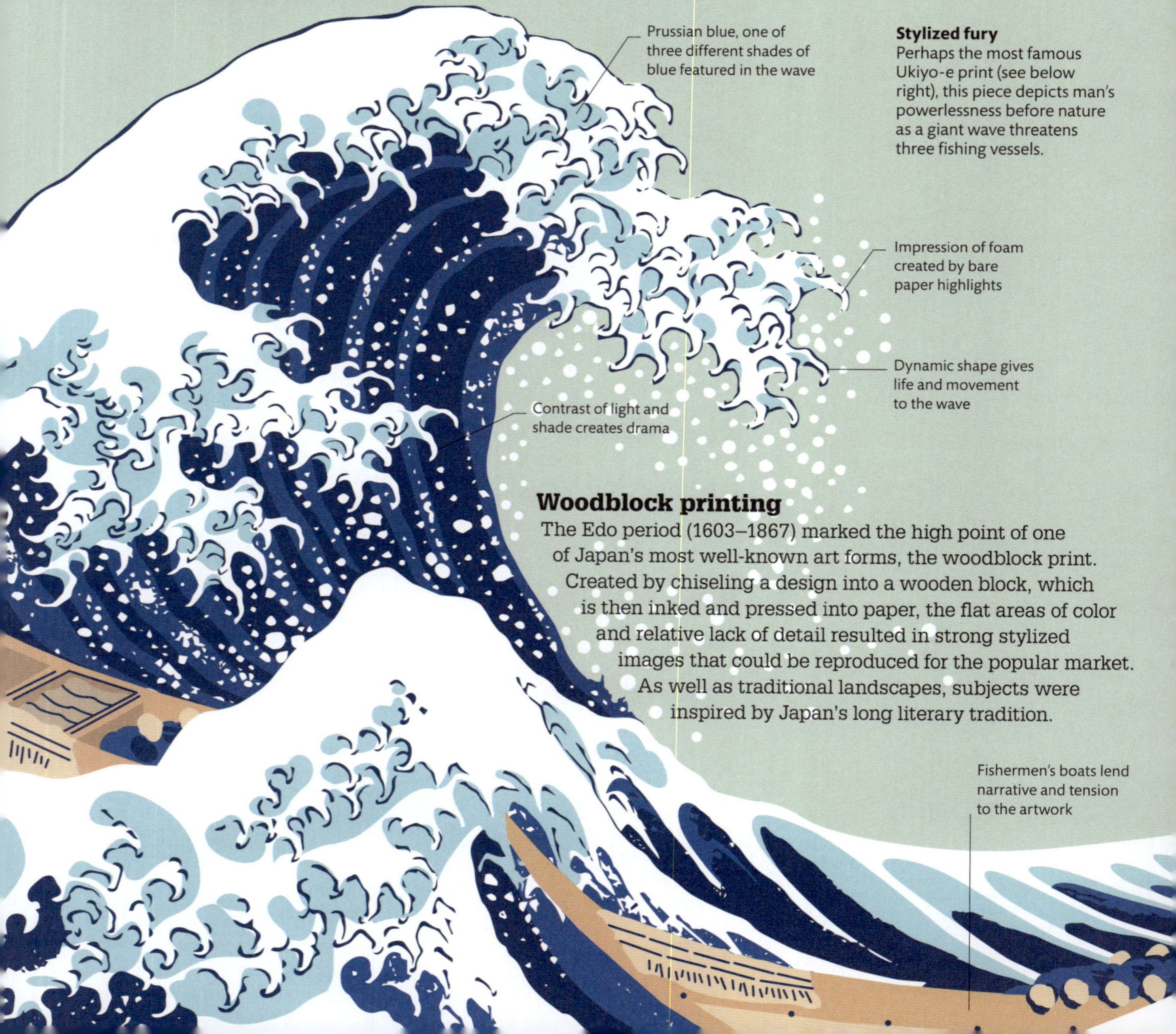

Stylized fury
Perhaps the most famous Ukiyo-e print (see below right), this piece depicts man's powerlessness before nature as a giant wave threatens three fishing vessels.

Woodblock printing

The Edo period (1603–1867) marked the high point of one of Japan's most well-known art forms, the woodblock print. Created by chiseling a design into a wooden block, which is then inked and pressed into paper, the flat areas of color and relative lack of detail resulted in strong stylized images that could be reproduced for the popular market. As well as traditional landscapes, subjects were inspired by Japan's long literary tradition.

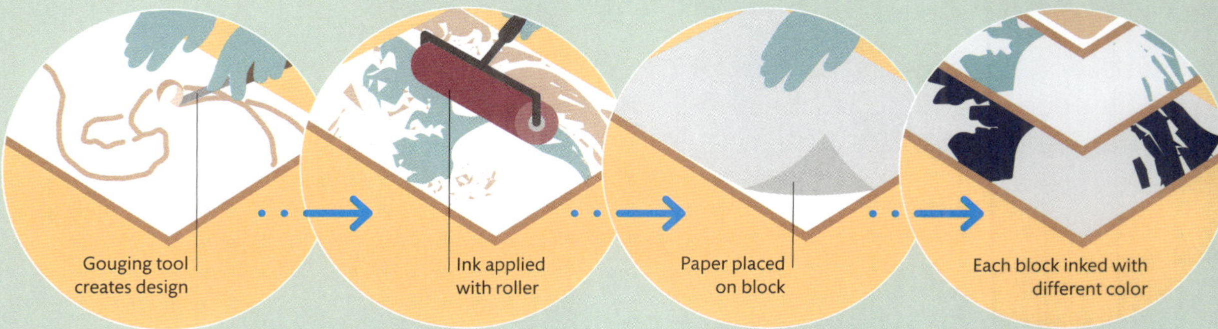

1 Each woodblock carefully carved
The artist uses chisels and other tools to cut the design into the woodblock, leaving raised areas to be inked. They repeat the process with each block.

2 Ink applied to carved surface
Using a roller, the artist spreads thick printing ink in a uniform layer over the first woodblock, leaving the recessed (cut out) areas blank.

3 Paper positioned over woodblock surface
The artist carefully lines up and positions the paper over the first block. They use weights or a press to make sure the ink makes contact with the paper.

4 Process repeated with each color
They repeat the process with a different woodblock for each color, which can then be layered on the same sheet of paper to build up the complete image.

Influences and heritage

Over the centuries, Japan's art absorbed some external cultural influences, despite its long periods of isolation. Monochrome ink painting shows the influence of Chinese art, with Japanese painters combining and refining Chinese techniques, using splashed ink and subtle washes to create Zen-inspired misty landscapes. Ceramics have been a major part of Japanese culture from prehistoric times, with some of the complex coil pots being produced by the Jômon people of Honshu as early as 2500 BCE.

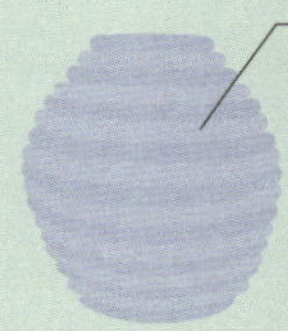

Coil pot
For millennia, Japanese potters made coil pots by coiling up rolled clay from a base in a spiral, then smoothing down the sides before firing.

8,000
THE ESTIMATED NUMBER OF **GREAT WAVE PRINTS** MADE IN THE **EDO** PERIOD

WHAT WAS UKIYO-E?

The Ukiyo-e ("floating world") school was a bold style of prints and paintings that catered for the hedonistic, newly affluent population of Edo (Tokyo) in the 17th–19th century.

ISOLATIONISM AND OPENING UP

By the mid-19th century, Japan had opened up to international trade after hundreds of years of self-imposed isolation, resulting in massive demand in Europe and the US for Japanese prints and other artworks. The craze was known as Japonisme, and it influenced many Western artists, including the Post-Impressionists (see pp.194–195).

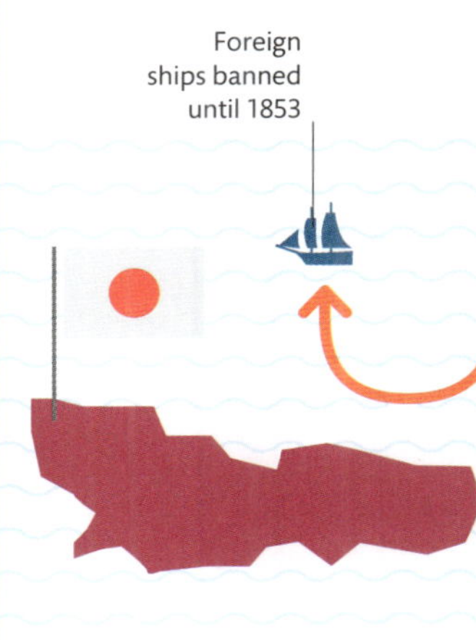

Mesoamerican Art

Mesoamerican art describes the art of the indigenous people of the Caribbean, and North, Central, and South America from c.13,000 BCE to the late 15th and early 16th centuries CE.

Aztecs

The Aztecs flourished from 1300 and grew to prominence in the 15th and 16th centuries. Although often viewed as a whole, they consisted of several distinct peoples, and their territory was organized into city-states. Aztec ideas about art and crafts (*toltecayotl*) spread via military conquests and trade expansion. These arts included writing, painting, sculpture, mosaics, ceramics, featherwork, and metalwork. Their capital city, Tenochtitlan, featured imposing buildings adorned with dramatic monumental sculptures; other artwork inclued masks and jewelry made of gold, silver, semiprecious stones, and shells.

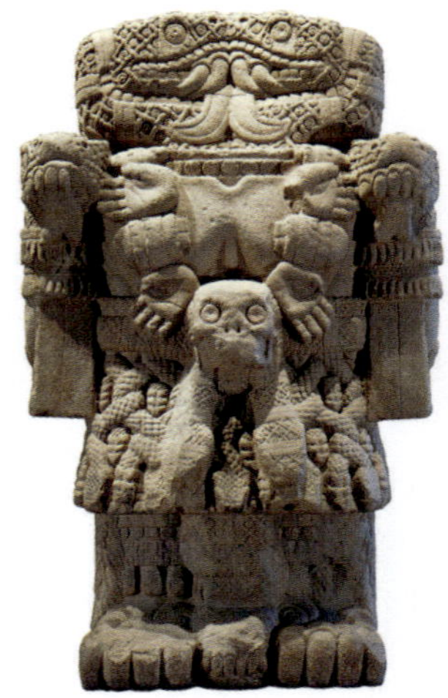

STATUE OF COATLICUE

Aztec snake goddess
Coatlicue represented Mother Earth. Her name translates as "the one with the skirt of serpents." Representations of gods and goddesses were frequent subject matter in Aztec art.

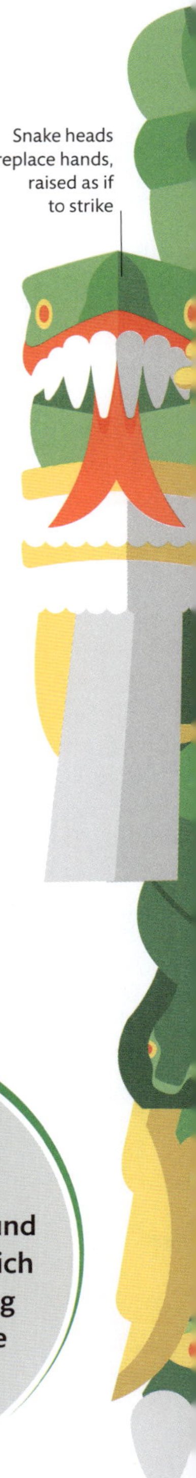

Inca

The Inca civilization flourished in Peru from c.1425–1532. Inca art included highly polished metalwork, ceramics, and textiles. Much of the art was influenced by the earlier Chimu civilization, blended with the Inca's own distinctive style and technical superiority. It featured standardized forms, colors, and proportions, including repeating, geometrical patterns.

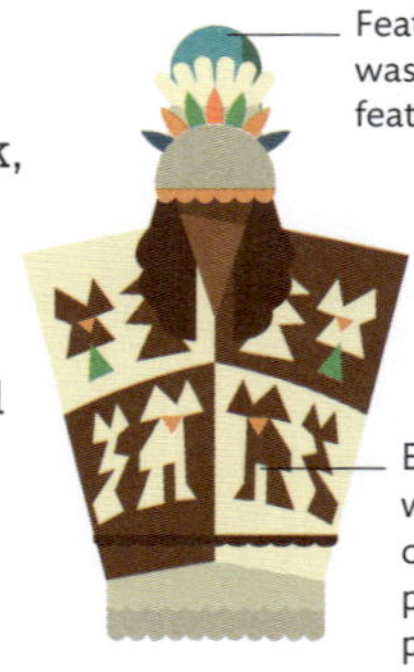

SHIRT AND HEADDRESS

COATLICUE REPRESENTS A MOTHER'S LOVE, AS WELL AS A DEADLY MONSTER

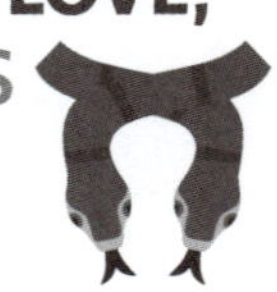

CHICHÉN ITZÁ

Containing 46 buildings, including stepped pyramids, temples, columned arcades, and other stone structures, Chichén Itzá was an active urban center, built by the Mayans from 750 to 1200. Linked to astronomy, the placement of the buildings represents the Mayan idea of the universe. For example, the temple of El Castillo has 365 steps; one for each day of the year.

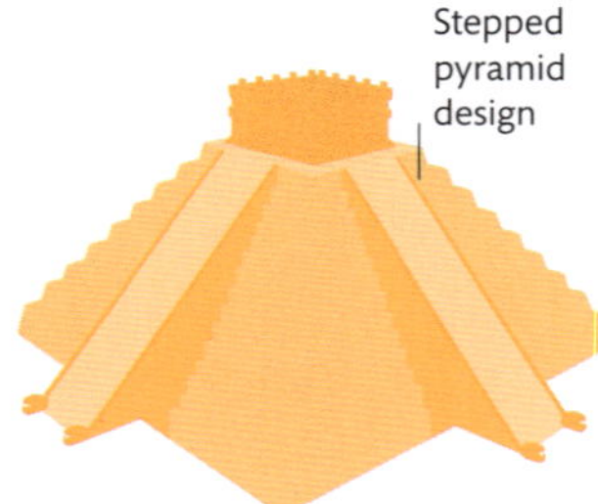

EL CASTILLO

WHAT WERE THE NAZCA LINES?

The Nazca lines were huge designs on the ground known as geoglyphs, which were made by removing rocks and dirt to create an image.

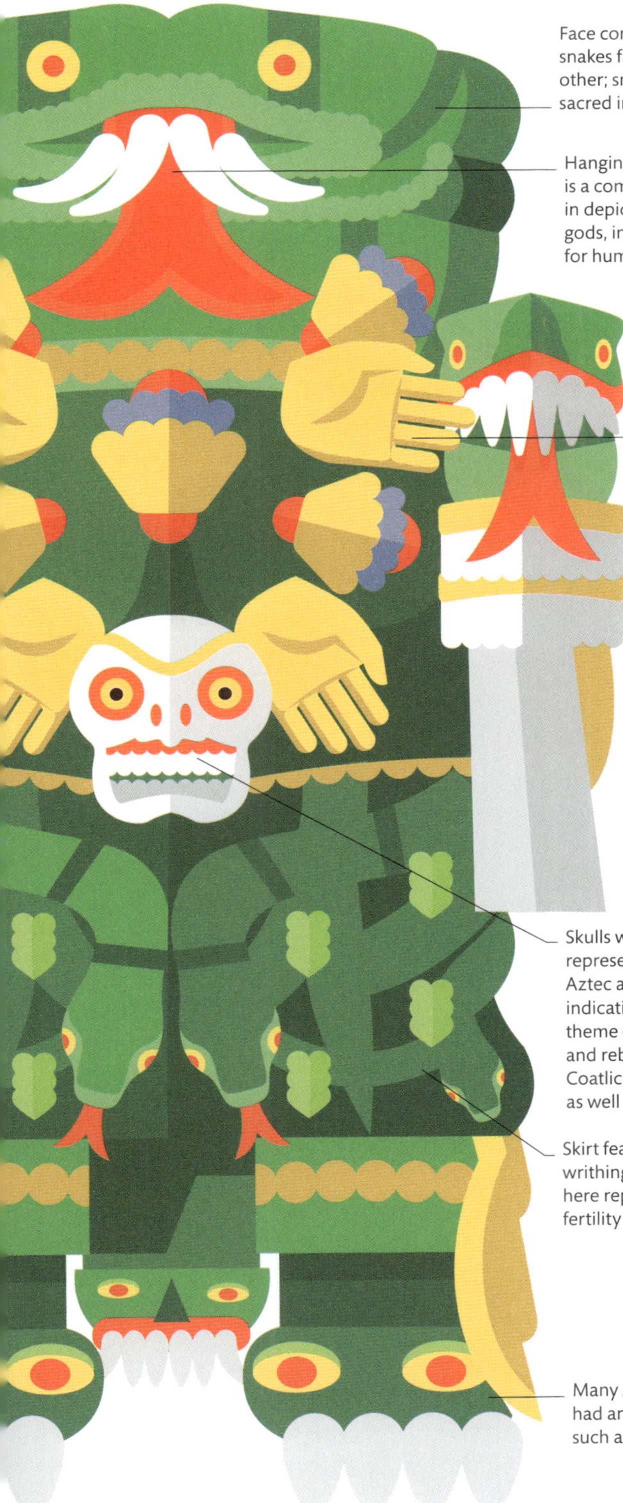

Other Mesoamerican civilizations

Mesoamerican cultures, including those listed below and the Aztecs and Inca, fall into three eras: the preclassic period (c.1200 BCE–200 CE); the classic period (c.200–900 CE); and the postclassic era (c.900–1580). These cultures' art reflected their beliefs and philosophies.

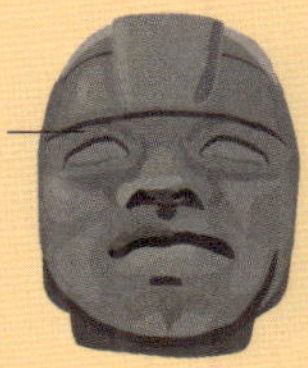

Olmec
In south central Mexico c.1200–400 BCE, the Olmec built pyramids and ceremonial complexes.

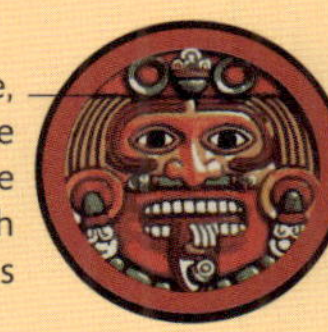

Maya
Flourishing in 200–900 CE, the Maya painted murals, made rock carvings, and sculpted in wood.

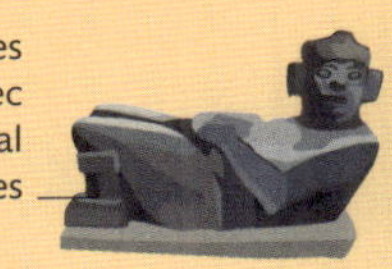

Toltec
Dominating central Mexico from 900–1150, the Toltec carved stone statues of their gods.

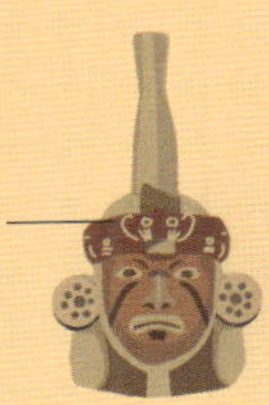

Moche
The Moche flourished in northern Peru around 100–700 CE. Common art includes pottery, metalwork, and textiles.

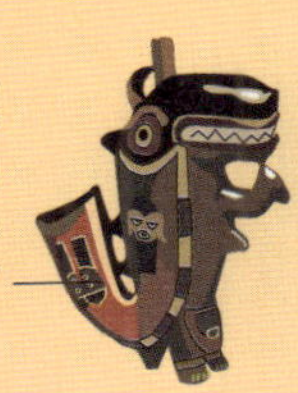

Nazca
Between 100 BCE and 650 CE, the Nazca of Peru made pottery, textiles, and geoglyphs (landscape art).

Other forms of art

Art was a means of communication in the largely illiterate medieval society. After Christianity became the Roman Empire's official religion in 330 CE, the focus of art was mostly in spreading the word of God. This carried over to the medieval period, with artworks in time becoming more stylized and sophisticated—and secular, as separate, often rival nation states began to develop. There was no distinction between "art" and "craft" at this time.

Sculpture
Medieval sculptures were modest in size, often in the form of reliefs, small statues, and crucifixes.

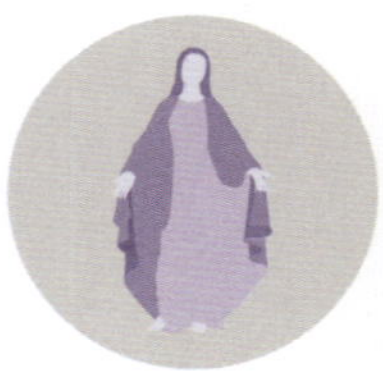

Illuminated manuscripts
Paid for by the Church or nobility, these were made by teams of scribes and illustrators.

Stained glass
Colored glass pieces were arranged into shapes and scenes held together by lead strips.

Tapestry
Providing insulation and decoration, large tapestries were created for the wealthy.

Metalwork
Items such as chalices, candlesticks, and crucifixes were finely wrought from gold, silver, and bronze.

Medieval Art

Also known as the Middle Ages, the medieval period saw important developments in painting, sculpture, and architecture between the end of the Roman Empire in 476 CE and the Renaissance almost 1,000 years later.

Art in a time of change

The art of the medieval age was for a long time sponsored—and controlled—by the Catholic Church, and its subject matter was almost entirely devotional. This changed as Europe's royalty, nobles, and merchants also became patrons of the arts. In *The Wilton Diptych*, for example, the secular figure of England's King Richard II kneels before the Virgin Mary and Jesus in its left-hand panel. In execution, medieval art is characterized by expensive materials, bold colors, and stylized figures. Over time, these figures became much more detailed and realistic.

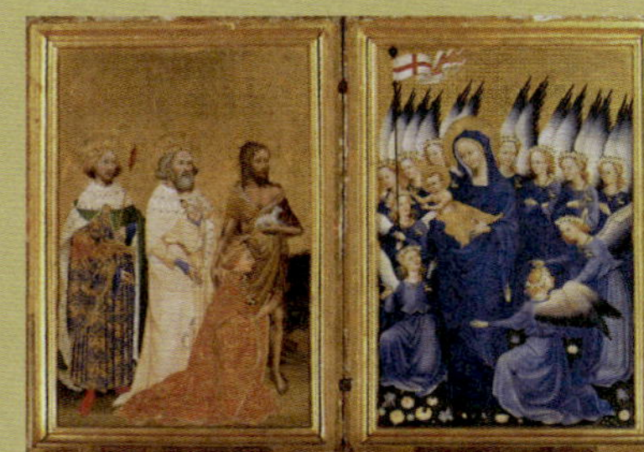

"THE WILTON DIPTYCH," C.1395–99

GOLD LEAF USED IN **MEDIEVAL ART** IS 100 TIMES THINNER THAN **HUMAN HAIR**

HOW IS MEDIEVAL ART CLASSIFIED?

The different styles of medieval art include Byzantine (see pp.162–163), Romanesque, early Christian, Viking, Anglo-Saxon, Carolingian, and Gothic (see pp.174–175).

END OF THE DARK AGES

The chaotic early medieval period in Europe after the fall of Rome was called the "Dark Ages." Stability began to return around 800 CE, as new states and the Church filled the power vacuum, allowing art and culture to flourish once more.

9TH-CENTURY CARVED IVORY PLAQUE

The Wilton Diptych
A small artwork made for King Richard II of England, this piece blends religious and secular imagery. The image below depicts part of the right-hand half of the diptych.

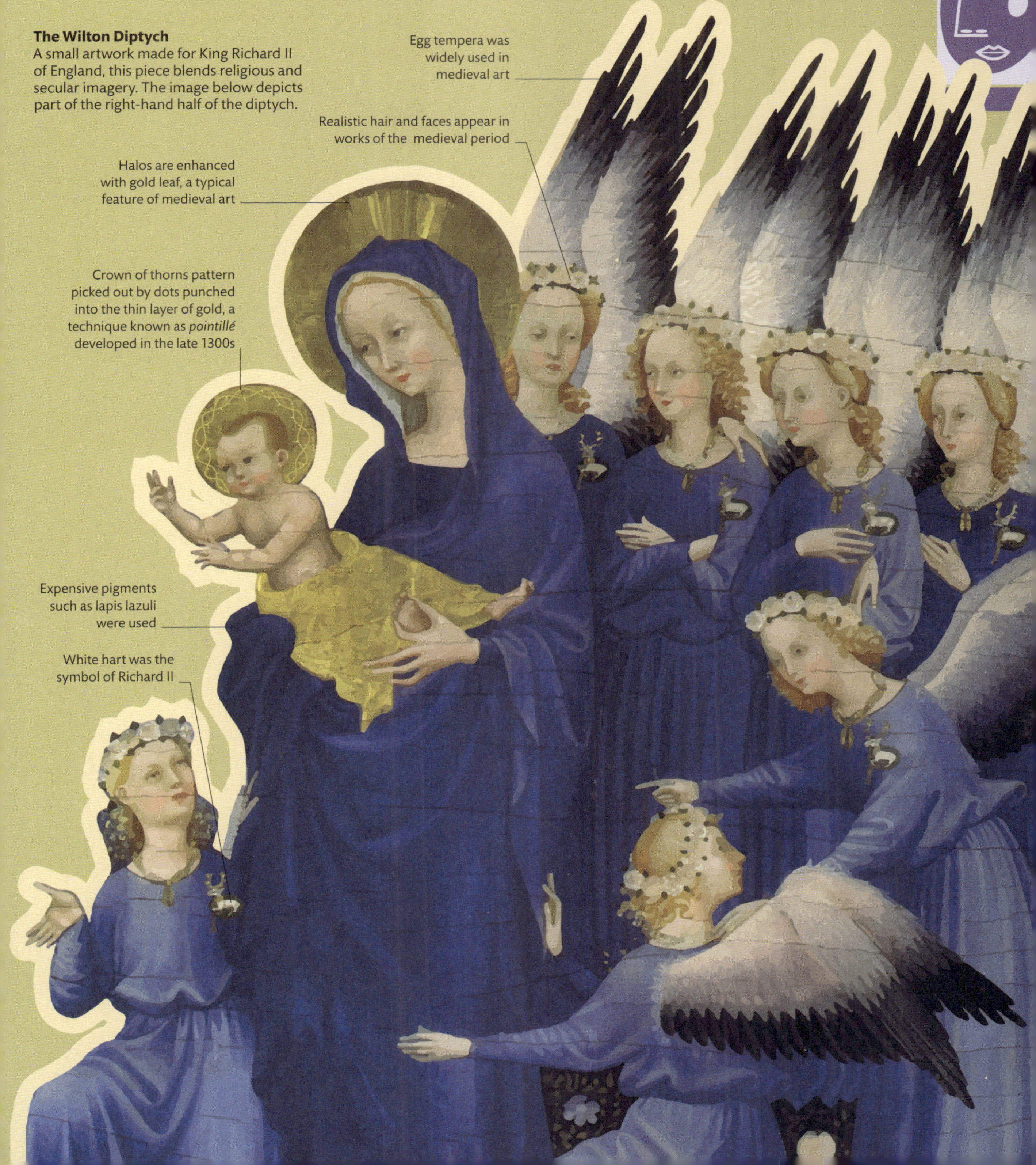

A sacred and secular art form

Tapestries, altar panels, stained glass, sculpture, reliefs, and illuminated manuscripts were the most valued art forms of the period, and a greater trend toward realism developed over time, especially in sculpture and relief. Here, figures generally had elongated proportions and an appearance of flowing elegance. Gothic art was created mostly in the service of the Church, although a style known as International Gothic developed that was used for secular buildings and royal portraiture and sculpture.

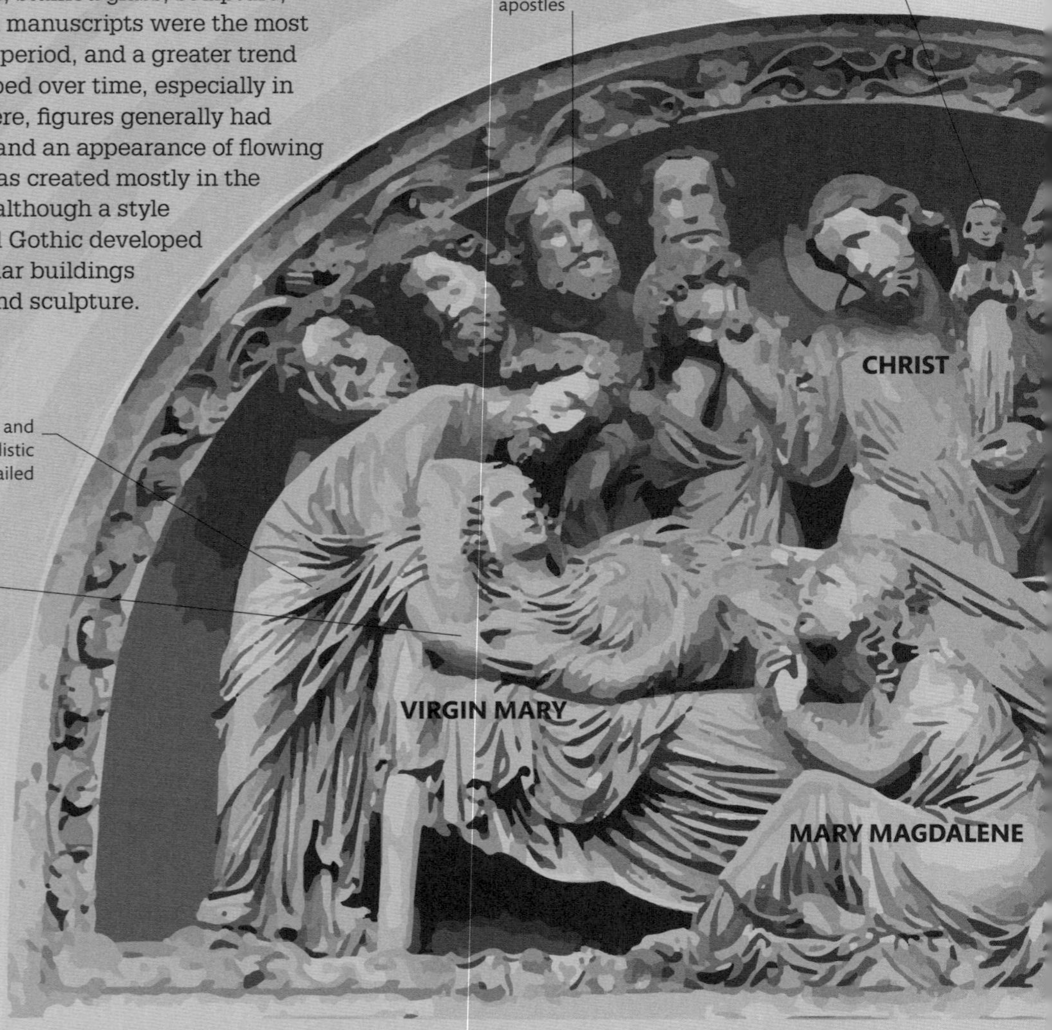

West Portal, Strasbourg Cathedral
Decorating an external recess (tympanum) of Strasbourg Cathedral, this relief depicts the death of the Virgin Mary, surrounded by Christ's apostles. Mary Magdalene symbolizes the repentant sinner.

Gothic Art

A forerunner to the Renaissance, Gothic art was a Christian style that emerged in 12th-century France and developed throughout Europe for several centuries. It brought a lighter touch, with a focus on light as a sign of God's grace.

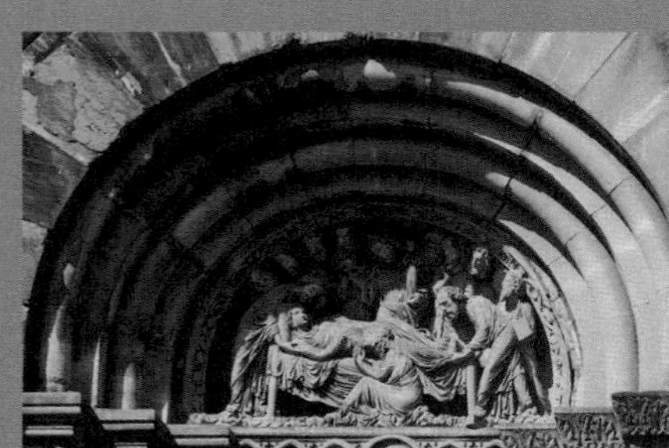

RELIEF OF THE VIRGIN MARY, ARTIST UNKNOWN (AFTER 1225)

THE INTERNATIONAL GOTHIC STYLE WAS BORN IN THE ROYAL COURTS OF EUROPE

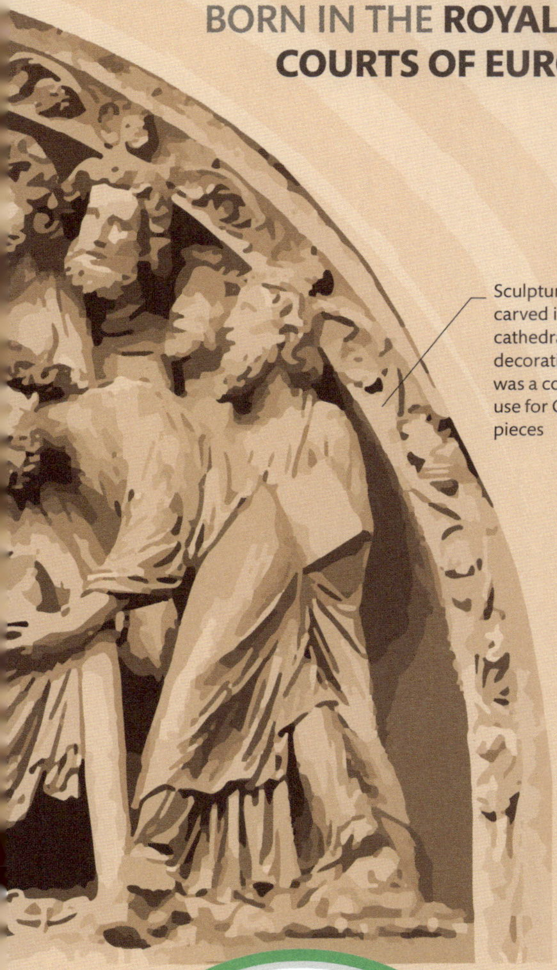

Architecture and stained glass

Gothic architecture employed a new skeletal system of construction that enabled large windows to take the place of solid areas of wall. As the style matured and glassmaking technology improved, Gothic stained glass developed and was widely used for windows in churches. Cathedrals such as Canterbury in the UK and Chartres in France are celebrated for their boldly colored, elaborate stained glass windows.

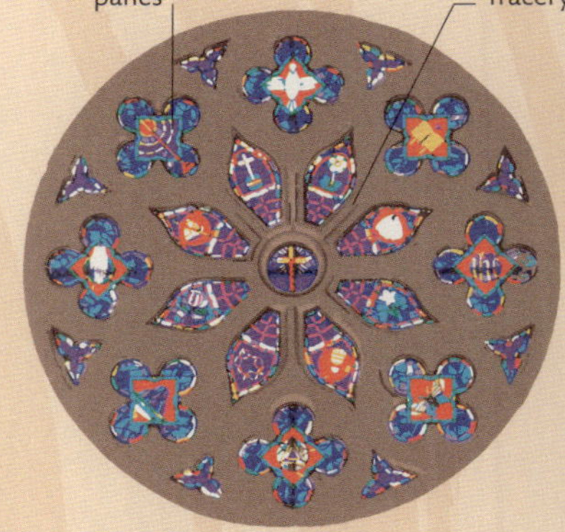

Stained glass
Tracery, or stone supports between sections of windows, helped support a wall's weight and allowed for large windows to be inserted. A common type of Gothic tracery is the rose window, where jewel-like stained glass shapes radiate from the center.

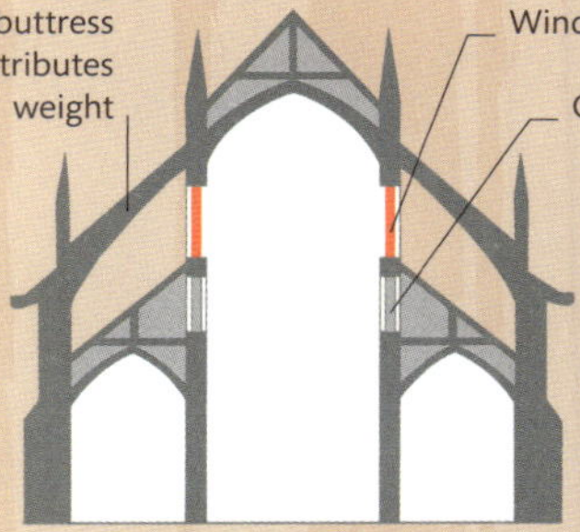

Architecture
In order to create greater interior heights and vertical space, architects utilized the equilateral arch, the vaulted ceiling, and, for added strength and stability, the flying buttress.

WAS GOTHIC ART ONE MOVEMENT?

Gothic art has been divided into three periods: Early, High, and International. Each style was more sophisticated than the last, with finer detailing and more realistic human and natural forms.

GOTHIC PAINTING

Gothic art was chiefly an instructional tool for Christianity. Paintings usually portrayed religious belief in simple but striking terms—of an eternal heavenly paradise for the just, and hellfire and damnation for unworthy sinners.

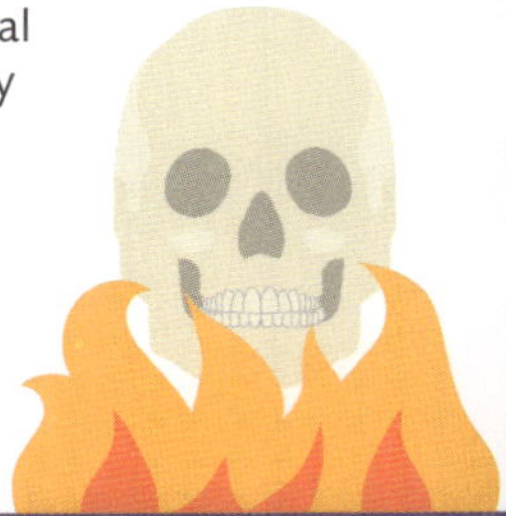

ETERNAL DAMNATION

Italian Renaissance

The Italian Renaissance was an explosion of culture, arts, and intellectual pursuits beginning in the 14th century. It was strongly inspired by Classical antiquity.

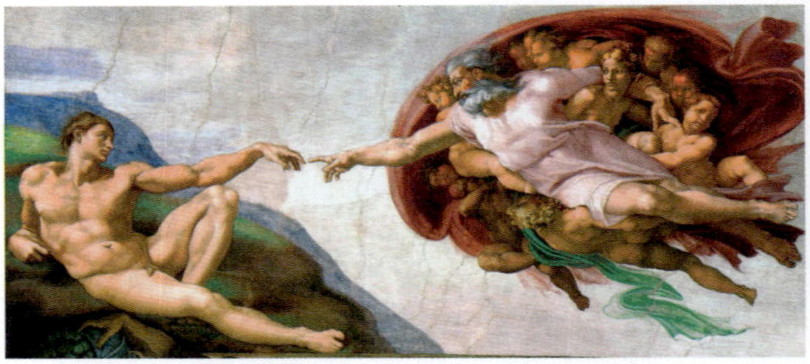

"THE CREATION OF ADAM", MICHELANGELO (C.1508–12)

Age of enlightenment

During the Italian Renaissance, sweeping changes took place across Italy. Political stability, a thriving mercantile economy, and new inventions such as the printing press brought art, literature, and philosophy to the fore. Architect Filippo Brunelleschi's mathematical understanding of linear perspective (see pp.104–105) gave paintings a realism never seen before, with Italian artists widely employing this to describe depth in their paintings. Religious works were no longer on gold backgrounds but in landscapes from the observable world. Artists were commissioned by powerful patrons, including popes, and individual rulers and monarchs.

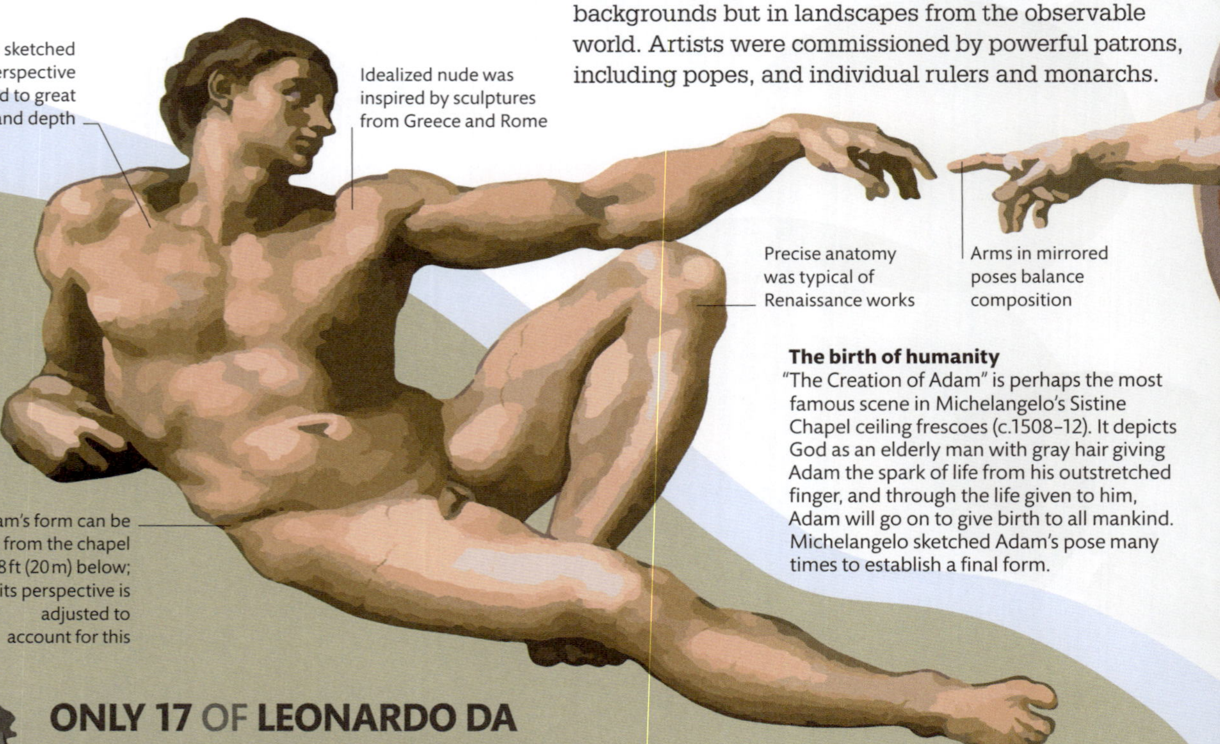

The birth of humanity

"The Creation of Adam" is perhaps the most famous scene in Michelangelo's Sistine Chapel ceiling frescoes (c.1508–12). It depicts God as an elderly man with gray hair giving Adam the spark of life from his outstretched finger, and through the life given to him, Adam will go on to give birth to all mankind. Michelangelo sketched Adam's pose many times to establish a final form.

ONLY 17 OF LEONARDO DA VINCI'S PAINTINGS SURVIVE, AND SEVERAL ARE UNFINISHED

HOW WAS THE SISTINE CHAPEL CEILING PAINTED?

It was painted using the buon (true) fresco technique. This means pigments are mixed with water and painted directly onto damp plaster.

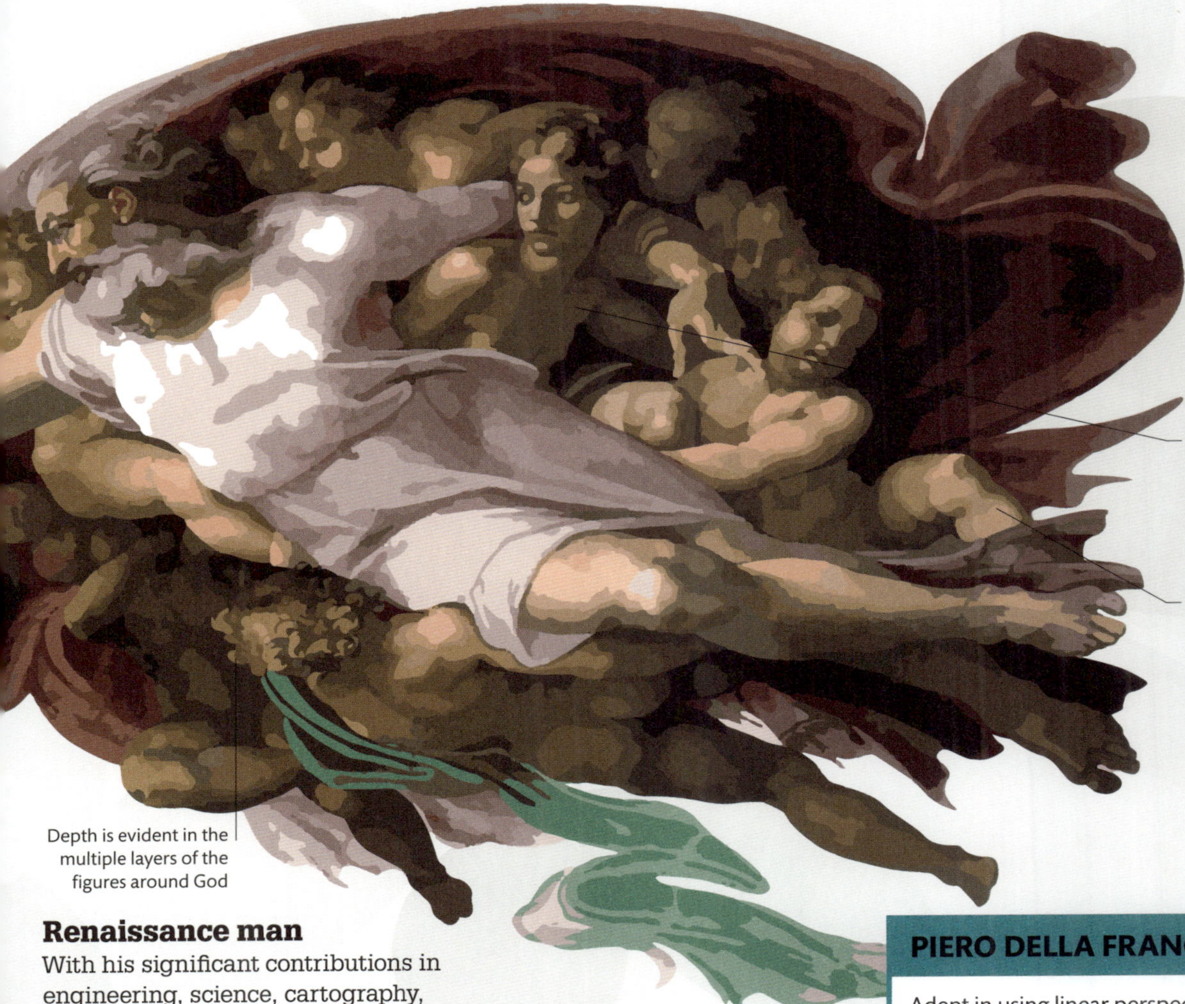

Renaissance man

With his significant contributions in engineering, science, cartography, philosophy, painting, and anatomy, the polymath Leonardo da Vinci personified Renaissance humanist ideals. Fascinated by anatomy, he went to great lengths to study it, performing dissections at hospitals all over Italy and recording his findings in detailed, anatomical drawings. Geometry was another interest, and his studies of proportion led him to compare the workings of the human body to those of the universe. He continues to be regarded as one of the greatest artists who ever lived.

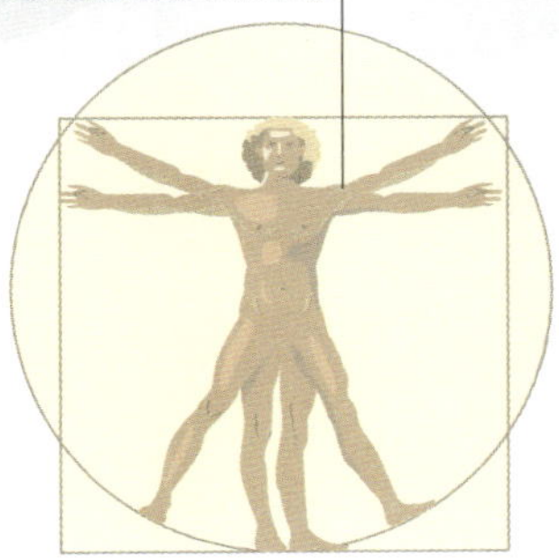

"Vitruvian Man" by Leonardo da Vinci
Created c. 1487, Da Vinci's drawing in pen and ink wash represents the ideal human proportions in two superimposed positions.

PIERO DELLA FRANCESCA

Adept in using linear perspective and foreshortening (see pp.104–107), Piero della Francesca combined geometrical compositions with naturalism. His cool color palette added to the refined nature and meditative quality of his works.

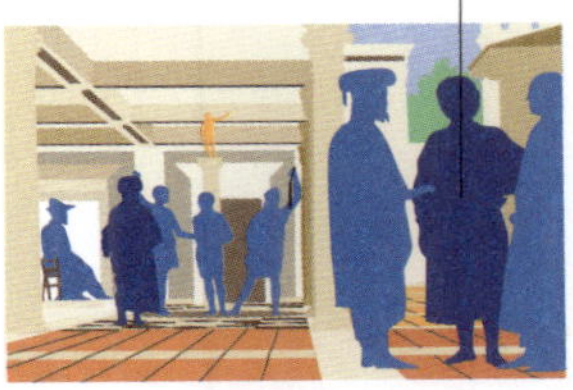

COMPOSITION USING PERSPECTIVE

Northern Renaissance

By early 1400, the spirit of the Italian Renaissance had spread to northern Europe. Like the Italian movement, it was inspired by Classical art but also blended influences of late Gothic art and ideas about observation.

Humble spectacle

Countries of the Northern Renaissance included Germany, France, England, Flanders, and the Low Countries (now the Netherlands), each with their own style. Northern artists were aware of Italian advances in perspective, humanism (a movement that focused on human learning), and naturalistic depictions (see pp.176–177). They also mainly replaced traditional glorifications with mundane, realistic scenes: art was commissioned largely by the merchant classes, and most portrayed holy figures as real people in domestic interiors rather than as visions of perfection in grand settings. A major innovation was oil paint (see pp.34–35).

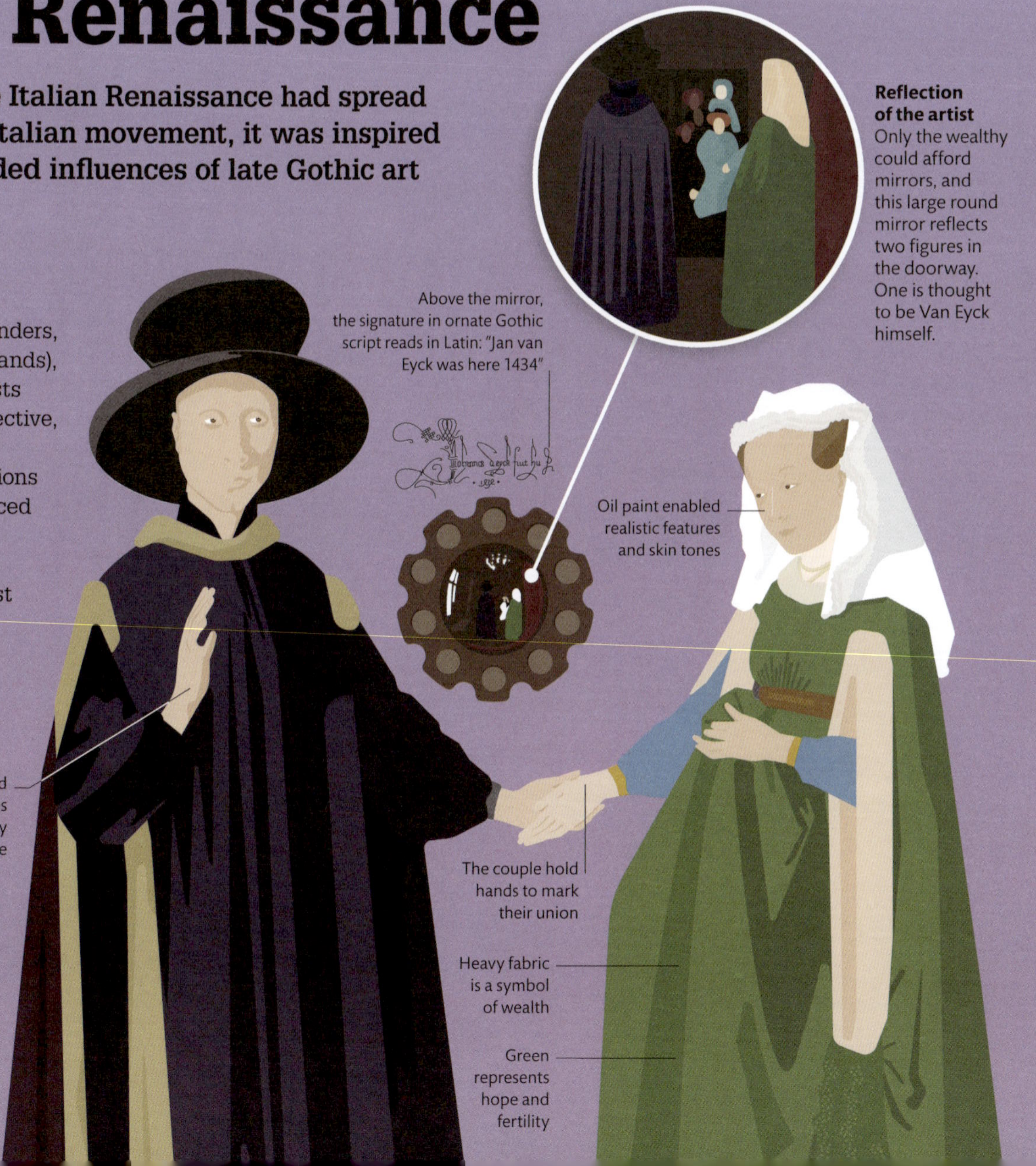

HOW DID JAN VAN EYCK BREAK NEW BOUNDARIES?

Van Eyck was famed as the founder of early Netherlandish painting due to his skill in melding naturalism and realism with rich, vibrant colors.

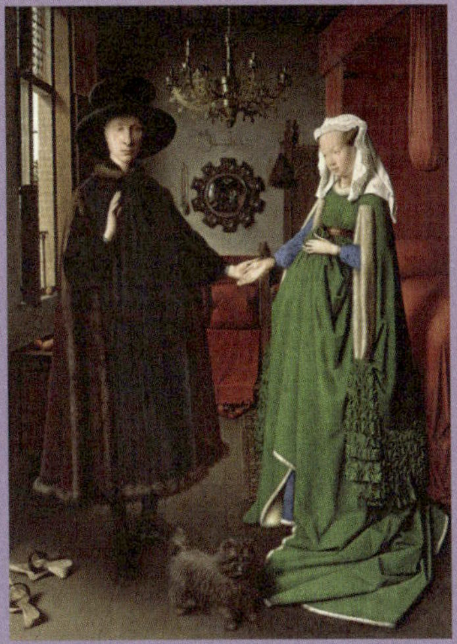

"THE ARNOLFINI PORTRAIT," JAN VAN EYCK (1434)

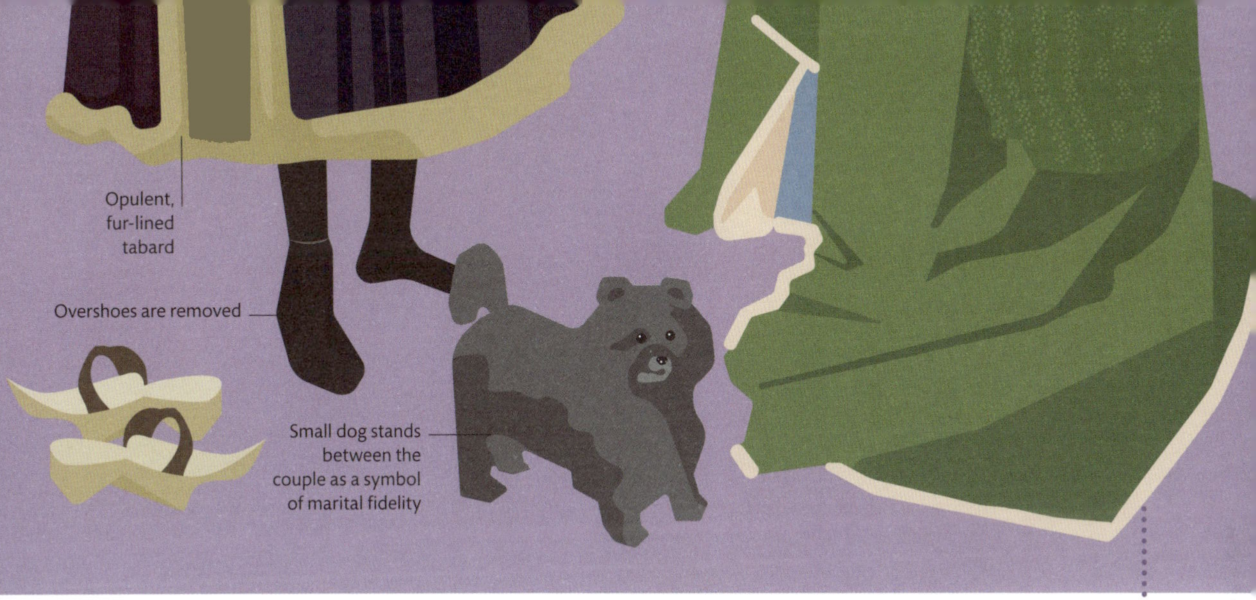

GUTENBERG PRESS

German inventor and goldsmith Johannes Gutenberg (1400–1468) originated a method of printing from movable type, making it possible to mass-produce books and other printed material quickly and cost-effectively. In 1455, in the town of Strasbourg, Gutenberg revealed the world's first working printing press that changed how knowledge and ideas were spread, facilitating the progress of learning.

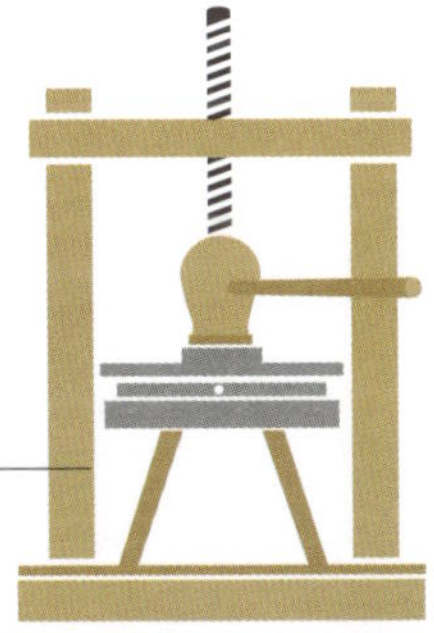

FIRST PRINTING PRESS

Characteristics

Northern European Renaissance artists became particularly skilled in a range of disciplines that included oil painting, printmaking, and wood carving. There was a proliferation of lifelike imagery depicting everyday scenes that featured moralizing messages, and works placed emphasis on elements such as realism, objective observation, precise details, and exacting use of linear and atmospheric perspective (see pp.104–07).

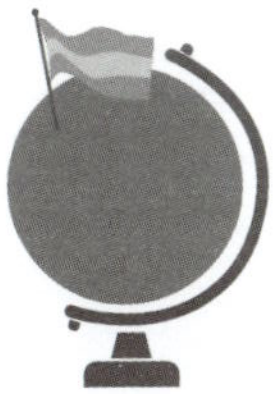

ANTWERP BECAME A CENTRE FOR ART IN THE 16TH AND 17TH CENTURIES

Use of oil paint
Among the first to use durable oil paint, artists of the Northern Renaissance applied it in glazes and thin layers as they explored light, form, colors, and texture.

Perspective and detail
Linear and aerial perspective conveyed depth and distance, and precise, minute details became essential aspects of Northern Renaissance art.

Erasmus and humanism
Humanists believed in human values rather than holy ones. The "Prince of Humanists" was Desiderius Erasmus, known for his influential, humanist writings.

Stories and subjects
The most popular subjects were naturalistic Biblical narratives that were made to resemble everyday life, as well as portraits and landscapes.

WHERE DOES THE NAME "MANNERISM" COME FROM?

The word "mannerism" is derived from the Italian word *maniera*, meaning "style" or "manner".

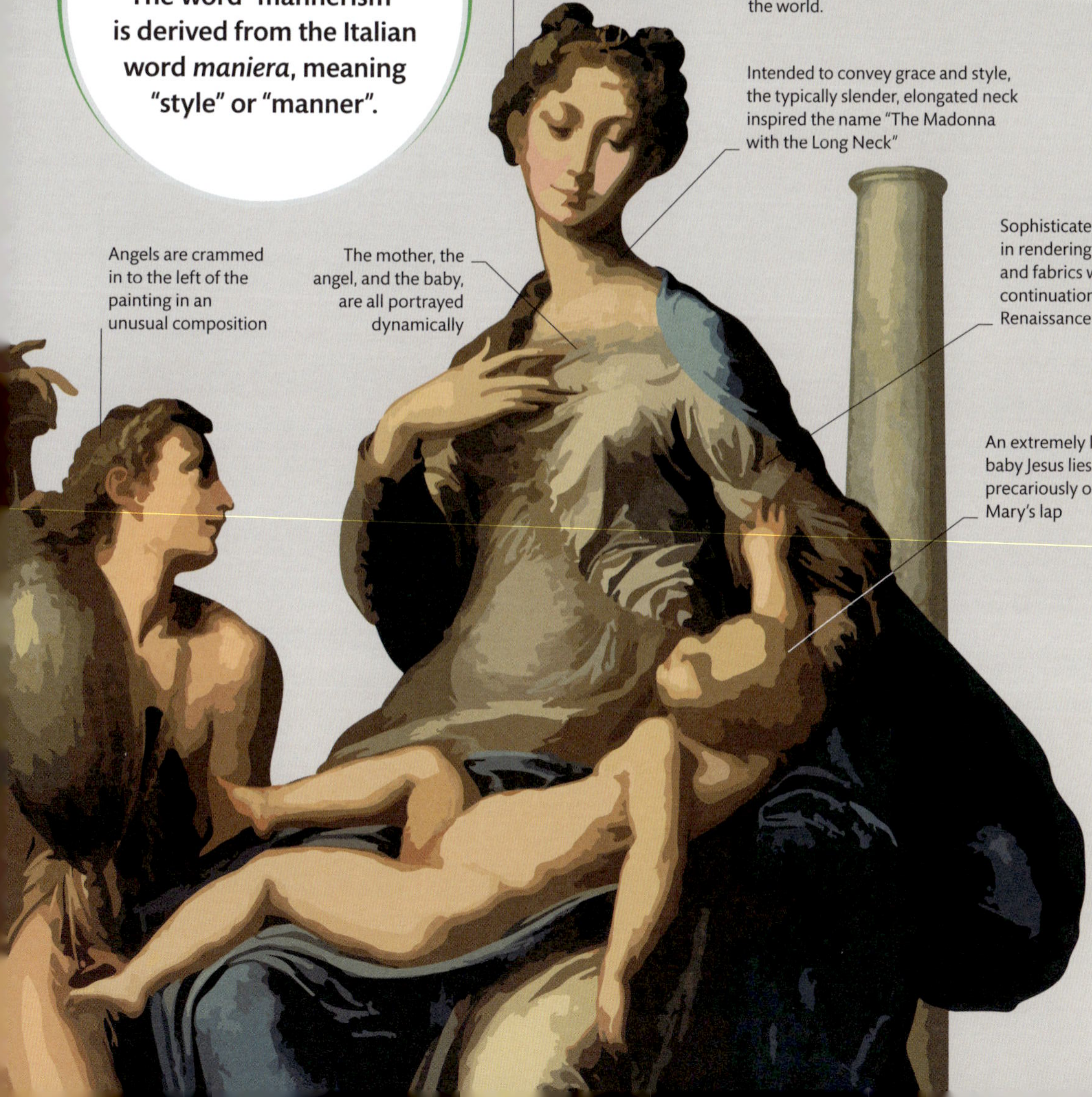

Mary looks down to admire her baby. Her hair, clothing, and jewels are those of a contemporary noblewoman

Angels are crammed in to the left of the painting in an unusual composition

The mother, the angel, and the baby, are all portrayed dynamically

"Madonna with the Long Neck"
Mannerists generally retained the painting and sculptural skills of their Renaissance predecessors. In an attempt to convey grace, elegance, and refinement, Parmigianino also extended the figures of his painting. Moving away from classical harmony, Mannerism was a dramatic new way of portraying the world.

Intended to convey grace and style, the typically slender, elongated neck inspired the name "The Madonna with the Long Neck"

Sophisticated skills in rendering textures and fabrics were a continuation of Renaissance ideals

An extremely large baby Jesus lies precariously on Mary's lap

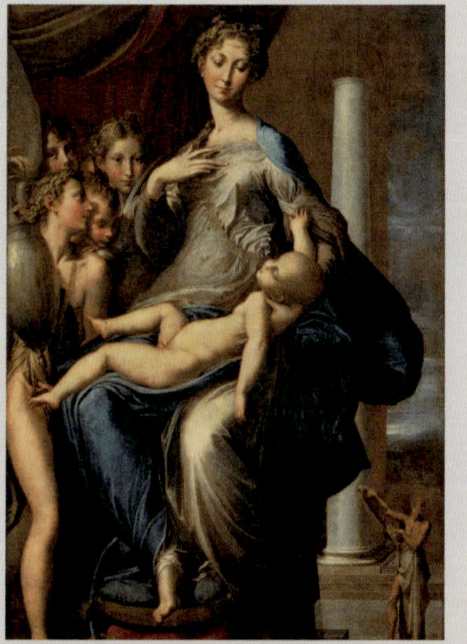

"MADONNA AND CHILD WITH ANGELS", FRANCESCO MAZZOLA, KNOWN AS PARMIGIANINO (1503–1540)

THE SPREAD OF MANNERISM

Mannerism emerged in Florence and Rome, and, while the movement was short-lived, its influence spread beyond Italy into Europe, partly due to its introduction at various royal courts. The King of France, Francis I, and Emperor Rudolf II in Prague both invited Italian artists to their courts. Artists from the Netherlands also adopted Mannerist styles.

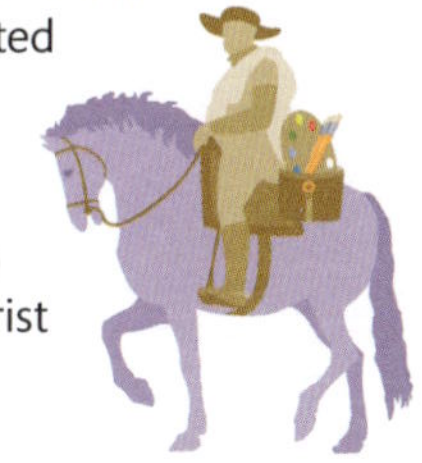

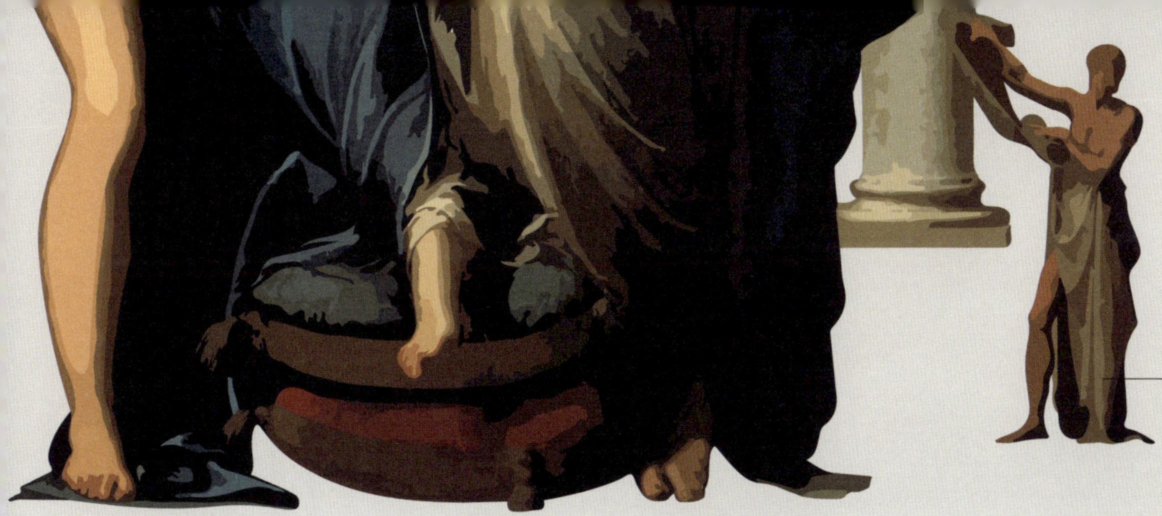

Mannerism often features unexplained contrasts in scale and perspective

MICHELANGELO'S HOUSE IS SAID TO HAVE BEEN BURGLED FOR DRAWINGS **BY RIVAL ARTISTS**

Mannerism

Emerging around 1520, during the later years of the Italian High Renaissance, Mannerists created distortions and asymmetrical compositions, especially elongations that evoked a sense of tension.

Distortion and asymmetry

Moving away from the naturalism of the Renaissance, especially from the harmonious styles of artists such as Raphael and Andrea del Sarto, with their emphasis on balance and ideal beauty, Mannerism spread from Italy across Europe and lasted until approximately the end of the 16th century, when it was replaced with the Baroque style. Paintings and sculpture often included the *figura serpentinata* or "serpentine figure": bodies twisted into fluid S-shapes. Mannerists were inspired by Michelangelo and the awe-inspiring grandeur of his work, and copied his paintings in the Sistine Chapel, especially *The Last Judgement* (1536–1541). The movement flourished first in Rome and then in Florence, Parma, Mantua, and other Italian cities, before spreading beyond Italy. During the period, patrons encouraged artists to compete with each other for commissions, so original art was noticed. This resulted in new approaches, with more stylized poses and altered proportions.

Characteristics

Mannerism was expressive and exaggerated, featuring a variety of approaches, including artifice, imbalance, and contrasting proportions, often set against artificial backgrounds.

Courtly elitism
The Mannerist style was seen as elegant and courtly—a style for the wealthy and well bred. Its complex symbolism required elite knowledge to interpret.

Bold colors and lighting
Decorative, unnatural colors—often bright or sharp—and clear, bright light all added to the distortions and tensions.

Tension and drama
Mannerists believed that they were conveying their sophistication and intellect by creating tension and drama through often unsettling distortions.

Elongated and exaggerated
Departing from the equilibrium of the High Renaissance, Mannerists elongated and exaggerated for elegant effect.

Characteristics and context

Although different Baroque artists interpreted the style using various different approaches, its common characteristics included powerful religious or mythological iconography, lavish and ambitious expression, technical brilliance, drama, theatricality, vitality, emotional intensity, vivid light, strong tones, and rich color.

Council of Trent
Held between 1545 and 1563, the Council of Trent was convened in response to the Protestant Reformation. Among other things, it decreed how art should celebrate Catholicism.

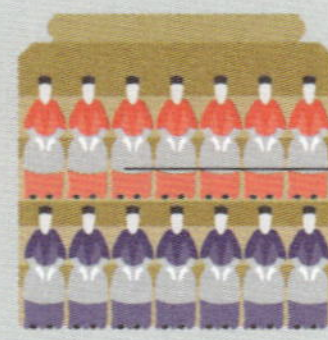
Religious leaders convened

Religious scenes
These had previously been banned by Protestants. The Catholic Church backed the style to inspire and uplift the population, reassert its authority, and reconnect ordinary people with Catholicism.

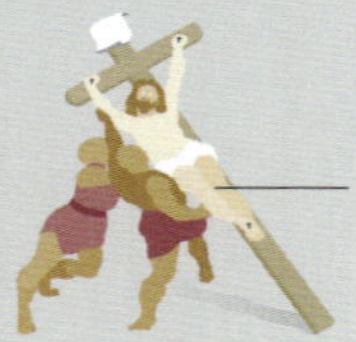
Dramatic scenes inspired awe

Easily understood
Baroque art was intended to evoke an emotional response in people. In order to achieve the aims of the Catholic Church, it also needed to be bold and easy to interpret, with instantly recognizable themes.

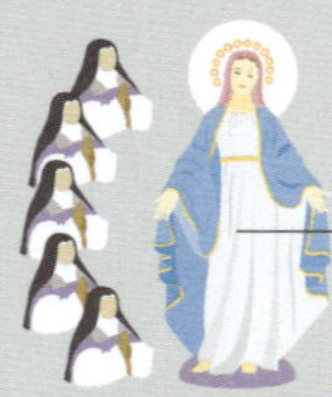
Familiar imagery appealed to the masses

Sensuality and color
Artists created awe-inspiring, sensual, richly colored paintings that appealed to ordinary people, often featuring dramatic themes, vividly depicted, with much contrast between dark and light.

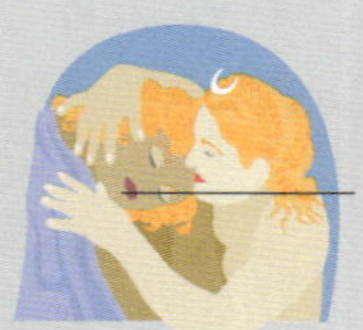
Vivid imagery and deep colors

Multiple perspectives
With some of the grandeur and dignity of the High Renaissance and the intellectual vigor of Mannerism, Baroque art often used multiple perspectives, creating movement and theatricality.

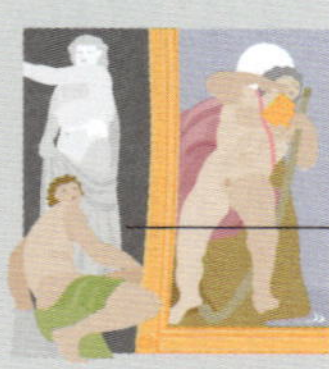
Views from different angles created dynamism

"BAROQUE" PROBABLY COMES FROM **THE PORTUGUESE** "BARROCCO"– DESCRIBING A **DEFORMED PEARL**

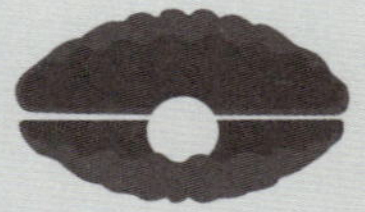

ELEMENTS OF BAROQUE SCULPTURE

In Baroque sculpture, dynamism and energy were important. Figure groups often twisted or stretched, with views from every angle conveying a fresh sense of drama. The foremost Baroque sculptor, Gian Lorenzo Bernini created works such as *The Ecstasy of Saint Theresa* (1647–52).

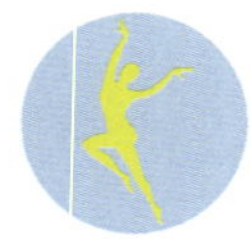
MOVEMENT

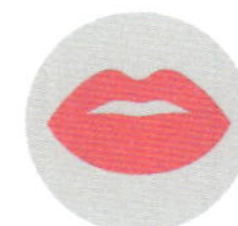
INTENSE EMOTION, SENSUALITY

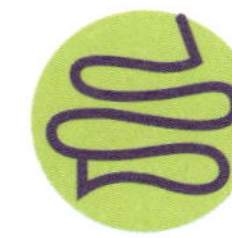
DRAPERY, FOLDS OF CLOTH

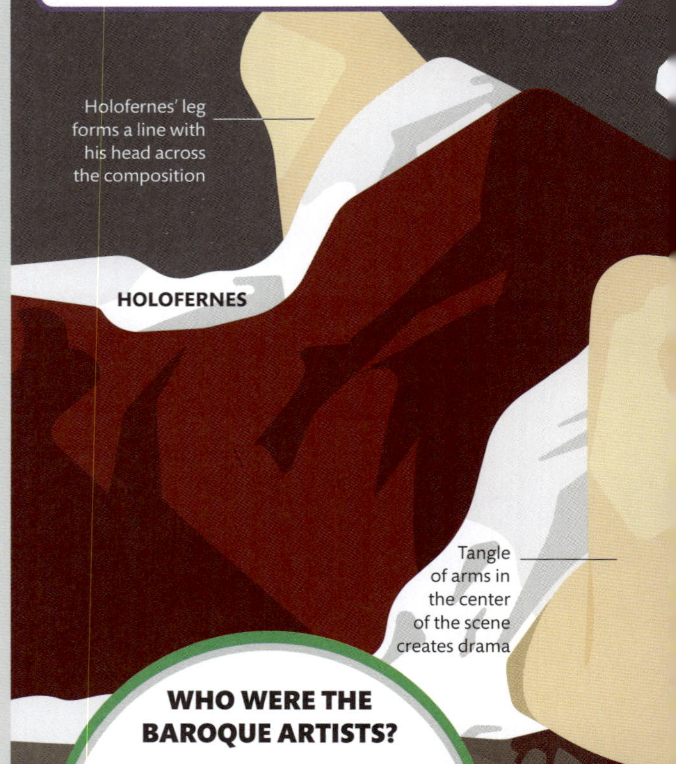

WHO WERE THE BAROQUE ARTISTS?

As well as Artemesia Gentileschi, some of the great Baroque artists include Caravaggio, Peter Paul Rubens, Anthony van Dyck, and Rembrandt van Rijn.

Baroque

Particularly associated with the Catholic Reformation, Baroque art aimed to reinvigorate followers of the Catholic Church with its dynamism, drama, and emotional appeal.

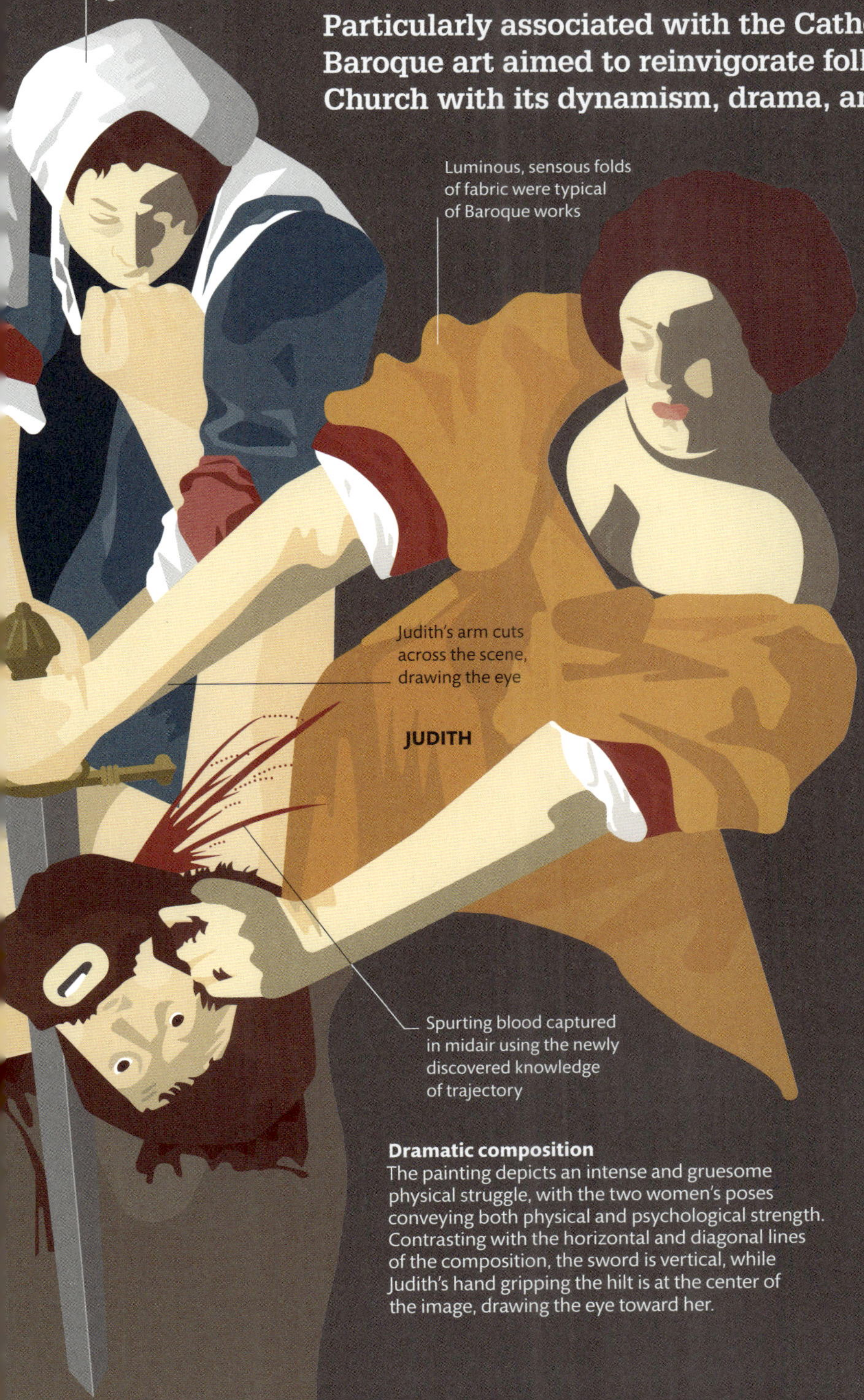

Allegorical art

Although it embraced many different styles, at its height from around 1630–80, Baroque art mainly depicted biblical and mythological allegories on a grand scale, using strong tonal contrasts and lighting, sumptuous colors, and a sense of action and awe. The movement began in Rome after the Council of Trent (see opposite), and then spread to Europe and beyond. As it spread, it changed and adapted to different needs, contexts, and tastes. This painting, by Artemisia Gentileschi, is based on a religious story of the Israelite Judith who kills her people's enemy, the Assyrian Holofernes, by seducing and decapitating him while he is in a drunken stupor.

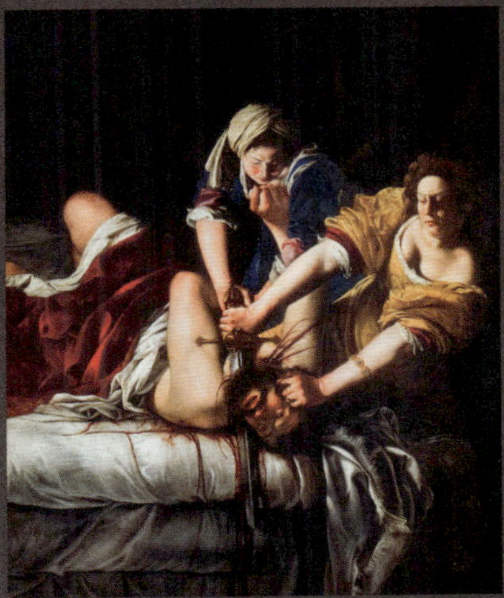

"JUDITH BEHEADING HOLOFERNES", ARTEMISIA GENTILESCHI (1620-21)

Dramatic composition

The painting depicts an intense and gruesome physical struggle, with the two women's poses conveying both physical and psychological strength. Contrasting with the horizontal and diagonal lines of the composition, the sword is vertical, while Judith's hand gripping the hilt is at the center of the image, drawing the eye toward her.

Ideal virtues

The most important aim of Neoclassicism was for art to portray ideal virtues, so helping viewers raise their morals. Art was required to include clarity of form, toned-down colors, marked horizontal and vertical angles, and a sense of the timelessness of ancient Greece and Rome. In this way, against the backdrop both of the French Revolution's upheavals and the Industrial Revolution's progress in science and invention, the movement sought to educate and improve.

"THE OATH OF THE HORATII", JACQUES-LOUIS DAVID (1785)

Dispute between cities, 669 BCE
In this painting, three Horatii brothers from Rome agree to fight three Curiatii brothers from Alba Longa. Swearing allegiance to Rome, the brothers take their swords from their father.

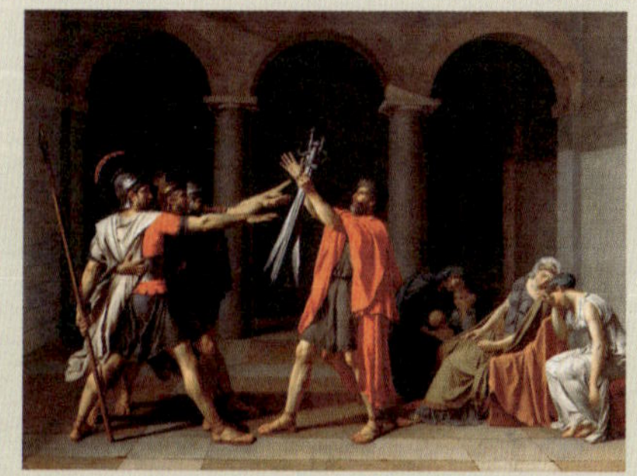

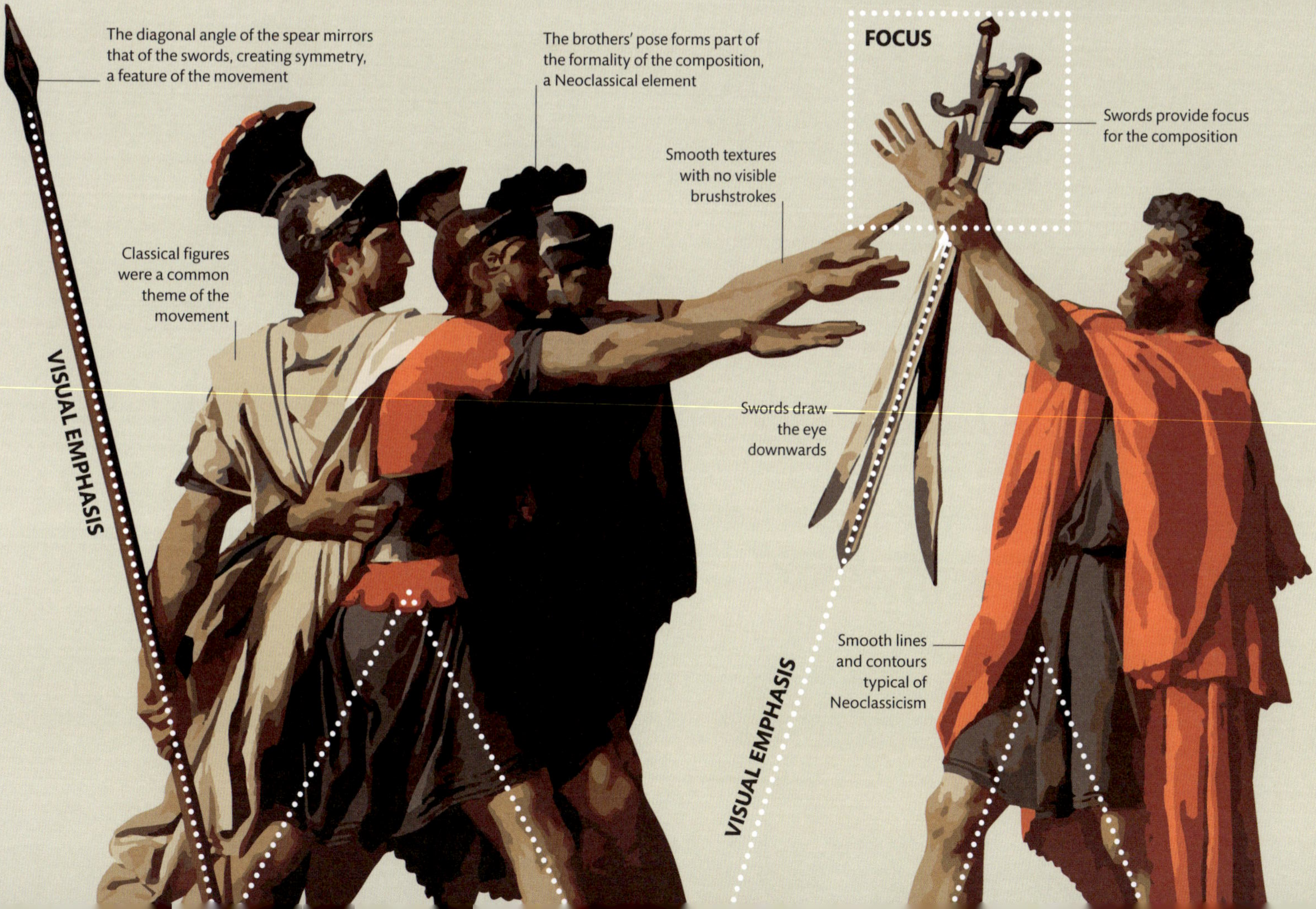

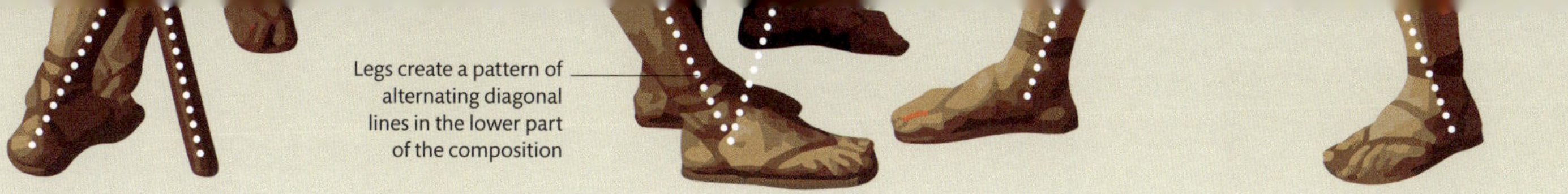

Neoclassicism

In reaction to the extravagances of the preceding Rococo styles, Neoclassicism revived many of the characteristics of classical antiquity, including solidity, formal composition, historic subject matter, and architecturally correct settings. The movement also promoted an underlying moral message through its works.

Ancient inspiration

Neoclassicism was influenced in part by the excavation of the ancient Roman cities of Herculaneum in 1738 and Pompeii in 1748 (see pp.156–157), which inspired artists to draw on the spirit of Greco-Roman antiquity. This rediscovery coincided with popular essays praising ancient Greek and Roman art, written by German philosopher and archaeologist Johann Winckelmann and Italian printmaker Giovanni Battista Piranesi.

THE "GRAND TOUR"

From around 1660 to 1820, young northern European aristocrats embarked on the "Grand Tour," visiting the great towns and cities of the Renaissance to complete their education. This trend further helped inspire Neoclassicism.

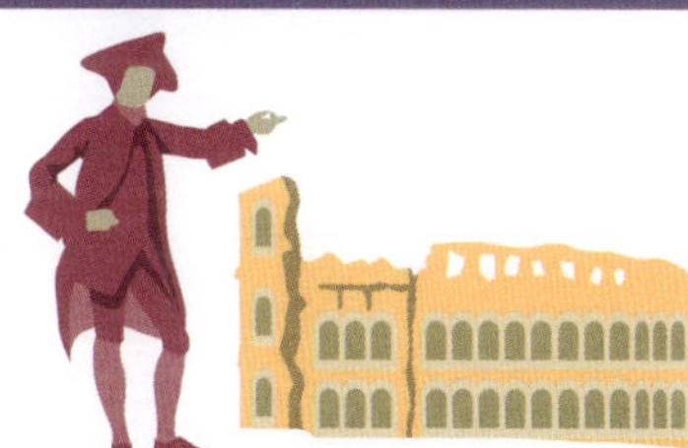

The hierarchy of painting

By the 17th century, the official art world had decreed that fine art painting should be categorized with a "hierarchy of genres" to reflect the innate moral power of each type of painting. Moral messages could be conveyed most effectively through history paintings, with the other genres arranged in the order below.

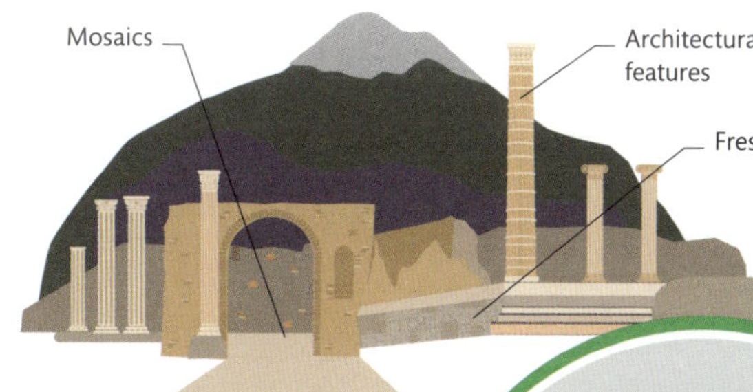

PRESERVED ROMAN CITY

NEOCLASSICAL ARTISTS **DREW GREATLY** FROM THE WORKS OF **HOMER**

HOW WAS NEOCLASSICISM LINKED TO THE FRENCH REVOLUTION?

Jacques-Louis David took part in the French Revolution and painted several Neoclassical works inspired by it.

Romanticism

An artistic, literary, musical, and intellectual movement that spread across Europe c.1780–1850, Romanticism conveyed emotion, intuition, subjectivity, and the imagination.

Emotion and passion

Developing alongside Neoclassicism (see pp.184–185), Romanticism rejected reason and discipline in favor of emotion, passion, spirituality, and mystery. The name derived from imaginative, medieval tales known as romances. Artists and writers explored contemporary themes and expressed their feelings, from revolutionary fervor to dreams or a love of the landscape and nature. They used loose brushstrokes, in contrast to the smooth precision of Neoclassical painting.

Against the backdrop of the Industrial Revolution, uprisings in North America and France inspired strong feelings and gave ordinary people a new power. Many Romanticists empathized with the oppressed, sharing notions of freedom, equality, and national pride, but some also protested the horrors of war.

SEEKING INSPIRATION, J.M.W. TURNER IS SAID TO HAVE HAD HIMSELF TIED TO A MAST IN A STORM

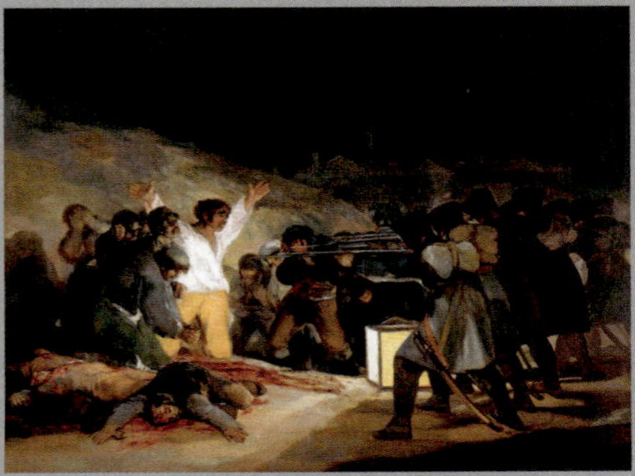

"THE THIRD OF MAY IN 1808 IN MADRID", FRANCISCO GOYA (1814)

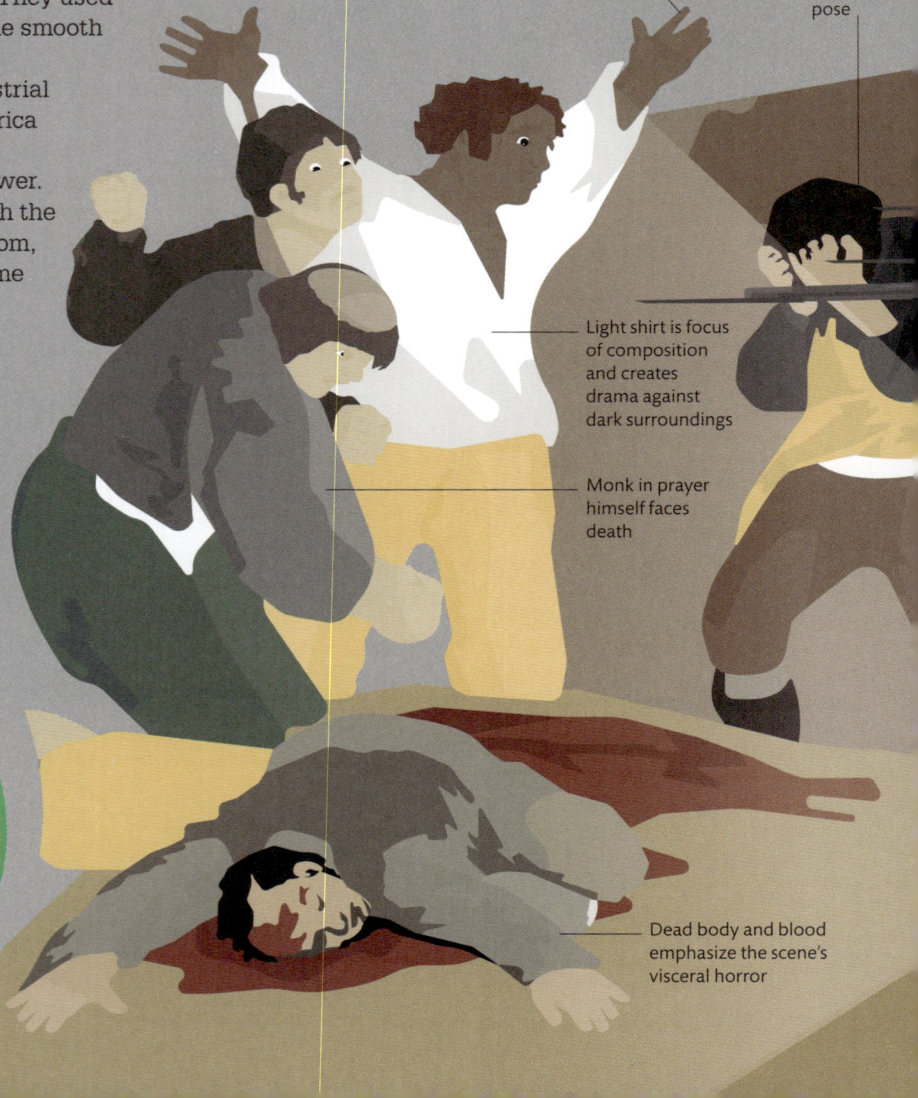

WHAT WAS ROMANTICISM'S LEGACY?

Romanticism promoted the idea of the creative act setting the artist apart from others. This contributed to the separation of arts and sciences.

HUDSON RIVER SCHOOL

In the mid-19th century, a group of New York-based landscape painters gained prominence. Influenced by Romanticism, their paintings typically depicted striking landscapes of the Hudson River Valley and surrounding area. Later artists of the school came from further afield, such as the American west, Canada, and South America.

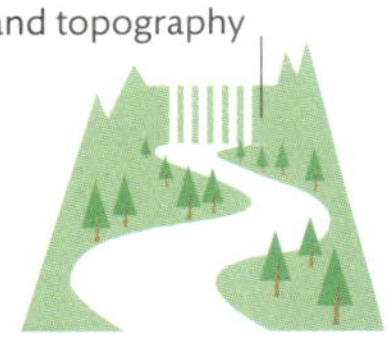

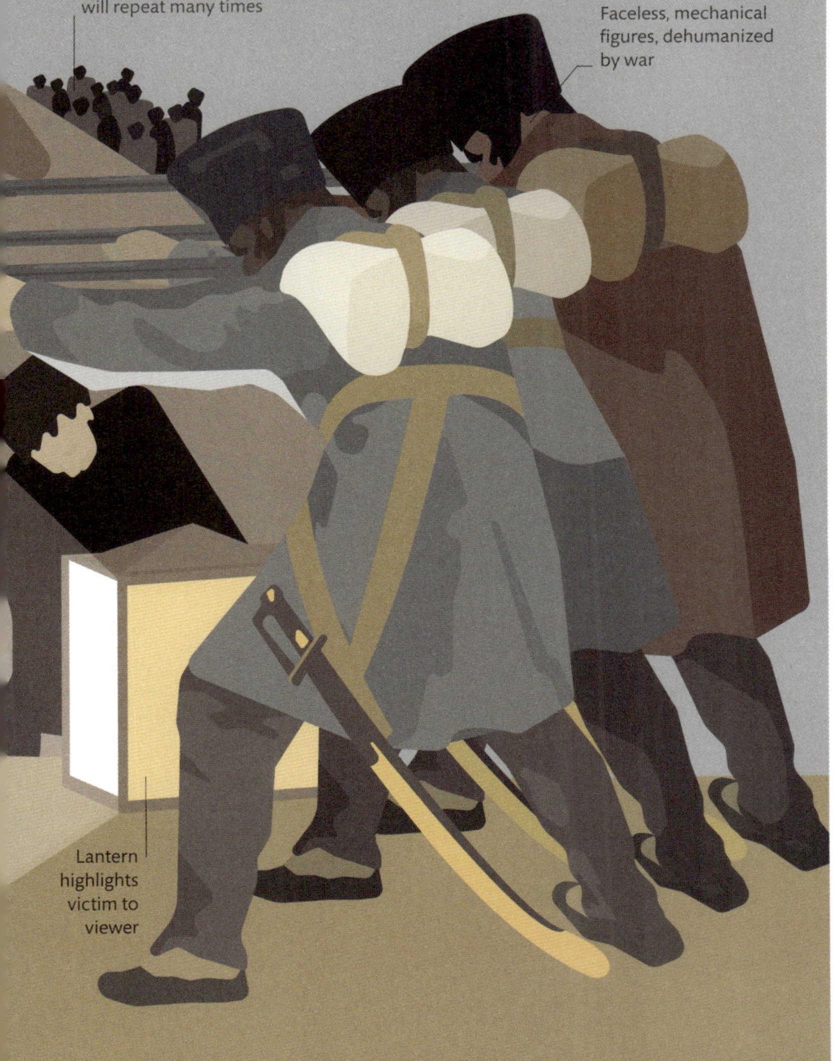

Goya's personal interpretation of war
Hailed as the first modern painting, this emotionally charged scene shows Spanish rebels facing a French firing squad in the Peninsular War.

Themes and characteristics

Romanticism had no single approach or viewpoint, but some common themes occurred within the movement's artworks, including a focus on nature, universal justice, and feelings over reason. Artists often used backgrounds to enhance the emotional intensity of their personal vision.

Artist's emotion
Romanticists intentionally depicted powerful emotions—such as anger, fear, or grief—to evoke strong reactions and feelings in the viewer.

Subjectivity
Moving away from Enlightenment's concepts of reasoning and logic, the Romantic artists emphasized individual subjectivity.

Nature's power over people
Romantic artists portrayed people in sweeping landscapes in a way that emphasized their insignificance in relation to God's omnipotence.

Affinity with nature
Reacting to the Industrial Revolution, many Romantic painters had an affinity with nature, perceiving it as a place for spiritual renewal.

Storms and shipwrecks
Artists such as J.M.W. Turner were known for inspiring intense emotions in the viewer with their depictions of violent storms and struggling ships.

Gothic architecture
In response to the Gothic revival, Romantic artists, such as Caspar David Friedrich, often featured Gothic ruins in their landscapes.

In music and literature
With its ability to be individual, spontaneous, visionary, and imaginative, the Romantic movement also influenced literature and music.

Pre-Raphaelites

Founded in 1848 by young British artists and a writer who were disillusioned with the ideas and teaching of the art establishment, the Pre-Raphaelite Brotherhood admired late medieval and early Renaissance art that was created before Raphael's time. They felt this style was more honest, and developed their own approaches and methods, advocating a return to the sincerity of subjects and styles of an earlier age.

Shocking content

The Pre-Raphaelites' paintings were often considered offensive. Traditional paintings idealised religious figures, but the Pre-Raphaelites did not. Their female models wore no corsets and their hair loose, and the works' vivid colors were seen as garish. The moral themes they often depicted, such as poverty and double standards in society, were considered objectionable. The artists also believed that Britain's Industrial Revolution had led to social and political problems, and they wanted to depict these modern realities. The shocking subject matter depicted by the artists, combined with their radical new style, caused quite a stir among both their contemporaries and the public.

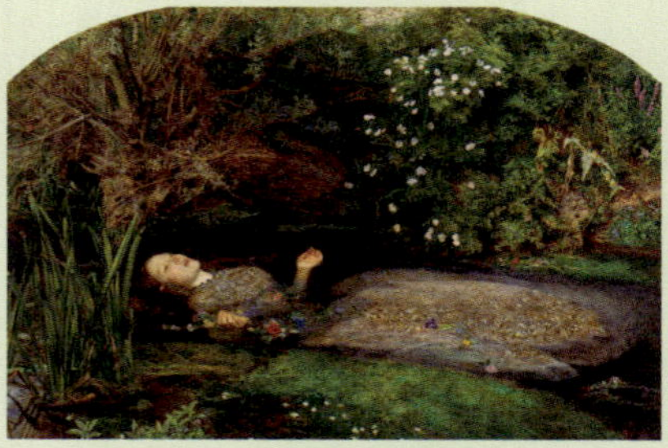

"Ophelia", John Everett Millais (1850–51)
This painting shows a scene from Shakespeare's *Hamlet* – this is the death of Ophelia. Millais painted the background on site, and the figure in his studio.

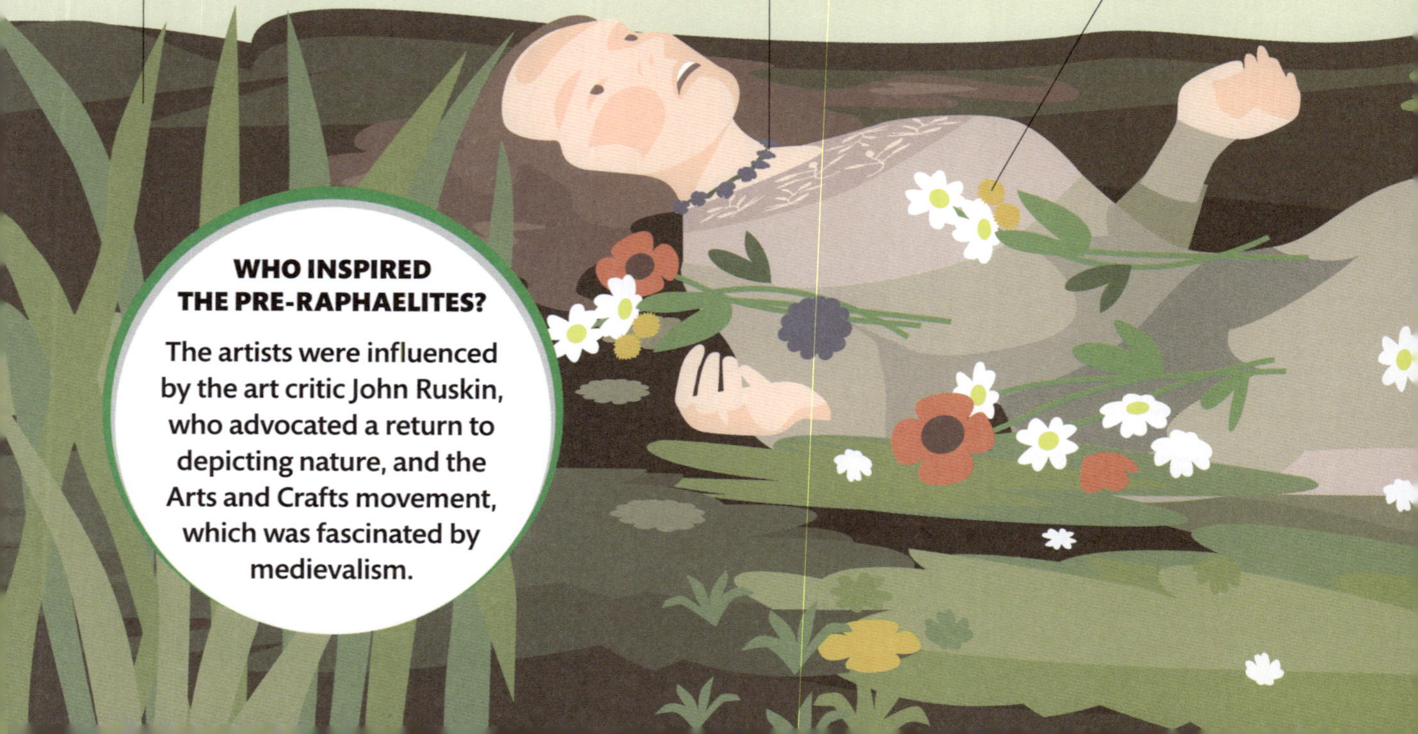

WHO INSPIRED THE PRE-RAPHAELITES?

The artists were influenced by the art critic John Ruskin, who advocated a return to depicting nature, and the Arts and Crafts movement, which was fascinated by medievalism.

Secret society

The group called themselves the Pre-Raphaelite Brotherhood, often signing their work with the initials PRB, maintaining secrecy by refusing to explain what this meant. This was because in defying the traditions of Britain's leading art school, the Royal Academy, they faced hostility from critics. They produced a journal called *The Germ*, featuring art, poetry and literature.

Genuine ideas
The PRB favoured realism over idealism and spurned established teachings.

Return to nature
Natural forms were depicted, as a response to industrial development.

Bright colors
Artists painted over white grounds with bright colors, drawing the eye.

Vibrant detail
Careful application of paint with small brushes created lively, detailed images.

CONDEMNATION

Because of their boldness, their depiction of social problems, and more, many reviled the Pre-Raphaelites, including the writer Charles Dickens, who criticized them as being "the lowest depths of what is mean, odious, repulsive, and revolting".

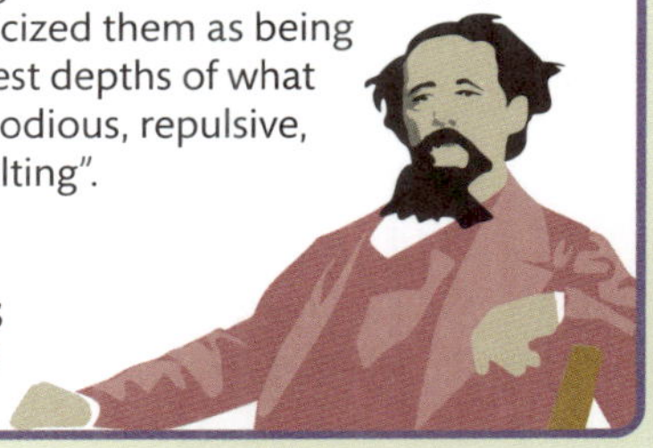

CHARLES DICKENS

ELIZABETH SIDDALL, **THE MODEL,** LAY IN A **WATER-FILLED BATH** EVERY DAY FOR **FOUR MONTHS** WHILE MILLAIS PAINTED, **AND NEARLY DIED**

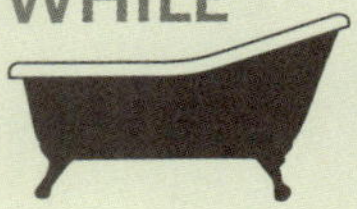

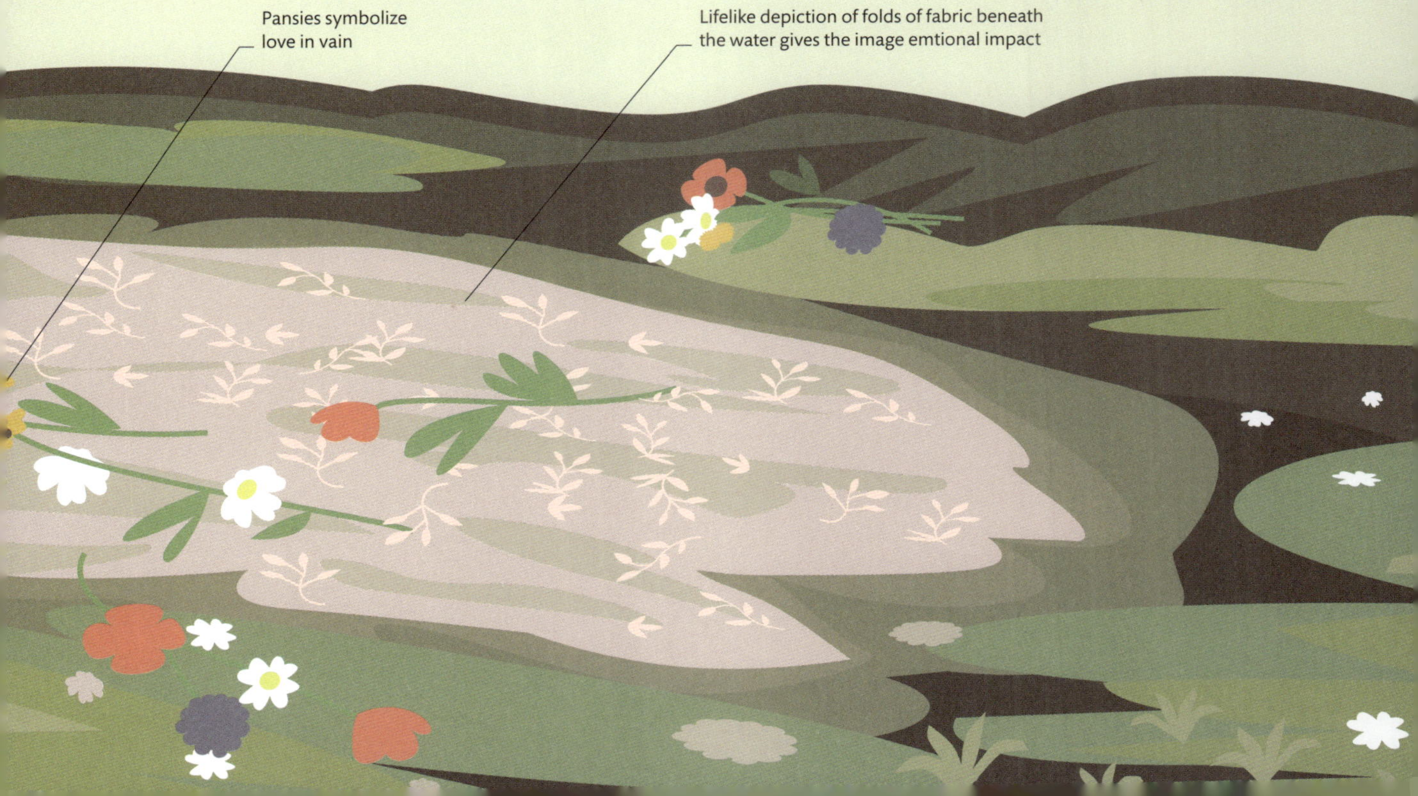

Realism

Often considered the first modern art movement, Realism developed in the mid-19th century when a diffuse group of artists rejected traditional subjects and methods, instead producing images of everyday life. Realists created candid, unglorified images of the modern world, including peasants and working-class life, expanding notions of what constituted art.

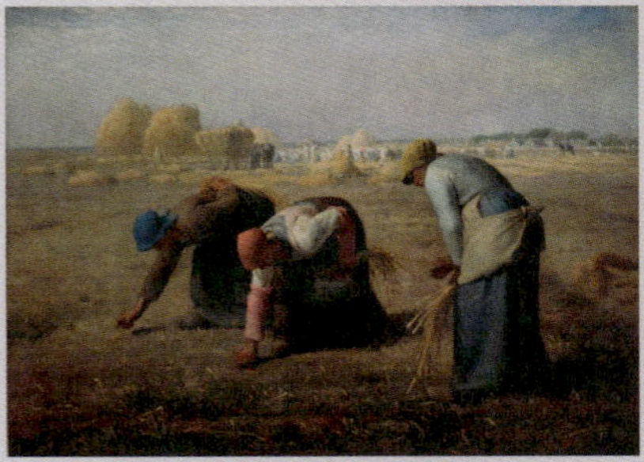

"THE GLEANERS", JEAN-FRANÇOIS MILLET (1857)

Rejecting Romanticism

After the 1848 revolution, Realism first emerged in France, rejecting the idealization and stylization of Romanticism (see pp.186–187) that had dominated Western art for years. By then, the modern, industrial world was becoming more established, and the working classes were gaining a newfound sense of worth. Romanticism, with its emotion, drama, and exotic scenes, seemed out of place, and Realists believed that everyday life, portrayed in lifelike styles with no "beautifying," was more honest.

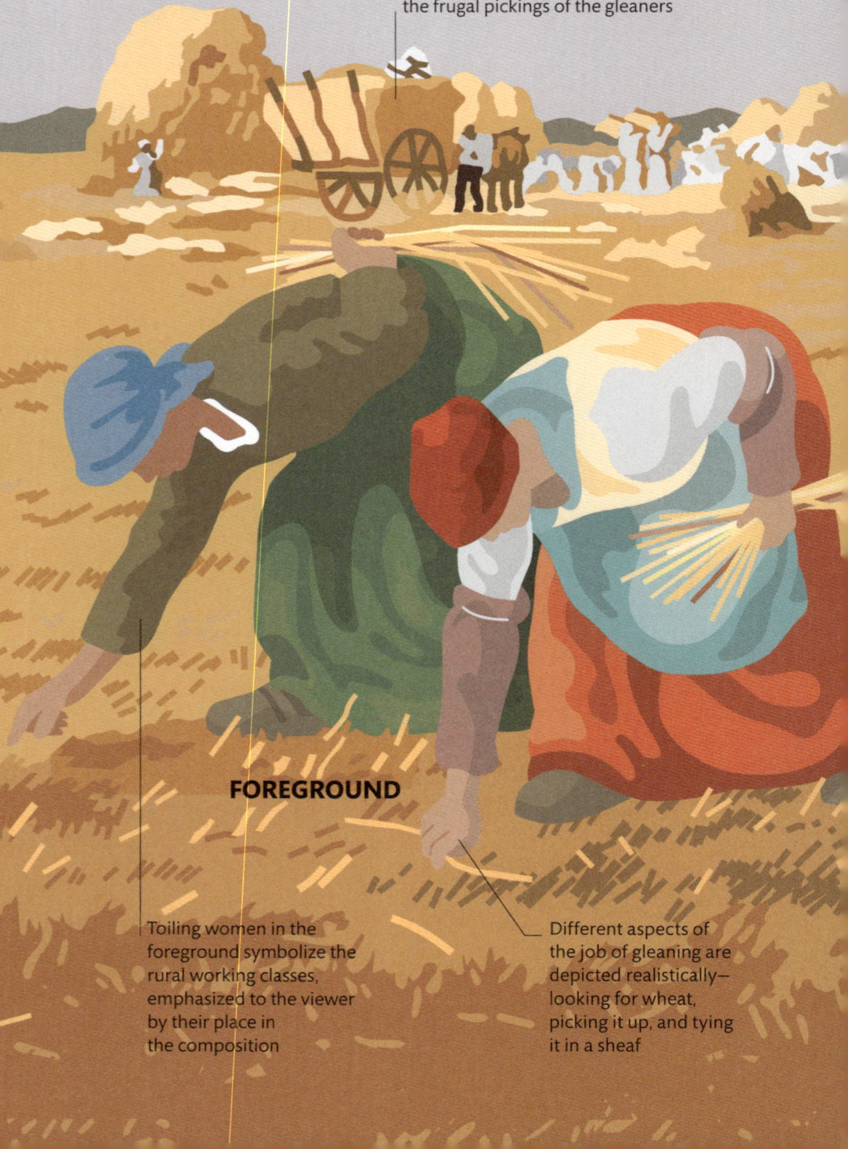

Lives of the workers
Millet's depiction of women working in the long-established job of "gleaning" (gathering leftover grain) conveys the dignity of human labor. The composition highlights the hard lives and humanity of the subjects.

THE **RED** AND **BLUE** HATS AND THE **WHITE** VEST IN MILLET'S **"THE GLEANERS"** FORM THE **COLORS** OF **THE FRENCH FLAG**

HOW DID REALISM REFLECT THE ERA?

Realism coincided with developments in photography and the rise of journalism, both of which increased interest in documenting real social conditions.

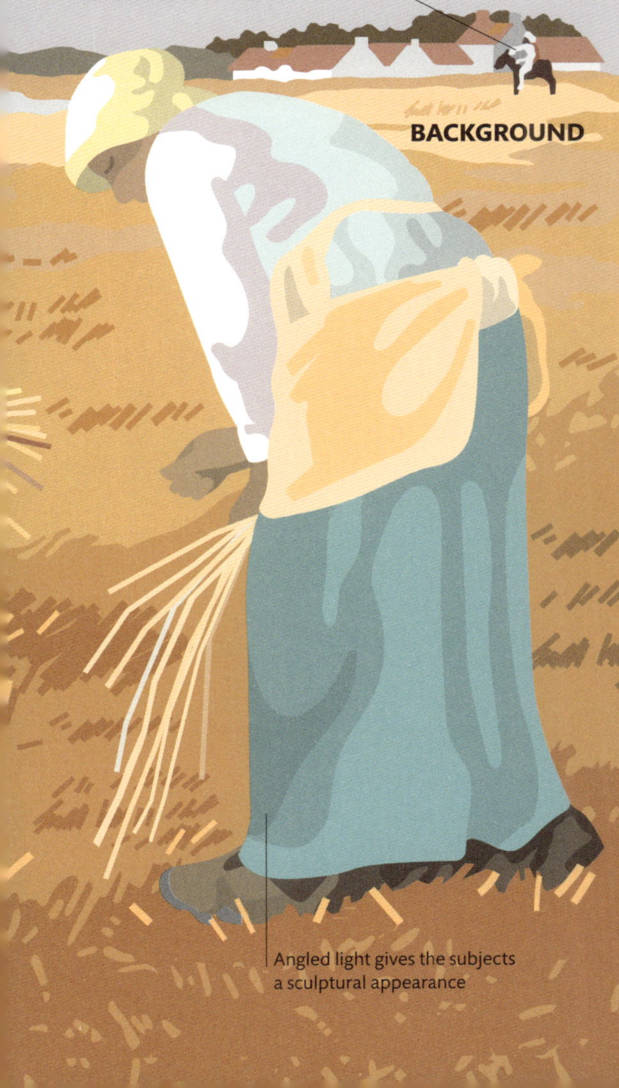

DIFFERING APPROACHES

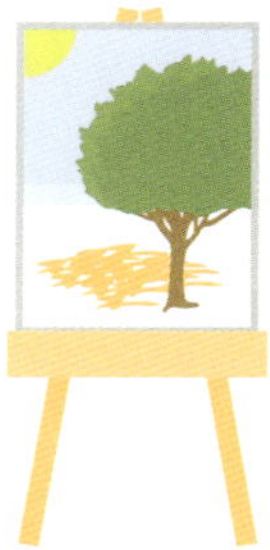

Both Realism and Impressionism (see pp.192–193) featured similar subjects, including rural landscapes, people, and scenes of modern life. While Realists focused on painting ordinary subjects with no artificiality, Impressionist painters aimed to capture the effects of light in a more interpretative way.

IMPRESSIONISM VS REALISM

Elements of realism

By the mid-19th century, industrialization was radically changing the Western world, leading to the rapid growth of cities and the middle classes. No longer commissioned to create art by wealthy patrons or institutions such as the Church, a new generation of artists searched for ways to express this changed world, reexamining and overturning traditional approaches and methods. Their subjects of everyday life and the modern world were all part of the progressive aims of Modernism.

Art rebels
Realism was the first art movement to rebel openly against contemporary conventions of art.

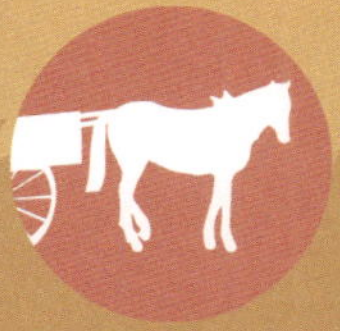

Everyday art
Realists promoted an interest in real-life subjects, more so than artists had done previously.

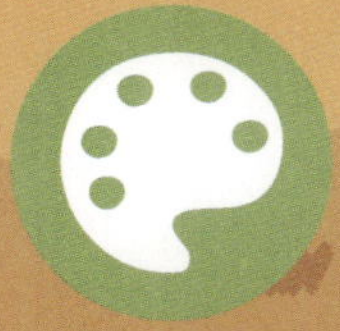

Dark colors
Realist painters often used dark color palettes that contrasted with popular ideals of beauty.

Famous artists
Realism introduced the concept of the artist as a celebrity, an idea that later increased in popularity.

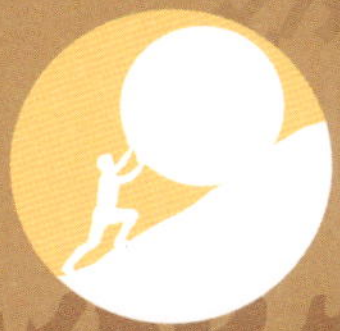

No embellishments
Realist artists aimed to depict its subjects in a clear and unadorned way to emphasize their plights.

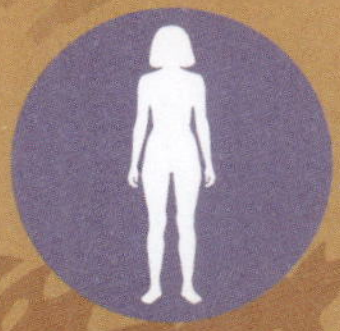

Sex and the body
Some realist works introduced a newfound frankness in depictions of the human body and sexuality.

Outdoor life

Many of the Impressionists were drawn to painting outside or "en plein air," in order to capture nature directly. Recent inventions such as screw-top paints, paint tubes, and portable easels allowed artists to easily carry their materials with them, giving them new flexibility and efficiency when painting outside. Artists such as Renoir were drawn to scenes from nature but also painted urban views featuring subjects from modern, everyday life that would have been wholly unacceptable to the Académie—from bars and prostitutes to steam trains and the seaside.

WHERE DID THE NAME "IMPRESSIONISM" COME FROM?

Taken from the title of a Claude Monet painting, the term was originally used by a disparaging art critic to denigrate this new style.

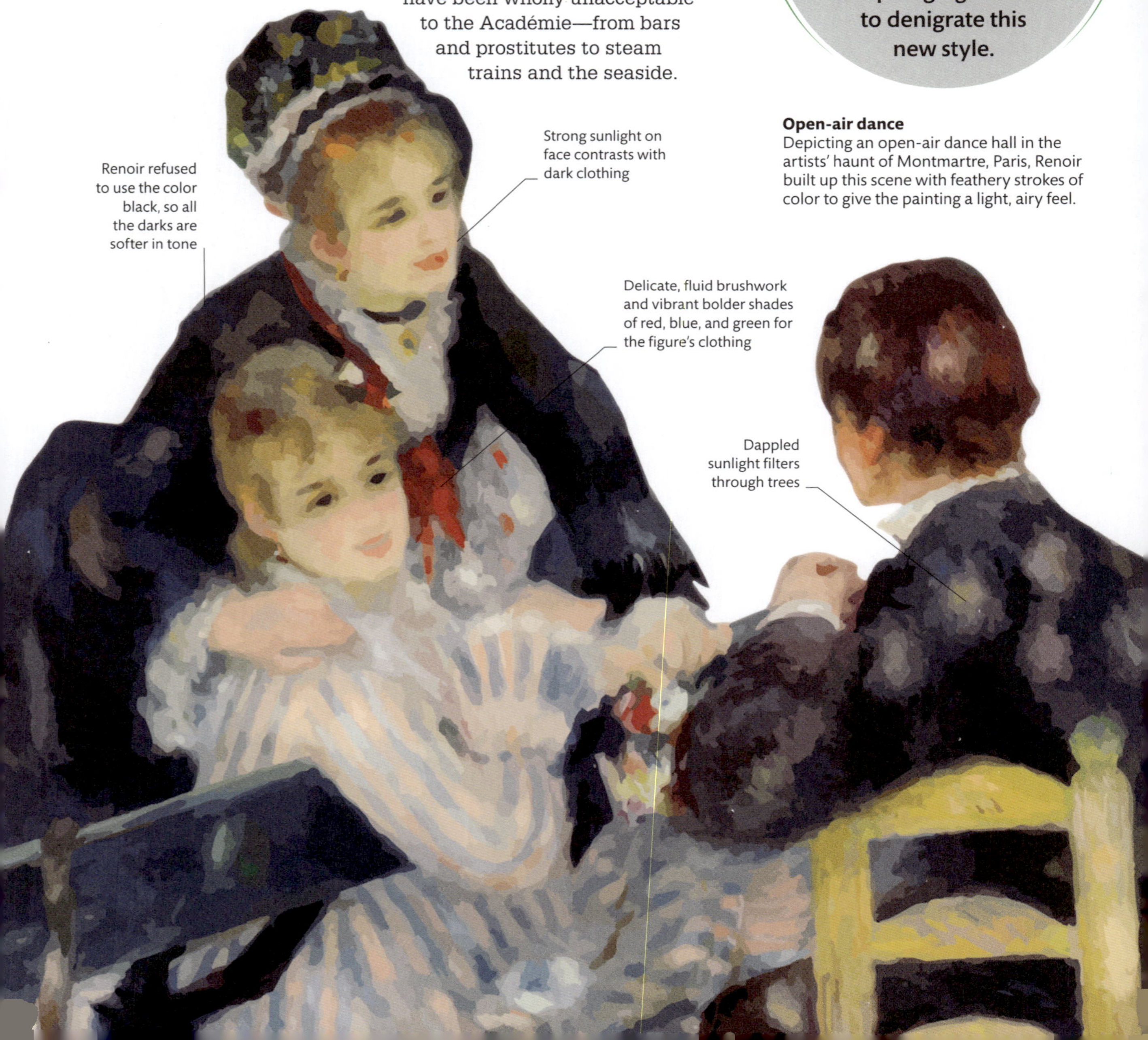

Open-air dance
Depicting an open-air dance hall in the artists' haunt of Montmartre, Paris, Renoir built up this scene with feathery strokes of color to give the painting a light, airy feel.

Impressionism

Impressionism developed in France in the 1860s when artists began recording the changing effects of light and color in the outside world, which they captured in quick brushstrokes to create "impressions."

In the second half of the 19th century, Impressionist artists, including Claude Monet, Mary Cassatt, and Pierre-Auguste Renoir, broke with artistic tradition and rejected the prevailing standards set out by the Académie des Beaux-Arts, a French society that preserved the painting of historical and moral scenes. Instead, the artists explored how paint could recreate their sensory experiences of everyday life. Using bright colors, often straight from the tube and applied in loose, sketchy brushstrokes, they worked to capture the fleeting sensations they felt while observing the world around them.

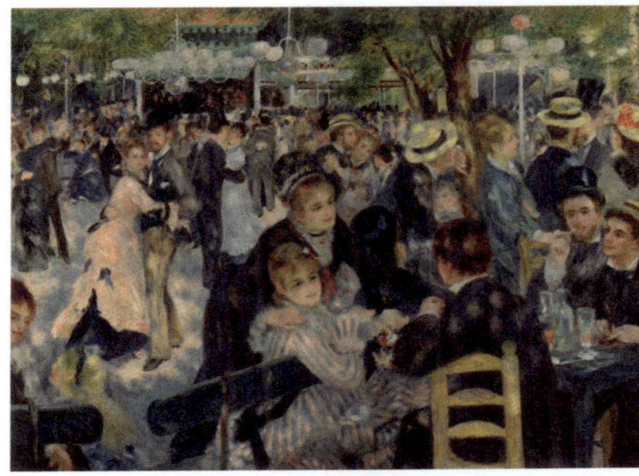

"BALL AT THE MOULIN DE LA GALETTE", PIERRE-AUGUSTE RENOIR (1876)

THE PAINT TUBE WAS INVENTED IN 1841 BY JOHN GOFFE RAND

Capturing light

Claude Monet (1840–1926) was a founding Impressionist who kept returning to the same subjects at different times of the day and changing seasons in the year. From haystacks and cathedrals, to the water lilies in his garden, he captured the varying effects of light on color, pushing his work to near abstraction.

Painting in situ
Monet's "Haystacks" series began in fall 1890 and continued for 18 months. He painted outside, carrying his painting equipment across fields.

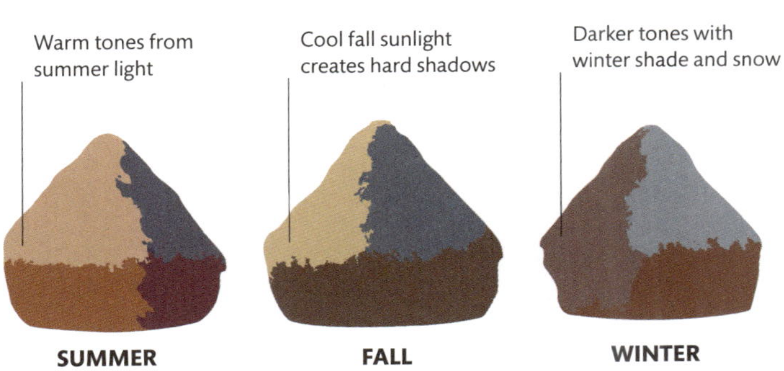

SALON DES REFUSÉS OF 1863

Many of the early Impressionist artists had their experimental works rejected by the Académie-sponsored annual exhibition, the Paris Salon, so in 1863 they set up their own "exhibition of rejects" at the Palais de L'industrie to showcase their works, causing uproar in the French art establishment.

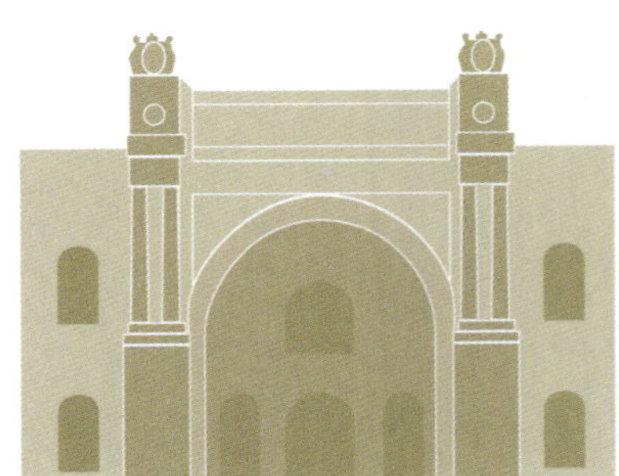

THE PALAIS DE L'INDUSTRIE

Post-Impressionism

Impressionism had a strong influence on several painters working mainly in France in the late 1880s. This diverse group came to be known collectively as the Post-Impressionists.

Individual visions

The Impressionists (see pp.192–193) opened the floodgates for the artistic experimentation that took place at the turn of the 19th century. The Post-Impressionist painters—a disparate group consisting of Paul Cézanne, Paul Gauguin, Vincent Van Gogh, and Georges Seurat—moved away from the Impressionists' idea of conveying light and color in a naturalistic way. Instead, they each experimented with different approaches to color, brush technique, and subject matter. In so doing, each of the painters recreated their own highly individual artistic visions. More interested in expressing emotions than reproducing what was in front of them, their works are rich in symbolism.

Mountain detail
Paul Cézanne used subtle variations in color and shifts in perspective to depict a landscape.

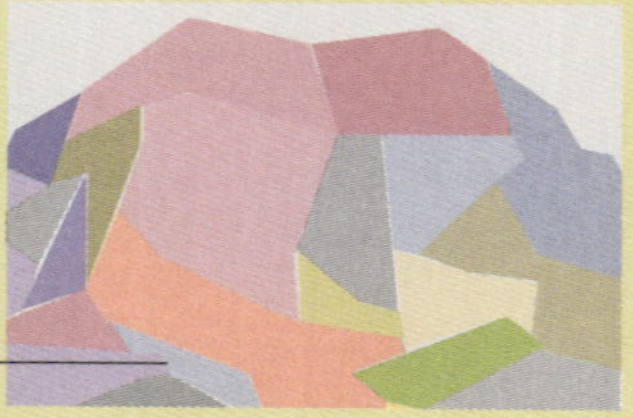

Flat planes of subtly graded color

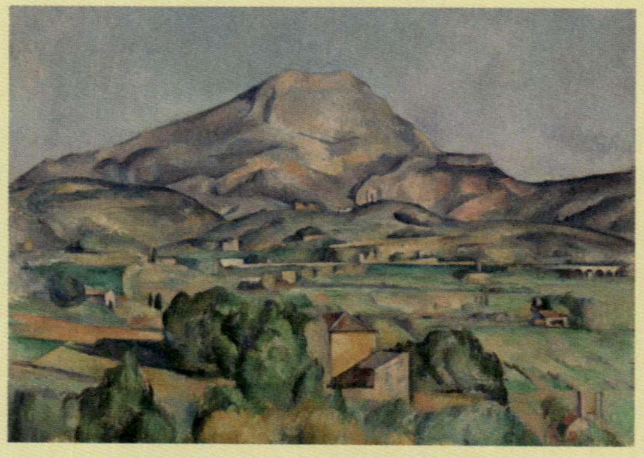

"Mont Sainte-Victoire", Paul Cézanne (1892–95)
Cézanne painted a series of pictures of this mountain in southern France. He used subtle outlines and implied geometric shapes to simplify the scene.

Vincent's sunflowers
Between 1888–1889, van Gogh painted a series of sunflower pictures. He used a limited palette of three types of chrome yellow, yellow ocher, and Veronese green oil paint.

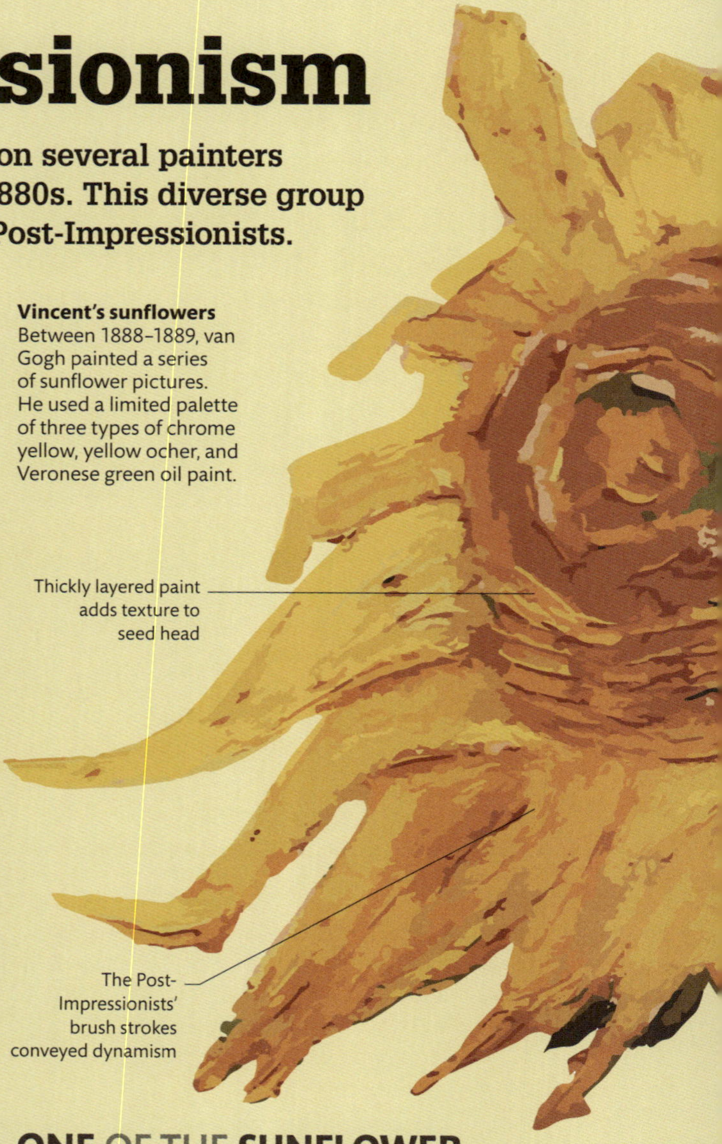

Thickly layered paint adds texture to seed head

The Post-Impressionists' brush strokes conveyed dynamism

ONE OF THE SUNFLOWER PAINTINGS WAS DESTROYED IN WORLD WAR II

Color and technique

Vincent van Gogh typified the Post-Impressionists' use of distorted form and unnatural coloring to recreate their subjects. Thanks to the invention of new paint pigments, he used vibrant oil colors in his pictures—in particular yellow—to provoke an emotional reaction in the viewer. His bold, thickly loaded brush strokes—a technique known as impasto—bring about an almost three-dimensional quality into his paintings of everyday scenes and objects.

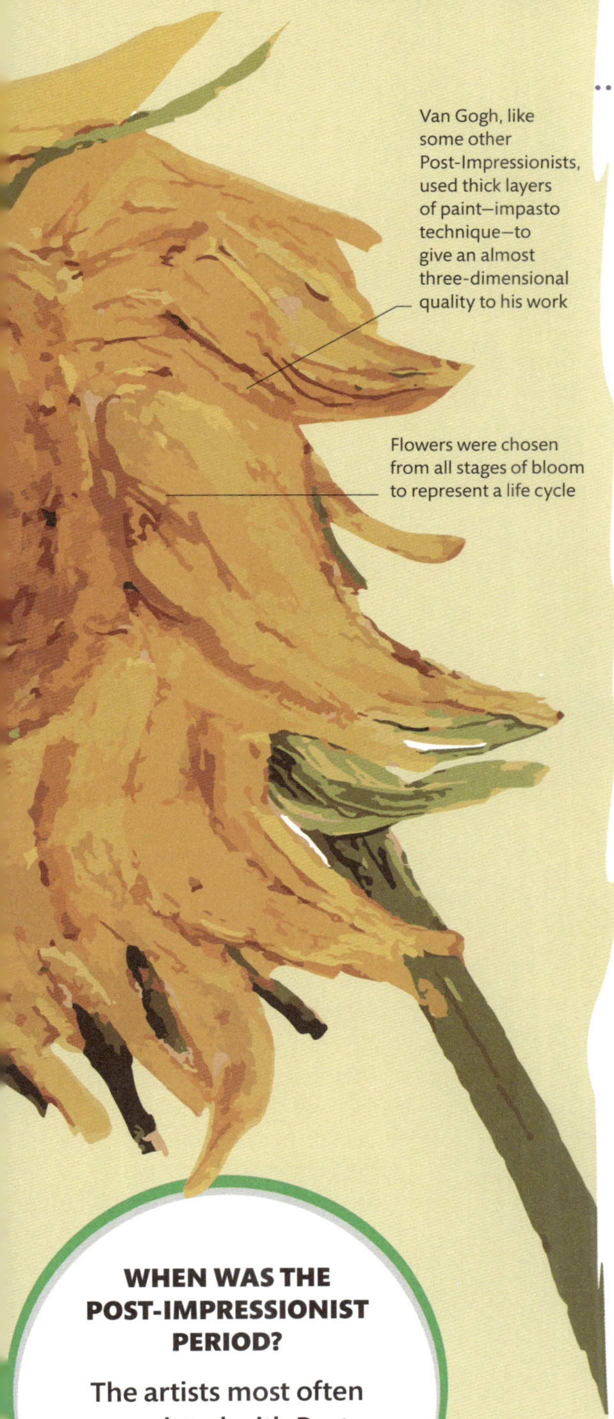

Gauguin and color

Inspired by the Impressionists, Paul Gauguin gave up his career as a stockbroker to pursue painting in 1883. His travels to Martinique in the Caribbean and the tropical islands of Tahiti in the South Pacific Ocean strongly influenced his use of bold color, which became a landmark of the Post-Impressionist movement. In his early works, he used broad areas of block color over graduated hues. Edging these areas with dark lines gave the impression of flattened forms.

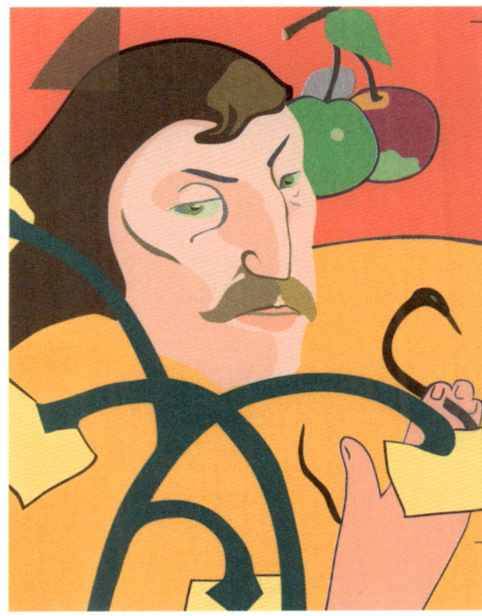

"Self-Portrait with Halo", Paul Gaugin (1889)
Gauguin often used colors symbolically—it has been debated whether the yellows and reds here suggest the heat of hell and creation.

VAN GOGH'S LETTERS

Vincent van Gogh was a prolific letter-writer. A total of 819 written by the artist survive today. Much of his correspondence was to his brother, Theo. In his letters, Van Gogh sometimes included sketches of the compositions he was working on at the time—often annotated with labels indicating where he would apply color.

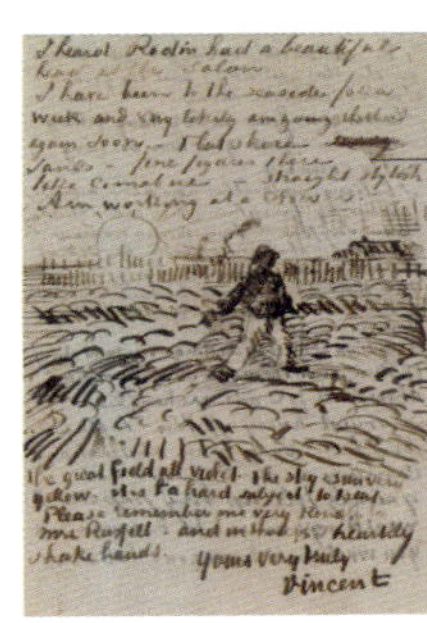

WHEN WAS THE POST-IMPRESSIONIST PERIOD?

The artists most often associated with Post-Impressionism mainly worked between 1880 and 1910.

The wallpaper process
Morris designed all his own wallpapers and had them hand-printed with pear-wood blocks. The motifs were made in a repeat pattern, using a foot-driven weight.

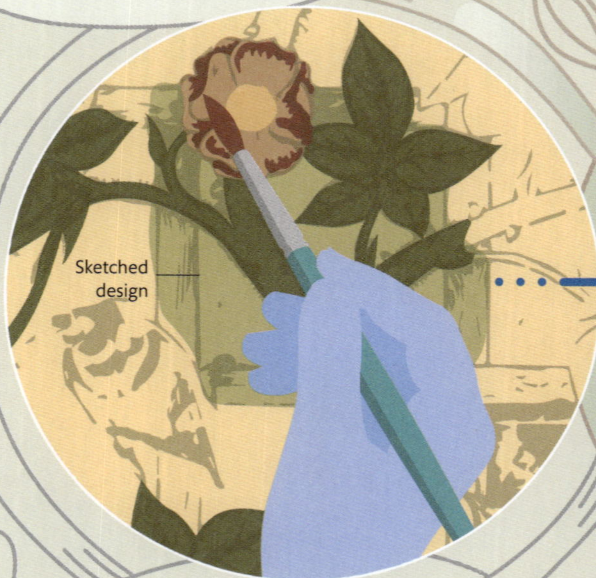

1 Create the wallpaper design
The design is sketched onto paper with a brush and then carefully transferred to the woodblock, often by tracing the design over carbon-transfer paper.

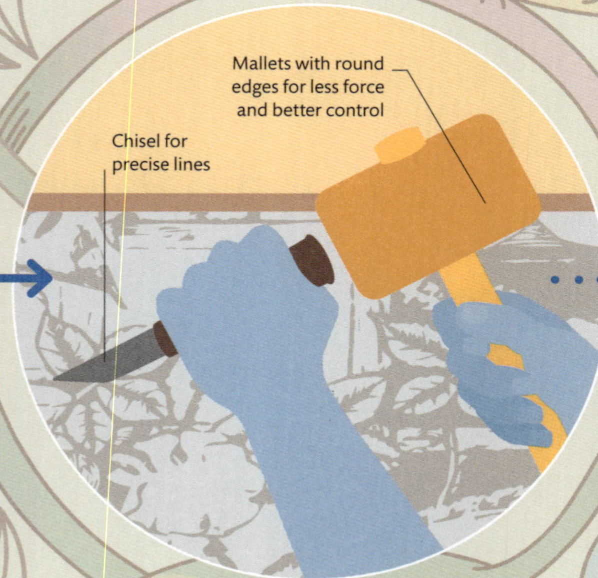

2 Carve the design in wood
Chisels and gouges incised the design into the wood, leaving the raised areas to take the ink. Morris sometimes added areas of metal or felt to create texture.

Arts and Crafts

The Arts and Crafts movement arose in England in the mid-1880s as a reaction to what was seen as the negative effects of the Industrial Revolution. Advocates of the movement, chiefly designer William Morris, instead wanted to create handmade artworks and objects that evoked the spirit of medieval traditions.

Furniture
Straight, simple lines were features of furniture.

Prints
Print designs were highly decorative and made using natural motifs and dyes.

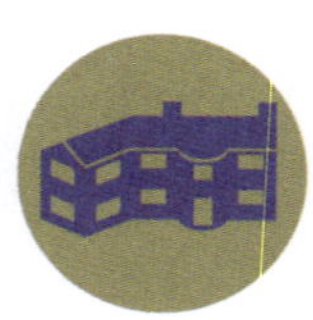

Architecture
Buildings were often asymmetrical with a focus on materials.

A reaction to industry

Overwhelmed by the amount of inferior, tasteless products on display at London's Great Exhibition of 1851, William Morris, and others who would become leading figures of the Arts and Crafts movement, opted instead to design objects that focused on simplicity, beauty, and practicality. As many Arts and Crafts designers had trained in architecture, the idea of a "total" interior, in which architecture, wallpaper, furniture, ceramics, and other objects combined to create a balanced whole, conformed to the modern, socially transformative ideal of domestic space.

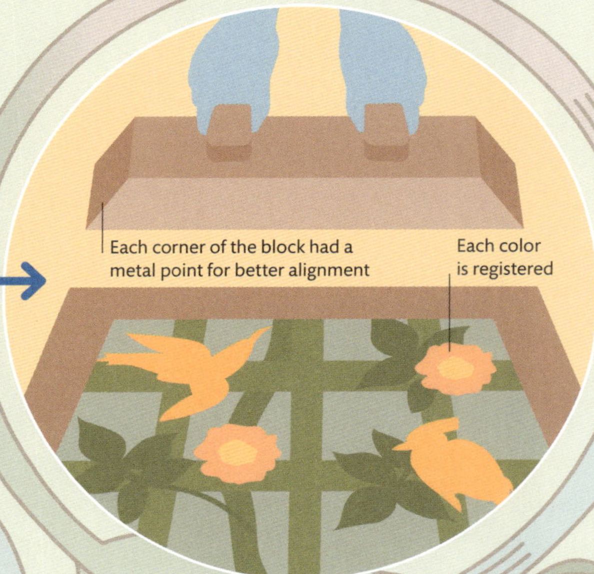

3 Print each color
A separate block must be carved for each color. Then, these are printed in turn over the same piece of paper, and the print is gradually built up into the completed design.

WHO WAS WILLIAM MORRIS?

William Morris was a poet, designer, and social reformer whose ideas on craft and its place in society made him a leading figure of the Arts and Crafts movement.

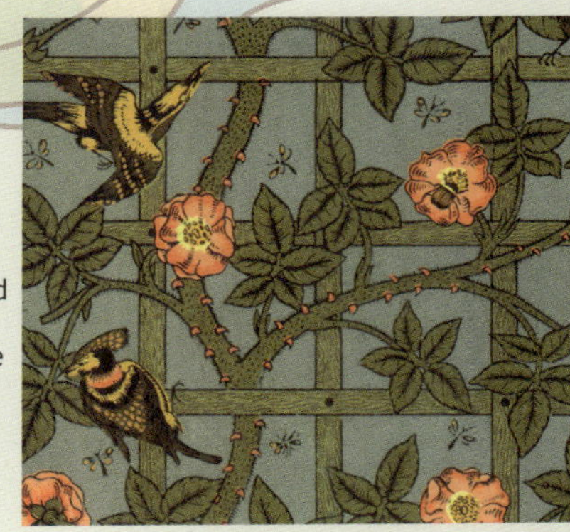

The finished wallpaper
Morris's "Trellis" wallpaper was inspired by the garden at his home, Red House. The pattern blends birds and roses on a pale background and is typical of his early designs.

Pugin's Parliament

English architect Augustus Pugin, like Morris, railed against the overt ornamentation of the Victorian age. Following a fire in 1834, Pugin was commissioned to design the clock tower and the interiors of the newly rebuilt Palace of Westminster in London. His finished designs combined Christian themes with Gothic interiors (see pp.174–175), furnishings, and wallpapers, all informed by an idyllic imagined past of the Middle Ages.

National icon
Elizabeth Tower or "Big Ben" is probably the most famous part of Pugin's design for the Palace of Westminster. Standing at 316 ft (96 m) tall, its hands and dials are painted in Prussian blue.

MORRIS'S "ACANTHUS" PATTERN WALLPAPER WAS PRINTED WITH 15 DIFFERENT COLORS

SOCIETIES AND GUILDS

The Arts and Crafts movement took its name from the Arts and Crafts Exhibition Society. It was made up of different groups, including the Exhibition Society, the Arts Workers Guild, and artisans in workshops and manufacturing companies.

Necessary tool
Traditional tools produced individual, high-quality items and put an end to the mechanization of the industrial age.

ODILON REDON

Odilon Redon was a French Symbolist painter and printmaker whose works explored fantastical, haunted, and often morbid themes. The sources for his artworks mainly came from his imagination rather than the observed world and were often inspired by poetry or dreams, invoking inner worlds of private torment as he delved deeper into his own psyche. Alongside these works, he also created numerous still life paintings of flowers, captured in vibrant, glowing colors using oils and pastels.

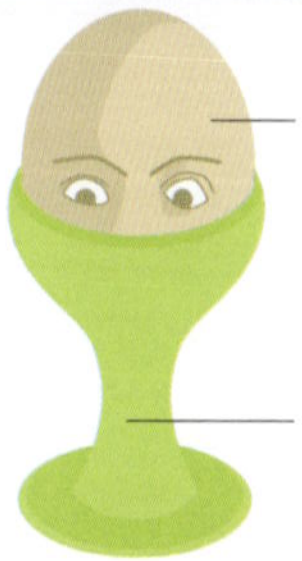

"THE EGG (L'ŒUF)", ODILON REDON (1885)

WHAT INSPIRED "THE SCREAM?"

One evening, Munch took a walk as the sun went down and the sky turned blood red. He described experiencing an "infinite scream passing through nature."

Red and orange sky dominates top part of the composition and creates an apocalyptic feel

Symbolism

The Symbolism movement was a reaction against the naturalism of earlier 19th-century painting and the Impressionists' attempts to recreate the effects of nature. Instead, the Symbolists were concerned with conveying emotional states of mind through their paintings.

Painting by intuition

Symbolist painters relied on their intuition rather than observation, using discordant colors and dreamlike compositions to suggest ideas, feelings, or moods that were often disturbing and nightmarish in tone. Although not united by a singular style, the Symbolists' exploration of the emotional power of art was internationally influential, prefiguring both Surrealism (see pp.206–207) and Expressionism (see pp.202–203).

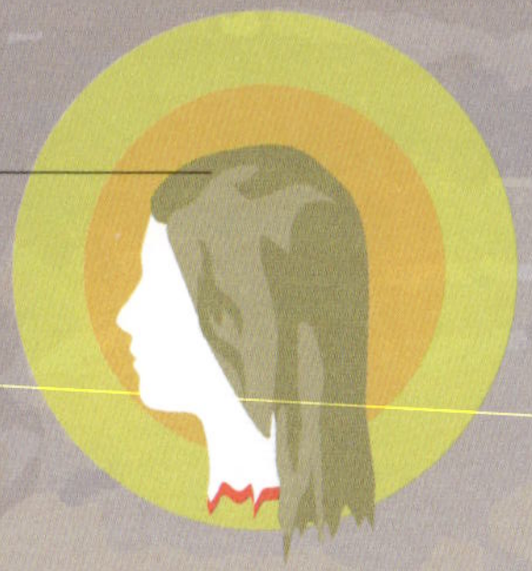

Severed or disembodied head
Heads appear in various forms of mythological, Biblical, and Classical art. The Symbolists revived it in their art, drawn to its power and mystery.

Recurrent themes

The Symbolists were interested in the unknown and the extraordinary, informed by the interest in spiritualism, the esoteric, and the anarchic that blossomed during the 1800s. Although they did not ascribe defined meanings to specific symbols in their work, there were several recurrent themes in Symbolist paintings, including the isolated figure, the androgyne, the severed head, and the femme fatale with long flowing locks. Color was also used symbolically. When nature does occur, it is often shown in a threatening, oppressive, or melancholy manner.

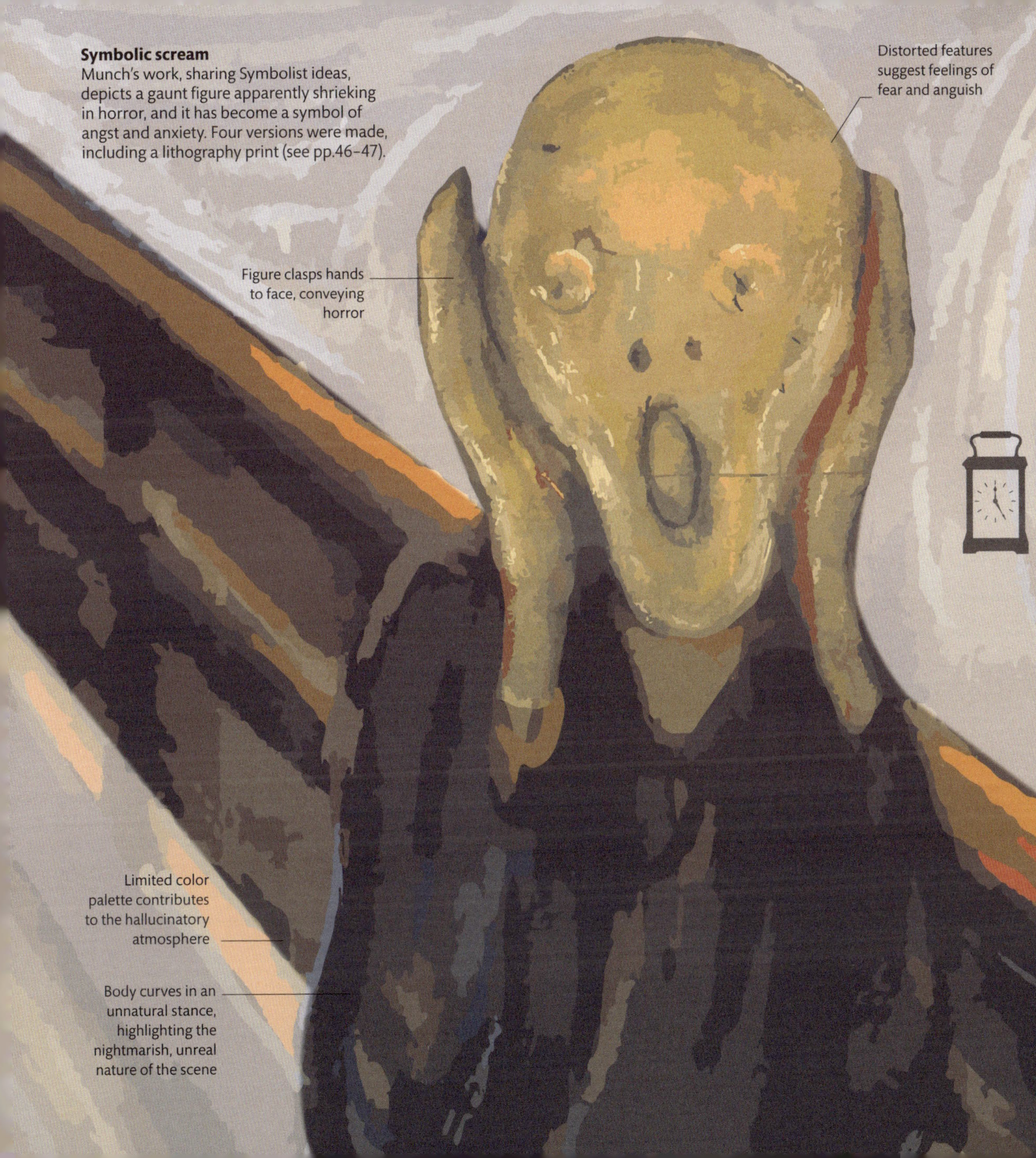

Symbolic scream
Munch's work, sharing Symbolist ideas, depicts a gaunt figure apparently shrieking in horror, and it has become a symbol of angst and anxiety. Four versions were made, including a lithography print (see pp.46–47).

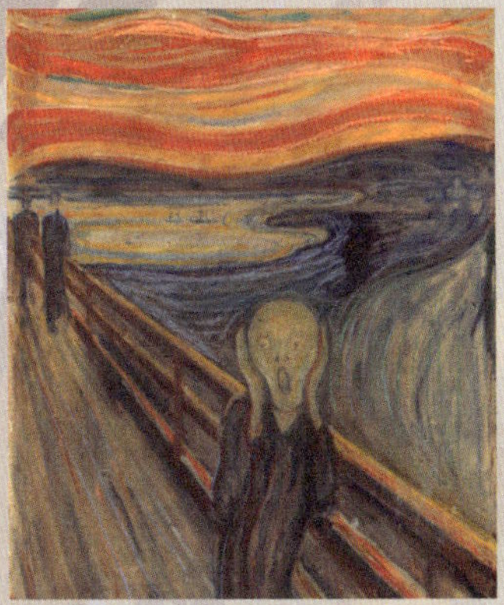

"THE SCREAM", EDVARD MUNCH (1893)

25 YEARS

THE **AMOUNT OF TIME REDON** WORKED ONLY IN **BLACK** CREATING HIS **"LES NOIRS" DRAWINGS**

Art Nouveau

Art Nouveau was an international, decorative style that developed in the final decades of the 19th century, influencing many artistic disciplines.

Style and sensuality

Art Nouveau broke from the historic emphasis of earlier 19th-century art to create a new style, characterized by stylized, flowing lines and organic motifs. Peaking in popularity between 1890 and 1910, it rapidly spread around Europe, where it was known as *Sezessionstil* in Austria and *Jugendstil* in Germany, and also became fashionable in the US. Art Nouveau's elegant lines and focus on decorative ornamentation, inspired by the natural world, spread beyond the walls of the art galleries to reach a mass audience via media such as advertising posters, glassware, jewelry, furniture, and building design.

Recurring themes

Art Nouveau artworks often made use of archetypes—typical examples of people or things. Common archetypes in Art Nouveau included the willowy, seductive woman; the image-obsessed, pleasure-seeking dandy; and various lovers. From the natural world, artists drew on the asymmetrical shapes of flower stalks, leaves, and vines, as well as subtle animal forms such as bird and insect wings.

DANDY

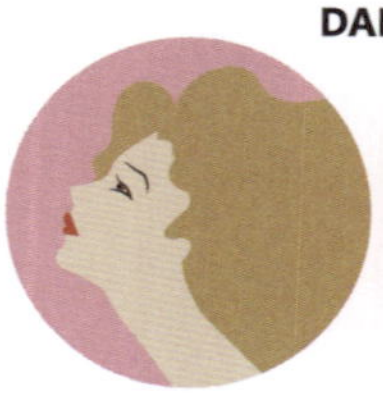

SEDUCTIVE WOMAN

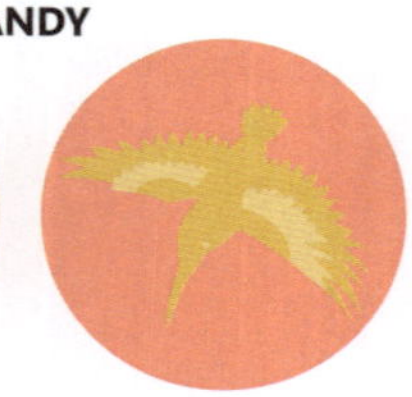

NATURAL FORM

KLIMT SOLD "THE KISS" TO A GALLERY BEFORE HE HAD COMPLETELY FINISHED IT

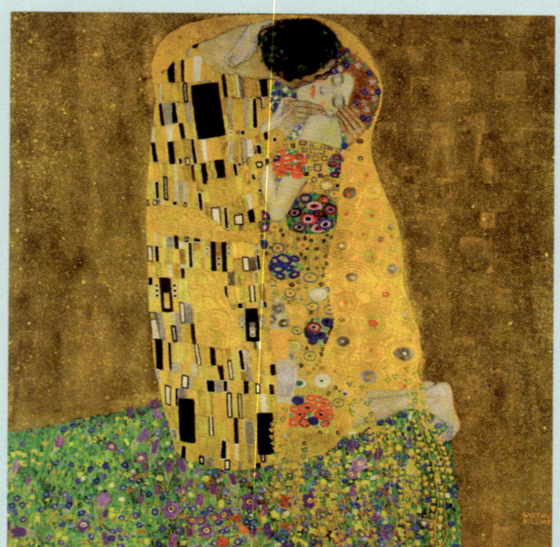

"THE KISS," GUSTAV KLIMT (1907)

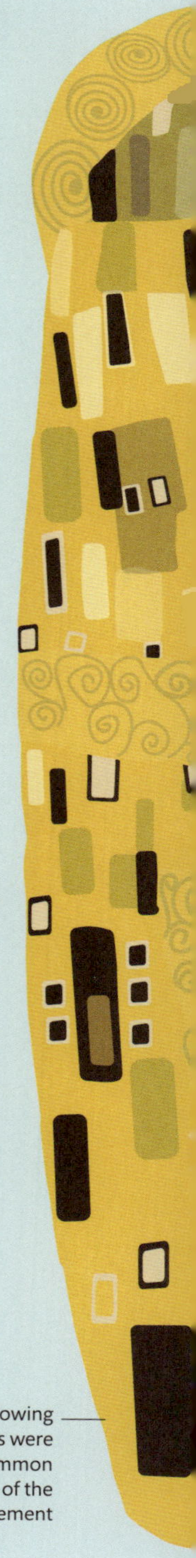

Flowing lines were a common feature of the movement

ARCHITECTURE

Art Nouveau architecture resulted in flowing, organic structures that featured vinelike lines and patterns, fusing form and ornament. This contrasted with the classically inspired building style that preceded it.

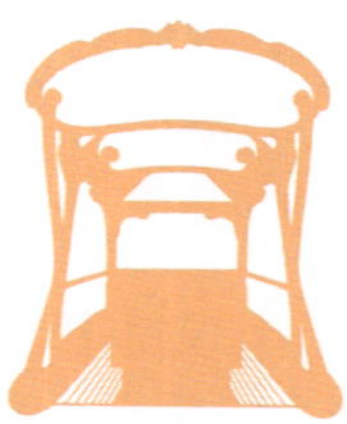

ORGANIC BUILDING STYLE

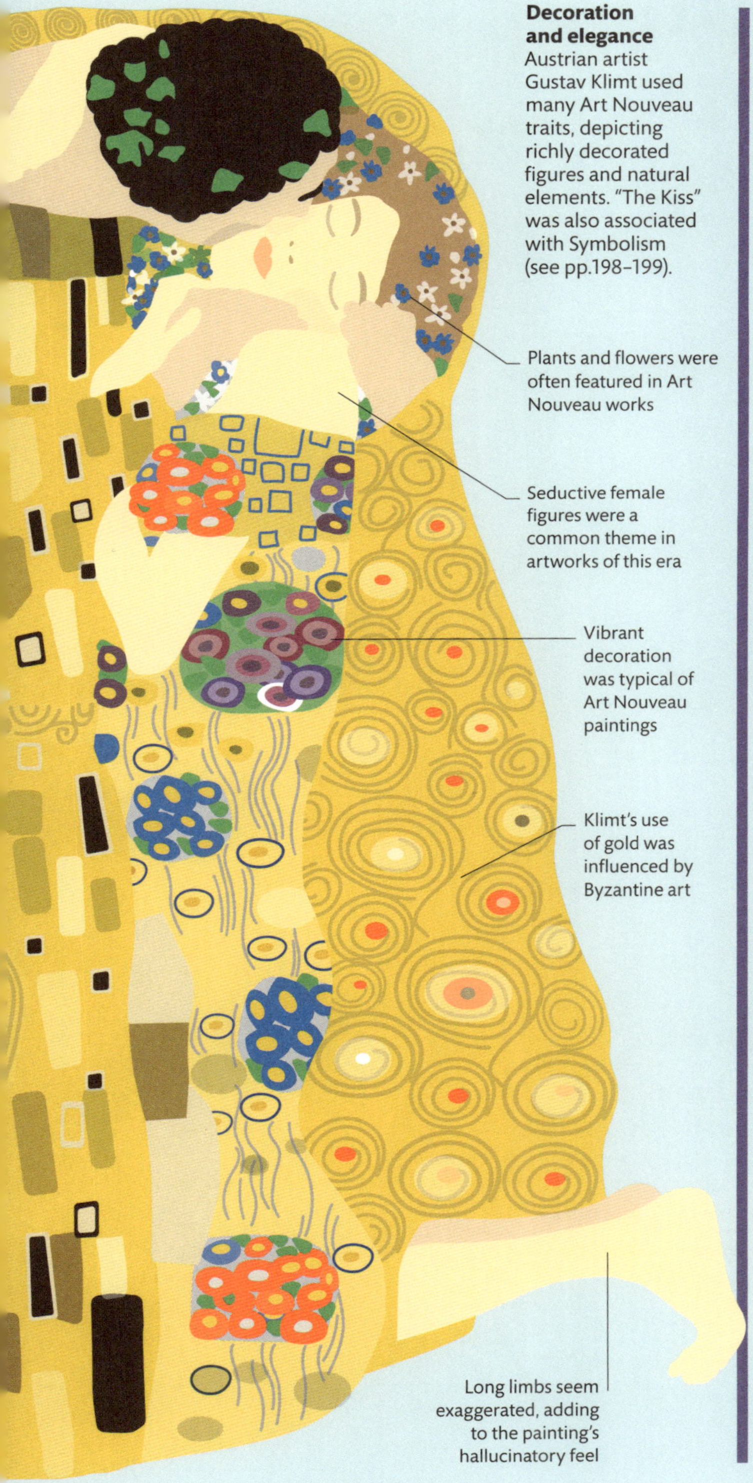

WHERE DID THE NAME "ART NOUVEAU" COME FROM?

The term was first used by Belgian magazine *L'Art Moderne* in the 1880s, referring to the pioneering work of a group of artists called "Les Vingts."

Main influences

Art Nouveau developed from a range of influences. Ukiyo-e Japanese prints (see p.169), with their strong linear aesthetic, were popular at the time, while the Arts and Crafts movement (see pp.196–197) had recently employed motifs from nature. Opulent Rococo furnishings and the interlacing patterns of Celtic design were also influential.

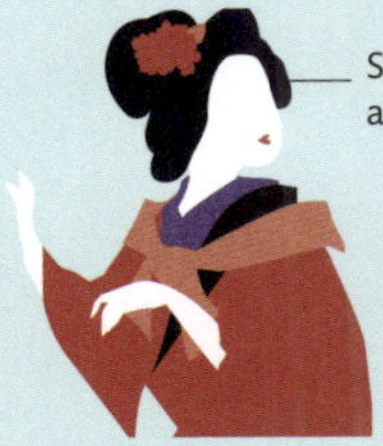

Japanese prints
Japanese prints were hugely influential when they arrived in Europe in the 1850s.

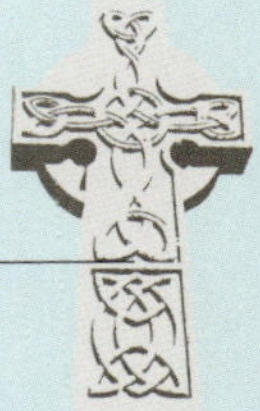

Celtic designs
The 1800s saw great interest in Celtic culture in the UK, seeking an idealized past in reaction to modernism.

Rococo
In the 1700s, Rococo used sculptural curves and ornamented decoration, often with natural forms.

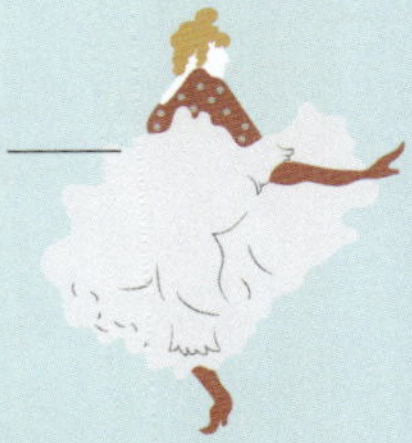

Advertising
Art Nouveau both influenced, and was influenced by, advertising's expressive linear works.

Expressionism and Fauvism

Expressionism and Fauvism developed in the first decade of the 20th century. Both employed strong color and nonnaturalistic compositions, but in differing ways.

A modern reaction

Expressionism and Fauvism were both born out of responses to the rapid technological change of the modern age in the early 1900s. Expressionism emerged across Europe but became particularly associated with artists in Germany such as Ernst Ludwig Kirchner, Karl Schmidt-Rottluff, and Emil Nolde. Using sickly, sometimes clashing color combinations, the German Expressionists made paintings that emphasized feelings rather than realism and addressed themes of alienation and social critique. The best-known German Expressionist artists were part of two groups—"Die Brücke" (The Bridge) and "Die Blaue Reiter" (The Blue Rider)—that both explored what they saw as society's ills through their distorted scenes.

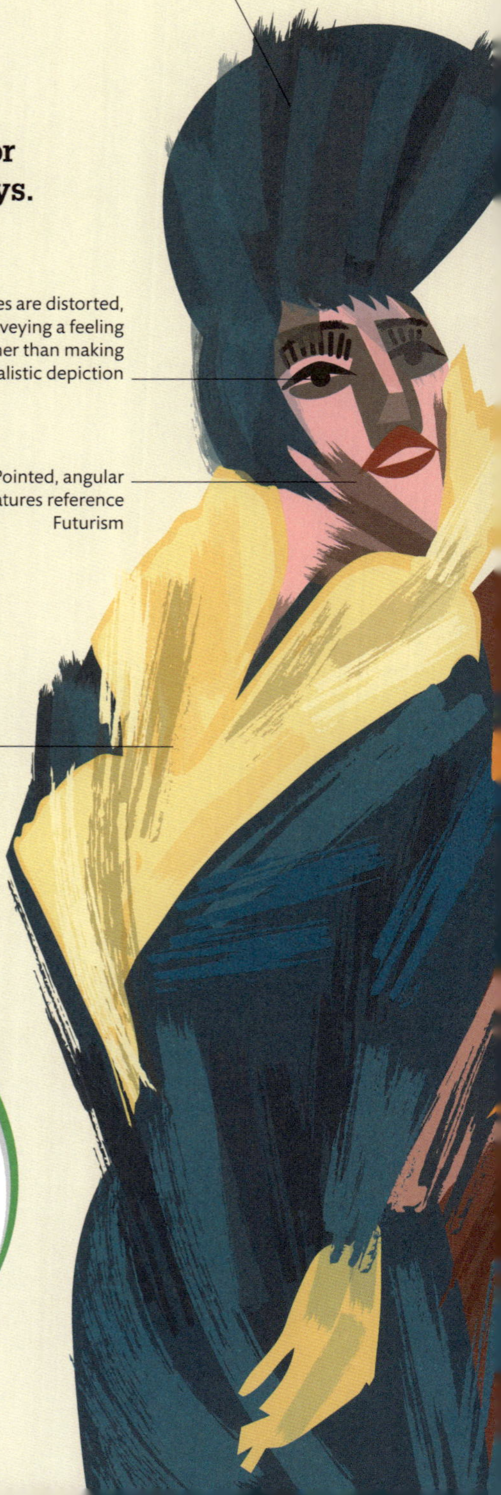

Urban street scenes
In 1913–1915, Kirchner made a series of works that highlighted modern society, and the crowded bustle and isolated individuals that characterized life in prewar Berlin.

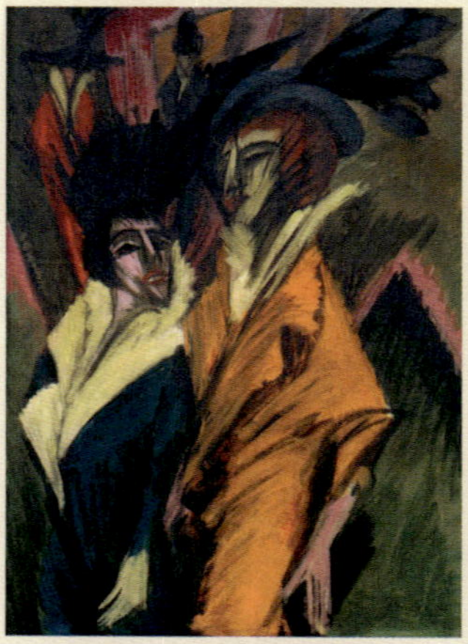

"TWO WOMEN IN THE STREET", ERNST LUDWIG KIRCHNER (1914)

HOW DID THE EXPRESSIONISTS GET THEIR NAME?

The Expressionists "expressed" their inner world of emotion through their paintings, using vivid colors and dramatic, jagged lines to convey the intensity of life.

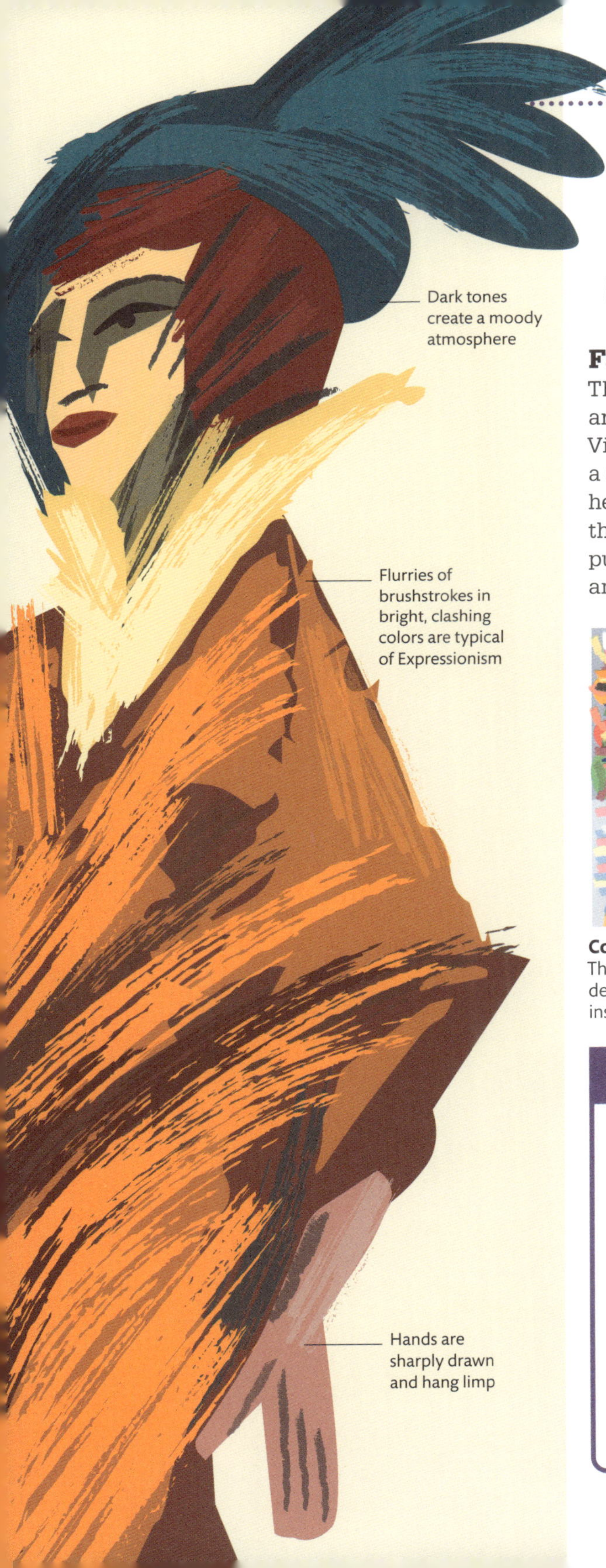

THE TERM **"FAUVES" (WILD CATS)** WAS ORIGINALLY MEANT AS AN INSULT BUT **THE NAME STUCK**

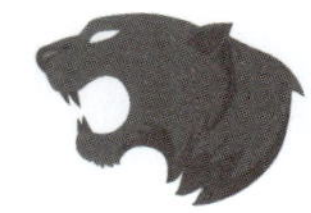

Fauvism

The Fauves were a group of Parisian painters, centered around Henri Matisse and André Derain. Influenced by Vincent van Gogh and Paul Gauguin, the Fauves embraced a sense of creative freedom, applying intense colors with heavy, thick brushstrokes. They reduced the world around them to simple shapes in solid colors, using flat areas of pure, bright color to create vibrant, pattern-like portraits and landscapes, prefiguring later abstract painting.

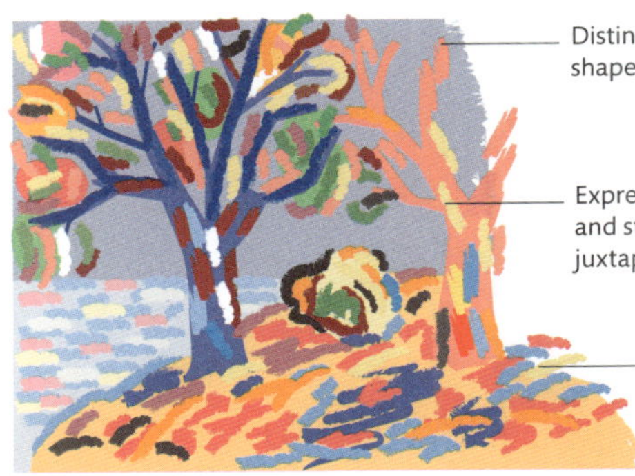

Color as a tool
The Fauves used color to illuminate rather than to describe, liberating it from the subject matter and, instead, examining its effects on their psyches.

MODERNISM

Both the Fauves and the Expressionists were experimenting with new ways of visually communicating the simmering feelings aroused by the rapid change of life around them in the early 20th century. The influences of new technologies, such as the camera, the automobile, and the telegraph called for fresh ways of art making to reflect the new "Modernism" of an increasingly industrialized world.

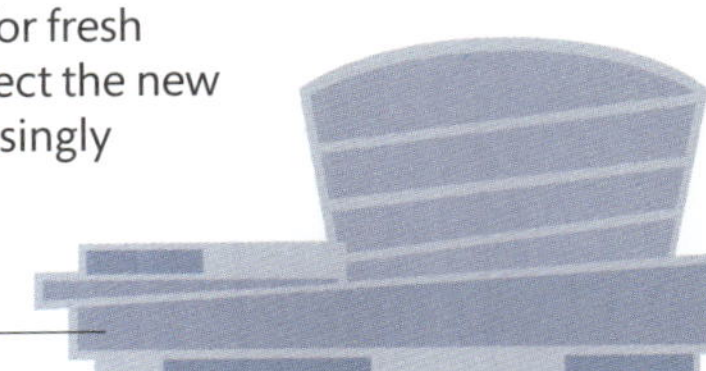

THE GUGGENHEIM MUSEUM

Analytic and Synthetic

Cubism moved through two stages. The first, of breaking down objects into constituent parts and viewpoints, became known as Analytic Cubism. In 1912, Braque and Picasso both began adding other materials to their paintings, such as colored paper, cardboard, and newsprint. This collage approach, Synthetic Cubism, emphasized the flatness of the canvas, abandoning attempts at creating illusionary, three-dimensional images.

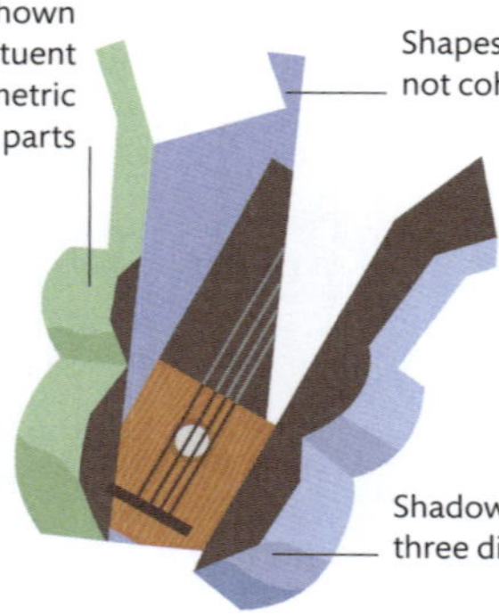

ANALYTIC

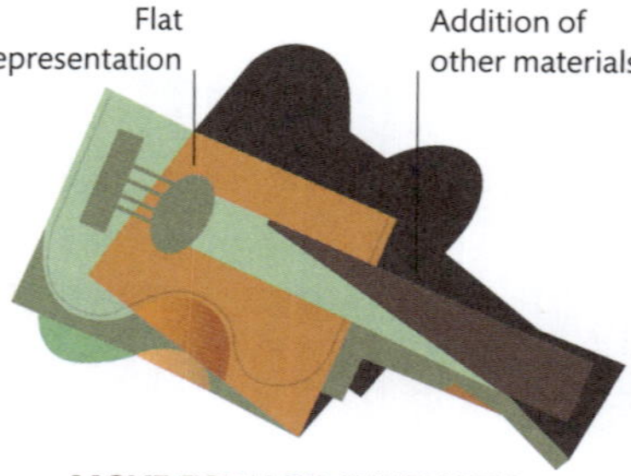

MOVE TOWARD SYNTHETIC

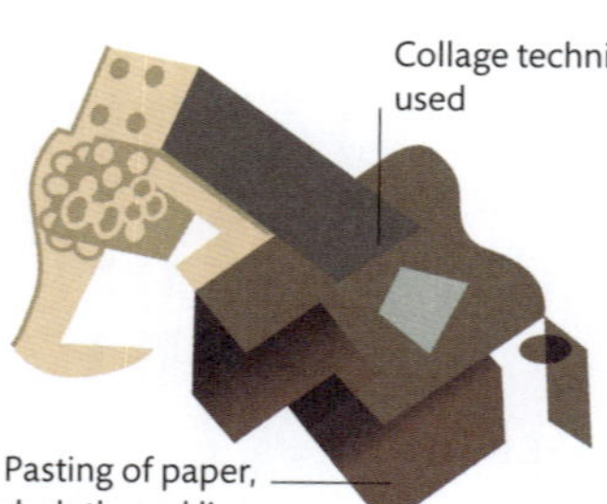

SYNTHETIC

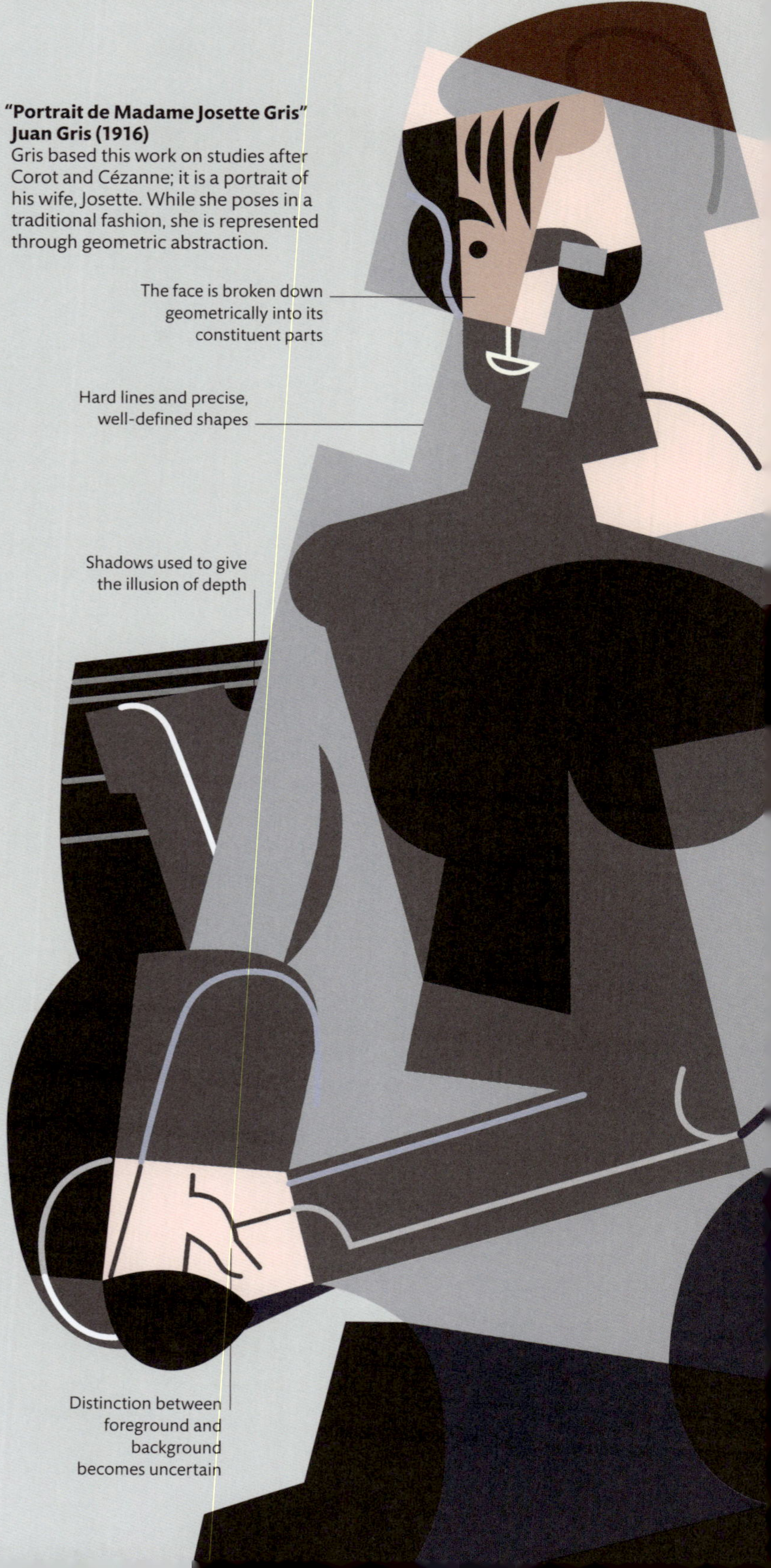

"Portrait de Madame Josette Gris" Juan Gris (1916)
Gris based this work on studies after Corot and Cézanne; it is a portrait of his wife, Josette. While she poses in a traditional fashion, she is represented through geometric abstraction.

Cubism and Futurism

The Cubists invented a new way of representing objects, abandoning the idea of a single fixed viewpoint that had been established in painting since the Renaissance.

Multiple viewpoints

Cubism was developed by Pablo Picasso and Georges Braque in 1907–1912. Their experimentation with perspective broke down subjects into multiple planes and shapes, in an effort to deconstruct the way the eye perceives objects in time and space. Multiple viewpoints spread out over a flat picture plane resulted in complicated, fragmented images.

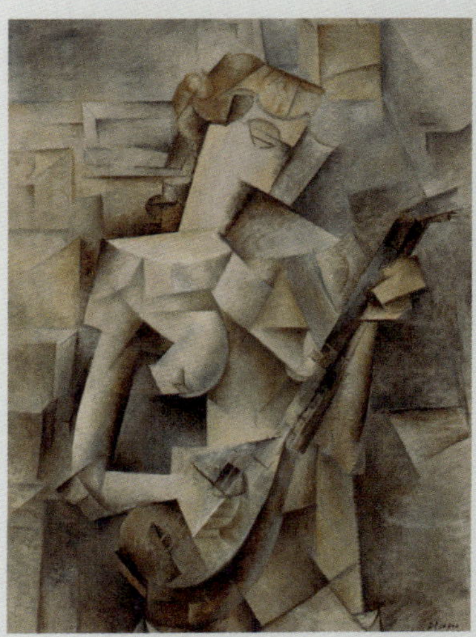

"Girl with Mandolin" Picasso (1910)
In this early example of Analytic Cubism, the figure and instrument are broken down into geometric elements.

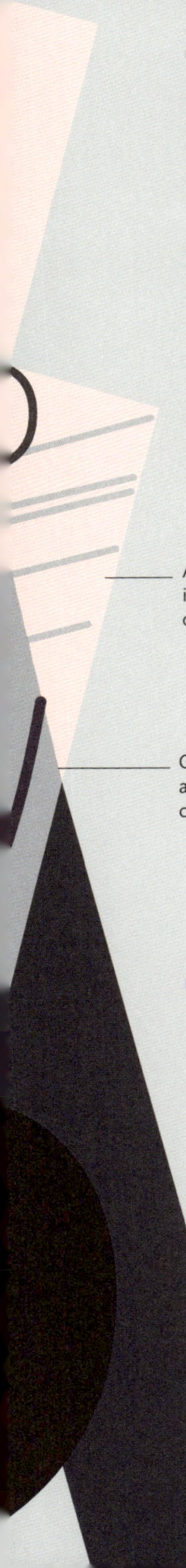

WHO INFLUENCED THE CUBISTS?

Post-Impressionist Paul Cézanne depicted subjects from different, slightly incompatible viewpoints and was a precursor to Cubism.

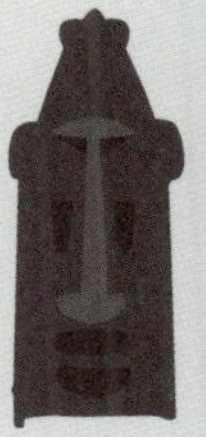

PICASSO WAS INSPIRED BY AFRICAN ART, INCLUDING MASKS

Futurism

Futurism emerged in Italy after Cubism. It appropriated the Cubist technique of using multiple viewpoints and fragmented forms in both painting and sculpture, to create dynamic representations of machines and people in energetic motion. Led by Filippo Tommaso Emilio Marinetti, the Futurists wanted to celebrate the mechanized technology and speed that characterized the modern world developing around them.

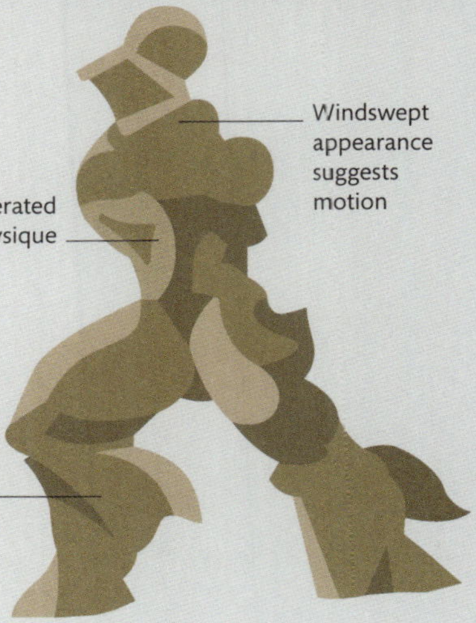

"Unique Forms of Continuity in Space" Umberto Boccioni (1913)
Futurists used new techniques such as repetition and lines of force, in an effort to show movement and dynamism, as in this striding figure.

Disrupting the making

The Surrealists pioneered many creative techniques to help them tap into the depths of their subconscious. Some were original, while others were adapted from childhood games or poetry. These aimed to disrupt the making process, undoing rational thought and opening the artist up to the unpredictable possibilities of random chance. This resulted in unexpected juxtapositions and uncanny, abstract, or rough imagery that stood in stark contrast to the styles and subjects of painting of the prewar period.

Automatic drawing
This was a technique in which the artist muted conscious decision making while in the act of drawing and painting, leaving the hand to move freely without thought.

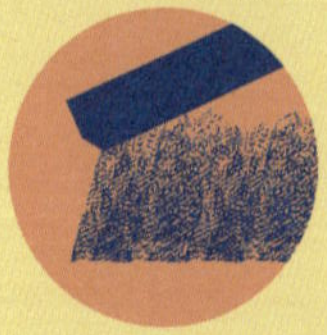

Frottage
A form of mark-making, frottage was achieved by rubbing crayon or pastel onto paper placed over textured surfaces, giving random, abstract effects.

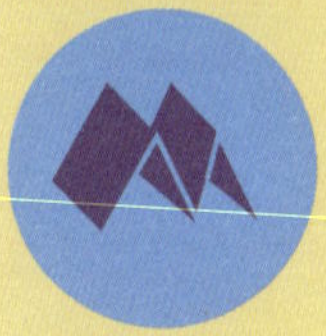

Exquisite corpse
Adapted from a parlor game, this technique involved drawing part of a subject on a piece of paper, folding it, and passing it on to the next artist, to create a jumble of parts.

WHO WERE THE KEY WOMEN OF THE SURREALIST MOVEMENT?

Important female artists in Surrealism included Dorothea Tanning, Leonora Carrington, and Eileen Agar.

SURREALISM IN FILM

Surrealism was one of the more influential art and literary movements, reaching wide audiences through film. Filmmakers such as Luis Buñuel created works filled with disturbing scenes, such as a "Un Chien Andalou," which featured a notorious sequence of an eyeball being sliced by a razor blade.

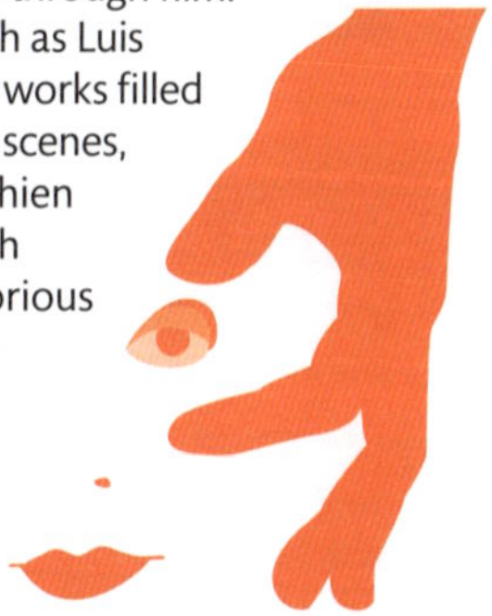

SHOCKING SCENES

SALVADOR DALÍ EXPERIMENTED WITH SLEEP TO UNLOCK HIS CREATIVITY

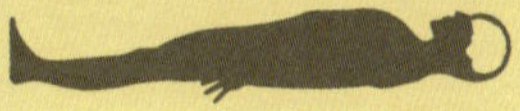

Distorted figures
Some surrealists, such as Salvador Dalí, made finely detailed, hyperrealist paintings depicting unrealistic subjects. Informed by the nonsensical narratives of dreams, Dalí painted dreamscapes that contained fantastic scenes, populated by uncanny figures with elongated limbs and distorted features. These works highlighted how lifelike the disturbing contents of dreams can sometimes feel when they are experienced.

Dreamlike scenes
The Surrealists were greatly influenced by the works of psychoanalyst Sigmund Freud, whose writings on interpreting dreams informed their ideas surrounding the subconscious. Freud believed dreams conveyed messages from the subconscious, and many Surrealist artists used the contents of their own dreams as subject matter for their paintings.

Bizarre arrangements of ordinary objects
Many Surrealist artists worked with sculpture, creating objects that combined unusual materials in bizarre configurations to form strange objects, such as Méret Oppenheim's fur-lined teacup and saucer.

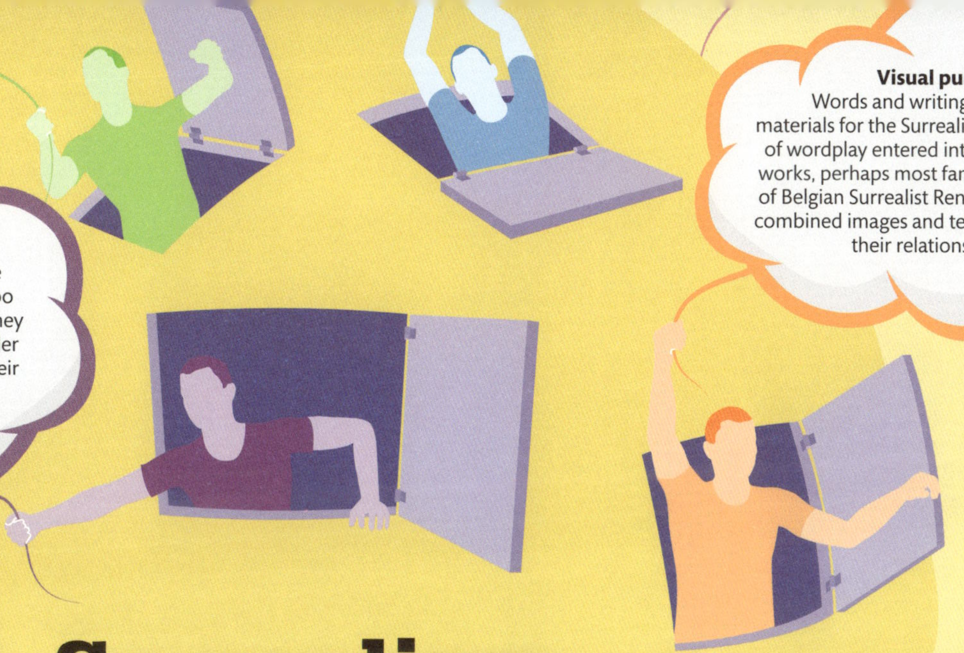

Taboo subjects and sexuality
Through their deep explorations of the human psyche, the Surrealists were drawn to subjects previously considered too taboo to be openly explored through art. They explored erotic fantasies, questions of gender identity, and modes of sexuality through their paintings, sculptures, and writings, to the shock of the art audiences of the time.

Visual puns
Words and writing were key materials for the Surrealists, and this love of wordplay entered into many of their works, perhaps most famously in the art of Belgian Surrealist René Magritte, who combined images and text to underscore their relationships.

Surrealism

Following World War I, in the 1920s the Surrealist movement took anarchic, anti-art ideals and combined them with experimental techniques to create art that explored the irrational and the subversive.

Playful subversion

The horrors of World War I had a major effect on the art that was produced in its wake. Many disillusioned artists believed the war had destroyed all former cultural values, and that a new kind of art and literature was required—a kind that playfully subverted existing standards. The Surrealists, led by French poet and writer André Breton, believed in tapping into the power of the subconscious mind, using a variety of probing, inventive methods to reveal a stream of hidden creative thoughts within themselves.

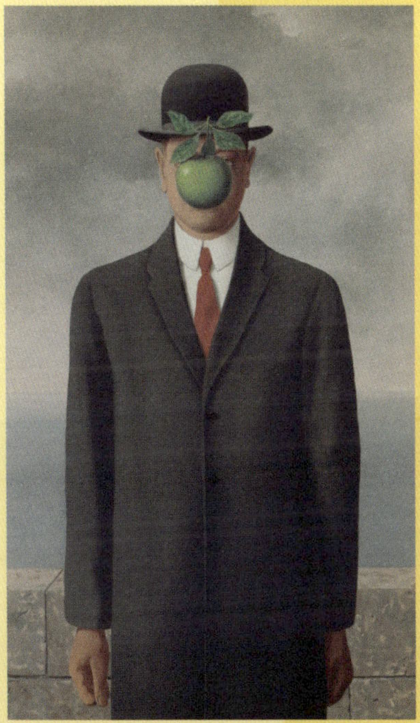

"The Son of Man", René Magritte (1946)
Magritte's subversive self-portrait shows a figure with the left arm bent backward and a mysterious, hovering apple.

Unity of disciplines

The Bauhaus taught that there should be no division between different creative endeavors, instead espousing a unified approach where all artists were craftsmen and vice versa. By uniting all disciplines—sculpture, painting, handicrafts, printing, furniture design, and architecture—the Bauhaus aimed to create total works of art where every object represented this unity. The school gave all its students a thorough grounding in technical skills as a foundation on which to build their future works. This approach was later copied by art schools around the world.

Sculpture
Mostly abstract and made from modern materials, sculptures explored shape, form, and color.

Painting
Painters Paul Klee, Josef Albers, and Wassily Kandinsky taught at the Bauhaus. Their approaches to color theory were influential.

Handicrafts
Traditionally seen as lesser than the fine arts of painting and sculpture, handicrafts were afforded equal importance.

Simple forms echo shapes found in Albers's geometric paintings

Frames made from oak

Bauhaus

Founded by architect Walter Gropius in Weimar, Germany, in 1919, the Bauhaus was one of the most important art schools of the 20th century. It fostered creative international cooperation, and established the use of a universal, geometric abstraction among its artists. It created a visual style and a practical mindset that remain influential today.

Form and function

The Bauhaus was a gathering place for avant-garde artists of a variety of different nationalities and became a center for a decidedly Modernist approach to education, combining art, design, and architecture. It taught that art and design should not be purely decorative and that form should arise harmoniously from the function it performs. Its students produced utilitarian objects, from chairs to teapots, that looked and felt modern, utopian, and futuristic.

Bright, simple colors added both aesthetic appeal and ease of use

Clear, geometric shapes with clean lines and angles

Printing
The pioneering textile and print artist Anni Albers, married to Josef, made many of her early works at the school.

Furniture design
Functional not decorative, furniture used materials such as metal and wood in innovative ways to make radical versions of chairs and tables.

Architecture
Bauhaus buildings were seen as "machines for living"—highly functional spaces with nothing extraneously ornamental.

WHY DID THE BAUHAUS CLOSE?

The school's radicalism and internationalism led to condemnation by the Nazi party, which closed it in 1933.

THE **BAUHAUS** WAS ALSO **FAMOUS** FOR ITS **FLAMBOYANT, THEMED COSTUME PARTIES**

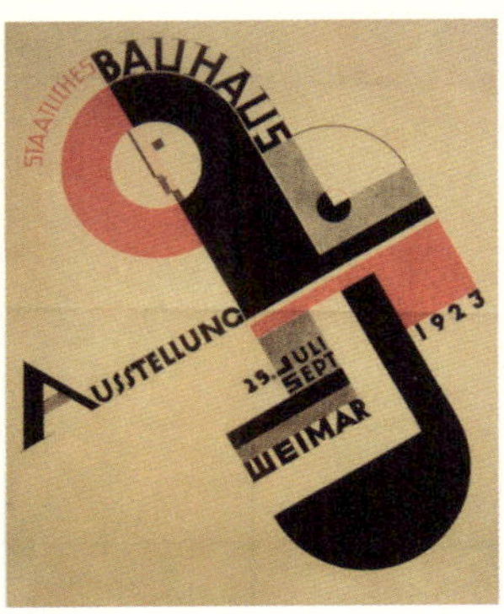

Poster, Joost Schmidt (1923)
The utopian and technology-driven attitude of the Bauhaus was expressed through the posters it produced to advertise the school, which combined shapes and text in a bold geometric, abstract style.

DE STIJL

De Stijl, or Neo-Plasticism, developed in the 1920s and 1930s by artists Piet Mondrian and Theo van Doesburg, furthered Bauhaus ideas of abstraction. Using blocks of primary colors in geometric grids, Mondrian explored how abstract painting could reveal the spiritual structure of the world.

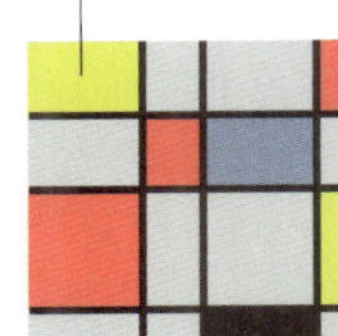

Geometric shapes

"Nesting" design is both visually pleasing and highly efficient

"Nesting Tables", Josef Albers (1926)
These tables exemplify the Bauhaus approach—simple, unadorned, produced easily with readily available materials and combining functionality and form to create affordable, aesthetically pleasing furniture for everyday use.

Abstract Expressionism

Developed in New York after World War II, the Abstract Expressionists aimed to capture emotions through their large-scale paintings, which explored physical gestures, unconscious symbols, and "fields" of color.

Gestural brushstrokes

Initially inspired by the European Surrealists and their explorations of the subconscious (see pp.206–207), the Abstract Expressionists were a group of artists primarily based in New York, whose work fell into two categories. In the first, artists such as Jackson Pollock and Willem de Kooning pursued "Action Painting," treating their works as emotional records of the spontaneous, improvised process of painting. Their large-scale canvases, which sometimes filled up an entire gallery wall, gave scope for the artist to explore a variety of gestures using their whole body, resulting in sweeping, rhythmic compositions that allowed the viewer to trace the moves the artist made in creating the work, and perhaps sense what they felt as they did so.

WHERE DID THE NAME "ACTION PAINTING" COME FROM?

In 1952, critic Harold Rosenberg wrote an article called "The American Action Painters" about Jackson Pollock and Willem de Kooning.

POLLOCK ONCE DEMOLISHED A WALL TO MAKE ROOM FOR A **19 FT (6 M) CANVAS**

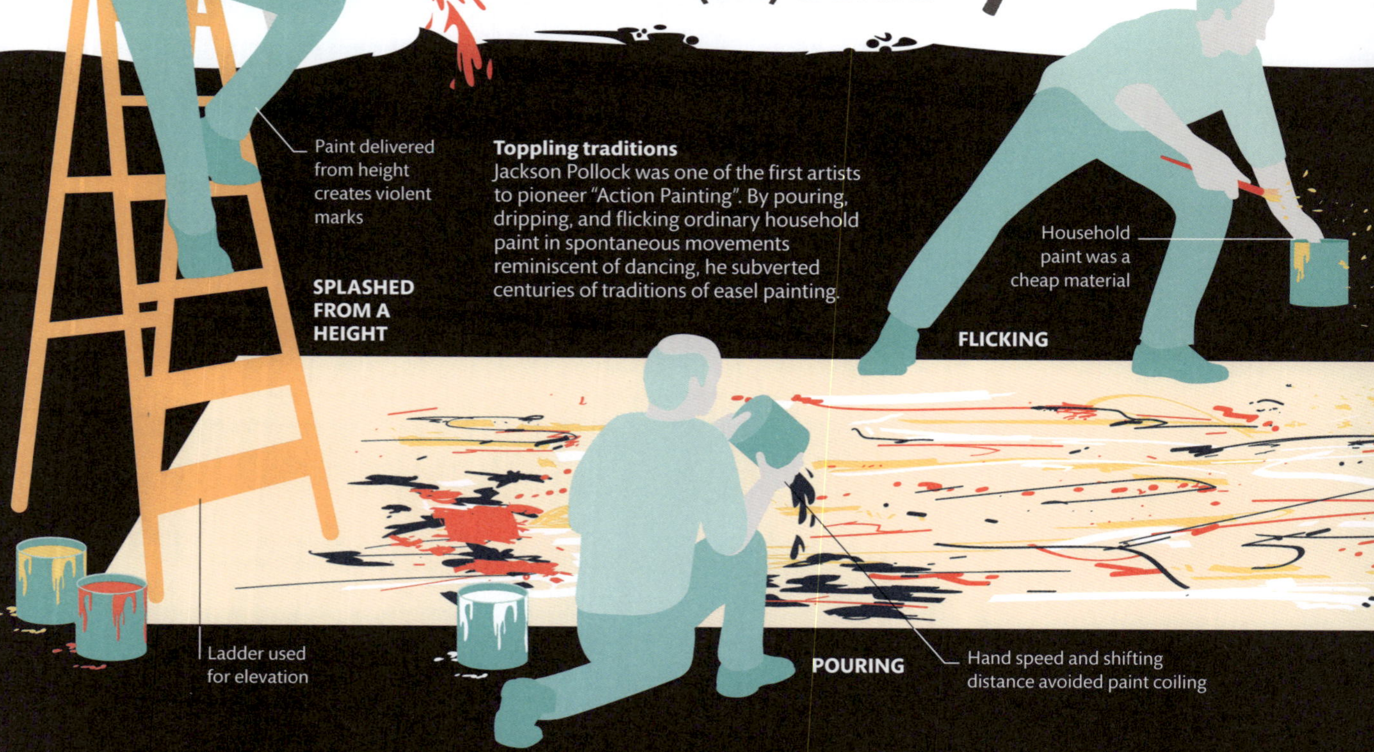

Toppling traditions
Jackson Pollock was one of the first artists to pioneer "Action Painting". By pouring, dripping, and flicking ordinary household paint in spontaneous movements reminiscent of dancing, he subverted centuries of traditions of easel painting.

Meditative paintings

The second group of Abstract Expressionists included Mark Rothko, Clyfford Still, and Barnett Newman, who painted simple, elemental abstract compositions with large areas of pure color as vehicles for conveying emotion. They aimed to produce paintings that a viewer could contemplate and engage with over long periods of time.

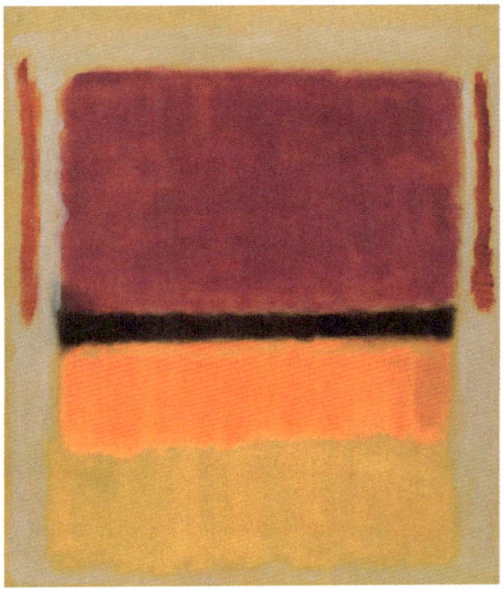

Mauve
Applied in thin glazes, mauve complements the black and provides warmth.

Black
Black acts as a contrasting dividing line that draws the viewer's eye.

Orange
Bright orange offsets the black, its irregular form seeming to ebb and flow.

Yellow
The outline of thinly applied white brings the warm yellow forward.

"Untitled (Violet, Black, Orange, Yellow on White and Red)," Mark Rothko (1949)
Blocks of contrasting colors or "multiforms" became Rothko's trademark.

LEE KRASNER

Artist Lee Krasner, married to Jackson Pollock until his death in 1956, took over his large studio at their remote home and created her own expansive canvases. Working with colorful collage techniques, she explored tonal contrasts and organic and geometric forms to create striking abstract works.

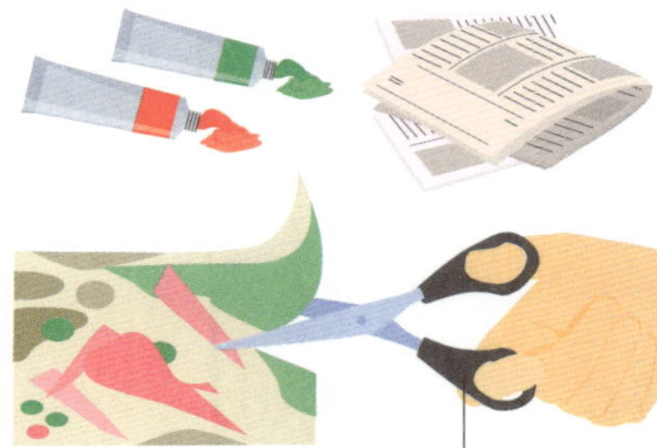

MIXTURE OF MEDIA

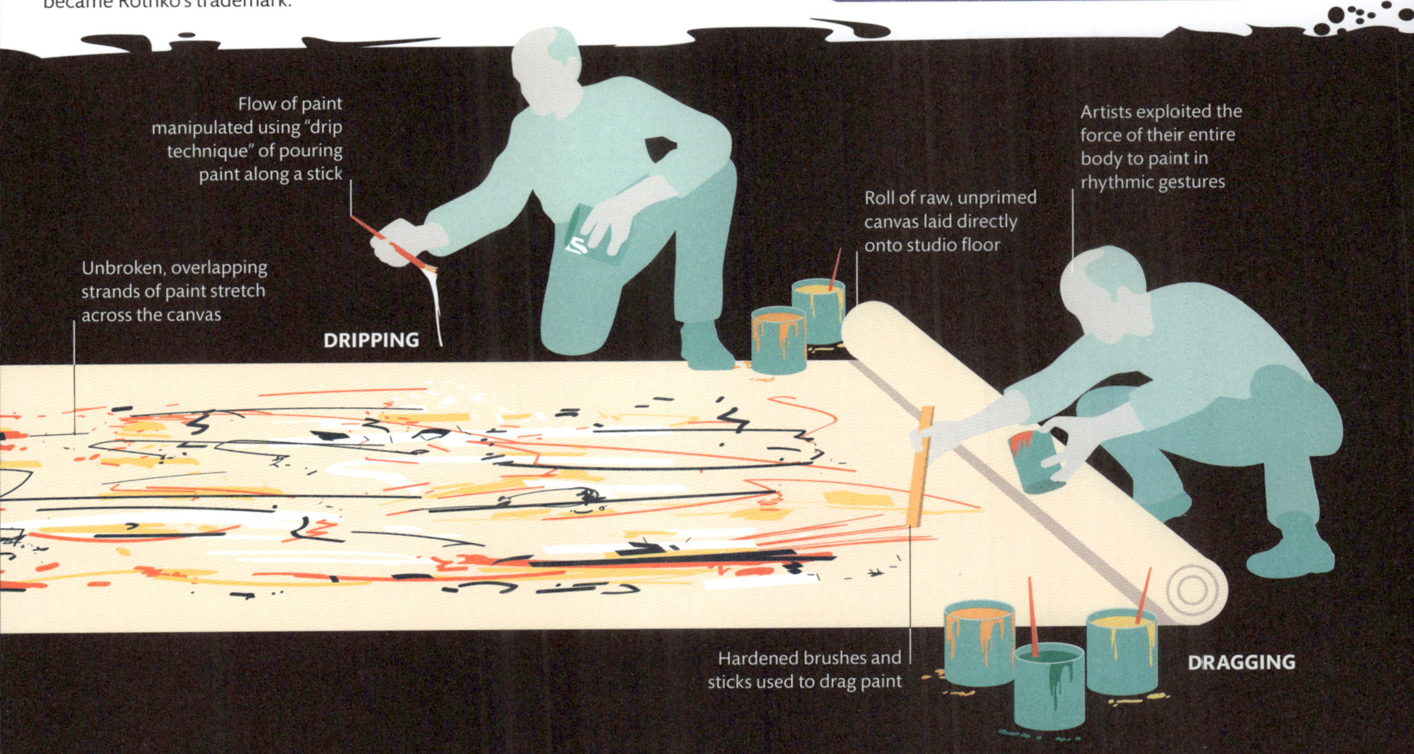

Pop Art

Pop Art arose in the late 1950s and '60s when artists began utilizing commercial production techniques to create works that blurred the line between pop culture and painting.

Satire and celebration

Taking images from everyday sources as a basis for their paintings, many Pop artists strove to reproduce them as mechanically as possible to create cool, slick artworks that trod a thin line between satirizing and celebrating consumerism. By employing production techniques used in advertising, such as silkscreen printing and sign writing, they made paintings that did away with a degree of artistic expression, instead creating a recognizable product for an eager marketplace.

WHAT WERE THE MOODS AND THEMES OF POP ART?

Pop Art was characterized as popular, transient, expendable, low cost, mass-produced, young, witty, glamorous, and commercially minded.

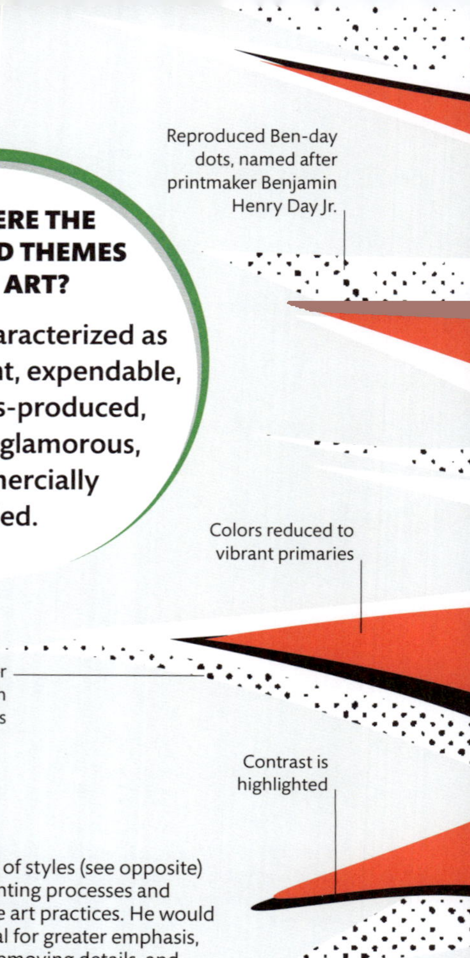

Industrial painting
Lichtenstein used a range of styles (see opposite) to imitate mechanical printing processes and interweave them with fine art practices. He would modify his source material for greater emphasis, adjusting compositions, removing details, and accentuating the clichés of the graphic world.

A 1956 COLLAGE BY **RICHARD HAMILTON** IS OFTEN DESCRIBED AS **THE FIRST WORK OF POP ART**

Warhol and mass production

Artists such as Andy Warhol and Roy Lichtenstein challenged traditional boundaries between materials and processes, blending painting with printmaking and photography, and combining handmade with ready-made elements to create new meaning. Warhol, who began his career in the 1950s as an advertising illustrator, was the most influential Pop artist, bridging the gap between the commercial and art worlds by mass-producing silkscreen prints of consumer products and figures from American pop culture. His New York studio was dubbed The Factory, the term a direct response to the media and popular culture of the time, and reflected his use of assistants and the assembly-line style of production methods he employed. He created many iconic celebrity prints.

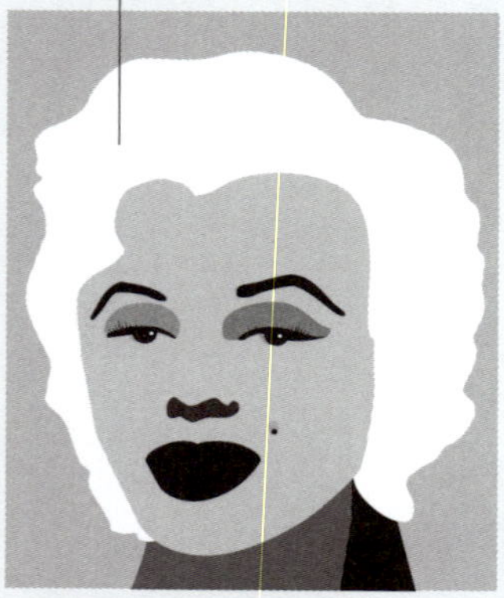

Monotone Marilyn Monroe
Warhol sourced a publicity shot of Marilyn Monroe to create a stencil for printing. This then became the basis for his series.

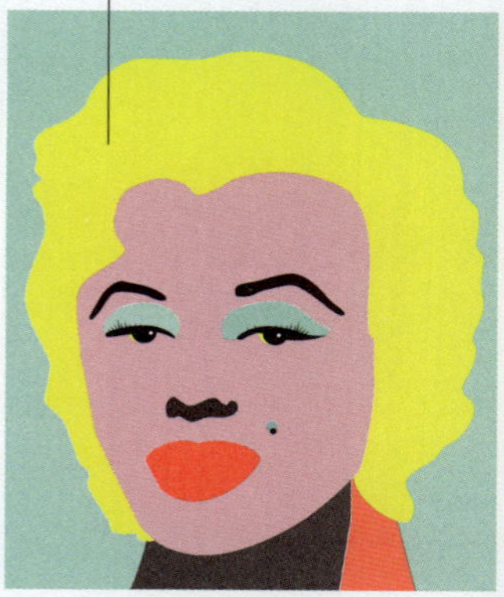

Loose brushstrokes
Vibrant areas of color were hand-painted directly onto the screen to accentuate the lips, eyeshadow, and hair.

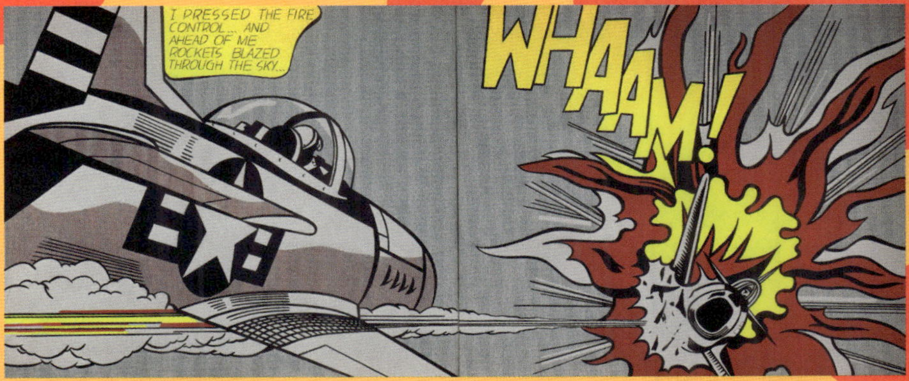

"WHAAM!" ROY LICHTENSTEIN (1963)

Pulp pictures

Initially an Abstract Expressionist (see pp.210–11), American artist Roy Lichtenstein turned to pop culture for inspiration, using images from cheap pulp comic books for the source material for his paintings. Taking comic panels that were originally only inches wide, he used a projector to transfer them onto large canvases, sizing up the image, and recreating the cheap printing dots that could be seen in the magnified image in paint by using stencils. This process removed any traces of individual artistic expression, in stark contrast to the works of the Abstract Expressionists of the decade before.

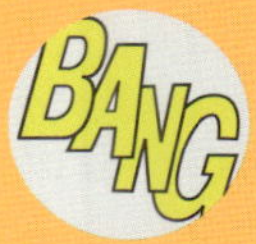

Text in painting
Taken out of context, the text becomes just another visual element of the painting.

Use of heavy black line
Heavy black lines give the image a bold, graphic power and define the individual features.

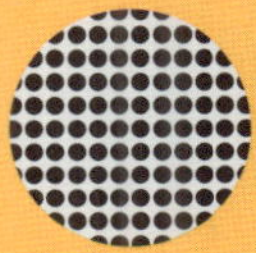

Ben-Day Dots
Lichtenstein originally painted these printers' dots by hand before moving to a stencil process.

Warhol saw ink blots as a good thing

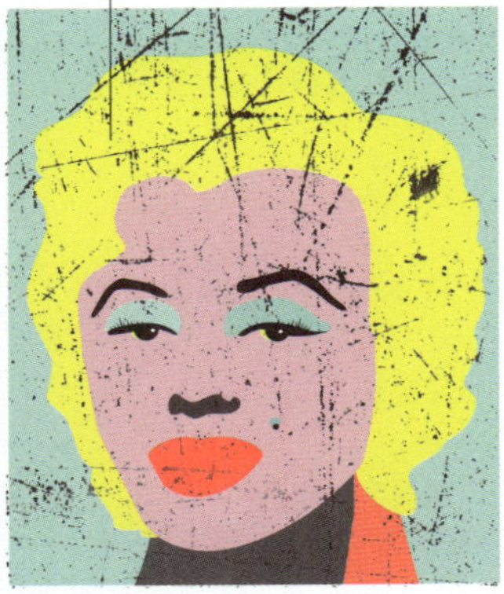

Black shadows
Warhol allowed chance to take over with the final layer of black ink, adding smudges, stains, and variations to the image.

A DIFFERENT VIEW ON POP ART

Pop art was also important in Britain in the 1950s and '60s, and as the only female artist in the British arm of the movement, the artist Pauline Boty provided a rare female perspective. She created colorful, energetic works that put women's desires at the forefront and explored their relationship with mass culture through the mythology of movie stars and contemporary pop songs. Boty also used her artworks to comment on ideas of culture and politics from a feminist perspective.

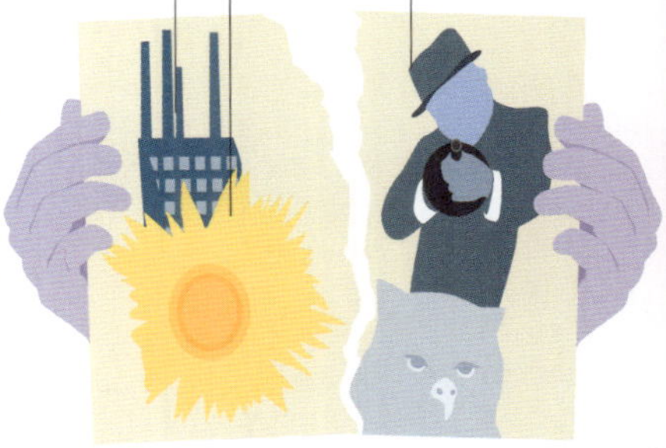

SUNFLOWER GIRL

Minimalism

Rather than a defined movement, Minimalism describes an approach to abstract art that was explored and adopted by a number of predominantly North American artists in the 1960s and 1970s. These artists made works with a highly simplified, austere approach to form in order to explore the conceptual limits of media.

Elemental simplicity

Key aspects of Minimalist art linked the works of several artists working in sculpture and painting. Sculptors such as Donald Judd, Carl Andre, and Robert Morris often made use of non-traditional or industrial materials, while painters including Robert Ryman, Frank Stella, and Agnes Martin produced works that were often characterized by simple rectilinear shapes or monochrome colors. Formats would often include repeated sequences of simple, self-contained, basic elements.

Exploring limits

Minimalist artists explored how basic, often geometric forms might arouse different emotions in a viewer, distilling the approach taken by Abstract Expressionists (see pp.210–211). However, in contrast to the Abstract Expressionists, Minimalist artists removed any trace of emotion or intuitive decision-making in the creative process, instead producing objects that emphasized their own objecthood and made the viewer aware of their color, materiality, and specific context in a gallery or museum space.

MATERIALS

Some minimalist sculptors turned to preexisting industrial materials such as bricks, tiles, or tubular lights, which they used in series to create their works. Others fabricated their works from scratch, but still followed an industrial aesthetic, often using metals, fiberglass, and plastics.

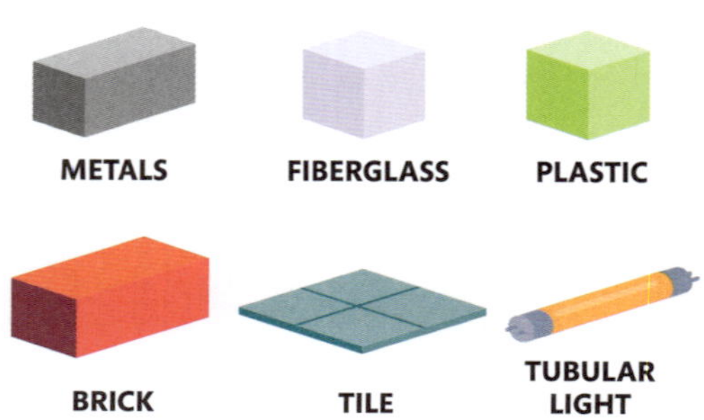

HOW IS MINIMALIST SCULPTURE MADE?

Minimalist sculptors often employed assistants, technicians, or manufacturers to physically make works to their specifications.

Escaping the real world
Pushing the idea of abstraction (see pp.78–79) even further, Minimalist artists often sought to create artworks that bore no relation to the real, familiar world, and instead encouraged the viewer to contemplate and respond to the work purely on its own terms.

IN 1965, **ART CRITIC BARBARA ROSE** FAMOUSLY DUBBED MINIMALISM **"ABC ART"**

"ART IS THE EXCLUSION OF THE UNNECESSARY" CARL ANDRE

"WHAT YOU SEE IS WHAT YOU SEE" FRANK STELLA

"ACTUAL SPACE IS INTRINSICALLY MORE POWERFUL AND SPECIFIC THAN PAINT ON A FLAT SURFACE" DONALD JUDD

"DON'T ASK WHAT THE WORK IS. RATHER, SEE WHAT THE WORK DOES" EVA HESSE

"ART IS THE CONCRETE REPRESENTATION OF OUR MOST SUBTLE FEELINGS" AGNES MARTIN

"IT IS WHAT IT IS AND IT AIN'T NOTHING ELSE" DAN FLAVIN

Conceptual Art

Conceptual art became a recognized movement during the 1960s, but its precedents lay in the work of earlier 20th century artist Marcel Duchamp, who was determined to create art that served the mind instead of stimulating the eye. His ideas were taken up and expanded by artists in the 1960s whose aim was to "dematerialize" art, creating works that were driven more by concepts and ideas than by aesthetics, techniques, or materials.

Ideas over material

Conceptualism holds that art is an idea rather than a physical object—the concept of the artwork realized in the mind of the audience is more important than the form the work takes and sometimes does not require it to take any form at all. The artist's intention and spectator's response are what matters, and conceptual artists blurred the lines between art objects and language to explore the ways they connect together.

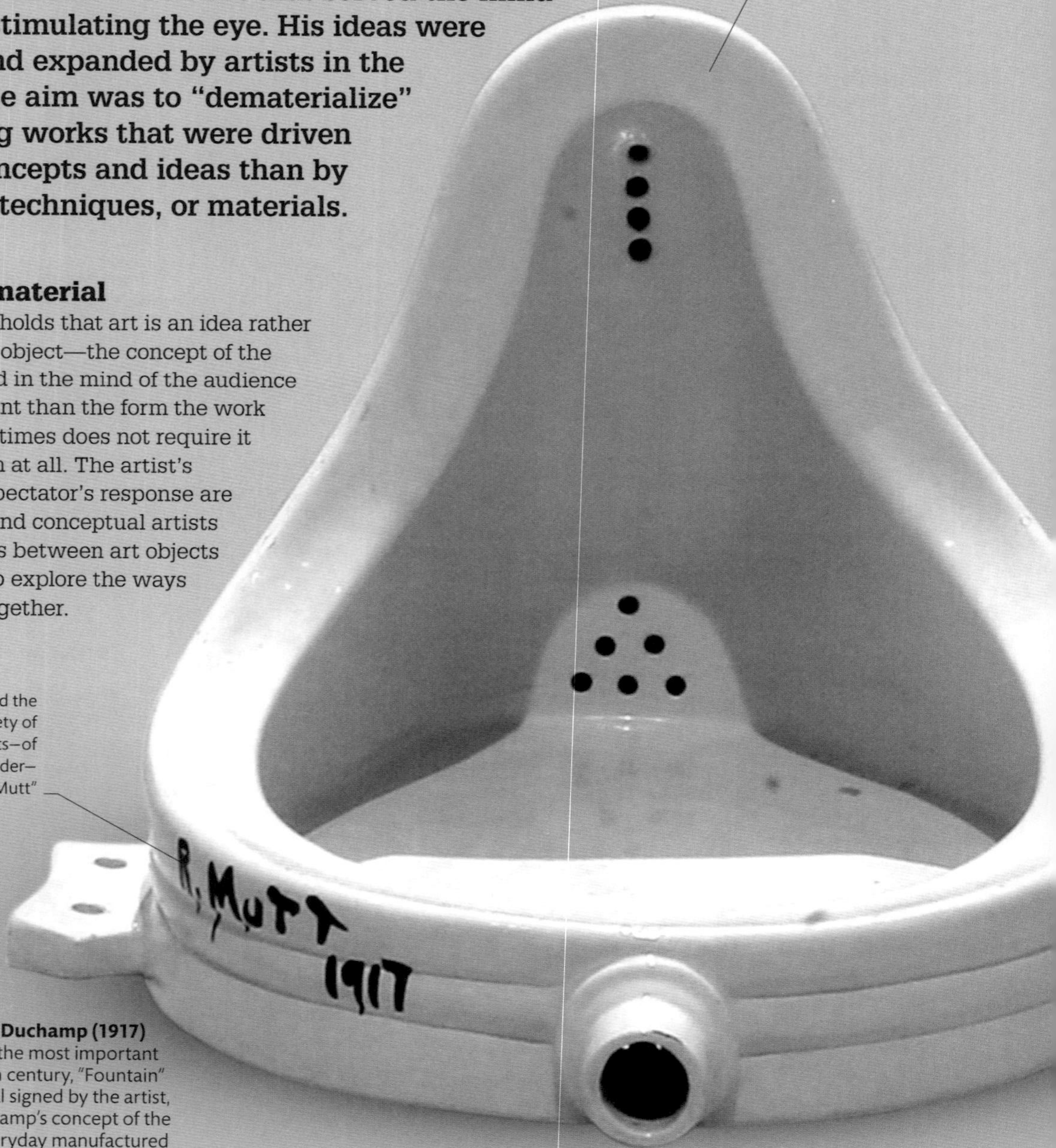

"Fountain," Marcel Duchamp (1917)
Regarded as one of the most important artworks of the 20th century, "Fountain" is an upturned urinal signed by the artist, an example of Duchamp's concept of the "readymade"—an everyday manufactured object designated as a work of art by the artist.

COUNTERCULTURE ART

Conceptual artists were part of the counterculture of the 1960s that aimed to disrupt traditional values and ideas. Conceptual art was an attack on the art market, as many pieces could not be meaningfully owned or sold. This idea continues today—Italian artist Maurizio Cattelan made a piece, "Comedian," consisting of a banana taped to a wall.

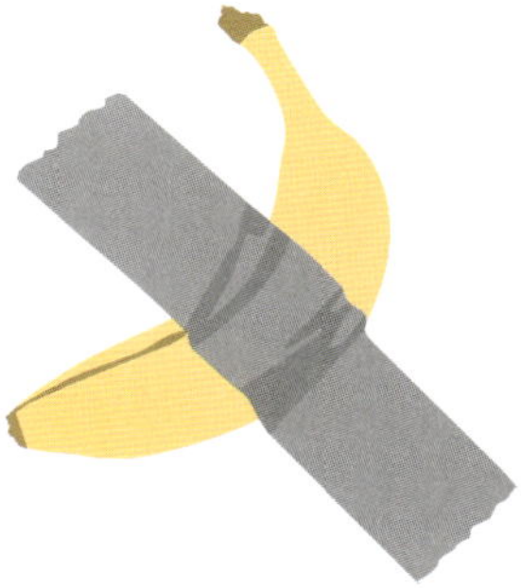

SUBVERSIVE ART

Instructions as art

Some modern and contemporary artists have sought to explore the idea that artists, instead of making something themselves, can issue instructions for the creation of art, which can take place with no further involvement from the artist. Notably, American artist Sol LeWitt, who was associated with the conceptual art movement, made pieces that consisted of simple instructions for ways of drawing on a wall. Other artists and members of the public may create pieces based on these works. In this way, the artist distills their art into a pure idea or concept that may or may not result in the creation of a physical artwork.

WHO IS THE FLUXUS GROUP?

Fluxus is a group of avante-garde artists and composers founded in 1960. It has been influential in promoting spontaneous and subversive art.

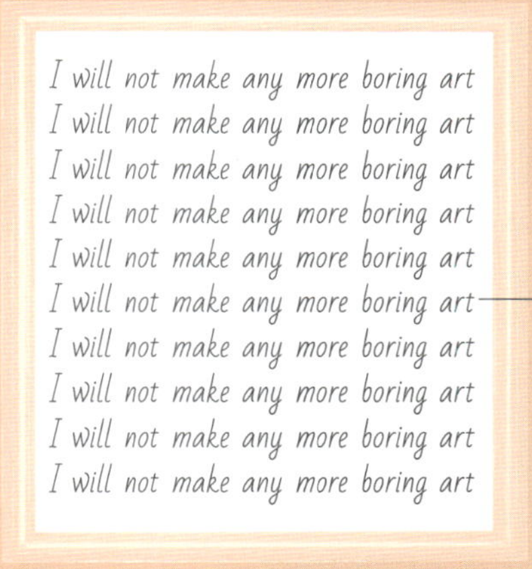

"Lines" raised questions about authorship and rules

The absent artist
American artist John Baldessari was unable to attend an installation in 1971. Instead, he instructed students to make a piece "by" him by writing, "I will not make any more boring art," over and over on the walls.

CONCEPTUAL ART IS SOMETIMES KNOWN AS **POST-OBJECT ART,** OR **ART-AS-IDEA**

New ways of making art

Conceptual artists upended the traditional "fine art" mediums of sculpture and painting, experimenting with breaking them down into their constituent elements to deconstruct how artworks functioned. As well as questioning existing forms, they also expanded their enquiries outward into other mediums, with conceptual artists making wall drawings and text-based pieces, and utilizing photography, film, installation, and performance to redefine what constituted art, laying the foundations for the multiple modes of expression that make up contemporary art today.

TEXT PIECES

PHOTOGRAPHS

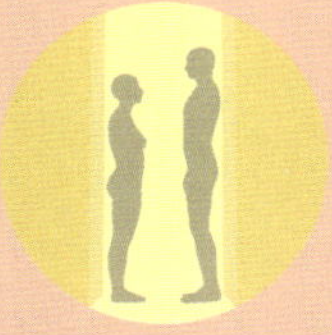

INSTALLATIONS

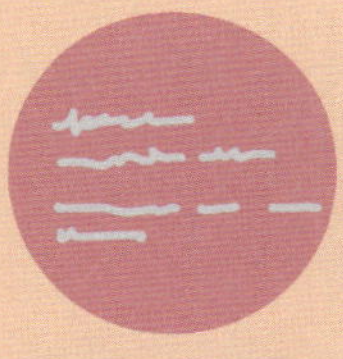

WALL DRAWINGS

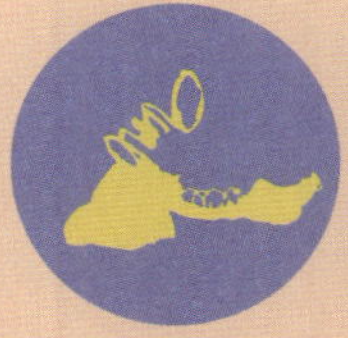

FOUND OBJECTS

FILM

Index

Picture credits

The publisher would like to thank the following for their kind permission to reproduce their photographs:

(Key: a-above; b-below/bottom; c-centre; f-far; l-left; r-right; t-top)

19 Alamy Stock Photo: Deco (br). 28-29 Julia Cassels. 31 Dreamstime.com: Gearstd (bc); Olga Khait (tl); Beata Kraus (tc); Sunfe17 (bl). 48 Dorling Kindersley: Tash Kahn (cra, cr, crb). 49 Dorling Kindersley: Stephen Bere (cr). Tash Kahn: (tc). 76 iStock: temizyurek (b). 77 Franco Clun. 98 Getty Images: Fine Art Images / Heritage Images. 99 123RF.com: archnoi1 (br/ Hessian); detchana wangkheeree (bl); mohsin majeed (br/Paper). Dreamstime.com: Vladimir Korostyshevskiy (c). 108 Dreamstime.com: Iryna Koliadzynska (br). 109 Dreamstime.com: Boyan Dimitrov (bl). 124 Dr. Wolfgang Beyer: (t). Dreamstime.com: Amicabel (bc); Tajra1 (br). 125 Alamy Stock Photo: Rachel Carbonell (cr); PRAWNS (c). Dreamstime.com: Funkyplayer (bc); Svetlana Urbanskaia (bl). 130 Dreamstime.com: Mullrich (l). 134, 135 (l) Bridgeman Images. 144 Getty Images: Eye Ubiquitous / Universal Images Group (t). 147 Getty Images: Richard I'Anson (c). 149 Alamy Stock Photo: Science History Images (cr). 151 Alamy Stock Photo: The Picture Art Collection (bl). 153 The Metropolitan Museum of Art: Gift of Edward S. Harkness, 1918 (br). 154-155 akg-images: Nimatallah (l). 157 Alamy Stock Photo: Heritage Image Partnership Ltd (c). 158 National Museum Lagos: (tl). 162 Alamy Stock Photo: funkyfood London - Paul Williams (tr). 165 Bridgeman Images: Christie's Images (cb). 167 Alamy Stock Photo: Universal Images Group North America LLC (tc). 170 Getty Images: DEA / G. Dagli Orti / De Agostini (tr). 172 Bridgeman Images. 173 Alamy Stock Photo: Peter Barritt. 176 Alamy Stock Photo: IanDagnall Computing (t). 179 Bridgeman Images: National Gallery, London, UK (l). 180 Bridgeman Images: Galleria degli Uffizi, Florence, Tuscany, Italy (tr). 183 Alamy Stock Photo: incamerastock. 184 Alamy Stock Photo: Artepics (t). 186 Alamy Stock Photo: FineArt (t). 188 Alamy Stock Photo: Album (t). 190 Alamy Stock Photo: Masterpics (tr). 193 Alamy Stock Photo: Granger Historical Picture Archive (tr). 194 Barnes Collection: Credit - Barnes Foundation (bl). 195 Alamy Stock Photo: Peter Barritt (br). 197 Alamy Stock Photo: V&A Images (cr). 199 Bridgeman Images: (r). 200 Alamy Stock Photo: Giorgio Morara (br). 202 akg-images. 205 Photo Scala, Florence: The Museum of Modern Art, New York / © Succession Picasso/DACS, London 2022 (tr). 207 Bridgeman Images: Christie's Images / © ADAGP, Paris and DACS, London 2022 (bl). 209 Alamy Stock Photo: Universal Art Archive (bl). 211 Bridgeman Images / © 1998 Kate Rothko Prizel & Christopher Rothko ARS, NY and DACS, London (tl). 212-213 Derivative Andy Warhol Artwork created by DK in 2022. © 2022 The Andy Warhol Foundation for the Visual Arts, Inc. / Licensed by DACS, London. (b). 213 akg-images / © Estate of Roy Lichtenstein/DACS 2022 (t). 216 Getty Images: Michael Macor / The San Francisco Chronicle / © Association Marcel Duchamp / ADAGP, Paris and DACS, London 2022

Acknowledgments

DK would like to thank the following people for help in preparing this book: Jo Walton for picture research; Elizabeth Wise for indexing; Joy Evatt for proofreading; Vaibhav Rastogi for design assistance; and Aarushi Dhawan and Dimple Desai for illustration assistance.